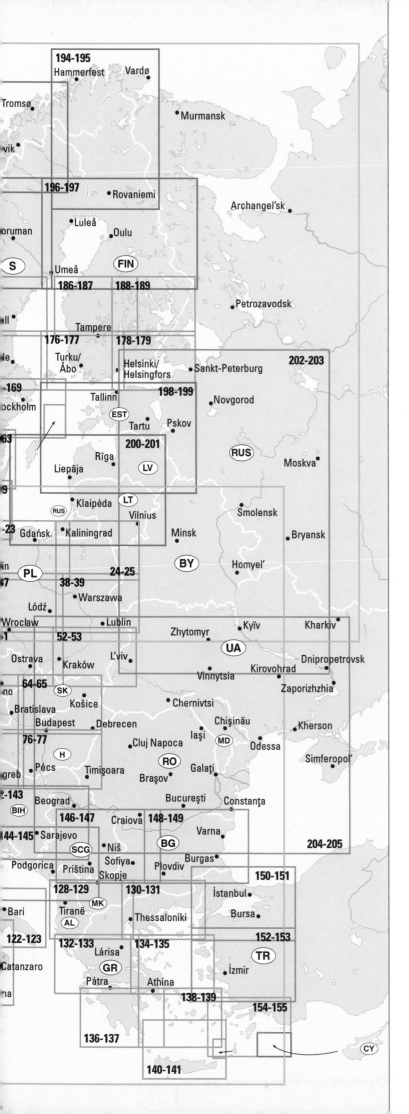

KEY TO MAPS
QUADRO D'U...
M...
TABLEAU
KARTE

Scale-Scala-Escala
Échelle-Maßstab
1 : 8 000 000

1 cm = 80 km   1 inch = 126.26 miles

| 0 | 100 | 200 | 300 | 400 | 500 km |

| 0 | 50 | 100 | 150 | 200 | 250 | 300 miles |

Scale-Scala-Escala
Échelle-Maßstab
1 : 3 000 000

1 cm = 30 km   1 inch = 47.35 miles

| 0 | 50 | 100 | 150 | 200 km |

| 0 | 25 | 50 | 75 | 100 miles |

Scale-Scala-Escala
Échelle-Maßstab
1 : 1 500 000
(Is. Canarias, Madeira, Açores 1 : 2 000 000)

1 cm = 15 km   1 inch = 23.67 miles

| 0 | 25 | 50 | 75 | 100 km |

| 0 | 20 | 40 | 60 miles |

Scale-Scala-Escala
Échelle-Maßstab
1 : 1 000 000

1 cm = 10 km   1 inch = 15.78 miles

| 0 | 10 | 20 | 30 | 40 | 50 | 60 km |

| 0 | 5 | 10 | 15 | 20 | 25 | 30 | 35 miles |

Scale-Scala-Escala
Échelle-Maßstab
1 : 800 000

1 cm = 8 km   1 inch = 12.63 miles

| 0 | 10 | 20 | 30 | 40 | 50 km |

| 0 | 5 | 10 | 15 | 20 | 25 | 30 miles |

ROAD ATLAS
ATLANTE STRADALE
ATLAS DE CARRETERAS
ATLAS ROUTIER
STRASSENATLAS
EUROPE
EUROPA

II

Contents

Sommario

Sumario

Sommaire

Inhaltsverzeichnis

GB Legend   I Legenda

GB Legend	I Legenda
Toll-free motorway, dual carriageway	Autostrada senza pedaggio a doppia carreggiata
Toll-free motorway, single carriageway	Autostrada senza pedaggio a singola carreggiata
Toll motorway, dual carriageway	Autostrada a pedaggio a doppia carreggiata
Toll motorway, single carriageway	Autostrada a pedaggio a singola carreggiata
Interchange; restricted interchange; service area	Svincolo; svincolo con limitazione; area di servizio
Motorway under construction (opening year)	Autostrada in costruzione (anno di apertura)
Motorway in tunnel	Autostrada in galleria
Number of motorway; european road; national road; regional or local road	Numero di autostrada; itinerario europeo; strada nazionale; strada regionale o locale
National road, dual carriageway	Strada nazionale a doppia carreggiata
National road, single carriageway	Strada nazionale a singola carreggiata
Regional road, dual carriageway	Strada regionale a doppia carreggiata
Regional road, single carriageway	Strada regionale a singola carreggiata
Local road, dual carriageway	Strada locale a doppia carreggiata
Local road, single carriageway	Strada locale a singola carreggiata
Secondary road	Strada secondaria
Road under construction (opening year)	Strada in costruzione (anno di apertura)
Road in tunnel	Strada in galleria
Motorway distances in kilometres (miles in United Kingdom and Ireland)	Distanze in chilometri (miglia nel Regno Unito e Irlanda) sulle autostrade
Road distances in kilometres (miles in United Kingdom and Ireland)	Distanze in chilometri (miglia nel Regno Unito e Irlanda) sulle strade
Gradient 14% and over; gradient 6%–13%	Pendenza maggiore del 14%; pendenza dal 6% al 13%
Panoramic routes	Percorsi panoramici
Pass with height and winter closure	Passo di montagna, quota e periodo di chiusura invernale
Toll point	Barriera di pedaggio
Railway and tunnel	Ferrovia e tunnel ferroviario
Ferry route (with car transportation) and destination	Linea di traghetto (con trasporto auto) e destinazione
Transport of cars by rail	Trasporto auto per ferrovia
National park, natural reserve	Parco nazionale, riserva naturale
International boundaries	Confini internazionali
Disputed boundary; internal boundary	Confine in contestazione; confine interno
International airport	Aeroporto internazionale
Religious building; Castle, fortress	Edificio religioso; Castello, fortezza
Isolated monument	Monumento isolato
Ruins, archaeological area; wall	Rovine, area archeologica; vallo, muraglia
Cave	Grotta
Natural curiosity	Curiosità naturale
Panoramic view	Punto panoramico
Other curiosities (botanical garden, zoo, amusement park etc.)	Altre curiosità (giardino botanico, zoo, parco divertimenti ecc.)
Town or place of great tourist interest	Città o luogo di grande interesse turistico
Interesting town or place	Città o luogo interessante
Other tourist town or place	Altra città o luogo turistico
Area covered and page number of more detailed maps in this atlas	Area e numero di pagina delle mappe di dettaglio presenti nell'atlante

E Leyenda   F Légende   D Zeichenerklärung

E Leyenda	F Légende	D Zeichenerklärung
Autopista de doble vía sin peaje	Autoroute sans péage à chaussées séparées	Zweibahnige Autobahn ohne Gebühr
Autopista de una vía sin peaje	Autoroute sans péage à chaussée unique	Einbahnige Autobahn ohne Gebühr
Autopista de doble vía de peaje	Autoroute à péage et chaussées séparées	Zweibahnige Autobahn mit Gebühr
Autopista de una vía de peaje	Autoroute à péage et chaussée unique	Einbahnige Autobahn mit Gebühr
Acceso; acceso parcial; estación de servicio	Échangeur; échangeur partiel; aire de service	Anschlussstelle; Autobahnein- und/oder -ausfahrt; Tankstelle
Autopista en construcción (año de apertura)	Autoroute en construction (année d'ouverture)	Autobahn in Bau (Fertigstellungsjahr)
Túnel en autopista	Tunnel autoroutier	Autobahntunnel
Número de autopista; carretera europea; carretera nacional; carretera regional o local	Numéro d'autoroute; route européenne; route nationale; route régionale ou locale	Straßennummer: Autobahn; Europastraße; Nationalstraße; Regional- oder Lokalstraße
Carretera nacional de doble vía	Route nationale à chaussées séparées	Zweibahnige Nationalstraße
Carretera nacional de vía unica	Route nationale à chaussée unique	Einbahnige Nationalstraße
Carretera regional de doble vía	Route régionale à chaussées séparées	Zweibahnige Regionalstraße
Carretera regional de vía unica	Route régionale à chaussée unique	Einbahnige Regionalstraße
Carretera local de doble vía	Route locale à chaussées séparées	Zweibahnige Lokalstraße
Carretera local de vía unica	Route locale à chaussée unique	Einbahnige Lokalstraße
Carretera secundaria	Route secondaire	Nebenstraße
Carretera en construcción (año de apertura)	Route en construction (année d'ouverture)	Straße in Bau (Fertigstellungsjahr)
Túnel en carretera	Tunnel routier	Straßentunnel
Distancias en kilómetros (millas en Gran Bretaña e Irlanda) en autopista	Distances autoroutières en kilomètres (miles en Royaume-Uni et Irlande)	Autobahnentfernungen in Kilometern (Meilen in Großbritannien und Irland)
Distancias en kilómetros (millas en Gran Bretaña e Irlanda) en carretera	Distances routières en kilomètres (miles en Royaume-Uni et Irlande)	Straßenentfernungen in Kilometern (Meilen in Großbritannien und Irland)
Pendientes superiores al 14%; pendientes entre 6%–13%	Pente 14% et outre; pente 6%–13%	Steigungen über 14%; Steigungen 6%–13%
Rutas panorámicas	Routes panoramiques	Aussichtsstraßen
Puerto de montaña con altura y cierre invernal	Col avec altitude et fermeture en hiver	Pass mit Höhe und Wintersperre
Peaje	Barrière de péage	Gebührenstelle
Ferrocarril y túnel	Chemin de fer et tunnel	Eisenbahn und Tunnel
Línea marítima (con transporte de coches) y destino	Ligne de navigation (bac pour voitures) et destination	Schiffahrtslinie (Autofähre) und Ziel
Transporte de coches por ferrocarril	Transport de voitures par chemin de fer	Autoverladung per Bahn
Parque nacional, reserva natural	Parc national, réserve naturelle	Nationalpark, Naturschutzgebiet
Límites internacionales	Frontières internationales	Staatsgrenzen
Frontera en disputa; límite interno	Frontière en contestation; frontière intérieure	Strittige Grenze; Verwaltungsgrenze
Aeropuerto internacional	Aéroport international	Internationaler Flughafen
Edificio religioso; Castillo, fortaleza	Édifice religieux; Château, château-fort	Religiösgebäude; Schloss, Festung
Monumento aislado	Monument isolé	Alleinstehendes Denkmal
Ruinas, zona arqueológica; muralla	Ruines, site archéologique; vallum, muraille	Ruinen, archäologisches Ausgrabungsgebiet; Wall, Mauer
Cueva	Grotte	Höhle
Paraje de interés natural	Curiosité naturelle	Natursehenswürdigkeit
Vista panorámica	Vue panoramique	Rundblick
Otras curiosidades (jardín botánico, zoo, parque de atracciones etc.)	Autres curiosités (jardin botanique, zoo, parc d'attractions etc.)	Andere Sehenswürdigkeiten (Botanischer Garten, Zoo, Freizeitpark usw.)
LONDON Ciudad o lugar de gran interés turístico	Localité ou site de grand intérêt touristique	Ortschaft oder Platz von großem touristischen Interesse
RAVENNA Ciudad o lugar interesante	Localité ou site remarquable	Sehenswerte Ortschaft oder Platz
MONTPELLIER Otra ciudad o lugar turístico	Autre localité ou site touristique	Andere touristischen Ortschaft oder Platz
216 Área geográfica cubierta y número de página de otros mapas más detallados en este atlas	Zone couverte et numéro de page pour des cartes plus détaillées dans cet atlas	Abgedecktes Gebiet und Seitennummer von ausführlicheren Karten in diesem Atlas

A11   E50   N13   D951

Col d'Izoard   2360   10-6

Bastia

EUROPEAN ROAD NETWORK   RETE STRADALE EUROPEA
RED EUROPEA DE CARRETERAS   RÉSEAU ROUTIER EUROPÉEN
EUROPÄISCHES STRASSENNETZ

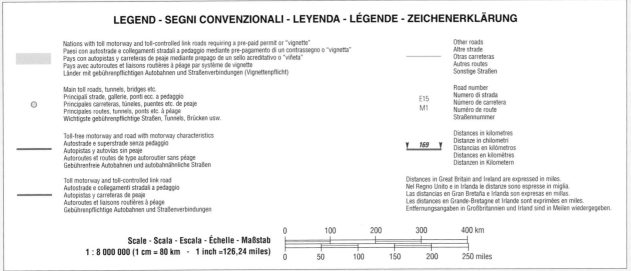

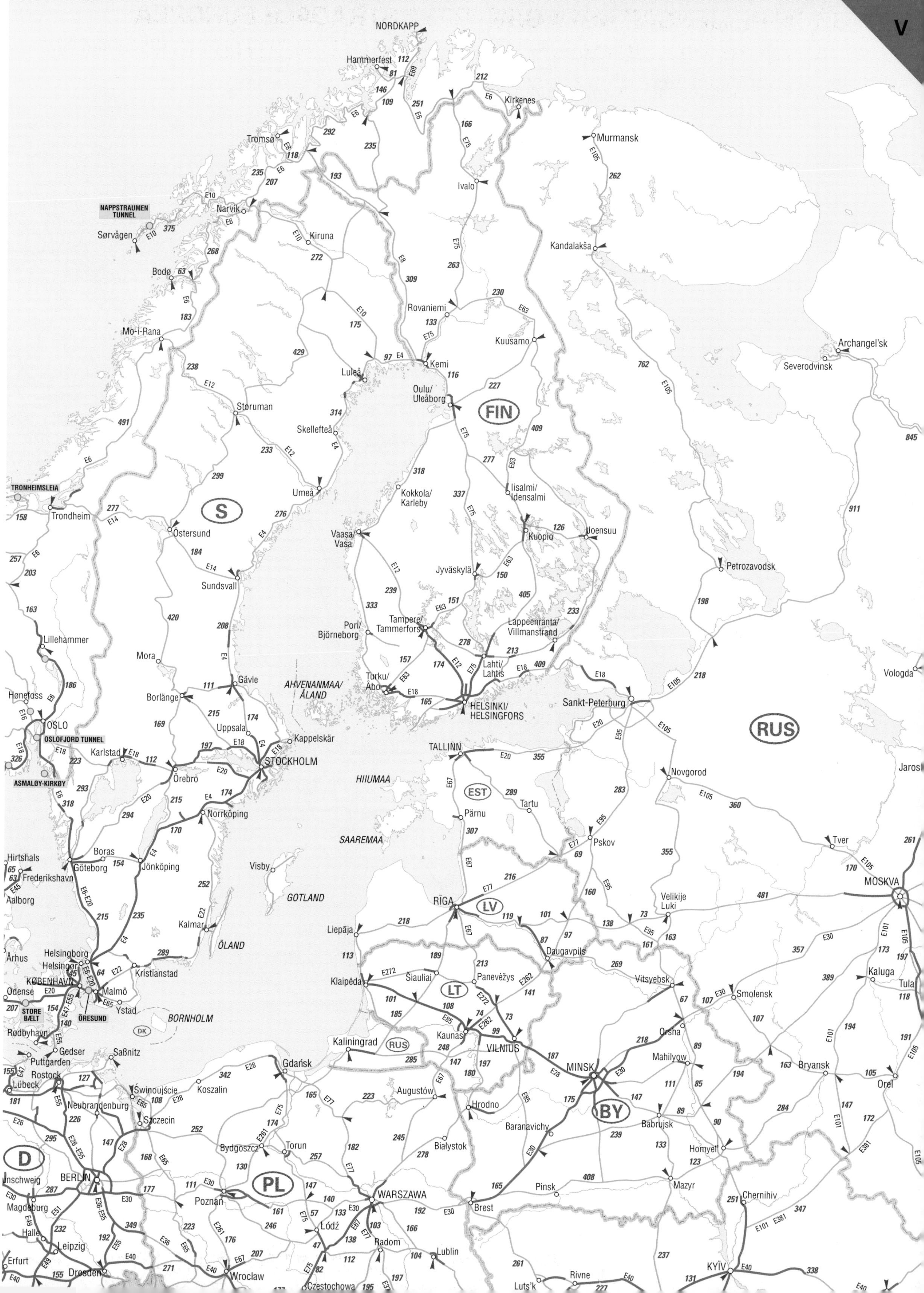

NORDKAPP

Hammerfest 112
E69
81
146
109 251
212
E6 Kirkenes
166
Tromsø 292
118 E8
193 235
E75 Murmansk
235 E6
207
E10 Narvik
E6
NAPPSTRAUMEN TUNNEL
Sørvågen E10 375
268
Ivalo
262
E105
Bodø 63
E6
183 Kandalakša
Mo-i-Rana
238
E12 Kiruna
272
E10
E8
309
263 Archangel'sk
Severodvinsk
762
E105
845
Rovaniemi 230
175 133 E63 Kuusamo
Storuman E12 E75
491 227
97 E4 Kemi
Luleå 116
314 Oulu/Uleåborg
FIN
Skellefteå
233 E12 E4
299 318 409
Umeå 277
276 E4 Kokkola/Karleby 337 E63 Iisalmi/Idensalmi
911
TRONHEIMSLEIA
158 Trondheim 277 E14
Östersund
184
E14
Vaasa/Vasa 126 Kuopio Joensuu
Sundsvall 318 E63 150
Jyväskylä 405
257 E6 420 239 151 233
203 208 E4 333 198
163 Mora E12 157 Tampere/Tammerfors
Lillehammer 111 Gävle Pori/Björneborg 278 Lappeenranta/Villmanstrand
186 215 AHVENANMAA/ÅLAND 174 213 E18 409
Hønefoss E6 Borlänge 174 Turku/Åbo E63 E75 Lahti/Lahtis
E16 169 Uppsala E12 218
OSLO 165 HELSINKI/HELSINGFORS Sankt-Peterburg
OSLOFJORD TUNNEL 197 E18 E18
E18 326 Karlstad 112 Örebro STOCKHOLM TALLINN E20 355 E105
ASMALØY-KIRKØY 293 E20 E4 HIIUMAA E67 Novgorod RUS
318 294 215 Norrköping EST 289 Tartu 283
Hirtshals 170 Pärnu 360 Jaros
Frederikshavn 63 Boras 154 Jönköping SAAREMAA 307 E95 Pskov
Aalborg E45 E6-E20 252 E77 69 355 Tver 261
215 235 E22 Kalmar 160 E105 170 MOSKVA
Århus Kalmar ÖLAND Visby RĪGA LV 216 101 Velikije Luki 481
Helsingborg 289 GOTLAND 218 119 138 73 E95 163 357
Helsingør 64 E22 Kristianstad Liepāja 113 189 213 87 97 Daugavpils 161 E30 389
KØBENHAVN E20 Malmö 101 Šiauliai 269 Vitsyebsk 173 197 Kaluga
Odense E20 ÖRESUND Klaipėda E272 LT 141 67 107 E30 Smolensk 194 Tula
207 STORE BÆLT 154 140 BORNHOLM Kaliningrad RUS 108 74 E262 73 218 Orsha 89 107 118
Rødbyhavn E55 285 248 Kaunas 99 VILNIUS 187 MINSK 111 85 191
Gedser Saßnitz 180 E30 Mahilyow E101
Puttgarden 127 Gdańsk 190 E85 175 BY 147 163 Bryansk 105
Lübeck 181 Świnoujście 342 E28 223 Augustów 239 133 89 90 Orel
E26 226 Szczecin 108 E28 165 E77 Hrodno Baranavichy Bābrujsk 284 147 172
295 E26-E55 252 174 245 Bialystok 123 Homyel' E381
BERLIN 147 E28 168 E261 Bydgoszcz 278 165 408 Mazyr Chernihiv
287 E30 177 111 E30 Torun 257 182 Pinsk 251 E101 347
Magdeburg 130 Poznań 147 WARSZAWA Brest 261 131 KYÏV E40 338
E49 232 192 161 140 E30 192 E30 237 E40
Halle Leipzig E36 223 176 57 133 Łódź 166 Rivne Luts'k 227
Erfurt 192 E55 271 E40 Wrocław 246 47 138 Radom Lublin
155 Dresden 195 82 112 104
Czestochowa 197

IRL · GB · NL · B · L · F · P · E · CH · MC · AND · CORSE · SARDEGNA

ISLE OF MAN · CHANNEL ISLANDS · ILLES BALEARS / ISLAS BALEARES

Ireland (IRL)
Galway/Gaillimh · Limerick/Luimneach · Cork/Corcaigh · Waterford/Port Lairge · Rosslare · DUBLIN/BAILE ÁTHA CLIATH

Great Britain (GB)
Holyhead · Liverpool · Leeds · York · Kingston upon Hull · Manchester · Birmingham · Norwich · Cambridge · Ipswich · Harwich · Fishguard · Cardiff · Bristol · Oxford · LONDON · Dover · Folkestone · Southampton · Portsmouth · Plymouth · Penzance · TYNE TUNNEL · HUMBER BRIDGE · MERSEY TUNNELS · SEVERN BRIDGES · TAMAR BRIDGE · DARTFORD TUNNEL · EUROTUNNEL

Netherlands (NL) / Belgium (B) / Luxembourg (L)
Groningen · Emden · Wilhelmshaven · AMSTERDAM · Den Haag · Rotterdam · Arnhem · Osnabrück · Duisburg · Dortmund · Köln · Bonn · Koblenz · Antwerpen · BRUSSEL/BRUXELLES · Lille · Liège · Luxembourg · Düsseldorf · PR. WILLEM ALEXANDERBRUG · KILTUNNEL · TUNNEL LIEFKENSHOEK · Oostende · Calais

France (F)
Brest · St-Malo · Cherbourg · Le Havre · Dieppe · Caen · Rouen · Amiens · Reims · Rennes · Nantes · Angers · Le Mans · Orléans · PARIS · Troyes · Metz · Nancy · Strasbourg · Saarbrücken · Mannheim · Karlsruhe · les Sables-d'Olonne · Poitiers · Tours · Bourges · Nevers · Dijon · Besançon · Basel · Zürich · BERN · La Rochelle · Limoges · Clermont-Ferrand · Lyon · Genève · Lausanne · Bordeaux · Brive-la-Gaillarde · le Puy-en-Velay · Grenoble · Torino · Milano · Genova · Mont-de-Marsan · Toulouse · VIADUCT DU MILLAU · Alès · Sisteron · Nice · Pau · Nîmes · Marseille · Toulon · Perpignan · TUNNEL MAURICE LEMAIRE (closed until 2007) · TUNNEL DU MONT BLANC · TUNNEL DU GRAND-ST-BERNARD · TUNNEL DU FRÉJUS · TUNNEL DE PUYMORENS · TUNNEL PRADO-CARENAGE · PONT DE NORMANDIE-PONTE DE TANCARVILLE

Spain (E) / Portugal (P)
A Coruña/La Coruña · Santiago de Compostela · Gijón · Oviedo · Santander · Vigo · Orense · León · Bilbao/Bilbo · Donostia-San Sebastián · Porto · Burgos · Pamplona/Iruña · Valladolid · Soria · Zaragoza · Salamanca · Segovia · Ávila · MADRID · Óbidos · Coimbra · Abrantes · LISBOA · Badajoz · Mérida · Toledo · Albacete · Valencia · Lleida/Lérida · Girona/Gerona · Barcelona · Sines · Lagos · Faro · Huelva · Sevilla · Córdoba · Granada · Murcia · Alicante/Alacant · Cartagena · Cádiz · Málaga · Almería · Algeciras · Gibraltar · Ceuta · Melilla · Palma de Mallorca · Alcúdia · Cala Ratjada · PONTE VASCO DA GAMA · 25 DE ABRIL · TÚNEL DEL CADÍ

Corse / Sardegna
Bastia · Ajaccio · Bonifacio · Porto Torres · Olbia · Iglésias · Cagliari

DRIVER INFORMATION - INFORMAZIONI UTILI
DIRECCIONES ÚTILES - INFORMATIONS UTILES
NÜTZLICHE AUSKÜNFTE

			🚗	☎	SOS	130	90	50	%‰
A	Österreich	A, C, E	0043	112	130	100	50	0,5 ‰
AL	Shqipëria	B, C, D	00355	b 113; 129	-	80	40	0,0 ‰
AND	Andorra, Andorre	A, C, D	00376	112	-	70-90	50	0,5 ‰
B	België, Belgique	A, C, E	0032	112	120	90-120	50	0,5 ‰
BG	Bălgarija	A, C, D	00359	146; 150	120	90	50	0,5 ‰
BIH	Bosna i Hercegovina	A, C, D	00387	92; 94	120	80	60	0,5 ‰
BY	Belarus'	B, C, D	00375	02; 03	110	90	60	0,0 ‰
CH	Schweiz, Suisse, Svizzera	A, C, E	0041	117; 140	120	80	50	0,5 ‰
CZ	Česká Republika	A, C, E	00420	112	130	90	50	0,0 ‰
CY	Kýpros, Kıbrıs	a A, C, E/D	00357	112	100	80	50	0,9 ‰
D	Deutschland	A, C, E	0049	112	130	100	50	0,5 ‰
DK	Danmark	A, C, E	0045	112	110	80	50	0,5 ‰
E	España	A, C, E	0034	112	120	90-100	50	0,3-0,5 ‰
EST	Eesti	A/B, C, D	00372	112	-	90-100	50	0,0 ‰
F	France	A, C, E	0033	112	130	90-110	50	0,5 ‰
FIN	Suomi, Finland	A, C, E	00358	112	120	80-100	50	0,5 ‰
FL	Fürstentum Liechtenstein	A, C, E	00423	112	-	80	50	0,8 ‰
GB	Great Britain and N. Ireland	A, C, E	0044	999 112 (70 mph)	96 (60 mph)	48 (30 mph)	0,8 ‰
GR	Hellas	A, C, E	0030	166; 171	120	90-110	50	0,5 ‰
H	Magyarország	A, C, E	0036	112	130	90-110	50	0,8 ‰
HR	Hrvatska	A, C, E	00385	987	130	80-100	50	0,0 ‰
I	Italia	A, C, E	0039	112	130	90-110	50	0,5 ‰
IRL	Ireland	A, C, E	00353	112 112 (70 mph)	96 (60 mph)	48 (30 mph)	0,8 ‰
IS	Ísland	A, C, E	00354	112	-	80-90	50	0,5 ‰
L	Lëtzebuerg, Luxembourg	A, C, E	00352	112; 26000	130	90	50	0,8 ‰
LT	Lietuva	A, C, D	00370	112	-	90-110	50	0,5 ‰
LV	Latvija	A/B, C, D	00371	112	-	90-100	50	0,4 ‰
M	Malta	A, C, D	00356	112	-	80	50	0,0 ‰
MC	Principauté de Monaco	A, C, E	00377	112	-	50	50	0,5 ‰
MD	Moldova	B, C, D	00373	902; 903	-	90	60	0,0 ‰
MK	Makedonija	A, C, D	00389	196	120	80-100	50-60	0,5 ‰
N	Norge	A, C, E	0047	112; 113	90-100	80	50	0,2 ‰
NL	Nederland	A, C, E	0031	112	120	80-100	50	0,5 ‰
P	Portugal	A, C, E	00351	112	120	90-100	50	0,5 ‰
PL	Polska	A, C, D	0048	112	130	80-90	60	0,2 ‰
RO	România	A/B, C, D	0040	112; 961	120	90	50	0,0 ‰
RUS	Rossija	B, C, E	007	02; 03	110	90	60	0,0 ‰
S	Sverige	A, C, E	0046	112	110	70	50	0,2 ‰
SCG	Srbija i Crna Gora	A, C, D	00381	92; 94	120	80-100	60	0,5 ‰
SK	Slovensko	A, C, E	00421	158; 155	130	90	60	0,0 ‰
SLO	Slovenija	A, C, E	00386	112	130	90-100	50	0,5 ‰
TR	Türkiye Cumhuriyeti	A, C, D	0090	112	130	90	50	0,5 ‰
UA	Ukraïna	B, C, D	00380	02; 03	130	90-110	60	0,0 ‰

UE
UE → 2007

a Green cards are not accepted in Northern Cyprus

b Tiranë

Key to table
Legenda
Leyenda
Légende
Zeichenerklärung

		€	
-	+1	Euro (€)	(43) 84 0999918
-	+1	Lek (ALL)	(355) 4 258323
-	+1	Euro (€)	(376) 827117
-	+1	Euro (€)	(32) 2 5138940
-	+2	Lev (BGN)	(359) 2 9874059
-	+1	Konvertabilna Marka (BAM)	(387) 33 532606
-	+2	Belarus Rouble (BYR)	(375) 17 2269840
-	+1	Schweizer Franken (CHF)	00800 10020030
ᶜ✓	+1	Koruna Česká (CZK)	(420) 2 21580111
-	+2	Cyprus Pound (CYP)	(357)22 313233
-	+1	Euro (€)	01805671920
✓	+1	Danske Krone (DKK)	(45) 32 889900
-	+1	Euro (€)	(34) 913 433 500
✓	+2	Kroon (EEK)	(372) 645 7777
✓	+1	Euro (€)	(33) 8 92683112
✓	+2	Euro (€)	(358) 9 4176911
-	+1	Schweizer Franken (CHF)	(423) 2396300
-	0	Pound Sterling (GBP)	(44) 020 8846 9000
-	+2	Euro (€)	(30) 210 3271300
✓	+1	Forint (HUF)	(36) 1 488 8700
-	+1	Kuna (HRK)	(385) 1 4556455
✓	+1	Euro (€)	(39) 06 49711
-	0	Euro (€)	(353) 1 6024000
✓	0	Íslensk Króna (ISK)	(354) 5623045
-	+1	Euro (€)	(352) 42 828210
ᶜ✓	+2	Litas (LTL)	(370) 2 622610
✓	+2	Lats (LVL)	(371) 7229945
-	+1	Maltese Lira (MTL)	(356) 22915000
-	+1	Euro (€)	(377) 92166166
-	+2	Leu (MDL)	(373) 2 210774
✓	+1	Denar (MKD)	(389) 2 118498
✓	+1	Norsk Krone (NOK)	(47) 24144600
-	+1	Euro (€)	(31) 20 2018800
-	0	Euro (€)	(351) 21 3466307
ᶜ✓	+1	Zloty (PLN)	(48) 22 8499361
-	+2	Leu (ROL)	(40) 1 3145160
✓	ᵈ+3	Russian Rouble (RUB)	(7) 95 7530003
✓	+1	Svensk Krona (SEK)	(46) 8 6679930
-	+1	Srpski Dinar (CSD)	(381) 11 3612754
✓	+1	Slovenská Koruna (SKK)	(421) 48 4136146
-	+2	Tolar (SIT)	(386) 1 3061215
-	+2	Türk Lirası (TRL)	(90) 212 2495153
-	+1	Hrivna (UAH)	(380) 44 2124215

ᶜ winter   ᵈ Moskva

Required driver's papers
Documenti di guida richiesti
Documentos requeridos para conducir
Papiers de conduire requis
Erforderliche Fahrzeugpapiere

A   Driver's licence
Patente di guida
Carné de conducir
Permis de conduire
Führerschein

B   International driver's licence
Patente di guida internazionale
Carné de conducir internacional
Permis international de conduire
Internationaler Führerschein

C   Log-book
Carta di circolazione
Carné de circulación
Permis de circulation
Kraftfahrzeugschein

D   Green card
Carta verde
Carta verde
Carte verte
Grüne Versicherungskarte

E   Special insurance
Assicurazione speciale
Seguro especial
Assurance spéciale
Spezialversicherung

International code
Prefisso internazionale
Prefijo telefónico internacional
Indicatif international
Internationale Vorwahl

Emergency numbers
Numeri d'emergenza
Números de emergencia
Numéros d'urgence
Notrufnummern

Tourist offices
Uffici turistici
Oficinas de turismo
Bureaux de tourisme
Touristenämter

 (km/h)

Speed limit on motorway
Limite di velocità in autostrada
Límite de velocidad en autopista
Limite de vitesse sur l'autoroute
Höchstgeschwindigkeit auf der Autobahn

 (km/h)

Speed limit outside the towns
Limite di velocità su strade extraurbane
Límite de velocidad en carreteras extraurbanas
Limite de vitesse sur les routes extra-urbaines
Höchstgeschwindigkeit außerhalb der Städte

 (km/h)

Speed limit in towns
Limite di velocità nei centri abitati
Límite de velocidad en ciudades
Limite de vitesse dans les villes
Höchstgeschwindigkeit innerhalb der Städte

Maximum permitted alcohol level
Tasso alcolemico massimo tollerato
Límite alcohólico màximo consentido
Taux d'alcoolémie maximum admis
Höchsterlaubte Blutalkoholgehalt

Lights on during the day
Obbligo luci accese di giorno
Encender los faros durante el dia
Feux allumés obligatoires de jour
Licht-Pflicht am Tag

Time zone from Greenwich
Fuso orario da Greenwich
Huso horario de Greenwich
Fuseaux horaires de Greenwich
Zeitzone gegenüber Greenwich

Local currency
Valuta locale
Divisa local
Devise locale
Lokalwährung

note: the table is indicative; it is advisable to check the information before leaving.
nota: la tabella è indicativa; si consiglia di verificare le informazioni prima della partenza.
nota: el prospecto es indicativo; se aconseja verificar las informaciones antes de partir.
nota: le tableau est indicatif; il est conseillé de vérifier les renseignements avant de partir.
Notiz: die Informationen sind als Hinweis gedacht; es empfiehlt sich,
       die Auskünfte vor der Abfahrt zu überprüfen.

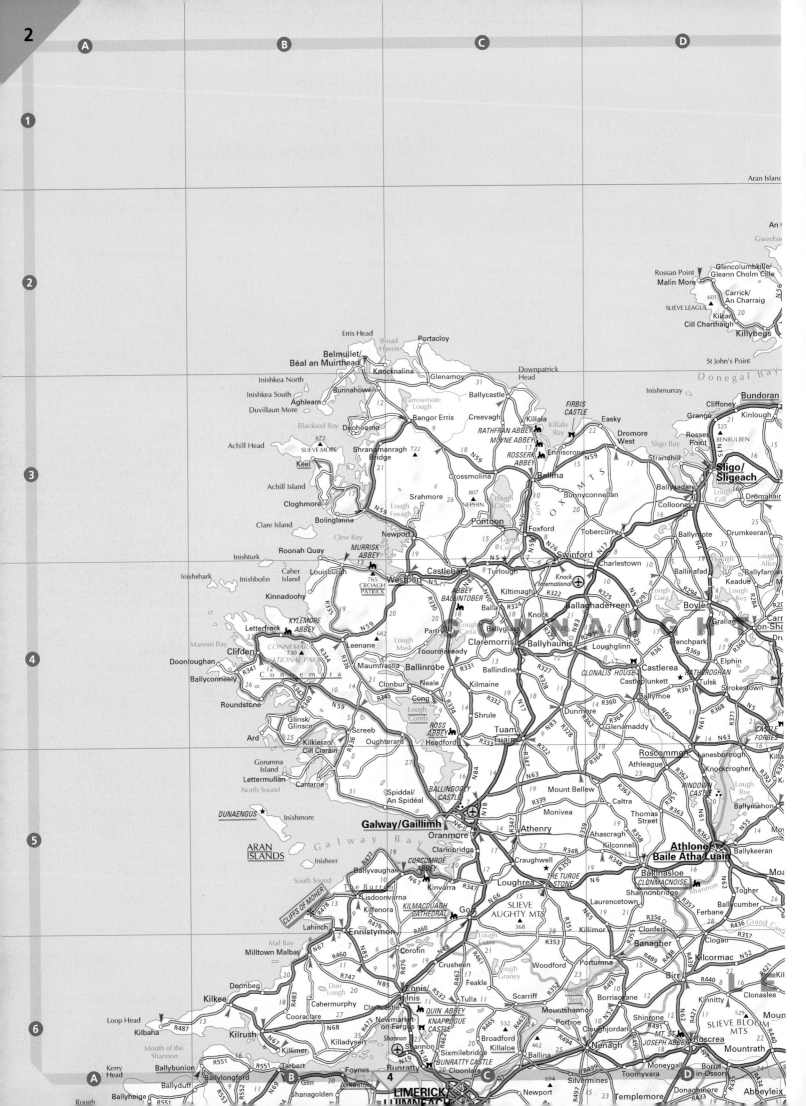

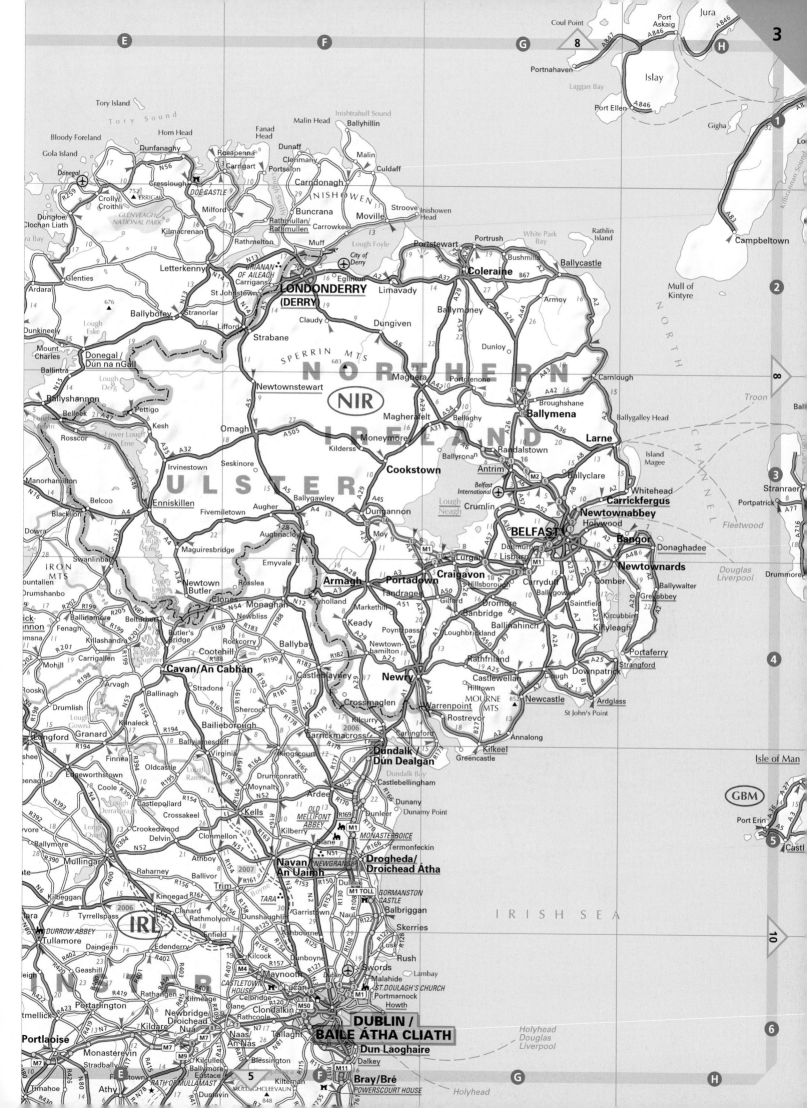

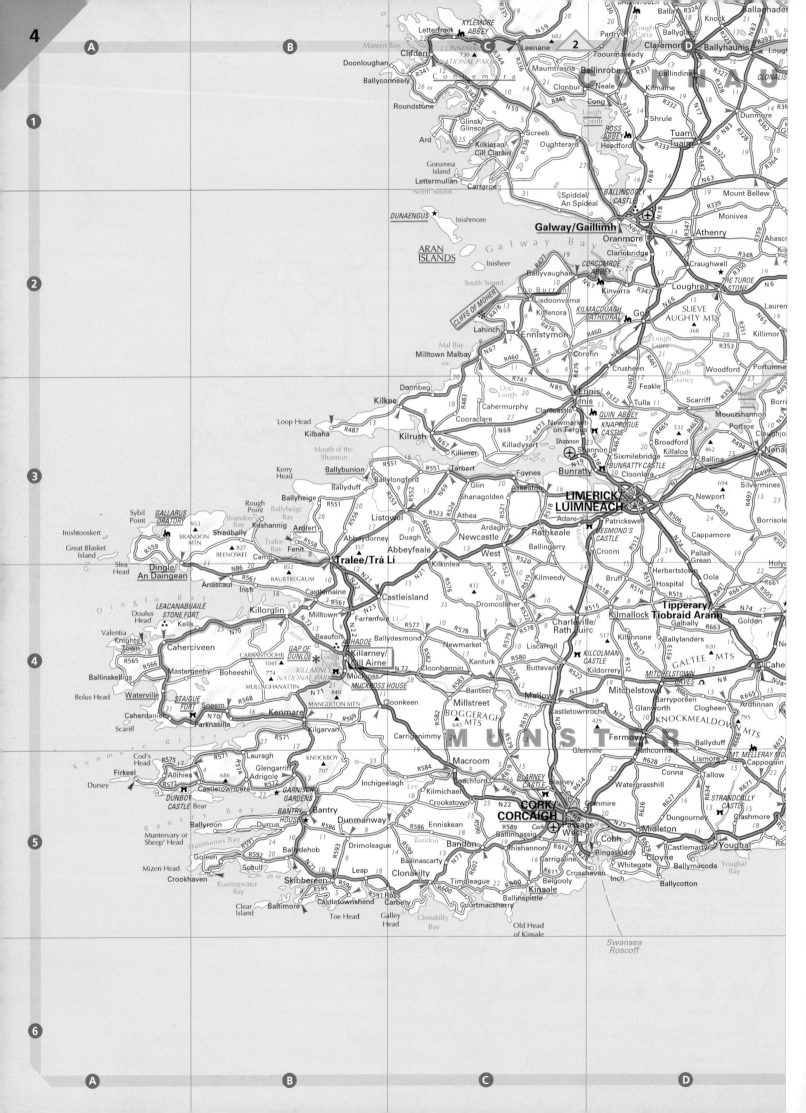

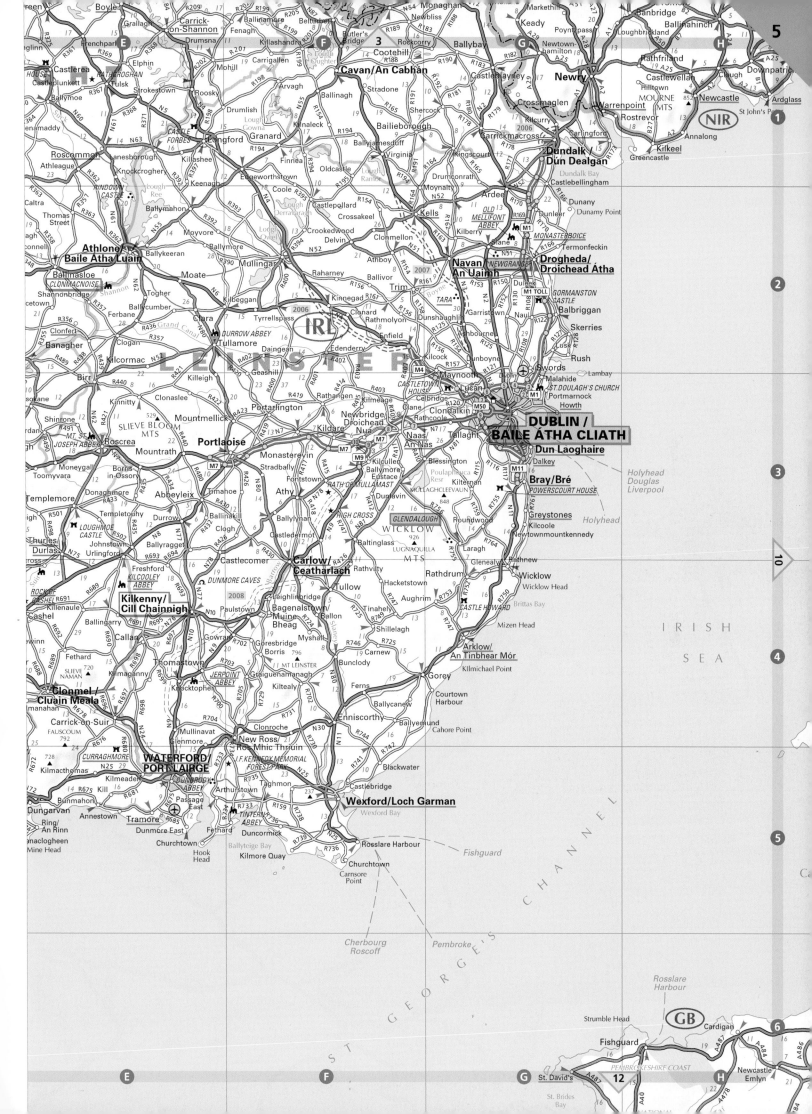

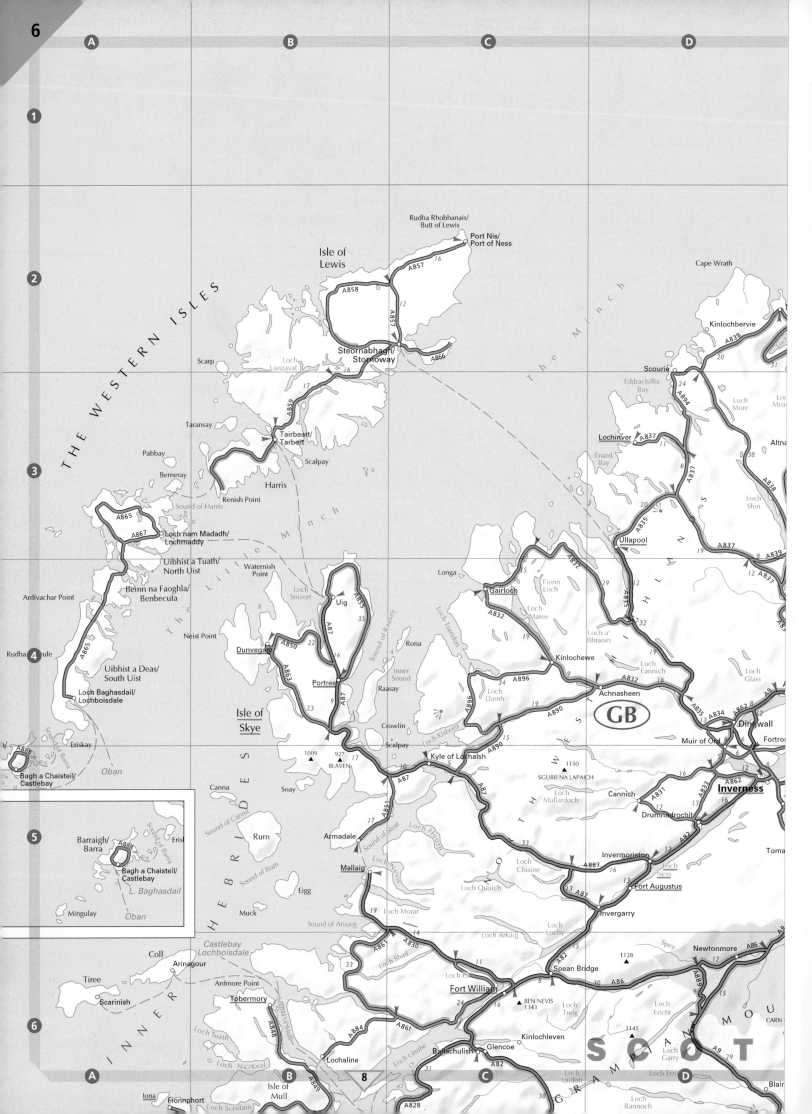

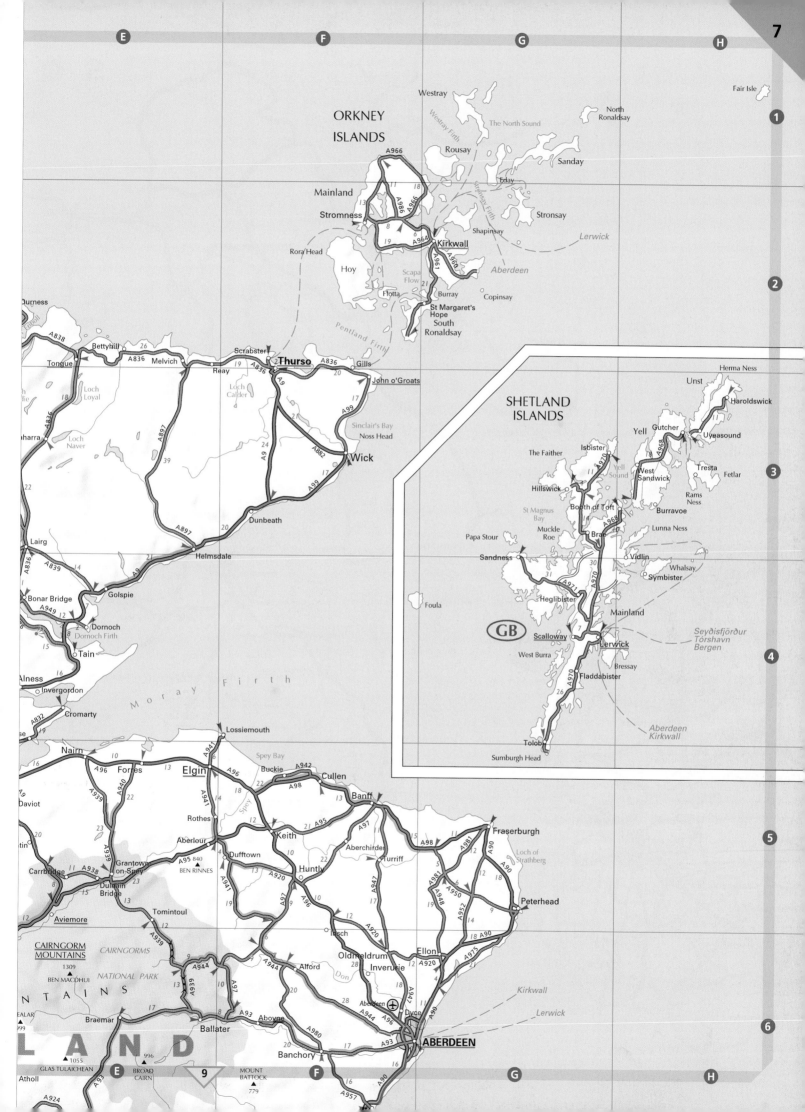

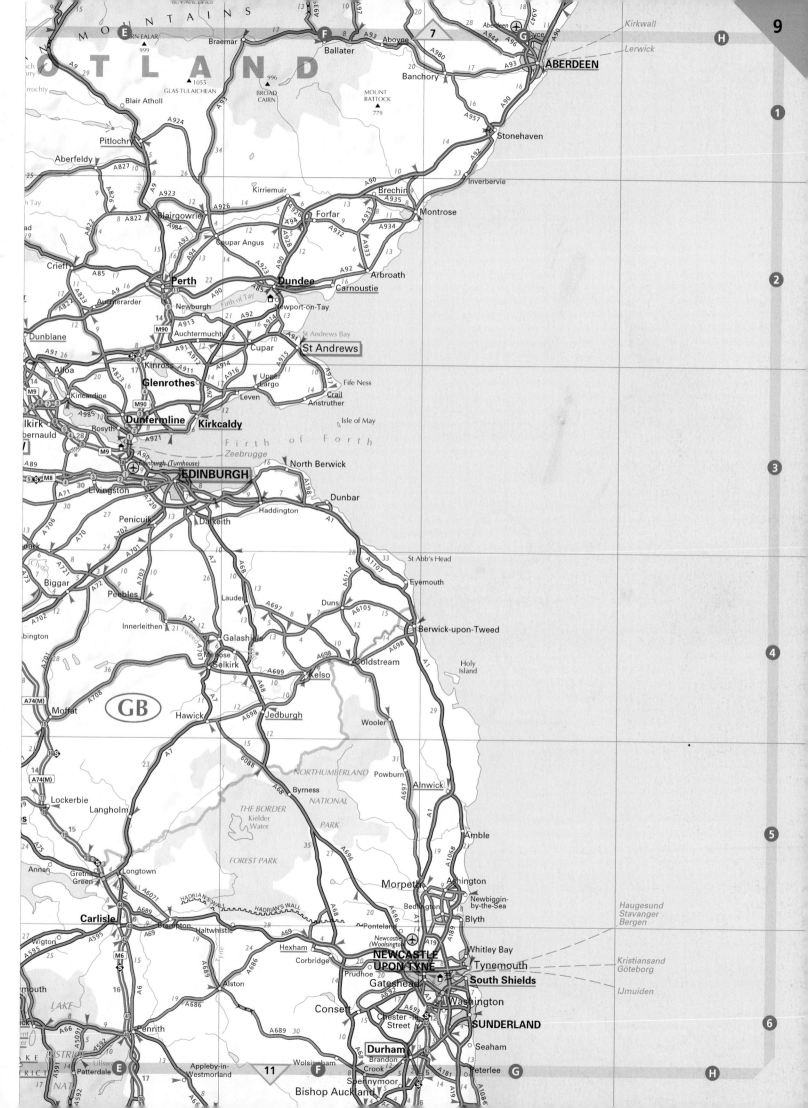

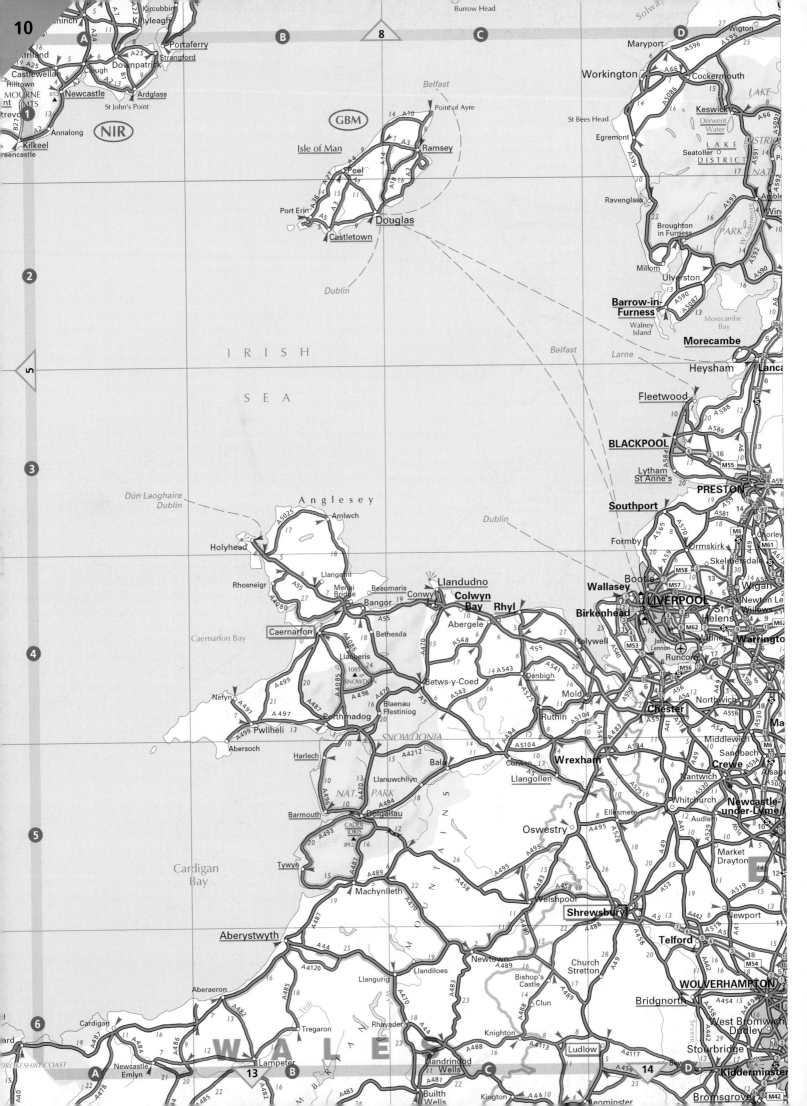

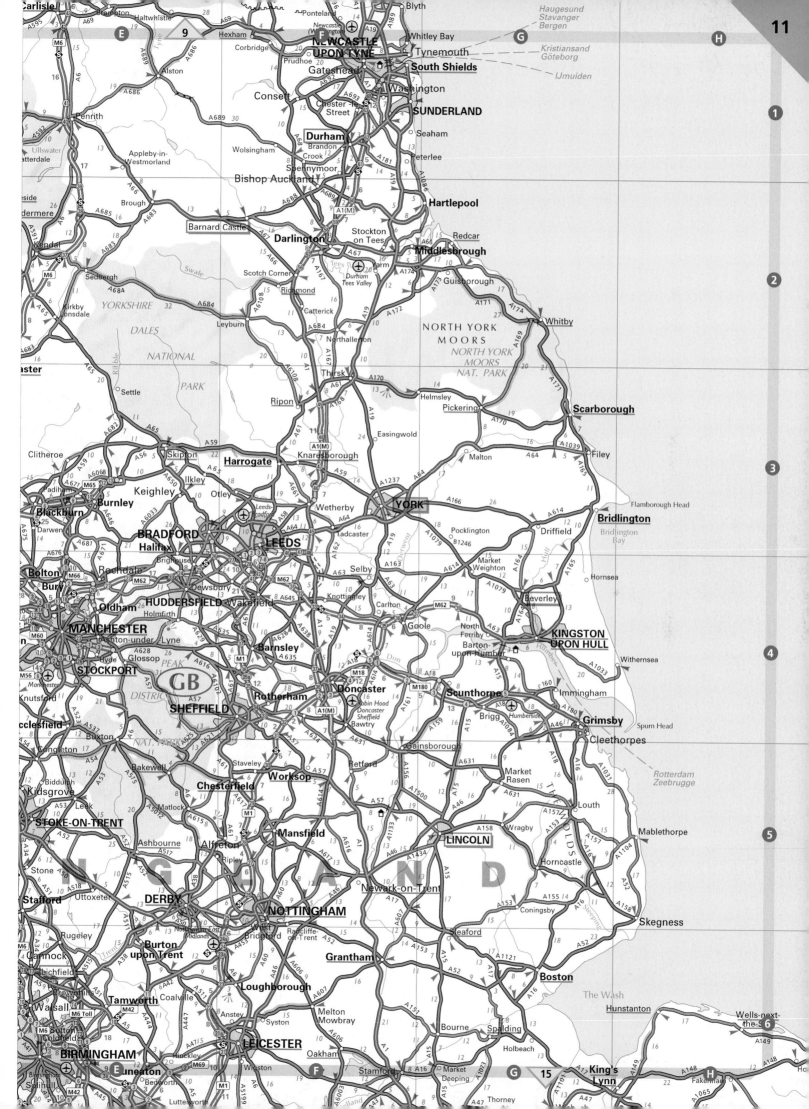

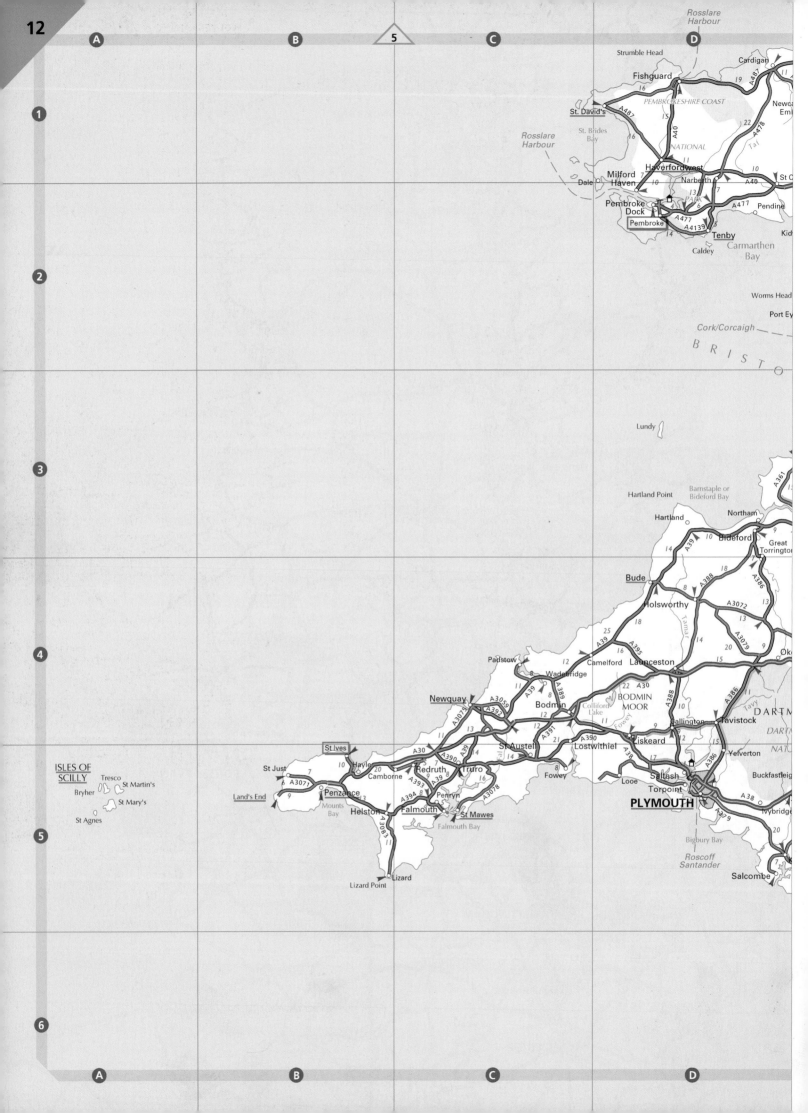

A   B   5   C   D

1

2

3

4

5

6

A   B   C   D

Rosslare
Harbour

Strumble Head
Cardigan
Fishguard
16
A487
19
A487
11
PEMBROKESHIRE COAST
St. David's
15
A40
Newca
Emb
St. Brides
Bay
22
A478
NATIONAL
Tai
Rosslare
Harbour
16
11
Haverfordwest
10
Dale
Milford
Haven
10
Narberth
A40
St C
Pembroke
Dock
13
7
A477
Pendine
Pembroke
6
A477
Kid
A4139
14
A477
Tenby
Caldey
Carmarthen
Bay
Worms Head
Port Ey
Cork/Corcaigh
B R I S T O

Lundy

Hartland Point
Barnstaple or
Bideford Bay
A361
Hartland
Northam
A39
10
Bideford
14
Great
Torrington
Bude
A388
18
7
A386
Holsworthy
8
A3072
13
25
18
Yamal
13
A39
A395
14
20
A3079
9
Oke
Padstow
12
Camelford
Launceston
16
15
11
A39
A389
22
A30
BODMIN
MOOR
A388
11
Newquay
A3059
Bodmin
Colliford
Lake
10
Tavy
A3075
A392
13
12
A391
11
Fowey
Callington
Tavistock
DART
St Ives
A30
13
12
21
A390
Liskeard
12
15
DARTM
Hayle
20
Redruth
Truro
14
St Austell
A391
A38
17
Yelverton
NAT
St Just
7
10
A30
A390
A39
8
Fowey
Looe
Saltash
Buckfastleig
A3071
Camborne
A393
A39
16
Torpoint
A38
Land's End
9
Penzance
A394
8
Penryn
A3078
PLYMOUTH
Ivybridge
6
13
St Mawes
A379
Mounts
Bay
Helston
Falmouth
Falmouth Bay
Bigbury Bay
A379
20
ISLES OF
SCILLY
A3083
Roscoff
Santander
Tresco   St Martin's
Bryher
11
7
St Mary's
St Agnes
Salcombe
Lizard
Lizard Point

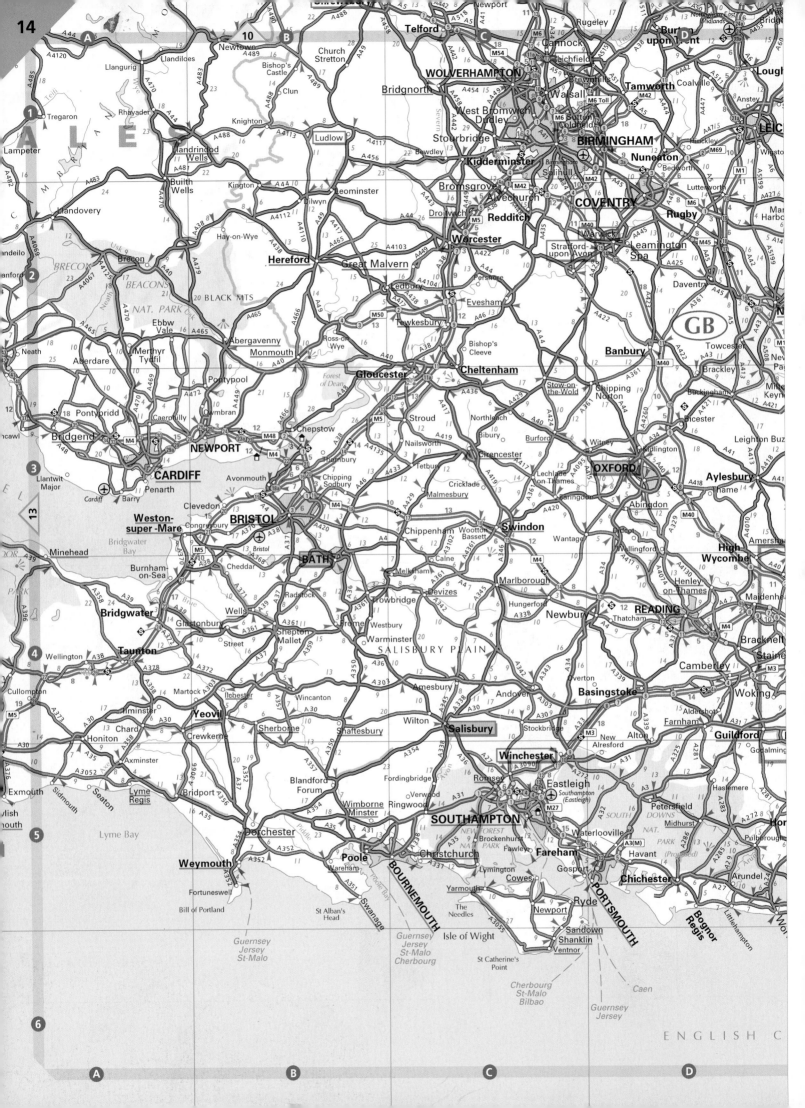

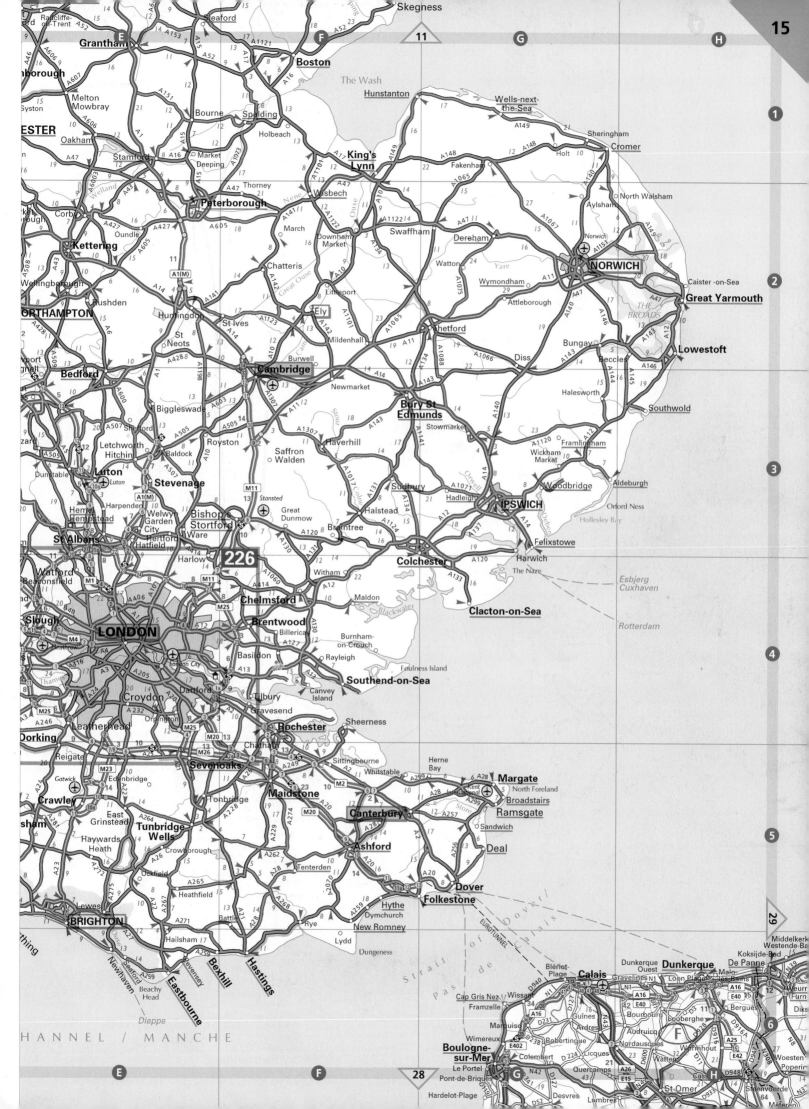

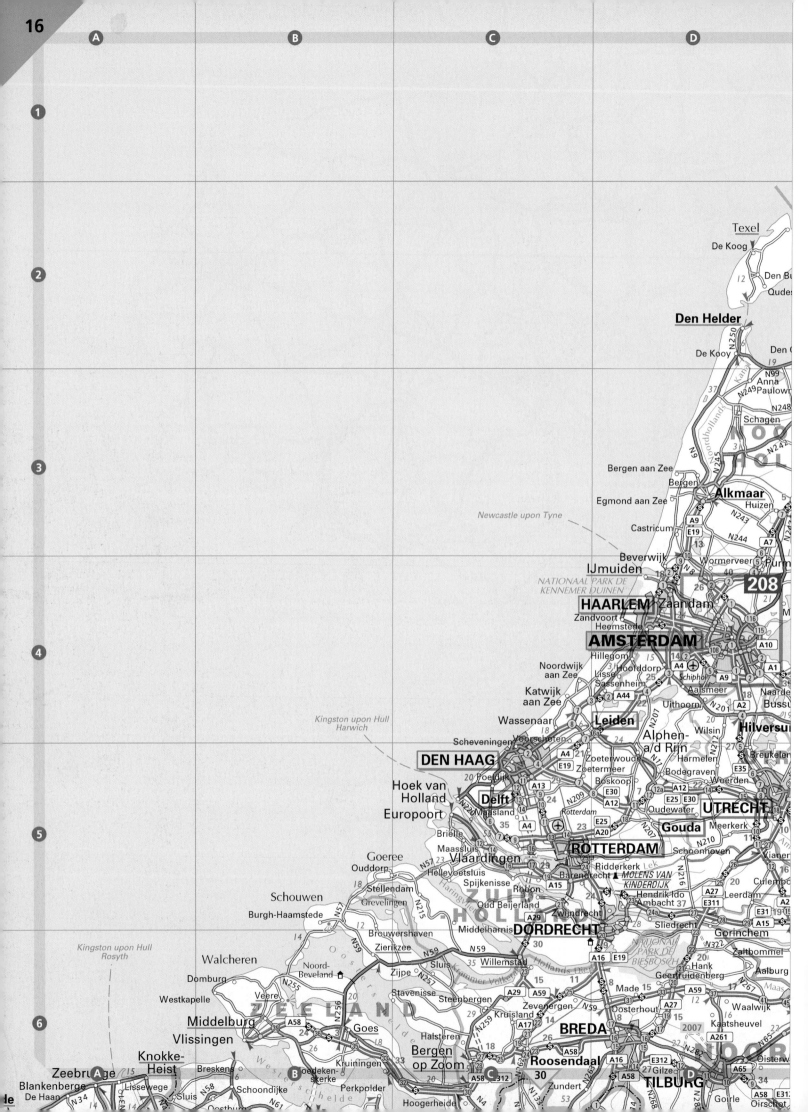

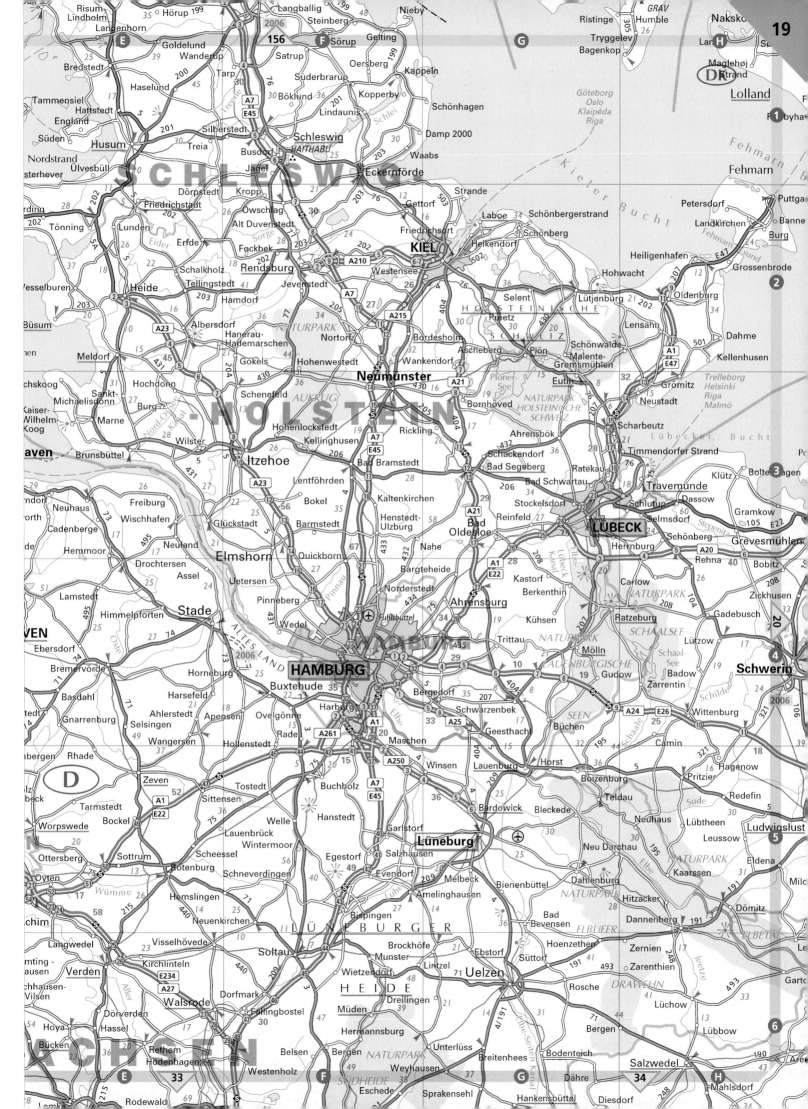

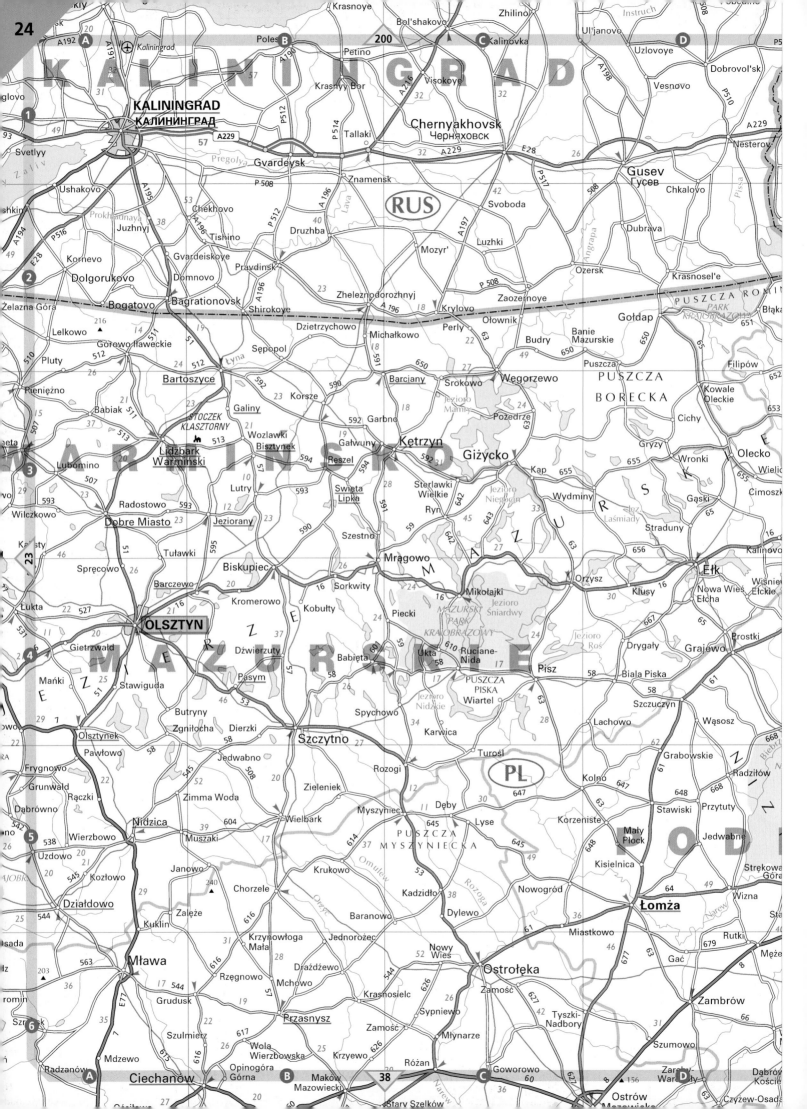

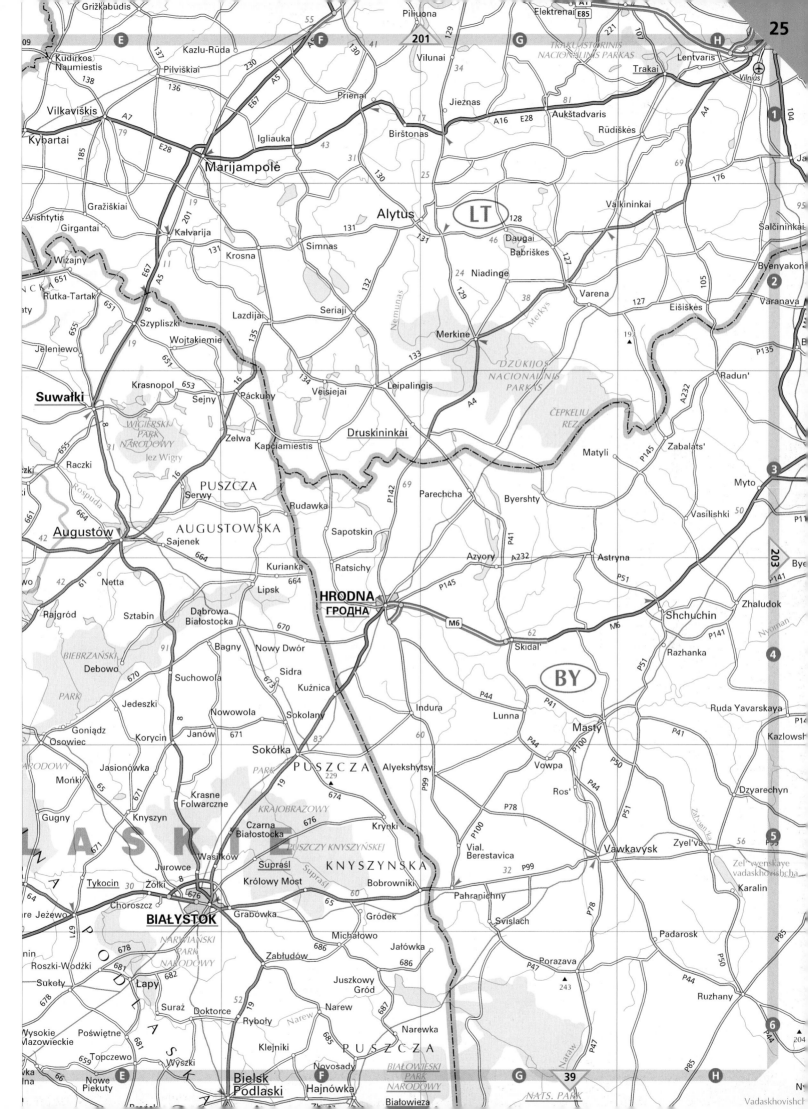

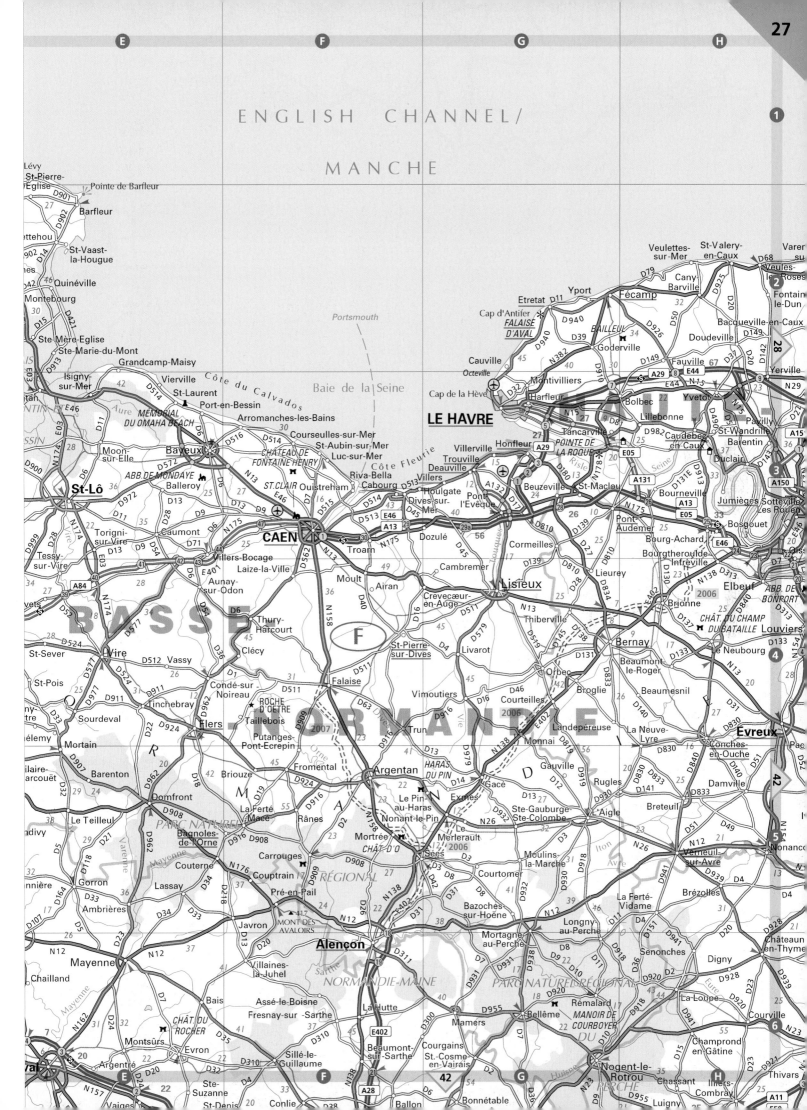

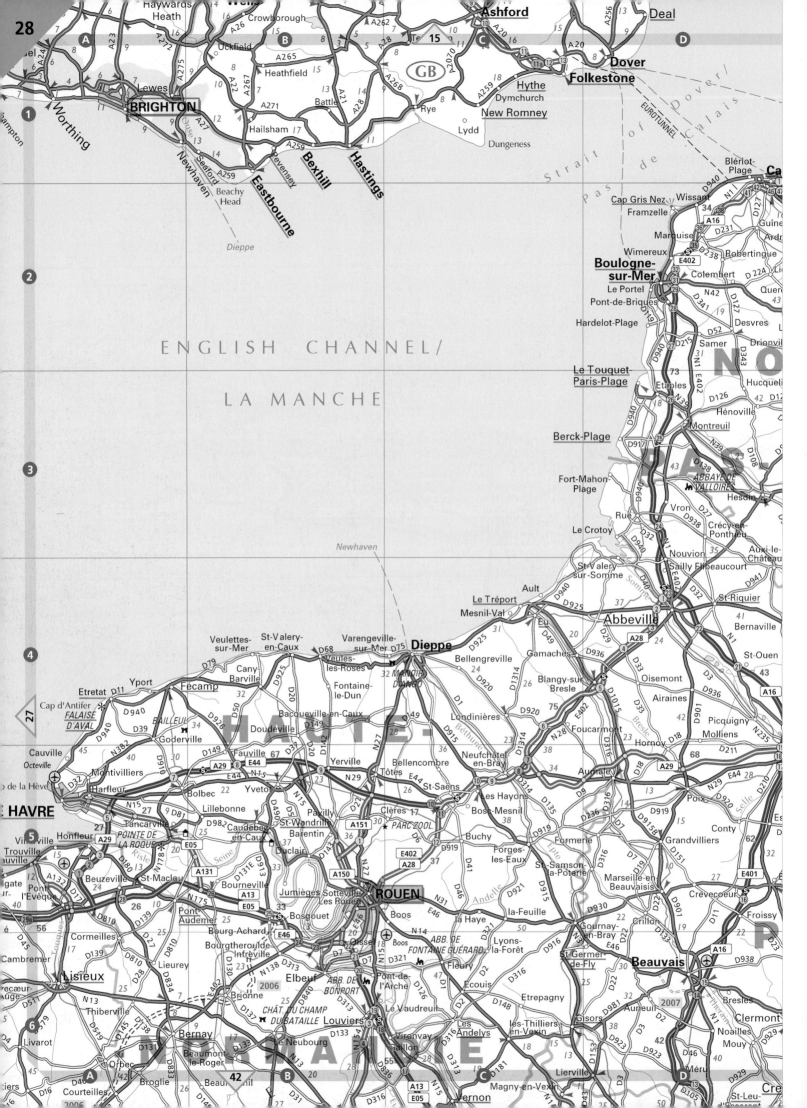

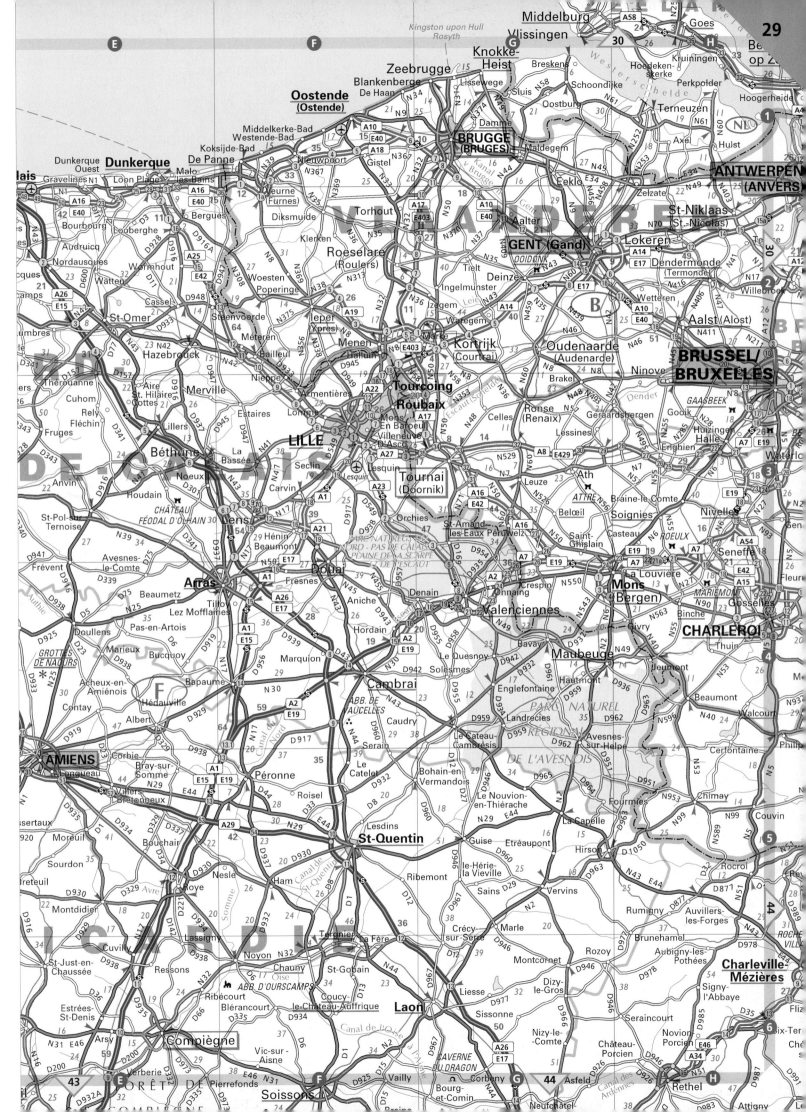

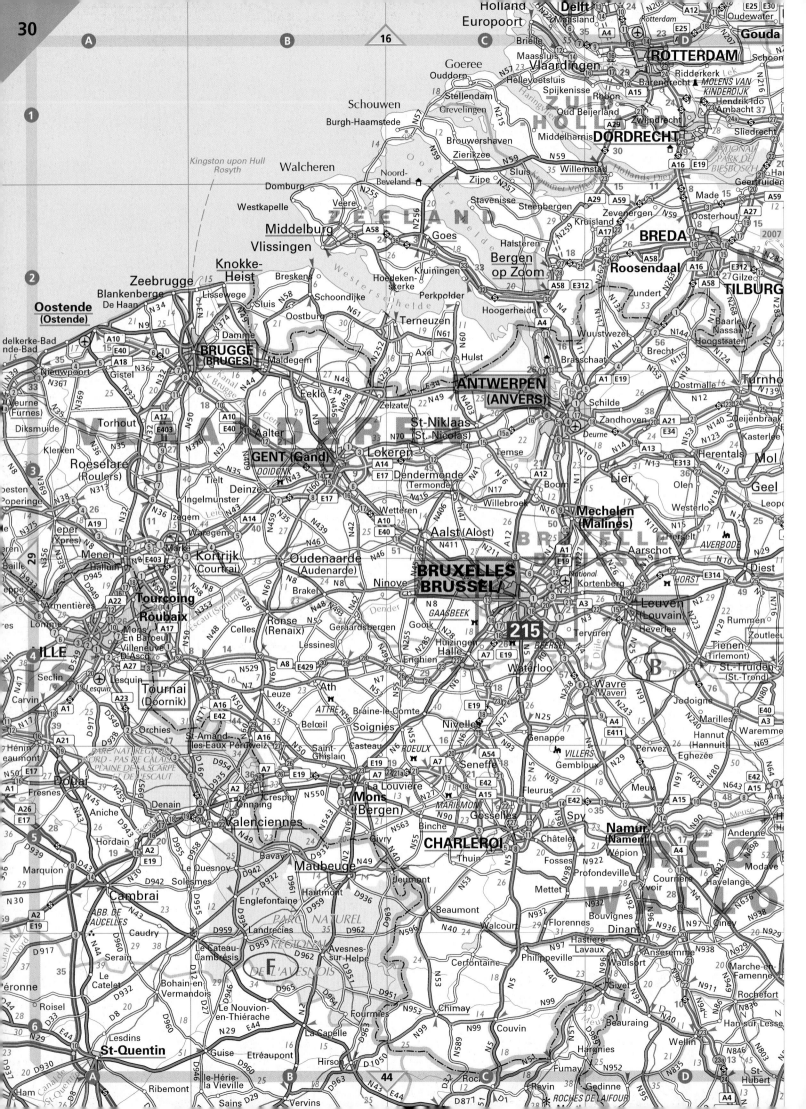

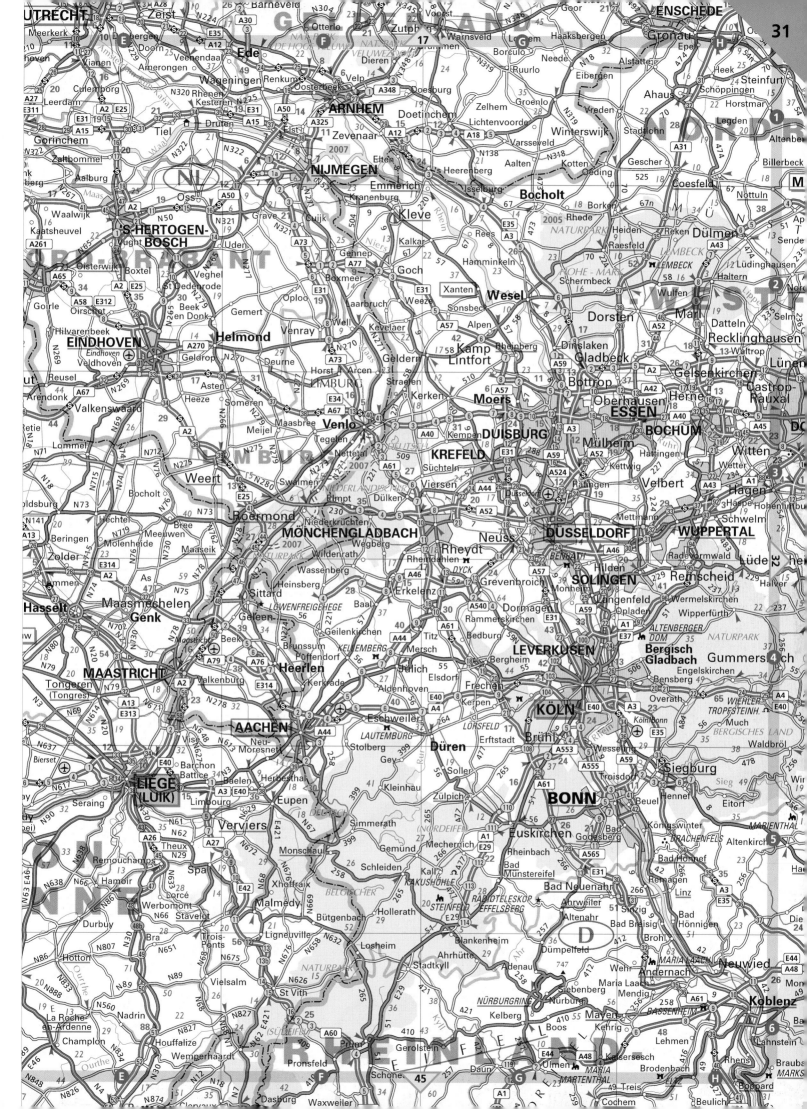

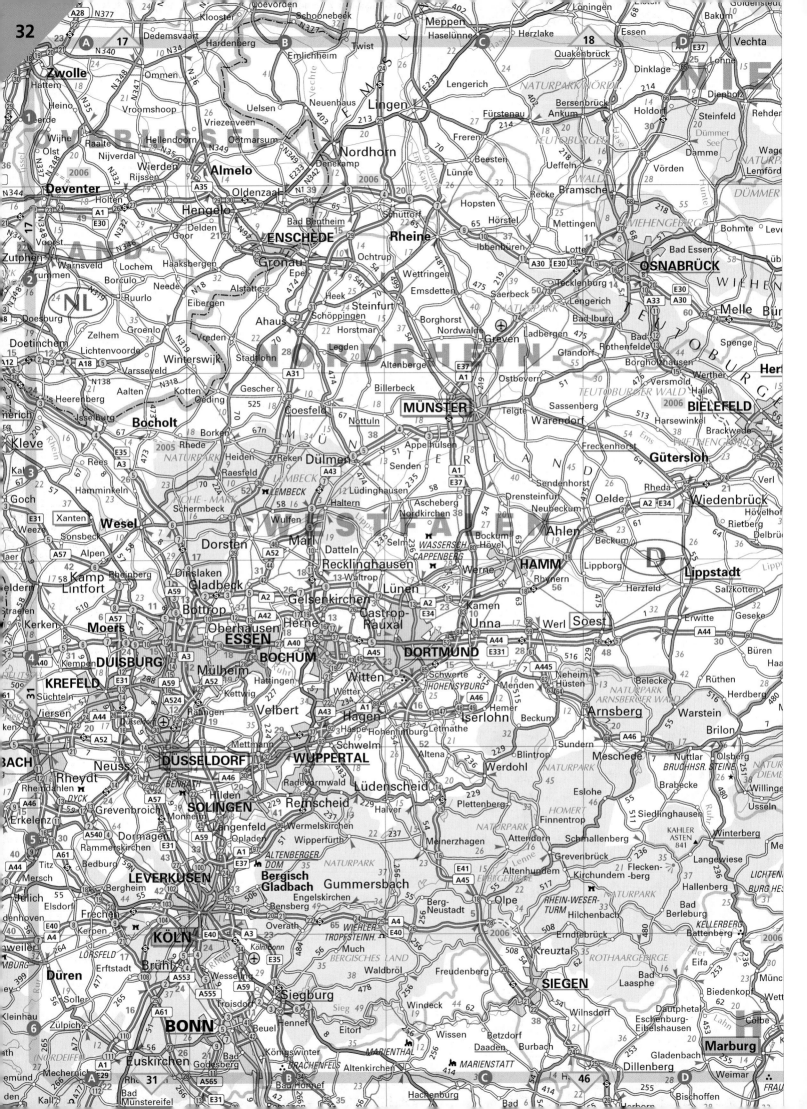

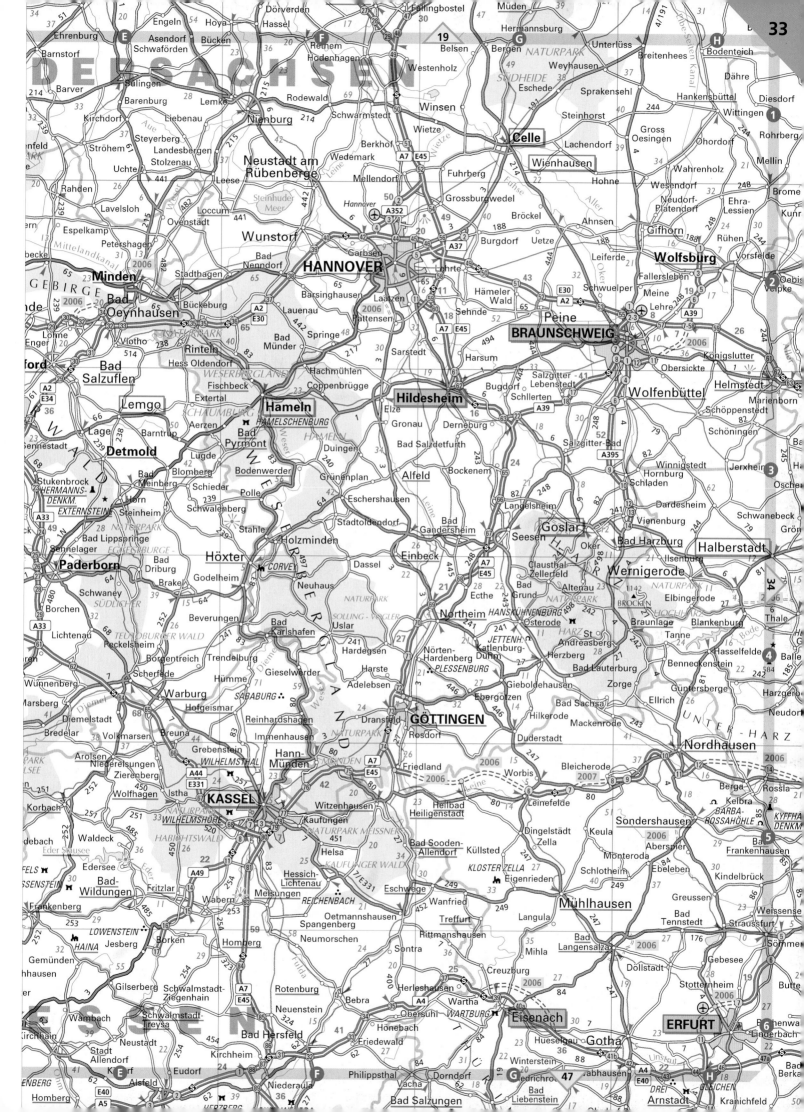

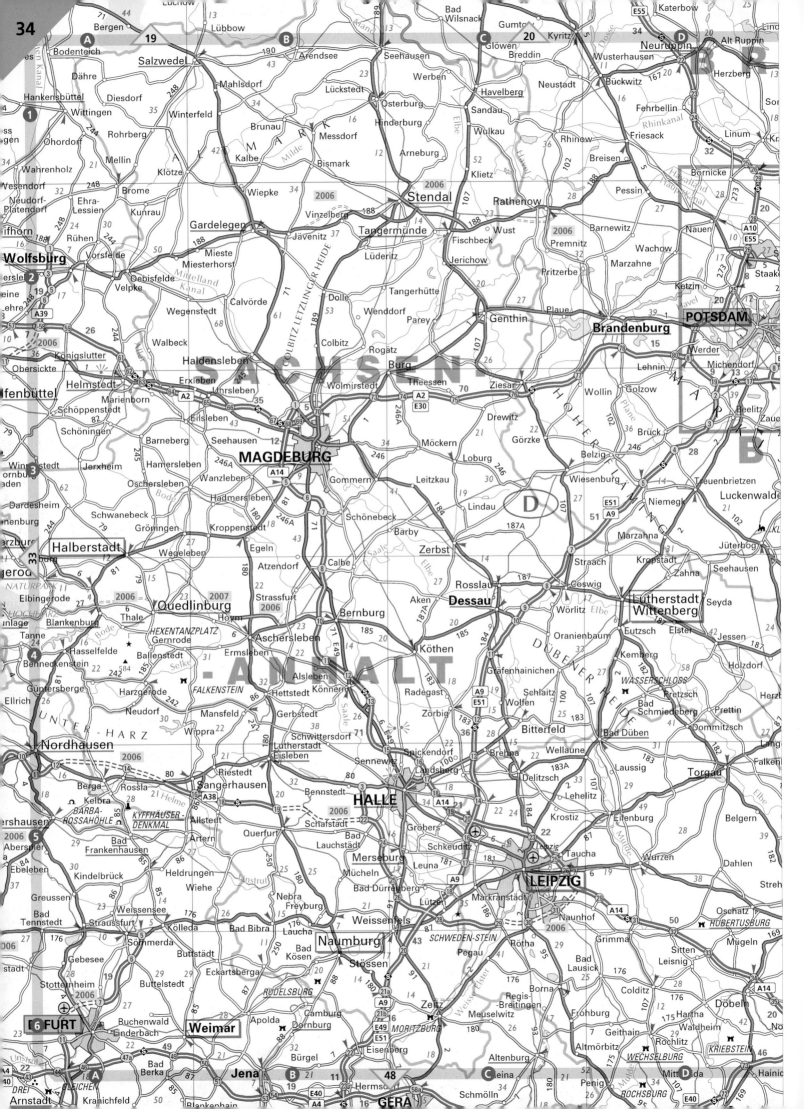

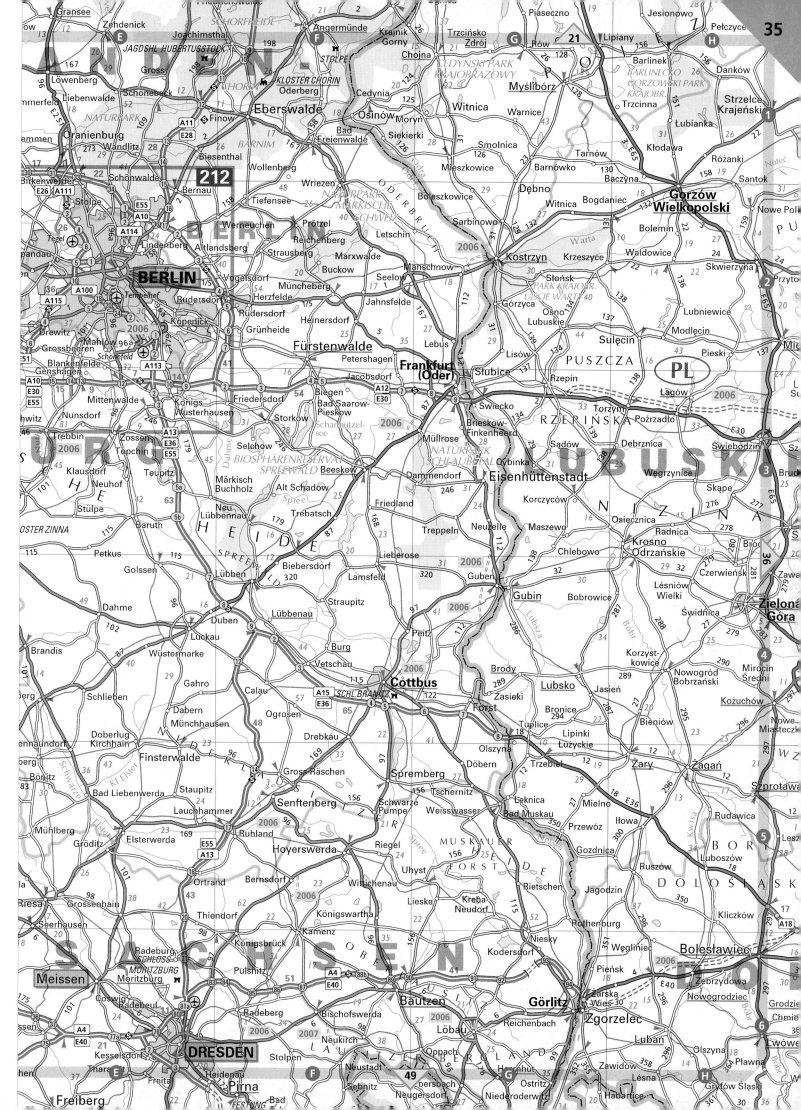

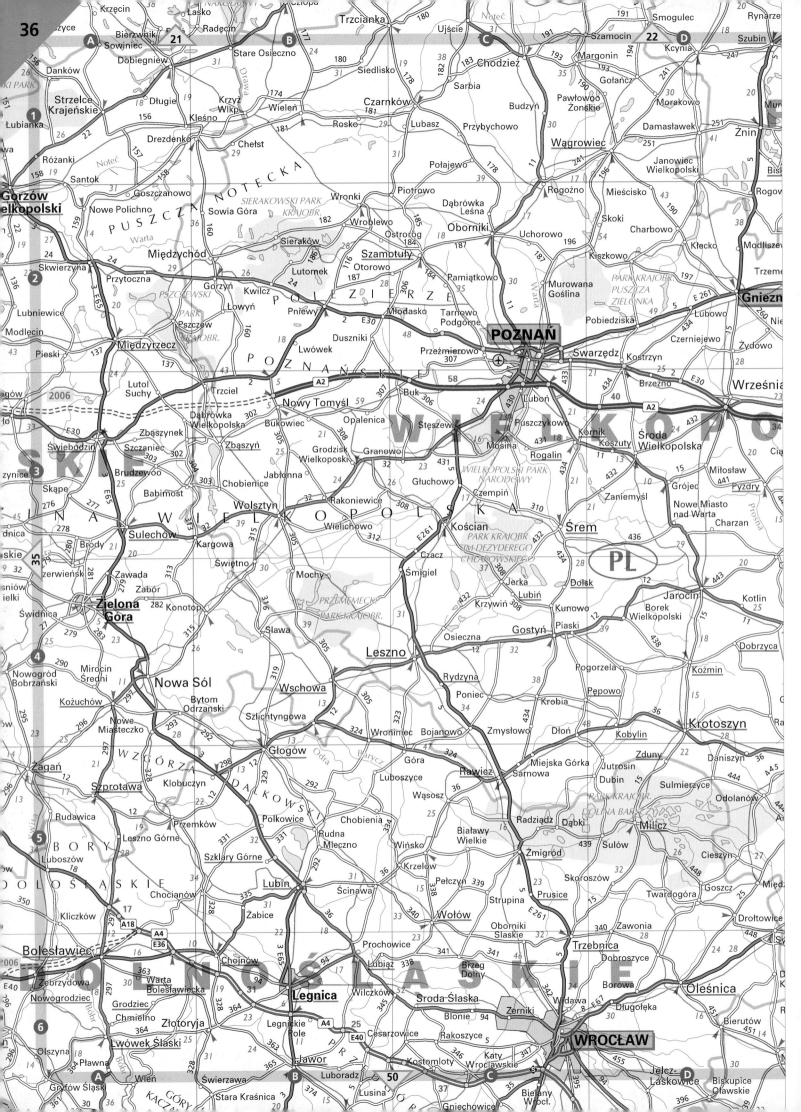

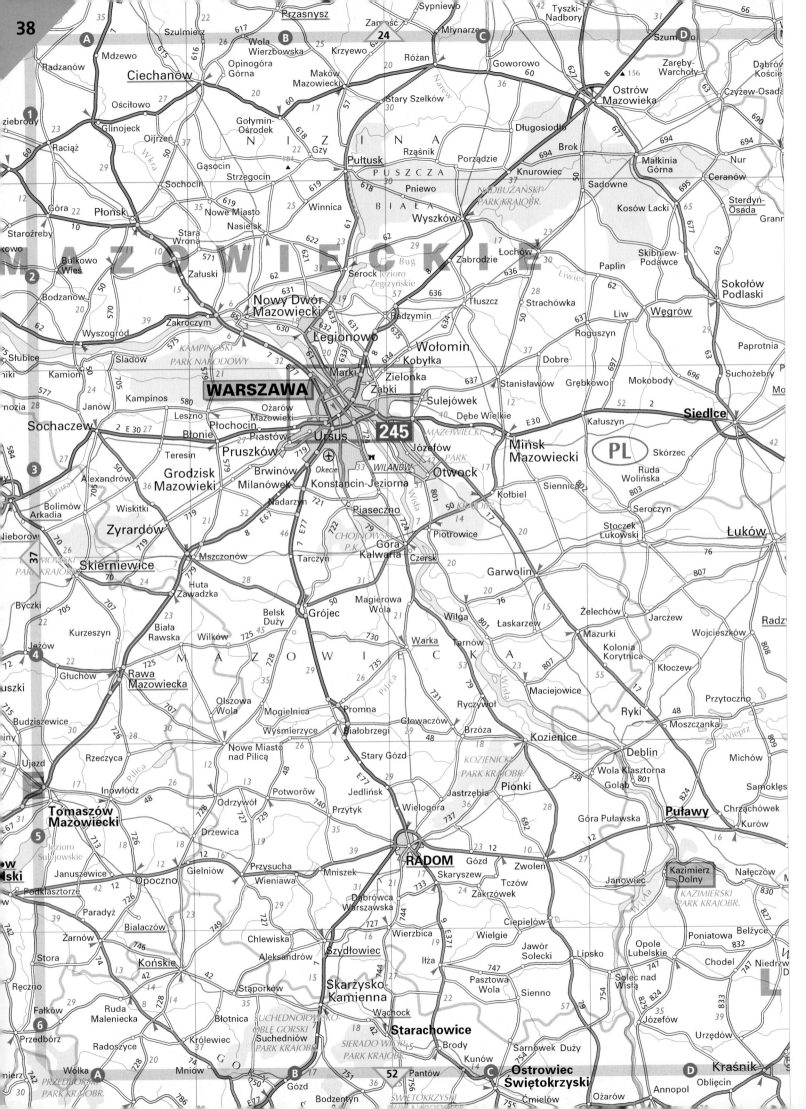

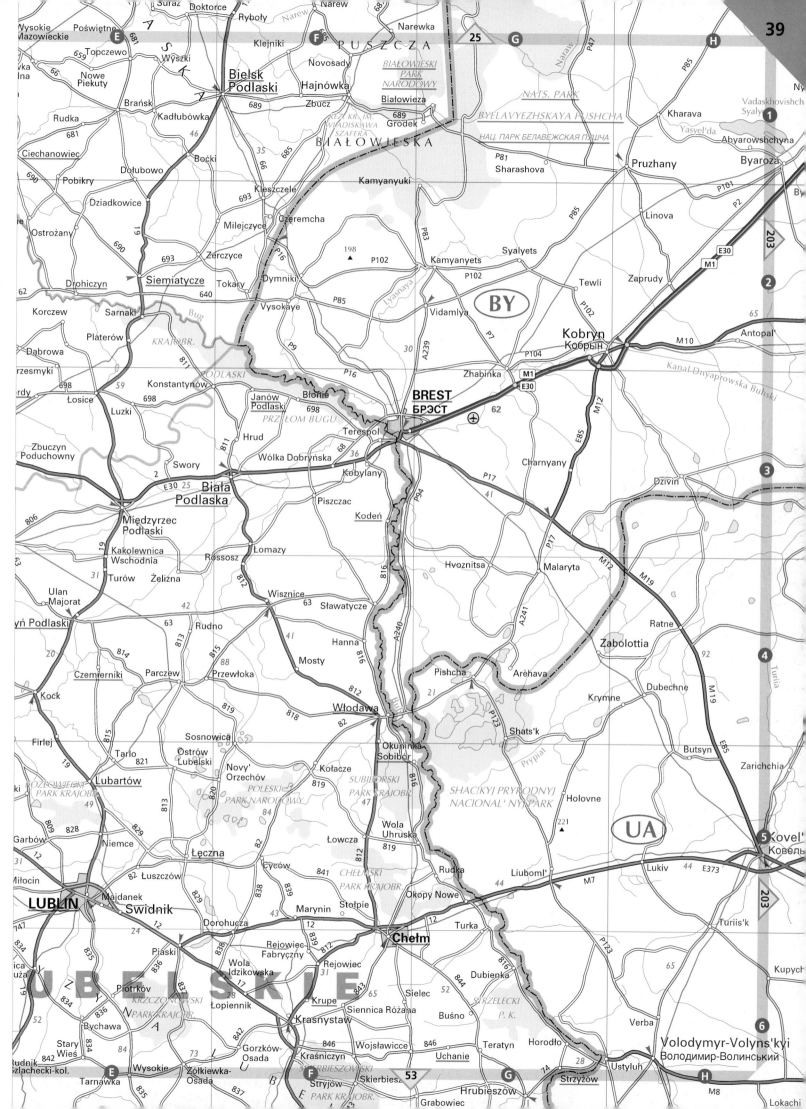

A B C D

Cork
Rosslare Harbour
Plymouth

1

Lampaul
Ile d'Ouessant

Ile de Molène

Ile de Beniguet

Le Conquet

POINTE DE
ST-MATHIEU

L'Aber-Wrac'h
Ploudalmézeau
Lampaul-Plouarzel
St-Renan

Guissény
Lannilis
le Folgoët
Lesneven
Plabennec
Guipavas

BREST

Brignogan Plage
Plouescat
St-Pol-de-Léon
Carantec

Ile de Batz
Roscoff

Primel-Trégastel
Plougasnou
Lanmeur
Locquirec
St-Michel-en-Grève
Plestin-les-Grèves

Trégastel
Trébeurden

Ploumanac'h
Perros-Guirec

Tréguier
Lézardrieux

CHÂTEAU DE KERJEAN
St-Thégonnec
Landivisiau
Landerneau
Guimiliau

Morlaix
Plouigneau
Plouaret

ROCHE DE KERGU
Bégard
Pontrieux

Lannion

Lanvollon

CHÂTEAU DE TONQUÉDEC

Plougastel-Daoulas
Daoulas

PARC NATUREL RÉGIONAL
D'ARMORIQUE

Pointe de Penhir
Camaret-sur-Mer
Crozon
Morgat
Landévennec

Sizun
Le Faou

MONTS D'ARRÉE
ROC TRÉVEZEL
MONTAGNE ST-MICHEL

Berrien
Huelgoat
Loqueffret

Scrignac
Callac
Bourbriac

Belle-Isle-en-Terre
Guingamp

St-B

2

PARC NATUREL RÉGIONAL D'ARMORIQUE

Ile de Sein
Pointe du Van
Pointe du Raz

Pentrez-Plage
MENEZ HOM
Ste-Anne-la-Palud
Châteaulin
Pleyben
Loqueffret

Carhaix-Plouguer

Kerien
St-Nicolas-du-Pélem

Cohiniac

Quintin

Tréboul
Douarnenez
Locronan

ROCHE DU FEU
Briec

Châteauneuf-du-Faou

MONTAGNES NOIRES

Rostrenen

BRE

Corlay

Gouarec

Uzel

Loudéac

3

Audierne
Pont-Croix
Landudec
Plozévet
Baie d'Audierne

CHAPELLE DE LANGUIDOU

Plonéour Lanvern
Pont-l'Abbé
St-Guénolé

POINTE DE PENMARCH
Guilvinec

Quimper
VIRE COURT
N.D. DE KERDEVOT
Fouesnant
Bénodet
Loctudy
Beg-Meil

Coray
Scaër
Rosporden
Bannalec
Concarneau

Gourin
Le Faouët
STE-BARBE
ST-FIACRE
Kernascléden
Guémené-sur-Scorff

Plouray

Mur-de-Bretagne

Lac de Guerlédan

BREBRE

Pontivy

ILES DE GLÉNAN

Pont-Aven
Port-Manec'h
Clohars-Carnoët
Le Pouldu

Quimperlé
Plouay
Pont-Scorff
Hennebont

Bubry
ST-NICODÈME

les Fo

4

Lorient
Merlévenez
Larmor
Port-Louis

Ile de Groix
Groix

Baud
Locminé

Pluvigner
Belz
Ste-Anne-d'Auray
Grand-Champ
Auray

St-Jean-Brévela

TOUR D'ELVEN

Vannes

N166

5

MENEC
Carnac
La Trinité
St-Pierre-Quiberon
Quiberon

TUMULUS DE GAVRINIS
Locmariaquer
Port-Navalo
Sarzeau

CHÂT. DE SUSCINIO

Ques

Pointe des Poulains
Sauzon
GROTTE DE L'APOTHICAIRERIE
Le Palais
Bangor
Belle-Ile
Locmaria

Ile de Houat

Ile de Hoedic

Piriac-sur-Mer
Penesti
La

6

Guérande
Le Croisic
Pointe du Croisic
Batz-sur-Mer

KORRIGANS
Côte d'Amour

A B C D

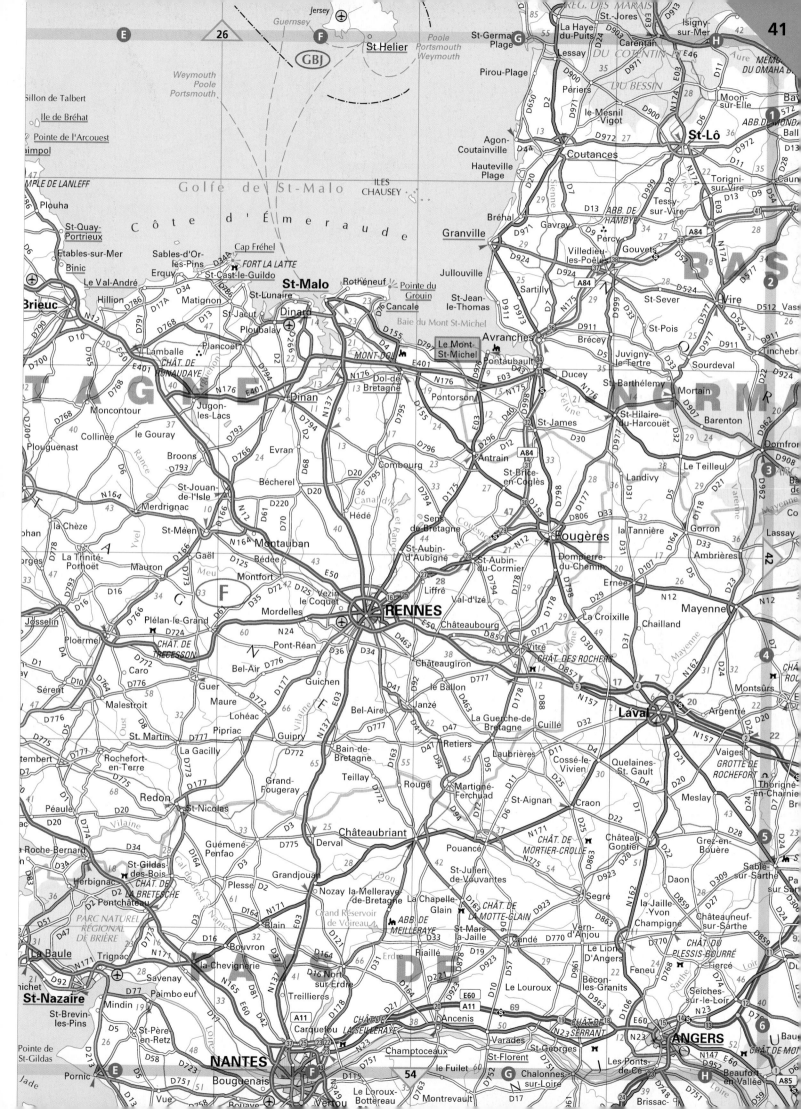

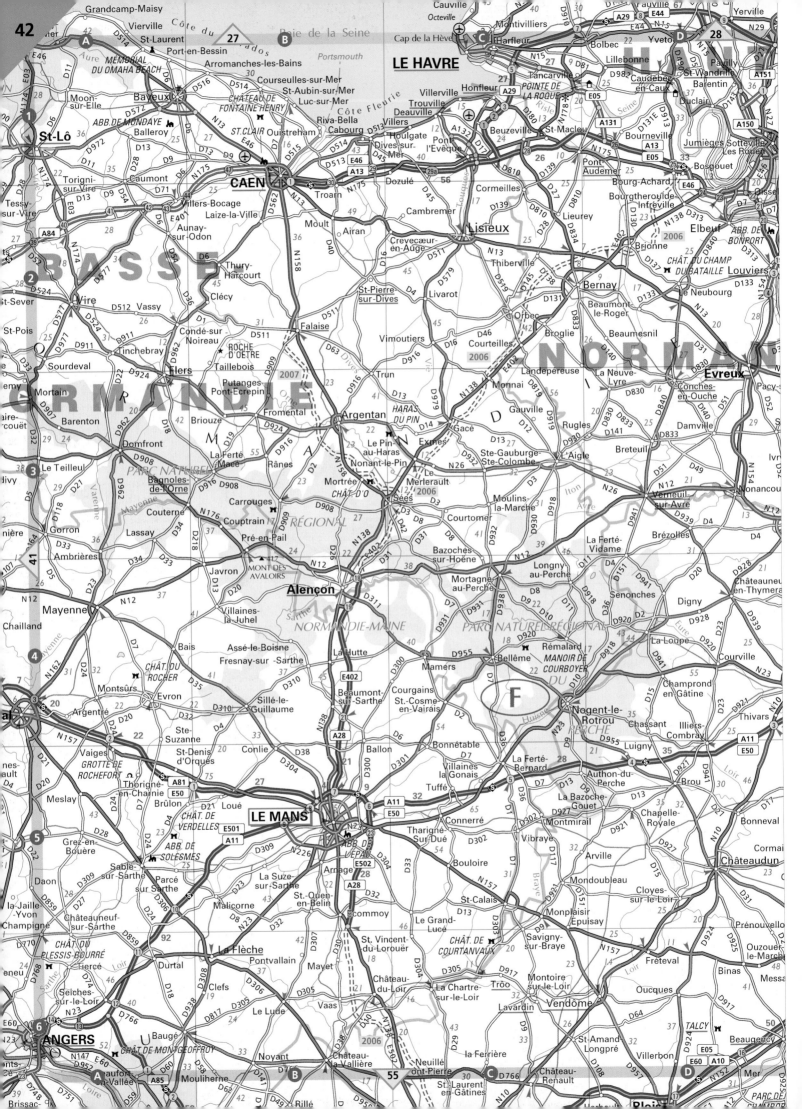

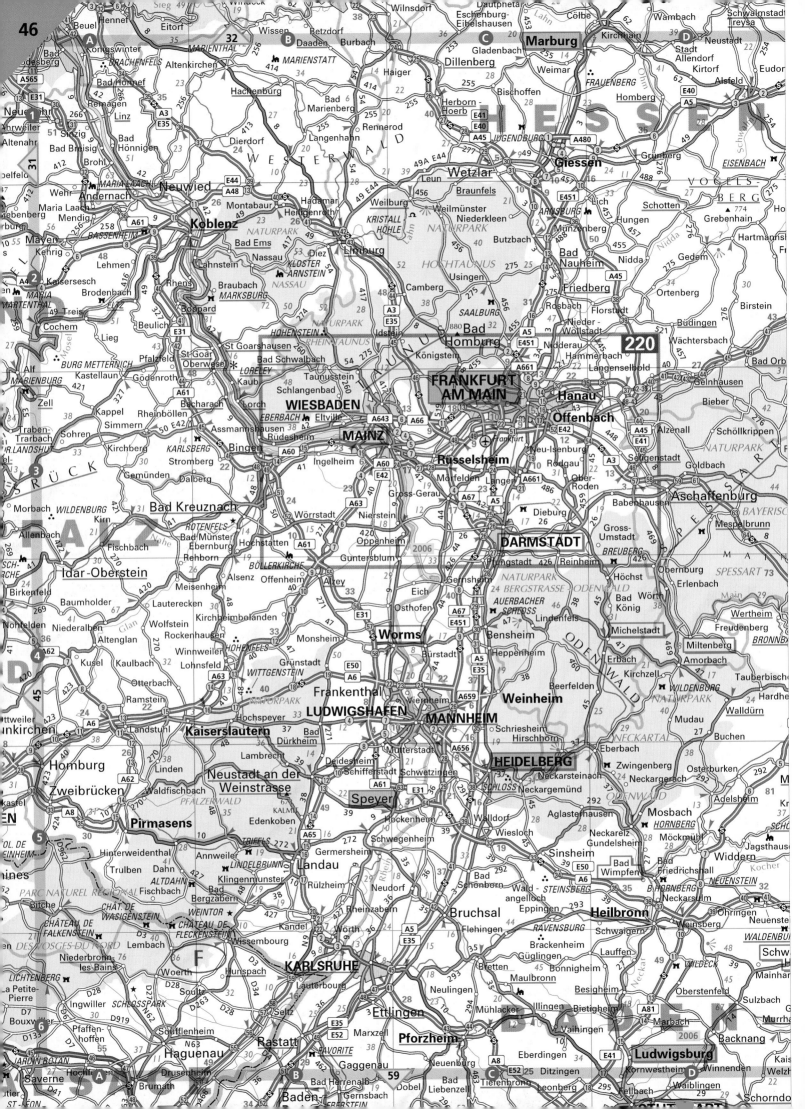

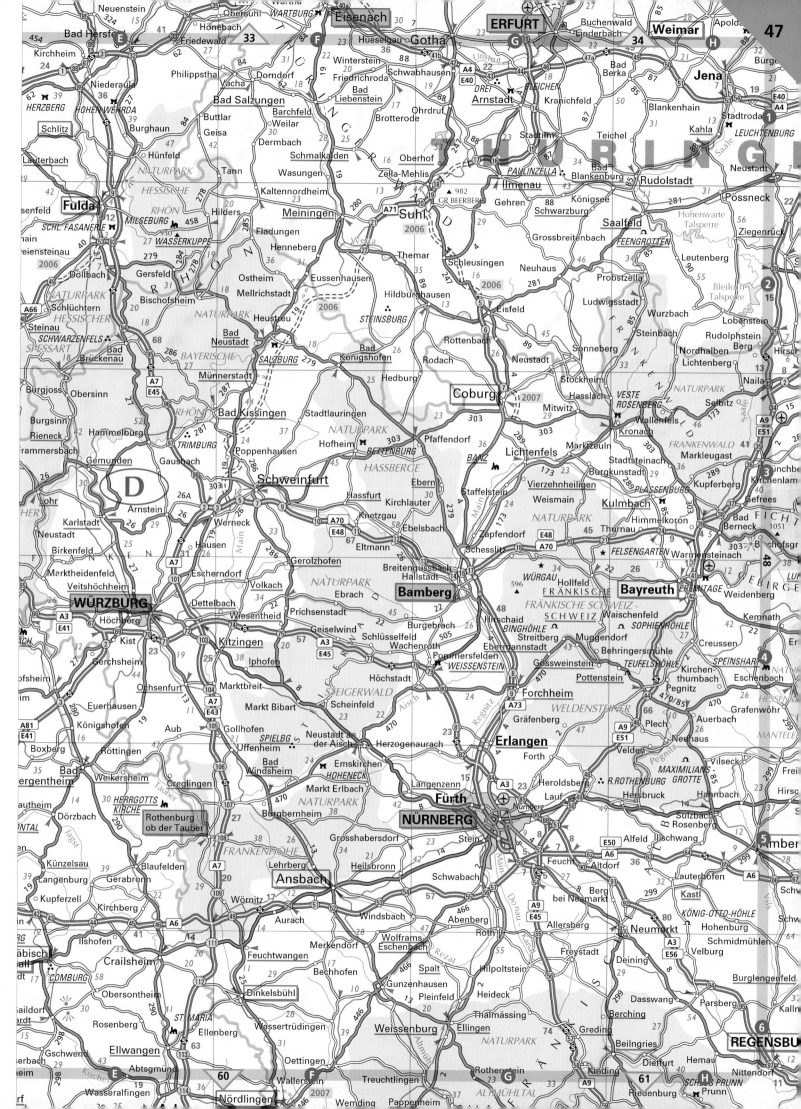

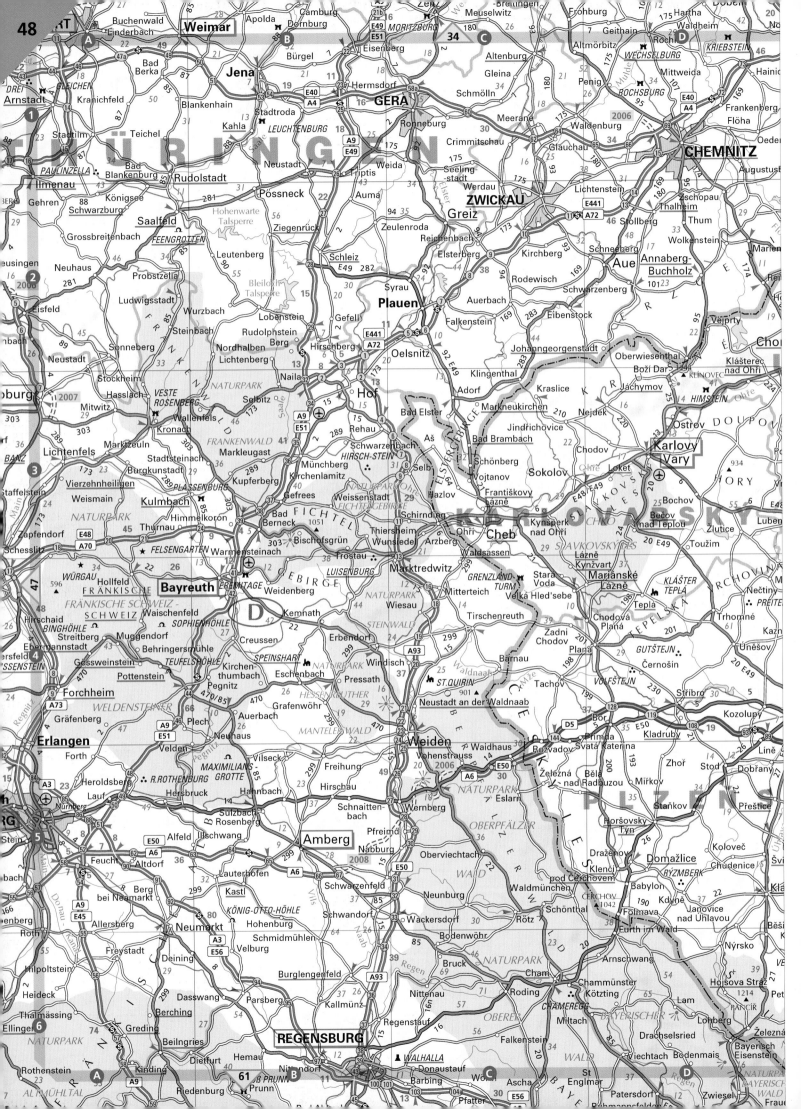

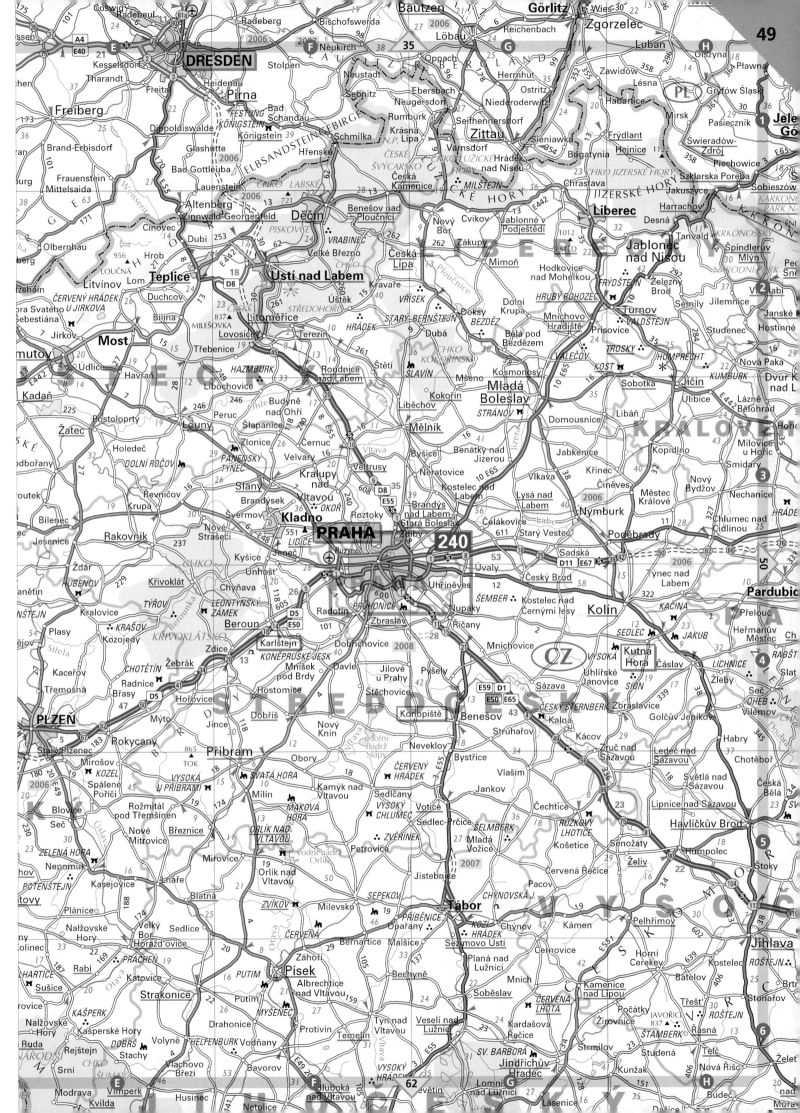

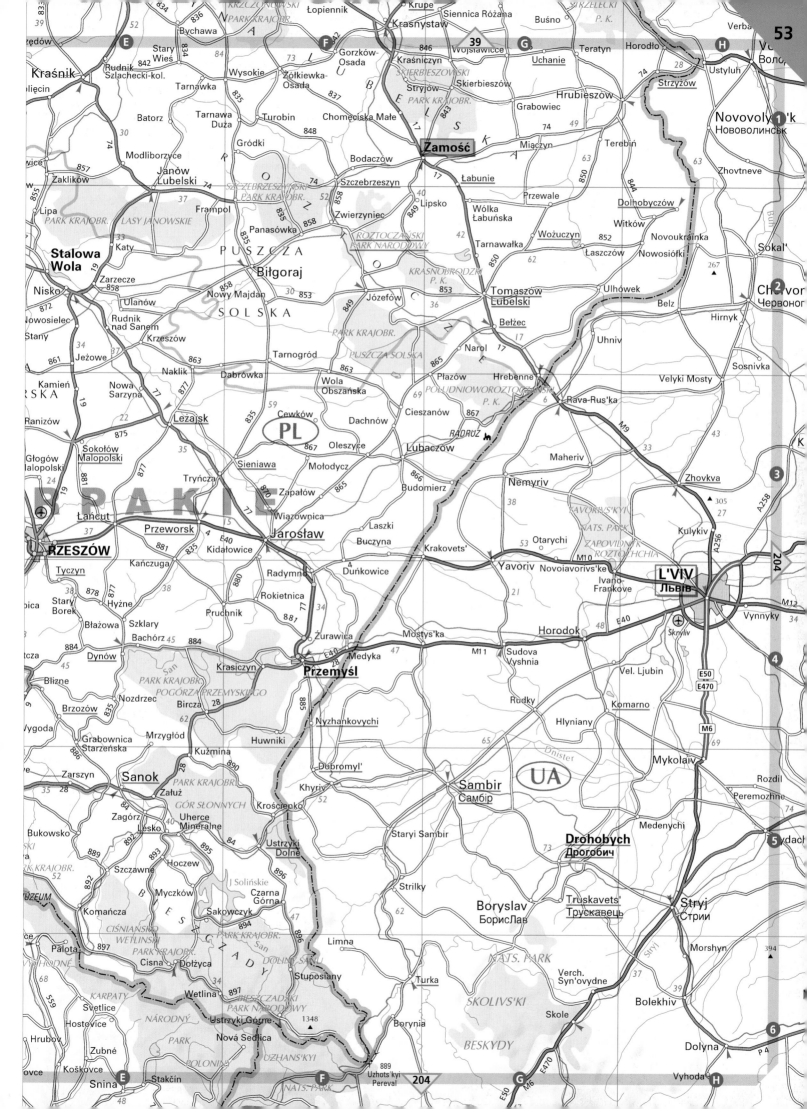

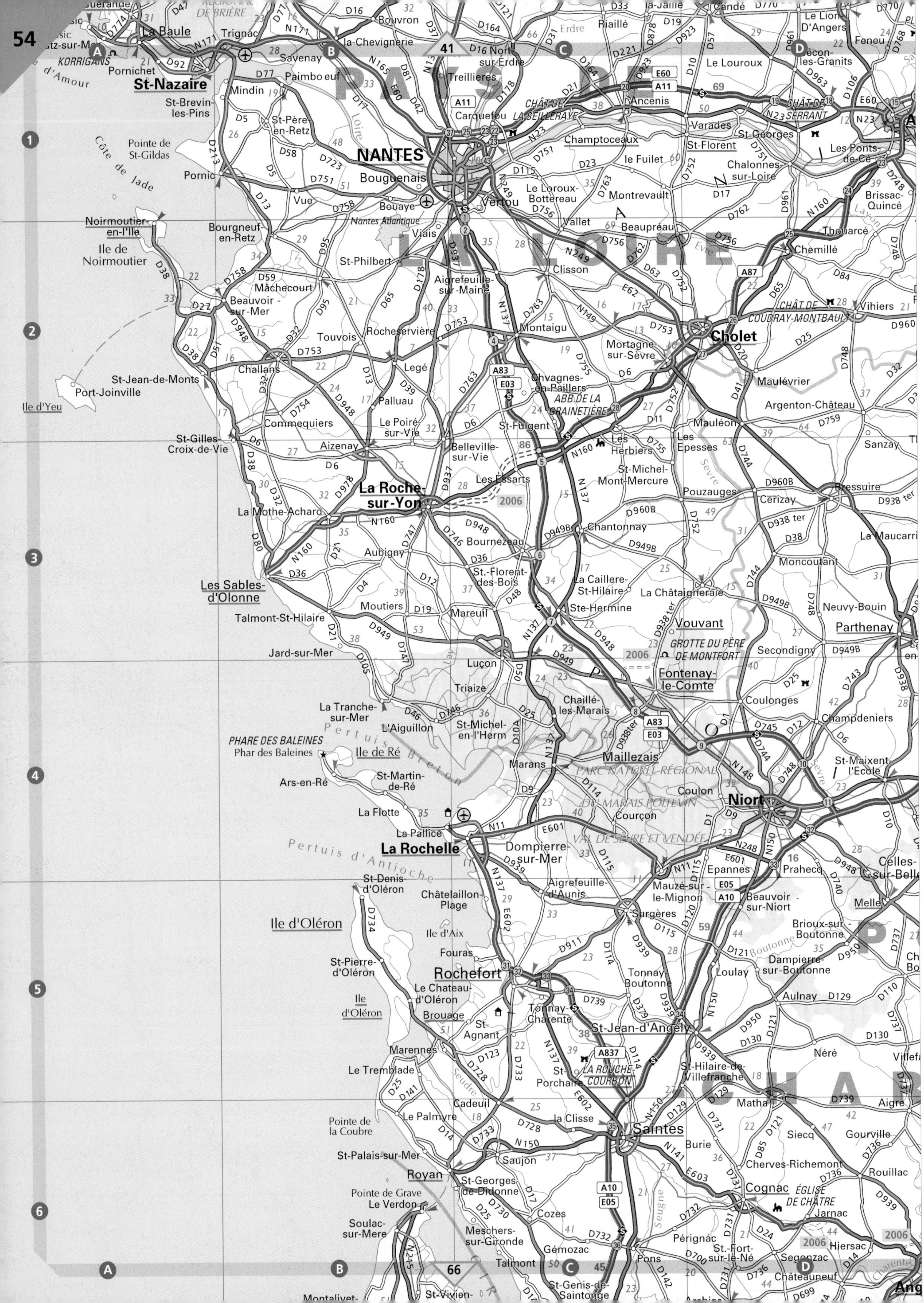

PAYS DE LA LOIRE

LA LOIRE

Korrigans d'Amour · La Baule · Pornichet · St-Nazaire · St-Brevin-les-Pins · Mindin · St-Père-en-Retz · Pornic · Pointe de St-Gildas · Côte de Jade · Noirmoutier-en-l'Ille · Ile de Noirmoutier · Bourgneuf-en-Retz · Machecourt · Beauvoir-sur-Mer · St-Jean-de-Monts · Port-Joinville · Ile d'Yeu · St-Gilles-Croix-de-Vie · Challans · Commequiers · Aizenay · La Mothe-Achard · Les Sables-d'Olonne · Talmont-St-Hilaire · Jard-sur-Mer · La Tranche-sur-Mer · L'Aiguillon · Phare des Baleines · Ile de Ré · Ars-en-Ré · St-Martin-de-Ré · La Flotte · La Pallice · La Rochelle · St-Denis-d'Oléron · Châtelaillon-Plage · Ile d'Oléron · St-Pierre-d'Oléron · Le Chateau-d'Oléron · Brouage · St-Agnant · Marennes · Le Tremblade · Le Palmyre · Pointe de la Coubre · St-Palais-sur-Mer · Royan · St-Georges-de-Didonne · Pointe de Grave · Le Verdon · Soulac-sur-Mer · Meschers-sur-Gironde · Talmont

Savenay · Paimbeuf · Bouaye · Vue · Bouguenais · NANTES · Vertou · Carquefou · Ancenis · Champtoceaux · St-Florent · Chalonnes-sur-Loire · Brissac-Quincé · Theouarcé · Chemillé · Beaupréau · Montrevault · Le Loroux-Bottereau · Vallet · Clisson · Aigrefeuille-sur-Maine · St-Philbert · Rocheservière · Montaigu · Mortagne-sur-Sèvre · Cholet · Maulévrier · Argenton-Château · Mauléon · Les Herbiers · St-Michel-Mont-Mercure · Les Epesses · Pouzauges · Cerizay · Bressuire · La Maucarrie · Legé · Palluau · Le Poiré-sur-Vie · St-Fulgent · Belleville-sur-Vie · Les Essarts · La Roche-sur-Yon · Aubigny · Bournezeau · Chantonnay · Moncoutant · St-Florent-des-Bois · La Caillere-St-Hilaire · La Châtaigneraie · Neuvy-Bouin · Parthenay · Moutiers · Mareuil · Ste-Hermine · Vouvant · Secondigny · Luçon · Triaize · Chaillé-les-Marais · Fontenay-le-Comte · Coulonges · Champdeniers · St-Michel-l'Herm · Marans · Maillezais · Coulon · Niort · St-Maixent-l'Ecole · Dompierre-sur-Mer · Aigrefeuille-d'Aunis · Mauzé-sur-le-Mignon · Epannes · Beauvoir-sur-Niort · Praheco · Melle · Celles-sur-Belle · Surgères · Brioux-sur-Boutonne · Dampierre-sur-Boutonne · Rochefort · Tonnay-Charente · Tonnay-Boutonne · Loulay · Aulnay · Néré · St-Jean-d'Angély · Villefagnan · Cadeuil · St-Porchaire · St-Hilaire-de-Villefranche · Matha · Aigre · Gourville · la Clisse · Saintes · Burie · Siecq · Cherves-Richemont · Rouillac · Cozes · Saujon · Pons · Pérignac · Cognac · Jarnac · Hiersac · Gémozac · St-Fort-sur-le-Né · Segonzac · Châteauneuf · St-Genis-de-Saintonge

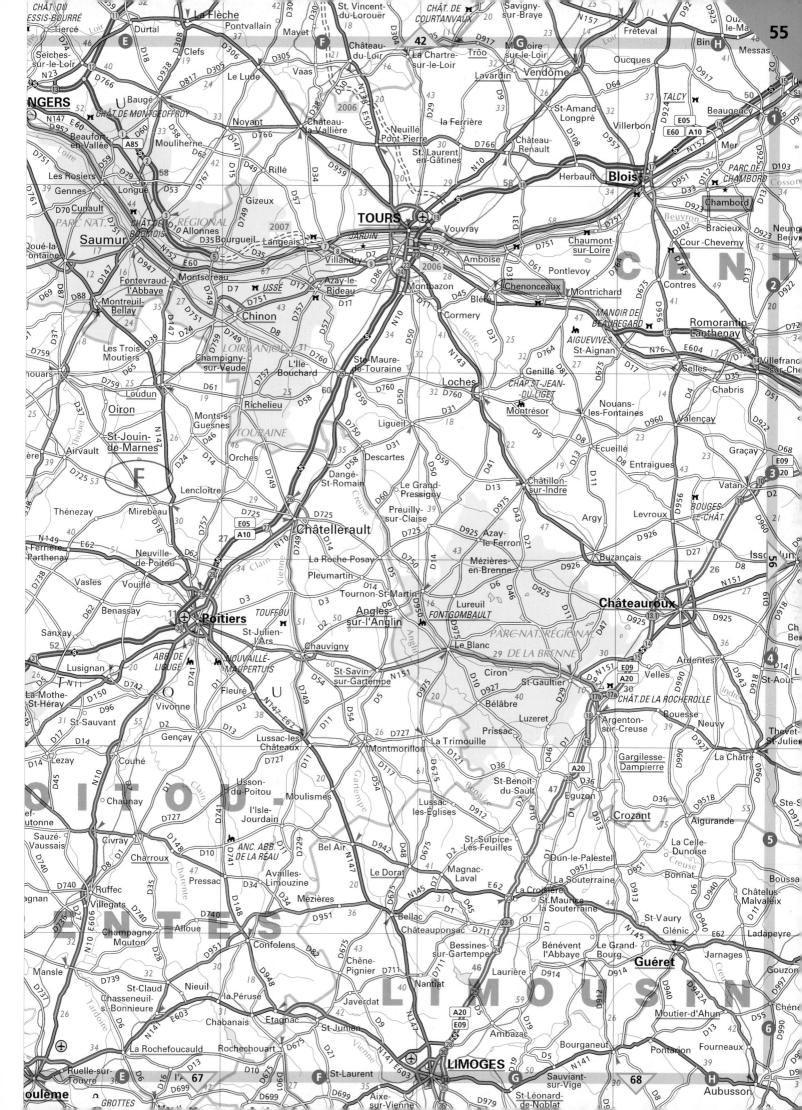

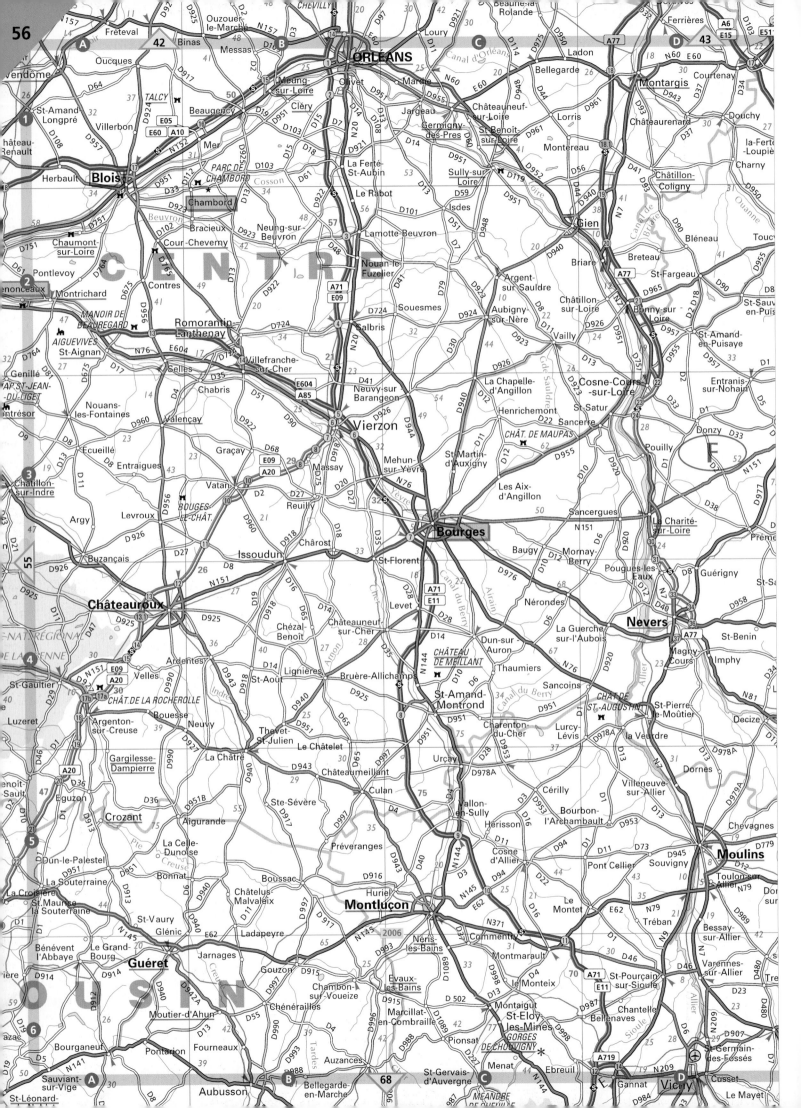

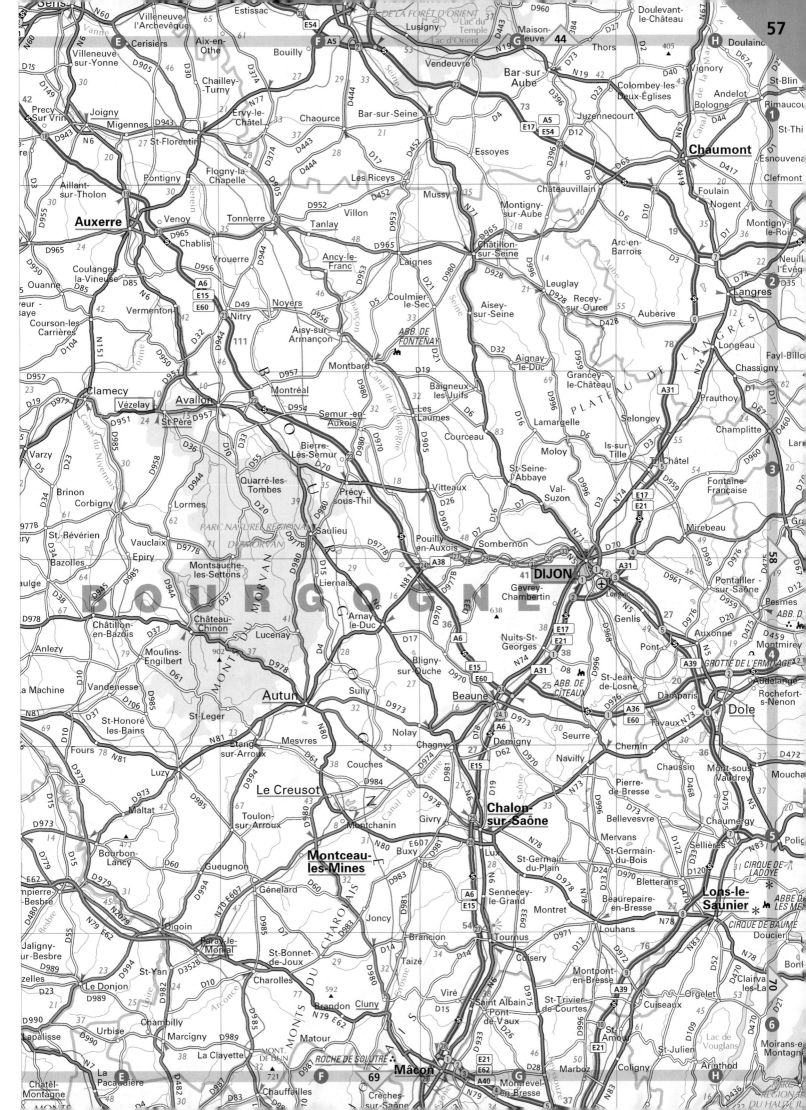

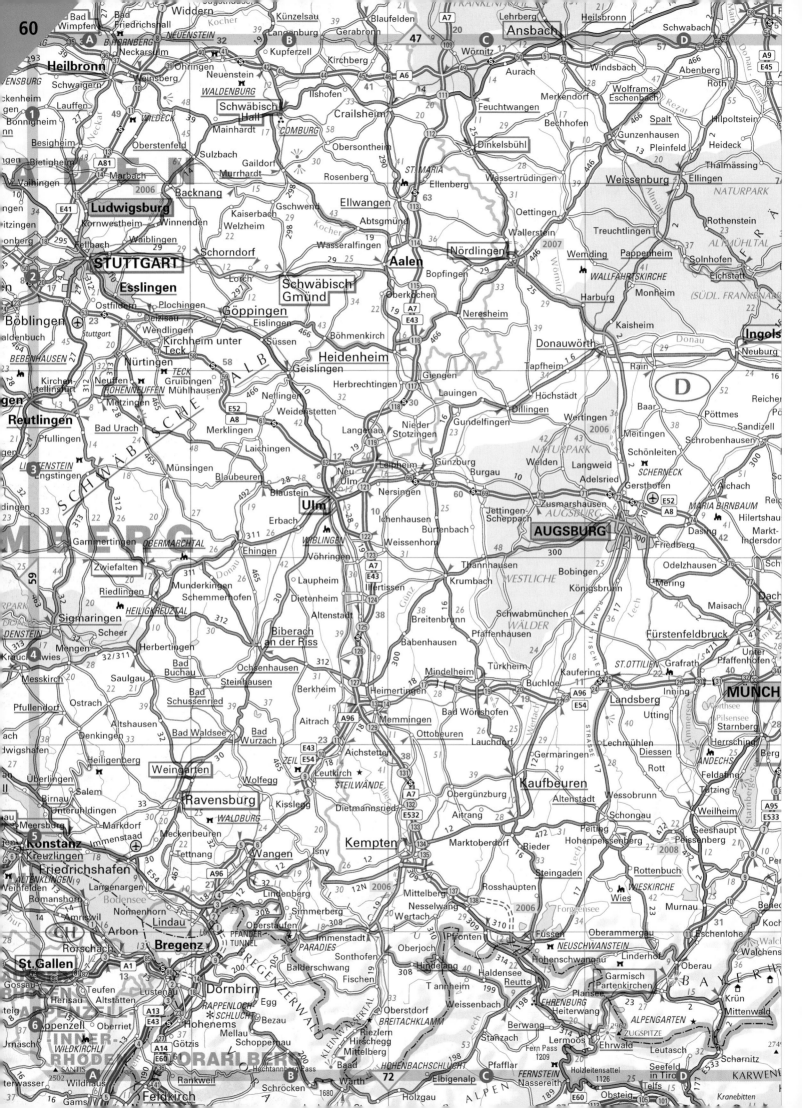

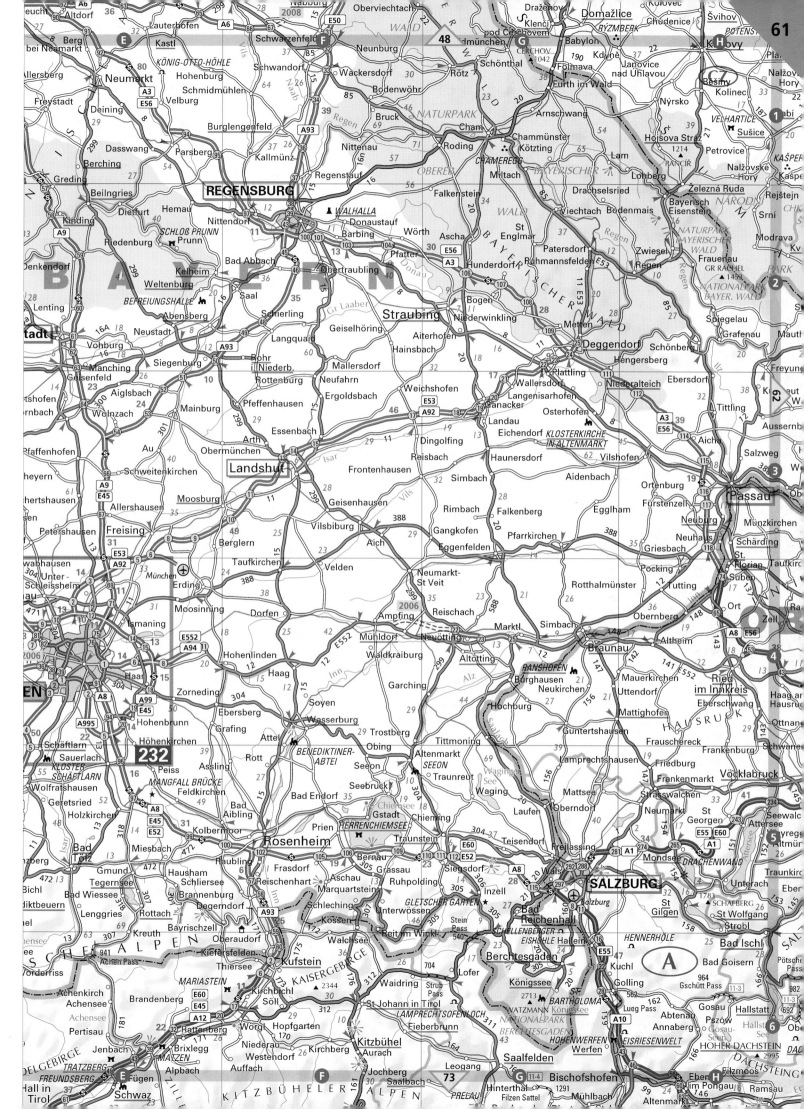

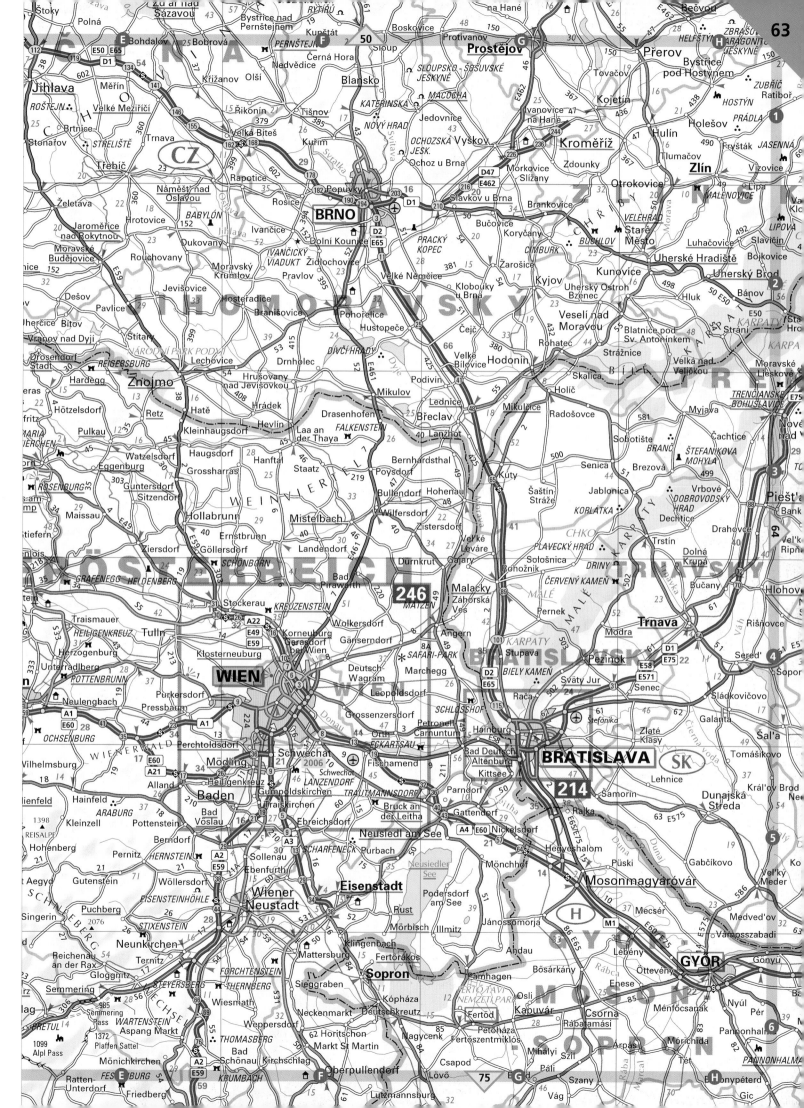

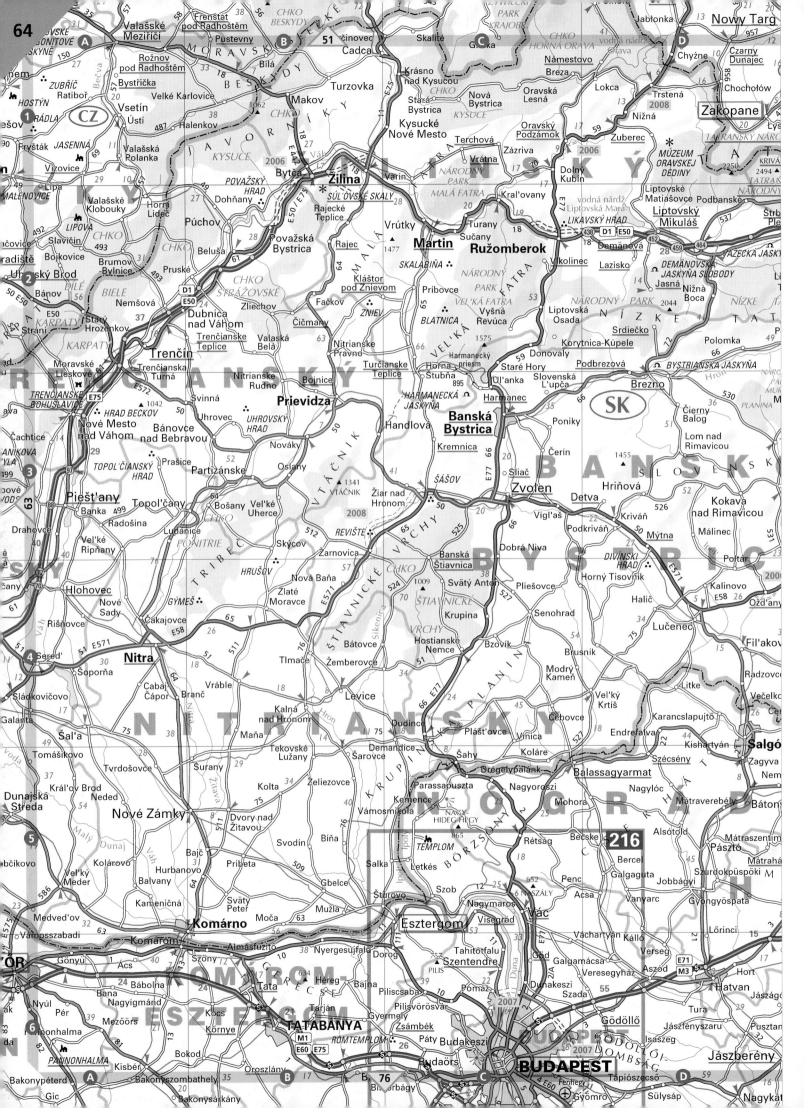

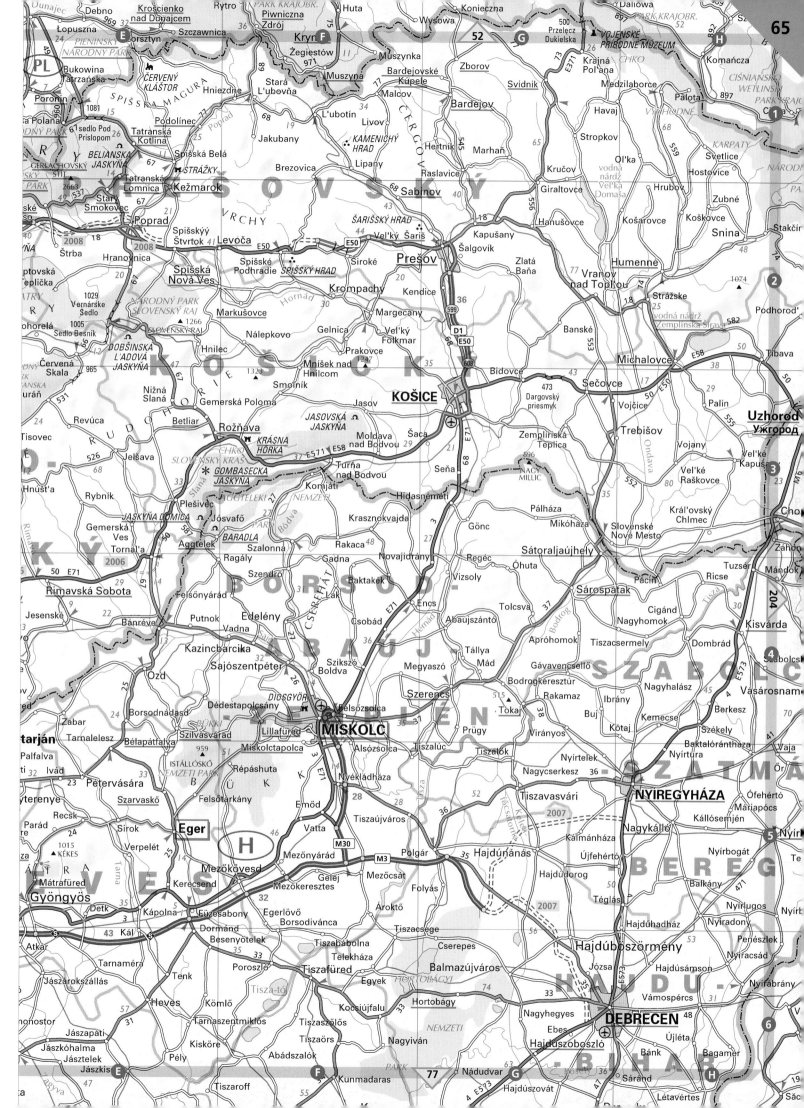

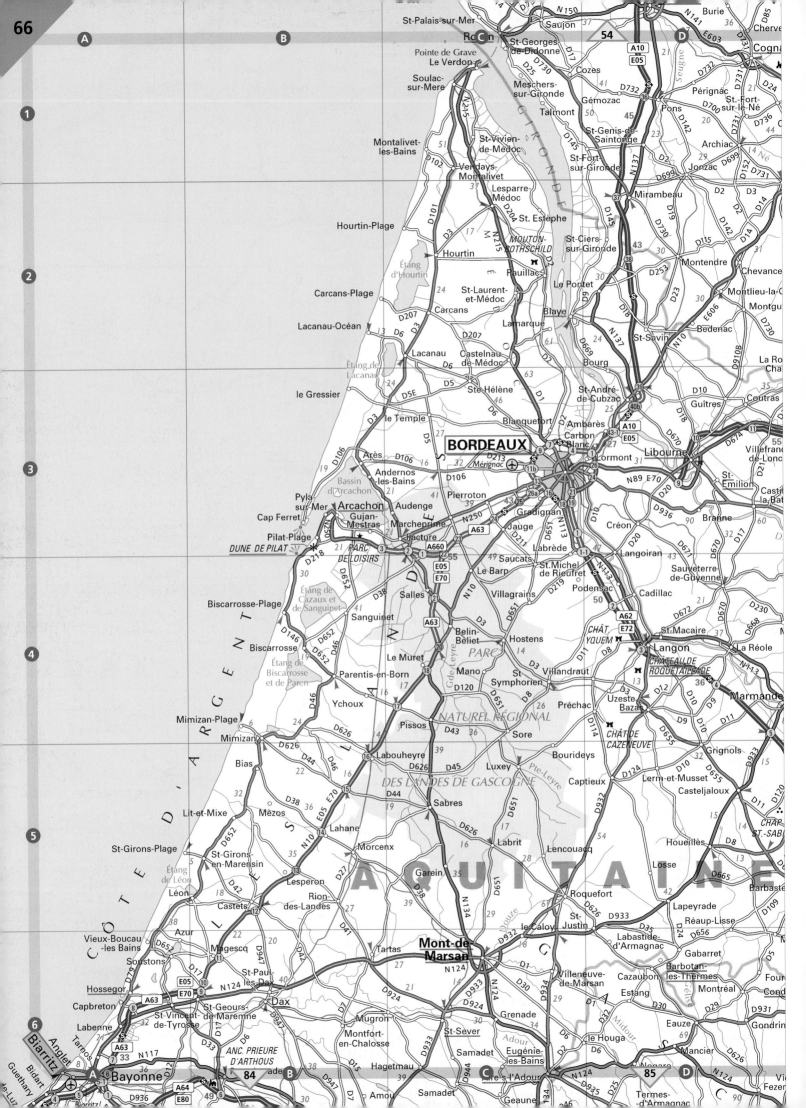

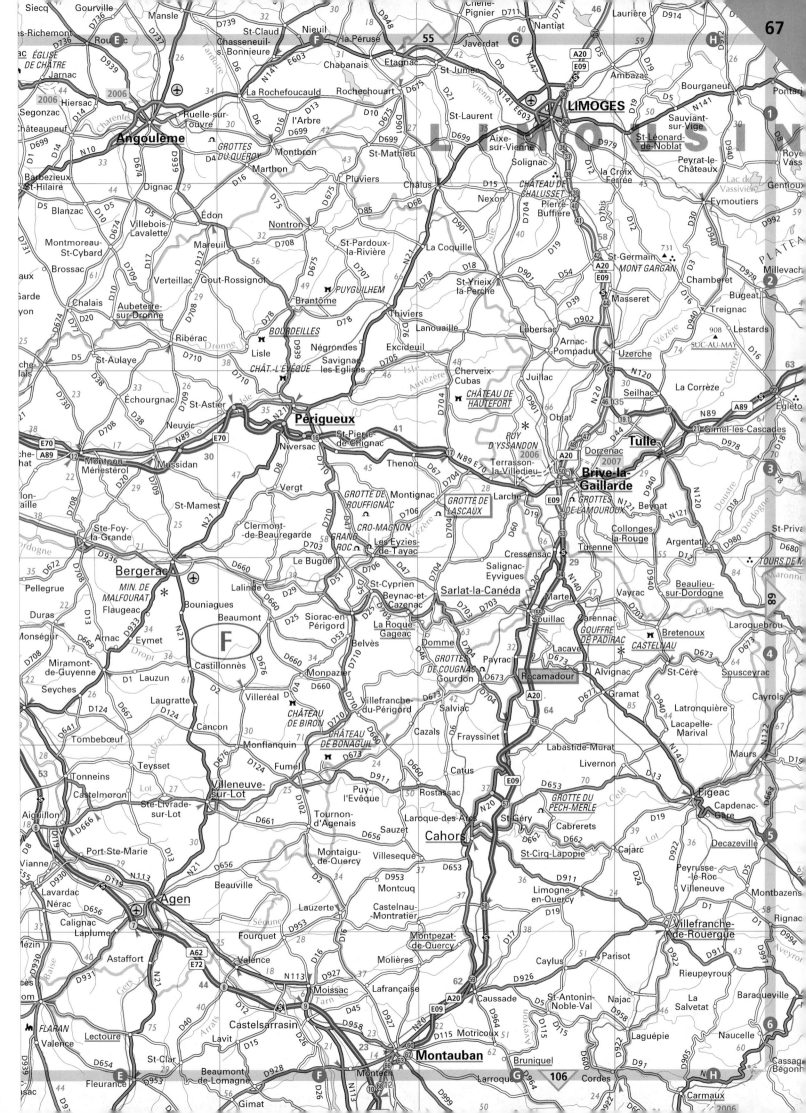

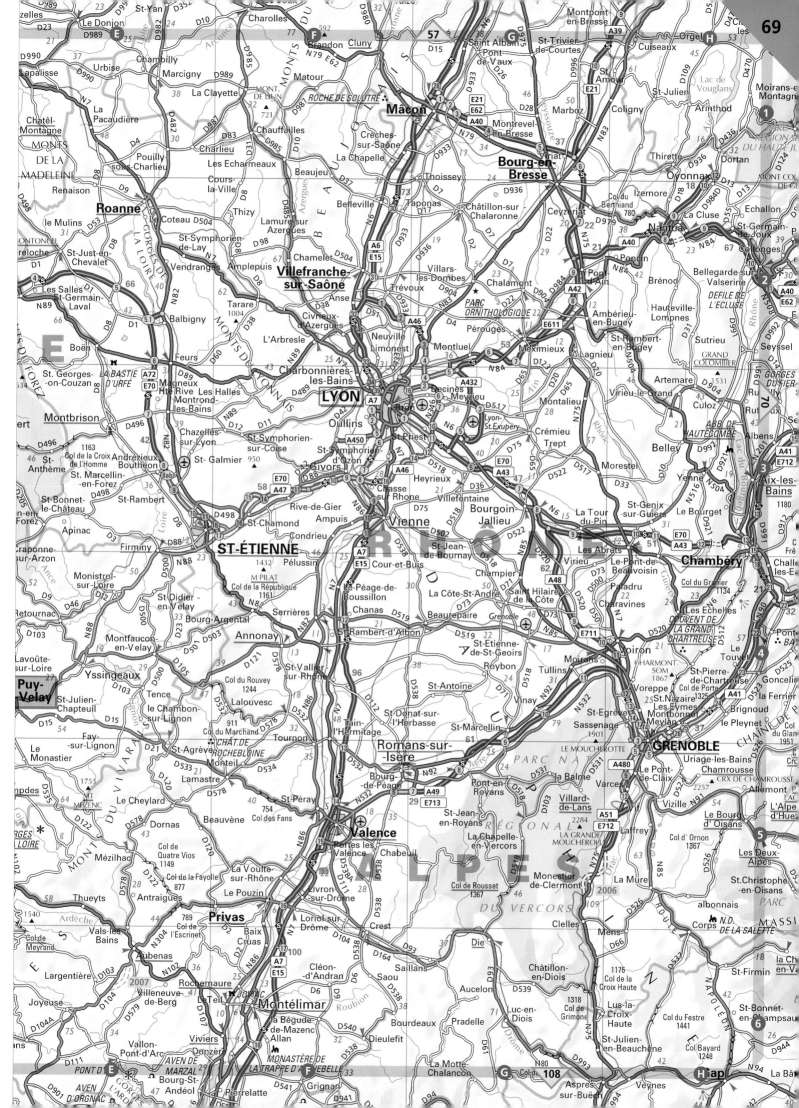

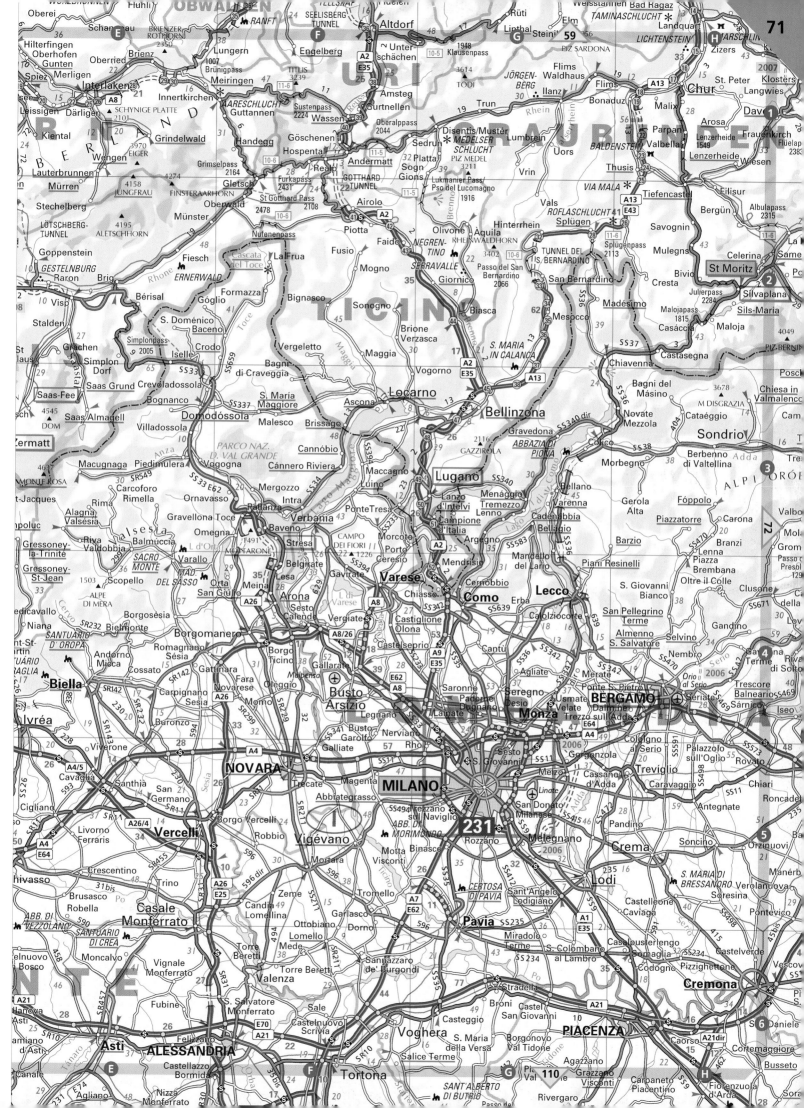

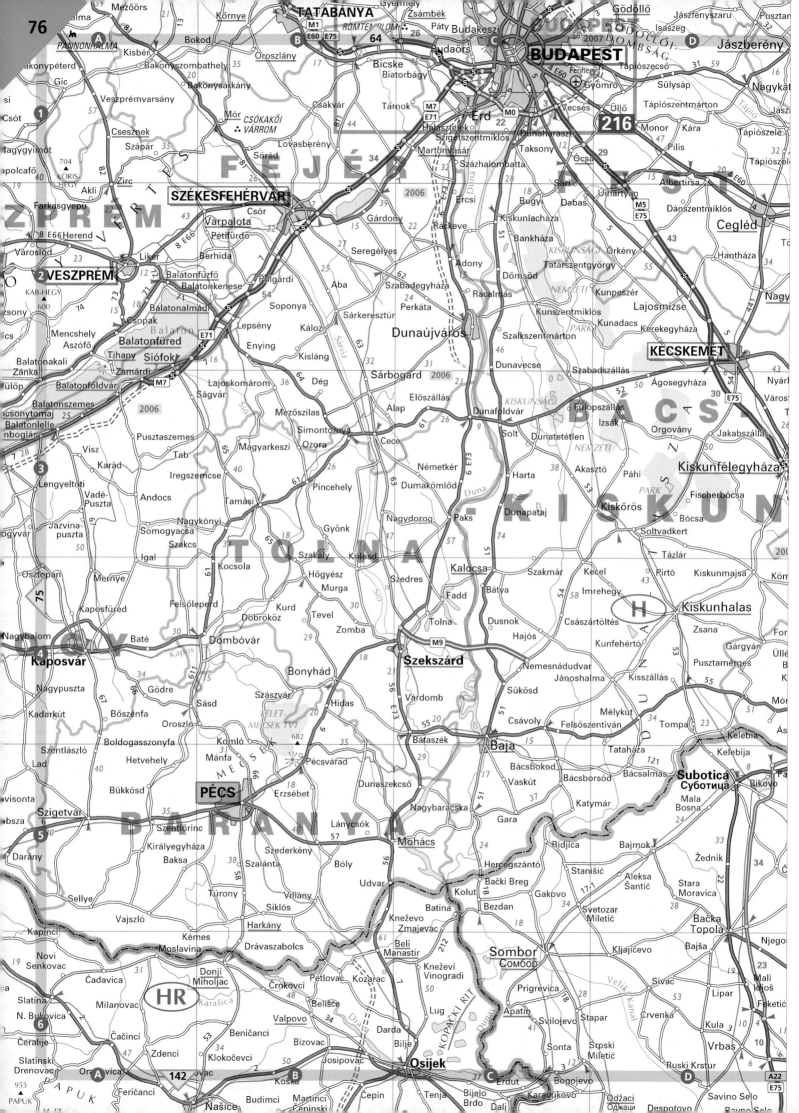

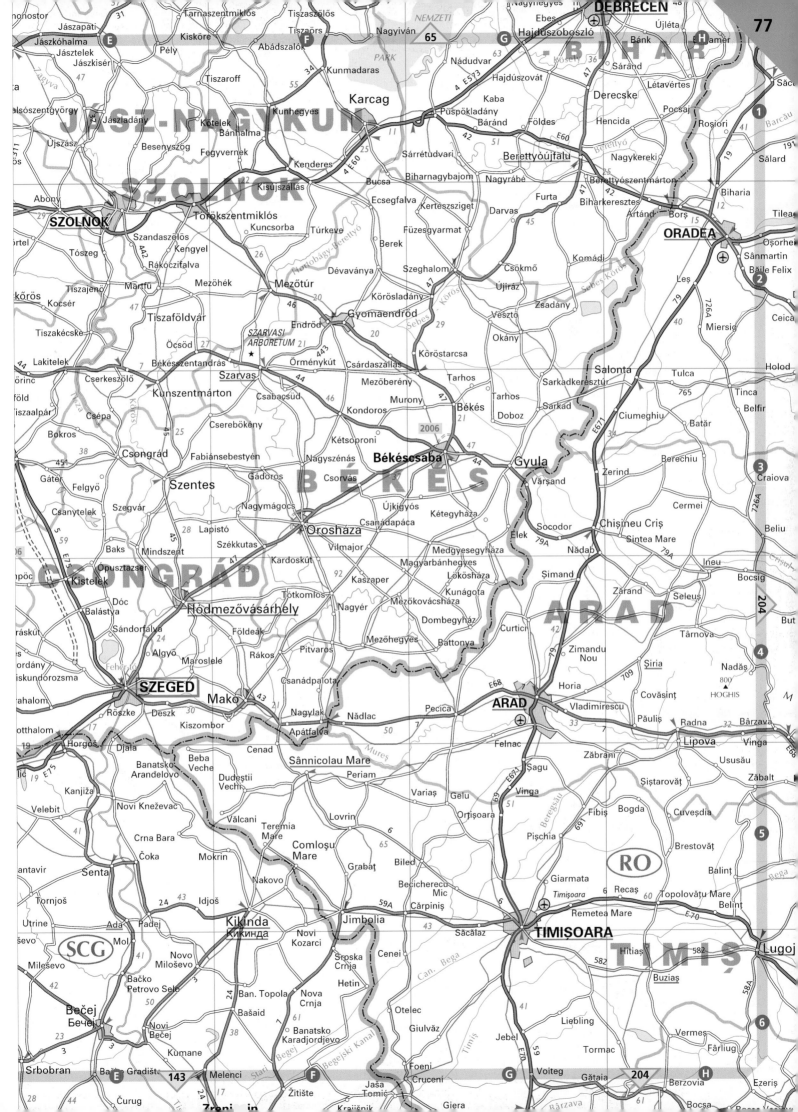

RÍAS

RÍAS S

A **B** **C** **D**

1

Punta
Candelaria

VIXÍA
HERBE

Cedeira

SAN
ANDRÉS

Cabo Prior

AC566

Valdoviño
Mera
de Boix

Cabo Prioriño **Ferrol**
NVI
Xubia
AC862
CASTILLO D
MOECHE

Illas
Sisargas

Cabo San Adrián
Malpica de
Bergantiños

Punta del
Roncudo

Ría de Betanzos

Murgados
Ares
Neda
San Sadurniño

25F
Fene
MONASTERIO
DE CAAVEIRO

CAST. DE
NARAIO

Laxe
Ponteceso

**A CORUÑA/
LA CORUÑA**

Pontedeume

21F
CAST. DE
ANDRADE

AG64

87

Arteixo

Oleiros

Cambre

Guisamo

As Pontes de García Rodrígu
Puentes de García Rodrigu

Cabo Vilán

Camariñas

Muxía

CEREIXO
DOLMEN
DE DOMBATE

CASTRO DE
BORNEIRO

Baio

33 29 222

Carballo

Laracha

Betanzos

54

Monfero

Pedreira

Embalse
de Eume

C640

2

Cabo Touriñán

Vimianzo

San Roque

Silva 65

Carral

Coiros

Irixoa

35

Zás

AC404

AC413

N550

AC13

Cerceda

Mesón do Vento

C542

AP9
E01

45

Curtis

Lourdes

Guitiriz

10

20

Fisterra/
Finisterre

AC445

Cee
Corcubión
Ézaro

Brandomil

Santa-Comba

Bembirre

Ordes

Trazo

Oroso

24

Lanzá

S

41

N634

30

Ru

Teixeiro

STA. MARIA DE MEZONZO

Baamonde

A6

Cabo Fisterra

AC550

Ponte
Oliveras

47

Portomouro

Sigüeiro

55

Pastor

SOBRADO DOS MONXES

Sobrado

21

27

Rabade

3

Pino do Val

A Baña

Negreira

Santiago

**Santiago de
Compostela**

STA. MARIA DE
CONXO

N634

Labacolla

45

N547

Arzúa

Melide

Friol

Toques

19

Lugo

Carnota

Outes

Muros

Ría
de Muros

Noia
Noya

AC543

Padrón

Teo
Ramallosa

El Pino

Fontedias

Embalse de
Portodemouros

15

22

Palas
de Rei

37

El Picato
660

Punta Carreiros

Porto do Son

AC550

Enfesta

AP53

Ponte Ulla

53

Cruces

N547

Guntín

CASTRO DE BAROÑA

36

VRG1.1

Catoira
Pontecesures

46

15

A Estrada

PAZO DE OCA

Silleda

24

Agolada

42

Monterroso

N640

26

Narón

Portomar

Pobra do Caramiñal/
Puebla del Caramiñal

Cimadevilla

Rianxo
Vilagarcía
de Arousa

PO548

N640

110

Cuntis

N640

39

33

Lalín

Rodeiro

CRG2.1

LU633

Cabo Corrubedo
Oleiros

Santa Uxía de Ribeira

Illa de
Arousa

Caldas
de Reis

Dozón /
Castro

Taboada

37

Embalse
de Belesar

G A L I C I

Punta de Couso

Ría de Arousa

O Grove

Vilanova
de Arousa

Cambados

55

A Lagoa /
Campo Lameiro

29

33

44

STA. MARIA DA REAL
DE RIBAS DO MIÑO
Escairón

Chantada

MONASTERIO

Bóve

Illa de Sálvora

PARQUE NACIONAL

A Toxa

E01
AP9

Forcarei

Soutelo

725

Alto de Santo
Domingo

63

La Barrela

N540

32

U656

LU652

4

Illa de Ons

DAS ILLAS

O Convento
Poio

PO550

PO301

129

N541

44

Cerdedo

1012

Piñor

Cea

37

Pantón

N120

Monforte
de Lemos

Sanxenxo

Combarro

Pontevedra

Ponte-
Caldelas

Beariz

Avión

O Carballiño

Maside

Embalse dos
Peares

48

Cambeo

Sober

Ría de Pontevedra

Marín

PO551

132

20

CAST. DE
SOUTOMAIOR

Berducido

Leiro

MONASTERIO
DE SAN CLODIO

Os Peares

ATLÁNTICAS

Hío

Moaña

23

45

146

61

SERRA DO SUIDO

Punxín

N120

Embalse de
San Esteban

Parada
del Sil

Illas
Cíes

Cangas

C551

148

Redondela

Mondariz-
Balneario

N120

Ribadavia

**OURENSE/
ORENSE**

SANTO ESTEVO

Ría de Vigo

VIGO

151

AS550

14

Mondariz

Ponteareas

40

A Cañiza

Cartelle

MONASTERIO
DE SANTO
ESTEVO

Castro
Caldelas

Puerto de A
de Cerdeir
890

Panxón

Nigrán

15

159

Areas

Cortegada

OU531

Esgos

C536

5

Cabo Silleiro

AG57

A52

Ramirás

A Merca

Maceda

Xunqueira
de Espadanedo

58

Baiona

Ramallosa

51

O Porriño

PO403

48

Salvaterra
de Miño

São
Gregório

OU410

44

Celanova

Allariz

950

Puerto de Alto
do Rodicio

Paredes

A Pobra d
Trives

Arrabal
Oia

Vilameán

E1

6

Tui

Monção

N202

Melgaço

25

Padrenda

Verea

OU531

39

Xunqueira
de Ambia

Embalse de
Chandrexa

1778

MANZANEDA

Valença
do Minho

14

18

A Guarda
La Guardia

PO552

28

Vila Nova
de Cerveira

13

28

Portela

Arcos de
Valdevez

39

1416

Bande

OU540

40

Vilar
de Barrio

SERRA DE Q

Caminha

MTE. DE STA. TEGRA

Lanhelas

N301

30

Paredes
de Coura

A3

SERRA DA PENEDA

Entrimo

Xinzo de Limia
Ginzo de Limia

Limia

60

Villariño
de Cons

Moledo
Vila Praia
de Âncora

Afife

Soajo

IP1

46

Muiños

Trasmiras

Laza

Campobecerros

VIANA DO CASTELO

Portela
do Home

849

**Viana do
Castelo**

STA. LUZIA

A1
IP9

Ponte
de Lima

A2
IC28

Lindoso

OU312

PARQUE NACIONAL
DA PENEDA-GERÊS

Cualedro

31

A Gudiña

Darque

Deão

N202

70

17

Ponte
da Barca

N203

Lobios

Baltar

Verín

N525

Castelo do Neiva

IC1

Balugães

N204

E1

10

Ponte da Barca

N203

P

SERRA DO GERÊS

Randín

N532

Ríos

Oimbra

6

Esposende

A28

Feitos

A3

N101

Covide

Montalegre

Gralhos

Vilardevós

N103

N205

Vila Verde
Caldelas

N. S. D'ABADIA

Gerês

Barragem
de Paradela

C103

Cávado

27

N103-1

TIBAES

N30

80

BOM

28

34

Nova

Barragem
de Venda

Alto Rabagão

N. SENHORA DA

Estela
N103-1

Barcelos

A11

19

20

205

JESUS DO MONTE

Loureda

Barragem do
Alto Rabagão

72

Vila Verde

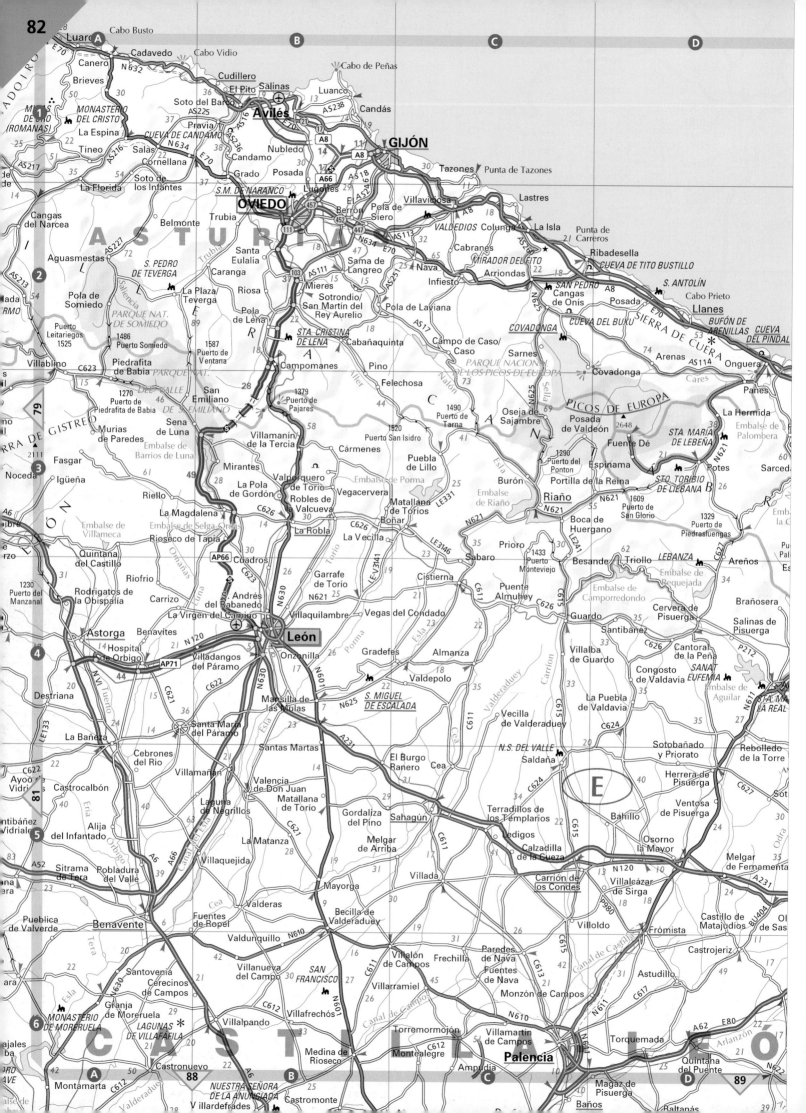

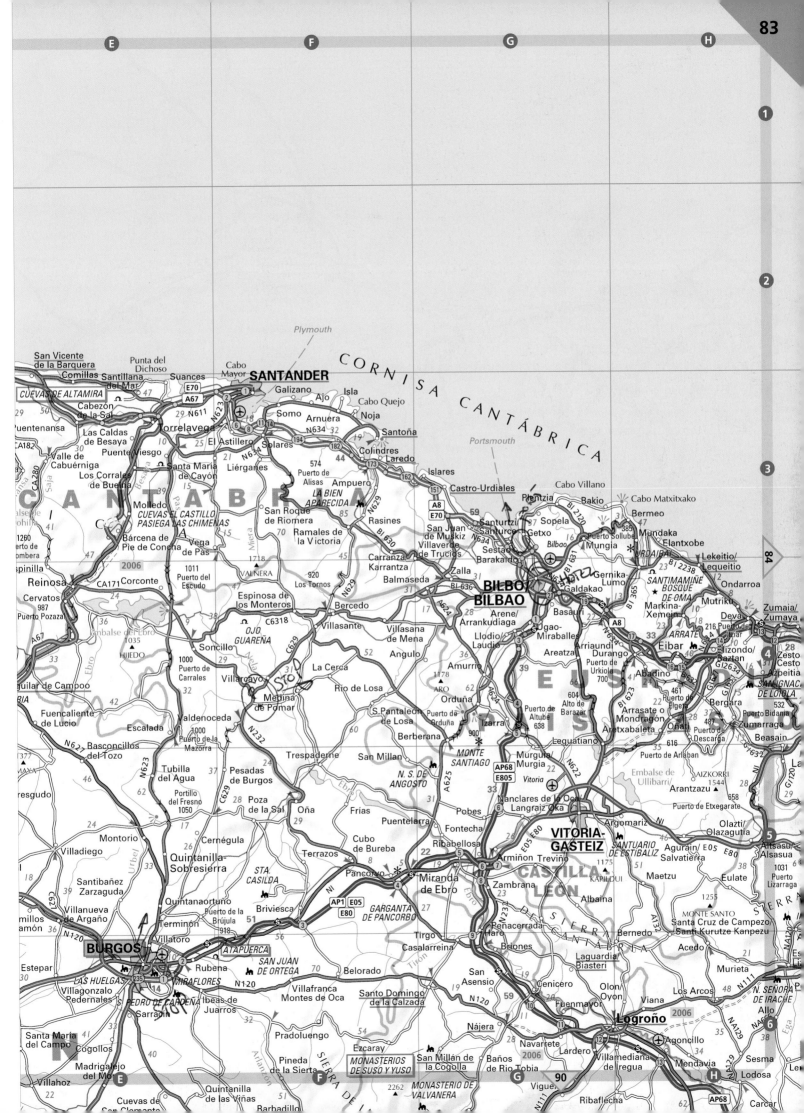

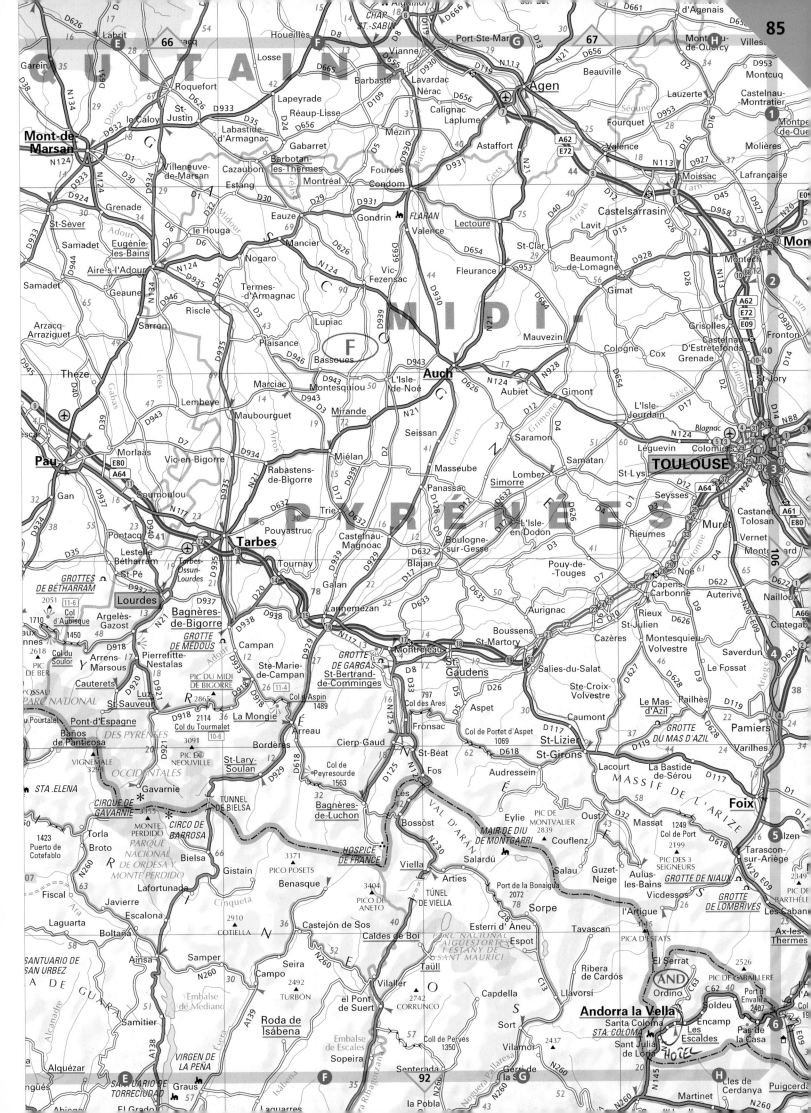

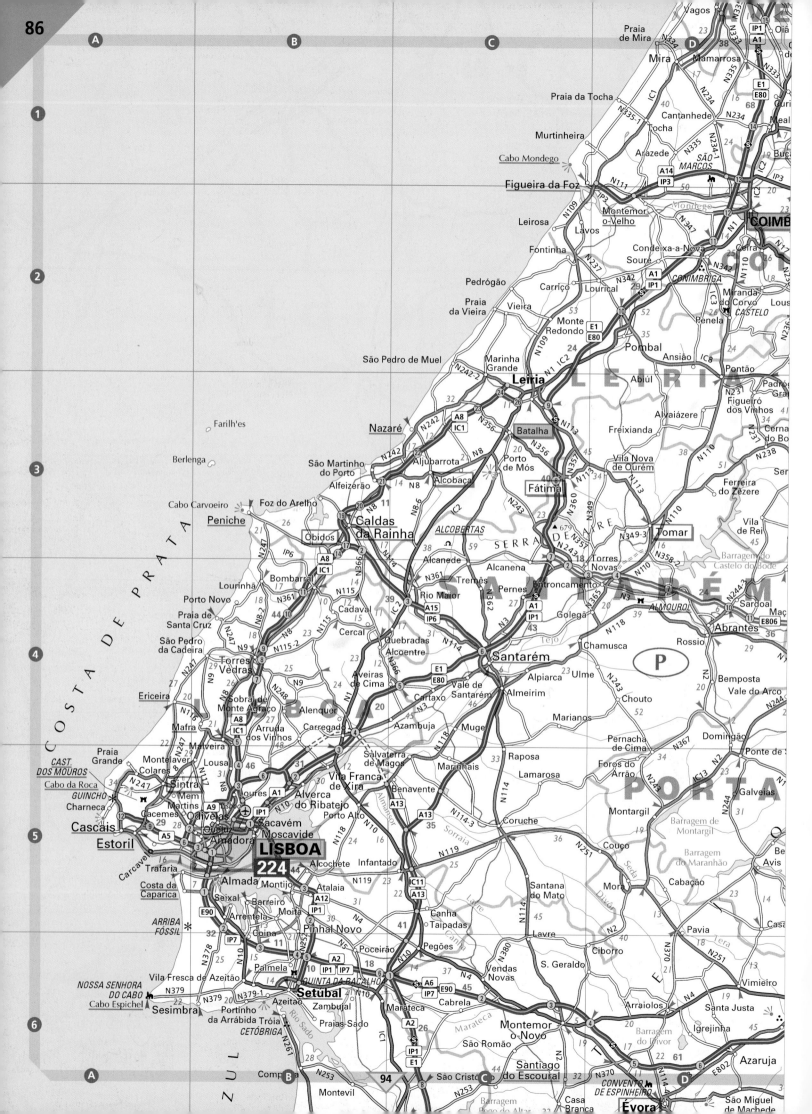

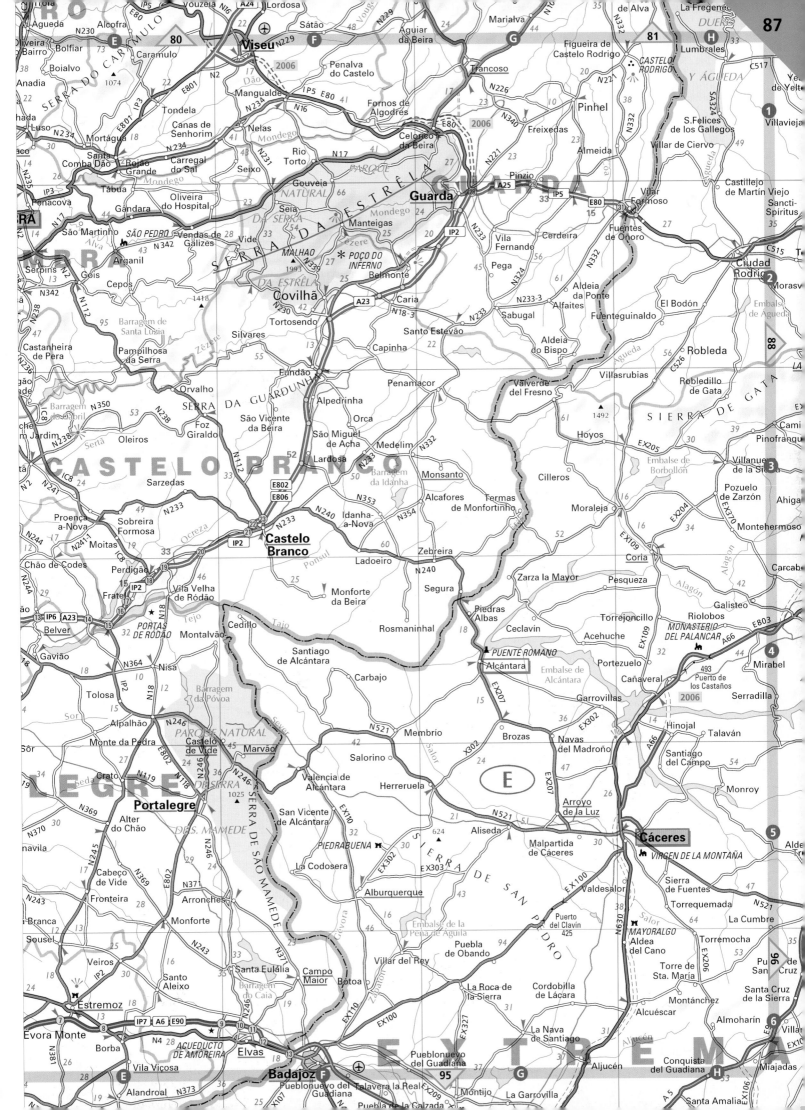

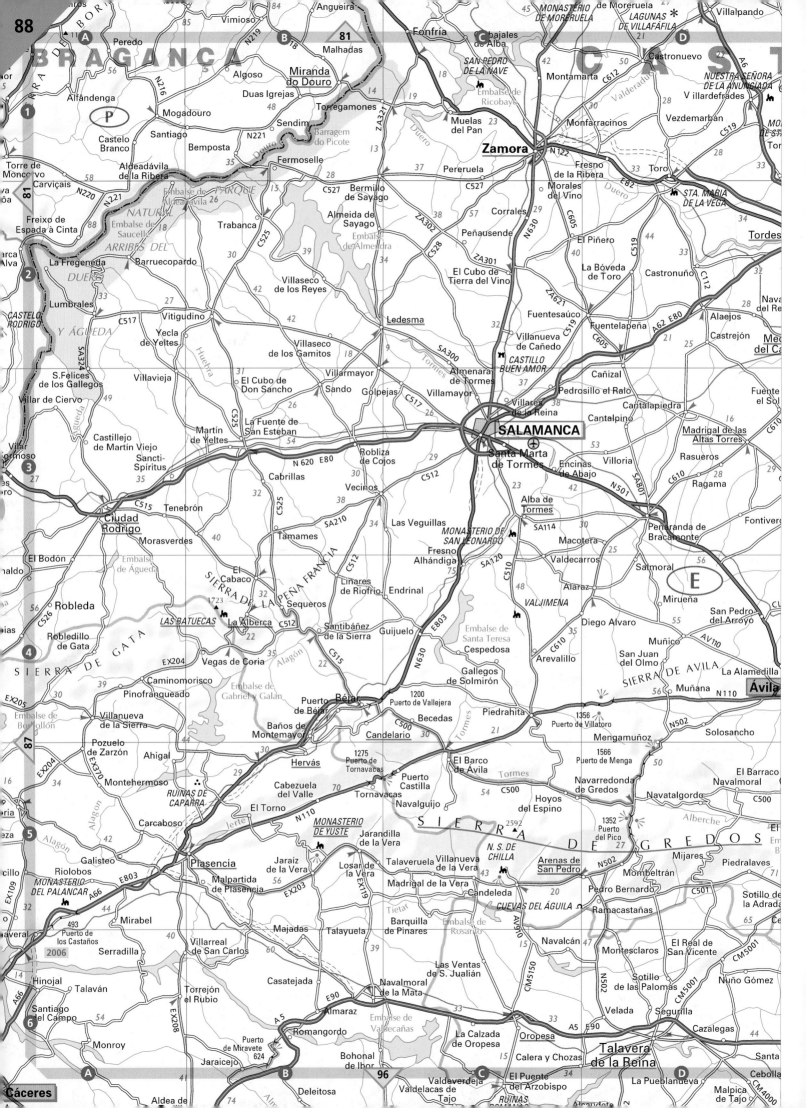

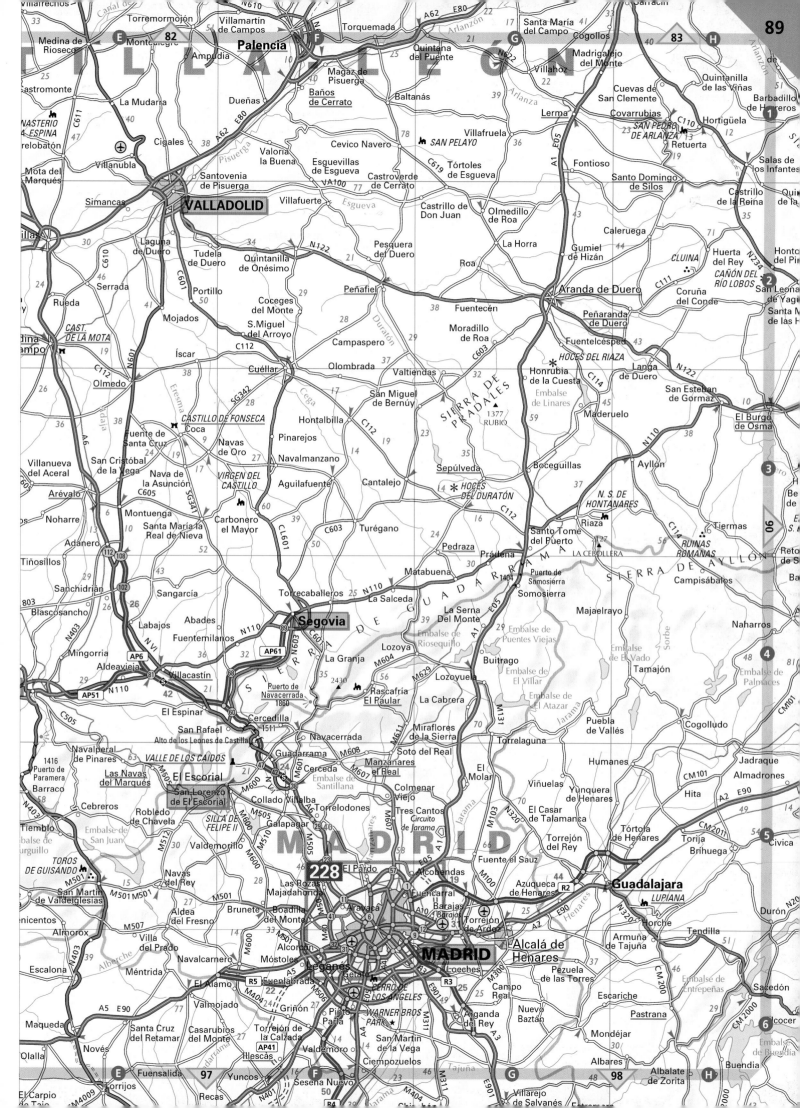

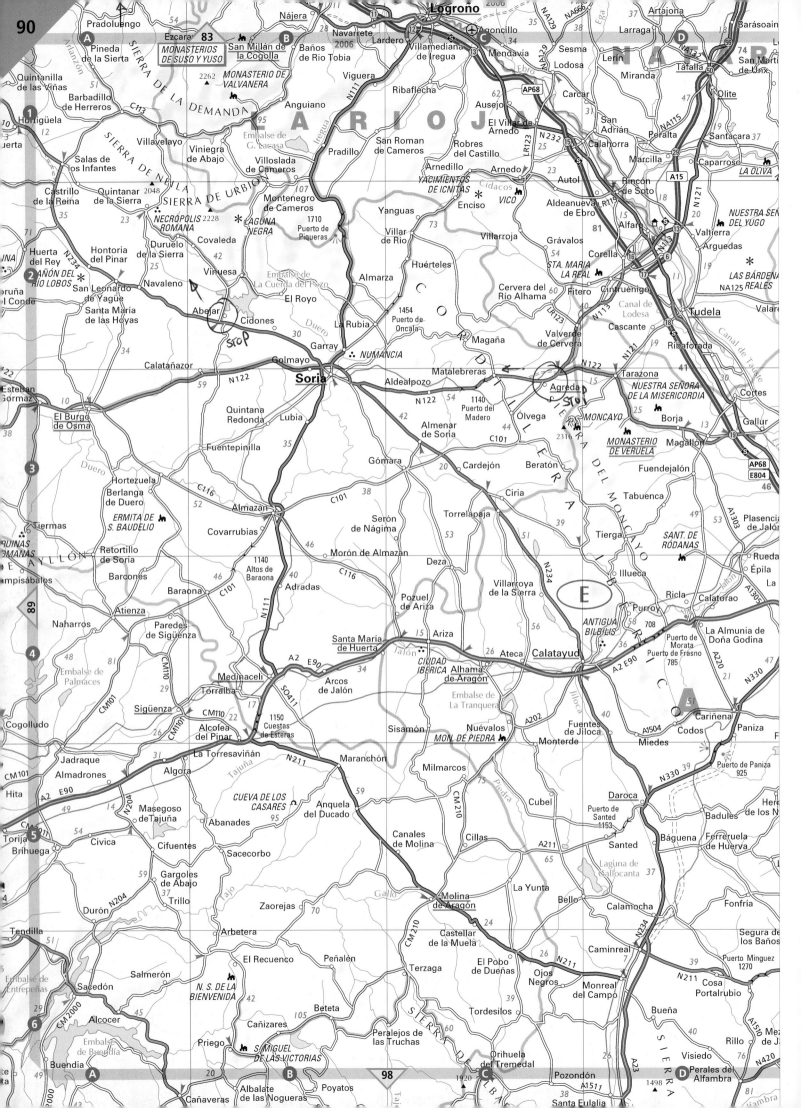

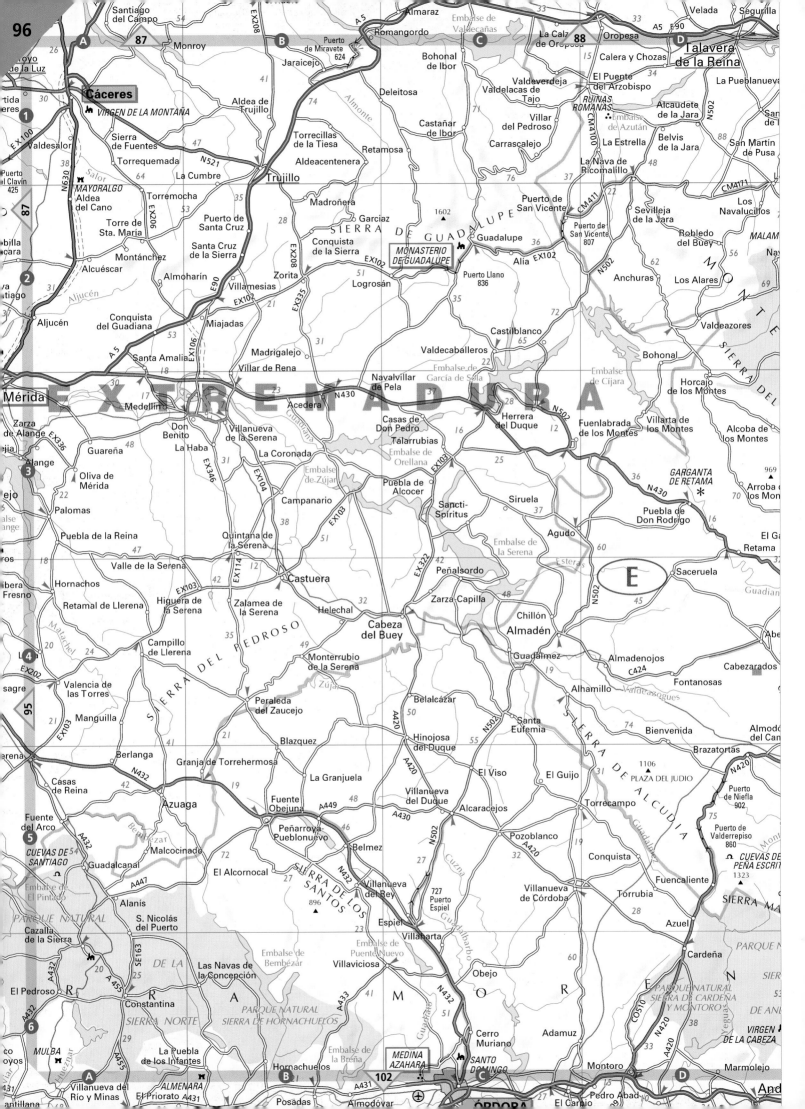

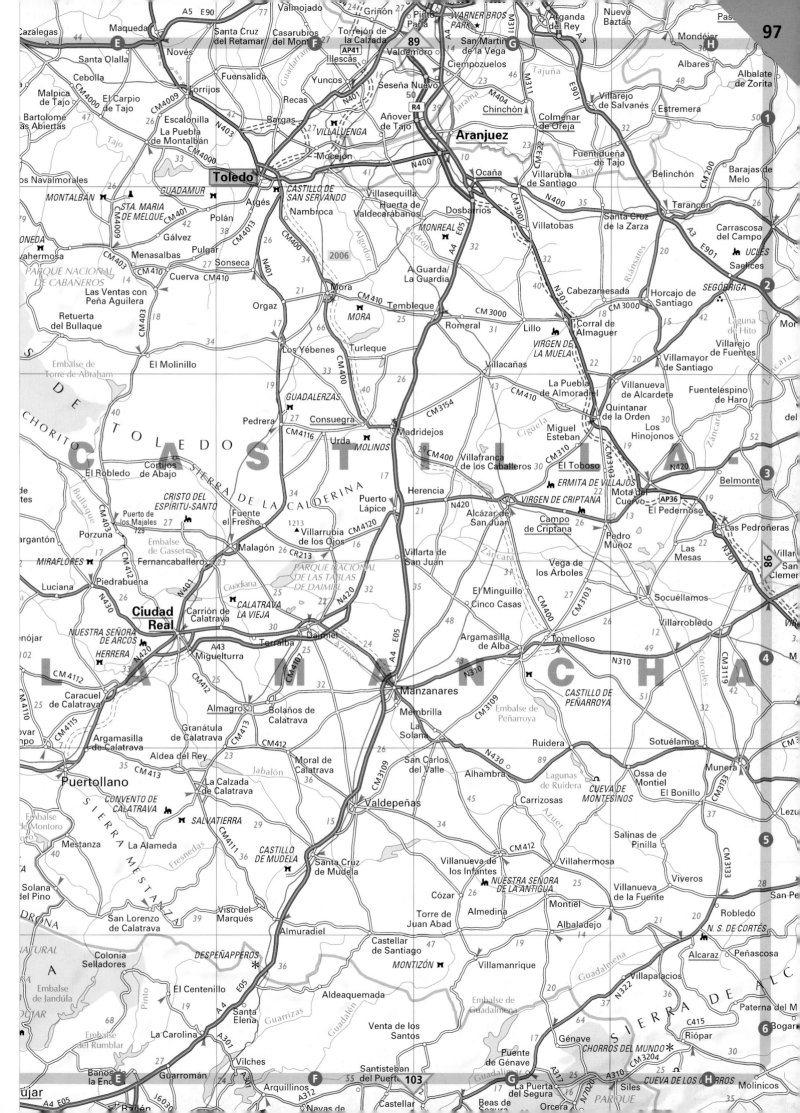

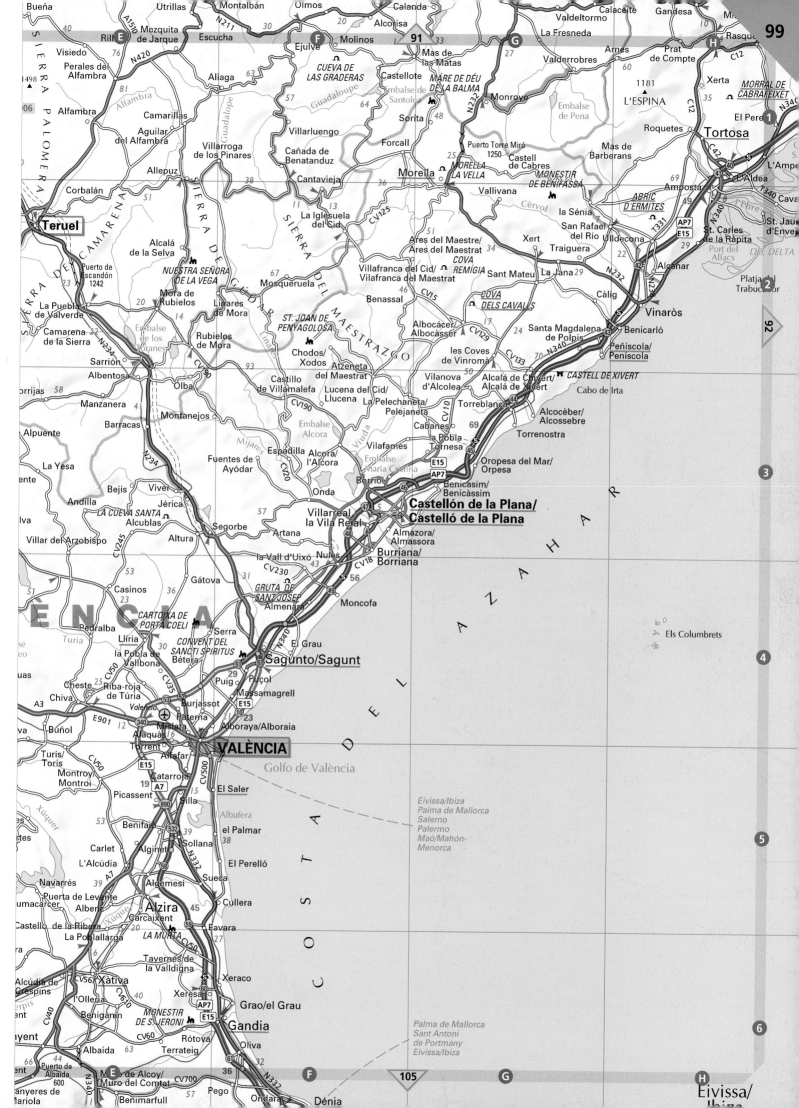

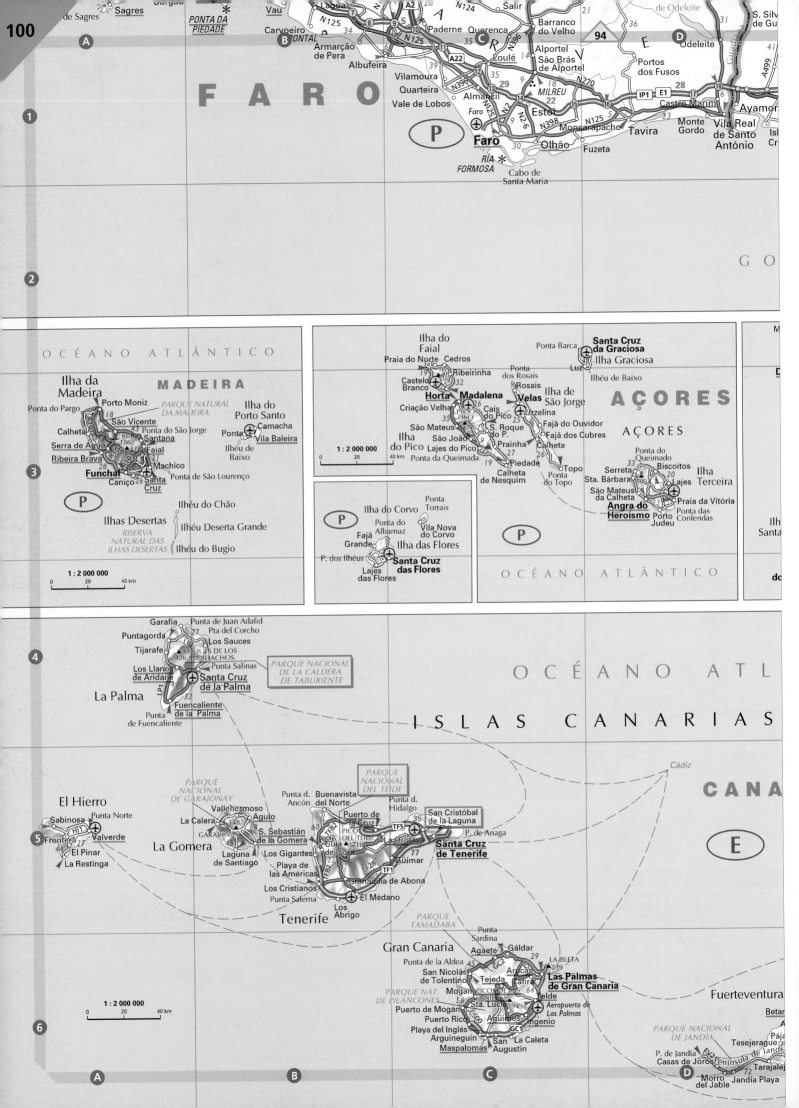

de Sagres Sagres Burgau
PONTA DA PIEDADE
Vau Lagoa A2 Salir N124 de Odeleite S. Silv
Carvoeiro N125 Paderne Querenca Barranco do Velho de Gu
Armação de Pera A22 Loulé Alportel São Brás de Alportel Portos dos Fusos Odeleite
Albufeira São Brás de Alportel Castro Marim
Vilamoura N396 Almancil MILREU IP1 E1 Ayamo
Quarteira N2 Estói Castro Marim Vila Real de Santo
Vale de Lobos Faro Monsarapacho Tavira Monte Gordo António
Faro Olhão Fuzeta Isl

F A R O

RIA FORMOSA Cabo de Santa Maria

G O

OCÉANO ATLÂNTICO

M A D E I R A

Ilha da Madeira
Ponta do Pargo Porto Moniz Parque Natural da Madeira
Calheta São Vicente Ilha do Porto Santo
Serra de Água Ponta do São Jorge Santana Ponta Camacha Vila Baleira
Ribeira Brava Faial Ilhéu de Baixo
Funchal Machico
Caniço Santa Cruz Ponta de São Lourenço
Ilhéu do Chão
Ilhas Desertas Ilhéu Deserta Grande
RISERVA NATURAL DAS ILHAS DESERTAS Ilhéu do Bugio

1 : 2 000 000

Ilha do Faial
Praia do Norte Cedros Ponta Barca **Santa Cruz da Graciosa**
Castelo Branco Ribeirinha Ponta dos Rosais Luz Ilha Graciosa Ilhéu de Baixo
Horta **Madalena** Rosais **Velas** Ilha de São Jorge
Criação Velha Cais do Pico Urzelina
São Mateus S. Roque Fajã do Ouvidor **AÇORES**
Ilha do Pico São João Fajã dos Cubres **AÇORES**
Lajes do Pico Prainha
Ponta da Queimada Piedade Calheta Ponta do Queimado Biscoitos
Calheta de Nesquim Ponta do Topo Topo Serreta Sta. Bárbara Ilha Terceira
São Mateus da Calheta Lajes
Angra do Heroísmo Porto Judeu Praia da Vitória
Ponta das Contendas
OCÉANO ATLÂNTICO

1 : 2 000 000

Ilha do Corvo Ponta Torrais
Ponta do Albarnaz Vila Nova do Corvo
Fajã Grande Ilha das Flores
P. dos Ilhéus **Santa Cruz das Flores**
Lajes das Flores

I S L A S   C A N A R I A S

Garafía Punta de Juan Adalid Pta del Corcho
Puntagorda Los Sauces
Tijarafe ROQUES DE LOS MUCHACHOS 2426 Punta Salinas
Los Llanos de Aridane **Santa Cruz de la Palma**
La Palma PARQUE NACIONAL DE LA CALDERA DE TABURIENTE
Fuencaliente de la Palma
Punta de Fuencaliente

OCÉANO ATL

Cádiz

C A N A

El Hierro
Sabinosa Punta Norte PARQUE NACIONAL DE GARAJONAY Buenavista del Norte Punta d. Hidalgo PARQUE NACIONAL DEL TEIDE San Cristóbal de la Laguna
Frontera Valverde Vallehermoso Agulo Punta d. Ancón Puerto de la Cruz TF5
El Pinar La Calera GARAJONAY 1487 Buenavista del Norte PICO DEL TEIDE 3718 La Orotava P. de Anaga
La Restinga **La Gomera** S. Sebastián de la Gomera Güía de Isora **Santa Cruz de Tenerife**
Laguna de Santiago Los Gigantes TF1 Güímar
Playa de las Américas TF28
Tenerife Granadilla de Abona **E**
Los Cristianos El Médano
Punta Salema Los Abrigos PARQUE TAMADABA Punta Sardina
Gran Canaria Agaete Gáldar LA ISLETA
Punta de la Aldea Arucas **Las Palmas de Gran Canaria**
San Nicolás de Tolentino Tejeda Tafira Telde **Fuerteventura**
PARQUE NAT. DE PILANCONES Mogán PICOS DE LAS NIEVES Aeropuerto de Las Palmas Betan
Puerto de Mogán Sta. Lucía Aguimes PARQUE NACIONAL DE JANDÍA
Puerto Rico Ingenio
Playa del Inglés GC1 P. de Jandía Teseierague
Arguineguin San La Caleta Casas de Joros Tarajalej
Maspalomas Agustín Morro del Jable Jandía Playa

1 : 2 000 000

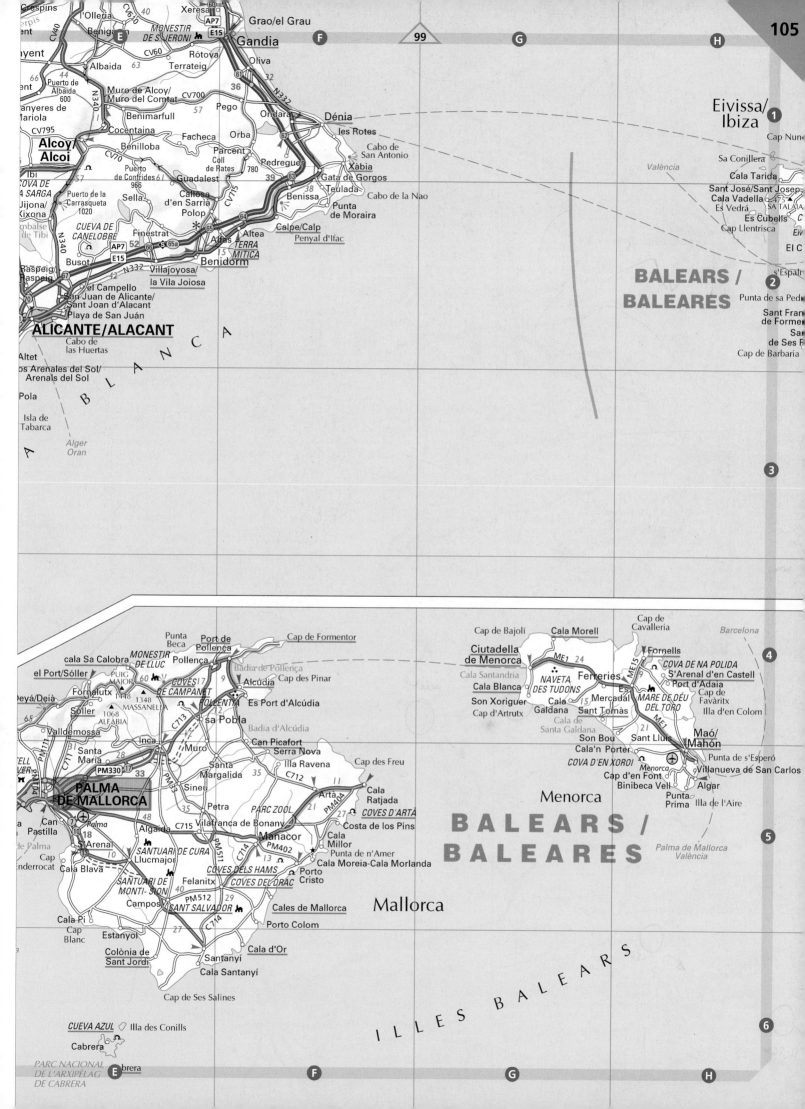

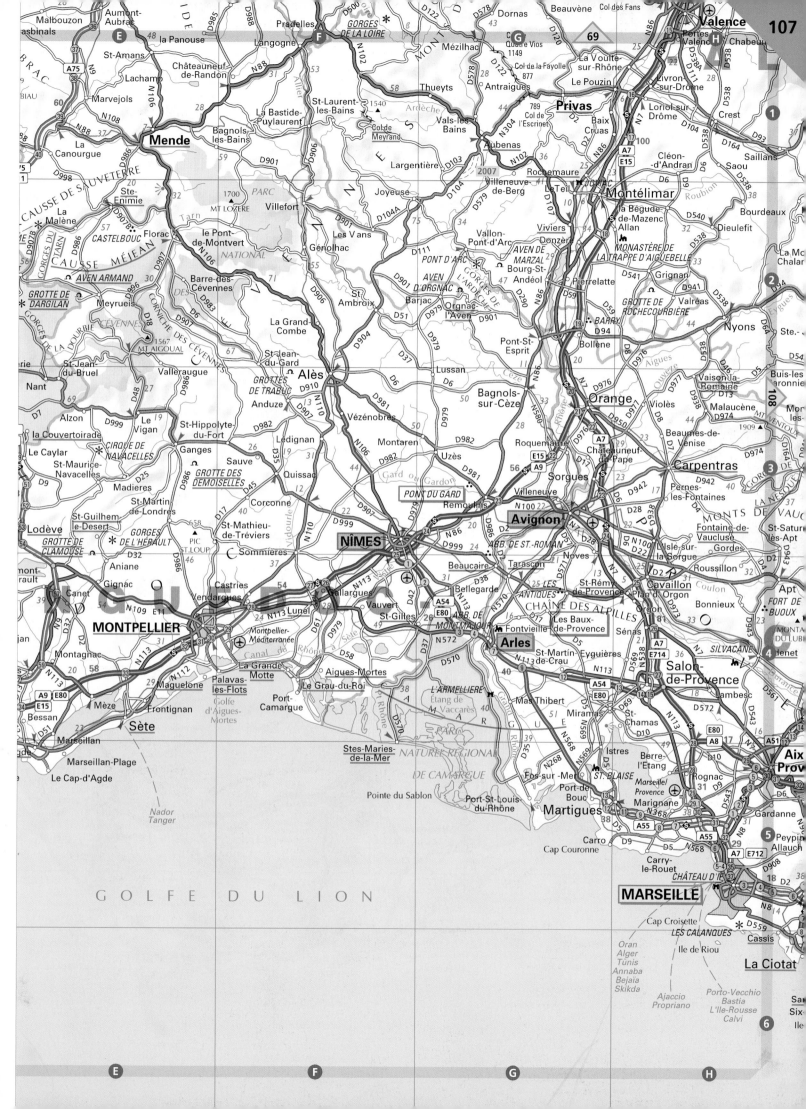

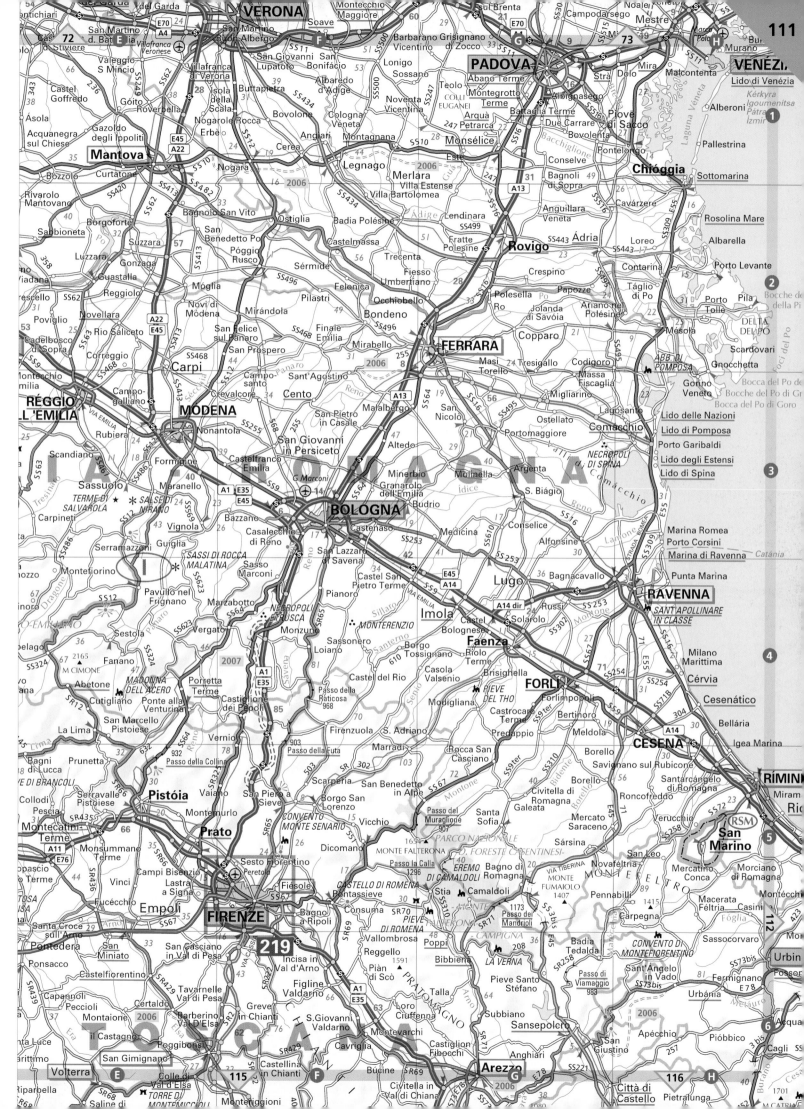

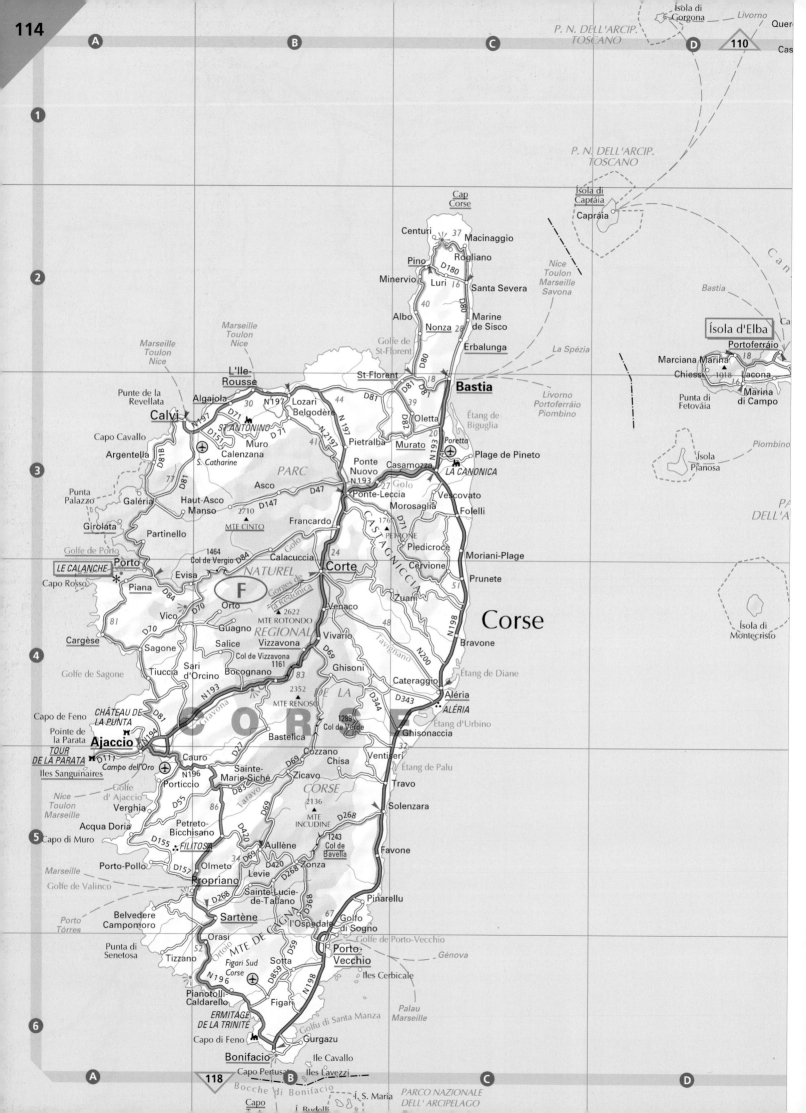

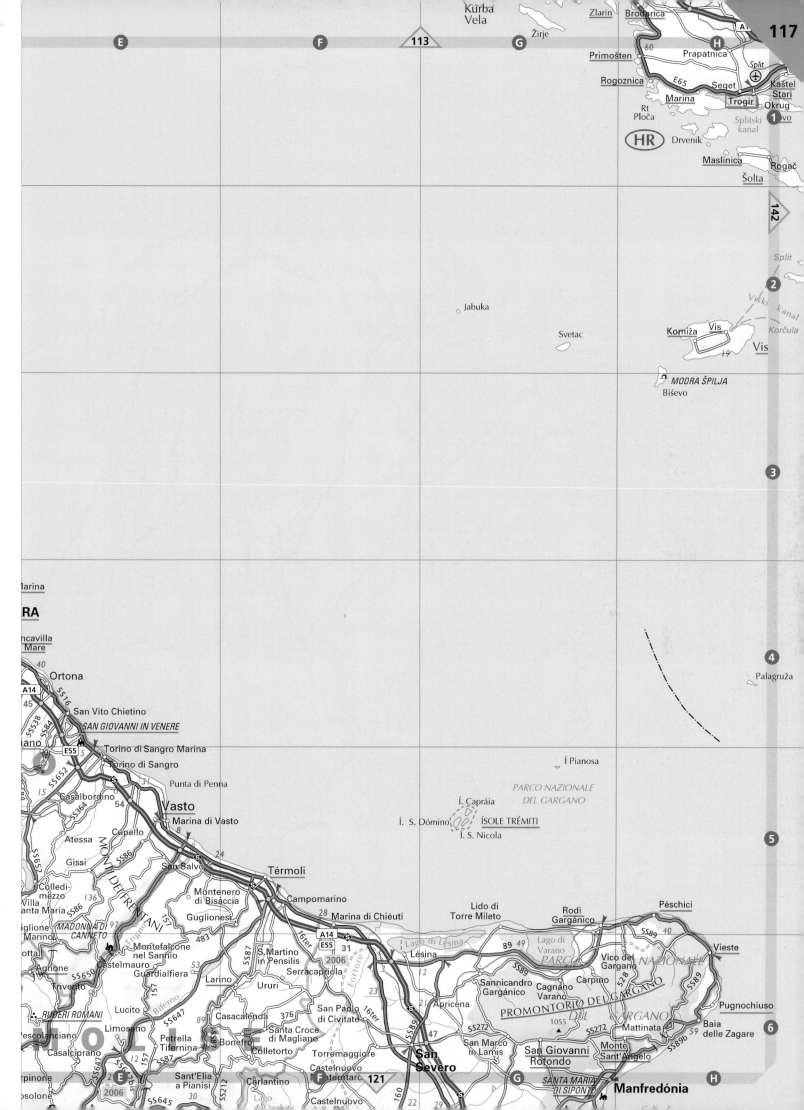

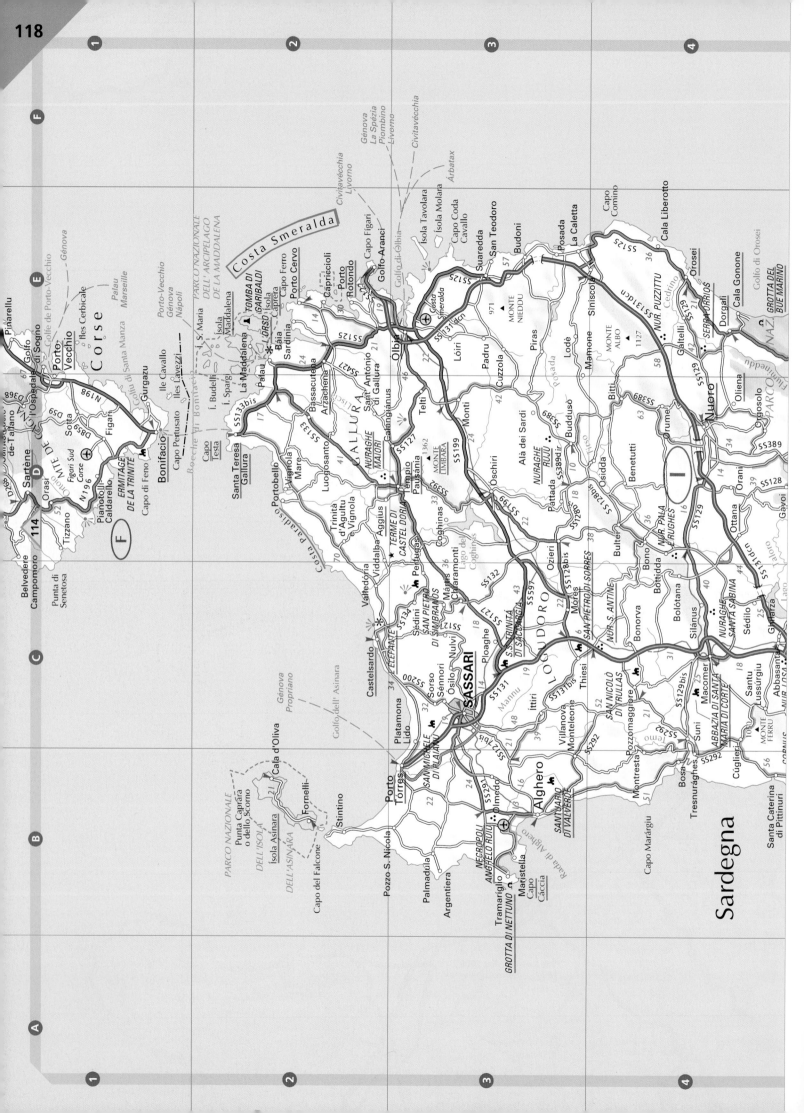

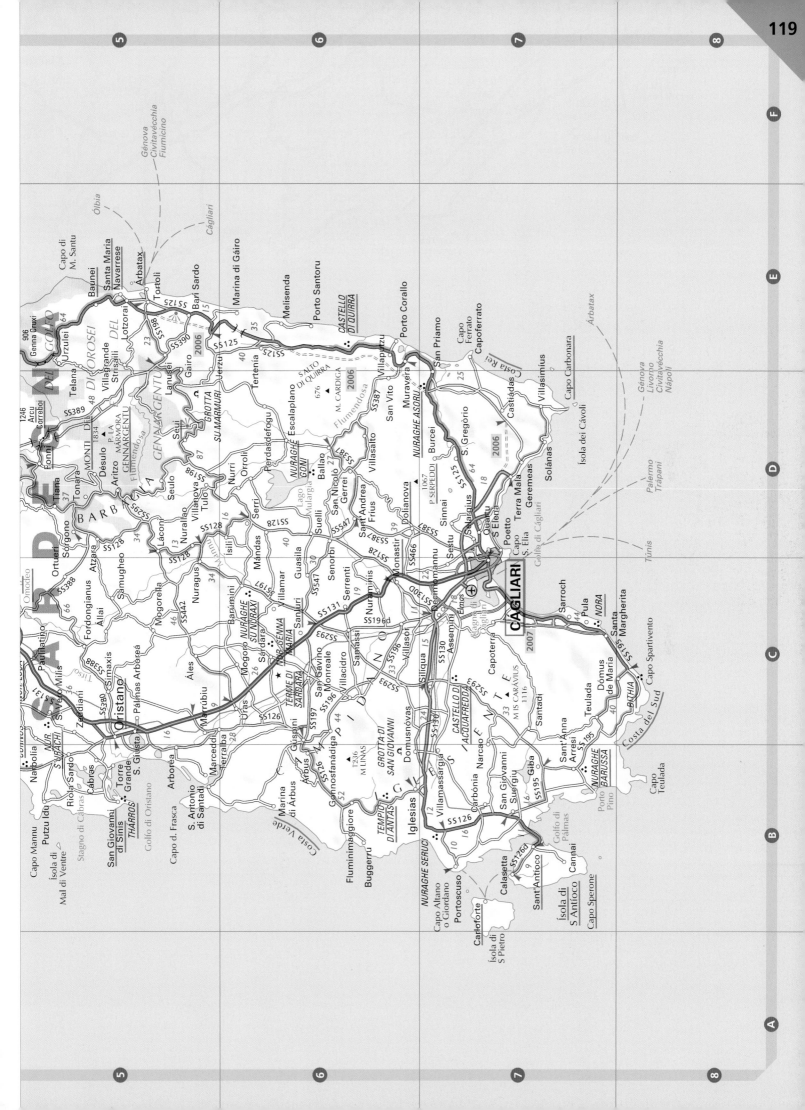

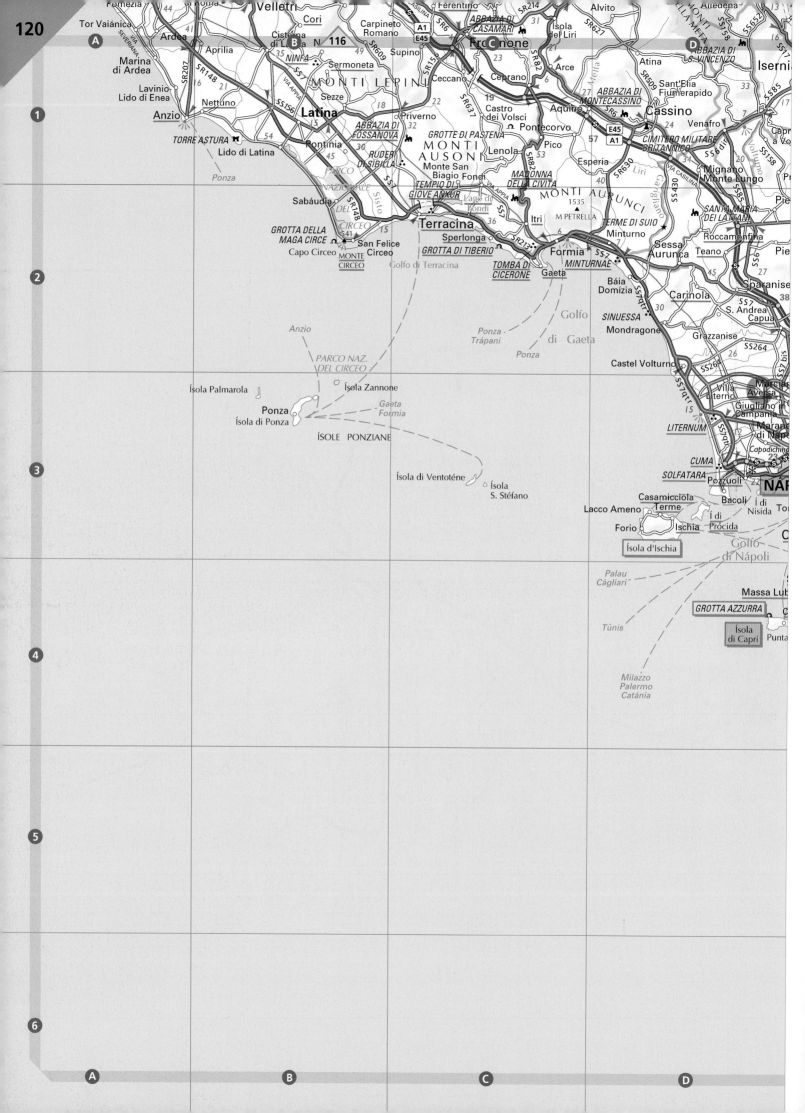

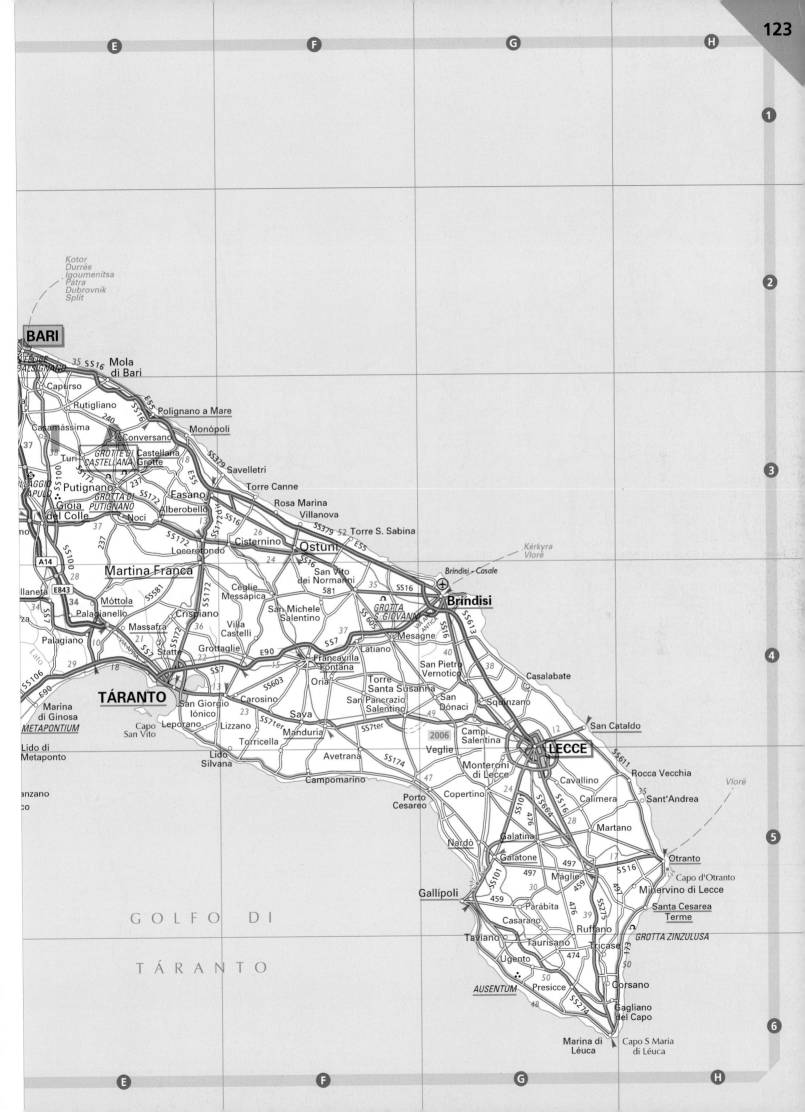

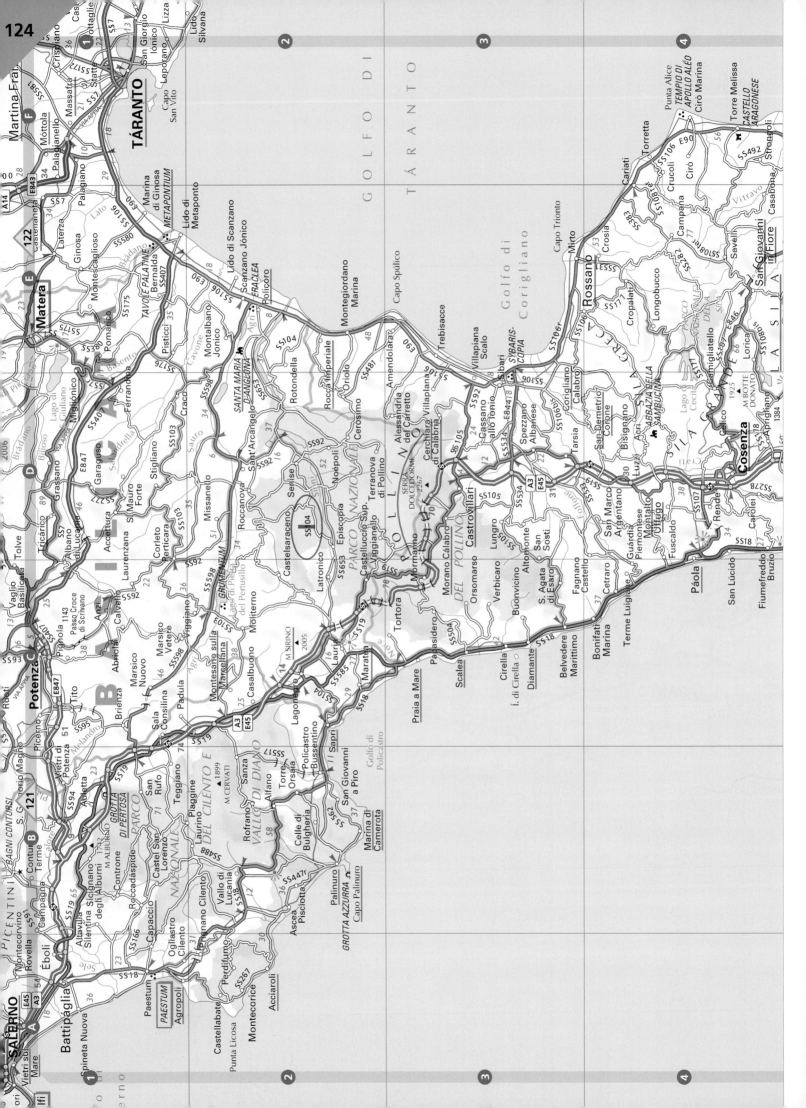

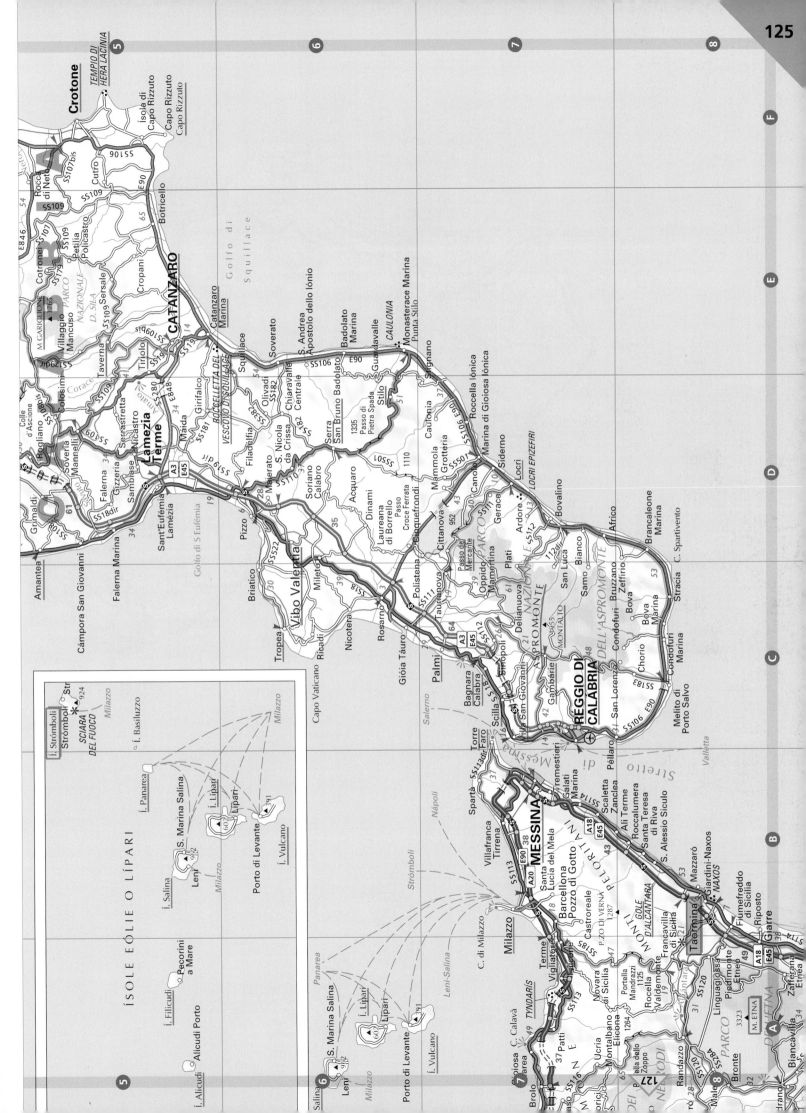

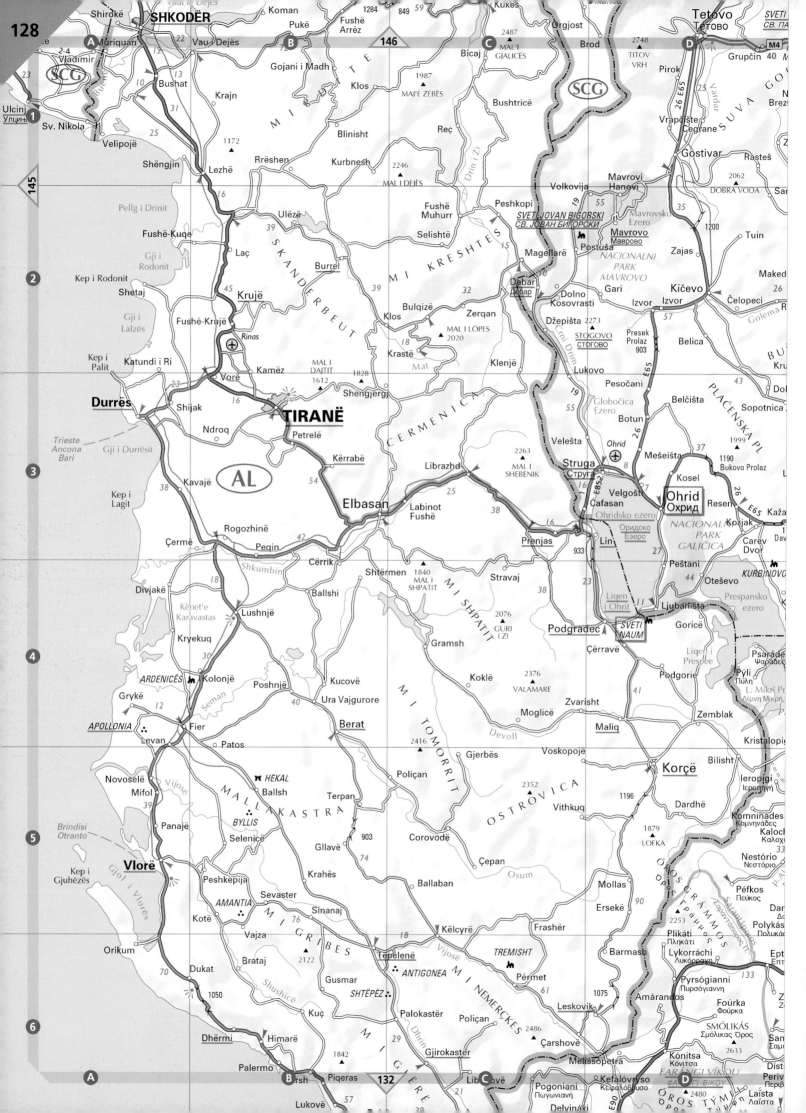

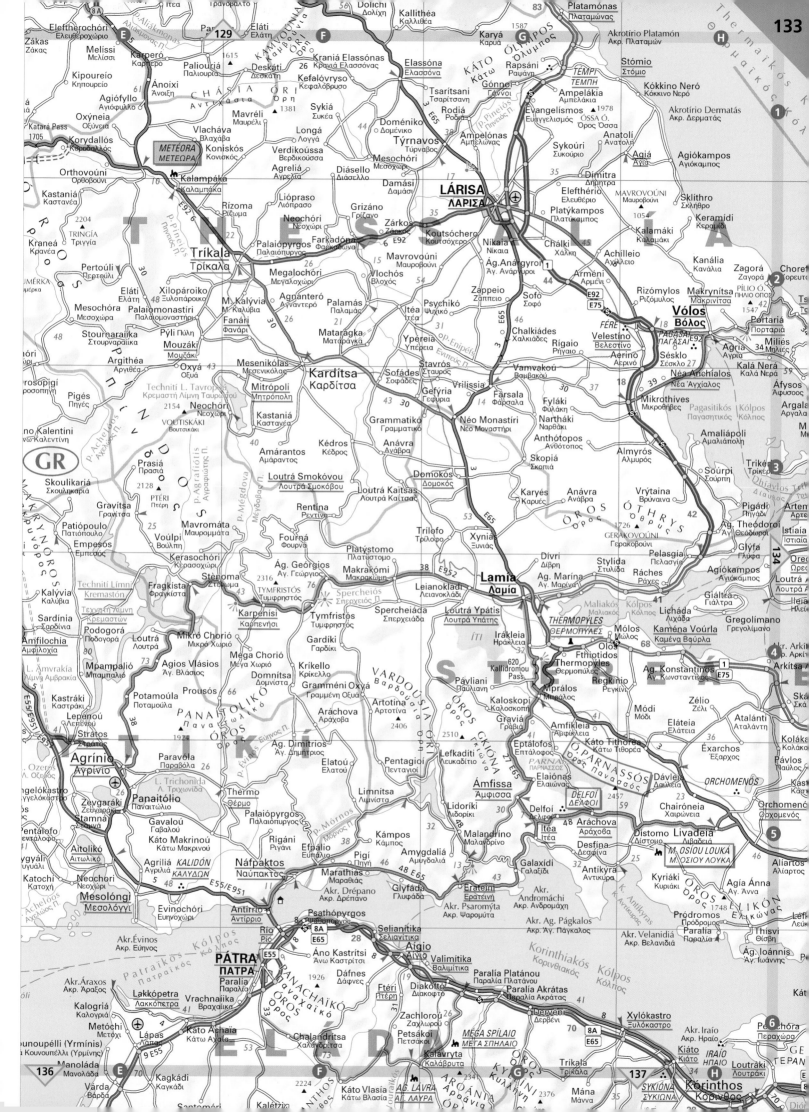

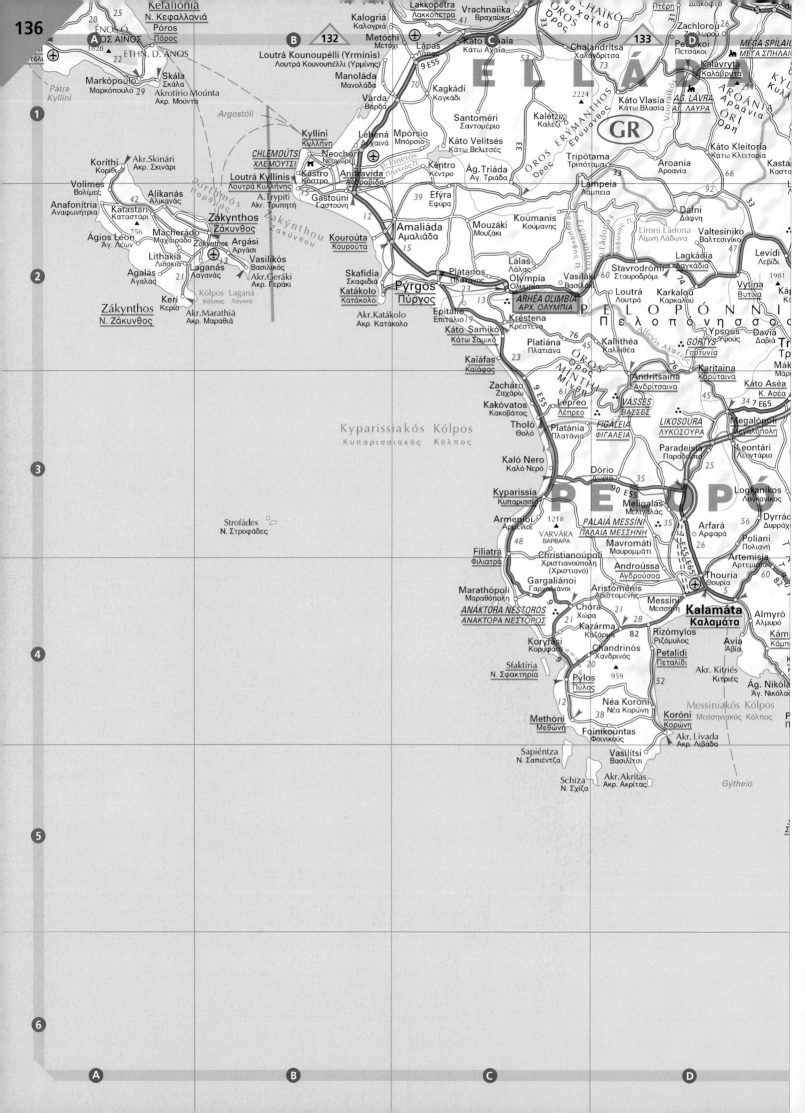

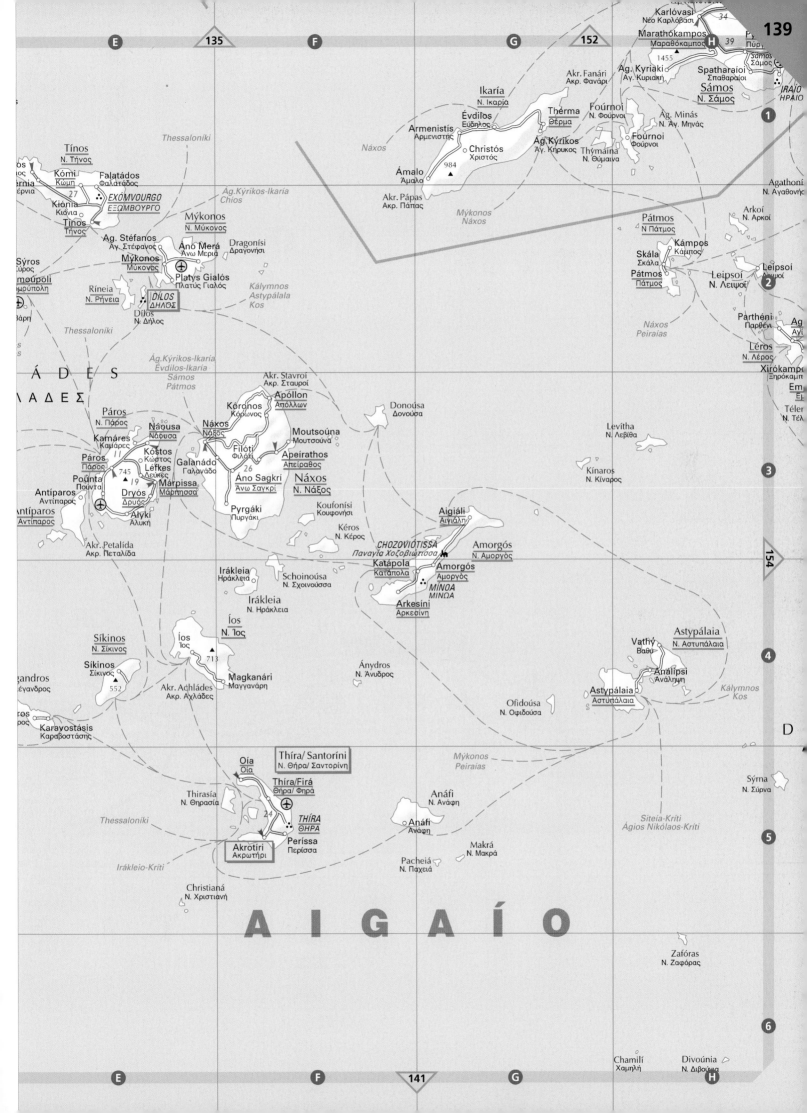

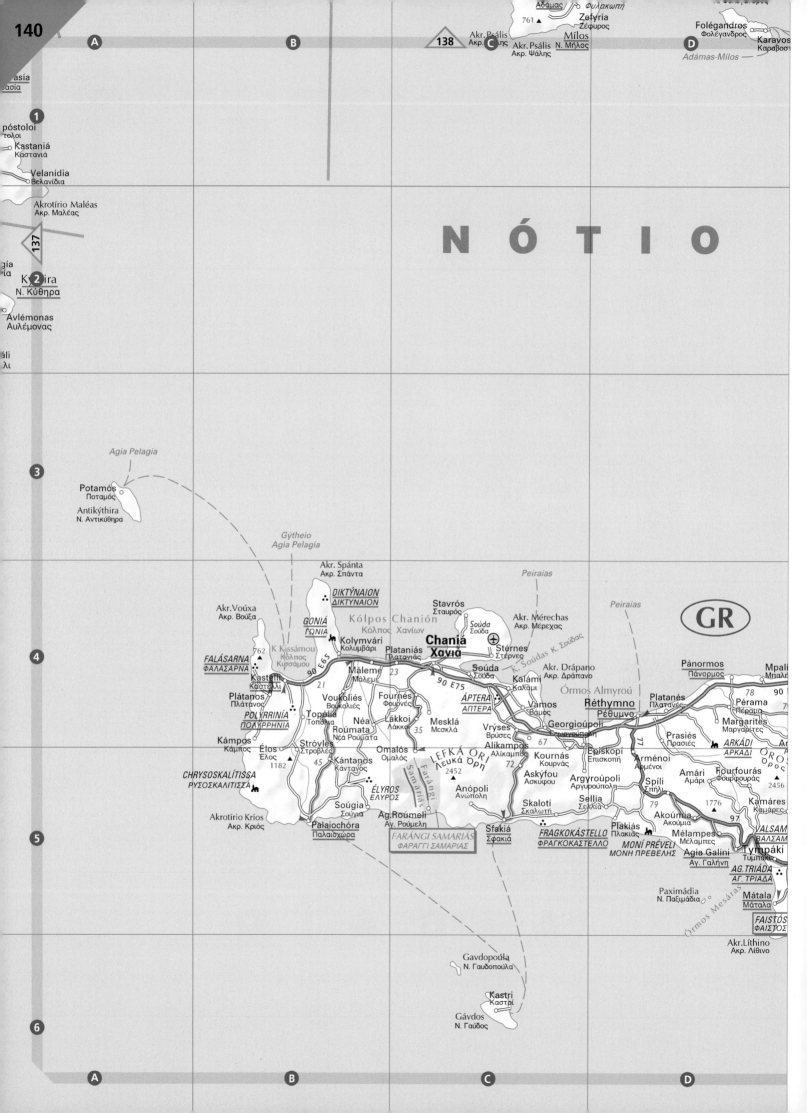

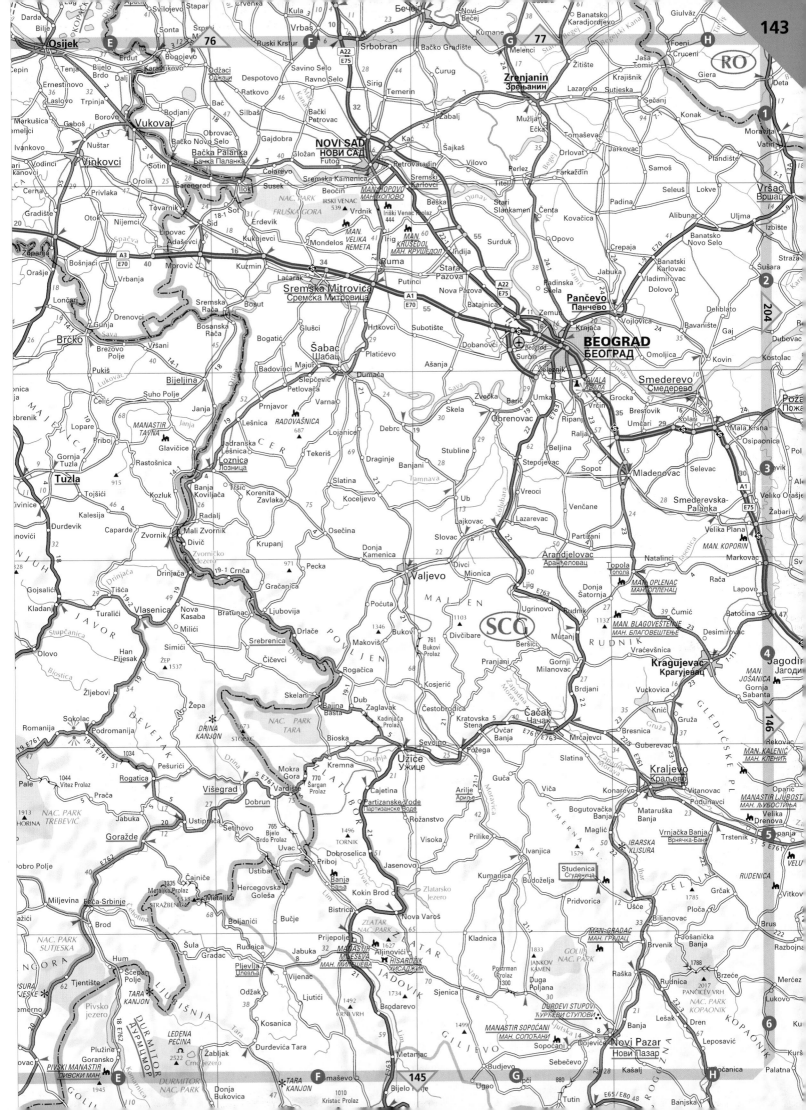

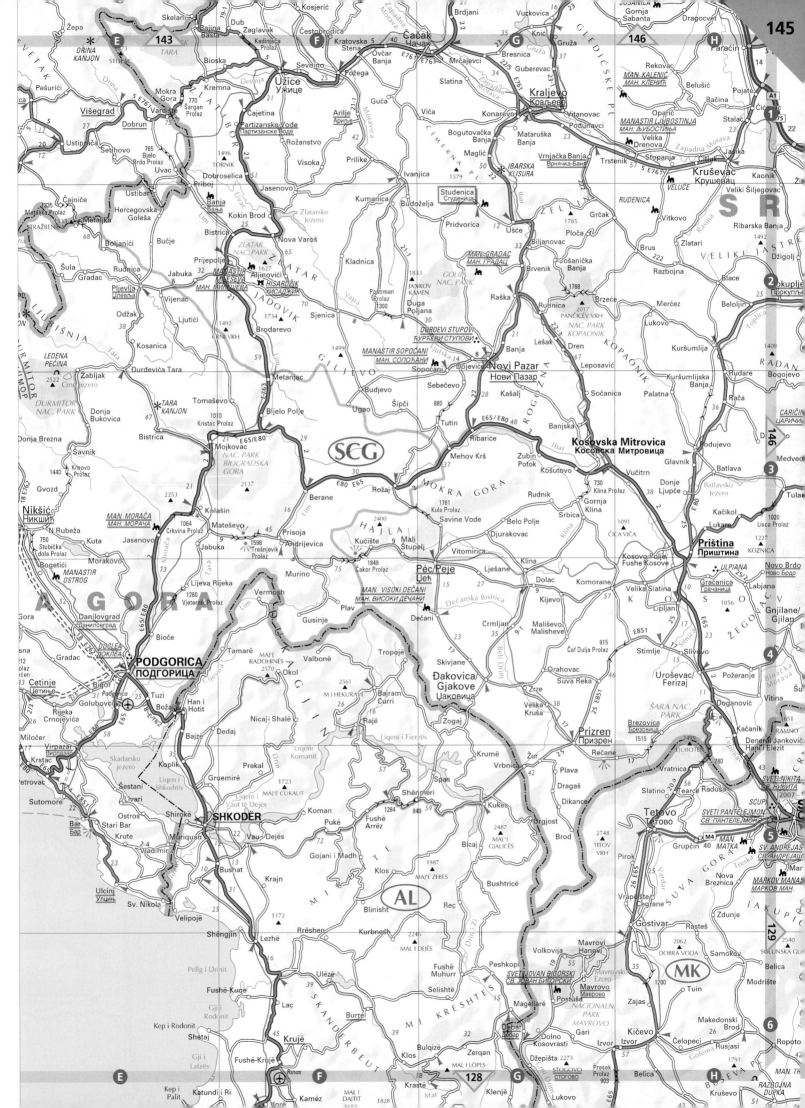

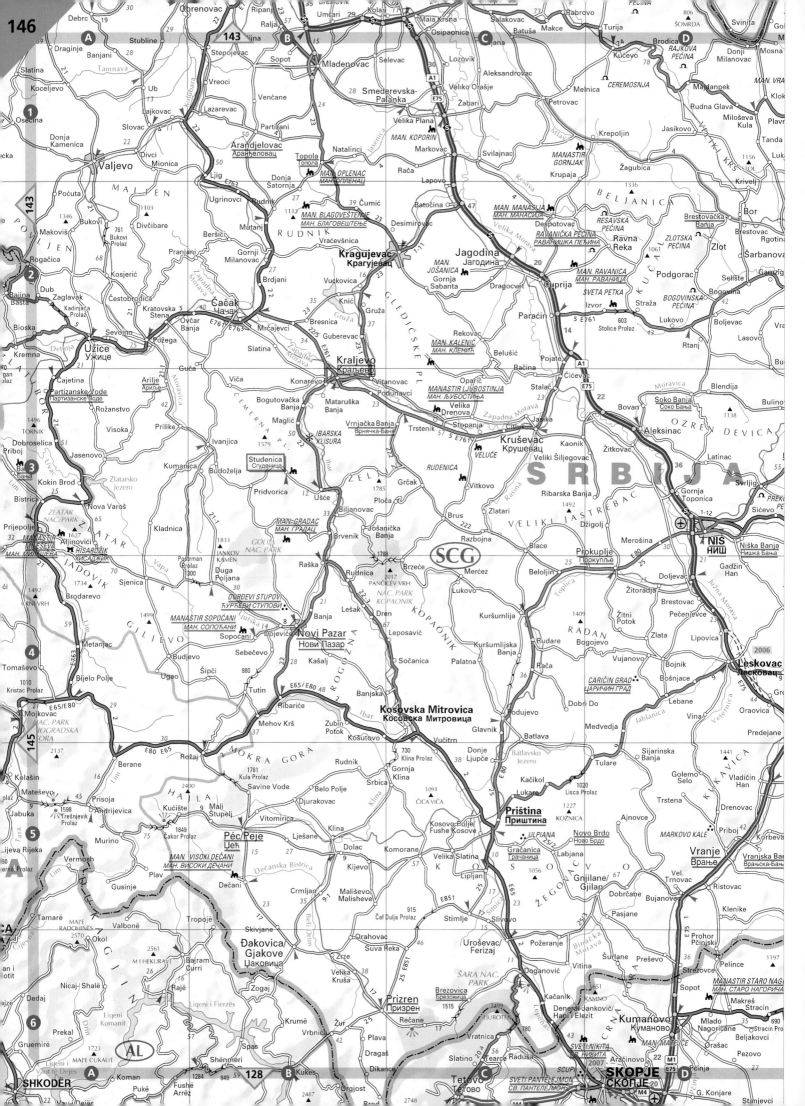

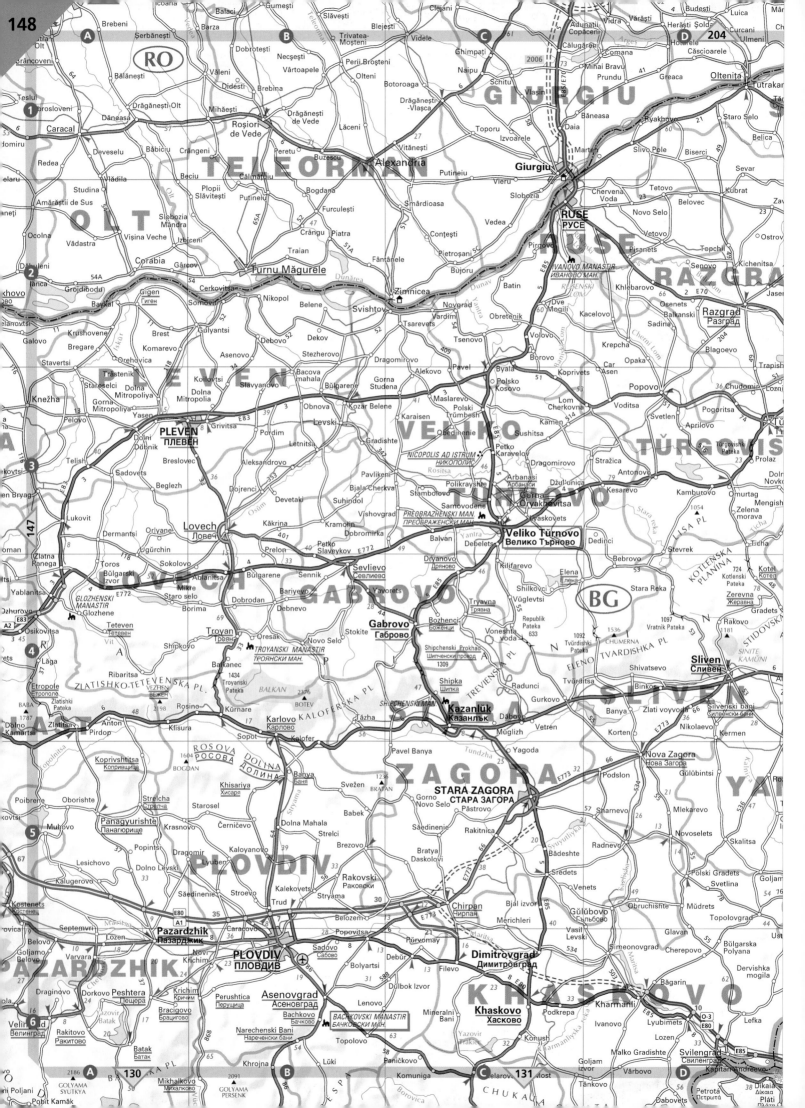

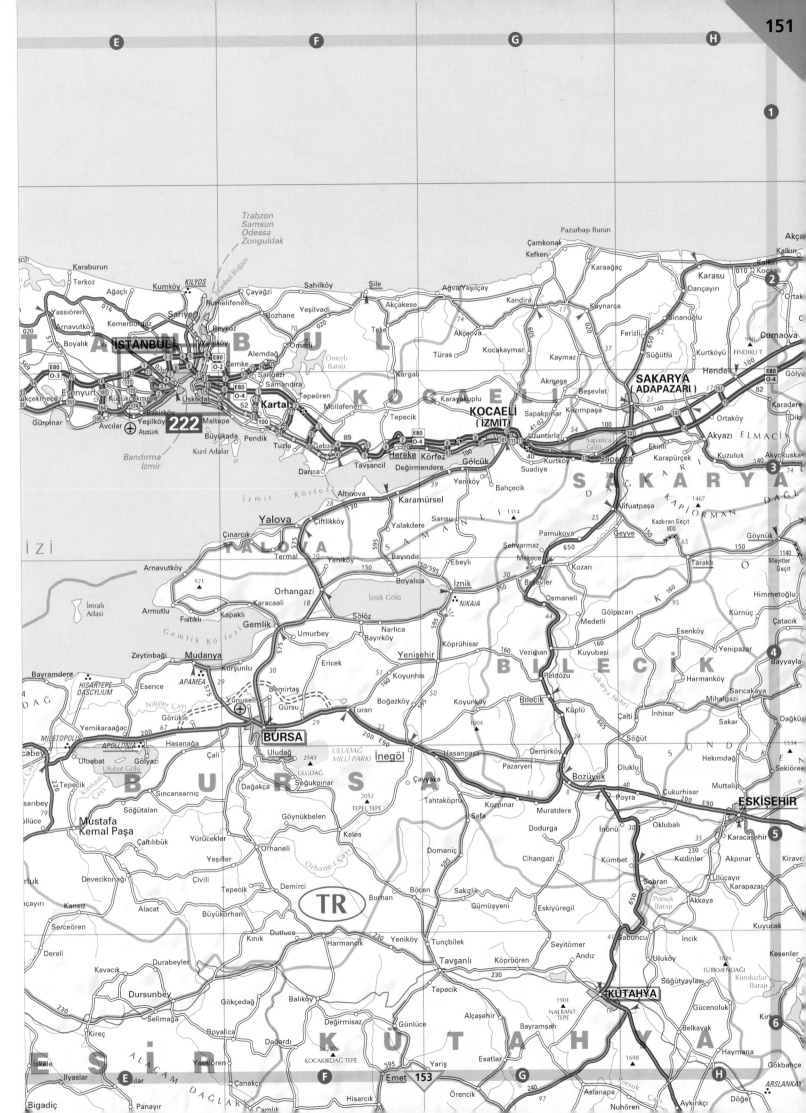

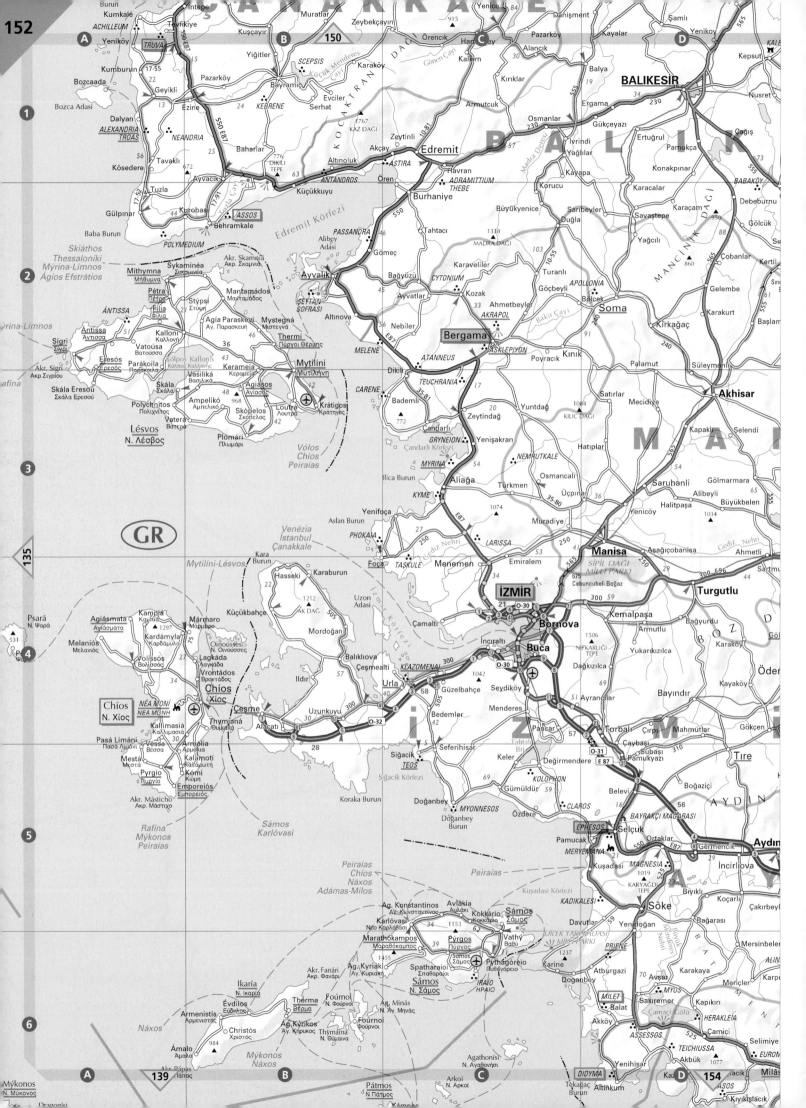

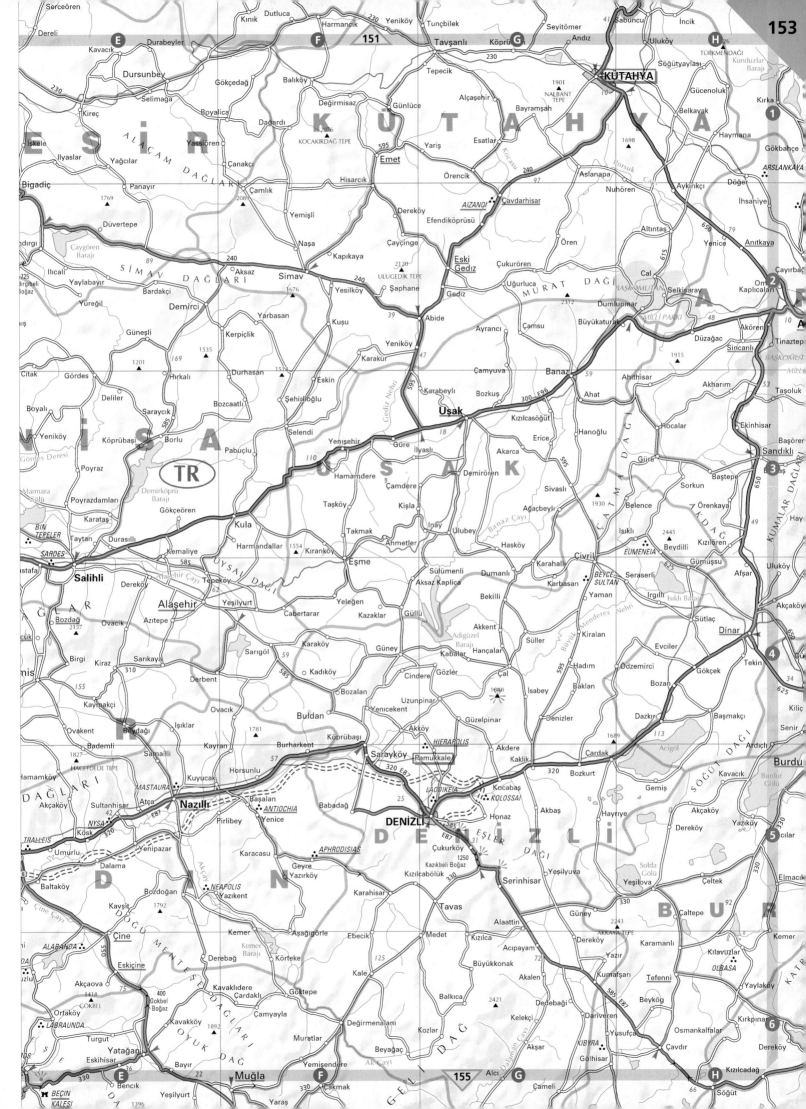

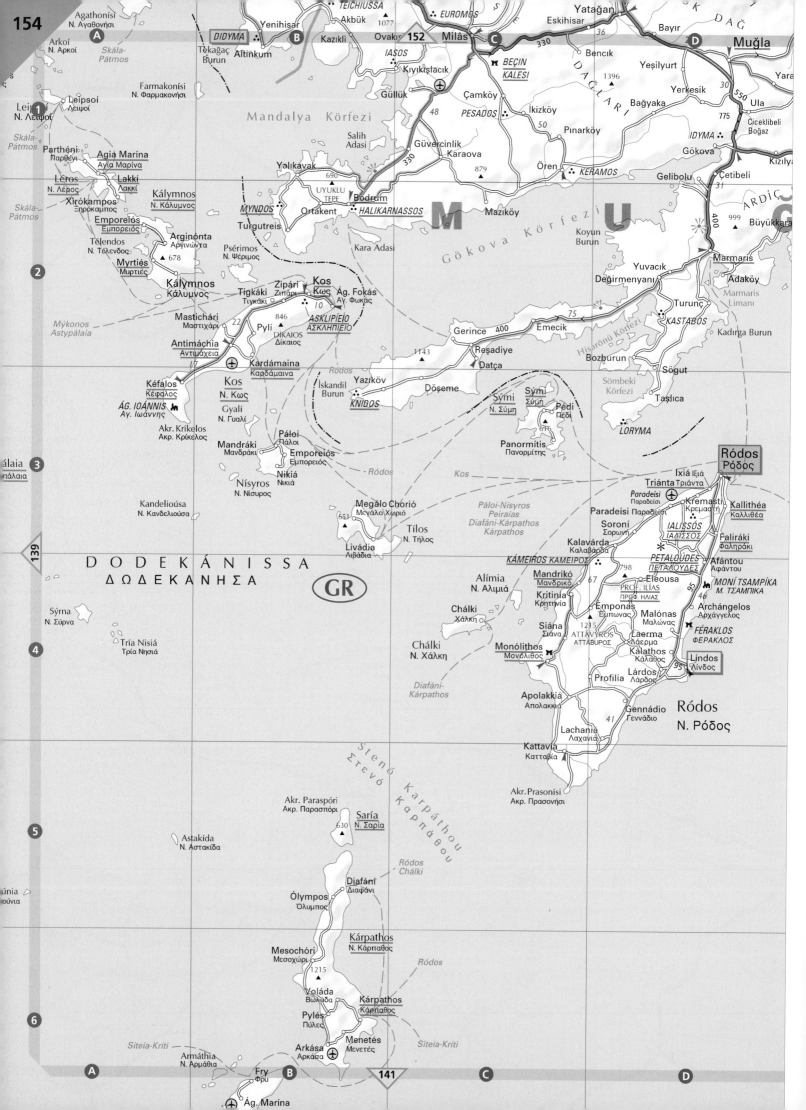

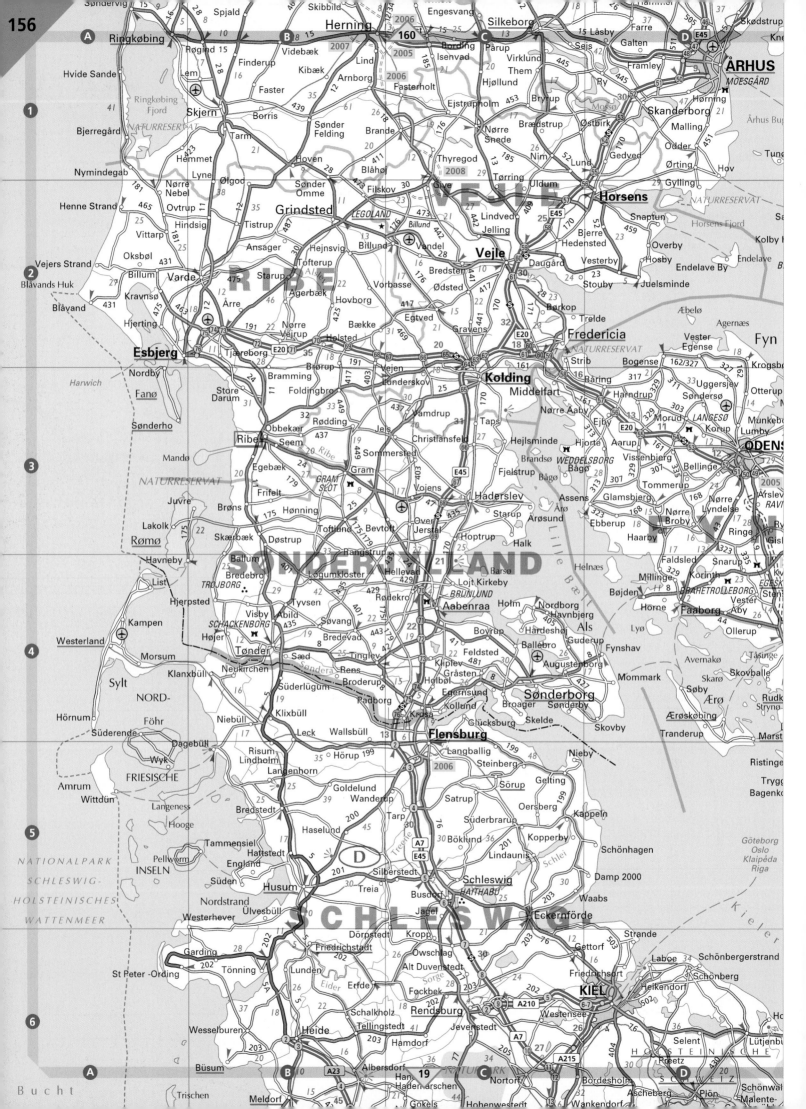

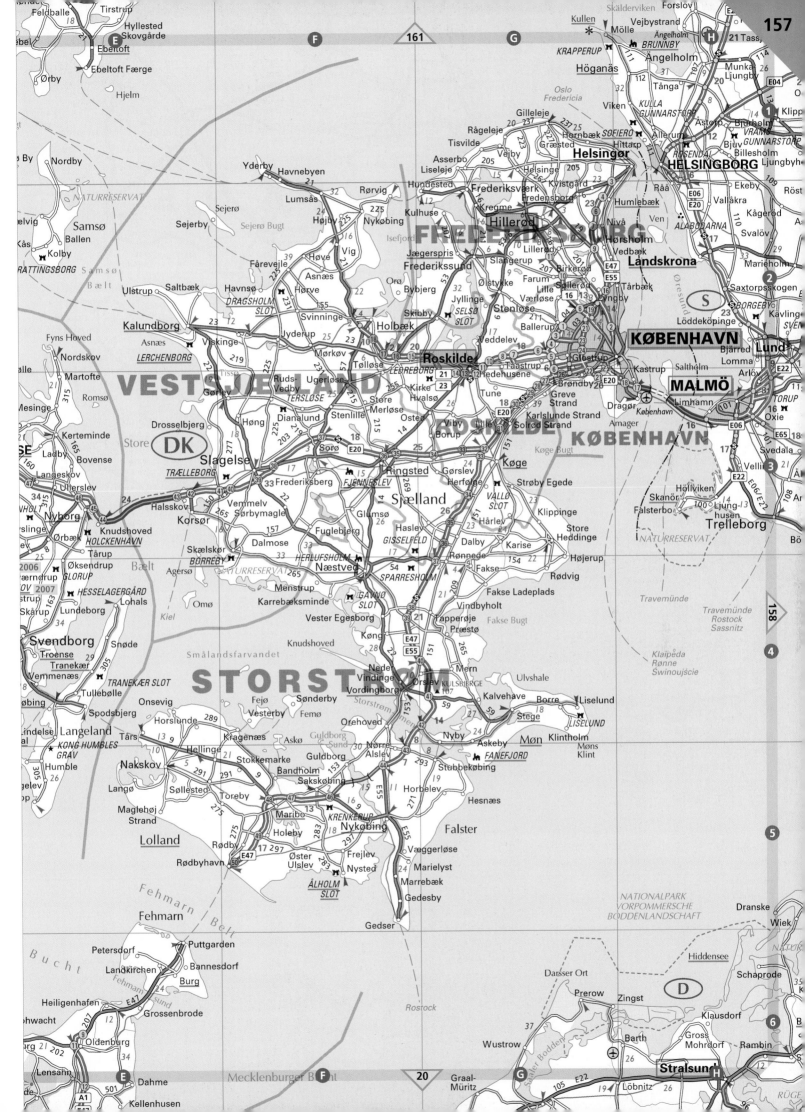

Kyrkhult
Hallábro
Eringsboda
Bidalite
Bergkvara
GETTLINGE
Stor
Segerstad

E
Ringamåla
Bökemåla
F
163
Tving
G
Degerhamn
H

B L E K I N G E

Olofström
Svängsta
Asarum
Bräkne-Hoby
Kallinge
Hjortsberga
Rödeby
Sälleryd
Brömsebro
Grönhögen

Mörrum
Ronneby
Nättraby
Kristianopel
Ottenby

Pukavik
Karlshamn
Sonekulla
Listerby
Jämjöslätt
LÅNGE JAN

1

Norje
Karlskrona
Lyckeby
Ölands södra udde

Sölvesborg
Mjällby
Kuggeboda
Tjurkö
Drottningskär
Forhamn

Nogersund
Pukaviksbukten
Liepāja
Klaipėda
Utlängan

2

nöbukten

VUDS
ALPARK

ishamn

Gdynia
3

Hammerodde
Christiansø

Sandvig
HAMMERSHUS
Allinge
Tejn
Bornholm

Hasle
Gudhjem
DK

Nyker
Klemensker
Østerlars
Svaneke

Rønne
Nylars
Østermarie
Helsinki
4

Arnager
Aakirkeby
Neksø

Pedersker
Snogebæk
Dueodde

R N H O L M

5

SŁOW
NA

Jezioro
Gardno
Rowy

PL
Ustka
Objazda
Gab

Jarosławiec
Jezioro
Wicko
22

Drozdowo
Postomino
Słupsk
6

Darłówko
Kanin
Wieprza
Lub

Dąbki
Darłowo
Staniewice
Warszkowo
Rę

E
F
G
22
H
Sławno

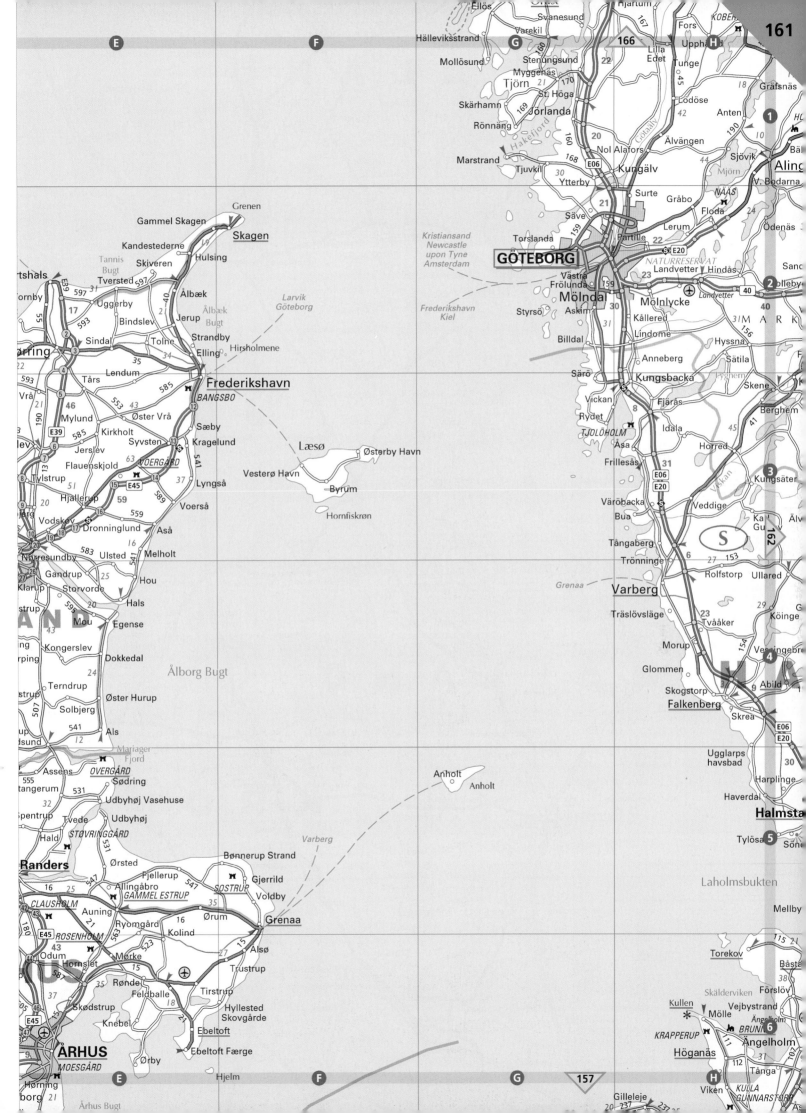

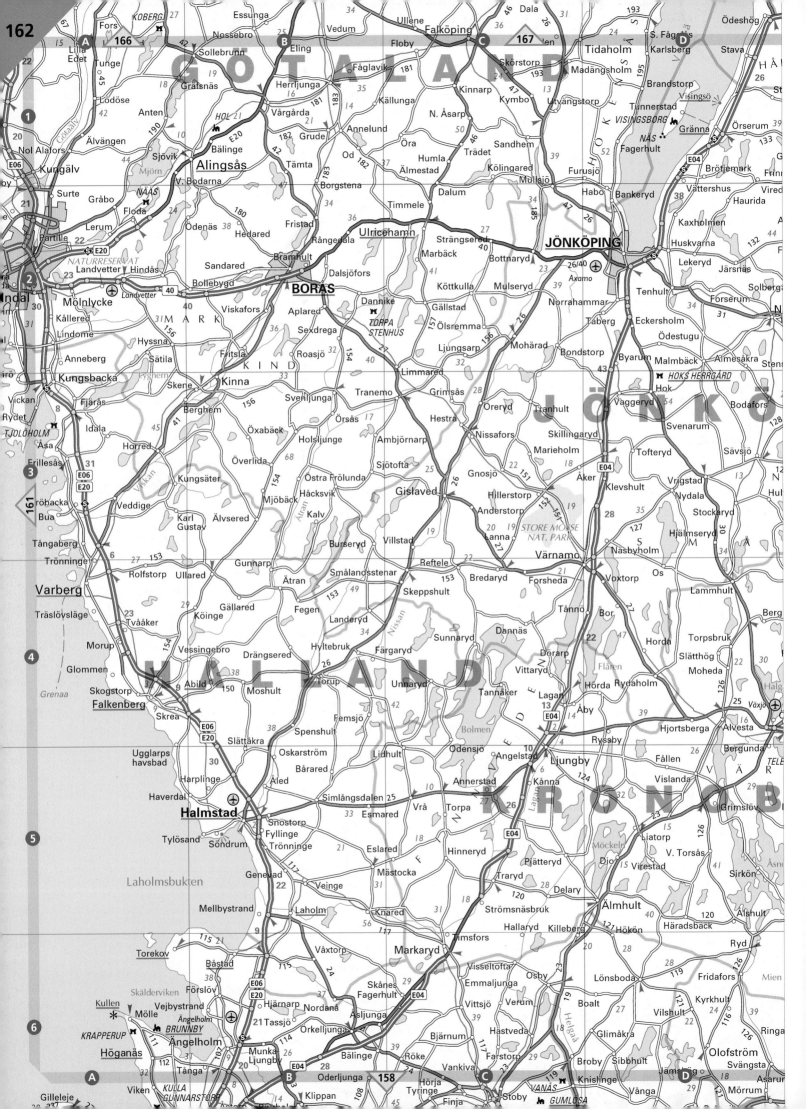

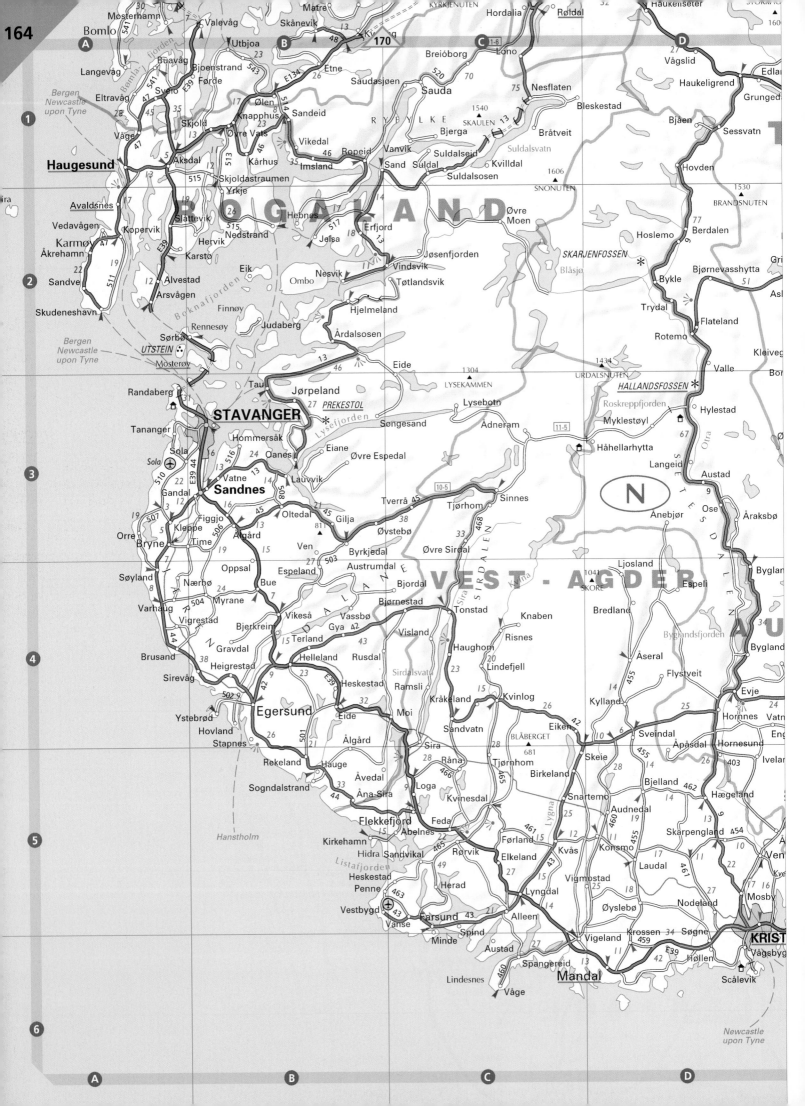

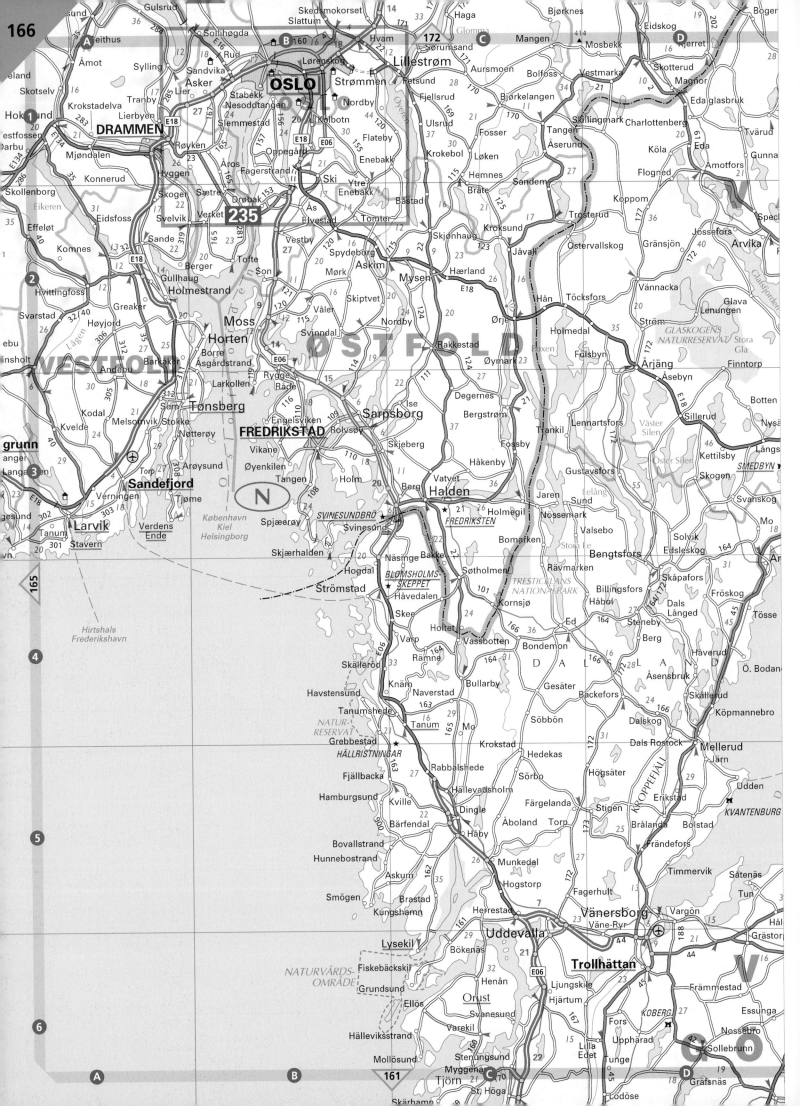

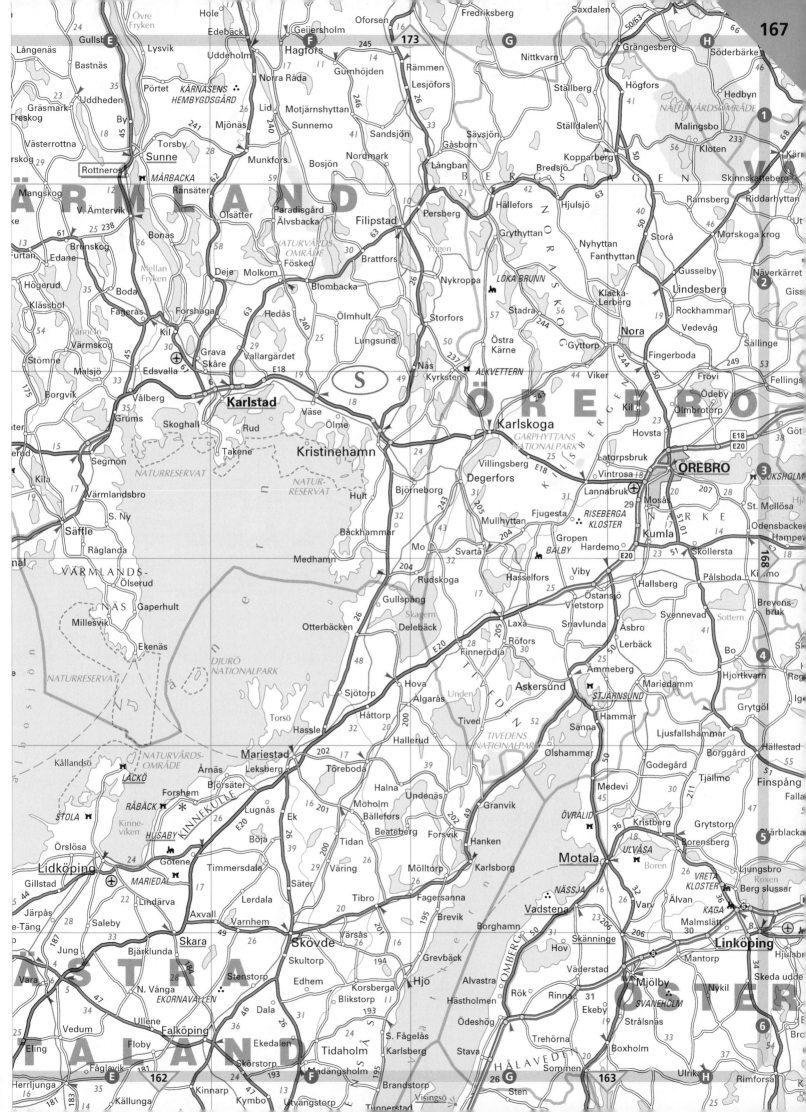

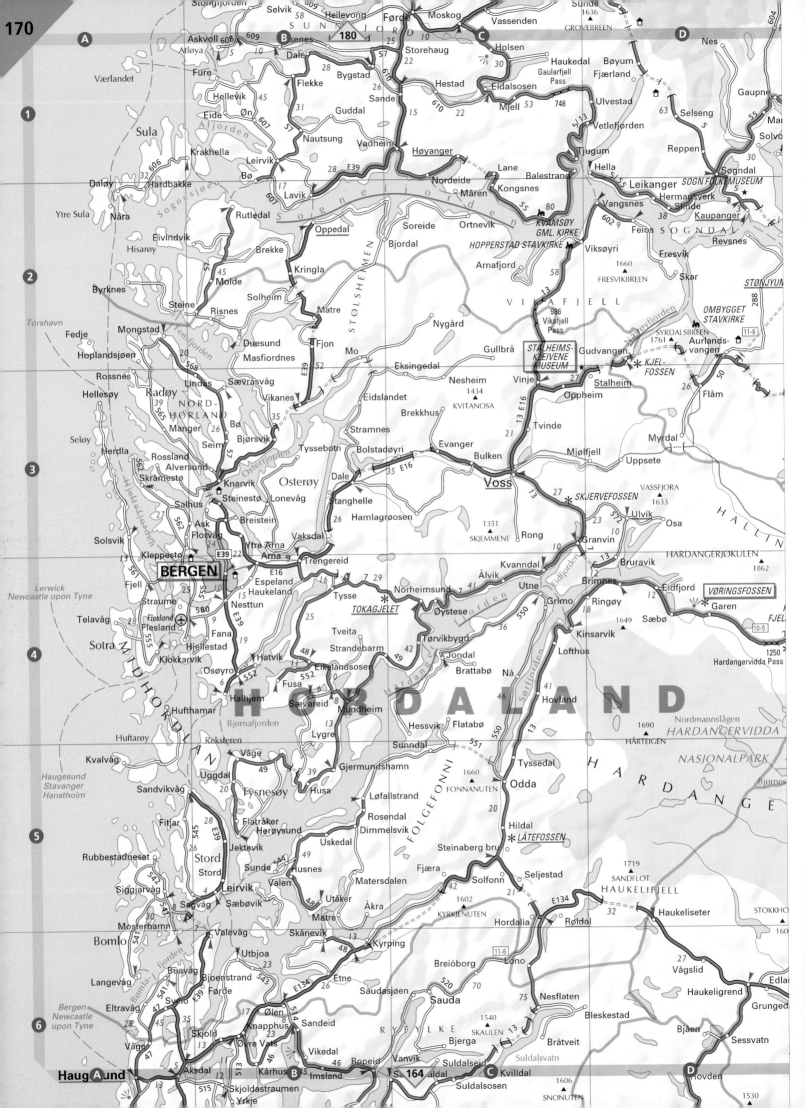

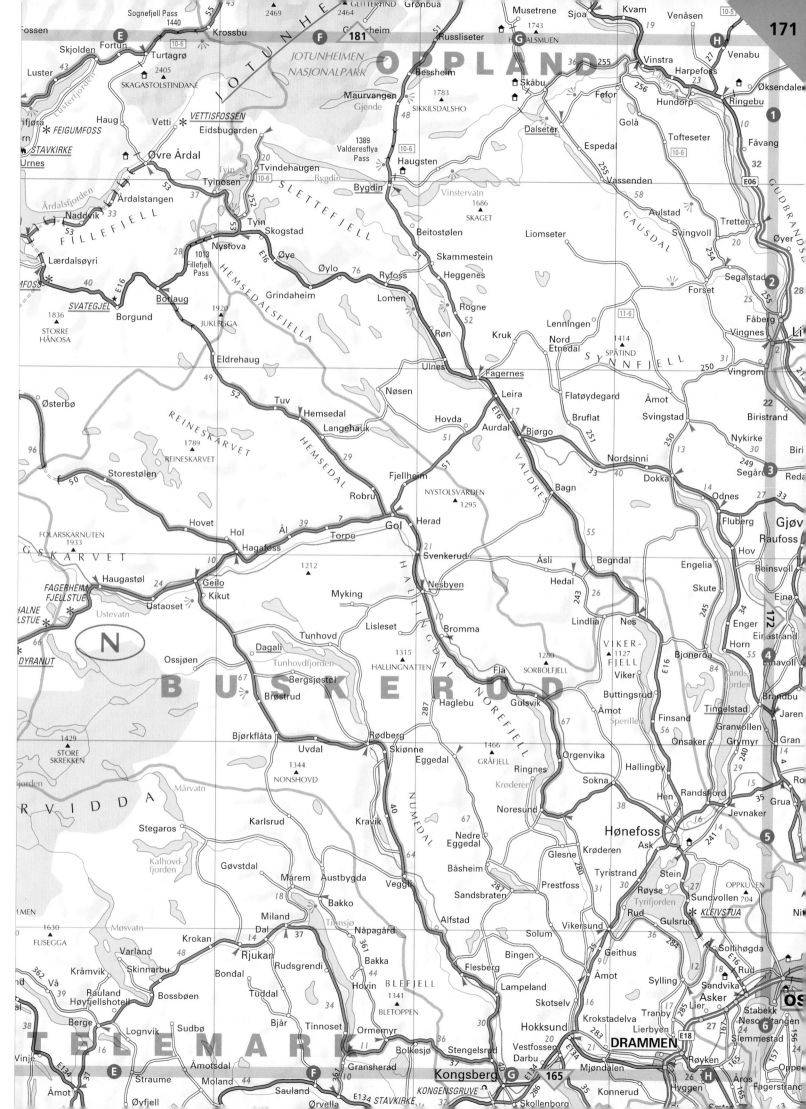

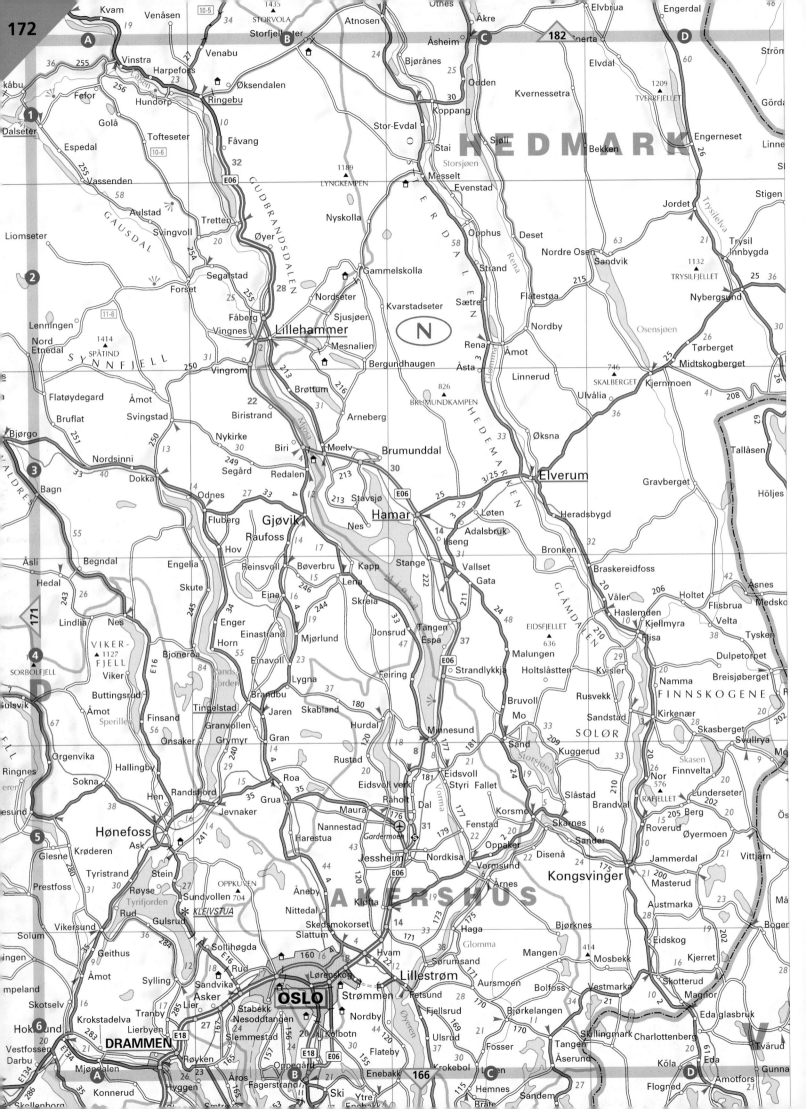

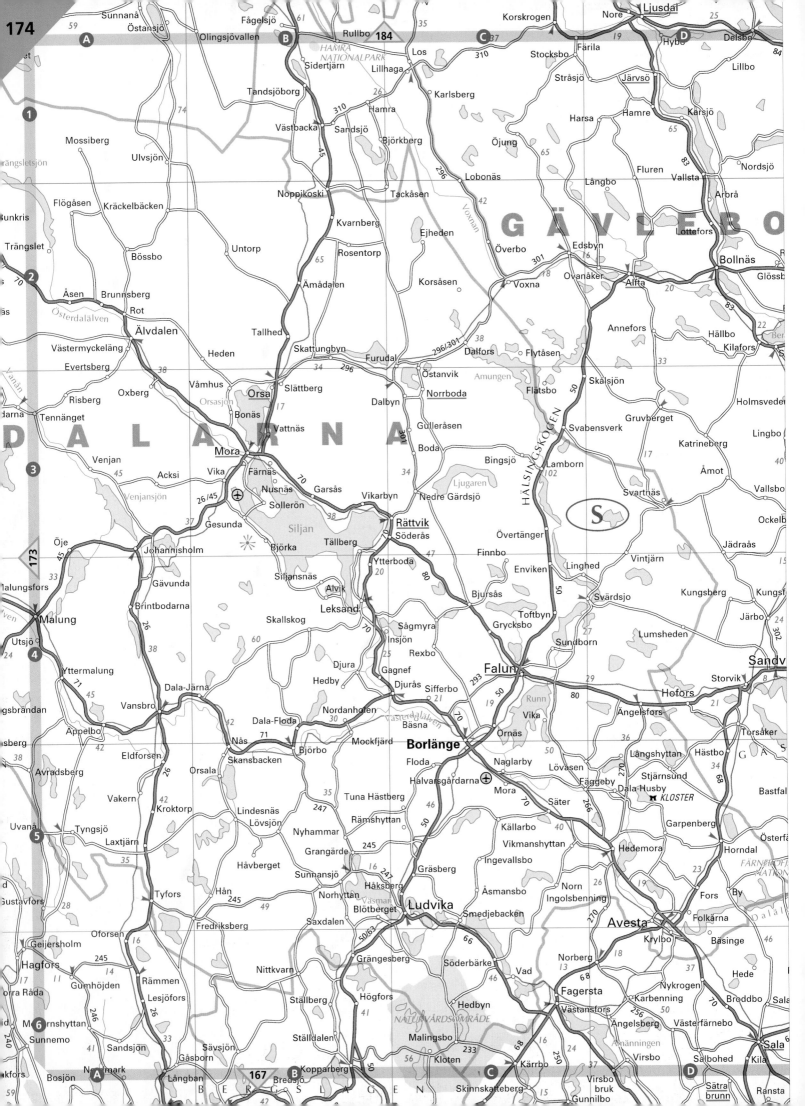

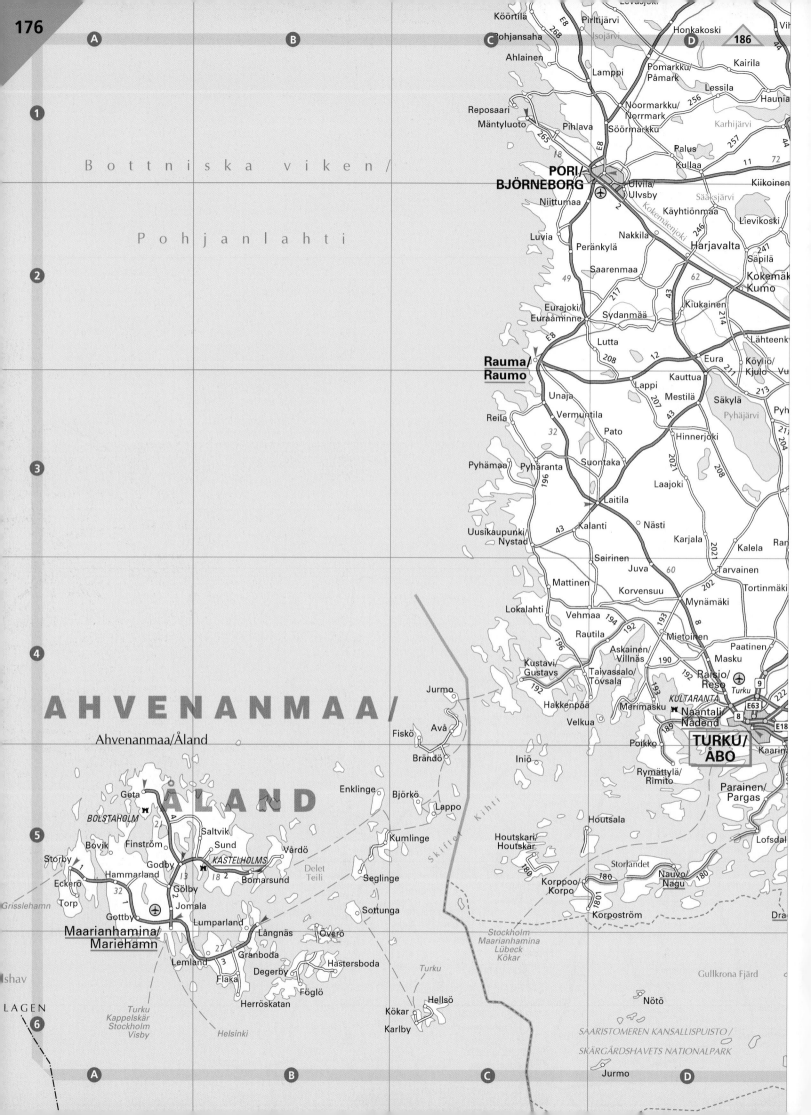

Bottniska viken/

Pohjanlahti

**PORI/
BJÖRNEBORG**

Kööртilä
Pohjansaha
Ahlainen
Lamppi
Reposaari
Mäntyluoto
Pihlava
Niittumaa
Luvia
Peränkylä
Saarenmaa
Eurajoki/
Euraåminne
**Rauma/
Raumo**
Unaja
Reila
Vermuntila
Pyhämaa
Pyhäranta
Suontaka
Uusikaupunki/
Nystad
Kalanti
Laitila
Sairinen
Mattinen
Korvensuu
Lokalahti
Vehmaa
Rautila
Kustavi/
Gustavs
Taivassalo/
Tövsala
Hakkenpää
Velkua
Poikko

Pirltijärvi
Honkakoski
Pomarkku/
Påmark
Kairila
Lessila
Haunia
Noormarkku/
Norrmark
Karhijärvi
Söörmarkku
Ulvila/
Ulvsby
Palus
Kullaa
Kiikoinen
Sääksjärvi
Käyhtiönmaa
Lievikoski
Nakkila
Harjavalta
Säpilä
Kokemäki
Kumo
Kiukainen
Sydanmää
Lutta
Eura
Köyliö/
Kjulo
Lähteenk
Kauttua
Lappi
Mestilä
Säkylä
Pyhäjärvi
Pato
Hinnerjoki
Laajoki
Nästi
Karjala
Kalela
Juva
Tarvainen
Tortinmäki
Mynämäki
Mietoinen
Paatinen
Askainen/
Villnäs
Masku
Merimasku
**Raisio/
Reso**
KULTARANTA
Naantali/
Nådend

Jurmo
Fiskö
Avå
Brändö
Enklinge
Björkö
Lappo
Kumlinge
Seglinge
Sottunga

AHVENANMAA/

Ahvenanmaa/Åland

Å L A N D

Geta
BOLSTAHOLM
Bovik
Finström
Saltvik
Sund
Vårdö
Storby
Godby
KASTELHOLMS
Eckerö
Hammarland
Bomarsund
Torp
Gölby
Delet
Teili
Gottby
Jomala
Lumparland
**Maarianhamina/
Mariehamn**
Långnäs
Överö
Lemland
Granboda
Flaka
Degerby
Föglö
Herröskatan
Håstersboda

Iniö
Rymättylä/
Rimito
**TURKU/
ÅBO**
Kaarin
Parainen/
Pargas
Houtsala
Houtskari/
Houtskär
Storlandet
Nauvo/
Nagu
Lofsdal
Korppoo/
Korpo
Korpoström
Dra

Stockholm
Maarianhamina
Lübeck
Kökar

Turku

Hellsö
Kökar
Karlby

Nötö
Gullkrona Fjärd

SAARISTOMEREN KANSALLISPUISTO /
SKÄRGÅRDSHAVETS NATIONALPARK

Grisslehamn
Turku
Kappelskär
Stockholm
Visby

Helsinki

Jurmo

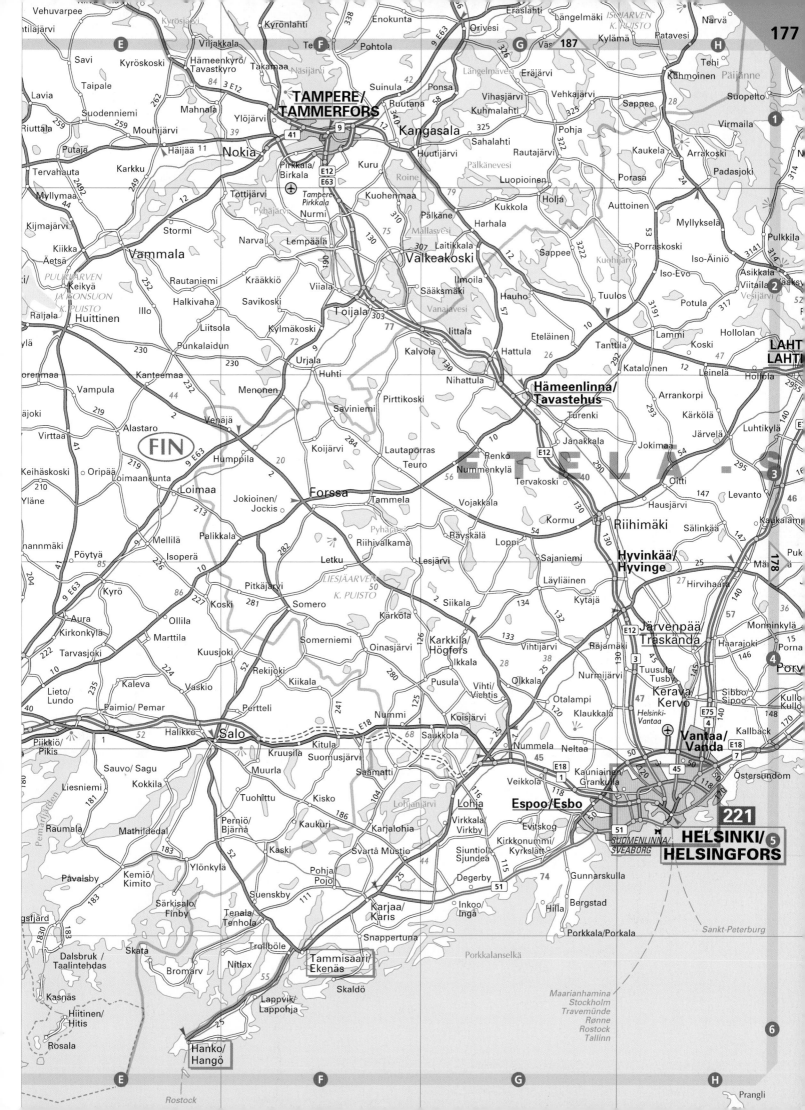

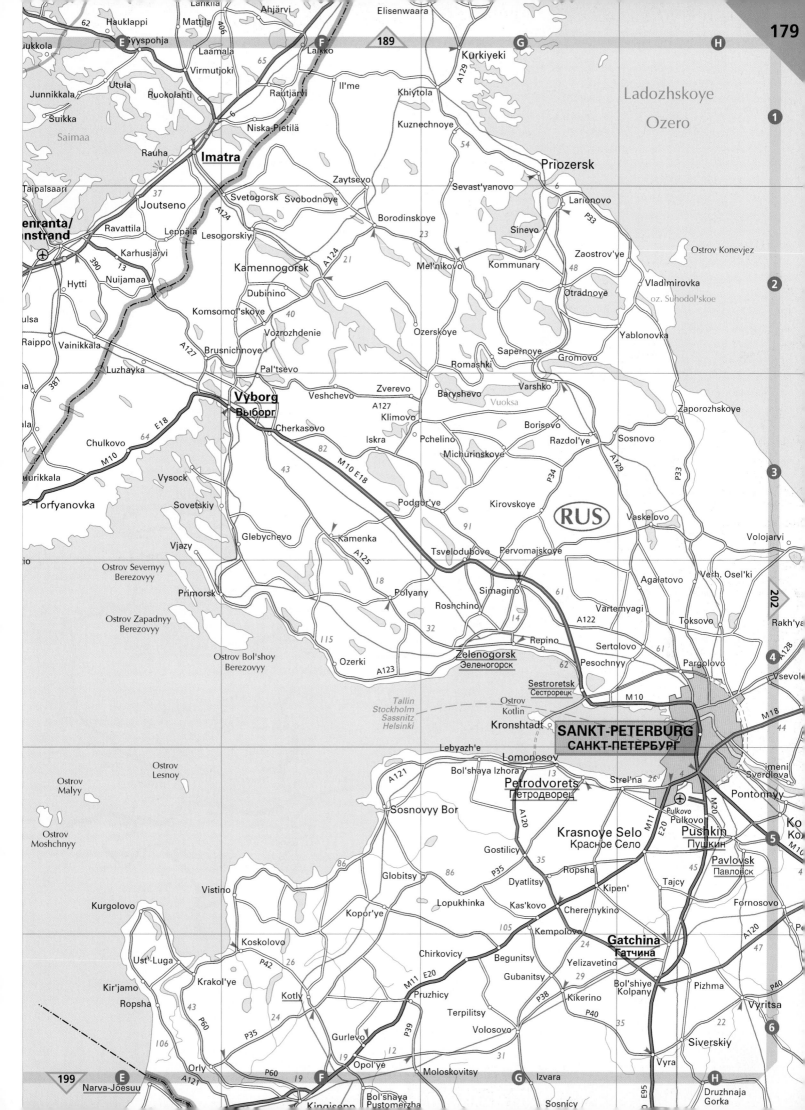

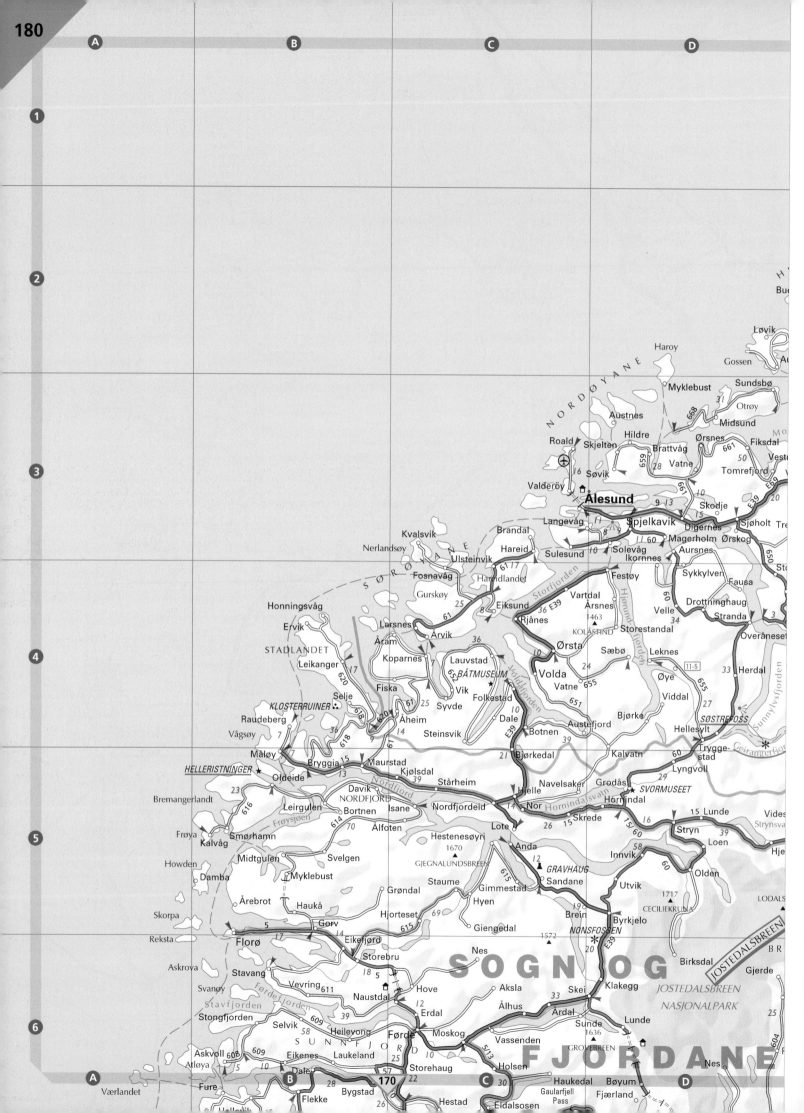

A B C D

1

2

Løvik
Haroy
Gossen A
Bud

NORDØYANE

Myklebust
Sundsbø
668 31 Otrøy
Austnes Midsund
Hildre 659 Ørsnes 661 Fiksdal
Roald Skjelten Brattvåg 50 Vest
Valderöy 16 Søvik 28 Vatne Tomrefjord Mo

3

Ålesund 9 13 Skodje E39 20 E69
Langevåg 11 15 E39
Kvalsvik Brandal Spjelkavik Sjøholt Tre
Nerlandsøy Hareid Digernes
Fosnavåg Sulesund Magerholm Ørskog 650 Sto
Gurskøy 61 17 Solevåg Aursnes
Hareidlandet Ikornnes Sykkylven Fausa
Honningsvåg 25 Eiksund Festøy 60 Drottninghaug
Ervik 61 8 Vartdal Velle Stranda 3
Larsnes 36 E39 Årsnes Storestandal Overåneset
STADLANDET Årvik 36 Rjånes 1463 Leknes
Leikanger 17 Koparnes Lauvstad KOLÅSTIND 34 Herdal
620 Åram 7 BÅTMUSEUM Volda 24 Øye 655 33
Fiska Vik 65 Vatne 655 Viddal 27
Selje 618 61 25 Folkestad 651 Bjørke SØSTREFOSS
KLOSTERRUINER 620 Syvde 10 Austefjord Hellesylt
Raudeberg 618 Åheim Dale E39 Geirangerfjo
Vågsøy 7 38 14 Steinsvik Botnen 39
Måløy 7 9 21 Bjørkedal Kalvatn Trygge- 60
HELLERISTNINGER Bryggia 15 Maurstad Bjørkedal stad Lyngvoll
Oldeide 13 Kjølsdal Stårheim Hjelle Navelsaker Grodås 29
23 Davik 39 Nor Hornindalsvatn Hornindal SVORMUSEET
Bremangerlandt 616 NORDFJORD Nordfjordeid 14 Skrede 15 60 15 Lunde
Leirgulen Bortnen Isane Nordfjordeid 26 15 16 Vides
Frøya 614 Ålfoten Lote 15 60 Stryn 39 Strynsva
Kalvåg Smørhamn 70 Hestenesøyri Anda 58 Loen Hje
Howden Midtgulen Svelgen 1670 12 Innvik 60 Olden
Damba Myklebust GJEGNALUNDSBREEN GRAVHAUG Utvik 1717
Skorpa Årebrot Haukå Staume Sandane CECILIEKRUNA LODALS
Gørv Grøndal Gimmestad Brein Byrkjelo NONSFOSSEN
Reksta 5 14 Hyen 615 198 20 E39 JOSTEDALSBREEN BR
Florø 17 Eikefjord Giengedal 1572 Birksdal Gjerde
Askrova Storebru Nes Skei Klakegg JOSTEDALSBREEN
Stavang 18 5 Aksla 33 JOSTEDALSBREEN
Svanøy Vevring 611 Hove Ålhus Ardal NASJONALPARK 25
Stongfjorden Naustdal 12 Erdal Sunde Lunde
Selvik 609 Heilevong Førde Moskog 1636 GROVEBREEN
Askvoll 60 609 SUNNFJORD Vassenden 604
Atløya 5 Eikenes Laukeland 25 Storehaug Holsen Nes
Værlandet Fure Dale 57 170 22 Haukedal Bøyum D
Flekke 28 Bygstad 30 Gaularfjell Fjærland
Hestad Pass Eldalsosen

SOGN OG
FJORDANE

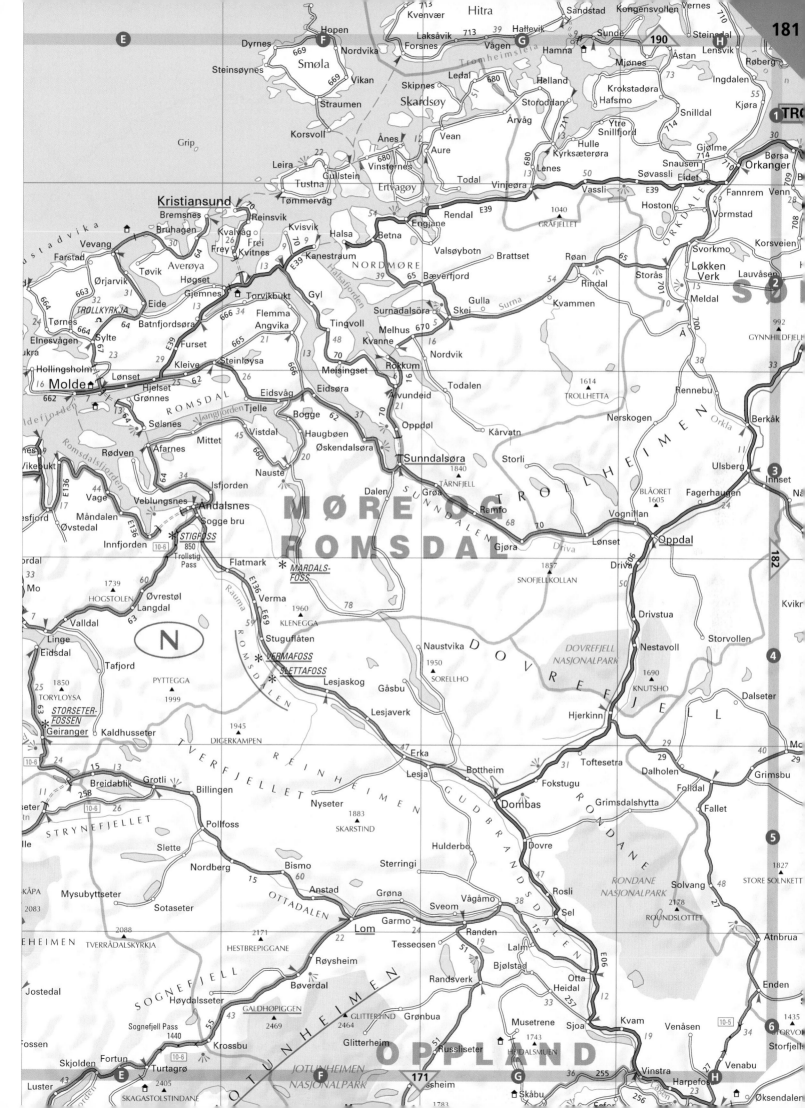

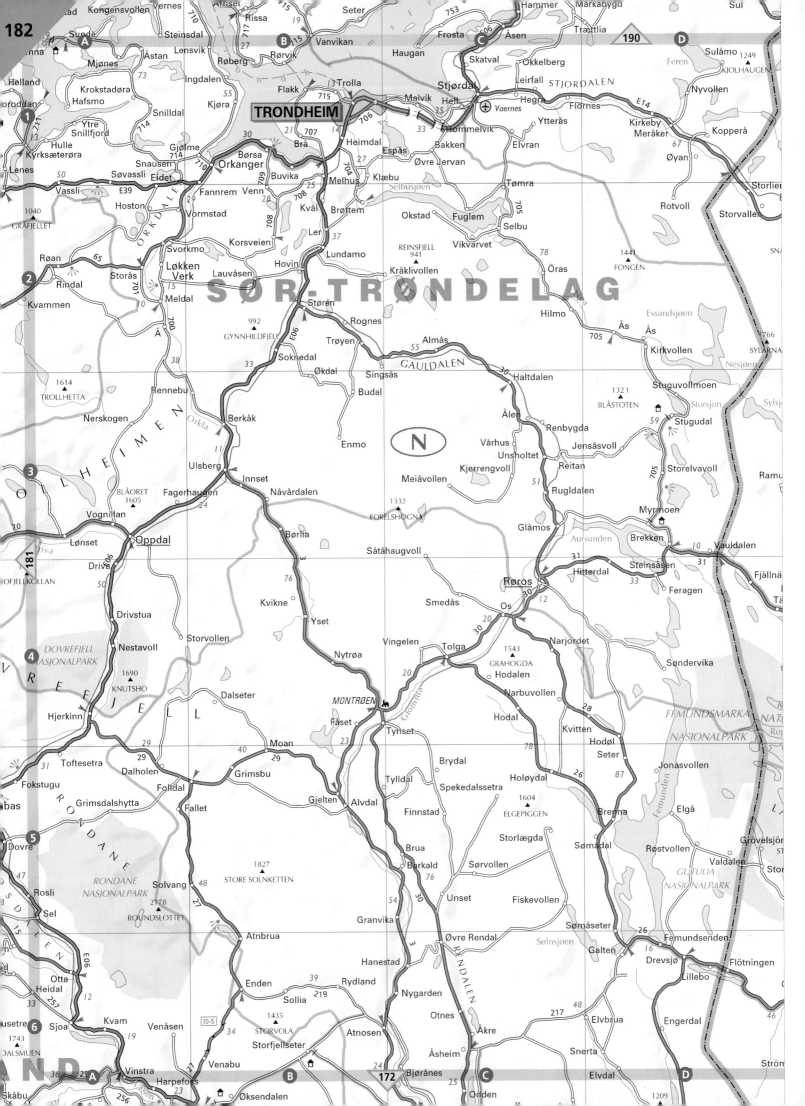

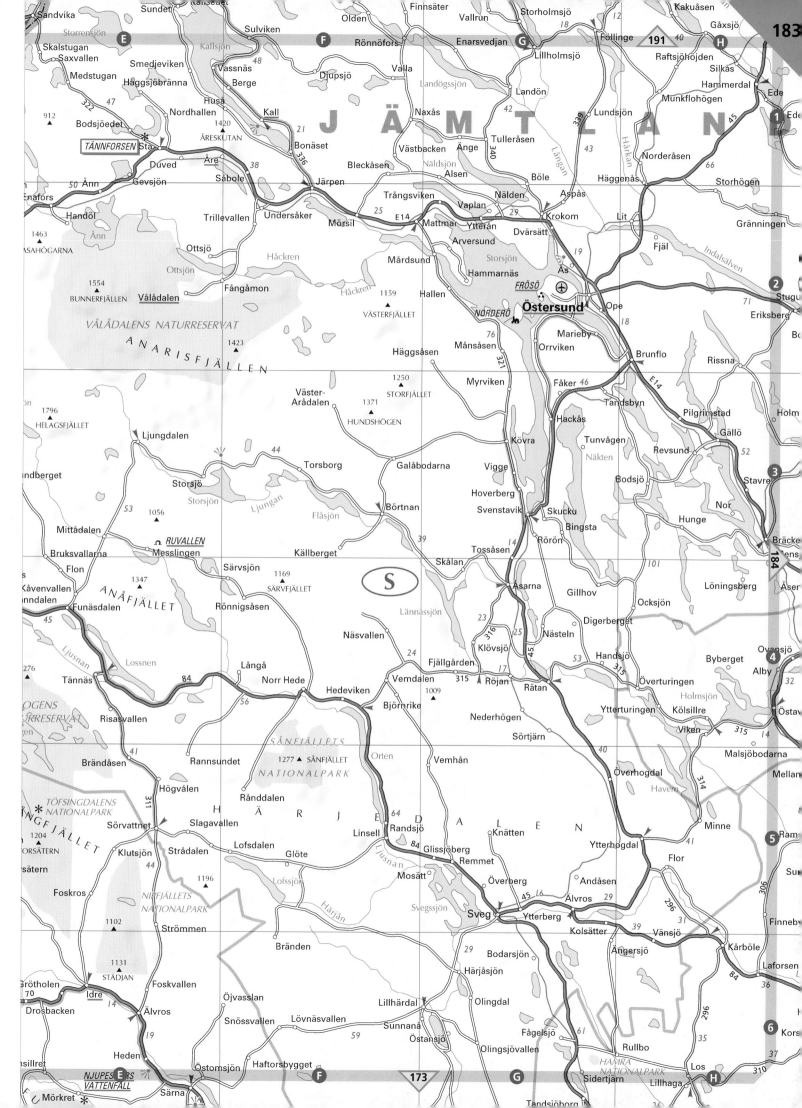

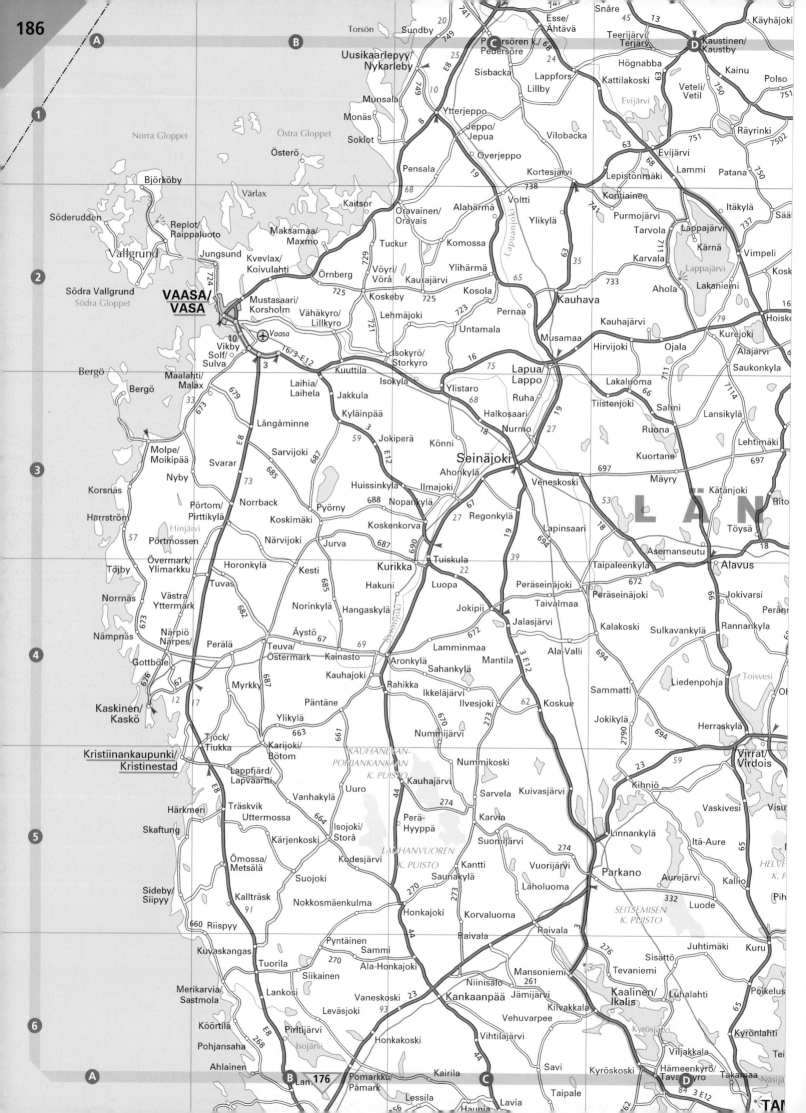

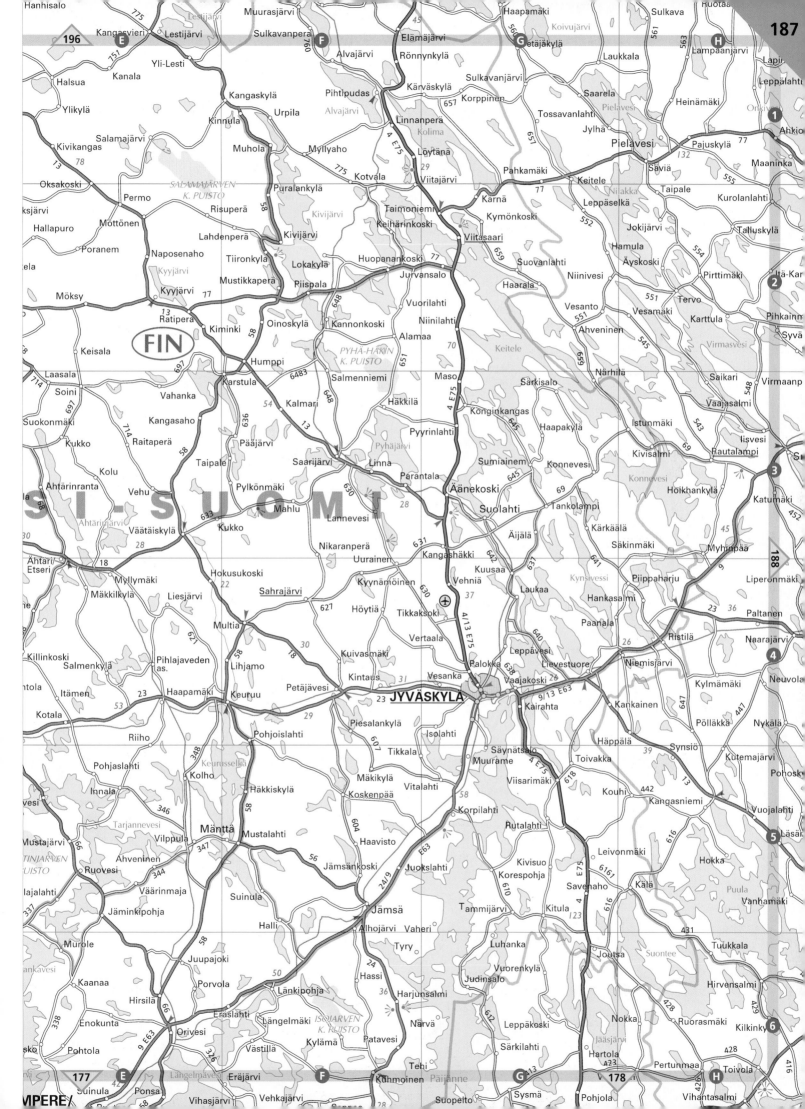

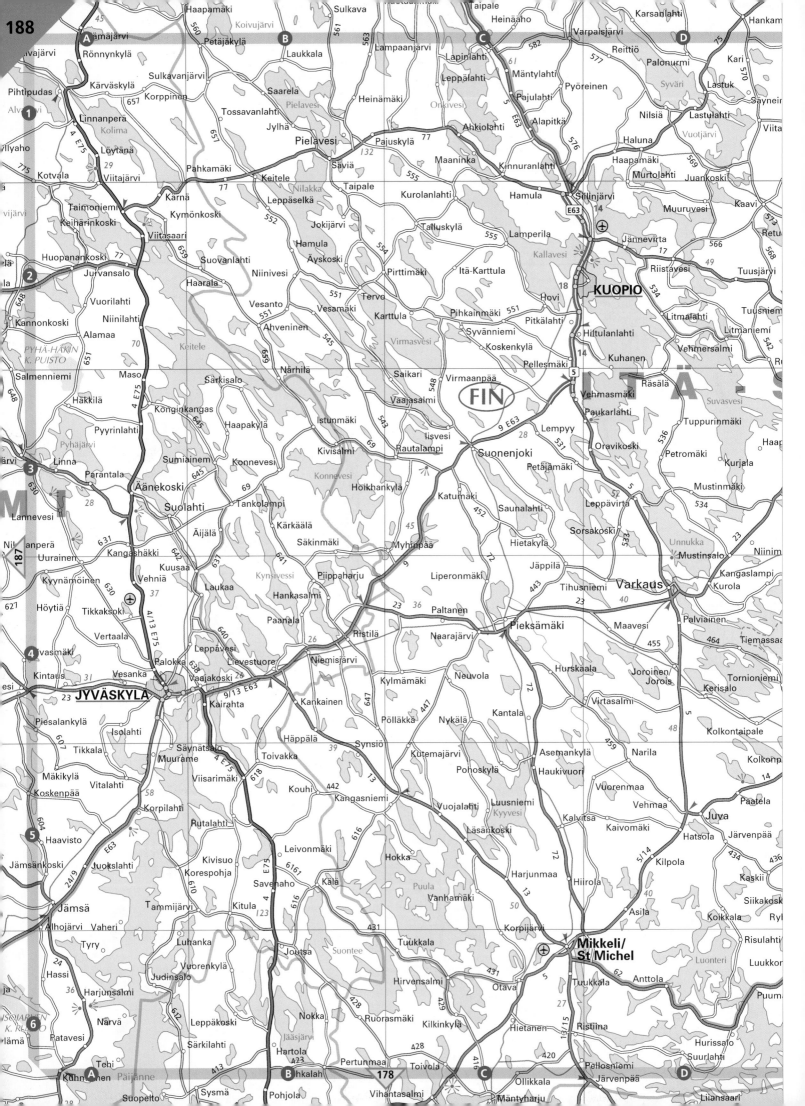

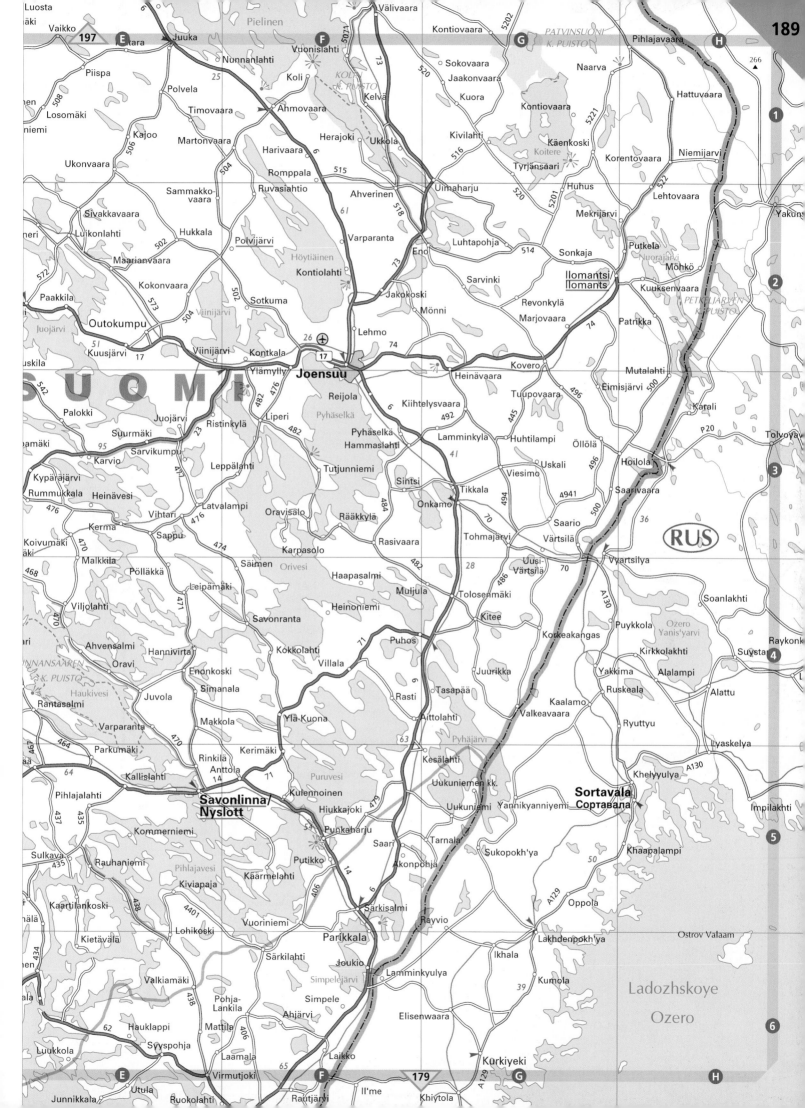

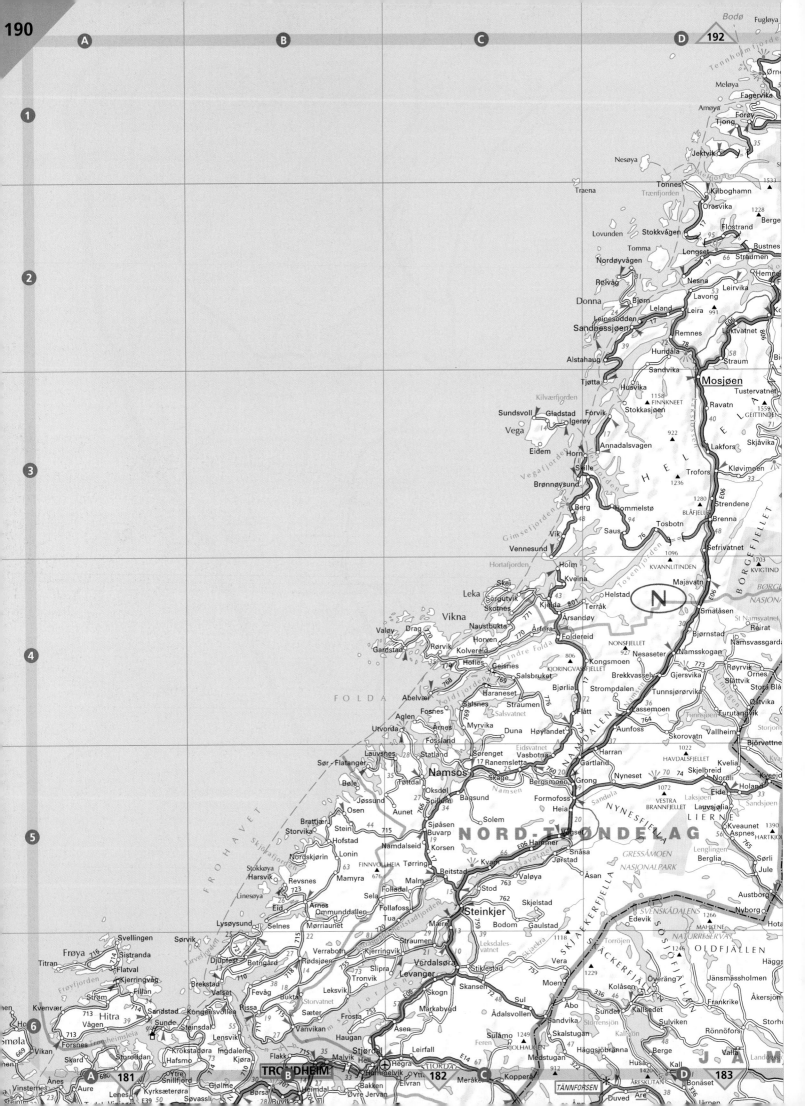

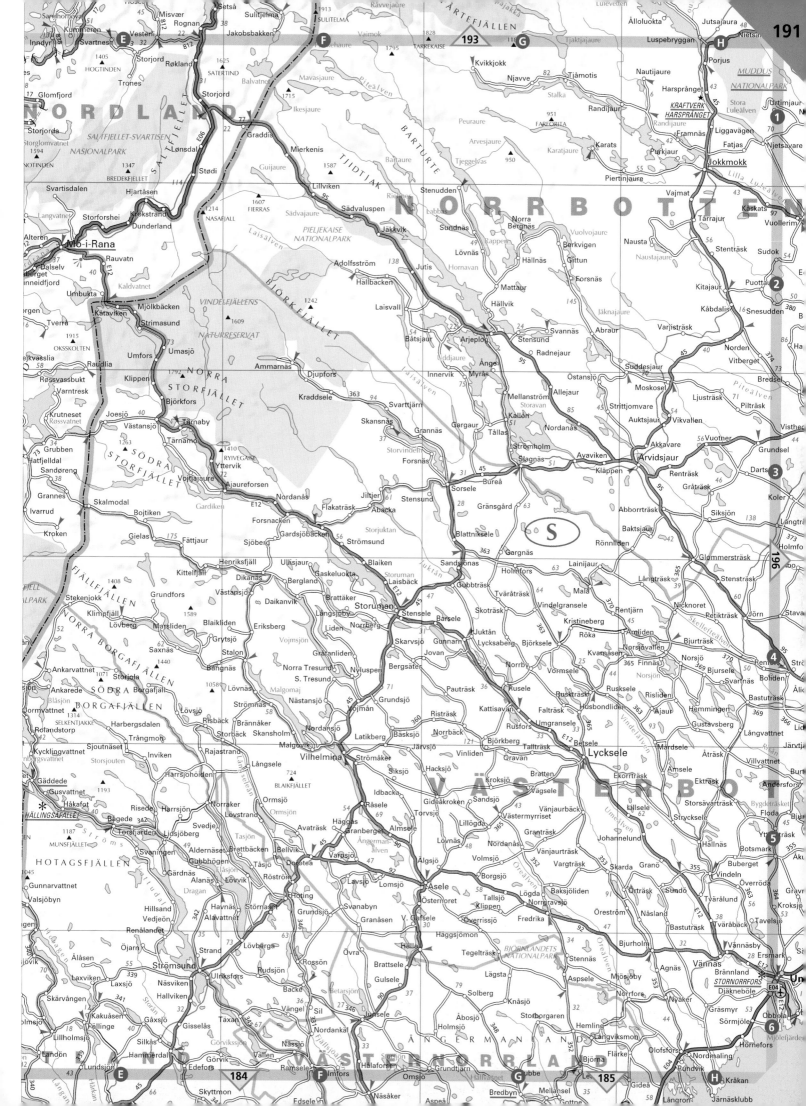

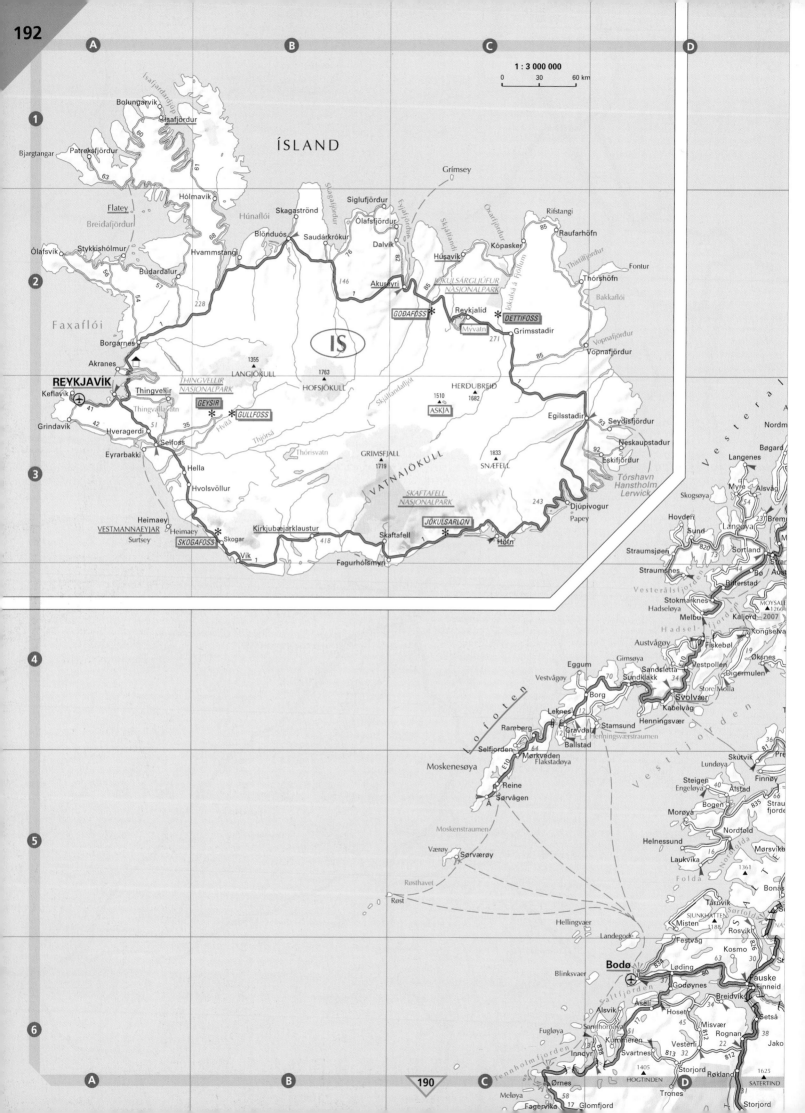

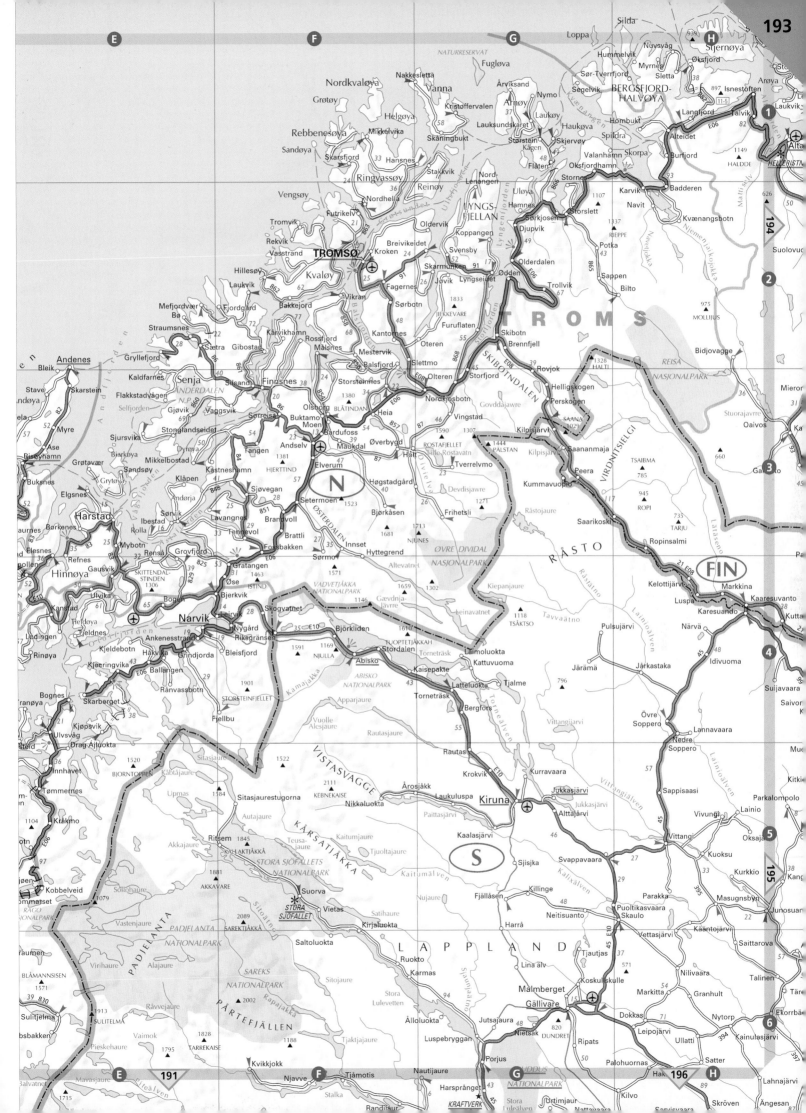

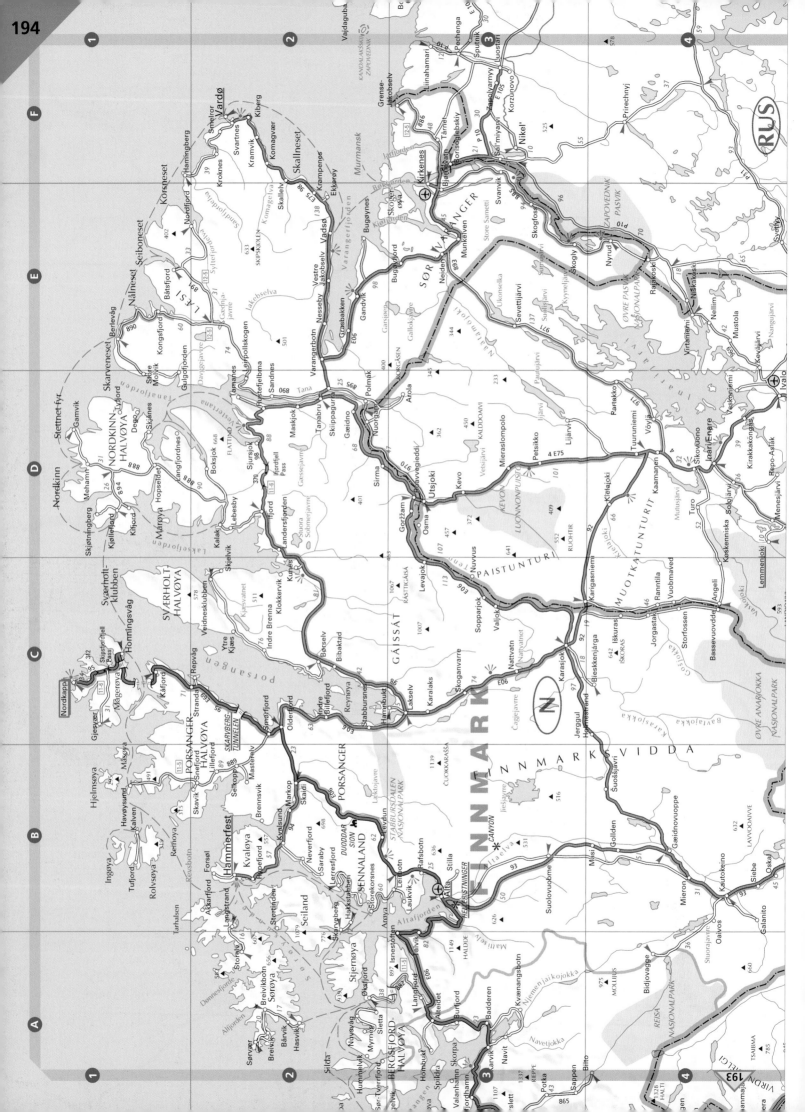

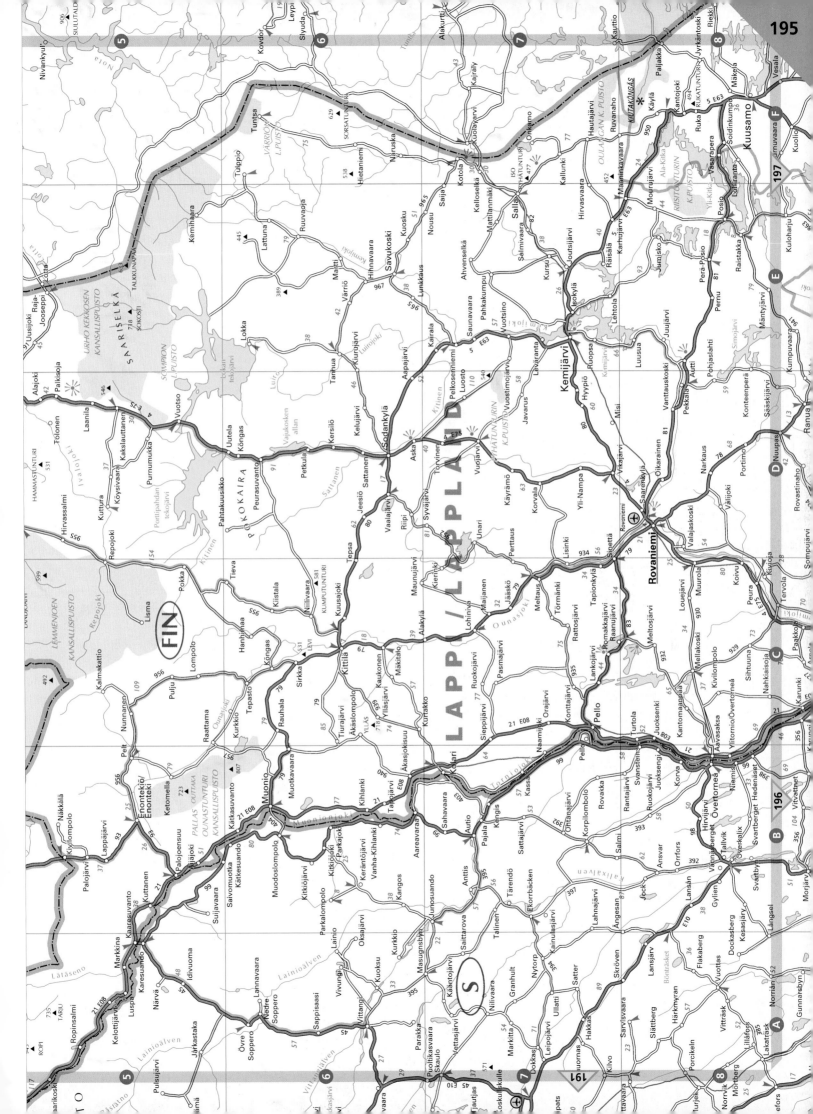

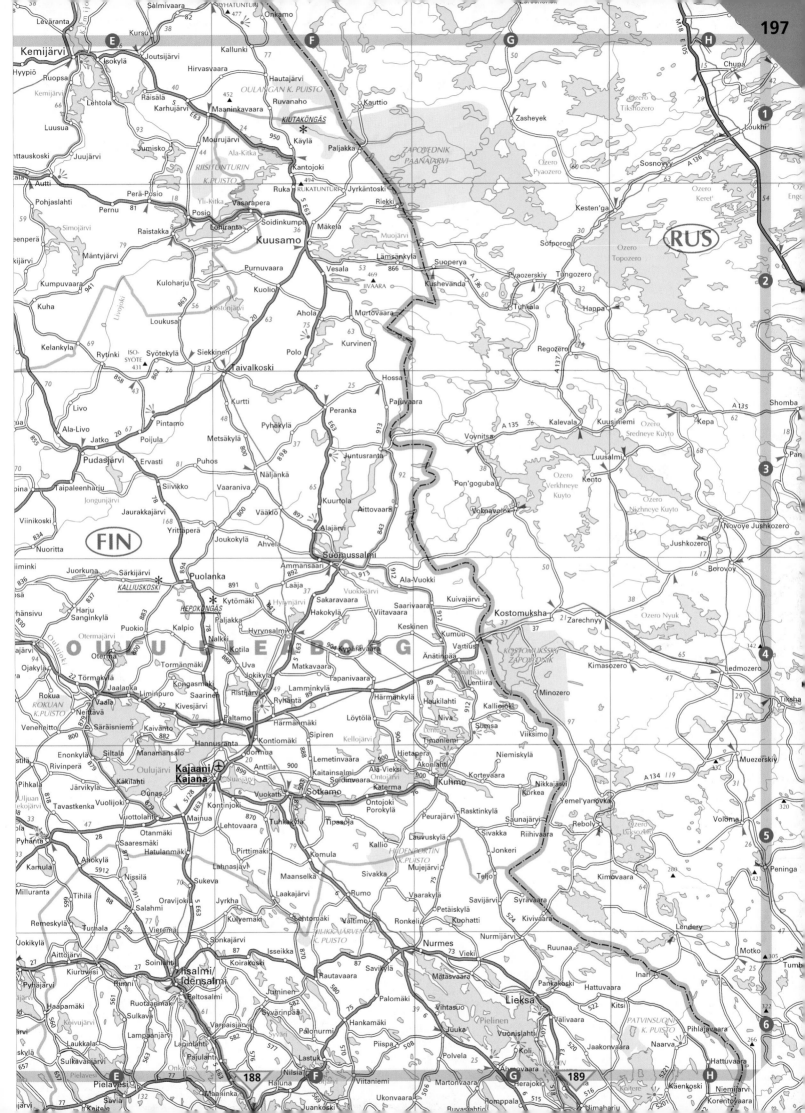

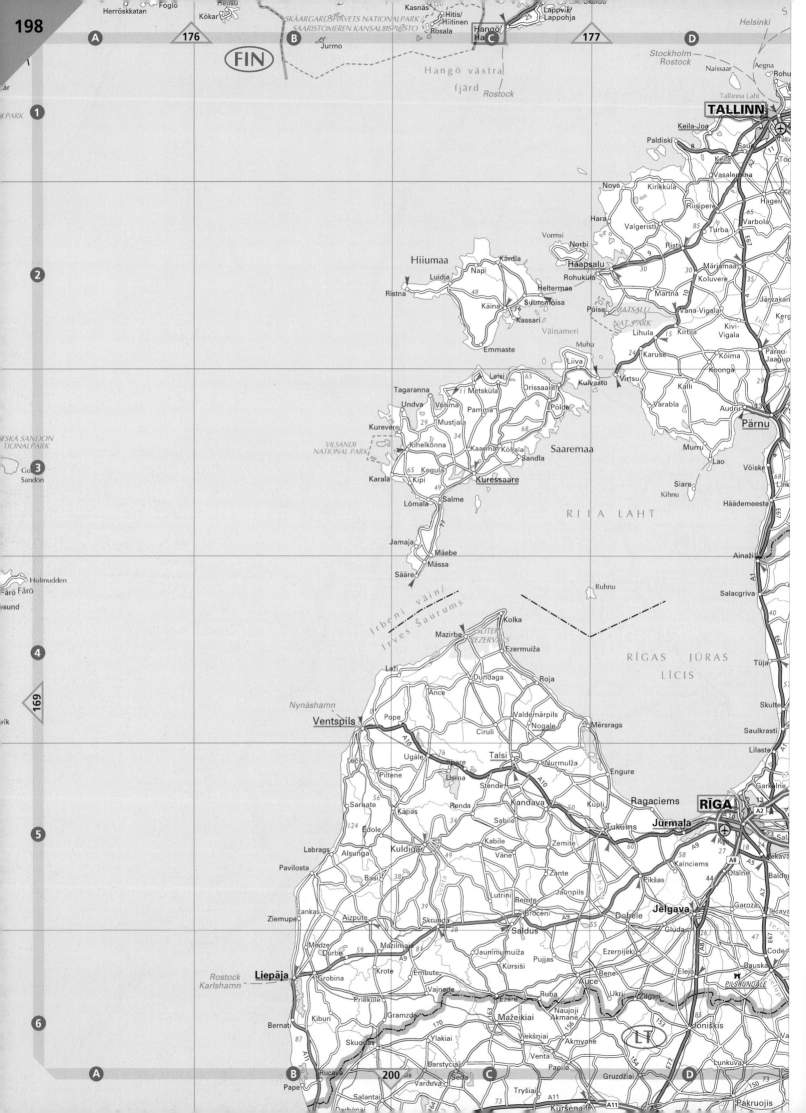

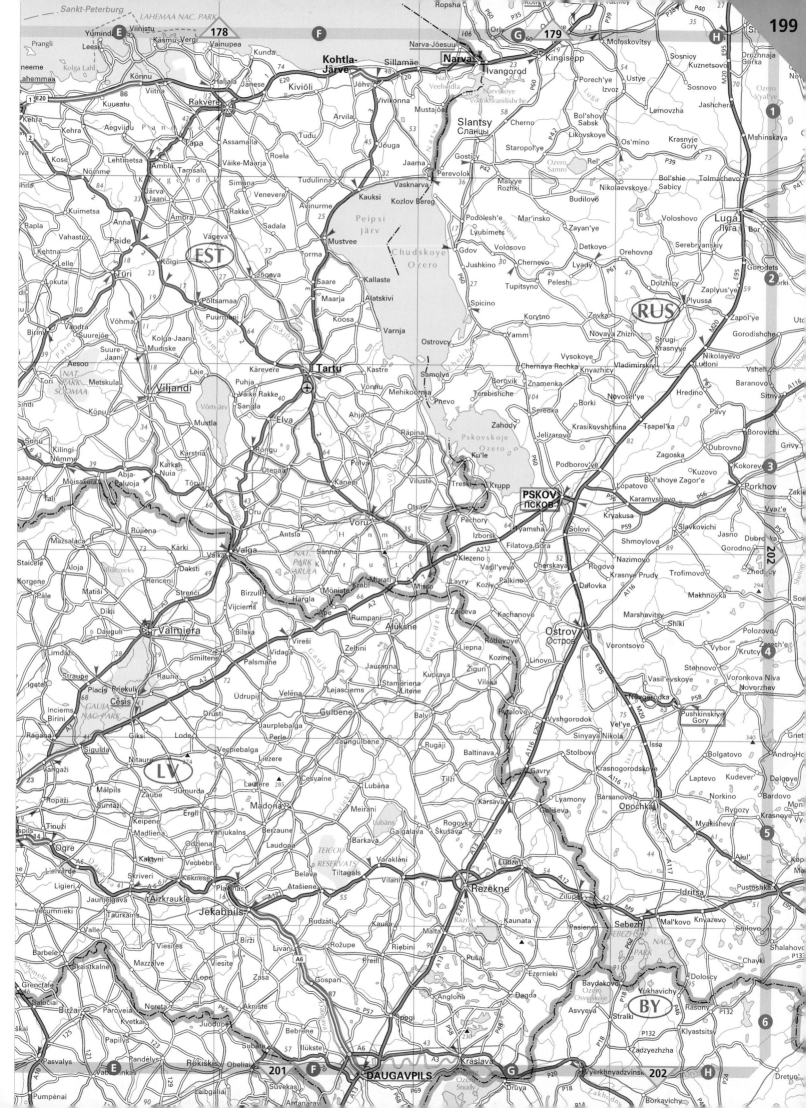

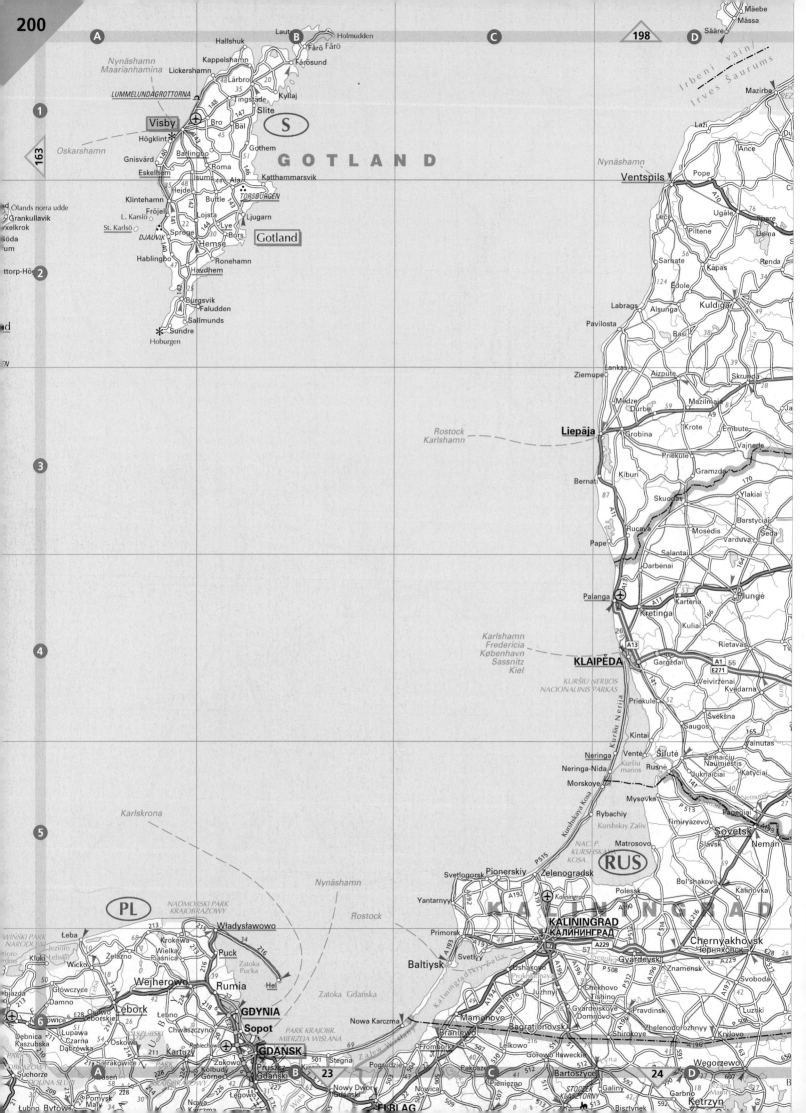

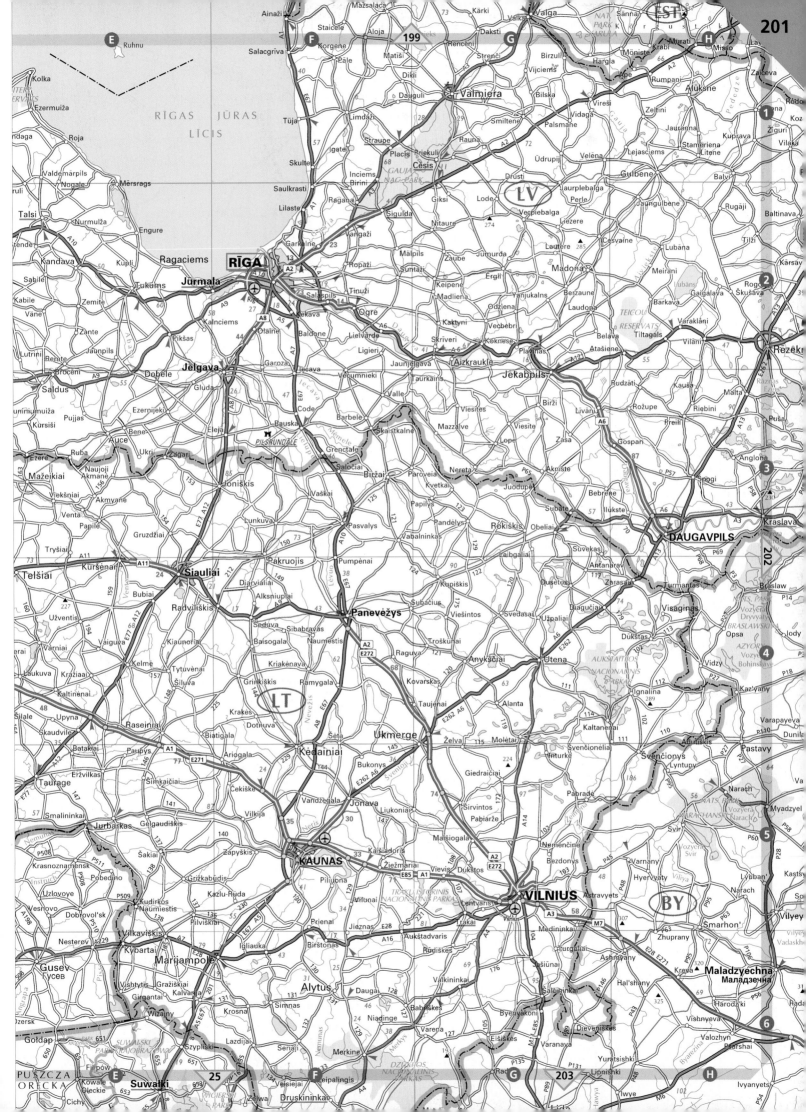

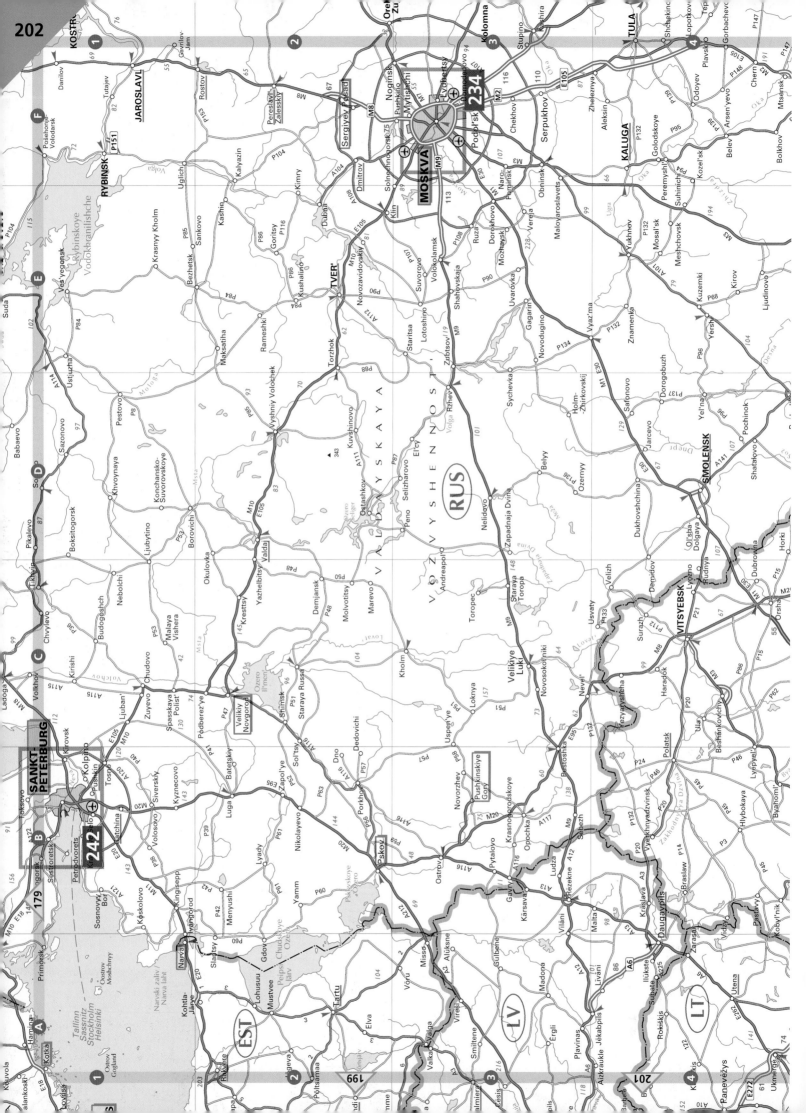

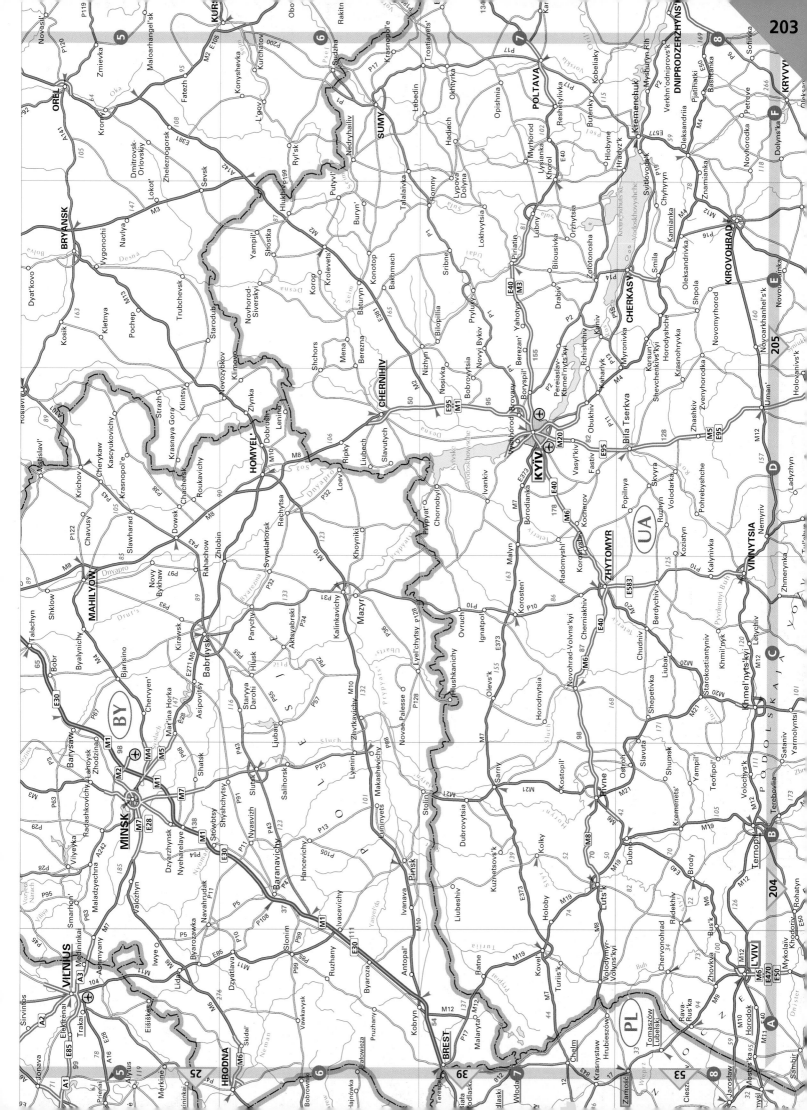

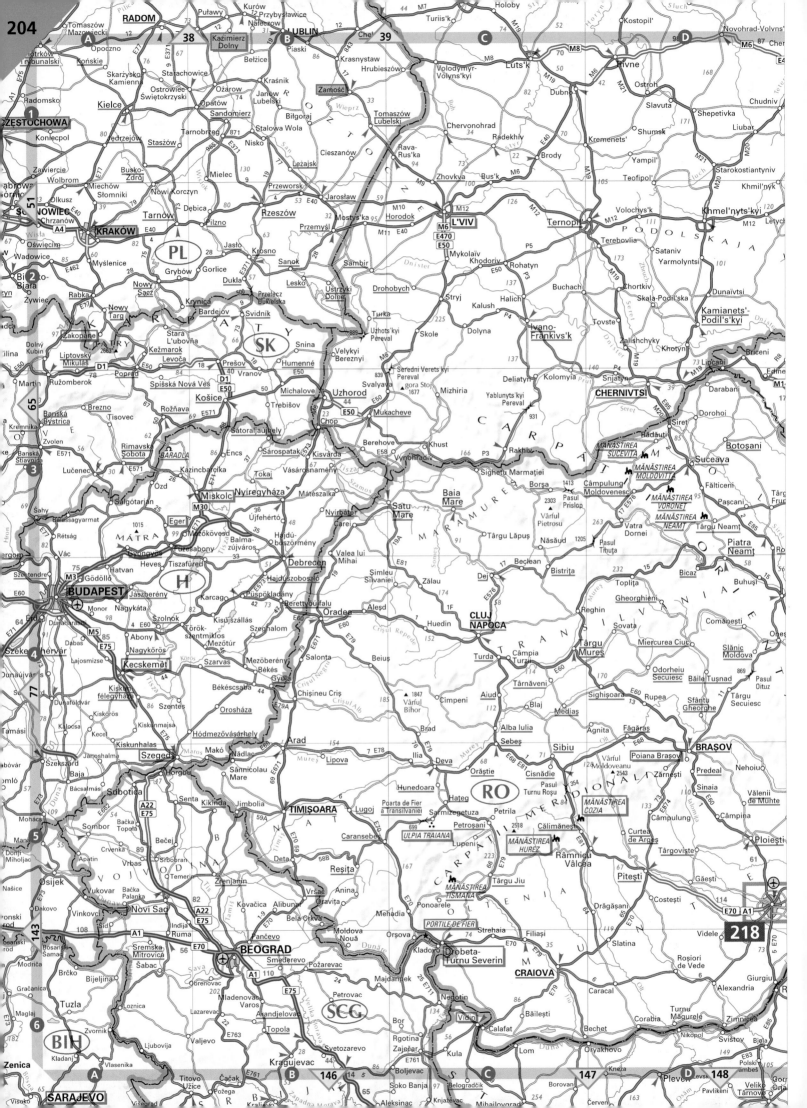

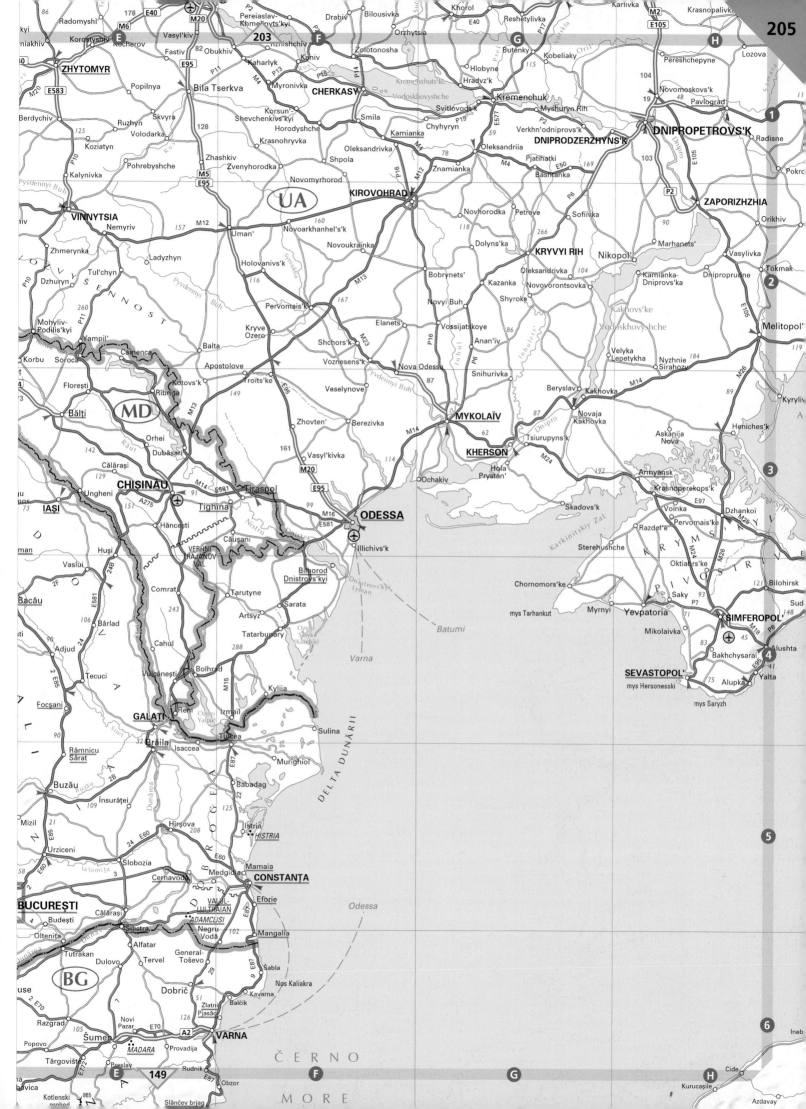

CITY AND URBAN ROUTES
CITTÀ E AREE URBANE
CIUDADES Y ÁREAS URBANAS
VILLES ET AIRES URBAINES
STÄDTE UND ZUFAHRTEN

City plans
Piante di città
Planos de ciudades
Plans de villes
Stadtpläne

Urban route maps
Aree urbane
Áreas urbanas
Aires urbaines
Stadtdurchfahrtspläne

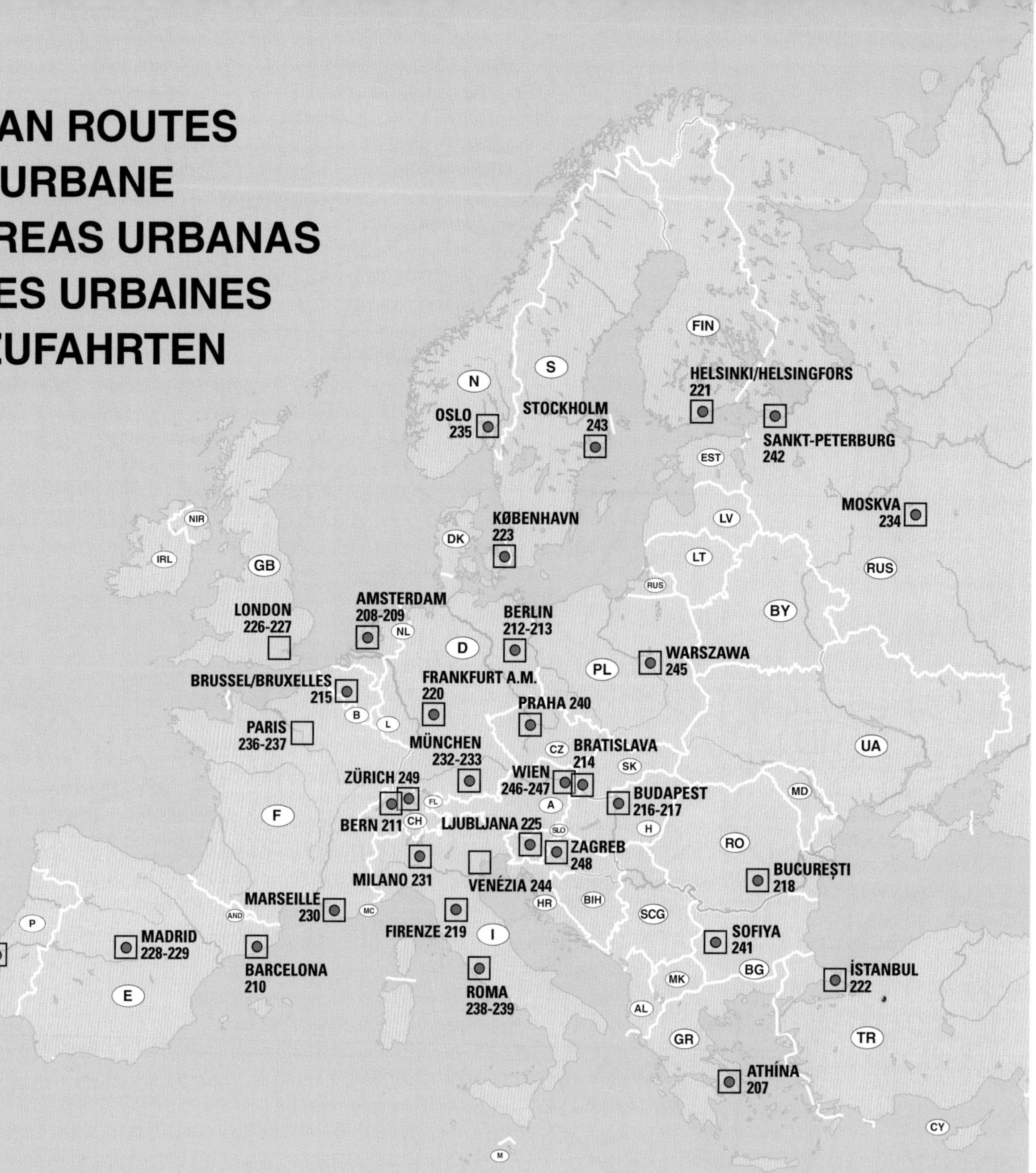

FIN

N S HELSINKI/HELSINGFORS 221

OSLO 235 STOCKHOLM 243

EST

SANKT-PETERBURG 242

LV MOSKVA 234

KØBENHAVN 223

DK

LT

NIR RUS RUS

IRL GB

BY

LONDON 226-227

AMSTERDAM 208-209 NL BERLIN 212-213 D

WARSZAWA 245

PL

BRUSSEL/BRUXELLES 215 FRANKFURT A.M. 220

PRAHA 240

B L

PARIS 236-237

MÜNCHEN 232-233 CZ BRATISLAVA 214 SK

UA

ZÜRICH 249 WIEN 246-247 A BUDAPEST 216-217 MD

F FL H

BERN 211 CH LJUBLJANA 225 SLO

RO

ZAGREB 248

MILANO 231 VENÉZIA 244 HR BIH SCG BUCUREȘTI 218

AND MARSEILLE 230 MC SOFIYA 241

P FIRENZE 219 I BG İSTANBUL 222

LISBOA 224 MADRID 228-229

BARCELONA 210 ROMA 238-239 MK AL GR TR

E ATHÍNA 207

M CY

Legend / Legenda / Leyenda / Légende / Zeichenerklärung

GB Legend	I Legenda	E Leyenda	F Légende	D Zeichenerklärung
Built-up area	Caseggiati	Zona edificada	Zones bâties	Bebauung
Building of interest	Edificio d'interesse	Edificio relevante	Édifice remarquable	Bemerkenswertes Gebäude
Motorway, access points, service area	Autostrada, caselli, stazione di servizio	Autopista, accesos, estación de servicio	Autoroute, accès, aire de service	Autobahn, Anschlüsse, Tankstelle
Road with motorway characteristics	Superstrada	Autovía	Route-express	Autobahnähnliche Schnellstraße
Through road	Strada di attraversamento	Travesía	Route de traversée	Hauptdurchfahrtsstraße
Other road	Altra strada	Otra carretera	Autre route	Sonstige Straße
A9 N202 Numbering of motorway and national roads	Numeri di autostrada e strade nazionali	Números de autopista y carreteras nacionales	Numéros d'autoroute et routes nationales	Autobahnnummer, Staatsstraßennummer
Road in tunnel	Galleria stradale	Túnel en carretera	Tunnel routier	Straßentunnel
2006 Motorway and road under construction (opening year)	Autostrada e strada in costruzione (anno di apertura)	Autopista y carretera en construcción (año de apertura)	Autoroute et route en construction (année d'ouverture)	Autobahn und straße in Bau (Fertigstellungsjahr)
Utrecht Destination	Direzione	Direccion	Direction	Richtung
Railway and station	Ferrovia e stazione	Ferrocarril y estacion	Chemin de fer et gare	Eisenbahn und Bahnhöf
Garden and park; cemeteries	Giardino e parco; cimiteri	Jardin y parque; cementerios	Jardin et parc; cimetières	Gärten und Park; Friedhöfe
Hospital; Parking	Ospedale; Parcheggio	Hospital; Aparcamiento	Hôpital; Parking	Krankenhaus; Parkplatz
Camping site	Campeggio	Cámping	Camping	Campingplatz
Vehicle ferry route	Trasporto auto su traghetto	Transbordador de automóviles	Bac pour autos	Autofähre
Panoramic view	Punto panoramico	Vista panorámica	Vue panoramique	Aussichtspunkt
M Underground railway station	Fermata della metropolitana	Estación del metro	Station de métro	U-Bahnhöfe
i Tourist information	Ufficio informazioni	Información turística	Informations touristiques	Touristische Auskünfte
Pedestrian area	Area pedonali	Área peatonales	Zone réservé aux piétons	Fußgängerzone

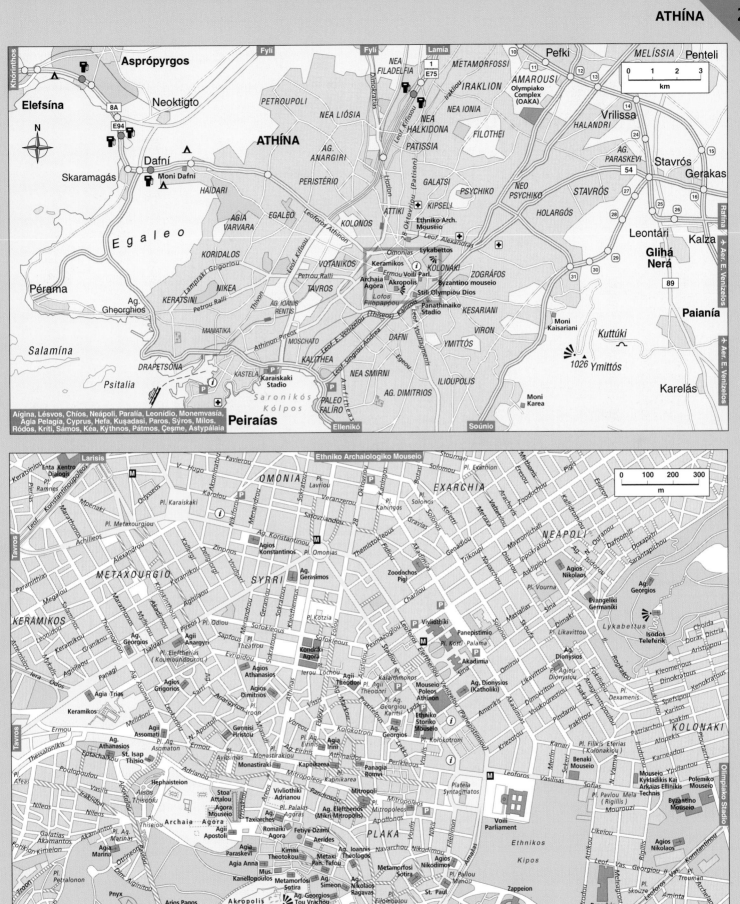

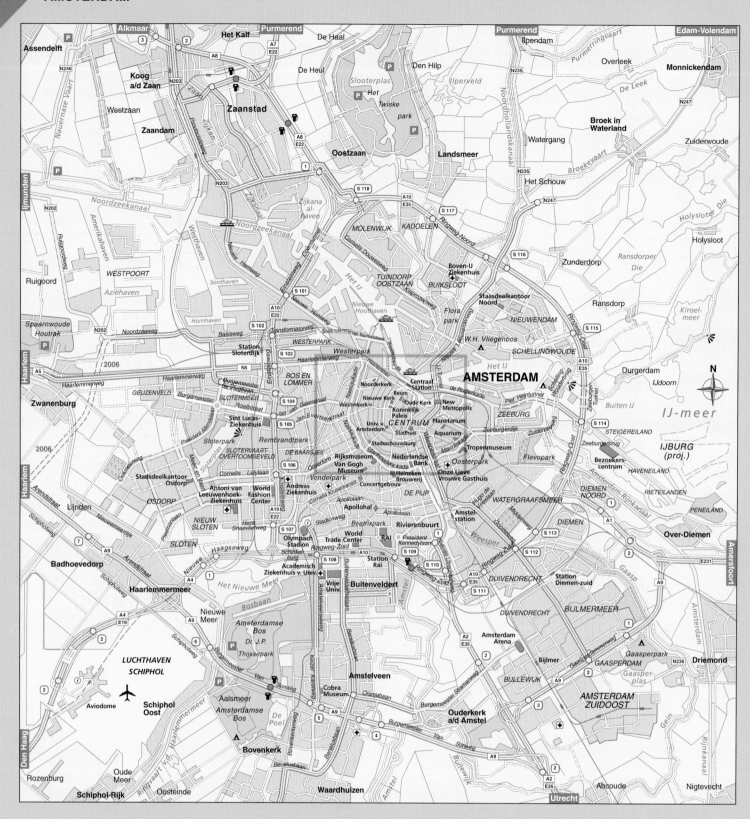

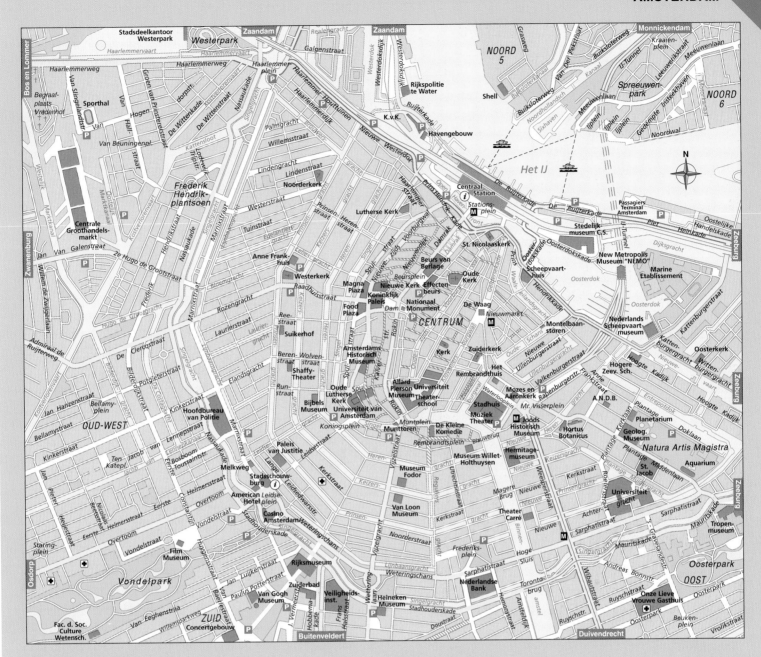

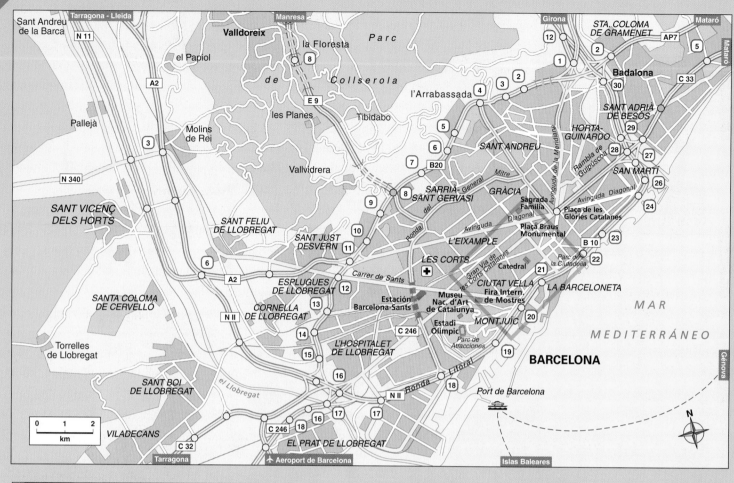

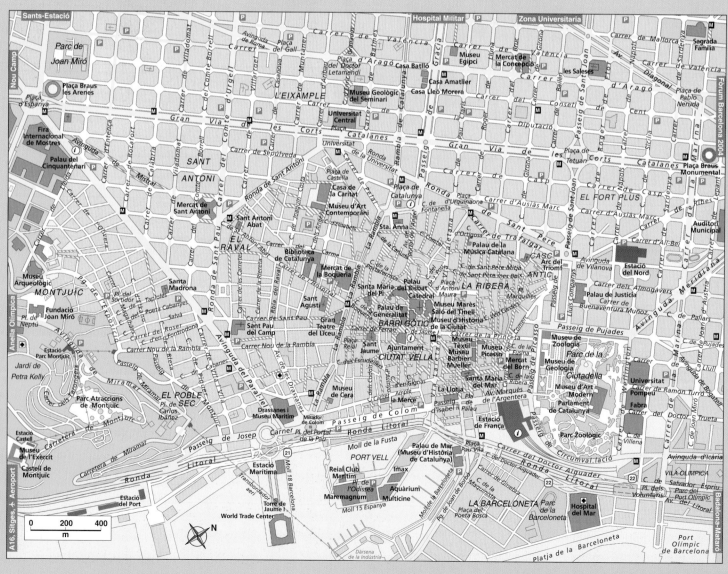

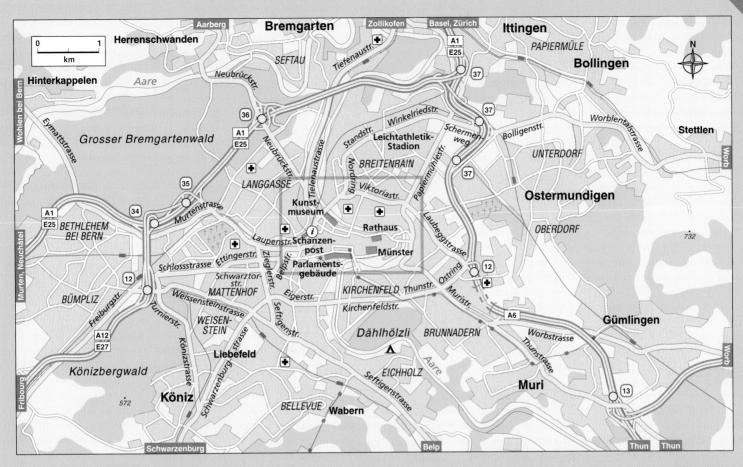

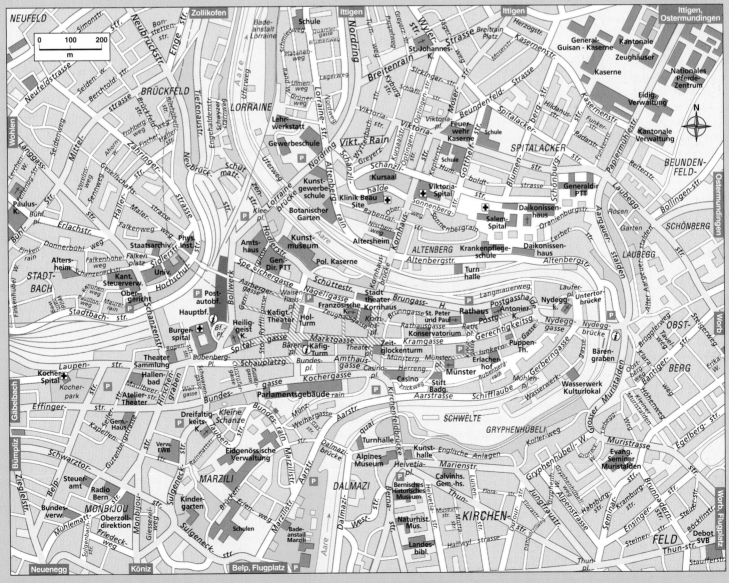

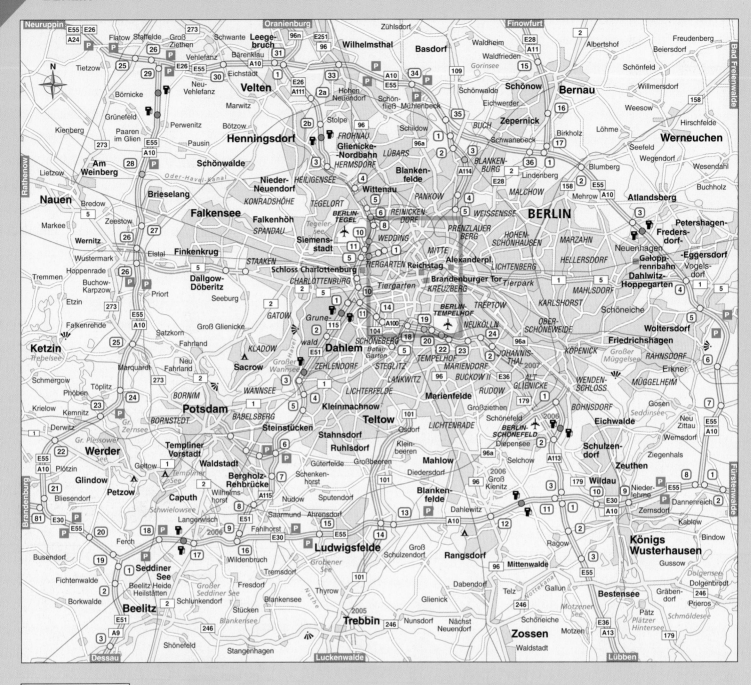

0 3 6 9
km

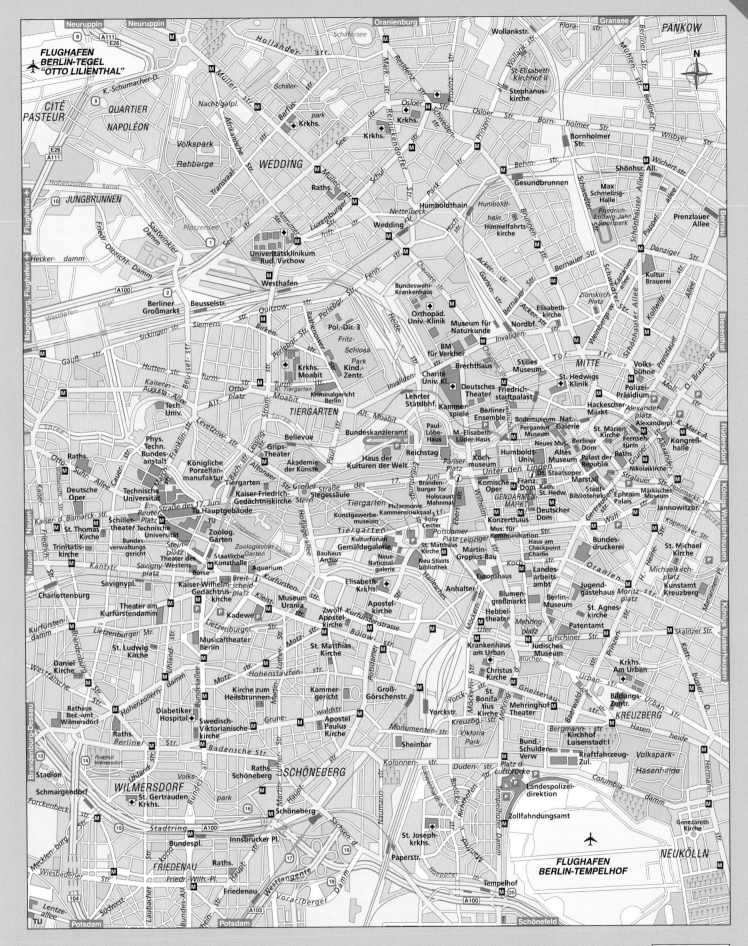

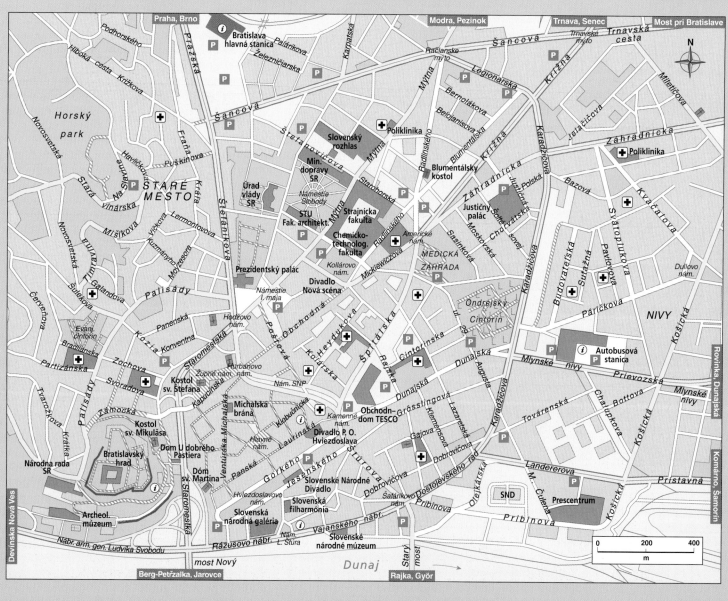

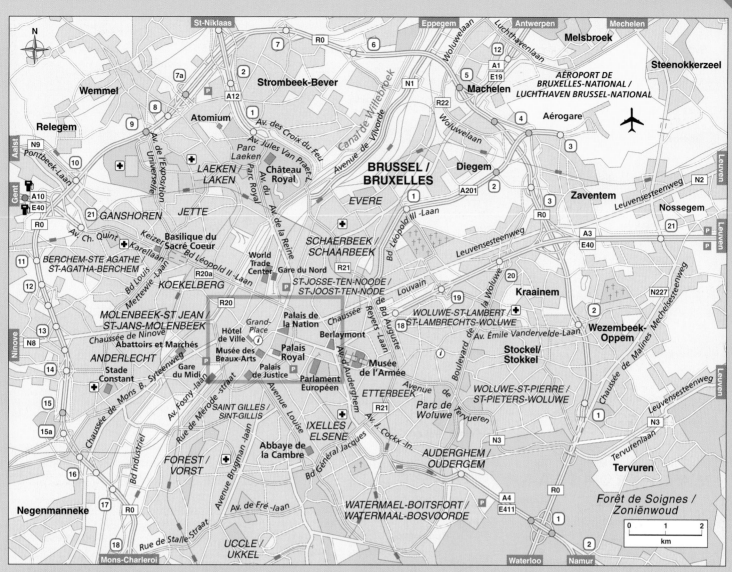

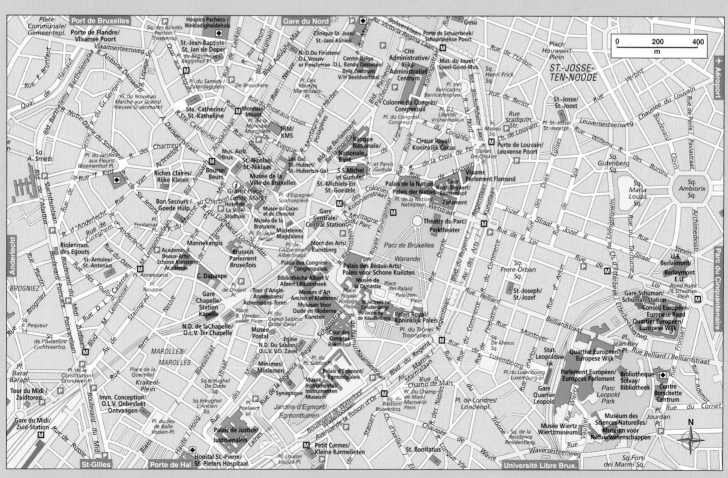

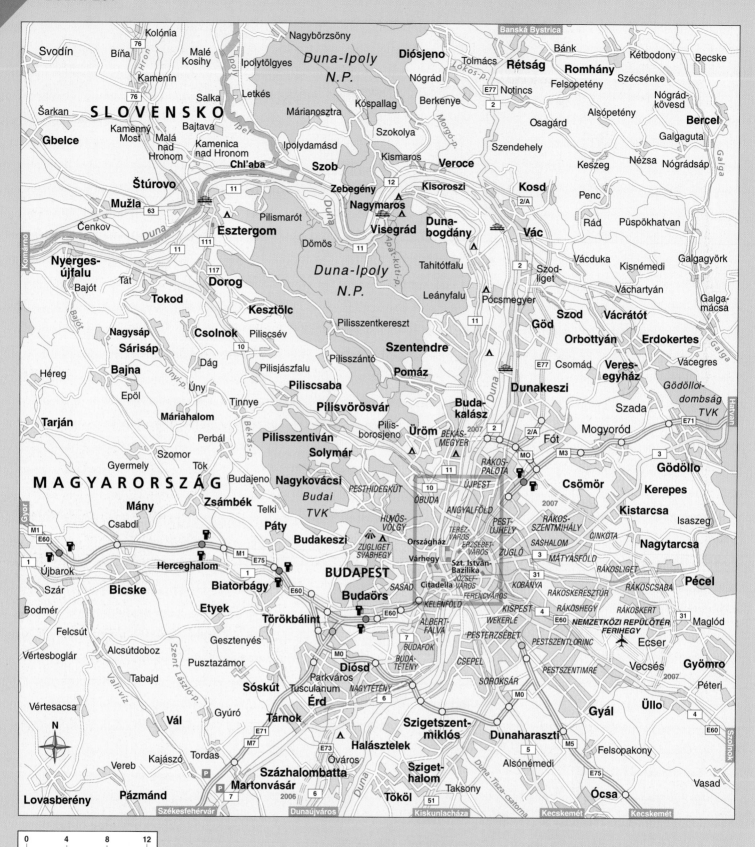

Svodín
Bína
Kolónia
76
Malé
Kosihy
Ipolytölgyes
Nagybörzsöny
Duna-Ipoly
N.P.
Diósjeno
Bánk
Kétbodony
Becske
Kamenín
Salka
Letkés
Nógrád
Tolmács
Rétság
Romhány
Szécsénke
E77 Notincs
Felsopetény
Nógrád-
kövesd

Šarkan
76
Kamenný
Most
Malá
nad
Hronom
Kamenica
nad Hronom
Márianosztra
Kóspallag
Berkenye
2
Osagárd
Alsópetény
Bercel

SLOVENSKO
Gbelce
Bajtava
Chl'aba
Szob
Ipolydamásd
Szokolya
Kismaros
Veroce
Szendehely
Keszeg
Nézsa
Nógrádsáp
Galgaguta

Štúrovo
Mužla
63
11
Zebegény
12
Kisoroszi
Kosd
2/A
Penc
Rád
Püspökhatvan
Osztergom

Čenkov
Pilismarót
Nagymaros
Duna-
bogdány
Vác
Vácduka
Kisnémedi
Galgagyörk

Nyerges-
újfalu
11
111
Esztergom
Dömös
11
Visegrád
Tahitótfalu
2
Szod-
liget
Váchartyán
Galga-
mácsa

Bajót
Tát
117
Dorog
Duna-Ipoly
N.P.
Leányfalu
Pócsmegyer
11
Szod
Vácrátót

Tokod
Kesztölc
Pilisszentkereszt
Szentendre
Göd
Orbottyán
Erdokertes

Nagysáp
Csolnok
Piliscsév
Pilisszántó
Pomáz
E77 Csomád
Veres-
egyház
Vácegres

Sárisáp
Dág
Pilisjászfalu
Dunakeszi
Szada
Gödölloi-
dombság
TVK

Héreg
Bajna
Epöl
Úny
Tinnye
Piliscsaba
Buda-
kalász
Üröm
Békás-
megyer
2007
2
2/A
Fót
Mogyoród
E71

Tarján
Máriahalom
Perbál
Pilisvörösvár
Pilis-
borosjeno
Rákos-
palota
MO
M3
3
Gödöllo

Szomor
Pilisszentiván
Solymár
ÚJPEST
Csömör
Kerepes

MAGYARORSZÁG
Gyermely
Tök
Budajeno
Nagykovácsi
PESTHIDEGKÚT
Budai
TVK
ÓBUDA
ANGYALFÖLD
PEST-
ÚJHELY
RÁKOS-
SZENTMIHÁLY
Kistarcsa
Isaszeg

Mány
Csabdi
Zsámbék
Telki
HÜVÖS-
VÖLGY
TERÉZ-
VÁROS
SASHALOM
CINKOTA
Nagytarcsa

Páty
Budakeszi
ZUGLIGET
SVÁBHEGY
Országház
ERZSÉBET-
VÁROS
ZUGLÓ
MÁTYÁSFÖLD
RÁKOSLIGET

M1
E60
Herceghalom
M1
E75
BUDAPEST
Várhegy
Szt. István-
Bazílika
JÓZSEF
VÁROS
31
KOBÁNYA
RÁKOSCSABA
Pécel

Újbarok
Szár
1
Bicske
Biatorbágy
E60
Budaörs
SASAD
Citadella
FERENCVÁROS
3
RÁKOSKERESZTÚR
RÁKOSHEGY

Bodmér
Etyek
Törökbálint
E60
KELENFÖLD
ALBERT-
FALVA
KISPEST
4
E60
RÁKOSKERT
31
Maglód

Felcsút
Gesztenyés
7
PESTERZSÉBET
WEKERLE
NEMZETKÖZI REPÜLOTÉR
FERIHEGY
Ecser

Vértesboglár
Alcsútdoboz
MO
BUDAFOK
BUDA-
TÉTÉNY
PESTSZENTLORINC
Vecsés
Gyömro

Tabajd
Pusztazámor
Diósd
Parkváros
CSEPEL
SOROKSÁR
PESTSZENTIMRE
2007
Péteri

Vértesacsa
Vál
Gyúró
Sóskút
Tusculanum
NAGYTÉTÉNY
6
MO
Üllo
4

N
Vereb
Kajászó
Tordas
Tárnok
Érd
Szigetszent-
miklós
Dunaharaszti
Gyál
E60

E71
M7
Óváros
E73
Halásztelek
Sziget-
halom
5
M5
Felsopakony

Lovasberény
Pázmánd
7
Martonvásár
2006
6
Százhalombatta
Tököl
51
Tököl
Taksony
Alsónémedi
E75
Vasad
Ócsa

0 4 8 12
km

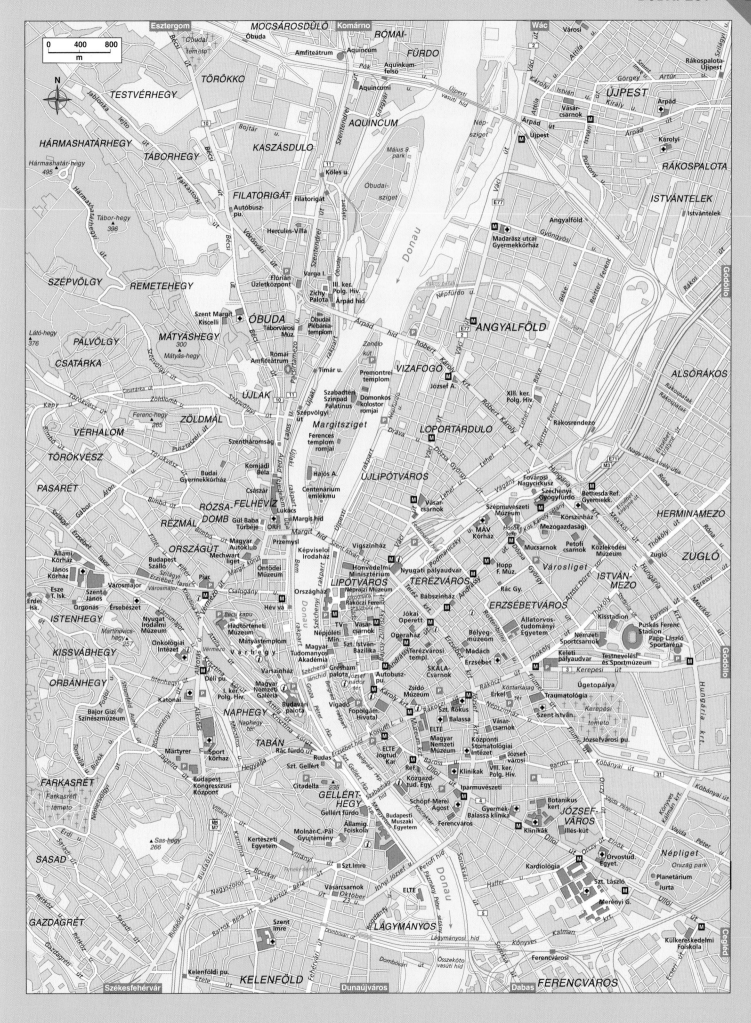

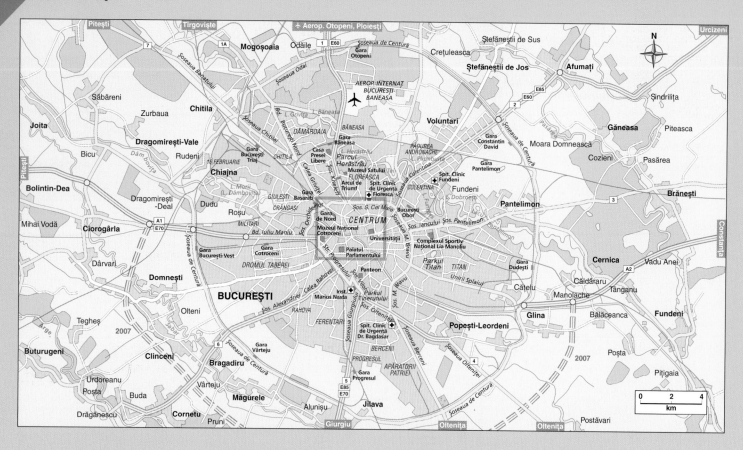

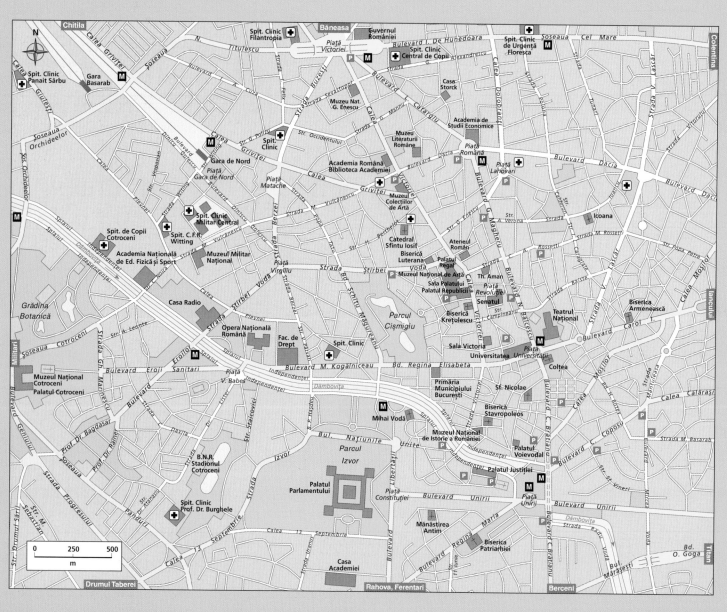

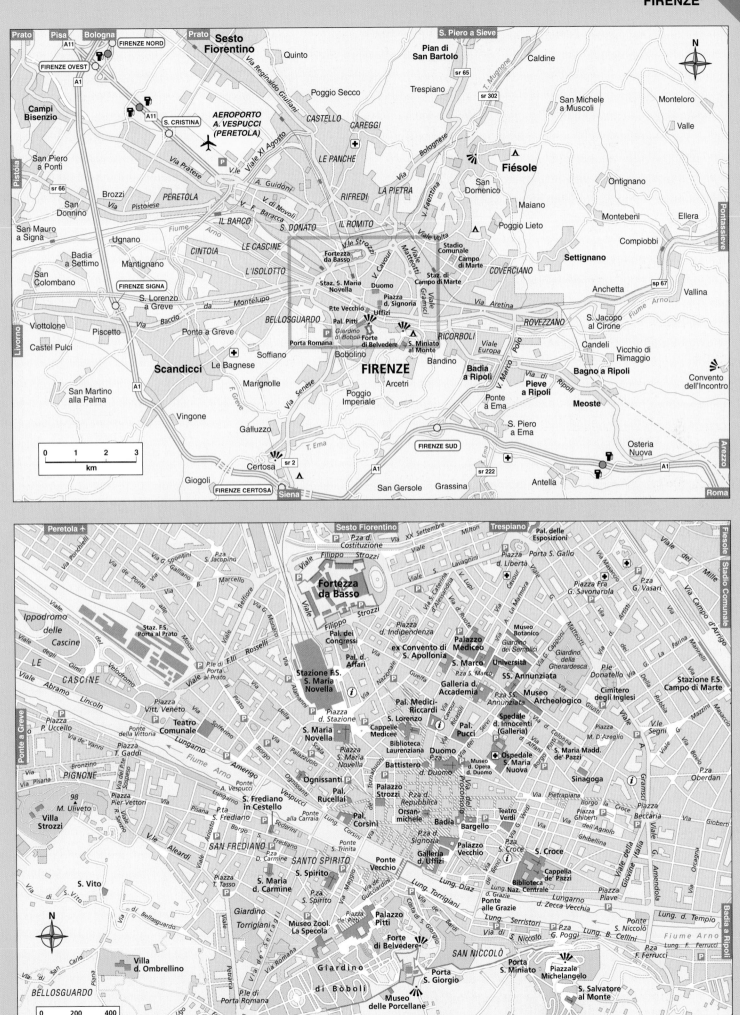

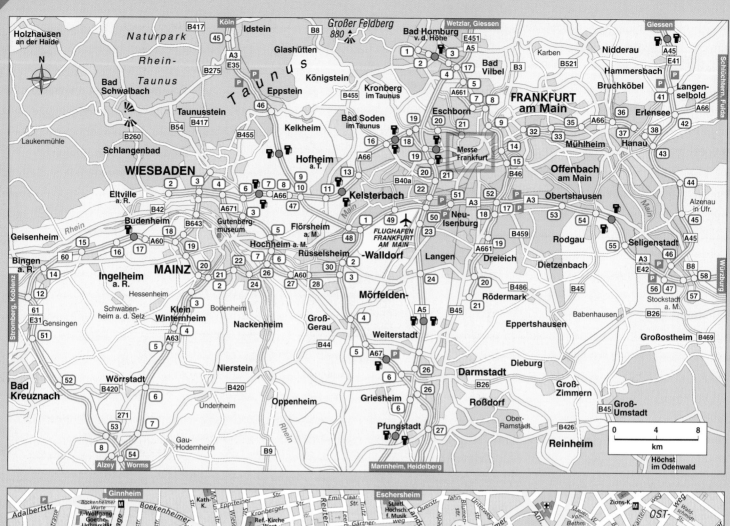

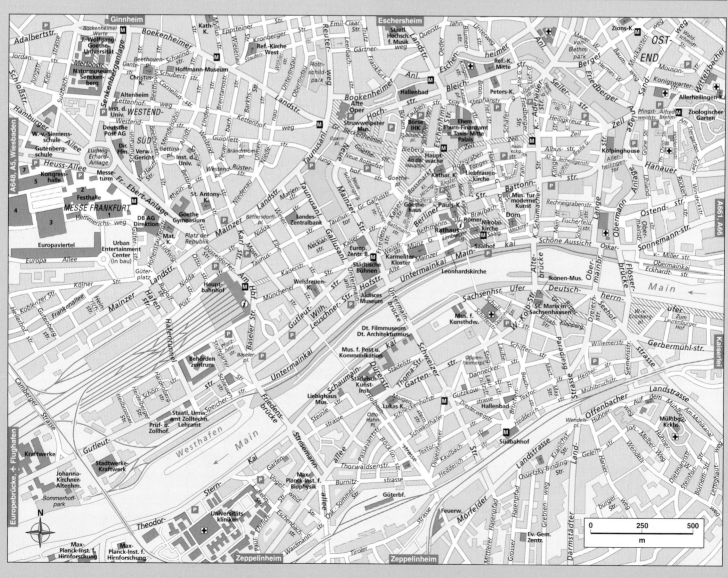

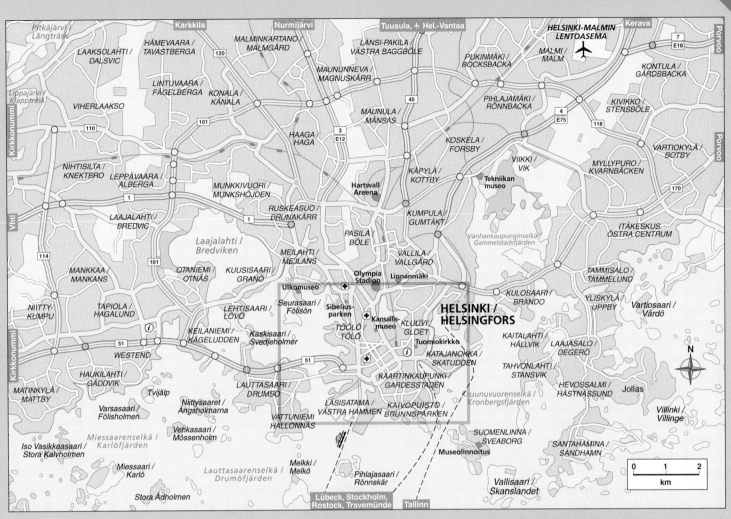

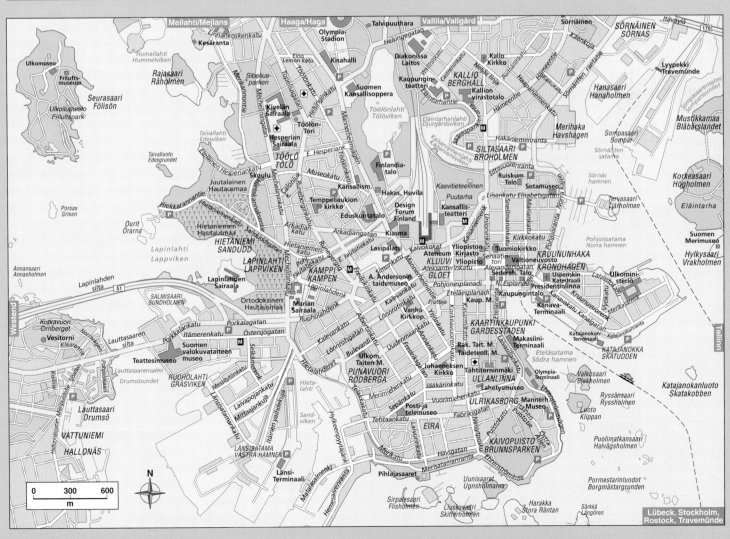

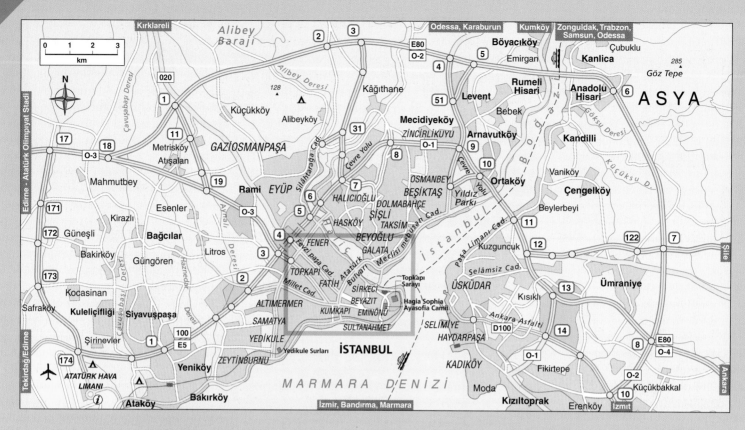

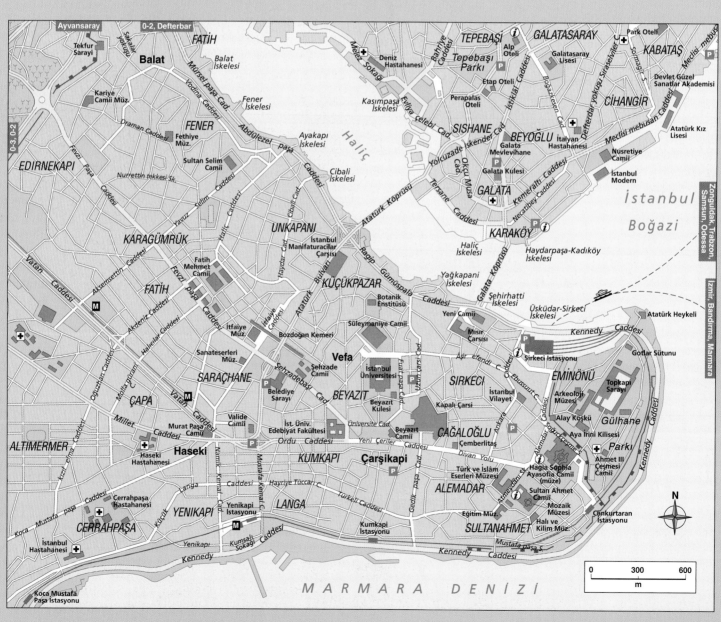

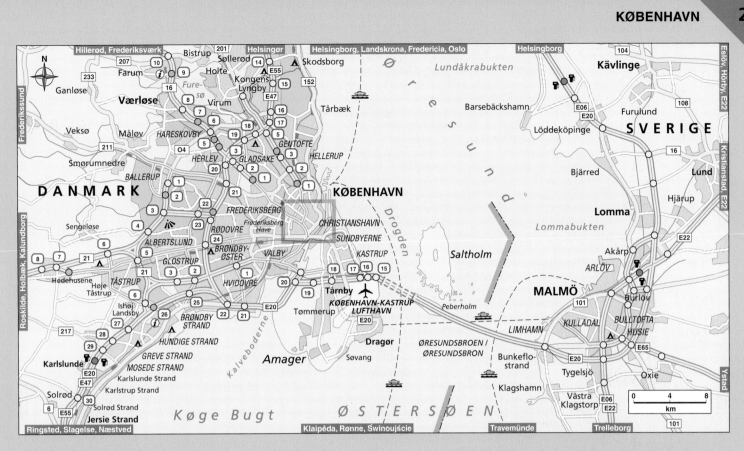

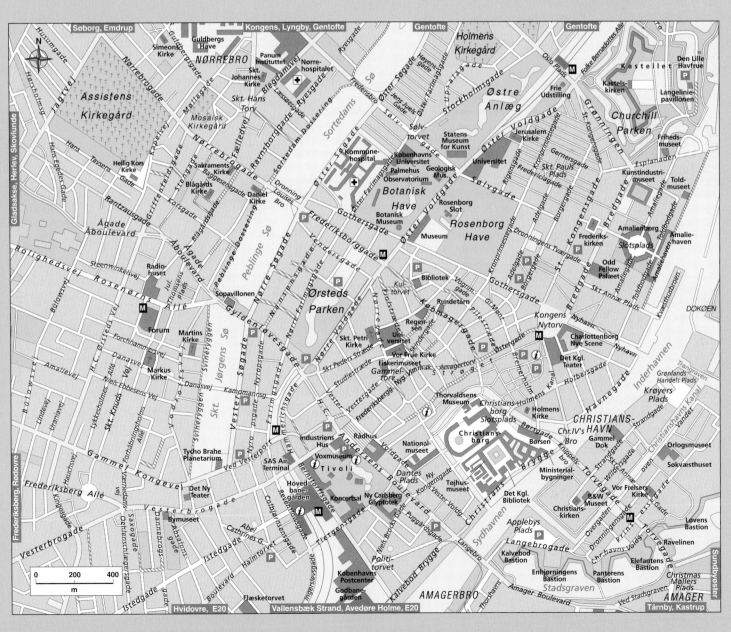

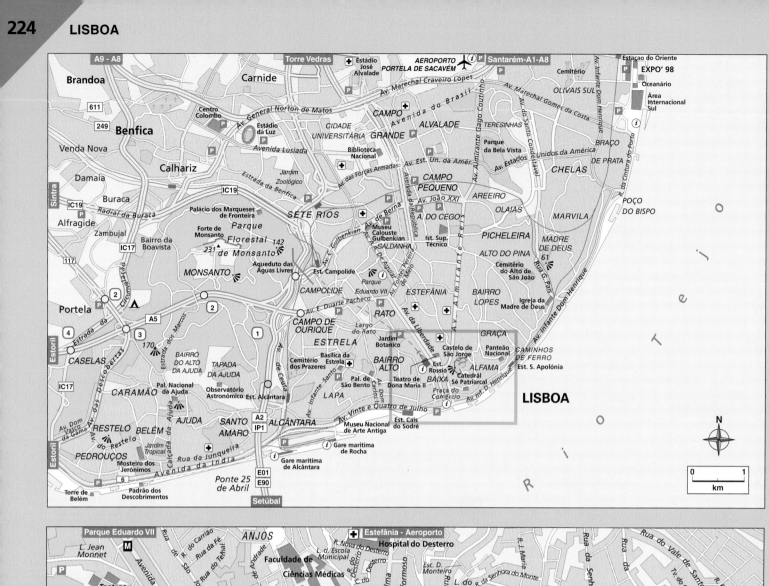

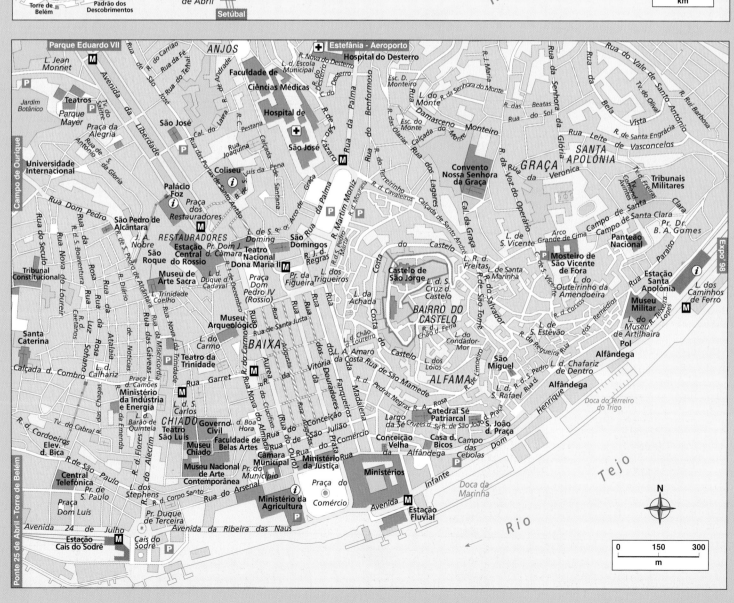

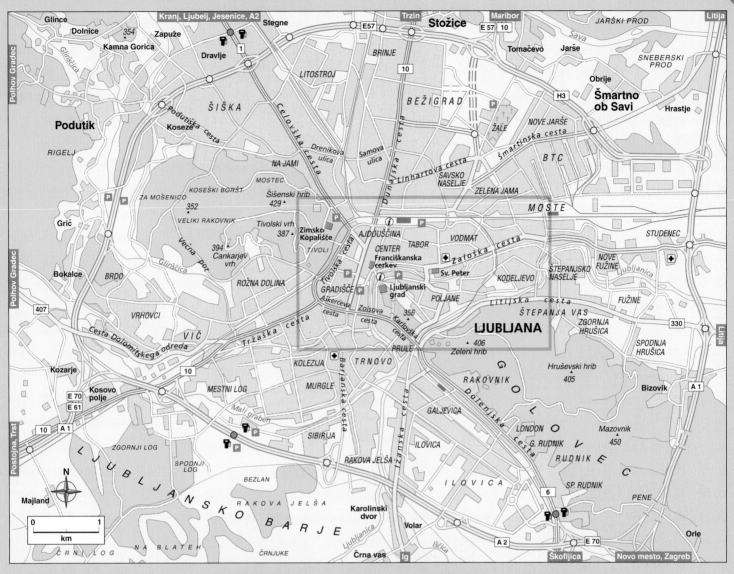

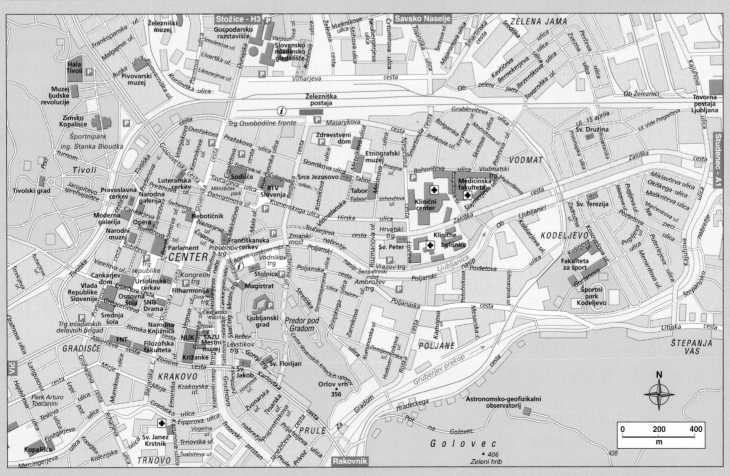

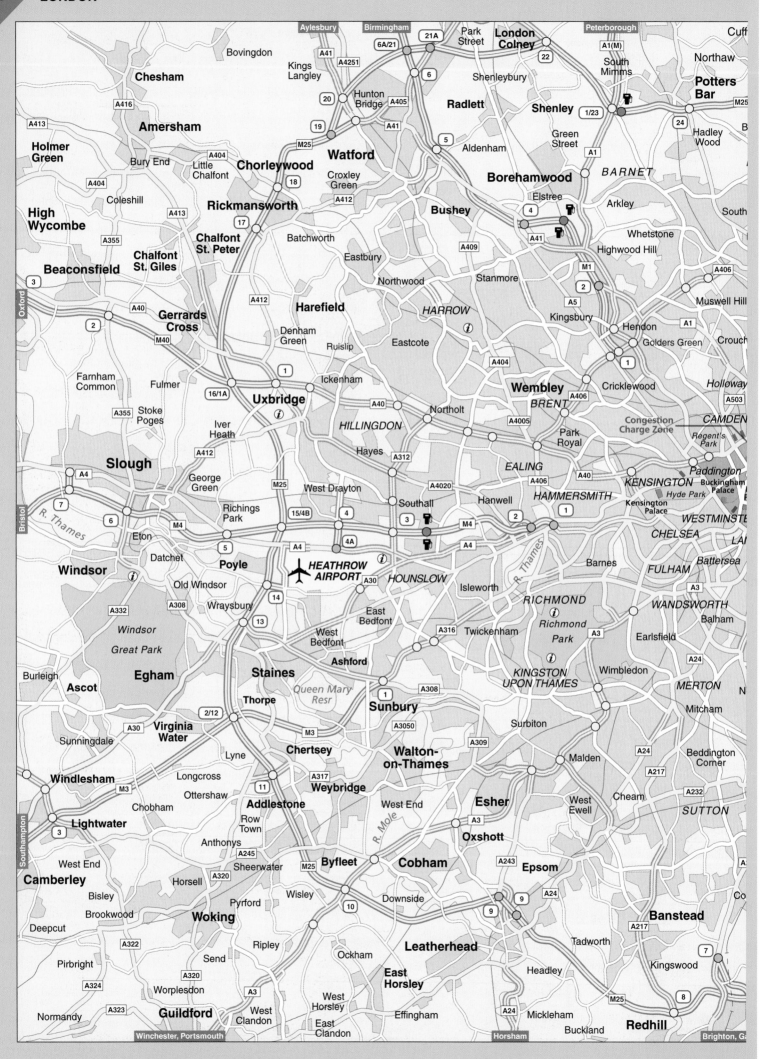

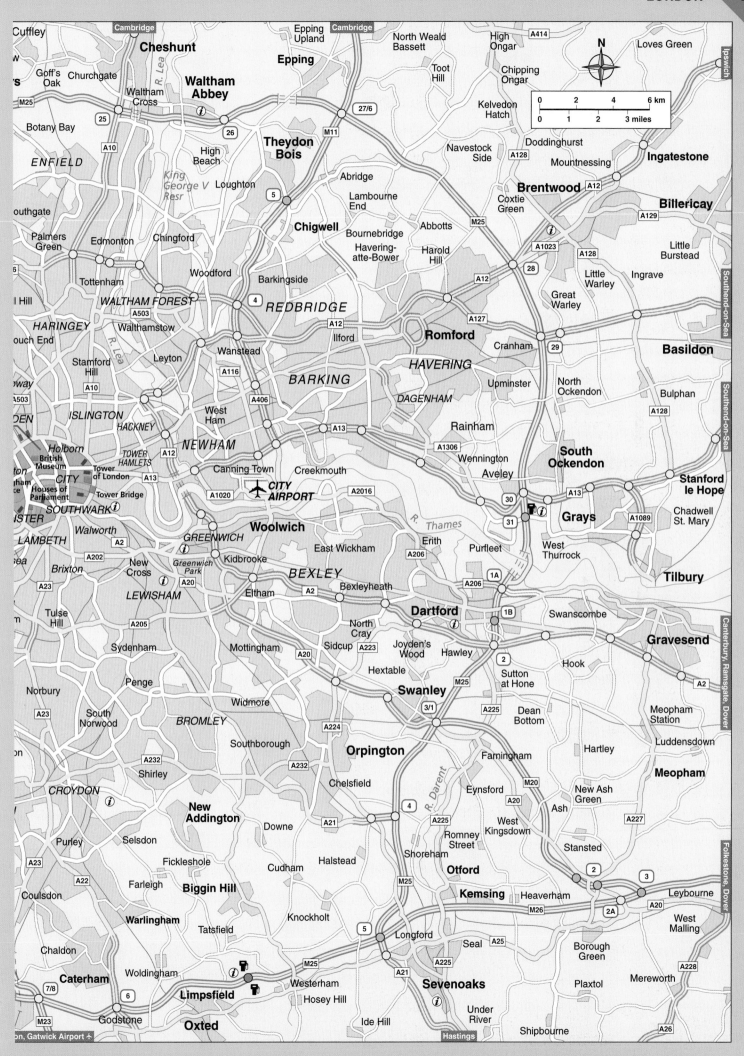

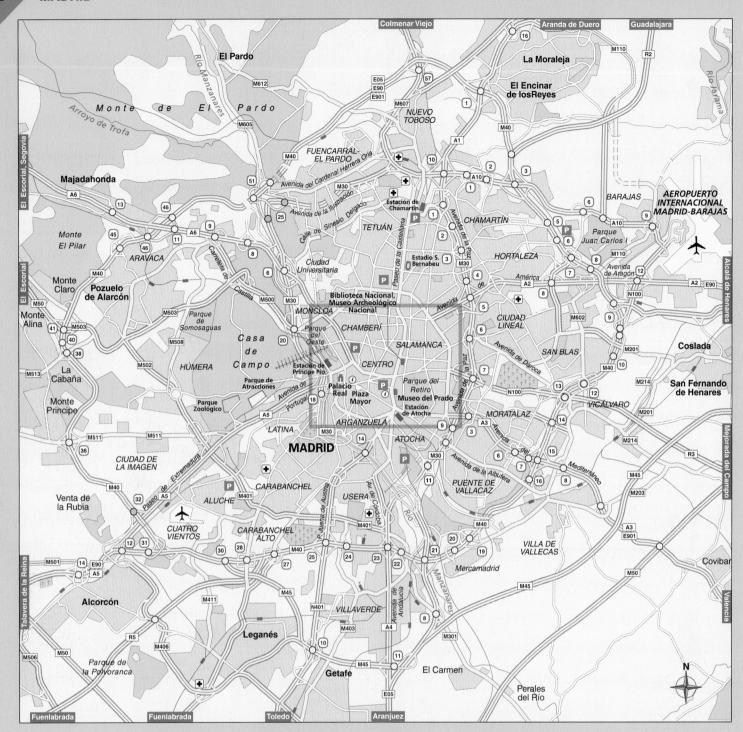

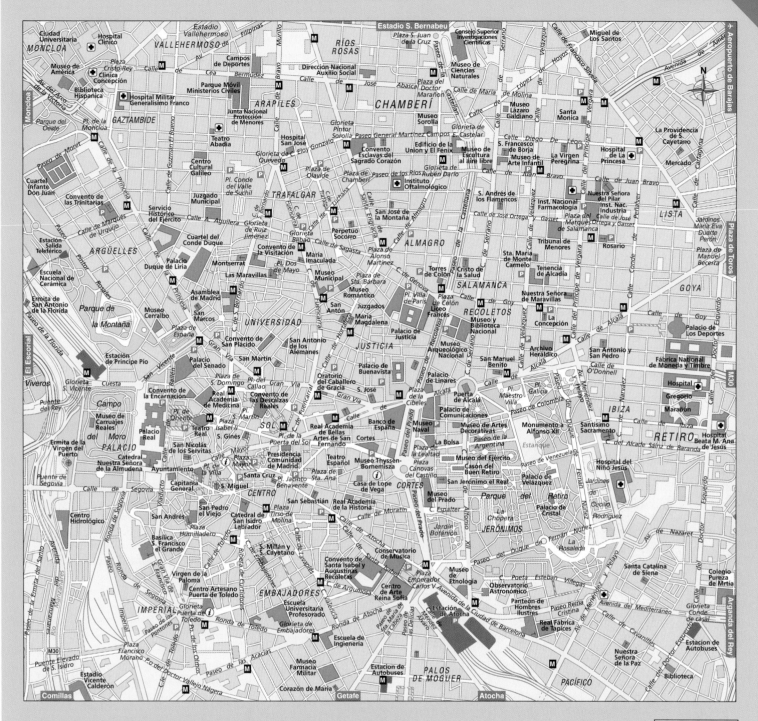

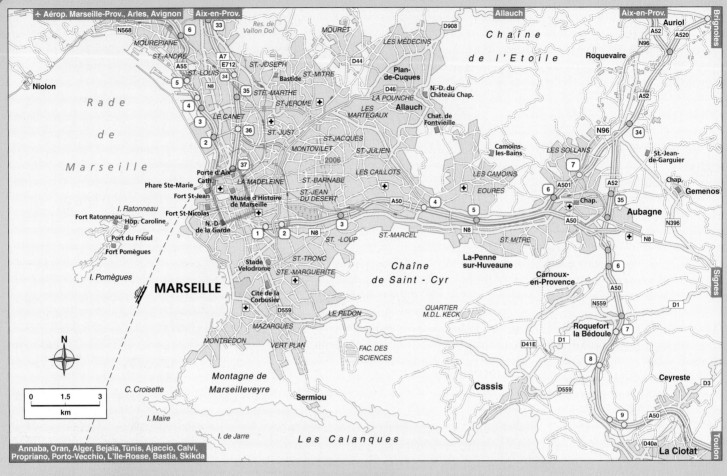

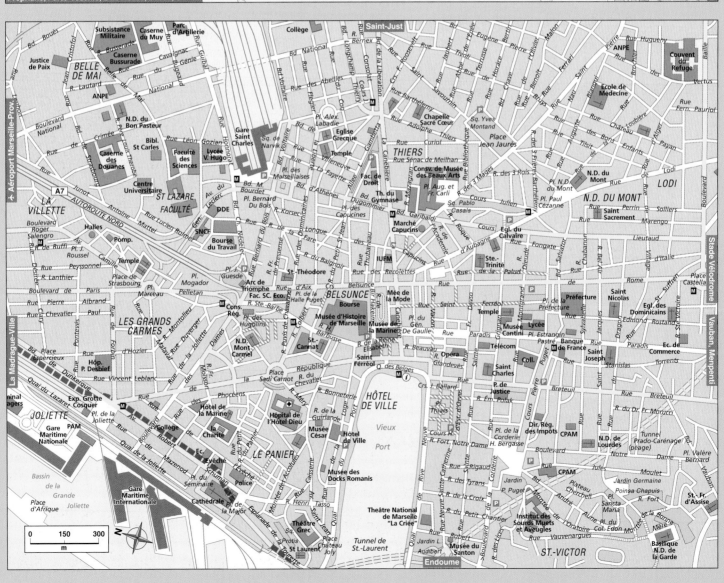

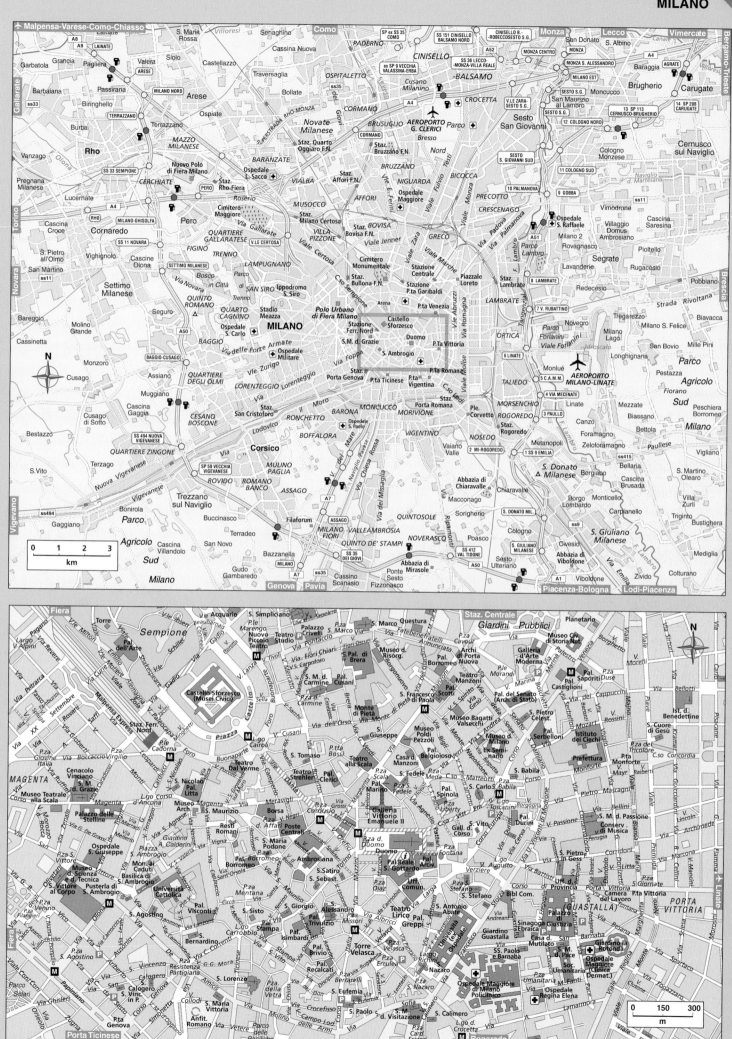

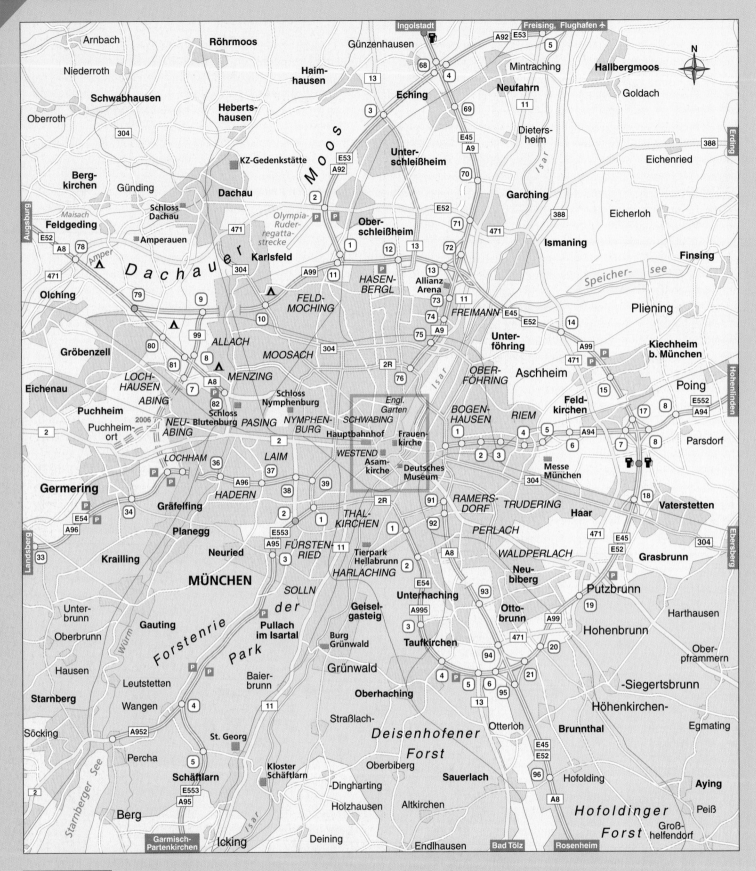

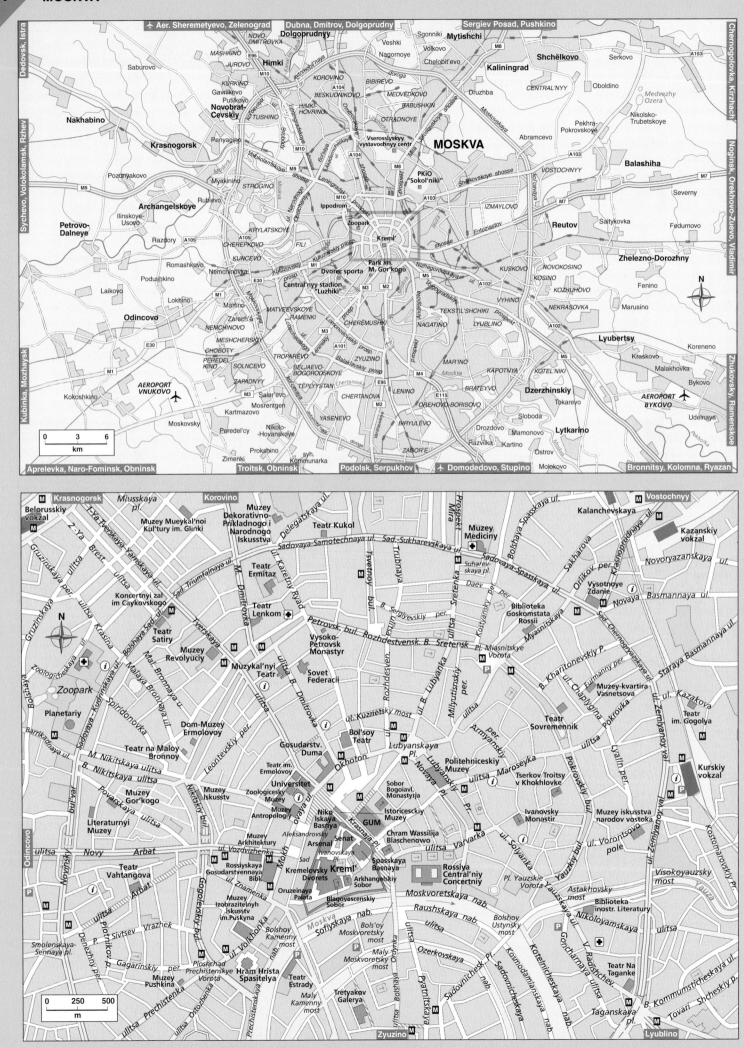

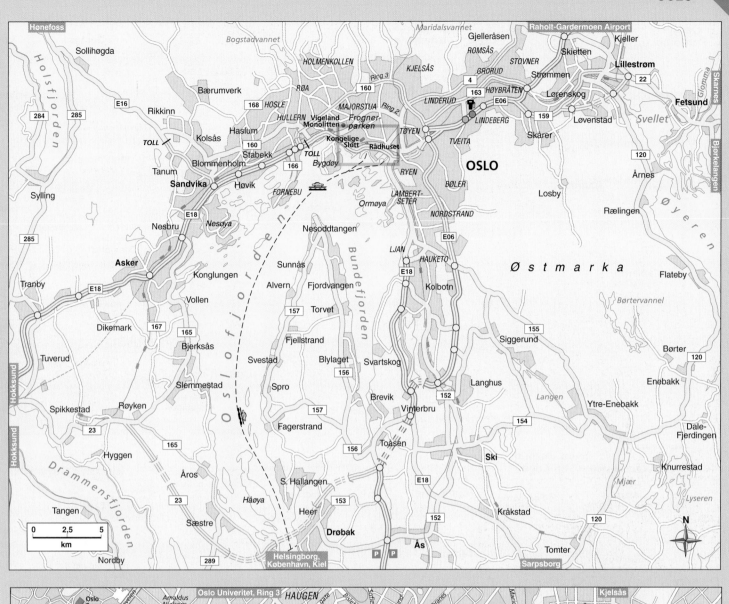

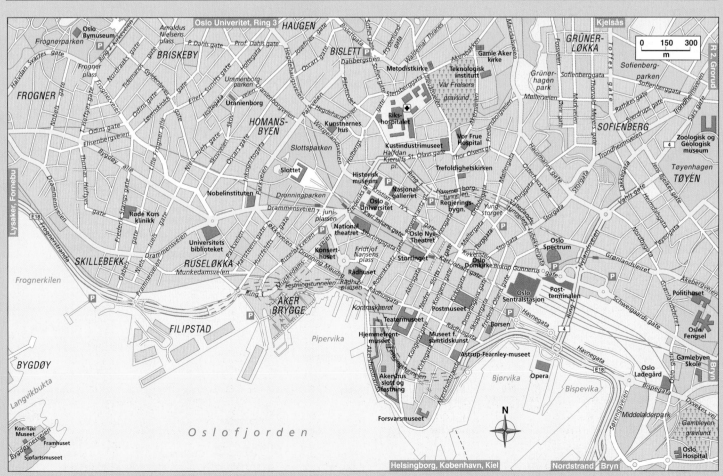

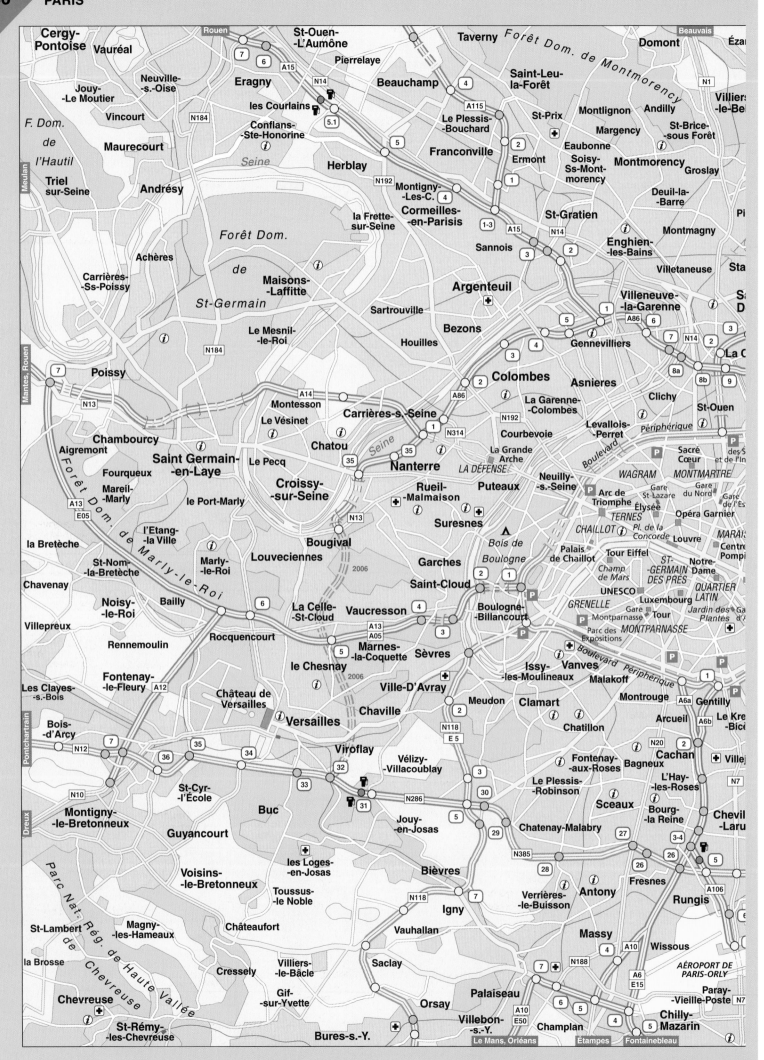

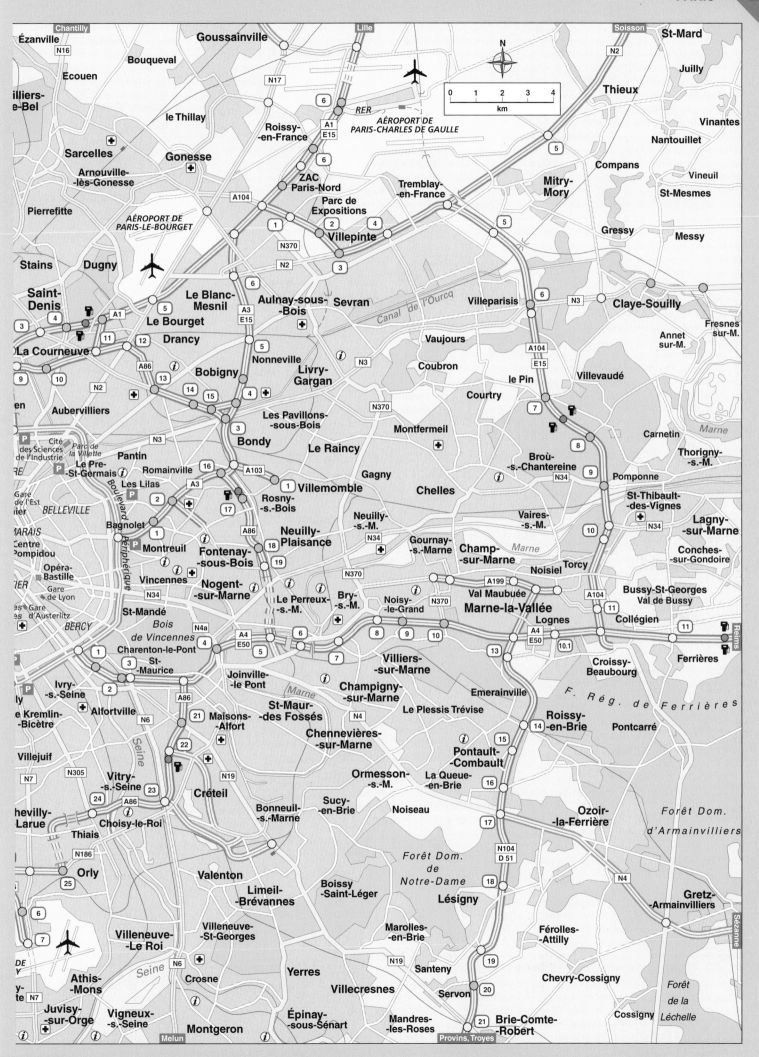

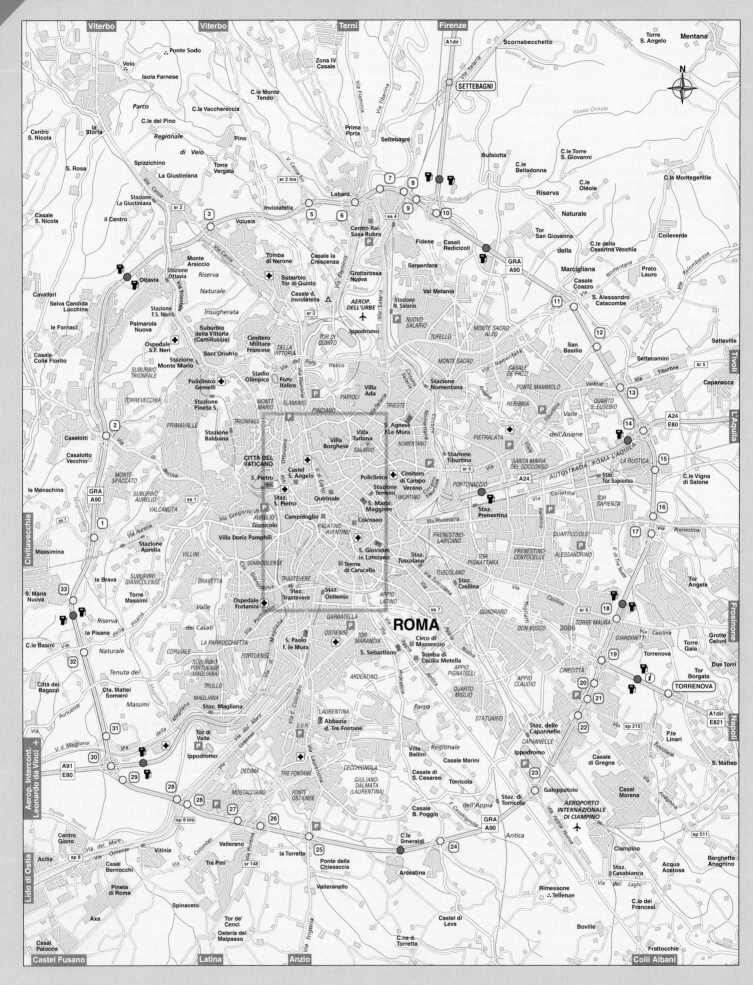

ROMA

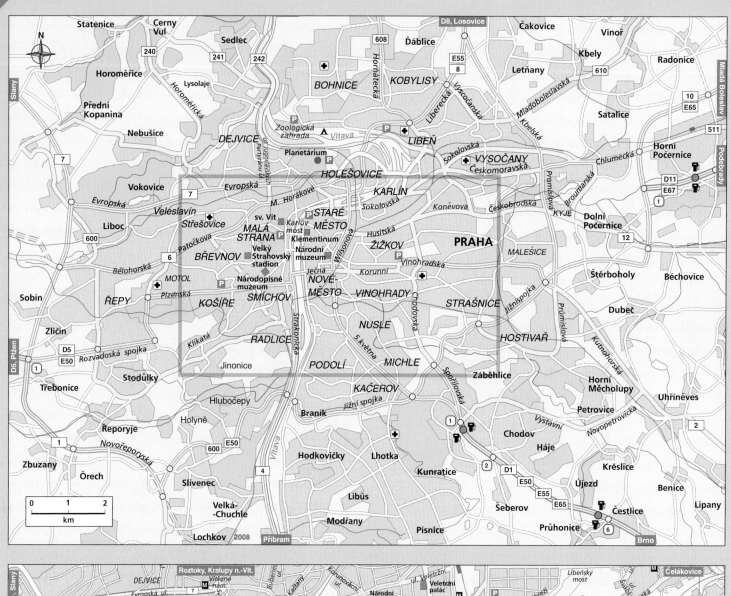

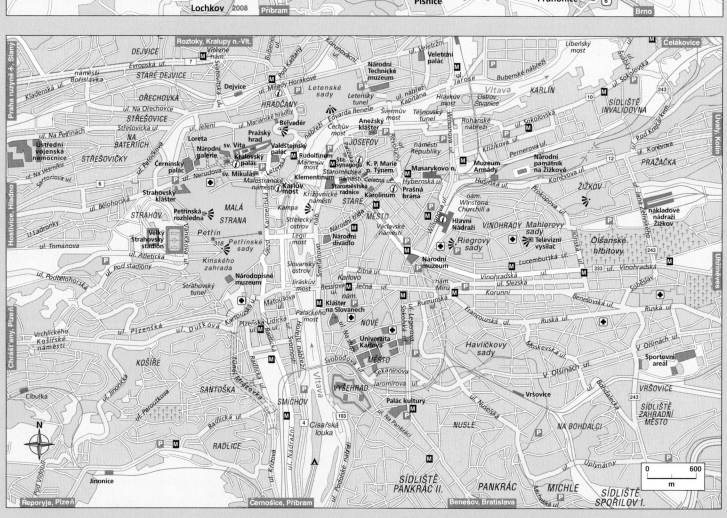

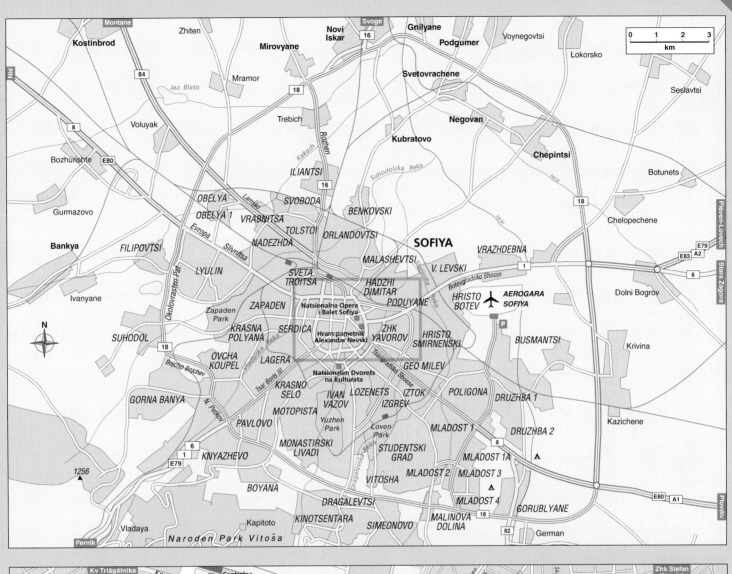

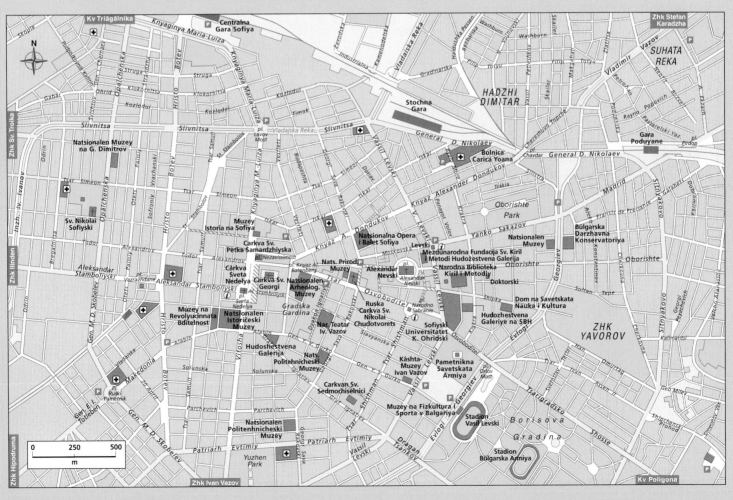

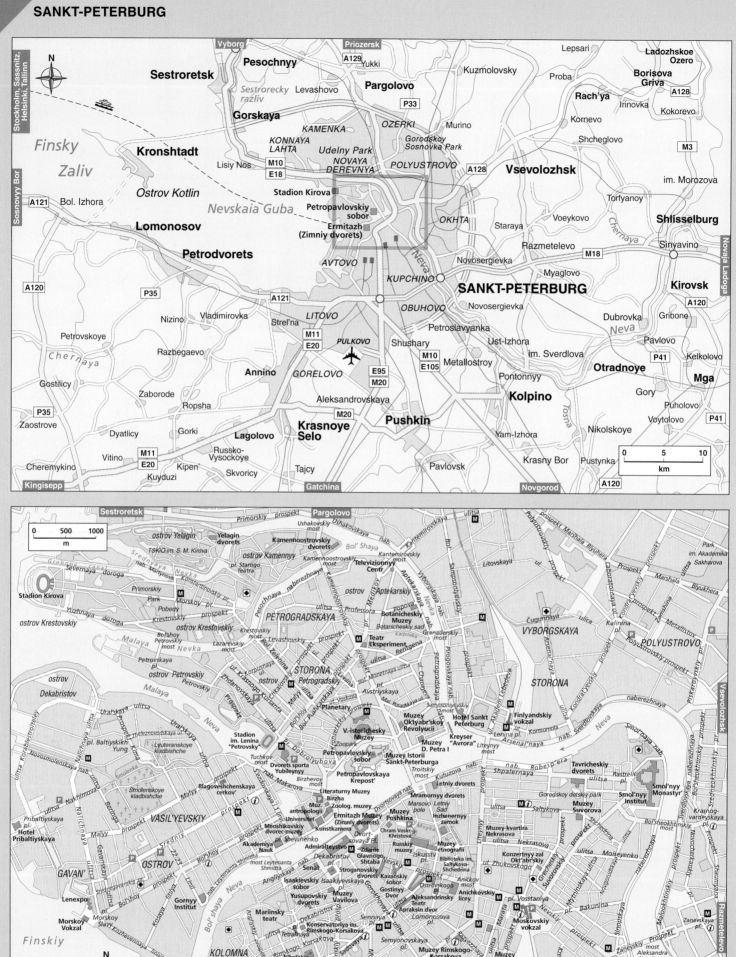

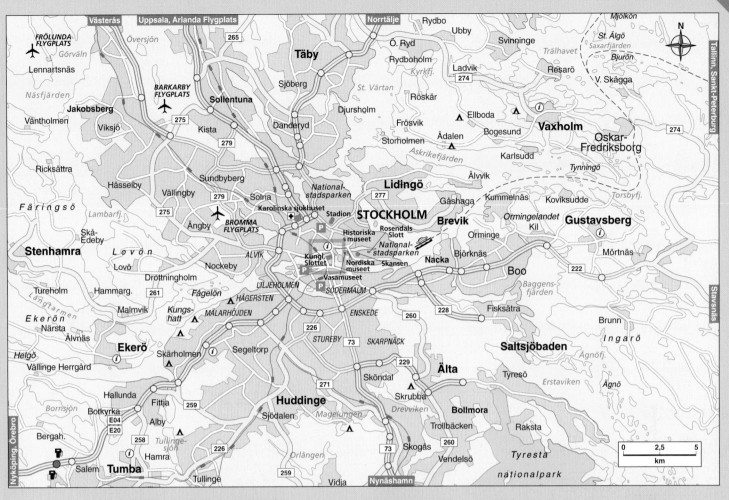

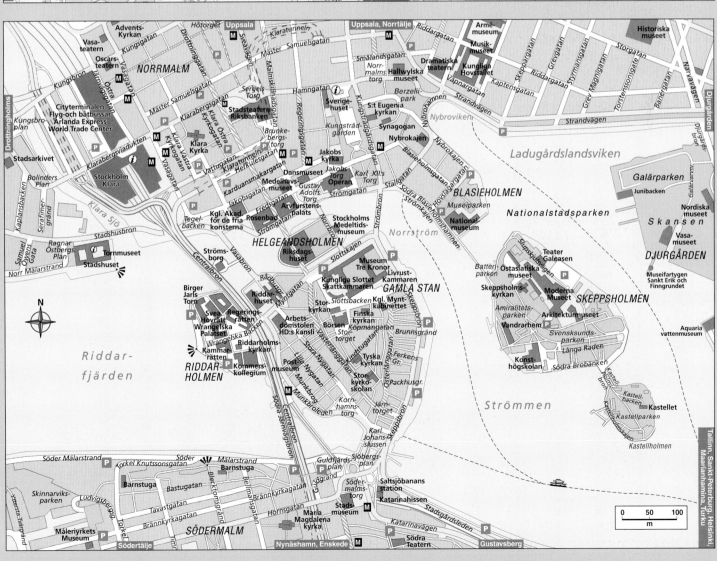

0 1 2 3

km

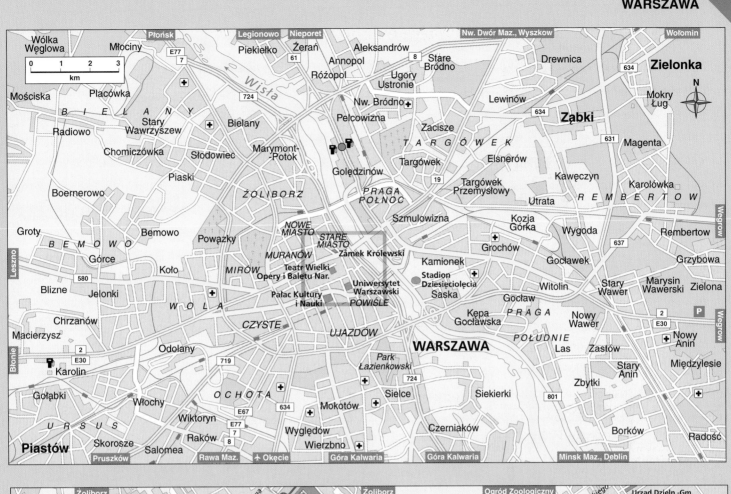

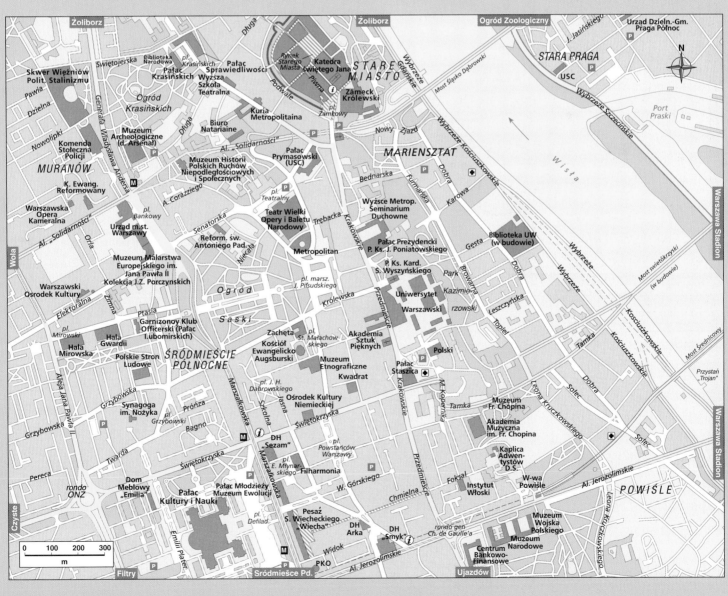

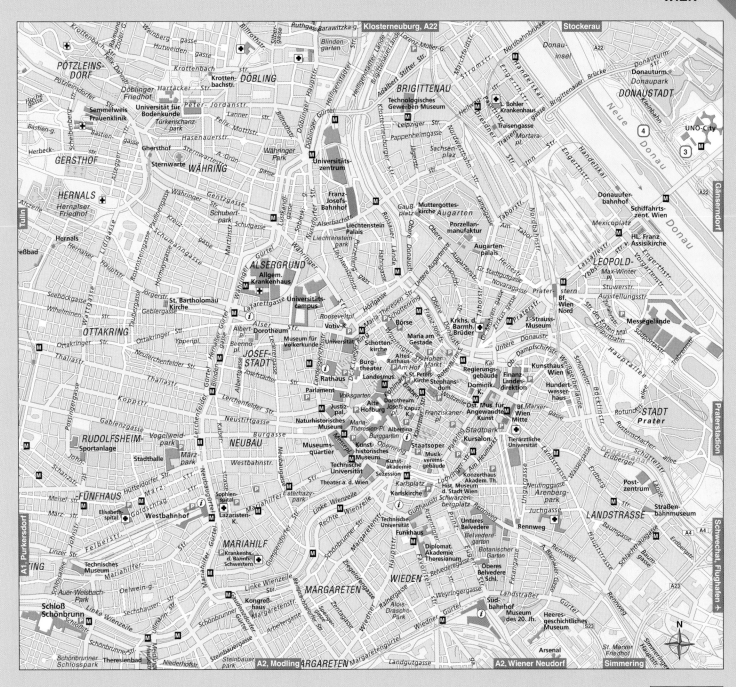

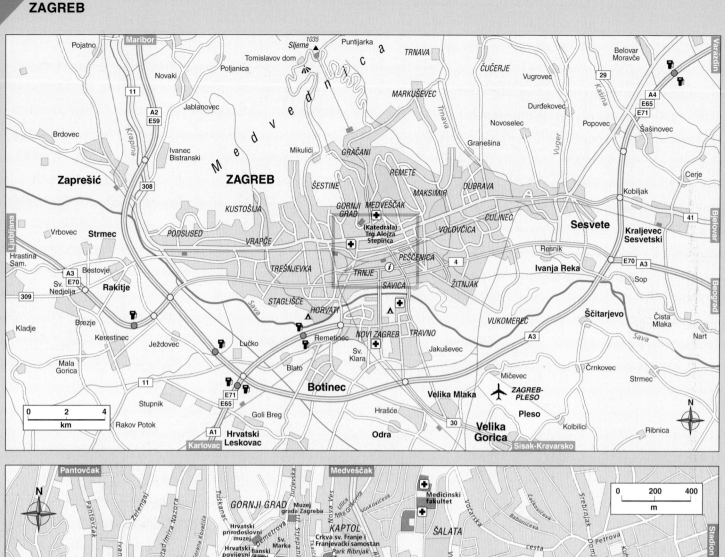

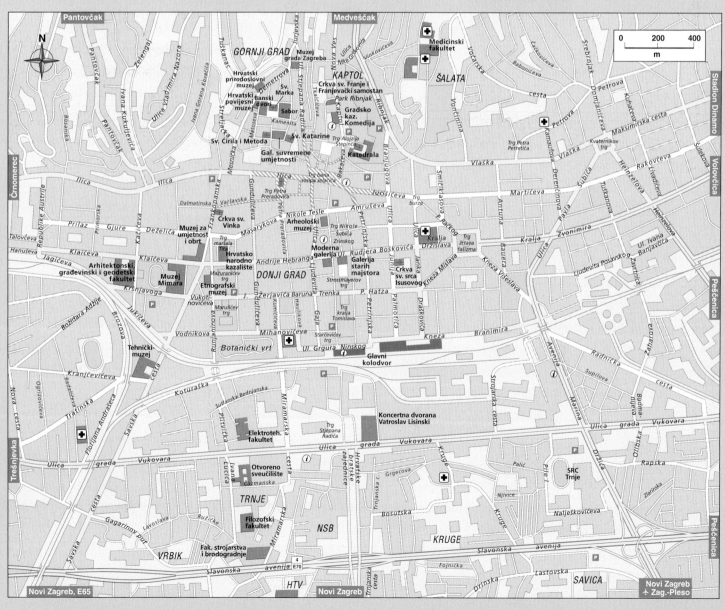

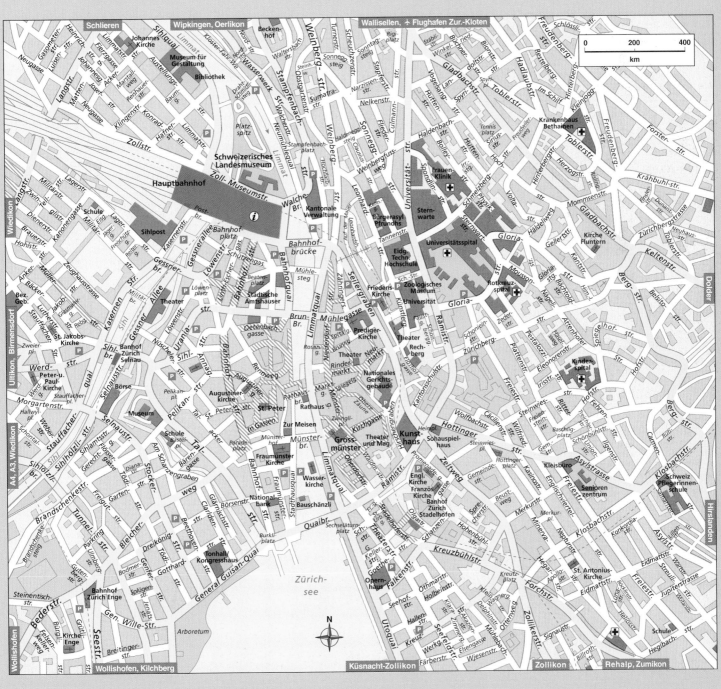

INDEX OF NAMES
INDICE DEI NOMI
ÍNDICE DE TOPÓNIMOS
INDEX DES NOMS
NAMENVERZEICHNIS

How to use the index • Avvertenze per la ricerca
Instrucciones para la consulta • Notices pour la recherche
Erläuterungen des Suchsystems

The index lists the place names, tourist sites, main tunnels and passes contained in the atlas, followed by the abbreviation of the country name to which they belong. All names contained in two adjoining pages are referenced to the even page number.

L'indice elenca i toponimi dei centri abitati, dei siti turistici, dei principali tunnel e passi presenti nell'atlante, accompagnati dalla sigla della nazione di appartenenza. Tutti i nomi contenuti in due pagine affiancate sono riferiti alla pagina di numero pari.

El índice presenta los topónimos de localidades, lugares turísticos, principales túneles y puertos de montaña que figuran en el atlas, seguidos de la sigla que indica el País de pertenencia. Todos los nombres contenidos en dos páginas juntas éstan referidos a la página de número par.

L'index récense les noms des localités, sites touristiques, principales tunnels et cols contenus dans l'atlas, suivis par le sigle qui indique le Pays d'appartenance. Tous les noms contenus dans deux pages l'une à côté de l'autre sont rapportés à la page avec nombre pair.

Der Index enthält die im Atlas vorhandenen Ortsnamen, Sehenswürdigkeiten, wichtigsten Tunnels und Pässe, von dem zugehörigen Staatskennzeichen gefolgt. Alle in zwei anliegenden Seiten enthaltenen Namen sind auf die Seite mit gerader Zahl bezogen.

A

23 August [RO] 148 G1
Å [N] 192 C5
Aabenraa [DK] 156 C4
Aabybro [DK] 160 D3
Aachen [D] 30 F4
Aakirkeby [DK] 158 E4
Aalborg [DK] 160 D4
Aalburg [NL] 16 D6
Aalen [D] 60 B2
Aalestrup [DK] 160 D4
Aalsmane [LV] 198 F4
Aalsmeer [NL] 16 D4
Aalst (Alost) [B] 28 H2
Aalten [NL] 16 G6
Aalter [B] 28 G2
Äänekoski [FIN] 186 G3
Aapajärvi [FIN] 194 D6
Aarau [CH] 58 E5
Aarberg [CH] 58 D5
Aarburg [CH] 58 E5
Aareavaraa [S] 194 B6
Aareschlucht [CH] 70 F1
Aars [DK] 160 D4
Aarschot [B] 30 D4
Aarup [DK] 156 D3
Aavasaksa [FIN] 194 B8
Aba [H] 76 B2
Åbacka [S] 190 F3
Abades [E] 88 F4
Abadín [E] 78 E2
Abadíno [E] 82 H4
Abádszalók [H] 64 F6
A Baña [E] 78 B2
Abanades [E] 90 B5
Abanilla [E] 104 C2
Abano Terme [I] 110 G1
Abarán [E] 104 C2
Abárzuza [E] 84 A4
Abaújszántó [H] 64 G4
Abbadia San Salvatore [I] 114 G2
Abbasanta [I] 118 C4
Abbaye d'Orval [B] 44 D2
Abbekås [S] 158 C3
Abbeville [F] 28 E4
Abbeydorney [IRL] 4 B3
Abbeyfeale [IRL] 4 C3
Abbeyleix [IRL] 4 E3
Abbiategrasso [I] 70 F5
Abborrträsk [S] 190 H3
Abdürrahim [TR] 130 H3
Abejar [E] 90 B2
Abela [P] 94 C2
Abéliéra [F] 108 E3
Abelnes [N] 164 C5
Abelvær [N] 190 C4
Abenberg [D] 46 G5
Abenójar [E] 96 D4

Abensberg [D] 60 E2
Aberaeron [GB] 10 B6
Aberchirder [GB] 6 F5
Aberdare [GB] 12 F2
Aberdeen [GB] 6 F6
Aberfeldy [GB] 8 E1
Abergavenny [GB] 12 F2
Abergele [GB] 10 C4
Aberlour [GB] 6 E5
Abersoch [GB] 10 B4
Aberspier [D] 32 H5
Aberystwyth [GB] 10 B6
Abetone [I] 110 E4
Abide [TR] 130 H5
Abide [TR] 152 G2
Abiego [E] 90 G3
Abild [DK] 156 B4
Abild [S] 162 B4
Abingdon [GB] 12 H3
Abington [GB] 8 D4
Abisko [S] 192 F4
Abiúl [P] 86 D2
Abja–Paluoja [EST] 198 E3
Abla [E] 102 F4
Ablanitsa [BG] 148 B4
Ablis [F] 42 E4
Åbo [S] 190 C6
Åbo / Turku [FIN] 176 D4
Åboland [S] 166 C5
Abondance [F] 70 C2
Abony [H] 76 E2
Åbosjö [S] 190 G6
Aboyne [GB] 6 F6
Abrantes [P] 86 D4
Abraur [S] 190 G2
Abreschviller [F] 44 G5
Abric d'Ermites [E] 92 A6
Abriès [F] 70 C6
Abrigo de la Peña del Escrito [E] 98 C3
Abriola [I] 120 H4
Abtei [A] 74 B3
Abtenau [A] 60 H6
Abtsgmünd [D] 60 B2
Abtshagen [D] 20 D3
Åby [S] 162 C4
Åby [S] 168 B5
Abyarowshchyna [BY] 38 H1
Åbyn [S] 196 B4
A Cañiza [E] 78 C5
Acate [I] 126 F5
Accadia [I] 120 G2
Acceglio [I] 108 E2
Accettura [I] 120 H4
Acciaroli [I] 120 H6
Accous [F] 84 D4
Accumoli [I] 116 B3
Acedera [E] 96 B3
Acedo [E] 82 H6

Acehuche [E] 86 G4
Acerenza [I] 120 H3
Acerno [I] 120 F3
Acerra [I] 120 E3
Aceuchal [E] 94 G2
Acey, Abbaye d'- [F] 58 A4
Acharnés [GR] 134 C6
Achenkirch [A] 60 E6
Achensee [A] 60 E6
Achern [D] 58 F1
Acheux-en-Amiénois [F] 28 E4
Achílleio [GR] 132 G2
Achílleum [TR] 130 H5
Achim [D] 18 E5
Achinós [GR] 130 C3
Achladochóri [GR] 130 B2
Achladókampos [GR] 136 E2
Achleiten [A] 62 B4
Achnasheen [GB] 6 D4
Aci Castello [I] 126 G3
Acipayam [TR] 152 G6
Acireale [I] 126 G3
Aci Trezza [I] 126 G3
Acksi [S] 172 G3
A Coruña / La Coruña [E] 78 C2
Acqua Doria [F] 114 A5
Acquafredda, Castello di– [I] 118 C7
Acqualagna [I] 112 B6
Acquanegra sul Chiese [I] 110 E1
Acquapendente [I] 114 G3
Acquaro [I] 124 D6
Acquasanta Terme [I] 116 C3
Acquasparta [I] 116 A3
Acquaviva delle Fonti [I] 122 D3
Acquedolci [I] 126 F2
Acqui Terme [I] 108 H2
Acri [I] 124 D4
Acropolis Iberica [E] 90 F5
Ács [H] 64 A6
Acsa [H] 64 D5
Ada [SCG] 76 E5
Adaköy [TR] 154 D2
Adalsbruk [N] 172 C3
Ådalsvollen [N] 190 C6
Adámas [GR] 138 D4
Adamuz [E] 96 C6
Adanero [E] 88 E3
Adapazari (Sakarya) [TR] 150 H3
Adare [IRL] 4 C3
Adelebsen [D] 32 F4
Adelboden [CH] 70 D2
Adelfia [I] 122 E3
Adelsheim [D] 46 D5
Adelsö [S] 168 D3
Adelsried [D] 60 C3
Ademuz [E] 98 D2

Adenau [D] 30 G6
Adjud [RO] 204 E4
Admont [A] 62 C6
Ådneram [N] 164 C3
Adolfsström [S] 190 F2
Adony [H] 76 C2
Adorf [D] 48 C3
Adra [E] 102 F5
Adradas [E] 90 B4
Adrall [E] 92 D1
Adramittium Thebe [TR] 152 C1
Adrano [I] 126 F3
Ádria [I] 110 G2
Adrigole [IRL] 4 B5
A. Drosiní [GR] 130 F2
Adutiškis [LT] 200 H4
Aegviidu [EST] 198 E1
Aerinó [GR] 132 H2
Ærøskøbing [DK] 156 D4
Aerzen [D] 32 F3
Aesoo [EST] 198 E2
A Estrada [E] 78 C3
Aetópetra [GR] 132 C1
Aetós [GR] 128 E4
Aetós [GR] 132 D5
Áetsä [FIN] 176 E2
Afántou [GR] 154 D4
Afife [P] 78 A6
Afiónas [GR] 132 A2
Aflenz [A] 62 D6
A Fonsagrada [E] 78 F3
Afoss [N] 164 G3
Africo [I] 124 D7
Afritz [A] 72 H3
Afşar [TR] 152 H4
Afsluitdijk [NL] 16 E2
Áfyssos [GR] 134 A3
Áfytos [GR] 130 B6
Ağaçbeyli [TR] 152 G3
Ağaçlı [TR] 150 E2
Agaete [E] 100 C6
Agalás [GR] 136 A2
Agalatovo [RUS] 178 H4
Ág.anárgyroi [GR] 132 G2
Ag. Antónios [GR] 130 B5
Ág. Athanásios [GR] 128 H4
Agay [F] 108 E5
Agazzano [I] 110 C2
Ag. Charálampos [GR] 130 F3
Agde [F] 106 E5
Ag. Dimítrios [GR] 132 F4
Ág. Dimítrios [GR] 128 G6
Ag. Dionysíou, Moní– [GR] 130 D5
Agen [F] 66 E5
Agéranos [GR] 136 E5
Agerbæk [DK] 156 B2

Ag. Fotiá [GR] 140 G5
Ág. Geórgios [GR] 132 F4
Agger [DK] 160 B4
Aggersund [DK] 160 D4
Ağla [TR] 154 E1
Aggsbach-Dorf [A] 62 D4
Aggsbach-Markt [A] 62 D4
Aggstein [A] 62 D4
Aggtelek [H] 64 E3
Aghadoe [IRL] 4 B4
Aghleam [IRL] 2 B3
Agiá [GR] 132 H1
Agía Ánna [GR] 132 H5
Agía Ánna [GR] 134 B4
Agía Efimía [GR] 132 C6
Agía Galíni [GR] 140 D5
Agia Marina [CY] 154 F5
Agía Marína [GR] 136 G1
Agia Marína [GR] 154 A1
Agía Nápa [CY] 154 G5
Agía Paraskeví [GR] 134 G2
Agia Pelagía [GR] 136 F6
Agiásmata [GR] 134 G4
Agiásos [GR] 134 H2
Agía Triáda [GR] 128 H5
Agía Triáda [GR] 132 D4
Agía Triáda [GR] 136 C1
Agía Varvára [GR] 140 D5
Ág. Ioánnis [GR] 154 A3
Agiófyllo [GR] 132 E1
Ágioi Déka [GR] 140 E5
Agiókampos [GR] 132 H4
Agiókampos [GR] 132 H1
Ágios Amvrósios (Esentepe) [CY] 154 G5
Ágios Andréas [GR] 136 E3
Ágios Apóstoloi [GR] 136 F5
Agios Athanásios [GR] 128 F4
Agios Dimítrios [GR] 128 G6
Agios Dimítrios [GR] 136 F4
Ágios Efstrátios [GR] 134 E1
Ágios Germanos [GR] 128 E4
Agios Konstantínos [GR] 132 H4
Agios Konstantínos [GR] 152 C5
Ágios Kýrikos [GR] 138 G1
Ágios Léon [GR] 136 A2
Ágios Matthaíos [GR] 132 B2
Ágios Mýron [GR] 140 E5
Ágios Nikítas [GR] 132 C4
Ágios Nikólaos [GR] 132 C2
Ágios Nikólaos [GR] 132 D4
Ágios Nikólaos [GR] 136 G2
Ágios Nikólaos [GR] 140 F4
Ágios Pétros [GR] 132 C5
Ágios Pétros [GR] 136 E3
Ágios Theodoros (Çayırova) [CY] 154 G5

Agios Vlásios [GR] 132 E4
Agira [I] 126 F3
Ág. Kyriakí [GR] 138 H1
Aglasterhausen [D] 46 C5
Ag. Lávra [GR] 136 D1
Aglen [N] 190 C4
Agliano [I] 108 H2
Agliate [I] 70 G4
Ag. Loukás [GR] 134 C5
Ag. Marína [GR] 132 G4
Ag. Marína [GR] 134 C5
Ág. Marína [GR] 140 G3
Agnánta [GR] 132 D2
Agnanteró [GR] 132 F2
Agnás [S] 190 H6
Ág. Nikólaos [GR] 130 C6
Agnita [RO] 204 D4
Agnone [I] 116 E6
Agnone Bagni [I] 126 G4
Agnóntas [GR] 134 B3
Agoitz / Aoiz [E] 84 C4
Agolada [E] 78 C3
Agoncillo [E] 82 H6
Agon–Coutainville [F] 26 D3
Agordo [I] 72 E4
Ágosegyháza [H] 76 D3
Agost [E] 104 D2
Ag. Panteleïmonas [GR] 128 F4
Ag. Pelagía [GR] 140 E4
Ag. Pétros [GR] 128 G4
Ág. Pródromos [GR] 130 B5
Agramón [E] 104 B1
Agramunt [E] 92 C3
Ágras [GR] 128 F4
Agreda [E] 84 A6
Agreliá [GR] 132 F1
Agriá [GR] 132 H2
Agriliá [GR] 132 E5
Agrínio [GR] 132 E5
Agriovótano [GR] 134 B3
Agrópoli [I] 120 F4
Ag. Roúmeli [GR] 140 C5
Ag. Stéfanos [GR] 138 E2
Ag. Theódoroi [GR] 132 H3
Ag. Theódoroi [GR] 136 F1
Ag. Thomás [GR] 140 E5
Ag. Triáda [GR] 134 C6
Agua, Cueva del– [E] 102 F2
Agua Amarga [E] 102 H5
Aguadulce [E] 102 G5
A Guarda / La Guardia [E] 78 A5
A Guarda / La Guardia [E] 92 G2
Aguasmestas [E] 78 G3
Aguas Nuevas [E] 98 B5
Aguda [P] 80 B4
A Gudiña [E] 78 D6

Agudo [E] 96 C3
Águeda [P] 80 B5
Agüero [E] 84 C5
Aguiar da Beira [P] 80 D5
Águila, Cuevas del– [E] 88 C5
Aguilafuente [E] 88 F3
Aguilar de Campoo [E] 82 D4
Aguilar de la Frontera [E] 102 C2
Aguilar del Alfambra [E] 98 E1
Águilas [E] 104 B4
Agüimes [E] 100 C6
Agulo [E] 100 B5
Agurain / Salvatierra [E] 82 H5
Aguzadera [E] 100 H3
Ağva / Yeşilçay [TR] 150 G2
Aha [D] 58 F3
Ahascragh [IRL] 2 D5
Ahat [TR] 152 G3
Ahaus [D] 16 G5
Åheim [N] 180 C4
Aheloy [BG] 148 F4
Ahigal [E] 88 A5
Ahithisar [TR] 152 H3
Ahja [EST] 198 F3
Ahlbeck [D] 20 E3
Ahlbeck [D] 20 B6
Ahlen [D] 32 C3
Ahlerstedt [D] 18 E4
Ahlhorn [D] 18 C6
Ahmetbey [TR] 150 C2
Ahmetbeyler [TR] 152 C2
Ahmetler [TR] 152 F3
Ahmetli [TR] 152 D3
Ahmovaara [FIN] 188 F1
Ahnsen [D] 32 H2
Ahokylä [FIN] 196 E5
Ahola [FIN] 186 D2
Ahola [FIN] 196 F2
Ahonkylä [FIN] 186 C3
Ahrensbök [D] 18 G3
Ahrensburg [D] 18 G4
Ahrhütte [D] 30 G6
Ahrweiler [D] 30 G5
Ähtäri / Etseri [FIN] 186 E4
Ahtärinranta [FIN] 186 E3
Ähtävä / Esse [FIN] 196 C6
Åhus [S] 158 D2
Ahvela [FIN] 196 F3
Ahveninen [FIN] 186 E5
Ahvenselkä [FIN] 194 E7
Aianí [GR] 128 F6
Aibar [E] 84 C4
Aich [D] 60 F3

Aicha [D] 60 H3
Aichach [D] 60 D3
Aichstetten [D] 60 B5
Aidenbach [D] 60 G3
Aidone [I] 126 F4
Aigiáli [GR] 138 G3
Aigialoúsa (Yenierenköy) [CY] 154 G4
Aigina [GR] 136 G2
Aigínio [GR] 128 G5
Áigio [GR] 132 F6
Aigle [CH] 70 C2
Aiglsbach [D] 60 E3
Aignay-le-Duc [F] 56 G2
Aigósthena [GR] 134 B6
Aigre [F] 54 D6
Aigrefeuille-d'Aunis [F] 54 C5
Aigrefeuille-sur-Maine [F] 54 C2
Aiguablava [E] 92 G3
Aiguebelle [F] 70 B4
Aiguebelle [F] 108 D6
Aigueperse [F] 68 D1
Aigues-Mortes [F] 106 F4
Aigues-Vives [F] 106 C4
Aiguevives [F] 54 G2
Aiguilles [F] 70 B6
Aigurande [F] 54 H5
Äijäjoki [FIN] 194 B5
Äijälä [FIN] 186 G3
Ailefroide [F] 70 B6
Aillant-sur-Tholon [F] 56 E1
Aime [F] 70 B4
Ainaži [LV] 198 D4
Ainet [A] 72 F2
Ainhoa [F] 84 C2
Ainsa [E] 84 E6
Airaines [F] 28 D4
Airan [F] 26 F4
Airasca [I] 70 D6
Aire [F] 28 E3
Aire-sur-l'Adour [F] 84 E2
Airolo [CH] 70 F2
Airvault [F] 54 E3
Aisey-sur-Seine [F] 56 G2
Aïssey [F] 58 B5
Aistaig [D] 58 G2
Aisými [GR] 130 G3
Aisy-sur-Armançon [F] 56 F2
Aiterhofen [D] 60 G2
Aitolikó [GR] 132 E5
Aitrach [D] 60 B4
Aitrang [D] 60 C5
Aittojärvi [FIN] 196 E6
Aittolahti [FIN] 188 F4
Aittoperä [FIN] 196 D5
Aittovaara [FIN] 196 F3
Aiud [RO] 204 C4
Áivo / Oivu [FIN] 196 C6

Aix-en-Othe [F] 42 H6
Aix-en-Provence [F] 108 B4
Aixe-sur-Vienne [F] 66 G1
Aix-les-Bains [F] 68 H3
Aizanoi [TR] 152 G2
Aizenay [F] 54 B3
Aizkraukle [LV] 198 E5
Aizpute [LV] 198 B5
Ajaccio [F] 114 A5
Ajaur [S] 190 H4
Ajaureforsen [S] 190 F3
Ajdovščina [SLO] 74 A5
Ajka [H] 74 H2
Ajnovce [SCG] 146 D5
Ajo [E] 82 F3
Ajos [FIN] 196 C3
Akáki [CY] 154 F5
Akalan [TR] 150 D2
Akalen [TR] 152 G6
Akanthoú (Tatlısu) [CY] 154 G5
Akarca [TR] 152 G3
Äkäsjokisuu [FIN] 194 B6
Äkäslompolo [FIN] 194 C6
Akasztó [H] 76 C3
Akbaş [TR] 152 G5
Akbük [TR] 152 D6
Akçakavak [TR] 154 E2
Akçakese [TR] 150 F2
Akçaköy [TR] 152 E5
Akçaköy [TR] 152 H5
Akçaova [TR] 150 G2
Akçaova [TR] 152 E6
Akçay [TR] 152 C1
Akçay [TR] 154 G2
Akdere [TR] 152 G5
Akdoğan (Lysi) [CY] 154 G5
Aken [D] 34 C4
Aker [S] 162 C3
Åkersberga [S] 168 E2
Akersjön [S] 190 D6
Åkers krutbruk [S] 168 C3
Akharım [TR] 152 H3
Akhisar [TR] 152 D3
Akhtopol [BG] 148 G5
Akine [TR] 154 F4
Akkarfjord [N] 194 B2
Akkavare [S] 190 H3
Akkaya [TR] 150 H5
Akkent [TR] 152 G4
Akköprü [TR] 154 E1
Akköy [TR] 152 D6
Akköy [TR] 152 F4
Akland [N] 164 F4
Akli [H] 76 A2
Akmeşe [TR] 150 G3
Akmyane [LT] 198 C6
Aknīste [LV] 198 F6
Akonlahti [FIN] 196 G5
Akonpohja [FIN] 188 F5
Akoúmia [GR] 140 D5
Akpınar [TR] 150 H5
Åkra [N] 170 B5
Akrai [I] 126 G5
Akraifia [GR] 134 B5
Akraífnio [GR] 134 B5
Åkran [N] 190 C6
Akranes [IS] 192 A2
Akrapol [TR] 152 C2
Åkre [N] 182 C6
Åkrehamn [N] 164 A2
Akrogiáli [GR] 130 C4
Akropótamos [GR] 130 C4
Akrōtíri [CY] 154 F6
Akrotíri [GR] 138 F5
Akrovoúni [GR] 130 D3
Aksakal [TR] 150 D5
Aksakovo [BG] 148 F2
Akşar [TR] 152 G6
Aksaz [TR] 150 C4
Aksaz [TR] 152 F2
Aksaz Kaplica [TR] 152 F4
Aksdal [N] 164 A1
Aksla [N] 180 C6
Aktsyabrski [BY] 202 C6
Åkullsjön [S] 196 A5
Akureyri [IS] 192 C2
Akyaka [TR] 154 F4
Akyazı [TR] 150 H3
Akyazı [TR] 154 G3
Ål [N] 170 F3
Ala [I] 72 C5
Ala [S] 168 G5
Alaattin [TR] 152 G5
Alabanda [TR] 152 E6
Alabodarna [S] 156 H2
Alacadağ [TR] 154 H2
Alacant / Alicante [E] 104 E2
Alacat [TR] 150 E5
Alaçatı [TR] 134 H5
Alà dei Sardi [I] 118 D3
Ala di Stura [I] 70 C5
Aladzha Manastir [BG] 148 G2
Alaejos [E] 88 D2
Alagna-Valsésia [I] 70 E3
A Lagoa / Campo Lameiro [E] 78 B4
Alagón [E] 90 E3
Alahärmä [FIN] 186 C2
Ala-Honkajoki [FIN] 186 C6
Alajärvi [FIN] 186 D2
Alajärvi [FIN] 196 F3
Alajoki [FIN] 194 D5
Alajoki [FIN] 196 D5
Alakylä [FIN] 194 C7
Alakylä [FIN] 196 C6
Alakylä [FIN] 196 D3
Alalampi [RUS] 188 H4
Ala-Livo [FIN] 196 E3
Alamaa [FIN] 186 F2
Alameda [E] 102 C3
Alamedilla [E] 102 F3
Alanäs [S] 190 E5
Alancık [TR] 152 C1
Åland [S] 168 D1
Alandroal [P] 94 E1
Ålandsbro [S] 184 F4
Alange [E] 94 H2
Alanís [E] 94 H4
Alanta [LT] 200 G4
Alap [H] 76 B3
Alapitkä [FIN] 188 C1
Alaquás [E] 98 E4
Alaraz [E] 88 D4
Alarcón [E] 98 B3
Alaşehir [TR] 152 E4
Ålåsen [S] 190 E6
Alássio [I] 108 G4
Alastaro [FIN] 176 E3
Ala-Temmes [FIN] 196 D4
Alatoz [E] 98 C5
Alatri [I] 116 C6
Alatskivi [EST] 198 F2
Alattu [RUS] 188 H4
Ala-Valli [FIN] 186 C4
Alavattnet [S] 190 E5
Alaveteli / Nedervetil [FIN] 196 C6
Ala-Vieksi [FIN] 196 F5
Alavieska [FIN] 196 C5
Ala-Vuokki [FIN] 196 F4
Alavus [FIN] 186 D4
Alba [I] 108 G2
Alba Adriatica [I] 116 D3
Albacete [E] 98 B5
Albacken [S] 184 D3
Alba de Tormes [E] 88 C3
Albæk [DK] 160 E2
Alba Fucens [I] 116 C5
Albaida [E] 98 E6
Albaina [E] 82 G5
Alba Iulia [RO] 204 C4
Albaladejo [E] 96 G5
Albalate de Cinca [E] 90 G4
Albalate de las Nogueras [E] 98 B1
Albalate de Zorita [E] 98 A1
Alban [F] 106 C3
Albánchez [E] 102 H4
Albano di Lucania [I] 120 H4
Albano Laziale [I] 116 A6
Albaredo d'Adige [I] 110 F1
Albarella [I] 110 H2
Albares [E] 88 H6
Albarracín [E] 98 D1
Albarracín, Cuevas de- [E] 98 D1
Albatana [E] 104 C1
Albena [BG] 148 G2
Albenga [I] 108 G4
Albens [F] 70 A3
Albentosa [E] 98 E3
Alberga [S] 168 B3
Albergaria-a-Velha [P] 80 B5
Alberic [E] 98 E5
Albernoa [P] 94 D3
Alberobello [I] 122 E3
Alberoni [I] 110 H1
Albersdorf [D] 18 E2
Albert [F] 28 E4
Albertirsa [H] 76 D1
Albertville [F] 70 B3
Albeşti [RO] 148 G1
Albi [F] 106 B2
Albignasego [I] 110 G1
Albissola Marina [I] 108 H3
Albo [F] 114 C2
Albocácer / Albocàsser [E] 98 G2
Albocàsser / Albocácer [E] 98 G2
Alböke [S] 162 G4
Alboraia / Alboraya [E] 98 E4
Alboraya / Alboraia [E] 98 E4
Alborea [E] 98 C4
Albox [E] 102 H4
Albrechtice nad Vltavou [CZ] 48 F6
Albrechtsburg [A] 62 D4
Albufeira [P] 94 C5
Albujón [E] 104 C4
Albuñol [E] 102 E5
Albuñuelas [E] 102 D4
Alburquerque [E] 86 F5
Alby [S] 162 G6
Alby [S] 184 C4
Alcácer do Sal [P] 94 C1
Alcáçovas [P] 94 D2
Alcadozo [E] 98 B6
Alcafores [P] 86 G3
Alcaide [E] 102 H3
Alcalá de Chivert / Alcalà de Xivert [E] 98 G2
Alcalá de Guadaira [E] 94 G6
Alcalá de Henares [E] 88 G6
Alcalá de la Selva [E] 98 E2
Alcalá del Júcar [E] 98 C5
Alcalá de los Gazules [E] 100 G4
Alcalá del Río [E] 94 G6
Alcalá del Valle [E] 102 A3
Alcalà de Xivert / Alcalá de Chivert [E] 98 G2
Alcalá la Real [E] 102 D3
Álcamo [I] 126 C2
Alcanar [E] 92 A6
Alcanede [P] 86 C4
Alcanena [P] 86 C4
Alcañices [E] 80 G4
Alcañiz [E] 90 F6
Alcántara [E] 86 G4
Alcantara, Gole d'- [I] 124 A8
Alcantarilla [E] 104 C3
Alcaracejos [E] 96 C5
Alcaraz [E] 96 H6
Alcaria Ruiva [P] 94 D4
Alcarràs [E] 90 H5
Alçaşehir [TR] 152 G1
Alcaudete [E] 102 D2
Alcaudete de la Jara [E] 96 D1
Alcázar de San Juan [E] 96 G3
Alcobaça [P] 86 C3
Alcoba de los Montes [E] 96 D3
Alcobendas [E] 88 F5
Alcobertas [P] 86 C3
Alcocèber / Alcossebre [E] 98 G3
Alcocer [E] 90 A6
Alcochete [P] 86 B5
Alcoentre [P] 86 B4
Alcofra [P] 80 C5
Alcoi / Alcoy [E] 104 E1
Alcolea [E] 102 F5
Alcolea del Pinar [E] 90 B4
Alconchel [E] 94 F2
Alcora / l'Alcora [E] 98 F3
Alcorcón [E] 88 F6
Alcorisa [E] 90 F6
Alcossebre / Alcocèber [E] 98 G3
Alcoutim [P] 94 D5
Alcover [E] 92 C4
Alcoy / Alcoi [E] 104 E1
Alcubierre [E] 90 F3
Alcublas [E] 98 E3
Alcúdia [E] 104 F4
Alcuéscar [E] 86 H6
Aldeacentenera [E] 96 B1
Aldeadávila de la Ribera [E] 80 F5
Aldea del Cano [E] 86 H6
Aldea del Fresno [E] 88 E5
Aldea del Rey [E] 96 E5
Aldea de Trujillo [E] 96 B1
Aldealpozo [E] 90 C3
Aldeanueva de Ebro [E] 84 A5
Aldeaquemada [E] 96 F6
Aldeavieja [E] 88 E4
Aldeburgh [GB] 14 G3
Aldeia da Ponte [P] 86 G2
Aldeia do Bispo [P] 86 G2
Aldenhoven [D] 30 F4
Aldernäset [S] 190 F5
Aldershot [GB] 14 D4
Aldinci [MK] 128 E1
Aldtsier [NL] 16 F2
Åled [S] 162 B5
Aledo [E] 104 B3
Alegranza [E] 100 E5
Alekovo [BG] 148 C3
Alekovo [BG] 148 E1
Aleksandrovac [SCG] 146 C1
Aleksandrovo [BG] 148 B3
Aleksandrów [PL] 38 B6
Aleksandrów Kujawski [PL] 36 F1
Aleksandrów Łódzki [PL] 36 G4
Aleksin [RUS] 202 F4
Aleksinac [SCG] 146 D3
Ålem [S] 162 G4
Alemdağ [TR] 150 F2
Ålen [N] 182 C3
Alençon [F] 26 F6
Alenquer [P] 86 B4
Aléria [F] 114 C4
Aléria [F] 114 C4
Áles [I] 118 C5
Aleşd [RO] 204 B4
Alessandria [I] 70 F6
Alessandria del Carretto [I] 122 D6
Alessándria della Rocca [I] 126 D3
Ålesund [N] 180 C3
Alexándreia [GR] 128 G4
Alexandria [RO] 148 B1
Alexandria Troas [TR] 130 H6
Alexandroúpoli [GR] 130 G3
Alexandrów [PL] 38 A3
Alf [D] 44 G2
Alfafar [E] 98 E5
Alfaites [P] 86 G2
Alfajarín [E] 90 E4
Alfambra [E] 98 E1
Alfambras [P] 94 B4
Alfândenga [P] 80 F4
Alfano [I] 120 G5
Alfarela de Jales [P] 80 E4
Alfaro [E] 84 B5
Alfarràs [E] 90 H4
Alfas [E] 104 F2
Alfatar [BG] 148 E1
Alfedena [I] 116 D6
Alfeizerão [P] 86 B3
Alfeld [D] 32 F3
Alfeld [D] 46 H5
Alfena [P] 80 C4
Alfonsine [I] 110 G3
Alford [GB] 6 F6
Alforja [E] 92 B4
Ålfoten [N] 180 C5
Alfreton [GB] 10 F5
Alfstad [N] 170 G5
Alfta [S] 174 D2
Algaida [E] 104 E5
Algajola [F] 114 B3
Algar [E] 100 G4
Algar [E] 104 H5
Älgarås [S] 166 F4
Älgård [N] 164 B3
Älgård [N] 164 B5
Algarinejo [E] 102 D3
Algarra [E] 98 D3
Algatocín [E] 100 H4
Algeciras [E] 100 G5
Algemesí [E] 98 E5
Älgered [S] 184 E5
Alghero [I] 118 B3
Älghult [S] 162 F4
Alginet [E] 98 E5
Algodonales [E] 100 H3
Algodor [P] 94 D4
Algora [E] 90 A5
Algoso [P] 80 F4
Älgsjö [S] 190 G5
Alguazas [E] 104 C3
Älgutsrum [S] 162 G5
Algyo [H] 76 E4
Alhama de Aragón [E] 90 C4
Alhama de Granada [E] 102 D4
Alhama de Murcia [E] 104 B3
Alhambra [E] 96 G5
Alhamillo [E] 96 C4
Alhaurín de la Torre [E] 102 B5
Alhaurín el Grande [E] 102 B4
Alhojärvi [FIN] 186 F5
Ålholm Slot [DK] 20 B1
Ålhus [N] 180 C6
Alía [E] 96 C2
Ália [I] 126 D3
Aliaga [E] 98 F1
Aliağa [TR] 152 C3
Alíartos [GR] 134 A5
Alibeyli [TR] 152 D3
Alibunar [SCG] 142 H2
Aliç [TR] 150 B3
Alicante / Alacant [E] 104 E2
Alicudi Porto [I] 124 A5
Åliden [S] 196 A4
Alife [I] 120 E2
Alifuatpaşa [TR] 150 G3
Alija del Infantado [E] 80 H3
Alijó [P] 80 E4
Alíkampos [GR] 140 C4
Alikanás [GR] 136 A2
Alikylä [FIN] 196 C6
Alimena [I] 126 E3
Alinci [MK] 128 E3
Alinda [TR] 152 E6
Alingsås [S] 162 B1
Alinyá [E] 92 D2
Aliseda [E] 86 G5
Ali Terme [I] 124 B7
Alivéri [GR] 134 C5
Aljaraque [E] 94 E5
Aljezur [P] 94 B4
Aljinovići [SCG] 146 A3
Aljubarrota [P] 86 C3
Aljucén [E] 86 G6
Aljustrel [P] 94 C3
Alkmaar [NL] 16 D3
Alkotz [E] 84 B3
Alkoven [A] 62 B4
Alksniupiai [LT] 200 F4
Alkvettern [S] 166 G2
Állai [I] 118 C5
Allaines [F] 42 E5
Allainville [F] 42 E4
Allan [F] 68 F6
Allanche [F] 68 C3
Alland [A] 62 E5
Allariz [E] 78 C5
Allauch [F] 108 B5
Alleen [N] 164 C5
Álleghe [I] 72 E4
Allejaur [S] 190 G3
Allemont [F] 68 H5
Allenbach [D] 44 G2
Allentsteig [A] 62 D3
Allepuz [E] 98 E1
Aller-Heiligen [D] 58 F1
Allersberg [D] 46 G6
Allershausen [D] 60 E3
Allerum [S] 156 H1
Alleuze, Château d'- [F] 68 C4
Allevard [F] 70 A4
Allgunnen [S] 162 F4
Allihies [IRL] 4 A5
Allingåbro [DK] 160 E5
Allinge [DK] 158 E4
Allo [E] 84 A4
Alloa [GB] 8 E3
Ållonuokta [S] 192 G6
Allonnes [F] 54 E2
Allonö [S] 168 B5
Allos [F] 108 D3
Allouе [F] 54 E5
Ällsjön [S] 184 E2
Allstedt [D] 34 B5
Almacelles [E] 90 H4
Almada [P] 86 B5
Almadén [E] 96 C4
Almadén de la Plata [E] 94 G5
Almadenojos [E] 96 D4
Almadrones [E] 90 A5
Almagreira [P] 100 E4
Almagro [E] 96 F4
Almancil [P] 94 C5
Almandoz [E] 84 B3
Almansa [E] 98 D6
Almanza [E] 82 C4
Almaraz [E] 88 B6
Almargen [E] 102 B3
Almarza [E] 90 B2
Almås [N] 182 C2
Almásfüzitő [H] 64 B6
Almassora / Almazora [E] 98 F3
Almazán [E] 90 B3
Almazora / Almassora [E] 98 F3
Almedina [E] 96 G5
Almeida [P] 80 E6
Almeida de Sayago [E] 80 G5
Almeirim [P] 86 C4
Almelo [NL] 16 G4
Almenar [E] 90 H4
Almenara [E] 98 F4
Almenara [E] 102 B1
Almenara de Tormes [E] 80 G6
Almenar de Soria [E] 90 C3
Almendra [P] 80 E5
Almendral [E] 94 G2
Almendralejo [E] 94 G2
Almenno S. Salvatore [I] 70 H4
Almere [NL] 16 E4
Almería [E] 102 G5
Almerimar [E] 102 F6
Almesåkra [S] 162 D2
Älmestad [S] 162 C1
Älmhult [S] 162 D5
Almodôvar [P] 94 C4
Almodóvar del Campo [E] 96 E4
Almodóvar del Río [E] 102 B1
Almogía [E] 102 C4
Almograve [P] 94 B3
Almoharín [E] 86 H6
Almonaster la Real [E] 94 F4
Almonte [E] 94 F6
Almoradí [E] 104 D3
Almoraima [E] 100 G5
Almorox [E] 88 E6
Almourol [P] 86 D4
Almsele [S] 190 F5
Älmsta-Väddö [S] 168 E1
Almudévar [E] 90 F3
Almuñécar [E] 102 D5
Almunge [S] 168 D1
Almuradiel [E] 96 F5
Almvik [S] 162 G2
Almyró [GR] 136 D4
Almyropótamos [GR] 134 D5
Almyrós [GR] 132 H3
Alness [GB] 6 E4
Alnwick [GB] 8 G5
Aloja [LV] 198 E4
Alol' [RUS] 198 H5
Alónnisos [GR] 134 C3
Álora [E] 102 B4
Alosno [E] 94 E5
Alost (Aalst) [B] 28 H2
Alozaina [E] 102 B4
Alp [E] 92 E2
Alpalhão [P] 86 E4
Alpbach [A] 60 E6
Alpedrinha [P] 86 F3
Alpen [D] 30 G2
Alpengarten [D] 60 D6
Alpera [E] 98 C5
Alphen-aan den Rijn [NL] 16 D5
Alpiarça [P] 86 C4
Alpirsbach [D] 58 F2
Alportel [P] 94 C5
Alpua [FIN] 196 D5
Alpuente [E] 98 D3
Alpullu [TR] 150 B2
Alqueva [P] 94 E3
Alquézar [E] 90 G3
Als [DK] 160 E4
Alsager [GB] 10 D5
Alsasua / Altsasu [E] 82 H5
Alsen [S] 182 G1
Alsenz [D] 46 B4
Alsfeld [D] 46 D1
Ålshult [S] 162 D5
Alsleben [D] 34 B4
Ålsø [DK] 160 F6
Alsótold [H] 64 D5
Alsózsolca [H] 64 F5
Ålstad [N] 192 D5
Alstad [S] 158 C3
Alstahaug [N] 190 D2
Alstätte [D] 16 G5
Alsterbro [S] 162 F4
Alstermo [S] 162 F4
Alston [GB] 8 F6
Alsunga [LV] 198 B5
Alsvåg [N] 192 D3
Alsvik [N] 192 D6
Alta [N] 194 B3
Altafulla [E] 92 C5
Altamira, Cuevas de- [E] 82 E3
Altamura [I] 122 D3
Altarejos [E] 98 B2
Altares [P] 100 D3
Altavilla Silentina [I] 120 F4
Altdahn [D] 44 H4
Altdorf [CH] 58 F6
Altdorf [D] 46 G5
Alt Duvenstedt [D] 18 F2
Altea [E] 104 F2
Altedo [I] 110 F3
Alteidet [N] 192 H1
Altena [D] 32 C5
Altenahr [D] 30 G5
Altenau [D] 32 G4
Altenberg [D] 48 E2
Altenberge [D] 16 H5
Altenberger Dom [D] 30 H4
Altenburg [A] 62 D3
Altenburg [D] 34 C6
Altenglan [D] 44 H3
Altenhundem [D] 32 C5
Altenkirchen [D] 20 D1
Altenkirchen [D] 32 C6
Altenklingen [CH] 58 G4
Altenmarkt [A] 62 C6
Altenmarkt [D] 60 F5
Altenstadt [D] 60 B4
Altenstadt [D] 60 D5
Altensteig [D] 58 G1
Altentreptow [D] 20 D4
Altenwalde [D] 18 D3
Alter do Chão [P] 86 E5
Alteren [N] 190 E2
Altheim [A] 60 H4
Althofen [A] 74 B2
Alti [TR] 154 B1
Altimir [BG] 146 G3
Altınoluk [TR] 152 B1
Altınova [TR] 150 F3
Altınova [TR] 152 B2
Altıntaş [TR] 152 H2
Altınyayla [TR] 154 G1
Altipiani di Arcinazzo [I] 116 B6
Altkirch [F] 58 D4
Altlandsberg [D] 34 E2
Altmörbitz [D] 34 C6
Altmünster [A] 62 A5
Altnaharra [GB] 6 E3
Alto de los Leones de Castilla [E] 88 F4
Altomonte [I] 124 D3
Alton [GB] 14 D4
Altopascio [I] 110 E5
Altorricón [E] 90 H4
Altötting [D] 60 G4
Altrier [L] 44 F2
Alt Ruppin [D] 20 C6
Altsasu / Alsasua [E] 82 H5
Alt Schadow [D] 34 F3
Altshausen [D] 58 H3
Altstätten [CH] 58 H5
Alttajärvi [S] 192 G5
Altuna [S] 168 C1
Altura [E] 98 E3
Altwarp [D] 20 E4
Altwindeck [D] 58 F1
Alūksne [LV] 198 F4
Ålum [DK] 160 D5
Ålund [S] 196 A4
Alunda [S] 168 D1
Alupka [UA] 204 H4
Aluste [EST] 198 E2
Alvaiázere [P] 86 D3
Alvajärvi [FIN] 186 F1
Alvalade [P] 94 C3
Älvan [S] 166 H5
Älvängen [S] 160 H1
Alvastra [S] 166 G6
Alvdal [N] 182 B5
Älvdalen [S] 172 F2
Alvechurch [GB] 12 H1
Alverca do Ribatejo [P] 86 B5
Alversund [N] 170 B3
Alvesta [S] 162 D4
Alvestad [N] 164 A2
Alvignac [F] 66 G4
Ålvik [N] 170 C4
Alvik [S] 172 G4
Alvik [S] 196 B3
Alvito [I] 116 C6
Alvito [P] 94 D2
Älvkarleby [S] 174 E4
Alvor [P] 94 B5
Älvros [S] 182 E6
Älvros [S] 182 G5
Älvsbacka [S] 166 F2
Älvsbyn [S] 196 A3
Alvsered [S] 162 B3
Alvsund [S] 184 E5
Ålvundeid [N] 180 F3
Alyekshytsy [BY] 24 G5
Alykí [GR] 130 E4
Alykí [GR] 130 E4
Alykí [GR] 138 E3
Alytus [LT] 24 G2
Alzenau [D] 46 D3
Alzey [D] 46 B4
Alzira [E] 98 E5
Alzon [F] 106 E3
Alzonne [F] 106 B4
Åmadalen [S] 172 G2
Amadora [P] 86 B5
Åmål [S] 166 D4
Amalfi [I] 120 E4
Amaliáda [GR] 136 C2
Amaliápoli [GR] 132 H3
Ámalo [GR] 138 G1
Amance [F] 58 B3
Amancey [F] 58 B5
Amandola [I] 116 C2
Amantea [I] 124 D5
Amantia [AL] 128 B5
Amarante [P] 80 C4
Amárantos [GR] 132 F3
Amărăştii de Sus [RO] 146 G2
Amareleja [P] 94 E3
Amári [GR] 140 D5
Amárynthos [GR] 134 C5
Amatrice [I] 116 C3
Amay [B] 30 E5
Ambarès [F] 66 D3
Ambazac [F] 54 G6
Amberg [D] 46 H5
Ambérieu-en-Bugey [F] 68 G2
Ambert [F] 68 D3
Ambiörnarp [S] 162 B3
Ambjörby [S] 172 E4
Ambla [EST] 198 E1
Amble [GB] 8 G5
Ambleside [GB] 10 D2
Amboise [F] 54 G2
Ämbra [EST] 198 E2
Ambrières [F] 26 E5
Åmdal [N] 164 D5
Ameixial [P] 94 C4
Amélia [I] 116 A3
Amélie-les-Bains [F] 92 F2
Amelinghausen [D] 18 F5
Amendolara [I] 122 D6
Amer [E] 92 F3
A Merca [E] 78 C5
Amerongen [NL] 16 E5
Amersfoort [NL] 16 E5
Amersham [GB] 14 E3
Amesbury [GB] 12 G4
A Mezquita [E] 78 E6
Amfiáreio [GR] 134 C5
Amfíkleia [GR] 132 G4
Amfilochía [GR] 132 D4
Amfípoli [GR] 130 C4
Ámfissa [GR] 132 G5
Amiens [F] 28 E5
Åmilden [S] 190 H4
Aminne [S] 168 G4
Amiternum [I] 116 C4
Åmli [N] 164 E3
Amlwch [GB] 10 B3
Ammanford [GB] 12 E2
Ämmänsaari [FIN] 196 F4
Ammarnäs [S] 190 F2
Åmmeberg [S] 166 G4
Ammóchostos (Gazimağusa) [CY] 154 G5
Ammótopos [GR] 132 D3
Ammoudára [GR] 140 E4
Ammoudára [GR] 140 F5
Åmnes [N] 164 F2
Amorbach [D] 46 D4
Amoreira, Acueducto de- [P] 86 E6
Amorgós [GR] 138 G4
Amorosi [I] 120 E2
Åmot [N] 164 E1
Åmot [N] 164 G1
Åmot [N] 170 G4
Åmot [N] 170 H3
Åmot [N] 172 C2
Åmot [S] 174 D3
Åmotfors [S] 166 D1
Åmotsdal [N] 164 E1
Amou [F] 84 D2
Ampelákia [GR] 132 G1
Ampelikó [GR] 134 H2
Ampelónas [GR] 132 G1
Ampezzo [I] 72 F4
Ampfing [D] 60 F4
Amphion [F] 70 B2
Amplepuis [F] 68 F2
Amposta [E] 92 A6
Ampudia [E] 82 C6
Ampuero [E] 82 F3
Ampuis [F] 68 F3
Ampus [F] 108 D4
Amriswil [CH] 58 H4
Am See [A] 72 C2
Amsele [S] 190 H5
Amsteg [CH] 70 F1
Amsterdam [NL] 16 D4
Amstetten [A] 62 C4
Ämtervik [S] 166 E2
Amtoft [DK] 160 C4
Amurrio [E] 82 G4
Amvrosía [GR] 130 F2
Amygdaleónas [GR] 130 D3
Amygdaliá [GR] 132 G5
Amýkles [GR] 136 E4
Amýntaio [GR] 128 F4
Amzacea [RO] 148 G1
Anadia [P] 80 B6
Anáfi [GR] 138 F5
Anafonítria [GR] 136 A2
Anagni [I] 116 B6
Anáktora Néstoros [GR] 136 C4
Análipsi [GR] 138 H4
Anamourion [TR] 154 F4
Anamur [TR] 154 F4
Anan'iv [UA] 204 G2
Anárgyroi [GR] 128 E5
Anarráchi [GR] 128 E5
Anascaul [IRL] 4 B4
Ånäset [S] 196 A5
Åna-Sira [N] 164 B5
Anastazewo [PL] 36 E2
Änätinpää [FIN] 196 G4
Anatolí [GR] 132 G1
Anatolikó [GR] 128 F5
Anávra [GR] 132 F3
Anávra [GR] 132 G3
Anávyssos [GR] 136 H1
An Cabhán / Cavan [IRL] 2 E4
Anc. Batterie [F] 108 D2
Ance [LV] 198 C4
Ancenis [F] 40 G6
Ancerville [F] 44 C5
An Charraig / Carrick [IRL] 2 D2
Anchuras [E] 96 D2
An Clochan Liath / Dungloe [IRL] 2 E2
Ancona [I] 112 C6
Ancy-le-Franc [F] 56 F2
Anda [N] 180 C5
An Daingean / Dingle [IRL] 4 A3
Andalo [I] 72 C4
Åndalsnes [N] 180 E3
Andåsen [S] 182 G5
Andau [A] 62 G6
Ändebol [S] 168 B4
Andebu [N] 164 H3
Andechs [D] 60 D5
Andelot [F] 44 D6
Andenes [N] 192 E2
Andenne [B] 30 D5
Andermatt [CH] 70 F1
Andernach [D] 30 H6
Andernos-les-Bains [F] 66 B3
Andersfors [S] 196 A5
Anderslov [S] 158 C3
Anderstorp [S] 162 C3
Andijk [NL] 16 E3
Andilla [E] 98 E3
Andız [TR] 150 G6
Andocs [H] 76 A3
Andolsheim [F] 58 E3
Andorno Micca [I] 70 E4
Andorra [E] 90 F6
Andorra la Vella [AND] 84 H6
Andover [GB] 12 H4
Andrade, Castelo de- [E] 78 D2
Andraitx [E] 104 D5
Andravída [GR] 136 B1
Andreapol' [RUS] 202 D3
Andrespol [PL] 36 G4
Andretta [I] 120 G3
Andrézieux-Bouthéon [F] 68 E3
Ándria [I] 122 C2
Andriake [TR] 154 H3
Andrijevica [SCG] 146 A5
Andrítsaina [GR] 136 D3
Ándros [GR] 134 E6
Androúsa [GR] 136 D4
Andrychów [PL] 50 G4
Andselv [N] 192 F3
Andújar [E] 102 D1
Anduze [F] 106 F3
Ånebjør [N] 164 D3
Aneby [N] 172 B5
Aneby [S] 162 E2
Ånes [N] 180 F1
Anet [F] 42 E3
Anfo [I] 72 B5
Anga [S] 168 G4
Ånge [S] 182 G1
Ånge [S] 184 C4
Ånge [S] 190 G2
Ångebo [S] 184 D6
Angeja [P] 80 B5
Ängelholm [S] 156 H1
Angeli [FIN] 194 C4
Angelókastro [GR] 132 E5
Angelókastro [GR] 136 F2
Angelsberg [S] 168 B1
Ängelsfors [S] 174 D4
Angelstad [S] 162 C5
Angenstein [CH] 58 E4
Angermünde [D] 20 E6
Angern [A] 62 G4
Angers [F] 40 H6
Ångersjö [S] 182 G6
Ångersjö [S] 184 H1
Angerville [F] 42 E5

Ängesan [S] 194 B8
Ängesbyn [S] 196 B3
Anghelo Ruiu, Necropoli- [I] 118 B3
Anghiari [I] 110 G6
Angiari [I] 110 F1
Anglès [E] 92 F3
Angles-sur-l'Anglin [F] 54 F4
Anglet [F] 84 C2
Anglona [LV] 198 G6
Anglure [F] 44 A5
Ango, Manoir d'- [F] 28 C4
Angoulême [F] 66 E1
Angra do Heroísmo [P] 100 D3
Ångskär [S] 174 F4
Ängsö [S] 168 C2
Angueira [P] 80 G4
Angüés [E] 90 G3
Anguiano [E] 90 B1
Anguillara Sabazia [I] 114 H5
Anguillara Veneta [I] 110 G2
Angulo [E] 82 G4
Angvik [N] 180 F2
Anholt [DK] 160 G5
Aniane [F] 106 E4
Aniche [F] 28 F4
Anina [RO] 204 B5
Anıtkaya [TR] 152 H2
Anjala [FIN] 178 C3
Anjalankoski [FIN] 178 C3
Anjan [S] 190 D6
Anjos [P] 100 E3
Anjum [NL] 16 F1
Ankaran [SLO] 72 H6
Ankarede [S] 190 E4
Ankarsrum [S] 162 G2
Ankarvattnet [S] 190 E4
Ankenesstrand [N] 192 E4
Anklam [D] 20 D4
Ankum [D] 32 D1
Anlezy [F] 56 E4
Ånn [S] 182 E2
Anna [EST] 198 E2
Annaberg [A] 60 H6
Annaberg [A] 62 D5
Annaberg-Buchholz [D] 48 D2
Annadalsvagen [N] 190 D3
Annalong [NIR] 2 G4
Annan [GB] 8 E5
Anna Paulowna [NL] 16 D3
An Nás / Naas [IRL] 2 F6
Anneberg [S] 160 H2
Anneberg [S] 162 E2
Annecy [F] 70 B3
Annefors [S] 174 D2
Annelund [S] 162 B1
Annemasse [F] 70 B2
Annenheim [A] 74 A3
Annerstad [S] 162 C5
Annestown [IRL] 4 E5
Annonay [F] 68 F4
Annopol [PL] 52 D1
Annot [F] 108 D3
Annweiler [D] 46 B5
Anógeia [GR] 140 E4
Ánoixi [GR] 132 E1
Áno Kalentíni [GR] 132 D3
Áno Kastrítsi [GR] 132 F6
Áno Merá [GR] 138 E2
Anópoli [GR] 140 C5
Áno Sagkri [GR] 138 F3
Áno Sýros [GR] 138 D2
Añover de Tajo [E] 96 F1
Áno Viánnos [GR] 140 F5
Áno Vrontoú [GR] 130 C2
Anquela del Ducado [E] 90 B5
An Rinn / Ring [IRL] 4 E5
Ans [DK] 160 D6
Ansager [DK] 156 B2
Ansbach [D] 46 F5
Anse [F] 68 F2
Ansedónia [I] 114 F4
Anseremme [B] 30 D6
Ansfelden [A] 62 B4
Ansião [P] 86 D2
Ansó [E] 84 D4
An Spidéal / Spiddal [IRL] 2 B5
Anstad [N] 180 F5
Anstey [GB] 10 F6
Anstruther [GB] 8 F3
Ansvar [S] 194 B8
Antanarav [LT] 200 G4
Antandros [TR] 134 H1
Antas [P] 80 D5
Antas, Tempio di- [I] 118 B6
Antegnate [I] 70 H5
Anten [S] 160 H1
Antequera [E] 102 C4
Anterselva / Antholz [I] 72 E2
Antey St. André [I] 70 D3
Anthéor [F] 108 E5
Anthí [GR] 130 B3
Antholz / Anterselva [I] 72 E2
Anthótopos [GR] 132 G3
Antibes [F] 108 E5
Antigonea [AL] 128 C6
Antigua [E] 100 E6
Antigua Bilbilis [E] 90 D4
Antikýra [GR] 132 H5
Antimáchia [GR] 154 B2
An Tinbhear Mór / Arklow [IRL] 4 G4
Antíparos [GR] 138 E3
Antírrio [GR] 132 F5
Ántissa [GR] 134 G2
Ántissa [GR] 134 G2
Antjärn [S] 184 F4
Antnäs [S] 196 B3
Anton [BG] 148 A4
Antonin [PL] 36 E5
Antoniów [PL] 52 D1
Antonovo [BG] 148 D3
Antopal' [BY] 38 H2
Antraigues [F] 68 E5
Antrain [F] 26 D5
Antrim [NIR] 2 G3
Antrodoco [I] 116 B4
Antsla [EST] 198 F3
Anttila [FIN] 196 F5
Anttis [S] 194 B7
Anttola [FIN] 188 D6
Anttola [FIN] 188 F5
Antwerpen (Anvers) [B] 30 C3
An Uaimh / Navan [IRL] 2 F5
Anundshögen [S] 168 C2
Anvers (Antwerpen) [B] 30 C3
Anvin [F] 28 E3
Anykščiai [LT] 200 G4
Anzi [I] 120 H4
Anzio [I] 120 A1
Aoiz / Agoitz [E] 84 C4
Aosta / Aoste [I] 70 D4
Aoste / Aosta [I] 70 D4
Apamea [TR] 150 E4
Åpåsdal [N] 164 D5
Apátfalva [H] 76 F4
Apatin [SCG] 76 C6
Apchon [F] 68 B3
Ape [LV] 198 F4
Apécchio [I] 110 H6
Apeírathos [GR] 138 F3
Apeldoorn [NL] 16 F5
Apen [D] 18 C5
Apensen [D] 18 F4
Aperlai [TR] 154 H3
Aphrodisias [TR] 152 F5
Apice [I] 120 F2
Apinac [F] 68 E3
Aplared [S] 162 B2
A Pobra de Brollón / Puebla del Brollón [E] 78 D4
A Pobra de Navia [E] 78 E4
A Pobra de Trives [E] 78 D5
Apoíkia [GR] 134 E6
Apolakkiá [GR] 154 C4
Apolda [D] 34 B6
Apollo Aléo, Tempio di- [I] 124 F4
Apóllon [GR] 138 F3
Apollonia [AL] 128 A4
Apollonía [GR] 130 B4
Apollonía [GR] 138 D3
Apollonía [GR] 138 D4
Apollonia [TR] 150 E4
Apollonia [TR] 152 D2
Apollonia [TR] 154 G3
A Pontenova [E] 78 E2
Apostolove [UA] 204 F3
Apothicairerie, Grotte de l'- [F] 40 C5
Äppelbo [S] 172 F4
Appelhülsen [D] 16 H6
Appenweier [D] 44 H6
Appenzell [CH] 58 H5
Appiano / Eppan [I] 72 D3
Appingedam [NL] 16 H2
Appleby-in-Westmorland [GB] 10 E1
Apremont, Gorges d'- [F] 42 F5
Aprica [I] 72 B4
Apricena [I] 116 G6
Aprigliano [I] 124 D4
Aprilia [I] 116 A6
Aprilovo [BG] 148 D3
Apróhomok [H] 64 G4
Ápsalos [GR] 128 F4
Apt [F] 108 B3
Áptera [GR] 140 C4
Aquila [CH] 70 G2
Aquileia [I] 72 G5
Aquilonia [I] 120 G3
Aquino [I] 120 C1
Arabba [I] 72 E3
Araburg [A] 62 E5
Araceli [E] 102 C3
Aracena [E] 94 F4
Aráchova [GR] 132 F4
Aráchova [GR] 132 G5
Aračinovo [MK] 128 E1
Arad [RO] 76 G4
Aradíppou [CY] 154 G5
Aragona [I] 126 D4
Arahal [E] 100 H2
Arakapás [CY] 154 F6
Åraksbø [N] 164 D3
Åram [N] 180 C4
Aramits [F] 84 D3
Araña, Cueva de la- [E] 98 D5
Aranda de Duero [E] 88 G2
Arandjelovac [SCG] 146 B1
Aranjuez [E] 96 G1
Arantzazu [E] 82 H5
Aras de Alpuente [E] 98 D3
Áratos [GR] 130 F2
Aravaca [E] 88 F5
Aravissós [GR] 128 G4
Arazede [P] 80 B6
Arbanasi [BG] 148 C3
Arbatax [I] 118 E5
Arbesbach [A] 62 C3
Arbetera [E] 90 B6
Arboga [S] 168 B3
Arbois [F] 58 A5
Arbon [CH] 58 H5
Arborèa [I] 118 B5
Arbrå [S] 174 D2
Arbroath [GB] 8 F2
Arbúcies [E] 92 F3
Árbus [I] 118 B6
Arc, Pont d'- [F] 106 G2
Arcachon [F] 66 B3
Arcas [E] 98 B2
Arc de Berà [E] 92 C5
Arce [I] 120 C1
Arcen [NL] 30 F3
Arc-en-Barrois [F] 56 H2
Arcévia [I] 116 B1
Archánes [GR] 140 E5
Archángelos [GR] 132 D3
Archángelos [GR] 154 D4
Archar [BG] 146 F2
Archena [E] 104 C2
Arches [F] 58 C2
Archiac [F] 66 D1
Archidona [E] 102 C3
Archivel [E] 104 A2
Arcidosso [I] 114 G2
Arcinazzo Romano [I] 116 B5
Arcis-sur-Aube [F] 44 B5
Arco [I] 72 C5
Arco de Baúlhe [P] 80 D3
Arcos de Jalón [E] 90 B4
Arcos de la Frontera [E] 100 G3
Arcos de la Sierra [E] 98 C1
Arcos de Valdevez [P] 78 B6
Ard [IRL] 2 B4
Ardagh [IRL] 4 C3
Årdal [N] 180 C6
Årdala [S] 168 C4
Ardales [E] 102 B4
Årdalsosen [N] 164 B2
Årdalstangen [N] 170 E2
Ardara [IRL] 2 E2
Ardea [I] 116 A6
Ardee [IRL] 2 F5
Arden [DK] 160 D4
Ardenicës [AL] 128 B4
Ardentes [F] 54 H4
Ardez [CH] 72 B2
Ardfert [IRL] 4 B3
Ardfinnan [IRL] 4 D4
Ardglass [NIR] 2 G4
Ardino [BG] 130 E1
Ardisa [E] 84 C6
Ardore [I] 124 D7
Ardres [F] 14 G6
Ardrossan [GB] 8 C3
Åre [S] 182 E1
Areas [E] 78 B5
Areatza [E] 82 G4
Årebrot [N] 180 B5
Arèhava [BY] 38 G4
Arenas [E] 82 D2
Arenas de San Pedro [E] 88 D5
Arendal [N] 164 F5
Arendonk [B] 30 D3
Arendsee [D] 20 A6
Arene / Arrankudiaga [E] 82 G4
Arenenberg [CH] 58 G4
Areños [E] 82 D3
Arenys de Mar [E] 92 F4
Arenzano [I] 108 H3
Areópoli [GR] 136 E5
Ares [E] 78 D2
Arès [F] 66 B3
Ares del Maestrat / Ares del Maestre [E] 98 F2
Ares del Maestre / Ares del Maestrat [E] 98 F2
Aréthousa [GR] 130 C4
Aretí [GR] 130 B4
Aretxabaleta [E] 82 H4
Arevalillo [E] 88 C4
Arévalo [E] 88 E3
Arezzo [I] 114 G1
Arfará [GR] 136 D3
Årfora [N] 190 C4
Argalastí [GR] 134 A3
Argamasilla de Alba [E] 96 G4
Argamasilla de Calatrava [E] 96 E5
Argancy [F] 44 F4
Arganda del Rey [E] 88 G6
Arganil [P] 86 E2
Argási [GR] 136 B2
Argegno [I] 70 G3
Argelès-Gazost [F] 84 E4
Argelès-Plage [F] 92 G1
Argelès-sur-Mer [F] 92 G1
Argenta [I] 110 G3
Argentan [F] 26 F5
Argentat [F] 66 H3
Argentella [F] 114 A3
Argentera [I] 108 E2
Argentiera [I] 118 B3
Argentière [F] 70 C3
Argenton-Château [F] 54 D2
Argenton-sur-Creuse [F] 54 G4
Argentré [F] 26 E6
Argent-sur-Sauldre [F] 56 C2
Argés [E] 96 F2
Argínónta [GR] 154 A2
Argithéa [GR] 132 E3
Argomariz [E] 82 H5
Árgos [GR] 136 E2
Árgos Orestikó [GR] 128 E5
Argostóli [GR] 132 C6
Arguedas [E] 84 B5
Arguís [E] 84 D6
Arguisuelas [E] 98 C3
Argy [F] 54 G3
Argyrádes [GR] 132 B3
Argyroúpoli [GR] 140 C5
Arhéa Olimbía [GR] 136 C2
Århus [DK] 156 D1
Ariano Irpino [I] 120 F2
Ariano nel Polésine [I] 110 H2
Aridaía [GR] 128 F3
Arif [TR] 154 H2
Arilje [SCG] 146 A3
Arinagour [GB] 6 A6
Ariño [E] 90 E5
Arinthod [F] 56 H6
Ariogala [LT] 200 F5
Aristoménis [GR] 136 D4
Aritzo [I] 118 D5
Ariza [E] 90 C4
Årjäng [S] 166 D2
Arjeplog [S] 190 G2
Arjona [E] 102 D1
Arkádi [GR] 140 D4
Arkadia [PL] 36 H3
Arkalochóri [GR] 140 E5
Arkása [GR] 140 H3
Arkesíni [GR] 138 F4
Arkitsa [GR] 132 H4
Arklow / An Tinbhear Mór [IRL] 4 G4
Arkösund [S] 168 C5
Arkutino [BG] 148 F5
Ärla [S] 168 C3
Arlanc [F] 68 D3
Arlberg Tunnel [A] 72 B1
Arlempdes [F] 68 D5
Arles [F] 106 G4
Arles-sur-Tech [F] 92 F2
Arlon (Aarlen) [B] 44 E2
Arlöv [S] 156 H3
Armadale [GB] 6 B5
Armagh [NIR] 2 F4
Armação de Pera [P] 94 B5
Arméni [GR] 132 G2
Armenioí [GR] 136 C3
Armenistís [GR] 138 G1
Arménoi [GR] 140 D5
Armentières [F] 28 F3
Armilla [E] 102 E4
Armiñon [E] 82 G5
Armólia [GR] 134 G5
Armoy [NIR] 2 G2
Armuña de Tajuña [E] 88 H6
Armutcuk [TR] 152 C1
Armutlu [TR] 150 C5
Armutlu [TR] 150 E4
Armutlu [TR] 152 D4
Armyansk [UA] 204 H3
Árna [GR] 136 E4
Arna [N] 170 B4
Arnac [F] 66 E4
Arnac-Pompadur [F] 66 G2
Arnafjord [N] 170 C2
Arnage [F] 42 B5
Arnager [DK] 158 E4
Arnaía [GR] 130 C5
Årnäs [S] 166 F5
Arnäs [S] 184 G2
Arnavutköy [TR] 150 E2
Arnavutköy [TR] 150 E4
Arnay-le-Duc [F] 56 F4
Arnborg [DK] 156 B1
Arneberg [N] 172 B3
Arneburg [D] 34 C1
Arnedillo [E] 90 C1
Arnedo [E] 84 A5
Arnes [E] 90 G6
Årnes [N] 172 C5
Årnes [N] 190 B5
Årnes [N] 190 C4
Arnhem [NL] 16 F5
Árnissa [GR] 128 F4
Arnoldstein [A] 72 H3
Arnön [S] 174 E1
Arnsberg [D] 32 C4
Arnsburg [D] 46 D2
Arnschwang [D] 48 D6
Årnset [N] 190 B6
Arnstadt [D] 46 G1
Arnstein [D] 46 E3
Arnuera [E] 82 F3
Aroanía [GR] 136 D1
Aroche [E] 94 F4
Árokto [H] 64 F5
Arolla [CH] 70 D3
Arolsen [D] 32 E5
Arona [I] 70 F4
Aronkylä [FIN] 186 B4
Åros [N] 164 H1
Arosa [CH] 70 H1
Årosjåkk [S] 192 F5
Årøsund [DK] 156 C3
Arouca [P] 80 C5
Arøysund [N] 164 H3
Arpacık [TR] 154 F2
Arpajon [F] 42 F4
Árpás [H] 62 H6
Arpela [FIN] 196 C2
Arquà Petrarca [I] 110 G1
Arquata del Tronto [I] 116 C3
Arquata Scrivia [I] 110 B2
Arquillinos [E] 102 F1
Arrabal / Oia [E] 78 A5
Arracourt [F] 44 F5
Arraiolos [P] 86 D6
Arrakoski [FIN] 176 H1
Arrankorpi [FIN] 176 H3
Arras [F] 28 F4
Arrasate o Mondragón [E] 82 H4
Arrate [E] 82 H4
Årre [DK] 156 B2
Arreau [F] 84 F4
Arrecife [E] 100 E6
Arrens-Marsous [F] 84 E4
Arrentela [P] 86 B5
Arriate [E] 102 A4
Arriaundi [E] 82 H4
Arriba Fóssil [P] 86 A5
Arrifana [P] 94 B4
Arriondas [E] 82 C2
Arroba de los Montes [E] 96 D3
Arromanches-les-Bains [F] 26 F3
Arronches [P] 86 F5
Arroyo de la Luz [E] 86 G5
Arroyo de la Miel-Benalmádena Costa [E] 102 B5
Arroyo de San Serván [E] 94 G2
Arruda dos Vinhos [P] 86 B4
Årsandøy [N] 190 C4
Ars-en-Ré [F] 54 B4
Arsen'yevo [RUS] 202 F4
Arsiè [I] 72 D5
Arsiero [I] 72 D5
Arslankaya [TR] 152 H1
Årslev [DK] 156 D3
Årsnes [N] 180 D4
Arsoli [I] 116 B5
Ars-sur-Moselle [F] 44 E4
Årsunda [S] 174 E4
Arsvågen [N] 164 A2
Arsy [F] 28 E6
Artà [E] 104 F5
Árta [GR] 132 D3
Artà, Coves d'- [E] 104 F5
Artajona [E] 84 B4
Artana [E] 98 F3
Ártánd [H] 76 H2
Arta Terme [I] 72 G3
Arteixo [E] 78 C2
Artemare [F] 68 H3
Artemisía [GR] 136 D4
Artemísio [GR] 134 A3
Artemónas [GR] 138 D3
Artena [I] 116 B6
Artenay [F] 42 E5
Artern [D] 34 A5
Artesa de Segre [E] 92 C3
Arth [CH] 58 F6
Arth [D] 60 F3
Arthous, Ancient Prieure d'- [F] 84 C2
Arthurstown [IRL] 4 E5
Arties [E] 84 G5
Artix [F] 84 E3
Artjärvi / Artsjö [FIN] 178 B3
Artotína [GR] 132 F4
Årtrik [S] 184 E2
Artsjö / Artjärvi [FIN] 178 B3
Artsyz [UA] 204 F4
A Rúa [E] 78 E5
Arucas [E] 100 C6
Arudy [F] 84 D3
Arundel [GB] 14 D5
Arva [E] 94 H6
Årvåg [N] 180 G1
Arvagh [IRL] 2 E4
Arversund [S] 182 G2
Árvi [GR] 140 F5
Arvidsjaur [S] 190 H3
Arvieux [F] 70 B6
Årvik [N] 180 C4
Arvika [S] 166 D2
Årviksand [N] 192 G1
Arvila [EST] 198 F1
Arville [F] 42 C5
Arykanda [TR] 154 H2
Arzachena [I] 118 E2
Arzacq-Arraziguet [F] 84 E2
Aržano [HR] 144 B2
Arzberg [D] 48 C3
Arzignano [I] 72 D6
Arzl [A] 72 C1
Arzúa [E] 78 C3
Aš [CZ] 48 C3
Ås [N] 166 B2
Ås [N] 182 D2
Ås [S] 182 G2
Aså [DK] 160 E3
Åsa [S] 160 H3
Asa [S] 162 E4
Aşağıçobanisa [TR] 152 D3
Aşağıgörle [TR] 152 F5
Aşağıinova [TR] 150 C5
Åsan [N] 190 C5
Åsäng [S] 184 E4
Ašanja [SCG] 142 G2
Åsarna [S] 182 G4
Asarum [S] 158 E1
Åsbro [S] 166 H4
Asby [S] 162 E2
Ascain [F] 84 C2
Ascea [I] 120 F5
Ascha [D] 60 G2
Aschach [A] 62 B4
Aschaffenburg [D] 46 D3
Aschau [A] 72 E1
Aschau [D] 60 F5
Aschbach Markt [A] 62 C5
Ascheberg [D] 16 H6
Ascheberg [D] 18 G2
Aschendorf [D] 16 H3
Aschersleben [D] 34 B4
Asciano [I] 114 G1
Ascó [E] 90 H6
Asco [F] 114 B3
Áscoli Piceno [I] 116 C3
Ascoli Satriano [I] 120 G2
Ascona [CH] 70 F3
Ase [N] 192 E3
Åsebyn [S] 166 D3
Åseda [S] 162 E4
Åsele [S] 190 G5
Åseli [N] 192 D6
Asemankylä [FIN] 188 C5
Asemanseutu [FIN] 186 D3
Åsen [N] 190 C6
Åsen [S] 172 F2
Åsen [S] 184 C4
Asendorf [D] 18 E6
Asenovgrad [BG] 148 B6
Asenovo [BG] 148 B2
Åsensbruk [S] 166 D4
Åseral [N] 164 D4
Åserund [N] 166 C1
Asfáka [GR] 132 C1
Asfeld [F] 44 B2
Åsgårdstrand [N] 164 H2
Asha (Pasaköy) [CY] 154 G5
Ashbourne [GB] 10 E5
Ashbourne [IRL] 2 F6
Åsheim [N] 182 C6
Ashford [GB] 14 F5
Ashington [GB] 8 G5
Ashmyany [BY] 200 H6
Ashton-under-Lyne [GB] 10 E4
Asiago [I] 72 D5
Asikkala [FIN] 176 H2
Asila [FIN] 188 D5
Asipovitsy [BY] 202 C5
Ask [N] 170 B3
Ask [N] 170 H5
Ask [S] 158 C2
Aska [FIN] 194 D6
Askainen / Villnäs [FIN] 176 D4
Askanija Nova [UA] 204 H3
Askeaton [IRL] 4 C3
Askeby [DK] 156 G4
Asker [N] 164 H1
Askersund [S] 166 G4
Askeryd [S] 162 E2
Askim [N] 166 C2
Askim [S] 160 G2
Askland [N] 164 E3
Asklepiyon [TR] 152 C2
Asklipieío [GR] 154 B2
Askola [FIN] 178 B4
Asköping [S] 168 B3
Askós [GR] 130 B4
Askum [S] 166 B5
Askvoll [N] 170 B1
Askýfou [GR] 140 C5
Aslanapa [TR] 152 G1
Aslestad [N] 164 E2
Åsli [N] 170 G4
Åsljunga [S] 162 B6
Åsmasbo [S] 172 H5
Asmunti [FIN] 196 E2
Asnæs [DK] 156 F2
Åsnes [N] 172 D4
As Nogais [E] 78 E4
Ásola [I] 110 E1
Asolo [I] 72 E5
Asopía [GR] 134 B5
Asopós [GR] 136 F4
Asoru, Nuraghe- [I] 118 D7
Ásos [GR] 132 C5
Ásotthalom [H] 76 D4
Aspa [S] 168 C4
Aspang Markt [A] 62 E6
Asparuhovo [BG] 148 E4
Asparukovo [BG] 148 F3
Aspås [S] 182 G2
Aspe [E] 104 D2
Aspeå [S] 184 F1
Aspet [F] 84 G4
Aspnes [N] 190 D5
Aspö [S] 168 C2
As Pontes de García Rodríguez / Puentes de García Rodríguez [E] 78 D2
Aspres-sur-Buëch [F] 108 C2
Asprópyrgos [GR] 134 B6
Asprόvalta [GR] 130 C4
Aspsele [S] 190 G6
Assel [D] 18 E4
Assé-le-Boisne [F] 26 F6
Assemini [I] 118 C7
Assen [NL] 16 G3
Assens [DK] 156 D3
Assens [DK] 160 E5
Asserbo [DK] 156 G1
Assergi [I] 116 C4
Asseria [HR] 112 G5
Assessos [TR] 152 D6
Ássiros [GR] 128 H4
Assisi [I] 116 A2
Assling [D] 60 F5
Assmannshausen [D] 46 B3
Assoro [I] 126 F3
Assos [TR] 134 H1
Åsta [N] 172 C3
Astaffort [F] 66 E6
Astakós [GR] 132 D5
Åstan [N] 180 H1
Asten [A] 62 B4
Asten [NL] 30 F3
Asti [I] 70 E6
Astira [TR] 152 C1
Astorga [E] 78 G6
Åstorp [S] 156 H1
Åstrand [S] 172 E5
Ástros [GR] 136 E3
Astrup [DK] 160 D4
Astryna [BY] 24 G3
Astudillo [E] 82 D6
Astura, Torre- [I] 120 B1
Astypálaia [GR] 138 H4
Asvyeya [BY] 198 G6
Aszód [H] 64 D6
Aszófo [H] 76 A2
Atalaia [P] 86 B5
Atalánti [GR] 132 H4
Atanneus [TR] 152 C2
Atapuerca [E] 82 E5
Atarfe [E] 102 E4
Atašiene [LV] 198 F5
Atburgazi [TR] 152 D6
Atça [TR] 152 E5
Ateca [E] 90 C4
Atella [I] 120 G3
Atessa [I] 116 E5
Ath [B] 28 G3
Athboy [IRL] 2 E5
Athea [IRL] 4 C3
Athenry [IRL] 2 C5
Athéras [GR] 132 C6
Athiénou [CY] 154 G5
Athína [GR] 134 C6
Athleague [IRL] 2 D5
Athlone / Baile Átha Luain [IRL] 2 D5
Athy [IRL] 4 F3
Atienza [E] 90 A4
Atina [I] 116 C6
Atkár [H] 64 E6
Atnbrua [N] 180 H6
Atnosen [N] 182 B6
A Toxa [E] 78 B4
Åtran [S] 162 B4
Åträsk [S] 190 H5
Atri [I] 116 D3
Atripalda [I] 120 F3
Atsalarma [EST] 198 F1
Áttali [GR] 134 C4
Attel [D] 60 F4
Attendorn [D] 32 C5
Attersee [A] 60 H5
Attigny [F] 44 C2
Attleborough [GB] 14 G2
Attmar [S] 184 E5
Attnang-Puchheim [A] 62 A5
Attre [B] 28 G3
Attrup [DK] 160 D3
Åtvidaberg [S] 168 B6
Atzara [I] 118 D5
Atzendorf [D] 34 B4
Atzeneta del Maestrat [E] 98 F3
Au [A] 62 D6
Au [D] 60 E3
Aub [D] 46 E4
Aubagne [F] 108 B5
Aubange [B] 44 E3
Aubenas [F] 68 E6
Aubérive [F] 44 C3
Auberive [F] 56 H2
Aubeterre-sur-Dronne [F] 66 E2
Aubiet [F] 84 G3
Aubigny [F] 54 B3
Aubigny-Les-Pothées [F] 28 H6
Aubigny-sur-Nère [F] 56 C2
Auboué [F] 44 E4
Aubrac [F] 68 C5
Aubusson [F] 68 B1
Auce [LV] 198 C6
Aucelon [F] 68 G6
Auch [F] 84 G2
Auchinleck [GB] 8 D4
Auchterarder [GB] 8 E2
Auchtermuchty [GB] 8 E2
Audelange [F] 56 H4
Audenge [F] 66 C3
Auderville [F] 26 D1
Audeux [F] 58 B4
Audierne [F] 40 A3
Audincourt [F] 58 C4
Audlem [GB] 10 D5
Audnedal [N] 164 D5
Audressein [F] 84 G5
Audru [EST] 198 D3
Audun-le-Roman [F] 44 E3
Aue [D] 48 D2
Auer / Ora [I] 72 D4
Auerbach [D] 46 H4
Auerbach [D] 48 C2
Auerbacher Schloss [D] 46 C4
Auffach [A] 60 F6
Augher [NIR] 2 F3
Aughnacloy [NIR] 2 F3
Aughrim [IRL] 4 G4
Augsburg [D] 60 D3
Augusta [I] 126 G4
Augustenborg [DK] 156 C4
Augustów [PL] 24 E3
Augustusburg [D] 48 D1
Aukra [N] 180 D2
Aukštadvaris [LT] 24 G1
Auktsjaur [S] 190 H3
Auletta [I] 120 G4
Aulla [I] 110 C4
Aullène [F] 114 B5
Aulnay [F] 54 D5
Aulstad [N] 170 H2
Ault [F] 28 C4
Aulus-les-Bains [F] 84 H5
Auma [D] 48 B2
Aumale [F] 28 D5
Aumetz [F] 44 E3
Aumont-Aubrac [F] 68 C5
Aunay-sur-Odon [F] 26 E4
Auneau [F] 42 E4
Aunet [N] 190 B6
Aunet [N] 190 C5
Auneuil [F] 28 D6
Aunfoss [N] 190 D4
Auning [DK] 160 E5
Aups [F] 108 D4
Aurach [A] 60 F6
Aurach [D] 46 F5
Auray [F] 40 D4
Aurdal [N] 170 G3
Aure [N] 180 G1
Aurejärvi [FIN] 186 D5
Aurich [D] 18 B4
Aurignac [F] 84 G4
Aurillac [F] 68 B4
Auriol [F] 108 B5
Auritz / Burguete [E] 84 C3
Aurlandsvangen [N] 170 D2
Auron [F] 108 E3
Auronzo di Cadore [I] 72 F3
Aursmoen [N] 166 C1
Aursnes [N] 180 D3
Áusa Corno [I] 72 G5
Ausejo [E] 84 A5
Ausentum [I] 122 G6
Aussernbrünst [D] 60 H3
Austad [N] 164 C6
Austad [N] 164 D3
Austanå [N] 164 E3
Austborg [N] 190 D5
Austbygda [N] 170 F5
Austbygdi [N] 170 F5
Austefjord [N] 180 C4
Austmarka [N] 172 D5
Austnes [N] 180 D3
Austpollen [N] 192 E4
Austrått [N] 190 B6
Austrumdal [N] 164 B4
Auterive [F] 84 H4
Authon [F] 108 D3
Authon-du-Perche [F] 42 C5
Autio [S] 194 B7
Autol [E] 84 A5
Autti [FIN] 194 E8
Auttoinen [FIN] 176 H2
Autun [F] 56 F4
Auve [F] 44 C4
Auvers-s-Oise [F] 42 F3
Auvillers-les-Forges [F] 28 H5
Auxerre [F] 56 E2
Auxi-le-Château [F] 28 D4
Auxonne [F] 56 H4
Auzances [F] 56 B6
Auzon [F] 68 D3
Avå [FIN] 176 C4
Ava [S] 184 H1
Avafors [S] 196 B2
Availles-Limouzine [F] 54 F5
Aval, Falaise d'- [F] 26 G2
Avala [SCG] 142 G3

Avaldsnes [N] 164 A2
Avallon [F] 56 E3
Ávas [GR] 130 G3
Avaträsk [S] 190 F5
Avaviken [S] 190 G3
Avcılar [TR] 150 E3
Avdímou [CY] 154 F6
Ávdira [GR] 130 E3
Ávdira [GR] 130 E3
Åvedal [N] 164 B5
A Veiga [E] 78 E6
Aveiras de Cima [P] 86 C4
Aveiro [P] 80 B5
Avelengo / Hafling [I] 72 D3
Avellino [I] 120 F3
Aven Armand [F] 106 E2
Avenches [CH] 58 C6
Aven de Marzal [F] 106 G2
Aven d'Orgnac [F] 106 G2
Averbode [B] 30 D3
Aversa [I] 120 D3
Avesnes-le-Comte [F] 28 E4
Avesnes-sur-Helpe [F] 28 G4
Avesta [S] 174 D5
Avetrana [I] 122 F4
Avezzano [I] 116 C5
Avgerinós [GR] 128 E6
Avía [GR] 136 D4
Aviano [I] 72 F5
Aviemore [GB] 6 E5
Avigliana [I] 70 D5
Avigliano [I] 120 G3
Avigna [I] 72 D3
Avignon [F] 106 G3
Ávila [E] 88 E4
Avilés [E] 78 H3
Avinurme [EST] 198 F2
Avinyó [E] 92 E3
Avio [I] 72 C5
Avión [E] 78 C4
Avis [P] 86 D5
Avlákia [GR] 152 C5
Avlémonas [GR] 136 F6
Avlí [GR] 130 D3
Avliótes [GR] 132 A2
Avlóna [GR] 134 C5
Avlonári [GR] 134 C5
Avlum [DK] 160 C6
Avola [I] 126 G5
Avonmouth [GB] 12 F3
Avoriaz [F] 70 C2
Avradsberg [S] 172 F5
Avramov [BG] 148 E4
Avranches [F] 26 D4
Avril [F] 44 E3
Avşar [TR] 152 D6
Avtovac [BIH] 144 D3
Axat [F] 106 B5
Axel [NL] 28 H1
Axioúpoli [GR] 128 G3
Ax-les-Thermes [F] 106 A6
Axmarby [S] 174 E3
Axminster [GB] 12 F4
Axós [GR] 140 E4
Axvall [S] 166 F5
Ay [F] 44 B3
Ayagalip [TR] 130 G5
Ayamonte [E] 94 D5
Ayas [I] 70 D3
Aydın [TR] 152 D5
Aydıncık [TR] 130 G5
Aydıncık [TR] 154 F4
Ayerbe [E] 84 D6
Aykırıkçı [TR] 152 H2
Aylesbury [GB] 14 D3
Ayllón [E] 88 H3
Aylsham [GB] 14 G2
Ayna [E] 98 B6
Ayoó de Vidriales [E] 80 H3
Ayora [E] 98 D5
Ayr [GB] 8 C4
Ayrancı [TR] 152 G2
Ayrancılar [TR] 152 C4
Ay. Seryios (Yenibogaziçi) [CY] 154 G5
Äyskoski [FIN] 186 H2
Äystö [FIN] 186 B4
Aytos [BG] 148 F4
Ayvacık [TR] 134 H1
Ayvalık [TR] 152 B2
Ayvatlar [TR] 152 C2
Azaila [E] 90 F5
Azambuja [P] 86 C4
Azannes-et-Soumazannes [F] 44 D3
Azanúy [E] 90 H3
Azaruja [P] 86 D6
Azath [TR] 150 B2
Azay-le-Ferron [F] 54 G3
Azay-le-Rideau [F] 54 F2
Azinheira dos Barros [P] 94 C2
Azıtepe [TR] 152 E4
Aznalcóllar [E] 94 G5
Azuaga [E] 96 A5
Azuara [E] 90 E5
Azuel [E] 96 D5
Azul, Cueva- [E] 104 E6
Azuqueca de Henares [E] 88 G5
Azur [F] 66 A6
Azyory [BY] 24 G4
Azzano Decimo [I] 72 F5
Azzurra, Grotta- [I] 120 D4
Azzurra, Grotta- [I] 120 F5

B

Baad [A] 60 B6
Baal [D] 30 F4
Baamonde [E] 78 D3
Baar [D] 60 D3
Baarle Nassau [NL] 30 D2
Baarn [NL] 16 E4
Babadag [RO] 204 F5
Babadağ [TR] 152 F5
Babaeski [TR] 150 B2
Babaköy [TR] 152 D2
Babek [BG] 148 B5
Babenhausen [D] 46 D3
Babenhausen [D] 60 C4
Babiak [PL] 22 G3
Babiak [PL] 36 F3
Babica [PL] 52 D4
Babice [PL] 50 G4
Băbiciu [RO] 148 A1
Babięta [PL] 24 B4
Babigoszcz [PL] 20 F4
Babimost [PL] 36 A3
Babin Potok [HR] 112 G3
BabnoPolje [SLO] 74 B6
Babócsa [H] 74 G5
Bábolna [H] 64 A6
Babruysk [BY] 202 C5
Babušnica [SCG] 146 E4
Babylon [CZ] 48 D5
Babylón [CZ] 62 E2
Bač [MK] 128 E4
Bač [SCG] 142 E1
Bač [SLO] 74 A6
Bača [SLO] 72 H4
Bacău [RO] 204 D4
Baccarat [F] 44 F6
Baceno [I] 70 F2
Bacharach [D] 46 B3
Bachkovo [BG] 148 B6
Bachkovski Manastir [BG] 148 B6
Bachórz [PL] 52 E4
Bačina [SCG] 146 C3
Backåkra [S] 158 D3
Bačka Palanka [SCG] 142 F1
Bäckaskog [S] 158 D1
Bačka Topola [SCG] 76 D5
Bäckby [FIN] 196 C6
Backe [S] 190 F6
Bäckebo [S] 162 F4
Bäckefors [S] 166 D4
Backen [S] 184 D4
Backen [S] 184 E4
Bäckhammar [S] 166 F3
Bački Breg [SCG] 76 C5
Bački Petrovac [SCG] 142 F1
Backnang [D] 46 D6
Bačko Gradište [SCG] 142 G1
Bačko Novo Selo [SCG] 142 E1
Bačko Petrovo Selo [SCG] 76 E6
Baćkowice [PL] 52 C1
Bacoli [I] 120 D3
Bacova mahala [BG] 148 B3
Bacqueville-en-Caux [F] 28 B4
Bácsalmás [H] 76 D5
Bácsbokod [H] 76 C5
Bácsborsód [H] 76 C5
Baczyna [PL] 34 H1
Bad Abbach [D] 60 F2
Badacsonytomaj [H] 74 H3
Bad Aibling [D] 60 F5
Badajoz [E] 86 F6
Badalona [E] 92 E4
Bad Aussee [A] 62 A6
Bad Bederkesa [D] 18 E4
Bad Bentheim [D] 16 H5
Bad Bergzabern [D] 46 B5
Bad Berka [D] 46 H1
Bad Berleburg [D] 32 D5
Bad Berneck [D] 46 H3
Bad Bertrich [D] 44 G1
Bad Bevensen [D] 18 G5
Bad Bibra [D] 34 B5
Bad Blankenburg [D] 46 H2
Bad Brambach [D] 48 C3
Bad Bramstedt [D] 18 F3
Bad Breisig [D] 30 H5
Bad Brückenau [D] 46 E2
Bad Buchau [D] 60 A4
Badderen [N] 192 H2
Bad Deutsch-Altenburg [A] 62 G5
Bad Doberan [D] 20 B3
Bad Driburg [D] 32 E4
Bad Düben [D] 34 D4
Bad Dürkheim [D] 46 B4
Bad Dürrenberg [D] 34 C5
Bad Dürrheim [D] 58 F3
Bad Elster [D] 48 C3
Bademli [TR] 152 E5
Bad Ems [D] 46 B2
Baden [A] 62 F5
Baden [CH] 58 F4
Baden-Baden [D] 58 F1
Bad Endorf [D] 60 F5
Badenweiler [D] 58 E3
Baderna [HR] 112 D2
Bădeshte [BG] 148 C5
Bad Essen [D] 32 D2
Bad Frankenhausen [D] 34 A5
Bad Freienwalde [D] 34 F1
Bad Friedrichshall [D] 46 D5
Bad Gandersheim [D] 32 G3
Badgastein [A] 72 G2
Bad Gleichenberg [A] 74 E3
Bad Godesberg [D] 30 H5
Bad Goisern [A] 60 H6
Bad Gottleuba [D] 48 F1
Bad Grund [D] 32 G4
Bad Hall [A] 62 B5
Bad Harzburg [D] 32 H3
Bad Herrenalb [D] 58 F1
Bad Hersfeld [D] 32 F6
Bad Hofgastein [A] 72 G1
Bad Homburg [D] 46 C2
Bad Honnef [D] 30 H5
Bad Hönningen [D] 30 H5
Badia Polésine [I] 110 F2
Badia Tedalda [I] 110 G6
Bad Iburg [D] 32 D2
Bad Ischl [A] 60 H5
Bad Karlshafen [D] 32 F4
Bad Kissingen [D] 46 E3
Bad Kleinen [D] 20 A4
Bad Kleinkirchheim [A] 72 H3
Bad König [D] 46 D4
Bad Königshofen [D] 46 F2
Bad Kösen [D] 34 B6
Bądkowo [PL] 36 F2
Bad Kreuznach [D] 46 B3
Bad Krozingen [D] 58 E3
Bad Laasphe [D] 32 D6
Bad Langensalza [D] 32 H6
Bad Lauchstädt [D] 34 B5
Bad Lausick [D] 34 D6
Bad Lauterburg [D] 32 G4
Bad Leonfelden [A] 62 B3
Bad Liebenstein [D] 46 F1
Bad Liebenwerda [D] 34 E5
Bad Liebenzell [D] 58 G1
Bad Lippspringe [D] 32 E3
Badljevina [HR] 142 C1
Bad Marienberg [D] 46 B1
Bad Meinberg [D] 32 E3
Bad Mergentheim [D] 46 E5
Bad Mitterndorf [A] 62 B6
Bad Münder [D] 32 F2
Bad Münster Ebernburg [D] 46 B3
Bad Münstereifel [D] 30 G5
Bad Muskau [D] 34 G5
Bad Nauheim [D] 46 C2
Bad Nenndorf [D] 32 E2
Bad Neuenahr [D] 30 G5
Bad Neustadt [D] 46 F2
Bad Oeynhausen [D] 32 E2
Badolato [I] 124 E6
Badolato Marina [I] 124 E6
Bad Oldesloe [D] 18 G3
Badonviller [F] 44 F6
Bad Orb [D] 46 D2
Badovinci [SCG] 142 F2
Badow [D] 18 H4
Bad Peterstal [D] 58 F2
Bad Pirawarth [A] 62 F4
Bad Pyrmont [D] 32 E3
Bad Radkersburg [A] 74 E3
Bad Ragaz [CH] 58 H6
Bad Reichenhall [D] 60 G5
Bad Rippoldsau [D] 58 F2
Bad Rothenfelde [D] 32 D2
Bad Saarow-Pieskow [D] 34 F3
Bad Sachsa [D] 32 G4
Bad Säckingen [D] 58 E4
Bad Salzdetfurth [D] 32 G3
Bad Salzuflen [D] 32 E3
Bad Salzungen [D] 46 F1
Bad Schallerbach [A] 62 B4
Bad Schandau [D] 48 F1
Bad Schmiedeberg [D] 34 D4
Bad Schönau [A] 74 F1
Bad Schönborn [D] 46 C5
Bad Schussenried [D] 60 B4
Bad Schwalbach [D] 46 B2
Bad Schwartau [D] 18 G3
Bad Segeberg [D] 18 G3
Bad Sooden-Allendorf [D] 32 F5
Bad St. Leonhard [A] 74 C2
Bad Sülze [D] 20 C3
Bad Tatzamannsdorf [A] 74 F1
Bad Tennstedt [D] 32 H5
Bad Tölz [D] 60 E5
Badules [E] 90 D5
Bad Urach [D] 58 H2
Bad Vöslau [A] 62 F5
Bad Waldsee [D] 60 B4
Bad Wiessee [D] 60 E5
Bad-Wildungen [D] 32 E5
Bad Wilsnack [D] 20 B6
Bad Wimpfen [D] 46 D5
Bad Windsheim [D] 46 F5
Bad Wörishofen [D] 60 C4
Bad Wurzach [D] 60 B5
Bad Zwischenahn [D] 18 C5
Bække [DK] 156 B2
Bækmarksbro [DK] 160 B5
Baelen [B] 30 F5
Baells [E] 90 H3
Baelo Claudia [E] 100 G5
Baena [E] 102 D2
Bæverfjord [N] 180 F2
Baeza [E] 102 F2
Bagà [E] 92 E2
Bagamér [H] 64 H6
Bağarası [TR] 152 D5
Bågede [S] 190 E5
Bagenalstown / Muine Bheag [IRL] 4 F4
Bagenkop [DK] 18 H1
Bagh Chaisteil / Castlebay [GB] 6 A5
Bagheria [I] 126 D2
Bagn [N] 170 G3
Bagnacavallo [I] 110 G4
Bagnara Calabra [I] 124 C7
Bagnères-de-Bigorre [F] 84 F4
Bagnères-de-Luchon [F] 84 F5
Bagni Contursi [I] 120 F4
Bagni del Másino [I] 70 H3
Bagni di Bormio [I] 72 B3
Bagni di Craveggia [I] 70 F3
Bagni di Lucca [I] 110 E5
Bagni di Rabbi [I] 72 C3
Bagni di Salomone [I] 72 E2
Bagni di Vinadio [I] 108 E3
Bagno A Ripoli [I] 110 F5
Bagno di Romagna [I] 110 G5
Bagnoles-de-l'Orne [F] 26 F5
Bagnoli di Sopra [I] 110 G1
Bagnolo Mella [I] 72 B6
Bagnolo Piemonte [I] 108 F1
Bagnolo San Vito [I] 110 E2
Bagnols-en-Forêt [F] 108 D5
Bagnols-les-Bains [F] 68 D6
Bagnols-sur-Cèze [F] 106 G3
Bagnone [I] 110 D4
Bagnoregio [I] 114 H3
Bagno Vignoni [I] 114 G2
Bagny [PL] 24 E4
Bågø [DK] 156 C3
Bagod [H] 74 F3
Bagolino [I] 72 B5
Bagrationovsk [RUS] 22 H2
Bagsund [N] 190 C5
Báguena [E] 90 D5
Bağyaka [TR] 154 D1
Bağyurdu [TR] 152 D4
Bağyüzü [TR] 152 C2
Baharlar [TR] 152 B1
Bahçecik [TR] 150 G3
Bahçeköy [TR] 150 B4
Bahçeköy [TR] 150 D2
Bahillo [E] 82 D5
Baia delle Zagare [I] 116 H6
Băia Domizia [I] 120 D2
Baia Mare [RO] 204 C3
Baiano [I] 120 E3
Baião [P] 80 C4
Băia Sardinia [I] 118 E2
Baiersbronn [D] 58 F2
Baigneux-les-Juifs [F] 56 G3
Baile Átha Cliath / Dublin [IRL] 2 F6
Baile Átha Luain / Athlone [IRL] 2 D5
Băile Felix [RO] 76 H2
Bailén [E] 102 E1
Băileşti [RO] 146 F2
Băile Tuşnad [RO] 204 D4
Bailieborough [IRL] 2 F4
Bailleul [F] 26 H2
Bailleul [F] 28 F2
Bain-de-Bretagne [F] 40 F5
Bains-les-Bains [F] 58 C2
Baio [E] 78 B2
Baiona [E] 78 A5
Bais [F] 26 E6
Baisogala [LT] 200 F4
Baix [F] 68 F5
Baixas [F] 92 G1
Baja [H] 76 C4
Bajánsenye [H] 74 F3
Bajč [SK] 64 B5
Bajina Bašta [SCG] 142 F4
Bajmok [SCG] 76 D5
Bajna [H] 64 B6
Bajram Curri [AL] 146 A6
Bajša [SCG] 76 D6
Bajzë [AL] 144 E4
Bak [H] 74 G3
Bakacak [TR] 150 C5
Bakar [HR] 112 E1
Bakewell [GB] 10 E5
Bakhchysarai [UA] 204 H4
Bakhmach [UA] 202 E6
Bakio [E] 82 G3
Bakırköy [TR] 150 E3
Bakka [N] 164 F1
Bakke [N] 164 F4
Bakke [N] 166 C4
Bakkejord [N] 192 F2
Bakken [N] 182 C1
Bakko [N] 170 F5
Baklan [TR] 152 G4
Bakonygyepes [H] 74 H2
Bakonypeterd [H] 76 A1
Bakonysárkány [H] 76 A1
Bakonyszombathely [H] 76 A1
Baks [H] 76 E3
Baksa [H] 76 A5
Baksjöliden [S] 190 G5
Baktakék [H] 64 F4
Baktalórántháza [H] 64 H5
Baktsjaur [S] 190 H3
Bakum [D] 18 C6
Bakvattnet [S] 190 D6
Bäl [S] 168 G4
Bala [GB] 10 C5
Balabancık [TR] 150 B4
Balaguer [E] 92 B3
Balanegra [E] 102 F5
Bălăneşti [RO] 148 A1
Balassagyarmat [H] 64 C5
Balástya [H] 76 E4
Balat [TR] 152 D6
Balatonakali [H] 74 H2
Balatonalmádi [H] 76 A2
Balatonboglár [H] 74 H3
Balatonederics [H] 74 H3
Balatonföldvár [H] 76 A3
Balatonfüred [H] 76 A2
Balatonfüzfo [H] 76 A2
Balatonkenese [H] 76 A2
Balatonkeresztúr [H] 74 H3
Balatonlelle [H] 74 H3
Balatonszemes [H] 76 A3
Balazote [E] 98 B5
Balbigny [F] 68 E2
Balboa [E] 78 E4
Balbriggan [IRL] 2 F5
Bålby [S] 166 G3
Balchik [BG] 148 G2
Balcon de Europa [E] 102 D5
Baldenstein [CH] 70 H1
Balderschwang [D] 60 B6
Baldock [GB] 14 E3
Baldone [LV] 198 E5
Bale [HR] 112 D2
Baleines, Phare des- [F] 54 B4
Baleira [E] 78 E3
Baleizão [P] 94 D3
Balestrand [N] 170 C1
Balestrate [I] 126 C2
Balewo [PL] 22 F4
Bălgarin [BG] 148 D6
Bälgviken [S] 168 B3
Balice [PL] 50 H3
Balıkesir [TR] 152 D1
Balıklıova [TR] 152 B4
Balıköy [TR] 152 F1
Bälinge [S] 158 C1
Bälinge [S] 162 B1
Bälinge [S] 168 D1
Balingen [D] 58 G2
Balinț [RO] 76 H5
Balio Chitarra [I] 126 B2
Baljvine [BIH] 142 B3
Balkanec [BG] 148 B4
Balkanski [BG] 148 D2
Balkány [H] 64 H5
Balkıca [TR] 152 G6
Balla [IRL] 2 C4
Ballaban [AL] 128 C5
Ballachulish [GB] 6 C6
Ballaghaderreen [IRL] 2 D4
Ballangen [N] 192 E4
Ballantrae [GB] 8 C4
Ballao [I] 118 D6
Ballater [GB] 6 E6
Ballebro [DK] 156 C4
Bällefors [S] 166 F5
Ballen [DK] 156 E2
Ballenstedt [D] 34 A4
Balleroy [F] 26 E3
Ballerup [DK] 156 G2
Ballı [TR] 150 B3
Ballina [IRL] 2 C3
Ballina [IRL] 2 C6
Ballinafad [IRL] 2 D4
Ballinagh [IRL] 2 E4
Ballinakill [IRL] 4 E3
Ballinamore [IRL] 2 E4
Ballinascarty [IRL] 4 C5
Ballinasloe [IRL] 2 D5
Ballindine [IRL] 2 C4
Ballindooly Castle [IRL] 2 C5
Ballingarry [IRL] 4 C3
Ballingarry [IRL] 4 E4
Ballinhassig [IRL] 4 C5
Ballinrobe [IRL] 2 C4
Ballinskelligs [IRL] 4 A4
Ballinspittle [IRL] 4 C5
Ballintober, Abbey- [IRL] 2 C4
Ballintra [IRL] 2 E3
Ballivor [IRL] 2 E5
Ballobar [E] 90 G4
Ballon [F] 42 B4
Ballon [IRL] 4 F4
Ballsh [AL] 128 B5
Ballshi [AL] 128 B4
Ballstad [N] 192 C4
Ballum [DK] 156 B3
Ballybay [IRL] 2 F4
Ballybofey [IRL] 2 E2
Ballybunion [IRL] 2 B6
Ballycanew [IRL] 4 F4
Ballycastle [IRL] 2 C3
Ballycastle [NIR] 2 G2
Ballyclare [NIR] 2 G3
Ballyconneely [IRL] 2 B4
Ballycotton [IRL] 4 D5
Ballycumber [IRL] 2 D5
Ballydehob [IRL] 4 B5
Ballydesmond [IRL] 4 C4
Ballyduff [IRL] 4 B3
Ballyduff [IRL] 4 D4
Ballyemund [IRL] 4 F4
Ballyfarnan [IRL] 2 D4
Ballygawley [NIR] 2 F3
Ballyglass [IRL] 2 C4
Ballygowan [NIR] 2 G4
Ballyhaunis [IRL] 2 C4
Ballyheige [IRL] 4 B3
Ballyhillin [IRL] 2 F1
Ballyjamesduff [IRL] 2 E4
Ballylanders [IRL] 4 D4
Ballylongford [IRL] 2 B6
Ballylynan [IRL] 4 F3
Ballymacoda [IRL] 4 D5
Ballymahon [IRL] 2 D5
Ballymena [NIR] 2 G3
Ballymoe [IRL] 2 D4
Ballymoney [NIR] 2 G2
Ballymore [IRL] 2 E5
Ballymore Eustace [IRL] 2 F6
Ballymote [IRL] 2 D3
Ballynahinch [NIR] 2 G4
Ballyragget [IRL] 4 E3
Ballyronan [NIR] 2 G3
Ballyroon [IRL] 4 B5
Ballysadare [IRL] 2 D3
Ballyshannon [IRL] 2 E3
Ballyvaughan [IRL] 2 C5
Ballywalter [NIR] 2 H4
Balmaseda [E] 82 G4
Balmazújváros [H] 64 G6
Balme [I] 70 C5
Balmúccia [I] 70 E3
Balogunyom [H] 74 F2
Balş [RO] 146 G1
Balsareny [E] 92 D3
Balsfjord [N] 192 F2
Balsicas [E] 104 C4
Balsjö [S] 190 H6
Balsorano [I] 116 C6
Bålsta [S] 168 D2
Balsthal [CH] 58 E5
Balta [UA] 204 E2
Baltaköy [TR] 152 E5
Baltanás [E] 88 F1
Baltar [E] 78 C6
Bălți [MD] 204 E3
Baltimore [IRL] 4 B5
Baltinava [LV] 198 G5
Baltinglass [IRL] 4 F3
Baltiysk [RUS] 22 G1
Baltrum [D] 18 B3
Balugães [P] 78 A6
Balvan [BG] 148 C3
Balvi [LV] 198 G4
Balya [TR] 152 D1
Balzers [FL] 58 H6
Bamberg [D] 46 G4
Bamble [N] 164 G3
Bana [H] 64 A6
Banafjäl [S] 184 G2
Banagher [IRL] 2 D6
Banarli [TR] 150 C3
Banatski Karlovac [SCG] 142 H2
Banatsko Aranđelovo [SCG] 76 E5
Banatsko Karadjordjevo [SCG] 76 F6
Banatsko Novo Selo [SCG] 142 H2
Banaz [TR] 152 G3
Banbridge [NIR] 2 G4
Banbury [GB] 14 D2
Banchory [GB] 6 F6
Bande [E] 78 C5
Bandholm [DK] 156 F5
Bandırma [TR] 150 D4
Bandol [F] 108 B5
Bandon [IRL] 4 C5
Băneasa [RO] 148 C1
Banff [GB] 6 F5
Bängnäs [S] 190 E4
Bangor [F] 40 C5
Bangor [GB] 10 B4
Bangor [NIR] 2 H3
Bangor Erris [IRL] 2 C3
Bangsbo [DK] 160 E3
Bangsund [N] 190 C5
Bánhalma [H] 76 F1
Banica [BG] 146 G3
Banie [PL] 20 F6
Banja [SCG] 144 E2
Banja [SCG] 146 B4
Banja Koviljača [SCG] 142 E3
Banjaloka [SLO] 112 F1
Banja Luka [BIH] 142 C3
Banjani [SCG] 146 A1
Banjska [SCG] 146 C4
Bánk [H] 64 H6
Banka [SK] 64 A3
Bankervd [S] 162 D2
Bankháza [H] 76 C2
Bankya [BG] 146 F5
Bannalec [F] 40 C3
Bannesdorf [D] 20 A2
Banon [F] 108 C3
Baños de Alicún de las Torres [E] 102 F3
Baños de Cerrato [E] 88 F1
Baños de la Encina [E] 96 E6
Baños de Montemayor [E] 88 B4
Baños de Panticosa [E] 84 E5
Baños de Rio Tobia [E] 82 G6
Bánov [CZ] 62 H2
Bánovce nad Bebravou [SK] 64 B3
Banovići [BIH] 142 D3
Bánréve [H] 64 E4
Bansin [D] 20 E3
Banská Bystrica [SK] 64 C3
Banská Štiavnica [SK] 64 C3
Banské [SK] 64 G2
Bansko [BG] 130 B1
Bansko [MK] 128 H2
Banteer [IRL] 4 C4
Bantheville [F] 44 D3
Ban. Topola [SCG] 76 F6
Bantry [IRL] 4 B5
Bantry House [IRL] 4 B5
Banya [BG] 148 B5
Banya [BG] 148 D4
Banya [BG] 148 F4
Banyalbufar [E] 104 D4
Banyeres de Mariola [E] 104 D1
Banyoles / Bañolas [E] 92 F3
Banyuls-sur-Mer [F] 92 G2
Banz [D] 46 G3
Bapaume [F] 28 F4
Bar [SCG] 144 E5
Baradla [H] 64 E3
Barajas [E] 88 G5
Barajas de Melo [E] 96 H1
Barakaldo [E] 82 G3
Baralla [E] 78 E4
Baranavichy [BY] 202 B6
Báránd [H] 76 G1
Baranowo [PL] 24 C5
Baranów Sandomierski [PL] 52 D2
Baraona [E] 90 B4
Baraqueville [F] 68 A6
Bårared [S] 162 B5
Barásoain [E] 84 B4
Barbadillo de Herreros [E] 90 A1
Barban [HR] 112 D2
Barbarano Vicentino [I] 72 D6
Barbaros [TR] 150 C3
Barba-Rossahöhle [D] 32 H5
Barbaste [F] 66 E5
Barbastro [E] 90 G3
Barbat [HR] 112 F3
Barbate [E] 100 F5
Bărbele [LV] 198 E6
Barberino Val D'Elsa [I] 110 F6
Barbezieux-St-Hilaire [F] 66 E2
Barbing [D] 60 F2
Barbizon [F] 42 F5
Barbotan-les-Thermes [F] 66 D6
Barby [D] 34 C3
Bårbyborg [S] 162 G6
Bârca [RO] 146 G2
Barca de Alva [P] 80 E5
Barcarrota [E] 94 F2
Barcellona-Pozzo di Gotto [I] 124 B7
Barcelona [E] 92 E4
Barcelonnette [F] 108 E2
Barcelos [P] 80 C3
Bárcena de Pie de Concha [E] 82 E3
Barchfeld [D] 46 F1
Barchon [B] 30 E5
Barciany [PL] 24 B3
Barcin [PL] 36 E1
Barcino [PL] 22 B3
Bárcis [I] 72 F4
Barcones [E] 90 A4
Barcs [H] 74 H5
Barczewo [PL] 22 H4
Bardakçi [TR] 152 E2
Bardejov [SK] 52 D6
Bardejovské Kúpele [SK] 52 C5
Bardi [I] 110 C3
Bardo [PL] 50 C2
Bardolino [I] 72 C6
Bardonécchia [I] 70 B5
Bardovo [RUS] 198 H5
Bardowick [D] 18 G5
Bardufoss [N] 192 F3
Bärenalm [A] 62 B6
Barenburg [D] 32 E1
Barendrecht [NL] 16 C5
Barentin [F] 26 H3
Barenton [F] 26 E5
Bärfendal [S] 166 C5
Barfleur [F] 26 E2
Barga [I] 110 D4
Bargas [E] 96 F1
Barge [I] 108 F2
Bargteheide [D] 18 G4
Bari [I] 122 E2
Barič [SCG] 142 G3
Bari Sardo [I] 118 E5
Barisciano [I] 116 C4
Bariyevo [BG] 148 B4
Barjac [F] 106 G2
Barjas [E] 78 E5
Barjols [F] 108 C4
Barkåker [N] 164 H2
Barkald [N] 182 C5
Barkarö [S] 168 B2
Barkava [LV] 198 F5
Barkowo [PL] 22 C4
Bârlad [RO] 204 E4
Bar-le-Duc [F] 44 D5
Barletta [I] 122 C2
Barlinek [PL] 20 G6
Barlingbo [S] 168 G4
Barmash [AL] 128 D6
Barmouth [GB] 10 B5
Barmstedt [D] 18 F3
Barnard Castle [GB] 10 F2
Bärnau [D] 48 C4
Barneberg [D] 34 A3
Barneveld [NL] 16 E5
Barneville-Carteret [F] 26 D2
Barnewitz [D] 34 D2
Barnówko [PL] 34 G1
Barnsley [GB] 10 F4
Barnstaple [GB] 12 E3
Barnstorf [D] 18 D6
Barntrup [D] 32 E3
Barovo [MK] 128 F2
Barquilla de Pinares [E] 88 C5
Barr [F] 44 G6
Barracas [E] 98 E3
Barraco [E] 88 E5
Barrafranca [I] 126 E4
Barranco do Velho [P] 94 C5
Barrancos [P] 94 F3
Barrax [E] 98 B5
Barre-des-Cévennes [F] 106 E2
Barreiro [P] 86 B5
Barrême [F] 108 D3
Barrosa [E] 100 F4
Barrow-in-Furness [GB] 10 D2
Barruecopardo [E] 80 F5
Barry [F] 106 G2
Barry [GB] 12 F3
Barryporeen [IRL] 4 D4
Barsanovo [RUS] 198 H5
Barsele [S] 190 G4
Barsinghausen [D] 32 F2
Barssel [D] 18 C5
Barstyciai [LT] 200 D3
Bar-sur-Aube [F] 44 C6
Bar-sur-Seine [F] 44 B6
Barsviken [S] 184 F4
Barth [D] 20 C2
Barton-upon-Humber [GB] 10 G4
Bartoszyce [PL] 22 H2
Barúmini [I] 118 C6
Barussa, Nuraghe- [I] 118 B7
Baruth [D] 34 E3
Barver [D] 32 E1
Bårvik [N] 194 A2
Barwice [PL] 22 A4
Barysaw [BY] 202 C5
Baryshevo [RUS] 178 G3
Bârzina [BG] 146 G3
Barzio [I] 70 G3
Bas [E] 92 F2
Bås [N] 164 E4
Bašaid [SCG] 76 E6
Başalan [TR] 152 F5
Basauri [E] 82 G4
Basconcillos del Tozo [E] 82 E5
Basdahl [D] 18 E4
Basel [CH] 58 E4
Baselga di Pinè [I] 72 D4
Båsheim [N] 170 G5
Bashtanka [UA] 202 F8
Basi [LV] 198 B5
Basildon [GB] 14 F4
Basilice [I] 120 F2
Båsinge [S] 174 D6
Basingstoke [GB] 14 D4
Baška [HR] 112 F2
Baška Voda [HR] 144 B2
Baške Ostarije [HR] 112 G4
Båsksjö [S] 190 F4
Başlamış [TR] 152 D2
Başmakçı [TR] 152 H4
Båsna [S] 172 H4
Bassacutena [I] 118 D2
Bassano del Grappa [I] 72 D5
Bassenheim [D] 30 H6
Bassevuovdde [N] 194 C4
Bassoues [F] 84 F2
Bassum [D] 18 D6
Båstad [N] 166 C2
Båstad [S] 162 B6
Bastelica [F] 114 B4
Baştepe [TR] 152 H3
Bastfallet [S] 174 E5
Bastia [F] 114 C3
Bastia [I] 116 A2
Bastnäs [S] 166 E1
Bastogne (Bastenaken) [B] 44 E1

Bastuny [BY] 200 G6
Bastuträsk [S] 190 H5
Bastuträsk [S] 190 H4
Batajnica [SCG] 142 G2
Batak [BG] 148 A6
Batakiai [LT] 200 E5
Batalha [P] 86 C3
Batanovtsi [BG] 146 F5
Batăr [RO] 76 H3
Bátaszék [H] 76 C4
Baté [H] 76 A4
Batea [E] 90 G6
Batelov [CZ] 48 H6
Batetskiy [RUS] 202 B2
Bath [GB] 12 G3
Batin [BG] 148 C2
Batina [HR] 76 C5
Batlava [SCG] 146 C4
Båtmuseum [N] 180 C4
Batnfjordsøra [N] 180 E2
Batočina [SCG] 146 C2
Bátonyterenye [H] 64 D5
Batorz [PL] 52 E1
Bátovce [SK] 64 B4
Båtsfjord [N] 194 E1
Båtsjaur [S] 190 G2
Battaglia Terme [I] 110 G1
Battenberg [D] 32 D6
Battice [B] 30 E5
Battipáglia [I] 120 F4
Battle [GB] 14 F5
Battonya [H] 76 G4
Batultsi [BG] 146 G4
Baturyn [UA] 202 E6
Bátya [H] 76 C4
Batyk [H] 74 G2
Batz-sur-Mer [F] 40 D6
Baud [F] 26 A6
Baugé [F] 42 A6
Baugy [F] 56 C3
Baume, Cirque de- [F] 56 H5
Baume, Grotte de la- [F] 58 B4
Baume-les-Dames [F] 58 B4
Baume-Les Messieurs, Abbeye de- [F] 56 H5
Baumholder [D] 44 H3
Baunei [I] 118 E5
Bauska [LV] 198 D6
Bautzen [D] 34 F6
Bavanište [SCG] 142 H2
Bavay [F] 28 G4
Baveno [I] 70 F3
Bavorov [CZ] 48 F6
Bawtry [GB] 10 F4
Bayard [F] 70 A4
Baydakovo [RUS] 198 H6
Bayerisch Eisenstein [D] 48 D6
Bayeux [F] 26 E3
Bayındır [TR] 150 F4
Bayındır [TR] 152 D4
Bayır [TR] 152 E6
Bayırköy [TR] 150 B5
Bayırköy [TR] 150 F4
Baykal [BG] 148 A2
Bayon [F] 44 E6
Bayonne [F] 84 C2
Bayrakçi Mağarasi [TR] 152 D5
Bayramdere [TR] 150 E4
Bayramiç [TR] 152 B1
Bayramşah [TR] 152 G1
Bayreuth [D] 46 H4
Bayrischzell [D] 60 F5
Baza [E] 102 G3
Bazas [F] 66 D4
Bazenheid [CH] 58 G5
Bazoches-sur-Hoëne [F] 26 G5
Bazolles [F] 56 E4
Baztan / Elizondo [E] 82 H4
Bazzano [I] 110 F3
Beaconsfield [GB] 14 D4
Béal an Mhuirhead / Belmullet [IRL] 2 B2
Beariz [E] 78 C4
Beas [E] 94 F5
Beasain [E] 84 A3
Beas de Segura [E] 102 G1
Beateberg [S] 166 F5
Beaucaire [F] 106 G4
Beaufort [IRL] 4 B4
Beaufort-en-Vallée [F] 54 E1
Beaufort-sur-Doron [F] 70 B3
Beaugency [F] 42 D6
Beaujeu [F] 68 F1
Beaulieu-sur-Dordogne [F] 66 H4
Beaulieu-sur-Mer [F] 108 F4
Beaumaris [GB] 10 B4
Beaumes de Venise [F] 106 H3
Beaumesnil [F] 26 H4
Beaumetz [F] 28 E4
Beaumont [B] 28 H4
Beaumont [F] 26 D1
Beaumont [F] 66 F4
Beaumont-de-Lomagne [F] 84 H2
Beaumont-le-Roger [F] 26 H4
Beaumont-sur-Sarthe [F] 26 F6
Beaune [F] 56 G4
Beaune-la-Rolande [F] 42 F6
Beaupréau [F] 54 C2
Beauraing [B] 30 D6
Beauregard, Manoir de- [F] 54 H2
Beaurepaire [F] 68 G4
Beaurepaire-en-Bresse [F] 56 H5
Beauvais [F] 28 D6
Beauvallon [F] 108 D5
Beauvène [F] 68 E5
Beauvezer [F] 108 D3
Beauville [F] 66 F5
Beauvoir-sur-Mer [F] 54 B2
Beauvoir-sur-Niort [F] 54 D5
Beba Veche [RO] 76 E5
Bebenhausen [D] 58 G2
Bebra [D] 32 F6
Bebrene [LV] 198 F6
Bebrovo [BG] 148 D4
Beccles [GB] 14 H2
Becedas [E] 88 C4
Bečej [SCG] 76 E6
Becerreá [E] 78 E4
Bécherel [F] 26 C5
Bechet [RO] 146 G2
Bechhofen [D] 46 F6
Bechyně [CZ] 48 F6
Becicherecu Mic [RO] 76 G5
Becilla de Valderaduey [E] 82 B5
Beçin Kalesi [TR] 154 C1
Beciu [RO] 148 A2
Beckenried [CH] 58 F6
Beckum [D] 32 C4
Beckum [D] 32 D3
Beclean [RO] 204 C4
Bécon-Les-Granits [F] 40 G6
Bečov nad Teplou [CZ] 48 D3
Becsehely [H] 74 G4
Becske [H] 64 D5
Bédarieux [F] 106 D4
Bedburg [D] 30 G4
Beddingestrand [S] 158 C3
Bédée [F] 26 C5
Bedemler [TR] 152 C4
Bedenac [F] 66 D2
Bedenica [HR] 74 F5
Bedford [GB] 14 E3
Będgoszcz [PL] 20 F5
Będków [PL] 36 H5
Bedlington [GB] 8 G5
Bednarka [PL] 52 D5
Bédole [I] 72 B4
Bedonia [I] 110 C3
Bedous [F] 84 D4
Bedsted [DK] 160 B4
Bedworth [GB] 14 D1
Będzin [PL] 50 G3
Będzino [PL] 20 H3
Beek [NL] 30 E4
Beek en Donk [NL] 30 E2
Beek Gem Bergh [NL] 16 F6
Beelitz [D] 34 D3
Beerfelden [D] 46 D4
Beersel [B] 30 C4
Beeskow [D] 34 F3
Beesten [D] 32 C1
Befreiungshalle [D] 60 E2
Bégard [F] 26 A4
Beglezh [BG] 148 A3
Beg-Meil [F] 40 B3
Begndal [N] 170 G4
Begov Han [BIH] 142 D3
Begunitsy [RUS] 178 G6
Begur [E] 92 G3
Behramkale [TR] 134 H1
Behramlı [TR] 130 H5
Behringersmühle [D] 46 G4
Beilen [NL] 16 G3
Beilngries [D] 46 H6
Beinwil [CH] 58 E5
Beith [GB] 8 D3
Beitostølen [N] 170 F2
Beiuş [RO] 204 B4
Beja [P] 94 D3
Béjar [E] 88 B4
Bejís [E] 98 E3
Bekçiler [TR] 154 G1
Békés [H] 76 G3
Békéscsaba [H] 76 G3
Békésszentandrás [H] 76 F2
Bekilli [TR] 152 G4
Bekken [N] 172 D1
Bélâbre [F] 54 G4
Bel Air [F] 54 F5
Bel-Aire [F] 26 C6
Belalcázar [E] 96 C4
Bělá Nad Radbuzou [CZ] 48 C5
Bela Palanka [SCG] 146 E4
Bélapátfalva [H] 64 E5
Bělá pod Bezdězem [CZ] 48 G2
Belava [LV] 198 F5
Belbaşı [TR] 154 H2
Belcaire [F] 106 A5
Bełchatów [PL] 36 G5
Belchin [BG] 146 G5
Belchite [E] 90 E5
Belčišta [MK] 128 D3
Belcoo [NIR] 2 E3
Belecke [D] 32 D4
Beled [H] 74 G1
Belej [HR] 112 E3
Belence [TR] 152 H3
Belene [BG] 148 B2
Belev [RUS] 202 F4
Belevi [TR] 152 D5
Belevren [BG] 148 F5
Belfast [NIR] 2 G3
Belfir [RO] 76 H3
Belfort [F] 58 C4
Belgern [D] 34 D5
Belgirate [I] 70 F4
Belgodère [F] 114 B3
Belgooly [IRL] 4 C5
Beli [HR] 112 E2
Belianes [E] 92 C3
Belianska Jaskyňa [SK] 52 B6
Belica [HR] 74 F4
Belica [MK] 128 D2
Belica [MK] 128 E2
Beli Iskăr [BG] 146 G5
Belikij Novgorod [RUS] 202 C2
Belıkliçeşme [TR] 150 C5
Beli Manastir [HR] 76 B6
Belimel [BG] 146 F3
Belin-Béliet [F] 66 C4
Belinchón [E] 96 H1
Belinţ [RO] 76 H5
Belišće [HR] 76 B6
Belitsa [BG] 146 G6
Beljakovci [MK] 146 D6
Beljina [SCG] 142 G3
Belkavak [TR] 152 H1
Bella [I] 120 G3
Bellac [F] 54 F5
Bellaghy [NIR] 2 G3
Bellágio [I] 70 G3
Bellamonte [I] 72 D4
Bellano [I] 70 G3
Bellante [I] 116 D3
Bellapaïs (Beylerbeyi) [CY] 154 G5
Bellária [I] 110 H4
Bellcaire d'Urgell [E] 92 C3
Belleek [NIR] 2 E3
Bellegarde [F] 106 G4
Bellegarde-en-Marche [F] 68 B1
Bellegarde-sur-Valserine [F] 70 A2
Belle-Isle-en-Terre [F] 40 D2
Bellême [F] 26 G6
Bellenaves [F] 56 D6
Bellencombre [F] 28 C5
Bellengreville [F] 28 C4
Bellevesvre [F] 56 H5
Belleville [F] 68 F2
Belleville-sur-Vie [F] 54 B2
Belley [F] 68 H3
Bellinge [DK] 156 D3
Bellinzona [CH] 70 G3
Bell-Lloc d'urgell [E] 90 H4
Bello [E] 90 D5
Bellö [S] 162 E2
Bellpuig [E] 92 C3
Belluno [I] 72 E4
Bellver de Cerdanya [E] 92 E2
Bellvik [S] 190 F5
Belmez [E] 96 B5
Belmez de la Moraleda [E] 102 F2
Belmonte [E] 78 G3
Belmonte [E] 96 H3
Belmonte [P] 86 F2
Belmont-sur-Rance [F] 106 D3
Belmullet / Béal an Mhuirhead [IRL] 2 B2
Beloeil [B] 28 G3
Belogradchik [BG] 146 E3
Belokamensk [UA] 204 H4
Beloljin [SCG] 146 C4
Belo Polje [SCG] 146 B5
Belopol'ye [UA] 202 F6
Belorado [E] 82 F6
Bělotín [CZ] 50 E5
Belovec [BG] 148 D2
Belovo [BG] 148 A6
Belozem [BG] 148 B5
Belpasso [I] 126 G3
Belsen [D] 18 F6
Belsk Duży [PL] 38 B4
Beltinci [SLO] 74 F3
Belturbet [IRL] 2 E4
Beluša [SK] 64 B2
Belušić [SCG] 146 C2
Belvedere Campomoro [F] 114 A5
Belvedere du Cirque [F] 108 E2
Belvedere Marittimo [I] 124 C3
Belver [P] 86 E4
Belvis de la Jara [E] 96 D1
Belyy [RUS] 202 D3
Belz [F] 40 C4
Belz [UA] 52 H2
Bełżec [PL] 52 G2
Belzig [D] 34 D3
Bełżyce [PL] 38 D6
Bembibre [E] 78 F5
Bembirre [E] 78 C2
Bemposta [P] 80 F5
Bemposta [P] 86 D4
Benabarre [E] 90 H3
Benalmádena [E] 102 B5
Benalup [E] 100 G5
Benamaurel [E] 102 G3
Benaojón [E] 100 H4
Benasque [E] 84 F5
Benassal [E] 98 F2
Benassay [F] 54 E4
Benátky nad Jezerou [CZ] 48 G3
Benavente [E] 82 A5
Benavente [P] 86 C5
Benavila [P] 86 D5
Benavites [E] 78 G6
Bencık [TR] 154 C1
Bene [LV] 198 D6
Benedikt [SLO] 74 E3
Benediktbeuern [D] 60 D5
Benediktiner-Abtei [D] 60 F4
Beneixama / Benejama [E] 104 D1
Benejama / Beneixama [E] 104 D1
Benešov [CZ] 48 G4
Benešov [CZ] 62 C3
Benešov nad Ploučnicí [CZ] 48 F2
Benestad [S] 158 D3
Benetutti [I] 118 D4
Bénévent l'Abbaye [F] 54 G6
Benevento [I] 120 F2
Benfeld [F] 58 E2
Bengtsfors [S] 166 D4
Beničanci [HR] 76 B6
Benicarló [E] 98 H2
Benicasim / Benicàssim [E] 98 G3
Benicàssim / Benicasim [E] 98 G3
Benidorm [E] 104 E2
Beniel [E] 104 C3
Benifaió [E] 98 E5
Beniganín [E] 98 E6
Benilloba [E] 104 E1
Benimarfull [E] 104 E1
Benissa [E] 104 F2
Benkovac [HR] 112 G5
Benkovski [BG] 148 F2
Benneckenstein [D] 32 H4
Bennstedt [D] 34 B5
Bénodet [F] 40 B3
Benrath [D] 30 G4
Bensafrim [P] 94 B5
Bensberg [D] 30 H4
Bensersiel [D] 18 C3
Bensheim [D] 46 C4
Bensjö [S] 184 C3
Benzú [MAR] 100 G6
Beočin [SCG] 142 F2
Beograd [SCG] 142 G2
Bera / Vera de Bidasoa [E] 84 B2
Berane [SCG] 146 A5
Berat [AL] 128 B4
Beratón [E] 90 C3
Berbenno di Valtellina [I] 70 H3
Berberana [E] 82 G4
Bercedo [E] 82 F4
Bercel [H] 64 D5
Berceto [I] 110 D3
Berchem [L] 44 F3
Berching [D] 46 G6
Berchtesgaden [D] 60 G6
Berck-Plage [F] 28 D3
Berdalen [N] 164 D2
Berducedo [E] 78 F3
Berducido [E] 78 B4
Berdún [E] 84 C5
Berdychiv [UA] 202 C8
Berechiu [RO] 76 H3
Berehove [UA] 204 B3
Berek [H] 76 F2
Berek [HR] 74 G6
Berest [PL] 52 C5
Berestowitsa [BY] 202 A6
Berettyószentmárton [H] 76 G1
Berettyóújfalu [H] 76 G1
Berezan' [UA] 202 E7
Berezivka [UA] 204 F3
Berezna [UA] 202 D6
Berg [CH] 58 F4
Berg [D] 46 H2
Berg [D] 60 D5
Berg [N] 166 C3
Berg [N] 172 D5
Berg [N] 190 C3
Berg [S] 162 D4
Berg [S] 166 D4
Berga [D] 32 H5
Berga [E] 92 E2
Berga [S] 162 F4
Bergama [TR] 152 C2
Bergamo [I] 70 H4
Bergara [E] 82 H4
Berg bei Neamarkt [D] 46 H5
Bergby [S] 174 E3
Berge [N] 164 E1
Berge [S] 182 F1
Bergedorf [D] 18 G4
Bergeforsen [S] 184 E4
Bergen [D] 18 F6
Bergen [D] 18 H6
Bergen [D] 20 D2
Bergen [D] 44 F3
Bergen [N] 170 B4
Bergen [NL] 16 D3
Bergen (Mons) [B] 28 G4
Bergen aan Zee [NL] 16 D3
Bergen op Zoom [NL] 16 C6
Berger [N] 164 H2
Bergerac [F] 66 E4
Berget [N] 190 B6
Berget [N] 190 E2
Bergfors [S] 192 G4
Bergheim [D] 30 G4
Berghem [S] 160 H3
Bergisch Gladbach [D] 30 H4
Bergkvara [S] 162 F6
Bergland [S] 190 F4
Berglern [D] 60 E3
Berglia [N] 190 D5
Berg-Neustadt [D] 32 C5
Bergö [FIN] 186 A3
Bergåsa [S] 162 E5
Bergsäter [S] 190 F4
Bergshamra [S] 168 E2
Bergsjö [S] 184 E6
Bergsjøstøl [N] 170 F4
Berg slussar [S] 166 H5
Bergsmoen [N] 190 C5
Bergstad [FIN] 176 G5
Bergstrøm [N] 166 C3
Bergsviken [S] 196 B3
Bergues [F] 14 H6
Bergum [NL] 16 F2
Bergün [CH] 70 H2
Bergunda [S] 162 D5
Bergundhaugen [N] 172 B2
Bergvik [S] 174 E2
Berhida [H] 76 B2
Beringel [P] 94 D3
Beringen [B] 30 E3
Bérisal [CH] 70 E2
Berja [E] 102 F5
Berkåk [N] 180 H3
Berkenthin [D] 18 G4
Berkesz [H] 64 H4
Berkheim [D] 60 B4
Berkhof [D] 32 F1
Berkovići [BIH] 144 C3
Berkovitsa [BG] 146 F3
Berkvigen [S] 190 G2
Berlanga [E] 94 H4
Berlanga de Duero [E] 90 A3
Berlevåg [N] 194 E1
Berlin [D] 34 E2
Bermeo [E] 82 H3
Bermillo de Sayago [E] 80 G5
Bern [CH] 58 D6
Bernalda [I] 122 D4
Bernartice [CZ] 48 F5
Bernati [LV] 198 B6
Bernau [D] 34 E2
Bernau [D] 60 F5
Bernaville [F] 28 E4
Bernay [F] 26 G4
Bernburg [D] 34 B4
Berndorf [A] 62 E5
Berne [D] 18 D5
Bernedo [E] 82 H6
Bernek [A] 72 C1
Bernhardsthal [A] 62 G3
Bernkastel-Kues [D] 44 G2
Bernsdorf [D] 34 F5
Bernstein [A] 74 F1
Beromünster [CH] 58 F5
Beronovo [BG] 148 E4
Beroun [CZ] 48 F4
Berovo [MK] 128 H1
Berre-l'Etang [F] 106 H5
Berrien [F] 40 C2
Berriozar [E] 84 B4
Berrocal [E] 94 F5
Berroquejo [E] 100 F4
Bersenbrück [D] 32 D1
Beršići [SCG] 146 B2
Bertinoro [I] 110 G4
Bertrix [B] 44 D2
Berwang [A] 60 C6
Berwick- upon-Tweed [GB] 8 F4
Beryslav [UA] 204 G3
Berzaune [LV] 198 F5
Berzence [H] 74 G4
Besalú [E] 92 F2
Besançon [F] 58 B5
Besande [E] 82 C3
Besenyotelek [H] 64 E6
Besenyszög [H] 76 E1
Beşevler [TR] 150 G4
Beşevler [TR] 150 G3
Besigheim [D] 46 D6
Běšiny [CZ] 48 D6
Beška [SCG] 142 G2
Bessan [F] 106 E4
Bessans [F] 70 C5
Bessay-sur-Allier [F] 56 D5
Besse-en-Chandesse [F] 68 C3
Besse-sur-Issole [F] 108 C5
Bessheim [N] 170 F1
Bessines-sur-Gartempe [F] 54 G6
Bestida [P] 80 B5
Bestorp [S] 168 A6
Beszowa [PL] 52 C2
Betancuria [E] 100 E6
Betanzos [E] 78 D2
Betelu [E] 84 B3
Bétera [E] 98 E4
Beteta [E] 90 B6
Bétharram, Grottes de- [F] 84 E4
Bethesda [GB] 10 B4
Béthune [F] 28 E3
Betliar [SK] 64 E3
Betna [N] 180 F2
Betna [N] 180 F2
Betsele [S] 190 G5
Bettenburg [D] 46 F3
Bettna [S] 168 C4
Bettola [I] 110 C2
Bettyhill [GB] 6 E2
Betws-y-Coed [GB] 10 C4
Betz [F] 42 G3
Betzdorf [D] 32 C6
Beuel [D] 30 H5
Beuil [F] 108 E3
Beulich [D] 44 H1
Beuron [D] 58 G3
Beuzeville [F] 26 G3
Bevagna [I] 116 A2
Beverley [GB] 10 G4
Beverstedt [D] 18 D4
Beverungen [D] 32 F4
Beverwijk [NL] 16 D4
Bevtoft [DK] 156 C3
Bewdley [GB] 12 G1
Bex [CH] 70 C2
Beyağaç [TR] 152 F6
Beyarmudu (Pergamos) [CY] 154 G5
Beyazköy [TR] 150 C2
Beycayırı [TR] 150 B5
Beyce Sultan [TR] 152 G4
Beydağı [TR] 152 E4
Beydilli [TR] 152 H3
Beykoğ [TR] 152 H6
Beykoz [TR] 150 E2
Beylerbeyi (Bellapaïs) [CY] 154 G5
Beynac-et-Cazenac [F] 66 F4
Beynat [F] 66 H3
Beyobaşı [TR] 154 E1
Bezau [A] 60 B6
Bezdan [SCG] 76 C5
Bezděz [CZ] 48 G2
Bezdonys [LT] 200 G5
Bezhetsk [RUS] 202 E2
Béziers [F] 106 D4
Béznar [E] 102 E4
Bezzecca [I] 72 C5
B. Hornberg [D] 46 D5
Biała [PL] 50 D3
Bialaczów [PL] 38 A5
Biała Piska [PL] 24 D4
Biała Podlaska [PL] 38 F3
Biała Rawska [PL] 38 A4
Białawy Wielkie [PL] 36 C5
Białobrzegi [PL] 38 B4
Białogard [PL] 20 H3
Białowieża [PL] 38 G1
Biały Bór [PL] 22 B4
Białystok [PL] 24 E5
Biancavilla [I] 126 G3
Bianco [I] 124 D7
Biar [E] 104 D1
Biarritz [F] 84 C2
Bias [F] 66 B5
Biasca [CH] 70 G2
Biasteri / Laguardia [E] 82 G6
Biatigala [LT] 200 E4
Biatorbágy [H] 76 C1
Bibaktad [N] 194 C2
Bibbiena [I] 110 G6
Bibbiona [I] 114 E1
Biberach [D] 58 F2
Biberach an der Riss [D] 60 B4
Bibione [I] 72 G6
Bibury [GB] 12 H3
Bič [SLO] 74 C5
Bicaj [AL] 128 C1
Bicaz [RO] 204 D4
Bicester [GB] 14 D3
Bichl [D] 60 D5
Bicos [P] 94 C3
Bicske [H] 76 B1
Bidache [F] 84 C2
Bidalite [S] 162 F6
Bidart [F] 84 C2
Biddulph [GB] 10 E5
Bideford [GB] 12 D3
Bidjovagge [N] 192 H2
Bidovce [SK] 64 G3
Bidziny [PL] 52 D1
Bie [S] 168 B4
Bieber [D] 46 D3
Biebersdorf [D] 34 F4
Biecz [PL] 52 C4
Biedenkopf [D] 32 D6
Biegen [D] 34 F3
Biejkvasslia [N] 190 D2
Biel [E] 84 C5
Biel / Bienne [CH] 58 D5
Bielany Wrocł. [PL] 50 C1
Bielawa [PL] 50 C2
Bielawy [PL] 36 G3
Bielczyny [PL] 22 E5
Bielefeld [D] 32 D3
Biella [I] 70 E4
Bielmonte [I] 70 E4
Bielopolje [HR] 112 H3
Bielowy [PL] 52 D4
Bielsa [E] 84 E5
Bielsa, Tunnel de- [EUR] 84 E5
Bielsk [PL] 36 H2
Bielsko-Biała [PL] 50 G4
Bielsk Podlaski [PL] 38 F1
Bienenbüttel [D] 18 G5
Bieniów [PL] 34 H4
Bienne / Biel [CH] 58 D5
Bienvenida [E] 94 G3
Bienvenida [E] 96 D4
Bierdzany [PL] 50 E2
Bierre-Lès-Semur [F] 56 F3
Bierutów [PL] 36 D6
Biescas [E] 84 D5
Biesenthal [D] 34 E1
Biesiekierz [PL] 20 H3
Bieskkenjárga [N] 194 C4
Bietigheim [D] 46 D6
Bieżuń [PL] 22 G6
Biga [TR] 150 C5
Bigadiç [TR] 152 D2
Biggar [GB] 8 E4
Biggleswade [GB] 14 E3
Bignasco [CH] 70 F2
Bigor [SCG] 144 E4
Bihać [BIH] 112 H3
Biharia [RO] 76 H2
Biharkeresztes [H] 76 H2
Biharnagybajom [H] 76 G1
Bijambarska Pećina [BIH] 142 D4
Bijeljani [BIH] 144 D3
Bijeljina [BIH] 142 E3
Bijelo Brdo [HR] 142 E1
Bijelo Polje [SCG] 146 A4
Bikava [LV] 198 G5
Bikovo [SCG] 76 D5
Bílá [CZ] 50 F5
Bila Tserkva [UA] 202 D8
Bilbao / Bilbo [E] 82 G4
Bilbo / Bilbao [E] 82 G4
Bileća [BIH] 144 D3
Bilecik [TR] 150 G4
Biled [RO] 76 G5
Bílenec [CZ] 48 E3
Biłgoraj [PL] 52 F2
Bilhorod Dnistrovs'kyi [UA] 204 F4
Bílina [CZ] 48 E2
Bilisht [AL] 128 D5
Biljanovac [SCG] 146 B3
Bilje [HR] 76 C6
Bilka [BG] 148 F3
Billdal [S] 160 G2
Billerbeck [D] 16 H6
Billericay [GB] 14 F4
Billesholm [S] 156 H1
Billingen [N] 180 E5
Billingsfors [S] 166 D4
Billom [F] 68 D2
Billsta [S] 184 G2
Billum [DK] 156 A2
Billund [DK] 156 C2
Bilopillia [UA] 202 E7
Bilousivka [UA] 202 E7
Bílovec [CZ] 50 E4
Bilska [LV] 198 F4
Bilsko [PL] 52 B4
Bilto [N] 192 H2
Biňa [SK] 64 B5
Binas [F] 42 D6
Binasco [I] 70 G5
Binche [B] 28 H4
Bindslev [DK] 160 E2
Binéfar [E] 90 G4
Bingen [D] 46 B3
Bingen [N] 170 G6
Binghöhle [D] 46 G4
Bingsjö [S] 174 C3
Bingsta [S] 182 G3
Binibeca Vell [E] 104 H5
Binic [F] 26 B4
Binkos [BG] 148 D4
Bin Tepeler [TR] 152 E3
Binz [D] 20 D2
Binzen [D] 58 E4
Bioče [SCG] 144 E4
Biograd [HR] 112 G5
Bionaz [I] 70 D3
Bioska [SCG] 144 F1
Bircza [PL] 52 E4
Birgi [TR] 152 E4
Birgittelyst [DK] 160 D5
Biri [N] 172 B3
Birini [EST] 198 E2
Birini [LV] 198 E4
Biristrand [N] 172 B3
Birkala / Pirkkala [FIN] 176 F1
Birkeland [N] 164 C5
Birkeland [N] 164 E5
Birkenfeld [D] 44 G3
Birkenfeld [D] 46 E4
Birkenhead [GB] 10 D4
Birkenwerder [D] 34 E2
Birkerød [DK] 156 G2
Birkfeld [A] 74 E1
Birksdal [N] 180 D6
Birmingham [GB] 10 E6
Birnau [D] 58 H4
Biron, Château de- [F] 66 F4
Birr [IRL] 2 D6
Birstein [D] 46 D2
Birštonas [LT] 24 F1
Biržai [LT] 198 E6
Birżebbuga [M] 126 C6
Birži [LV] 198 F6
Birzuli [LV] 198 F4
Bisaccia [I] 120 G3
Bisacquino [I] 126 C3
Bisbal d'Empordà, la- [E] 92 G3
Biscarrosse [F] 66 B4
Biscarrosse-Plage [F] 66 B4
Bisceglie [I] 122 D2
Bischoffen [D] 46 C1
Bischofsgrün [D] 46 H3
Bischofsheim [D] 46 E2
Bischofshofen [A] 72 G1
Bischofswerda [D] 34 F6
Biscoitos [P] 100 D3
Biserci [BG] 148 D1
Bishop Auckland [GB] 10 F2
Bishop's Castle [GB] 10 C6
Bishop's Cleeve [GB] 12 G2
Bishop's Stortford [GB] 14 F3
Bisignano [I] 124 D4
Bisko [HR] 144 A2
Biskupice Oławskie [PL] 50 D1
Biskupice Radłowskie [PL] 52 C3
Biskupiec [PL] 22 F5
Biskupiec [PL] 22 H4
Biskupin [PL] 36 D1
Bisław [PL] 22 D5
Bislev [DK] 160 D4
Bismark [D] 34 B1
Bismo [N] 180 F5
Bispingen [D] 18 F5
Bistreţ [RO] 146 F2
Bistrica [SCG] 144 E3
Bistrica [SCG] 146 A3
Bistriţa [RO] 204 C4
Bistritsa [BG] 146 F5
Bisztynek [PL] 22 H3
Bitburg [D] 44 F2
Bitche [F] 44 G4
Bitetto [I] 122 D3
Bithia [I] 118 C8
Bitola [MK] 128 E3
Bitonto [I] 122 D2
Bítov [CZ] 62 E2
Bitterfeld [D] 34 C4
Bitterstad [N] 192 D4
Bitti [I] 118 D4
Bivio [CH] 70 H2
Bivona [I] 126 D3
Bıyıklı [TR] 152 D5
Bizovac [HR] 76 B6
Bjåen [N] 164 D1
Bjala Cherkva [BG] 148 C3
Bjalizvor [BG] 148 C5
Bjår [N] 164 F1
Bjarisino [BY] 202 C5
Bjärklunda [S] 166 E6
Bjärnå / Perniö [FIN] 176 F5
Bjärnum [S] 158 D1
Bjärred [S] 156 H2
Bjärträ [S] 184 F3
Bjästa [S] 184 G2
Bjelland [N] 164 D5
Bjelovar [HR] 74 G5
Bjerga [N] 164 C1
Bjergby [DK] 160 C5
Bjerkreim [N] 164 B4
Bjerkvik [N] 192 E4
Bjerre [DK] 156 D2
Bjerregård [DK] 156 A1
Bjerringbro [DK] 160 D5
Bjoenstrand [N] 164 B1
Bjølstad [N] 180 G6
Bjoneroa [N] 170 H4
Bjørånes [N] 172 C1
Björbo [S] 172 G5
Bjordal [N] 164 C4
Bjordal [N] 170 B2
Bjørgo [N] 170 G3
Björka [S] 172 G3
Bjørkåsen [N] 192 F3
Björkattnet [S] 190 D5
Björkberg [S] 172 H1
Björkberg [S] 190 G4
Bjørke [N] 180 D4
Bjørkedal [N] 180 C4
Björkefors [S] 162 F1
Bjørkelangen [N] 166 C1
Bjørkflåta [N] 170 F4
Björkfors [S] 190 E3
Björkhöjden [S] 184 D2
Björkliden [S] 192 F4
Björklinge [S] 168 D1
Bjørknes [N] 172 C6
Björkö [FIN] 176 C5
Björkö [S] 162 E3
Björkö [S] 168 F1
Björköby [FIN] 186 A2
Björksele [S] 190 G4

Breitenbrunn [D] 60 C4
Breitengussbach Hallstadt [D] 46 G4
Breitenhees [D] 18 G6
Breivik [N] 194 A2
Breivikbotn [N] 194 A2
Breivikeidet [N] 192 G2
Brekke [N] 170 B2
Brekken [N] 182 D3
Brekkhus [N] 170 C3
Brekkvassely [N] 190 D4
Brekovica [BIH] 112 H3
Brekstad [N] 190 B6
Bremen [D] 18 D5
Bremerhaven [D] 18 D4
Bremervörde [D] 18 E4
Bremnes [N] 192 D3
Bremsnes [N] 180 E2
Breń [PL] 20 H6
Brenes [E] 94 H6
Brenna [N] 182 D5
Brenna [N] 190 D3
Brenner Pass [EUR] 72 D2
Brennfjell [N] 192 G2
Brennsvik [N] 194 B2
Breno [I] 72 B5
Brénod [F] 68 H2
Brentwood [GB] 14 F4
Brenzone [I] 72 C5
Brescello [I] 110 E2
Bréscia [I] 72 B6
Breskens [NL] 28 G1
Bresles [F] 28 D6
Breslovec [BG] 148 B3
Bresnica [SCG] 146 B2
Bressanone / Brixen [I] 72 D3
Bressuire [F] 54 D3
Brest [BG] 148 A2
Brest [BY] 38 F3
Brest [F] 40 B2
Brestova [HR] 112 E2
Brestovac [HR] 142 C1
Brestovac [SCG] 146 D4
Brestovac [SCG] 146 D2
Brestovačka Banja [SCG] 146 D2
Brestovăț [RO] 76 H5
Brestovik [SCG] 142 H3
Breteau [F] 56 D2
Bretenoux [F] 66 H4
Bretesche, Château de la- [F] 40 E5
Breteuil [F] 26 H5
Breteuil [F] 28 D5
Bretten [D] 46 C6
Breuberg [D] 46 D4
Breuil-Cervínia [I] 70 D3
Breukelen Ut [NL] 16 D5
Breuna [D] 32 E4
Brevens Bruk [S] 166 H4
Brevik [N] 164 G3
Brevik [S] 166 G5
Brevik [S] 168 E3
Breza [BIH] 142 D4
Breza [SK] 50 G5
Brežice [SLO] 74 D5
Brežiški Grad [SLO] 74 D5
Breznica [BG] 130 C1
Breznica [HR] 74 F5
Breznica Đak. [HR] 142 D1
Březnice [CZ] 48 E5
Breznik [BG] 146 F5
Brezno [SK] 64 D3
Brézolles [F] 26 H5
Brezová [SK] 62 H3
Brezovica [SCG] 146 C6
Brezovica [SK] 52 C6
Brezovica [SLO] 74 B5
Brezovo [BG] 148 B5
Brezovo Polje [BIH] 142 E2
Brezovo Polje [HR] 142 A2
Briançon [F] 70 B6
Briare [F] 56 D2
Briatico [I] 124 C6
Bribirske Mostine [HR] 112 H5
Briceni [MD] 204 D2
Bricquebec [F] 26 D2
Bridgend [GB] 12 E3
Bridgnorth [GB] 10 D6
Bridgwater [GB] 12 F4
Bridlington [GB] 10 G3
Bridport [GB] 12 F5
Brie-Comte-Robert [F] 42 G4
Brielle [NL] 16 C5
Brienne-le-Château [F] 44 B5
Brienz [CH] 70 E1
Brienza [I] 120 G4
Brieskow-Finkenheerd [D] 34 G3
Brieves [E] 78 G3
Briey [F] 44 E3
Brig [CH] 70 E2
Brigg [GB] 10 G4
Brighouse [GB] 10 E4
Brighton [GB] 14 E5
Brignogan-Plage [F] 40 B1
Brignoles [F] 108 C5
Brignoud [F] 68 H4
Brihuega [E] 88 H5
Brijesta [HR] 144 B3
Brilon [D] 32 D4
Brimnes [N] 170 D4
Brinches [P] 94 E3
Bríndisi [I] 122 G4
Brinje [HR] 112 F2
Brinkum [D] 18 D5
Brinon [F] 56 E3
Brintbodarna [S] 172 F4
Briones [E] 82 G6
Brione Verzasca [CH] 70 F2
Brionne [F] 26 H4
Brioude [F] 68 D3
Brioux-sur-Boutonne [F] 54 D5
Briouze [F] 26 F5
Brisighella [I] 110 G4
Brissac-Quincé [F] 54 D1
Brissago [CH] 70 F3
Bristol [GB] 12 G3
Brive-la-Gaillarde [F] 66 G3
Briviesca [E] 82 F5
Brixen / Bressanone [I] 72 D3
Brixham [GB] 12 E5
Brixlegg [A] 60 E6
Brnaze [HR] 144 A1
Brněnec [CZ] 50 C5
Brno [CZ] 50 C6
Bro [S] 168 D2
Bro [S] 168 G4
Broadford [IRL] 2 C6
Broadstairs [GB] 14 G5
Broager [DK] 156 C4
Broby [S] 158 D1
Broby [S] 168 B4
Broćanac [HR] 112 G2
Broceni [LV] 198 C5
Brock [D] 32 C2
Bröckel [D] 32 G2
Brockenhurst [GB] 12 G5
Brockhöfe [D] 18 F6
Brod [BIH] 144 D2
Brod [SCG] 128 D1
Brodarevo [SCG] 146 A4
Brodarica [HR] 112 H6
Broddbo [S] 168 B1
Broddebo [S] 162 F1
Brode [SLO] 74 B5
Brodenbach [D] 44 H1
Broderup [DK] 156 B4
Brodestorf [D] 20 B3
Brodica [SCG] 146 D1
Brodick [GB] 8 C3
Brod na Kupi [HR] 112 F1
Brodnica [PL] 22 F5
Brody [PL] 34 G4
Brody [PL] 34 H3
Brody [PL] 38 C6
Broglie [F] 26 G4
Brohl [D] 30 H6
Brojce [PL] 20 G3
Brok [PL] 38 C1
Brokind [S] 168 A6
Brolo [I] 124 B6
Bromarv [FIN] 176 E6
Brome [D] 32 H2
Bromma [N] 170 G4
Brommat [F] 68 B5
Bromölla [S] 158 E1
Brömsebro [S] 158 G1
Bromsgrove [GB] 12 H1
Bron [F] 68 G3
Brønderslev [DK] 160 E3
Broni [I] 70 G6
Bronice [PL] 34 G4
Bronikowo [PL] 20 H5
Bronken [N] 172 C4
Bronnbach [D] 46 E4
Brønnøysund [N] 190 C3
Brøns [DK] 156 B3
Bronte [I] 126 F3
Broons [F] 26 B5
Brørup [DK] 156 B2
Brösarp [S] 158 D2
Brossac [F] 66 E2
Brossasco [I] 108 F2
Brøstrud [N] 170 F4
Brötjemark [S] 162 D1
Broto [E] 84 E5
Brottby [S] 168 E2
Brøttem [N] 182 B2
Brotterode [D] 46 F1
Brøttum [N] 172 B3
Brou [F] 42 D5
Brouage [F] 54 C5
Brough [GB] 10 E2
Broughshane [NIR] 2 G3
Broughton in Furness [GB] 10 D2
Brouis, Col de- [F] 108 F4
Broumov [CZ] 50 B2
Brouvelieures [F] 58 C2
Brouwershaven [NL] 16 B5
Brovary [UA] 202 D7
Brovst [DK] 160 D3
Brownhills [GB] 10 E6
Brozas [E] 86 G4
Brseč [HR] 112 E2
Brtnice [CZ] 50 A6
Brua [N] 182 C5
Bruchhausen-Vilsen [D] 18 E6
Bruchhauser Steine [D] 32 D5
Bruchsal [D] 46 C5
Bruck [A] 72 F2
Brück [D] 34 D3
Bruck [D] 48 C6
Bruck an der Grossglocknerstrasse [A] 72 G1
Bruck an der Leitha [A] 62 G5
Bruck an der Mur [A] 74 D1
Brückl [A] 74 C3
Brudzeń Duży [PL] 36 G2
Brudzewoo [PL] 36 A3
Brüel [D] 20 A4
Bruère-Allichamps [F] 56 C4
Bruff [IRL] 4 D4
Bruflat [N] 170 G3
Brugg [CH] 58 F4
Brugge [B] 28 G1
Brugnato [I] 110 C4
Bruhagen [N] 180 E2
Brühl [D] 30 G4
Brújula, Puerto de- [E] 82 F6
Bruksvallarna [S] 182 E3
Brûlon [F] 42 A5
Brumath [F] 44 H5
Brummen [NL] 16 F5
Brumov Bylnice [CZ] 64 A2
Brumunddal [N] 172 B3
Brunau [D] 34 B1
Brune [N] 180 D4
Bruneck / Brunico [I] 72 E2
Brunehamel [F] 28 H5
Brunete [E] 88 F5
Brunflo [S] 182 H2
Brunheda [P] 80 E4
Brunico / Bruneck [I] 72 E2
Bruniquel [F] 66 G6
Brunkeberg [N] 164 E2
Brunlund [DK] 156 C4
Brunna [S] 168 D1
Brunnby [S] 160 H6
Brunnen [CH] 58 F6
Brunnsberg [S] 172 F2
Brunsbüttel [D] 18 E3
Brunskog [S] 166 E2
Brunssum [NL] 30 F4
Bruntál [CZ] 50 D4
Bruravik [N] 170 D4
Brus [SCG] 146 C3
Brusand [N] 164 A4
Brušane [HR] 112 G4
Brusarci [BG] 146 F2
Brusasco [I] 70 E5
Brúsio [CH] 72 B4
Bruška [HR] 112 H5
Brusnichnoye [RUS] 178 E2
Brusník [SK] 64 D4
Brussel / Bruxelles [B] 30 C4
Brüssow [D] 20 E5
Brusy [PL] 22 C4
Bruvno [HR] 112 H4
Bruvoll [N] 172 C4
Bruxelles / Brussel [B] 30 C4
Bruyères [F] 58 C2
Bruzaholm [S] 162 E2
Bruzzano Zeffirio [I] 124 D8
Brvenik [SCG] 146 B3
Brwinów [PL] 38 B3
Bryansk [RUS] 202 E5
Brydal [N] 182 C5
Bryggja [N] 180 B5
Bryne [N] 164 A3
Bryrup [DK] 156 C1
Brza Palanka [SCG] 146 E1
Brzeće [SCG] 146 C4
Brzeg [PL] 50 D1
Brzeg Dolny [PL] 36 C6
Brześć Kujawski [PL] 36 F2
Brzesko [PL] 52 B4
Brzeszcze [PL] 50 G4
Brzezie [PL] 22 B4
Brzezie [PL] 36 E4
Brzeziny [PL] 36 E5
Brzeziny [PL] 36 H4
Brzeźnica [PL] 50 H4
Brzeźnica [PL] 52 D3
Brzeżno [PL] 36 D3
Brzostek [PL] 52 D4
Brzoza [PL] 22 D6
Brzóza [PL] 38 C4
Brzozie Lubawskie [PL] 22 F5
Brzozów [PL] 52 E4
Bua [S] 160 H3
Buavåg [N] 164 A1
Buberget [S] 190 H5
Bubiai [LT] 200 E4
Bubry [F] 40 D3
Buca [TR] 152 C4
Buçaco [P] 80 B6
Bučany [SK] 62 H4
Buccheri [I] 126 F4
Bucchianico [I] 116 D4
Buchach [UA] 204 C2
Büchen [D] 18 G4
Buchen [D] 46 D4
Buchenwald [D] 34 A6
Buchholz [D] 18 F5
Buchin Prohod [BG] 146 F4
Buchloe [D] 60 C4
Buchlov [CZ] 62 G2
Buchs [CH] 58 H6
Buchy [F] 28 C5
Bučin [MK] 128 E3
Bùcine [I] 110 F6
Bučište [MK] 128 F1
Bučje [SCG] 144 E2
Bučje [SCG] 146 D2
Bückeburg [D] 32 E2
Bücken [D] 18 E6
Buckfastleigh [GB] 12 E5
Buckie [GB] 6 F5
Buckingham [GB] 14 D3
Buckow [D] 34 F2
Bückwitz [D] 34 D1
Bučovice [CZ] 50 C6
Bucquoy [F] 28 E4
Bucsa [H] 76 F1
Bucureşti [RO] 204 D5
Buczek [PL] 36 G5
Buczyna [PL] 52 F3
Bud [N] 180 E2
Budakeszi [H] 64 C6
Budakovo [MK] 128 E3
Budal [N] 182 B3
Budal [N] 182 B3
Budaörs [H] 64 C6
Budapest [H] 64 C6
Búðardalur [IS] 192 A2
Buddusò [I] 118 D3
Bude [GB] 12 D4
Budeč [CZ] 62 D2
Budeşti [RO] 204 E5
Budilovo [RUS] 198 G2
Budimci [HR] 142 D1
Budimić Japra [BIH] 142 A2
Budimir [HR] 144 A2
Büdingen [D] 46 D2
Budišov nad Budišovkou [CZ] 50 D4
Budjevo [SCG] 146 A4
Budmirici [MK] 128 F3
Budogoshch [RUS] 202 C1
Budomierz [PL] 52 G3
Budoni [I] 118 E3
Budowo [PL] 22 C2
Budoželja [SCG] 146 B3
Budrio [I] 110 F3
Budrovci [HR] 142 D1
Budry [PL] 24 C2
Budva [SCG] 144 D4
Budyně nad Ohří [CZ] 48 F3
Budziszewice [PL] 36 H4
Budzyń [PL] 36 C1
Bue [N] 164 B4
Bue Marino, Grotta del- [I] 118 E4
Bueña [E] 90 D6
Buen Amor, Castillo- [E] 80 H6
Buenavista del Norte [E] 100 B5
Buendia [E] 88 H6
Bufón De Arenillas [E] 82 D2
Buğdayli [TR] 150 D5
Bugeat [F] 66 H2
Buggerru [I] 118 B6
Bugojno [BIH] 142 C4
Bugøyfjord [N] 194 E3
Bugøynes [N] 194 E2
Buguchwałów [PL] 50 E3
Bugyi [H] 76 C2
Bühl [D] 58 F1
Buhuşi [RO] 204 D4
Builth Wells [GB] 12 F1
Buis-les-Baronnies [F] 108 B2
Buitenpost [NL] 16 F2
Buitrago [E] 88 G4
Buj [H] 64 G4
Bujalance [E] 102 D1
Bujanovac [SCG] 146 D5
Bujaraloz [E] 90 F4
Buje [HR] 112 D1
Bujoru [RO] 148 C2
Buk [PL] 20 E5
Buk [PL] 36 C3
Bükkösd [H] 76 A5
Bukonys [LT] 200 F5
Bukovi [SCG] 146 A2
Bukovice [CZ] 50 C4
Bukovo, Manastir- [SCG] 146 E1
Bukowiec [PL] 36 B3
Bukowina Tatrzańska [PL] 52 B6
Bukowo Morskie [PL] 22 A2
Bukowsko [PL] 52 E5
Buksnes [N] 192 E3
Bukta [N] 190 B6
Buktamo [N] 192 F3
Bülach [CH] 58 F4
Buldan [TR] 152 F4
Bülgarene [BG] 148 B3
Bülgarene [BG] 148 B4
Bülgarene [BG] 148 G2
Bülgarovo [BG] 148 F4
Bülgarska Polyana [BG] 150 A1
Bülgarski Izvor [BG] 148 A4
Bulinac [HR] 74 G6
Bulinovac [SCG] 146 D3
Bulken [N] 170 C3
Bulkowo Wieś [PL] 36 H2
Bullarby [S] 166 C4
Bullas [E] 104 B2
Bulle [CH] 70 C1
Bullendorf [A] 62 F3
Bullmark [S] 196 A5
Bulqizë [AL] 128 C2
Bultei [I] 118 D4
Buna [BIH] 144 C2
Bunclody [IRL] 4 F4
Buncrana [IRL] 2 F2
Bunde [D] 16 H2
Bünde [D] 32 E2
Bundoran [IRL] 2 D3
Bunessan [GB] 8 B1
Bungay [GB] 14 G2
Bunge [S] 168 G3
Bunić [HR] 112 G3
Bunkris [S] 172 F2
Bunleix [F] 68 B2
Bunmahon [IRL] 4 E5
Bunnahowen [IRL] 2 B3
Bunnyconnellan [IRL] 2 C3
Buñol [E] 98 E4
Bunratty [IRL] 2 C6
Bunratty Castle [IRL] 2 C6
Buonalbergo [I] 120 F2
Buonconvento [I] 114 G2
Buonfornello [I] 126 D2
Buonvicino [I] 124 C3
Buoux, Fort de- [F] 108 B3
Bur [DK] 160 B5
Burano [I] 72 F6
Burbach [D] 32 C6
Burcei [I] 118 D7
Bureå [S] 190 G3
Bureå [S] 196 A4
Burela [E] 78 E2
Büren [CH] 58 D5
Büren [D] 32 D4
Burfjord [N] 192 H1
Burford [GB] 12 H3
Burg [D] 18 E3
Burg [D] 18 H2
Burg [D] 34 C3
Burgas [BG] 148 F4
Burgau [A] 74 E2
Burgau [D] 60 C3
Burgau [P] 94 B5
Burgbernheim [D] 46 F5
Burgdorf [CH] 58 E5
Burgdorf [D] 32 G2
Burgebrach [D] 46 F4
Bürgel [D] 34 B6
Burgeln [D] 58 E4
Burgelu / Elburgo [E] 102 B4
Burghaun [D] 46 E1
Burghausen [D] 60 G4
Burg Hessenstein [D] 32 E5
Burgh-Haamstede [NL] 16 B5
Búrgio [I] 126 C3
Burgistein [CH] 58 D6
Burgjoss [D] 46 E3
Burg Klam [A] 62 C4
Burgkunstadt [D] 46 G3
Burglengenfeld [D] 48 B6
Burg Metternich [D] 44 G1
Burgos [E] 82 E6
Burgsinn [D] 46 E3
Burg Stargard [D] 20 D5
Burgsvik [S] 168 G6
Burguete / Auritz [E] 84 C3
Burguillos [E] 94 G5
Burguillos del Cerro [E] 94 G3
Burhan [TR] 150 F5
Burhaniye [TR] 152 C2
Burharkent [TR] 152 F5
Burie [F] 54 D6
Burila Mare [RO] 146 E1
Burjassot [E] 98 E4
Burlada [E] 84 B4
Burladingen [D] 58 G2
Burnham-on-Crouch [GB] 14 F4
Burnham-on-Sea [GB] 12 F3
Burnley [GB] 10 E3
Burón [E] 82 C3
Buron, Château de- [F] 68 D3
Buronzo [I] 70 E4
Burravoe [GB] 6 H3
Burrel [AL] 128 B2
Burriana / Borriana [E] 98 F3
Burs [S] 168 G5
Burs [S] 168 G4
Bursa [TR] 150 F4
Burseryd [S] 162 B3
Bürstadt [D] 46 C4
Burtenbach [D] 60 C3
Burton upon Trent [GB] 10 E6
Burträsk [S] 196 A5
Burvik [S] 196 B5
Burwell [GB] 14 F2
Bury [GB] 10 E4
Buryn' [UA] 202 E6
Bury St Edmunds [GB] 14 F3
Burzenin [PL] 36 F5
Burziya [BG] 146 F3
Busalla [I] 110 B3
Busana [I] 110 D4
Busca [I] 108 F2
Busdorf [D] 18 F1
Buseto Palizzolo [I] 126 B2
Buševec [HR] 74 E6
Bushat [AL] 128 A1
Bushmills [NIR] 2 G2
Bushtricë [AL] 128 C1
Bus'k [UA] 202 B8
Busko-Zdrój [PL] 52 B2
Bušno [PL] 38 G6
Busot [E] 104 E2
Busovača [BIH] 142 D4
Bussang [F] 58 D3
Bussang, Col de- [F] 58 D3
Busseto [I] 110 D2
Bussolengo [I] 72 C6
Bussoleno [I] 70 C5
Bussum [NL] 16 E4
Bustnes [N] 190 E2
Busto Arsízio [I] 70 F4
Busto Garolfo [I] 70 F4
Büsum [D] 18 E2
Butan [BG] 146 G3
Butenky [UA] 202 F7
Butera [I] 126 E4
Bütgenbach [B] 30 F5
Buthrotum [AL] 132 B2
Butler's Bridge [IRL] 2 E4
Butrint [AL] 132 B2
Butryny [PL] 22 H4
Butsyn [UA] 38 H5
Buttapietra [I] 110 F1
Buttelstedt [D] 34 A6
Buttevant [IRL] 4 C4
Buttingsrud [N] 170 H4
Buttlar [D] 46 E1
Buttle [S] 168 G5
Buttstädt [D] 34 B6
Butzbach [D] 46 C2
Bützow [D] 20 B3
Buvarp [N] 190 C5
Buvik [N] 182 B1
Buvika [N] 182 D5
Buxtehude [D] 18 F4
Buxton [GB] 10 E5
Buxu, Cueva del- [E] 82 C2
Buxy [F] 56 F5
Büyükada [TR] 150 F3
Büyükaturak [TR] 152 H2
Büyükbelen [TR] 152 D3
Büyükçekmece [TR] 150 E3
Büyükkaraağaç [TR] 154 E2
Büyükkarıştıran [TR] 150 C2
Büyükkonak [TR] 152 G6
Büyükkonuk (Komi Kebir) [CY] 154 G4
Büyükorhan [TR] 150 F5
Büyüksöğle [TR] 154 H2
Büyükyenice [TR] 152 C2
Buzançais [F] 54 G3
Buzancy [F] 44 D3
Buzău [RO] 204 E5
Buzescu [RO] 148 B1
Buzet [HR] 112 D1
Buziaş [RO] 76 H6
Buzyakovtsi [BG] 146 G5
By [S] 166 E1
By [S] 174 D5
Byahoml' [BY] 202 B4
Byala [BG] 148 C2
Byala [BG] 148 F3
Byala Slatina [BG] 146 G3
Byal Izvor [BG] 130 E1
Byalynichy [BY] 202 C5
Byaroza [BY] 202 A6
Byarozawka [BY] 202 A5
Byarum [S] 162 D2
Byberget [S] 182 H4
Bybjerg [DK] 156 F2
Bychawa [PL] 38 E6
Byczki [PL] 36 H4
Byczyna [PL] 36 E6
Bydgoszcz [PL] 22 D6
Bye [S] 184 F4
Byenyakoni [BY] 200 G6
Byershty [BY] 24 G3
Bygdeå [S] 196 A5
Bygdeträsk [S] 196 A5
Bygdin [N] 170 F2
Bygdsiljum [S] 196 A5
Bygland [N] 164 D4
Byglandsfjord [N] 164 D4
Bygstad [N] 170 B1
Bykle [N] 164 D2
Byllis [AL] 128 B5
Byrkjedal [N] 164 B3
Byrkjelo [N] 180 D5
Byrknes [N] 170 A2
Byrness [GB] 8 F5
Byrum [DK] 160 F3
Byrum [S] 162 H3
Byšice [CZ] 48 G3
Byske [S] 196 A4
Bystré [CZ] 50 B5
Bystrianska Jaskyňa [SK] 64 D2
Bystřice [CZ] 48 G4
Bystřice nad Pernštejnem [CZ] 50 B5
Bystřice pod Hostýnem [CZ] 50 D6
Bystřička [CZ] 50 E5
Bystrzyca Kłodzka [PL] 50 C3
Byszki [PL] 22 B5
Byszyno [PL] 20 H4
Bytča [SK] 50 F6
Bytom [PL] 50 F3
Bytom Odrzański [PL] 36 A4
Bytonia [PL] 22 D4
Bytów [PL] 22 C3
Byvattnet [S] 184 F1
Byxelkrok [S] 162 H3
Bzenec [CZ] 62 G2
Bzovík [SK] 64 C4

C

Cabação [P] 86 D5
Cabaj-Čápor [SK] 64 A4
Cabañaquinta [E] 78 H4
Cabañas [E] 78 D2
Cabanes [E] 98 G3
Čabar [HR] 74 C6
Cabeço de Vide [P] 86 E5
Cabertarar [TR] 152 F4
Cabeza del Buey [E] 96 C4
Cabezamesada [E] 96 G2
Cabezarados [E] 96 E4
Cabezas Rubias [E] 94 E4
Cabezo de Torres [E] 104 C3
Cabezón de la Sal [E] 82 E3
Cabezuela del Valle [E] 88 B5
Cabo de Gata [E] 102 G6
Cabo de Palos [E] 104 D4
Cabourg [F] 26 F3
Cabra [E] 102 C2
Cabra del Santo Cristo [E] 102 F2
Cabranes [E] 82 C2
Cábras [I] 118 B5
Cabreiros [E] 78 D2
Cabrela [P] 86 C6
Cabrera [E] 104 E6
Cabrerets [F] 66 G5
Cabrillas [E] 88 B3
Cacabelos [E] 78 F5
Čačak [SCG] 146 B2
Cáccamo [I] 126 D2
Cacemes [P] 86 A5
Cáceres [E] 86 H5
Cachopo [P] 94 D5
Čachtice [SK] 62 H3
Čačini [HR] 76 A6
Cadaqués [E] 92 G2
Cadaval [P] 86 B4
Cadavedo [E] 78 G2
Čađavica [BIH] 142 B3
Čađavica [HR] 76 A6
Čadca [SK] 50 F5
Cadelbosco di Sopra [I] 110 E2
Cadenábbia [I] 70 G3
Cadenberge [D] 18 E3
Cadenet [F] 106 H4
Cadeuil [F] 54 C6
Cádiar [E] 102 E5
Cadillac [F] 66 D4
Cadipietra [I] 72 E2
Cádiz [E] 100 F4
Cadrete [E] 90 E4
Caen [F] 26 F3
Caernarfon [GB] 10 B4
Caerphilly [GB] 12 F3
Čafasan [MK] 128 C3
Çağış [TR] 152 D1
Cagli [I] 112 B6
Cágliari [I] 118 C7
Çağman [TR] 154 H3
Cagnano Varano [I] 116 G6
Cagnes-sur-Mer [F] 108 E4
Caherciveen [IRL] 4 A4
Caherdaniel [IRL] 4 A4
Cahermurphy [IRL] 2 B6
Cahir [IRL] 4 D4
Cahors [F] 66 G5
Cahul [MD] 204 E4
Caiazzo [I] 120 E2
Cairnryan [GB] 8 C5
Cairo Montenotte [I] 108 G3
Cais do Pico [P] 100 C3
Caister-on-Sea [GB] 14 H2
Caivano [I] 120 E3
Cajarc [F] 66 G5
Čajetina [SCG] 146 A3
Čajniče [BIH] 144 E2
Čakajovce [SK] 64 A4
Çakılı [TR] 150 C2
Çakır [TR] 150 C5
Çakırbeyli [TR] 152 E5
Çakmak [TR] 154 E1
Čakovec [HR] 74 F4
Çal [TR] 152 G4
Cal [TR] 152 H2
Cala [E] 94 G4
Cala Blanca [E] 104 G4
Cala Blava [E] 104 E5
Calabor [E] 80 F3
Calabritto [I] 120 F3
Calaceite [E] 90 G6
Calacuccia [F] 114 B3
Cala del Moral, La- [E] 102 B5
Cala d'Oliva [I] 118 B2
Cala d'Or [E] 104 F6
Calaf [E] 92 D3
Calafat [RO] 146 F2
Calafell [E] 92 D5
Cala Galdana [E] 104 G4
Cala Gonone [I] 118 E4
Calahonda [E] 102 B5
Calahonda-Chaparral [E] 102 E5
Calahorra [E] 84 A5
Calais [F] 14 G6
Cala Liberotto [I] 118 E4
Cala Millor [E] 104 F5
Calamocha [E] 90 D5
Calamonte [E] 94 H2
Cala Moreia-Cala Morlanda [E] 104 F5
Cala Morell [E] 104 G4
Calañas [E] 94 F5
Calanda [E] 90 F6
Calangiánus [I] 118 D3
Cala'n Porter [E] 104 H5
Cala Pi [E] 104 E5
Călăraşi [MD] 204 E3
Călăraşi [RO] 204 E5
Cala Ratjada [E] 104 F5
cala Sa Calobra [E] 104 E4
Cala Santanyí [E] 104 E6
Calascibetta [I] 126 E3
Calasetta [I] 118 B7
Calasparra [E] 104 B2
Calatafimi [I] 126 B2
Calatañazor [E] 90 B3
Cala Tarida [E] 104 B5
Calatayud [E] 90 D4
Calatorao [E] 90 D4
Calatrava, Convento de- [E] 96 E5
Calatrava la Vieja [E] 96 F4
Calau [D] 34 F4
Cala Vadella [E] 104 B5
Calbe [D] 34 B4
Caldarola [I] 116 C2
Caldas da Rainha [P] 86 B3
Caldas de Reis [E] 78 B3
Caldas de Vizela [P] 80 C3
Caldelas [P] 78 B6
Caldes de Boí [E] 84 F6
Caldes de Malavella [E] 92 F3
Caldes de Montbui [E] 92 E4
Caldes d'Estrac [E] 92 F4
Caldirola [I] 110 B2
Calella [E] 92 F4
Calella de Palafrugell [E] 92 G3
Calenzana [F] 114 B3
Calera y Chozas [E] 88 C6
Caleruega [E] 88 H2
Cales de Mallorca [E] 104 F5
Calheta [P] 100 A3
Calheta [P] 100 C3
Çali [TR] 150 F5
Càlig [E] 92 A6
Calignac [F] 66 E5
Çalıklı [TR] 152 F3
Călimăneşti [RO] 204 C5
Calimera [I] 122 G5
Calitri [I] 120 G3
Callac [F] 40 D2
Callan [IRL] 4 E4
Callander [GB] 8 D2
Callington [GB] 12 D4
Callosa d'en Sarrià [E] 104 E2
Callosa de Segura [E] 104 D3
Călmăţuiu [RO] 148 B2
Calne [GB] 12 G3
Calnegre, Puntas de- [E] 104 B4
Calolziocorte [I] 70 G4
Calonge [E] 92 G3
Calpe / Calp [E] 104 F2
Çalpınar [TR] 154 H1
Caltabellotta [I] 126 C3
Caltagirone [I] 126 F4
Caltanissetta [I] 126 E3
Caltavuturo [I] 126 E2
Çaltepe [TR] 152 H5
Çaltı [TR] 150 H4
Çaltılıbük [TR] 150 E5
Caltra [IRL] 2 D5
Călugăreni [RO] 148 C1
Caluso [I] 70 D5
Calvello [I] 120 H4
Calvi [F] 114 A3
Calvià [E] 104 D5
Calvörde [D] 34 B2
Calw [D] 58 G1
Calzadilla de la Cueza [E] 82 C5
Camacha [P] 100 B3
Camaiore [I] 110 D5
Camaldoli [I] 110 G5
Camaldoli, Eremo di- [I] 110 G5
Çamaltı [TR] 152 C4
Camarena de la Sierra [E] 98 E2
Camarès [F] 106 D3
Camaret-sur-Mer [F] 40 B2
Camarillas [E] 98 E1
Camariñas [E] 78 B2
Camarzana de Tera [E] 80 H3
Camas [E] 94 G6
Cambados [E] 78 B4
Cambeo [E] 78 C5
Camberg [D] 46 C2
Camberley [GB] 14 D4
Cambo-les-Bains [F] 84 C2
Camborne [GB] 12 C5
Cambrai [F] 28 F4
Cambre [E] 78 C2
Cambremer [F] 26 G4
Cambridge [GB] 14 F3

Červený Kameň [SK] 62 G4
Červený Kláštor [SK] 52 B5
Červený Kostelec [CZ] 50 B2
Cervera [E] 92 C3
Cervera del Llano [E] 98 B3
Cervera del Río Alhama [E] 84 A6
Cervera de Pisuerga [E] 82 D4
Cerveteri [I] 114 H5
Cérvia [I] 110 H4
Cervignano del Friuli [I] 72 G5
Cervinara [I] 120 E3
Cervione [F] 114 C4
Cervo [E] 78 E1
Cervo [I] 108 G4
Cesana Torinese [I] 70 B6
Cesarica [HR] 112 F3
Cesarò [I] 126 F2
Cesarzowice [PL] 36 C6
Cesena [I] 110 H4
Cesenático [I] 110 H4
Cēsis [LV] 198 E4
Česká Bělá [CZ] 50 A5
Česká Kamenice [CZ] 48 F2
Česká Lípa [CZ] 48 G2
Česká Skalice [CZ] 50 B3
Česká Třebová [CZ] 50 B4
České Budějovice [CZ] 62 C2
České Velenice [CZ] 62 C3
Český Brod [CZ] 48 G4
Český Krumlov [CZ] 62 B2
Český Šternberk [CZ] 48 G4
Český Těšín [CZ] 50 F5
Çeşme [TR] 134 H5
Çeşmealti [TR] 152 C4
Cespedosa [E] 88 C4
Cessalto [I] 72 F5
Cessenon-sur-Orb [F] 106 D4
Čestimensko [BG] 148 E1
Čestobrodica [SCG] 146 A2
Cestona / Zestoa [E] 84 A2
Cesvaine [LV] 198 F5
Cetate [RO] 146 F1
Çetibeli [TR] 154 D1
Cetinje [SCG] 144 E4
Cetóbriga [P] 86 B6
Cetona [I] 114 G2
Cetraro [I] 124 C4
Ceuta [E] 100 G6
Ceutí [E] 104 C3
Ceva [I] 108 G3
Cevico Navero [E] 88 F1
Čevo [SCG] 144 E4
Cewków [PL] 52 F3
Ceylan [TR] 154 G2
Ceyzériat [F] 68 G2
Chaalis, Abbaye de- [F] 42 G3
Chabanais [F] 54 F6
Chabeuil [F] 68 F5
Chablis [F] 56 E2
Chabreloche [F] 68 D2
Chabris [F] 54 H3
Chachersk [BY] 202 D5
Chagny [F] 56 G5
Chailland [F] 26 E6
Chaillé-les-Marais [F] 54 C4
Chailley-Turny [F] 42 H6
Chailluz, Fort de- [F] 58 B4
Chairóneia [GR] 132 H5
Chajkola [RUS] 196 H3
Chalabre [F] 106 B5
Chalais [F] 66 E2
Chalamont [F] 68 G2
Chalampé [F] 58 E3
Chalandritsa [GR] 132 F6
Chálki [GR] 132 G2
Chálki [GR] 154 C4
Chalkiádes [GR] 132 G2
Chalkída [GR] 134 B5
Chalkidóna [GR] 128 G4
Challans [F] 54 B2
Challes-les-Eaux [F] 70 A4
Chalonnes-sur-Loire [F] 54 D1
Châlons-en-Champagne [F] 44 B4
Chalon-sur-Saône [F] 56 G5
Châlus [F] 66 G2
Chalusset, Château de- [F] 66 G1
Cham [CH] 58 F5
Cham [D] 48 C6
Chamberet [F] 66 H2
Chambéry [F] 68 H3
Chambilly [F] 56 E6
Chambley-Bussières [F] 44 E4
Chambon-sur-Lac [F] 68 C2
Chambon-sur-Voueize [F] 56 B6
Chambord [F] 54 H2
Chambord, Parc de- [F] 54 H2
Chameregg [D] 48 C6
Chammünster [D] 48 C6
Chamonix-Mont-Blanc [F] 70 C3
Champagnac-le-Vieux [F] 68 D3
Champagne-Mouton [F] 54 E5
Champagnole [F] 58 B6
Champaubert [F] 44 A4
Champdeniers [F] 54 D4
Champ du Bataille, Château du- [F] 26 H4
Champ du Feu [F] 44 G6
Champeix [F] 68 C3
Champéry [CH] 70 C2
Champex [CH] 70 C3
Champier [F] 68 G4
Champigné [F] 40 H6
Champigny-sur-Veude [F] 54 F2
Champillon [F] 44 B3
Champlitte [F] 58 A3
Champlon [B] 30 E6
Champoluc [I] 70 D3
Champrond-en-Gâtine [F] 26 H6
Champtoceaux [F] 40 F6
Champvent [CH] 58 C6
Chamrousse [F] 68 H5
Chamusca [P] 86 C4
Chanas [F] 68 F4
Chandrinós [GR] 136 C4
Chaniá [GR] 140 C4
Chaniótis [GR] 130 C6
Chantada [E] 78 D4
Chantelle [F] 56 D6
Chantemerle [F] 70 B6
Chantilly [F] 42 G3
Chantonnay [F] 54 C3
Chão de Codes [P] 86 D4
Chaource [F] 44 B6
Chapelle-Royale [F] 42 D5
Chárakas [GR] 140 E5
Charavgí [GR] 128 F5
Charavines [F] 68 G4
Charbonnières-les-Bains [F] 68 F3
Charbowo [PL] 36 D2
Chard [GB] 12 F4
Charenton-du-Cher [F] 56 C4
Charité, Abbaye de la- [F] 58 B4
Charleroi [B] 30 C5
Charlestown [IRL] 2 D4
Charleville / Rath Luirc [IRL] 4 C4
Charleville-Mézières [F] 44 C2
Charlieu [F] 68 E1
Charlottenberg [S] 166 D1
Charly [F] 42 H3
Charmes [F] 44 E6
Charneca [P] 86 A5
Charny [F] 56 D1
Charnyany [BY] 38 G3
Charolles [F] 56 F6
Chârost [F] 56 B3
Charpentry [F] 44 D3
Charrières [CH] 70 C1
Charroux [F] 54 E5
Chartres [F] 42 E4
Charvarica [BG] 146 F6
Charzan [PL] 36 D3
Chassant [F] 42 D4
Chasseneuil-s.-Bonnieure [F] 54 E6
Chasse sur Rhone [F] 68 F3
Chassigny [F] 56 H3
Château-Arnoux [F] 108 C3
Châteaubourg [F] 26 D6
Châteaubriant [F] 40 F5
Château-Chinon [F] 56 E4
Château d'Oex [CH] 70 C1
Château-du-Loir [F] 42 B6
Châteaudun [F] 42 D5
Châteaugiron [F] 26 C6
Château-Gontier [F] 40 H5
Château-Landon [F] 42 F5
Château-la-Vallière [F] 42 B6
Château-L'Évêque [F] 66 F3
Châteaulin [F] 40 B2
Châteaumeillant [F] 56 B5
Châteauneuf [F] 66 E1
Châteauneuf-de-Randon [F] 68 D5
Châteauneuf-du-Faou [F] 40 C3
Châteauneuf-du-Pape [F] 106 G3
Châteauneuf-en-Thymerais [F] 26 H6
Châteauneuf-sur-Cher [F] 56 C4
Châteauneuf-sur-Sarthe [F] 40 H6
Châteauponsac [F] 54 G5
Château-Porcien [F] 28 H6
Château-Queyras [F] 70 B6
Château-Regnault [F] 44 C1
Châteaurenard [F] 42 G6
Château-Renault [F] 54 G1
Châteauroux [F] 54 H4
Château-Salins [F] 44 F5
Château-Thierry [F] 42 H3
Châteauvillain [F] 56 G2
Châtel [F] 70 C2
Châtelaillon-Plage [F] 54 C5
Châtelet [B] 30 C5
Châtelguyon [F] 68 C2
Châtellerault [F] 54 F3
Châtel-Montagne [F] 68 E1
Châtel-St-Denis [CH] 70 C1
Châtelus-Malvaleix [F] 54 H5
Châtenois [F] 44 E6
Chatham [GB] 14 F4
Châtillon [I] 70 D4
Châtillon-Coligny [F] 56 D1
Châtillon-en-Bazois [F] 56 E4
Châtillon-en-Diois [F] 68 G6
Châtillon-sur-Chalaronne [F] 68 G2
Châtillon-sur-Indre [F] 54 G3
Châtillon-sur-Loire [F] 56 D2
Châtillon-sur-Marne [F] 44 A3
Châtillon-sur-Seine [F] 56 G2
Châtre, Église de- [F] 54 D6
Chatteris [GB] 14 F2
Chaudes-Aigues [F] 68 C5
Chauffailles [F] 68 F1
Chaufour-lès-Bonnières [F] 42 E3
Chaumergy [F] 56 H5
Chaumont [F] 56 H1
Chaumont-sur-Aire [F] 44 D4
Chaumont-sur-Loire [F] 54 G2
Chaunay [F] 54 E5
Chauny [F] 28 F6
Chaussin [F] 56 H5
Chauvigny [F] 54 F4
Chaux-Neuve [F] 58 B6
Chavdar [BG] 130 D1
Chaves [P] 80 E3
Chavusy [BY] 202 D5
Chayki [RUS] 198 H6
Chazelles-sur-Lyon [F] 68 F3
Cheb [CZ] 48 C3
Chęciny [PL] 52 B1
Cheddar [GB] 12 F3
Chef-Boutonne [F] 54 D5
Chekhov [RUS] 202 F3
Chekhovo [RUS] 22 H2
Cheles [E] 94 F2
Chełm [PL] 38 F6
Chełmek [PL] 50 G3
Chełmno [PL] 22 D5
Chelmsford [GB] 14 F4
Chełmża [PL] 22 E6
Chełst [PL] 36 B1
Cheltenham [GB] 12 G2
Chelva [E] 98 D3
Chémery-sur-Bar [F] 44 C2
Chemillé [F] 54 D2
Chemin [F] 56 H5
Chemnitz [D] 48 D1
Chenaux [CH] 58 C6
Chêne-Pignier [F] 54 F6
Chénérailles [F] 56 B6
Chenonceaux [F] 54 G2
Chepelare [BG] 130 E1
Chepstow [GB] 12 G3
Chera [E] 98 D4
Cherasco [I] 108 G2
Cherbourg [F] 26 D2
Cheremykino [RUS] 178 G5
Cherepovo [BG] 148 D6
Cherkasovo [RUS] 178 F3
Cherkasy [UA] 202 E8
Chern [RUS] 202 F4
Cherna Mesta [BG] 146 G6
Chernaya Rechka [RUS] 198 G3
Chernevo [RUS] 198 G2
Cherniakhiv [UA] 202 C7
Chernihiv [UA] 202 D6
Cherni rid [BG] 130 G1
Chernivtsi [UA] 204 D3
Chernomorets [BG] 148 F4
Chernyakhovsk [RUS] 24 C1
Chéroy [F] 42 G5
Cherskaya [RUS] 198 G4
Chérso [GR] 128 H3
Cherveix-Cubas [F] 66 G3
Chervena Voda [BG] 148 D2
Cherven Bryag [BG] 148 A3
Cherves-Richemont [F] 54 D6
Chervonohrad [UA] 52 H2
Chervyen' [BY] 202 C5
Cherykaw [BY] 202 D5
Cheste [E] 98 E4
Chester [GB] 10 D4
Chesterfield [GB] 10 F5
Chester-le-Street [GB] 8 F6
Chevagnes [F] 56 D5
Chevanceaux [F] 66 D2
Chevenez [CH] 58 D4
Chevilly, Château de- [F] 42 E6
Chevreuse [F] 42 F4
Chézal-Benoît [F] 56 B4
Chiampo [I] 72 D6
Chianca, Dolmen di- [I] 122 D2
Chianciano Terme [I] 114 G2
Chiaramonti [I] 118 C3
Chiaramonti Gulfi [I] 126 F5
Chiaravalle [I] 112 C6
Chiaravalle Centrale [I] 124 D6
Chiaravalle della Colomba [I] 110 D2
Chiari [I] 70 H5
Chiasso [CH] 70 G4
Chiavari [I] 110 B3
Chiavenna [I] 70 G2
Chichester [GB] 14 D5
Chiclana de la Frontera [E] 100 F4
Chieming [D] 60 F5
Chieri [I] 70 D6
Chiesa in Valmalenco [I] 70 H3
Chiessi [I] 114 D2
Chieti [I] 116 D4
Chiewo [PL] 36 F4
Chiliadoú [GR] 134 C4
Chiliandaríou, Moní- [GR] 130 D5
Chiliomódi [GR] 136 F1
Chillarón de Cuenca [E] 98 B2
Chillon [CH] 70 C2
Chillón [E] 96 C4
Chimay [B] 28 H5
Chinadievo [UA] 204 B3
Chinchilla de Monte-Aragón [E] 98 C5
Chinchón [E] 96 G1
Chinon [F] 54 F2
Chióggia [I] 110 H1
Chíos [GR] 134 G4
Chipiona [E] 100 F3
Chippenham [GB] 12 G3
Chipping Norton [GB] 12 H2
Chipping Sodbury [GB] 12 G3
Chiprovtsi [BG] 146 F3
Chirivel [E] 102 H3
Chirpan [BG] 148 C5
Chisa [F] 114 B5
Chişinău [MD] 204 E3
Chişineu Criş [RO] 76 G3
Chiusa / Klausen [I] 72 D3
Chiusa di Pesio [I] 108 F3
Chiusaforte [I] 72 G4
Chiusa Sclâfani [I] 126 C3
Chiusi [I] 114 H2
Chiva [E] 98 E4
Chivasso [I] 70 D5
Chkalovo [PL] 24 D3
Chlebowo [PL] 34 G3
Chlemoútsi [GR] 136 B1
Chlewice [PL] 50 H2
Chlewiska [PL] 38 B6
Chlmec [SK] 64 H4
Chlumec nad Cidlinou [CZ] 48 H3
Chlum u Třeboně [CZ] 62 C2
Chmielnik [PL] 52 B2
Chmielno [PL] 36 A6
Chobienia [PL] 36 B5
Chobienice [PL] 36 B3
Choceň [CZ] 50 B4
Choceń [PL] 36 F2
Chochołów [PL] 50 H5
Chocianów [PL] 36 B5
Chociwel [PL] 20 G5
Choczewo [PL] 22 D1
Chodecz [PL] 36 F2
Chodel [PL] 38 D6
Chodová Planá [CZ] 48 D4
Chodzież [PL] 22 B6
Chojna [PL] 20 F6
Chojnice [PL] 22 C4
Chojnów [PL] 36 B6
Cholet [F] 54 D2
Chomakovtsi [BG] 146 G3
Chomęciska Małe [PL] 52 F1
Chomutov [CZ] 48 E2
Chop [UA] 204 B3
Chóra [GR] 136 C4
Choreftó [GR] 134 A2
Chorges [F] 108 D2
Chorio [I] 124 C8
Choristí [GR] 130 D3
Chorley [GB] 10 D3
Chornobyl [UA] 202 D7
Chornomors'ke [UA] 204 G4
Choroszcz [PL] 24 E5
Chorro, Garganta del- [E] 102 B4
Chorros, Cueva de los- [E] 96 H6
Chorros del Mundo [E] 96 H6
Chortkiv [UA] 204 D2
Chorzele [PL] 22 H5
Chorzów [PL] 50 G3
Chorzyna [PL] 36 F5
Choszczno [PL] 20 G6
Chotěboř [CZ] 50 A5
Chotětín [CZ] 48 E4
Choumnikó [GR] 130 C3
Chouto [P] 86 D4
Chouvigny, Gorges de- [F] 56 C6
Choye [F] 58 A4
Chozoviótissa [GR] 138 G3
Chrast [CZ] 50 B4
Chrastava [CZ] 48 G1
Chrepiski Manastir [BG] 146 G4
Christchurch [GB] 12 G5
Christianoúpoli [GR] 136 C3
Christiansfeld [DK] 156 C3
Christinehof [S] 158 D2
Christkindl [A] 62 B5
Christós [GR] 138 G1
Chrudim [CZ] 50 A4
Chrýsafa [GR] 136 E4
Chrysochóri [GR] 130 E3
Chrysoskalítissa [GR] 140 B5
Chrysoúpoli [GR] 130 E3
Chrząchówek [PL] 38 D5
Chrzanów [PL] 50 G3
Chudenice [CZ] 48 D5
Chudniv [UA] 202 C8
Chudoba [PL] 50 E1
Chudomir [BG] 148 D3
Chudovo [RUS] 202 C1
Chulkovo [RUS] 178 E3
Chupa [RUS] 196 H1
Chuprene [BG] 146 E3
Chur [CH] 70 H1
Church Stretton [GB] 10 D6
Churchtown [IRL] 4 E5
Churchtown [IRL] 4 F5
Churek [BG] 146 G4
Chvagnes-en-Paillers [F] 54 C2
Chvylevo [RUS] 202 C1
Chwaszczyno [PL] 22 D2
Chyhyryn [UA] 202 E8
Chyňava [CZ] 48 F4
Chýnov [CZ] 48 G5
Chýnovská Jeskyně [CZ] 48 G5
Chyžne [PL] 50 H5
Cianciana [I] 126 D3
Ciasna [PL] 50 F2
Ciążeń [PL] 36 E3
Ciborro [P] 86 D6
Ciboure [F] 84 B2
Cicciano [I] 120 E3
Cicerone, Tomba di- [I] 120 C2
Ćićevac [SCG] 146 C3
Čičevci [BIH] 142 F4
Cichy [PL] 24 D3
Čiciuk [SCG] 146 C3
Ciclopi, Isole dei- [I] 126 G3
Čičmany [SK] 64 B2
Cide [TR] 204 H6
Cidones [E] 90 B2
Ciechanów [PL] 38 B1
Ciechanowiec [PL] 38 D1
Ciechocinek [PL] 36 F1
Ciemnik [PL] 20 G5
Ciempozuelos [E] 96 G1
Ciepielów [PL] 38 C5
Cieplice Śląskie-Zdrój [PL] 50 A1
Cierp-Gaud [F] 84 F4
Cieszanów [PL] 52 F3
Cieszyn [PL] 36 D5
Cieszyn [PL] 50 F4
Cieza [E] 104 C2
Ciężkowice [PL] 52 C4
Çiftlikköy [TR] 150 F3
Cifuentes [E] 90 A5
Cigales [E] 88 E1
Cigánd [H] 64 H4
Cigliano [I] 70 E5
Cihangazi [TR] 150 G5
Cilipi [HR] 144 D4
Cill Airne / Killarney [IRL] 4 B4
Cillas [E] 90 C5
Cill Chaínnigh / Kilkenny [IRL] 4 E4
Cill Charthaigh / Kilcar [IRL] 2 D2
Cill Chiaráin / Kilkieran [IRL] 2 B4
Cilleros [E] 86 G3
Cimadevilla [E] 78 B3
Cimburk [CZ] 50 C5
Cimburk [CZ] 62 G2
Cimino, Monte- [I] 114 H4
Cimoláis [I] 72 F4
Cimoszki [PL] 24 E3
Cîmpeni [RO] 204 C4
Çınarcık [TR] 150 F3
Cinco Casas [E] 96 G4
Cindere [TR] 152 F4
Çine [TR] 152 E6
Činěves [CZ] 48 H3
Ciney [B] 30 D5
Cinfães [P] 80 C4
Cingoli [I] 116 C1
Cinigiano [I] 114 F2
Cinisi [I] 126 C1
Cínovec [CZ] 48 E2
Cinquefrondi [I] 124 D6
Cintegabelle [F] 84 H4
Cintruénigo [E] 84 A6
Ciółkowo [PL] 36 H2
Circo de Barrosa [E] 84 E5
Cirella [I] 124 C3
Cirencester [GB] 12 G3
Cirey [F] 44 G6
Ciria [E] 90 C3
Ciriè [I] 70 D5
Čirkovicy [RUS] 178 G6
Cirò [I] 124 F4
Cirò Marina [I] 124 F4
Ciron [F] 54 G4
Çirpı [TR] 152 D4
Ciruli [LV] 198 C4
Cisa, Passo della- [I] 110 C3
Cisna [PL] 52 E6
Cisnădie [RO] 204 C5
Cista Provo [HR] 144 B2
Cista Velika [HR] 144 A2
Cisterna di Latina [I] 116 B6
Cisternino [I] 122 F3
Cistierna [E] 82 C4
Citak [TR] 152 E2
Cîteaux, Abbaye de- [F] 56 G4
Çıtlık [TR] 154 D1
Cittadella [I] 72 D6
Città della Pieve [I] 114 H2
Città del Vaticano [V] 116 A5
Città di Castello [I] 114 H1
Cittaducale [I] 116 B4
Cittanova [I] 124 D7
Città Sant'Angelo [I] 116 D4
Ciudad Iberica [E] 90 C4
Ciudad Real [E] 96 E4
Ciudad Rodrigo [E] 86 H2
Ciumeghiu [RO] 76 H3
Ciutadella de Menorca [E] 104 G4
Civica [E] 90 A5
Cividale del Friuli [I] 72 G5
Çivili [TR] 150 E5
Civita [I] 114 H3
Cívita Castellana [I] 116 A4
Civitanova Marche [I] 116 C1
Civitavécchia [I] 114 G5
Civitella del Tronto [I] 116 C3
Civitella di Romagna [I] 110 G5
Civitella in Val di Chiana [I] 114 G1
Civitella Paganico [I] 114 F2
Civitella Roveto [I] 116 C5
Civray [F] 54 E5
Civrieux-d'Azergues [F] 68 F2
Çivril [TR] 152 G4
Clacton-on-Sea [GB] 14 G4
Clairvaux-les-Lacs [F] 70 A1
Clamecy [F] 56 E3
Clamouse, Grotte de- [F] 106 E3
Clane [IRL] 2 F6
Clara [IRL] 2 D5
Clarecastle [IRL] 2 C6
Claremorris [IRL] 2 C4
Clarinbridge [IRL] 2 C5
Claros [TR] 152 C5
Clashmore [IRL] 4 D5
Claudy [NIR] 2 F2
Clausholm [DK] 160 E5
Clausthal-Zellerfeld [D] 32 G4
Claviere [I] 70 B6
Cleanovu [RO] 146 F1
Clécy [F] 26 F4
Cleethorpes [GB] 10 G4
Clefmont [F] 58 A2
Clefs [F] 42 B6
Clelles [F] 68 G5
Clementino, Porto- [I] 114 G4
Cléon-d'Andran [F] 68 F6
Clères [F] 28 C5
Clermont [F] 28 E6
Clermont-de-Beauregarde [F] 66 F3
Clermont-en-Argonne [F] 44 D4
Clermont-Ferrand [F] 68 C2
Clermont-l'Hérault [F] 106 E4
Clerval [F] 58 C4
Clervaux [L] 44 F1
Cléry [F] 42 E6
Cles [I] 72 C3
Clevedon [GB] 12 F3
Clifden [IRL] 2 B4
Cliffoney [IRL] 2 D3
Clisson [F] 54 C2
Clitheroe [GB] 10 E3
Clitunno, Fonti del- [I] 116 B3
Clitunno, Tempio del- [I] 116 B3
Clogan [IRL] 2 D6
Clogh [IRL] 4 F3
Clogheen [IRL] 4 D4
Cloghmore [IRL] 2 B3
Clohars-Carnöet [F] 40 C4
Clonakilty [IRL] 4 C5
Clonalis House [IRL] 2 D4
Clonard [IRL] 2 E5
Clonaslee [IRL] 2 D6
Clonbur [IRL] 2 C4
Clondalkin [IRL] 2 F6
Clones [IRL] 2 E4
Clonfert [IRL] 2 D5
Clonmacnoise [IRL] 2 D5
Clonmany [IRL] 2 F1
Clonmel / Cluain Meala [IRL] 4 E4
Clonmellon [IRL] 2 E5
Clonroche [IRL] 4 F4
Cloonbannin [IRL] 4 C4
Cloonkeen [IRL] 4 B4
Cloonlara [IRL] 4 D3
Cloppenburg [D] 18 C6
Clough [NIR] 2 G4
Cloughjordan [IRL] 2 D6
Cloyes-sur-le-Loir [F] 42 D5
Cloyne [IRL] 4 D5
Cluain Meala / Clonmel [IRL] 4 E4
Cluina [E] 88 H2
Cluj Napoca [RO] 204 C4
Clun [GB] 10 C6
Cluny [F] 56 F6
Cluses [F] 70 B2
Clusone [I] 72 A5
Ćmielów [PL] 52 D1
Cmolas [PL] 52 D3
Coachford [IRL] 4 C5
Coalville [GB] 10 E6
Coaña [E] 78 F2
Çobanisa [TR] 154 H1
Çobanlar [TR] 152 D2
Cobh [IRL] 4 D5
Coburg [D] 46 G3
Coca [E] 88 E3
Coceges del Monte [E] 88 F2
Cocentaina [E] 104 E1
Cochem [D] 44 G1
Cockermouth [GB] 8 D6
Code [LV] 198 D6
Codigoro [I] 110 G2
Codogno [I] 70 H6
Codos [E] 90 D4
Codróipo [I] 72 G5
Coesfeld [D] 16 H6
Coflans [F] 70 B4
Cofrentes [E] 98 D5
Coghinas [I] 118 D3
Cognac [F] 54 D6
Cogne [I] 70 D4
Cogolin [F] 108 D5
Cogollos [E] 82 E6
Cogolludo [E] 88 H4
Cogul, Cova del- [E] 90 H5
Cohiniac [F] 26 A4
Coimbra [P] 86 D2
Coín [E] 102 B4
Coina [P] 86 B6
Coirós [E] 78 D2
Čoka [SCG] 76 E5
Colares [P] 86 A5
Cölbe [D] 32 D6
Colbitz [D] 34 B2
Colcerasa [I] 116 B1
Colchester [GB] 14 F3
Colditz [D] 34 D6
Coldstream [GB] 8 F4
Colembert [F] 14 G6
Coleraine [NIR] 2 G2
Colfiorito [I] 116 B2
Colfosco [I] 72 E3
Colico [I] 70 G3
Coligny [F] 56 H6
Colindres [E] 82 F3
Colintraive [GB] 8 C2
Collado Villalba [E] 88 F5
Coll de Nargó [E] 92 D2
Collécchio [I] 110 D2
Colledimezzo [I] 116 E5
Colle di Val d'Elsa [I] 114 F1
Colleferro [I] 116 B6
Collegno [I] 70 D5
Colle Isarco / Gossensass [I] 72 D2
Collesalvetti [I] 110 D6
Colle Sannita [I] 120 F2
Collesano [I] 126 E2
Colletorto [I] 116 F6
Colliano [I] 120 G3
Collinée [F] 26 B5
Cóllio [I] 72 B5
Collioure [F] 92 G2
Collodi [I] 110 E5
Collonges [F] 70 A2
Collonges-la-Rouge [F] 66 G3
Collooney [IRL] 2 D3
Colmar [F] 58 D3
Colmars [F] 108 D3
Colmenar [E] 102 C4
Colmenar de Oreja [E] 96 G1
Colmenar Viejo [E] 88 F5
Cologna Véneta [I] 110 F1
Cologne [F] 84 G2
Cologno al Serio [I] 70 H5
Colombey-les-Belles [F] 44 E5
Colombey-les-Deux-Églises [F] 44 C6
Colomiers [F] 84 H3
Colònia de Sant Jordi [E] 104 E6
Colonia Selladores [E] 96 E6
Colorno [I] 110 D2
Colosimi [I] 124 D5
Colunga [E] 82 C2
Colwyn Bay [GB] 10 C4
Comácchio [I] 110 H3
Comana [RO] 148 D1
Comana [RO] 148 G1
Comăneşti [RO] 204 D4
Comano Terme [I] 72 C4
Coma-ruga [E] 92 C5
Combarro [E] 78 B4
Combeaufontaine [F] 58 B3
Comber [NIR] 2 G4
Combourg [F] 26 C5
Combronde [F] 68 C1
Comburg [D] 46 E6
Comeglians [I] 72 G3
Comelico Superiore [I] 72 F3
Comillas [E] 82 E3
Cómiso [I] 126 F5
Comloşu Mare [RO] 76 F5
Commentry [F] 56 C6
Commequiers [F] 54 B2
Commercy [F] 44 D5
Como [I] 70 G4
Cómpeta [E] 102 D4
Compiègne [F] 28 E6
Comporta [P] 94 C1
Comps-sur-Artuby [F] 108 D4
Comrat [MD] 204 E4
Comunanza [I] 116 C2
Concarneau [F] 40 B3
Concesio [I] 72 B5
Conches-en-Ouche [F] 26 H4
Concordia Sagittaria [I] 72 F5
Condat [F] 68 C3
Condé-en-Brie [F] 42 H3
Condeixa-a-Nova [P] 86 D2
Condé-sur-Noireau [F] 26 E4
Condino [I] 72 B5
Condofuri [I] 124 C8
Condofuri Marina [I] 124 C8
Condom [F] 66 E6
Condove [I] 70 C5
Condrieu [F] 68 F3
Conegliano [I] 72 E5
Conflans En Jarnisy [F] 44 E4
Conflans-sur-Lanterne [F] 58 B3
Confolens [F] 54 F6
Cong [IRL] 2 C4
Congleton [GB] 10 E5
Congosto de Valdavia [E] 82 D4
Congresbury [GB] 12 F3
Conil de la Frontera [E] 100 F5
Conímbriga [P] 86 D2
Coningsby [GB] 10 G5
Conlie [F] 42 B5
Conna [IRL] 4 D5
Connerré [F] 42 C5
Conques [F] 68 B5
Conquista [E] 96 D5
Conquista de la Sierra [E] 96 B2
Conquista del Guadiana [E] 96 A2
Conselice [I] 110 G3
Conselve [I] 110 G1
Consett [GB] 8 F6
Constanţa [RO] 204 F5
Constantí [E] 92 C5
Constantina [E] 96 A6
Consuegra [E] 96 F3
Consuma [I] 110 F5
Contarina [I] 110 H2
Contay [F] 28 E4
Conţeşti [RO] 148 C2
Contigliano [I] 116 B4
Contres [F] 54 H2
Contrexéville [F] 58 B2
Controne [I] 120 F4
Contursi Terme [I] 120 F4
Conty [F] 28 D5
Conversano [I] 122 E3
Conwy [GB] 10 C4
Cookstown [NIR] 2 F3
Coole [IRL] 2 E5
Cooraclare [IRL] 2 B6
Cootehill [IRL] 2 F4
Cope [E] 104 B4
Copertino [I] 122 G5
Çöpköy [TR] 150 B3
Copparo [I] 110 G2
Coppenbrügge [D] 32 F3
Corabia [RO] 148 A2
Corato [I] 122 D2
Coray [F] 40 C3
Corbalán [E] 98 E2
Corbeil-Essonnes [F] 42 F4
Corbeny [F] 28 G6
Corbie [F] 28 E5
Corbigny [F] 56 E3
Corbridge [GB] 8 F6
Corby [GB] 14 E2
Corcaigh / Cork [IRL] 4 C5
Corciano [I] 114 H2
Corcieux [F] 58 D2
Corcomroe Abbey [IRL] 2 C5
Corconne [F] 106 F3
Corconte [E] 82 E4
Corcubión [E] 78 B2
Cordenons [I] 72 F5
Cordes [F] 106 B2
Córdoba [E] 102 C1
Cordobilla de Lácara [E] 86 G6
Corella [E] 84 A6
Cori [I] 116 B6
Coria [E] 86 H3
Coria del Río [E] 94 G6
Corigliano Calabro [I] 124 E3
Corinaldo [I] 112 C6
Coripe [E] 100 H3
Cork / Corcaigh [IRL] 4 C5
Corlătel [RO] 146 E1
Corlay [F] 26 A4
Corleone [I] 126 C2
Corleto Perticara [I] 120 H4
Çorlu [TR] 150 C3
Cormainville [F] 42 E5
Cormeilles [F] 26 G3
Cormery [F] 54 G2
Cornellana [E] 78 G3
Córniglio [I] 110 D3
Cornimont [F] 58 D3
Cornuda la Valle [I] 72 E5
Cornus [I] 118 B5
Corofin [IRL] 2 C6
Corovodë [AL] 128 C5
Corps [F] 68 H6
Corral de Almaguer [E] 96 G2
Corralejo [E] 100 E6
Corrales [E] 80 H5
Corre [F] 58 B3
Corrèggio [I] 110 E2
Corridonia [I] 116 C2
Corsano [I] 122 G6

Corte [F] 114 B4
Cortegada [E] 78 C5
Cortegana [E] 94 F4
Cortemaggiore [I] 70 H6
Cortemilia [I] 108 G2
Cortes [E] 90 D3
Cortes de la Frontera [E] 100 H4
Cortes de Pallás [E] 98 D5
Cortijos de Abajo [E] 96 E3
Cortina d'Ampezzo [I] 72 E3
Cortona [I] 114 H1
Coruche [P] 86 C5
Coruña del Conde [E] 88 H2
Corvara in Badia [I] 72 E3
Corvera [E] 104 C3
Corvey [D] 32 F4
Cosa [E] 90 D6
Cosa [I] 114 F4
Cosenza [I] 124 D4
Cosne-Cours-sur-Loire [F] 56 D3
Cosne d'Allier [F] 56 C5
Coşoveni [RO] 146 G1
Cospeito [E] 78 E3
Cossato [I] 70 E4
Cossé-le-Vivien [F] 40 G5
Cossonay [CH] 70 B1
Costa da Caparica [P] 86 A5
Costa de los Pins [E] 104 F5
Costa Nova do Prado [P] 80 B5
Costeşti [RO] 204 D5
Costigliole Saluzzo [I] 108 F2
Coswig [D] 34 C4
Coswig [D] 34 E6
Cote [E] 100 H3
Cotignac [F] 108 C5
Cotronei [I] 124 E5
Cottbus [D] 34 F4
Couches [F] 56 F5
Couço [P] 86 D5
Coucy-le-Château-Auffrique [F] 28 F6
Coudray-Montbault, Château de- [F] 54 D2
Couflenz [F] 84 G5
Cougnac, Grottes de- [F] 66 G4
Couhé [F] 54 E5
Couilly [F] 42 G3
Couiza [F] 106 B5
Coulanges-la-Vineuse [F] 56 E2
Coulmier-le-Sec [F] 56 G2
Coulommiers [F] 42 G4
Coulon [F] 54 D4
Coulonges [F] 54 D4
Coupar Angus [GB] 8 E2
Couptrain [F] 26 F5
Courboyer, Manoir de- [F] 26 G6
Courceau [F] 56 G3
Courchevel [F] 70 B4
Cour-Cheverny [F] 54 H2
Courçon [F] 54 C4
Cour-et-Buis [F] 68 G4
Courgains [F] 26 F6
Courmayeur [I] 70 C3
Courpière [F] 68 D2
Courriere [B] 30 D5
Coursan [F] 106 D5
Courseulles-sur-Mer [F] 26 F3
Cours-la-Ville [F] 68 F2
Courson-les-Carrières [F] 56 E2
Courtacon [F] 42 H4
Courtanvaux, Château de- [F] 42 C6
Courteilles [F] 26 G4
Courtenay [F] 42 G6
Courtmacsherry [IRL] 4 C5
Courtomer [F] 26 G5
Courtown Harbour [IRL] 4 G4
Courtrai (Kortrijk) [B] 28 G2
Courville [F] 26 H6
Coutances [F] 26 D3
Couterne [F] 26 E5
Coutevroult [F] 42 G4
Coutras [F] 66 D3
Couvet [CH] 58 C6
Couvin [B] 28 H5
Covadonga [E] 82 C2
Covadonga [E] 82 C2
Covaleda [E] 90 B2
Covarrubias [E] 88 H1
Covarrubias [E] 90 B3
Covăsinţ [RO] 76 H4
Covci [RO] 146 F2
Coventry [GB] 14 D2
Covide [P] 78 B6
Covilhã [P] 86 F2
Cowes [GB] 12 H5
Cox [F] 84 H2
Cózar [E] 96 G5
Cozes [F] 54 C6
Cozzano [F] 114 B5
Craco [I] 122 D4
Craigavon [NIR] 2 G4
Crail [GB] 8 F3
Crailsheim [D] 46 E6
Craiova [RO] 76 H3
Craiova [RO] 146 G1
Crângeni [RO] 148 B1
Crângu [RO] 148 B2
Crans [CH] 70 D2
Craon [F] 40 G5
Craponne-sur-Arzon [F] 68 D3
Crato [P] 86 E5
Craughwell [IRL] 2 C5
Crawley [GB] 14 E5
Crea, Santuario di- [I] 70 E6
Crêches-sur-Saône [F] 68 F1
Crécy [F] 42 G4
Crécy-en-Ponthieu [F] 28 D3
Crécy-sur-Serre [F] 28 G6
Crediton [GB] 12 E4
Creevagh [IRL] 2 C3
Creglingen [D] 46 E5
Creil [F] 42 G2
Crema [I] 70 H5
Cremaste [TR] 150 B5
Crémieu [F] 68 G3
Cremona [I] 110 D1
Črenšovci [SLO] 74 F3
Créon [F] 66 D3
Crepaja [SCG] 142 G2
Crépy-en-Valois [F] 42 G3
Cres [HR] 112 E2
Crescentino [I] 70 E5
Crespin [F] 28 G4
Crespino [I] 110 G2
Cressensac [F] 66 G3
Cresslough [IRL] 2 E1
Crest [F] 68 F6
Cresta [CH] 70 H2
Creussen [D] 46 H4
Creutzwald [F] 44 F4
Creuzburg [D] 32 G6
Crevalcore [I] 110 F3
Crevecæur-en-Auge [F] 26 G4
Crevecoeur [F] 28 D5
Crevillent / Crevillente [E] 104 D2
Crevillente / Crevillent [E] 104 D2
Crevoladossola [I] 70 E3
Crewe [GB] 10 D5
Crewkerne [GB] 12 F4
Criação Velha [P] 100 C3
Crianlarich [GB] 8 D2
Cricklade [GB] 12 H3
Crieff [GB] 8 E2
Crikvenica [HR] 112 F2
Crillon [F] 28 D5
Crimmitschau [D] 48 C1
Čišnjeva [HR] 112 F2
Crispiano [I] 122 E4
Crissolo [I] 108 F2
Cristo, Monasterio del- [E] 78 G3
Cristo del Espíritu-Santo [E] 96 E3
Crivitz [D] 20 A4
Crkvina Prolaz [SCG] 144 E3
Crmljan [SCG] 146 B5
Črmošnjice [SLO] 74 C6
Črna [SLO] 74 C4
Crna Bara [SCG] 76 E5
Crna Trava [SCG] 146 E4
Crnča [SCG] 142 F4
Crni Lug [BIH] 142 B4
Crni Vrh [SLO] 74 B5
Črnkovci [HR] 76 B6
Črnomelj [SLO] 74 D6
Crocq [F] 68 B1
Crodo [I] 70 F2
Croithlí / Crolly [IRL] 2 E2
Croix Haute, Col de la- [F] 68 G6
Crolly / Croithlí [IRL] 2 E2
Cro-Magnon [F] 66 F3
Cromarty [GB] 6 E4
Cromer [GB] 14 G1
Crook [GB] 10 F1
Crookedwood [IRL] 2 E5
Crookhaven [IRL] 4 B5
Crookstown [IRL] 4 C5
Croom [IRL] 4 D3
Cropalati [I] 124 E4
Cropani [I] 124 E5
Crosia [I] 124 E4
Crossakeel [IRL] 2 E5
Crosshaven [IRL] 4 D5
Crossmaglen [NIR] 2 F4
Crossmolina [IRL] 2 C3
Crotone [I] 124 F5
Crowborough [GB] 14 E5
Croydon [GB] 14 E4
Crozant [F] 54 G5
Crozon [F] 40 B2
Cruas [F] 68 F6
Cruceni [RO] 142 H1
Cruces [E] 78 C3
Crucoli [I] 124 F4
Crumlin [NIR] 2 G3
Cruseilles [F] 70 B2
Crusheen [IRL] 2 C6
Cruzy [F] 106 D4
Crvenka [SCG] 76 D6
Csabacsüd [H] 76 F3
Csákánydoroszlo [H] 74 F2
Csakvár [H] 76 B1
Csanádapáca [H] 76 F3
Csanádpalota [H] 76 F4
Csanytelek [H] 76 E3
Csapod [H] 62 G6
Csárdaszállás [H] 76 F2
Császártöltés [H] 76 C4
Csávoly [H] 76 C4
Csépa [H] 76 E3
Cserebökény [H] 76 E3
Cserepes [H] 64 G6
Cserkeszolo [H] 76 E2
Csesznek [H] 76 A1
Csobád [H] 64 F4
Csókakoi Varrom [H] 76 B1
Csökmo [H] 76 G2
Csokonyavisonta [H] 74 H5
Csongrád [H] 76 E3
Csopak [H] 76 A2
Csór [H] 76 B2
Csorna [H] 62 G6
Csorvás [H] 76 F3
Csót [H] 74 H1
Csurgó [H] 74 G4
Cuadros [E] 78 H5
Cualedro [E] 78 D6
Cuba [P] 94 D2
Cubel [E] 90 C5
Cubo de Bureba [E] 82 F5
Çubukdağı [TR] 152 F5
Çubuklu [TR] 154 F1
Cudillero [E] 78 G3
Cuéllar [E] 88 F2
Cuenca [E] 98 B2
Cuers [F] 108 C5
Cuerva [E] 96 E2
Cuesta Blanca de Arriba [E] 104 C4
Cuestas de Esteras [E] 90 B4
Cueva de Don Juan [E] 98 D5
Cuevas del Almanzora [E] 102 H4
Cuevas del Becerro [E] 102 B4
Cuevas de San Clemente [E] 88 H1
Cuevas de San Marcos [E] 102 C3
Cúglieri [I] 118 C4
Cuhom [F] 28 E3
Cuijk [NL] 16 E6
Cuillé [F] 40 G4
Cuiseaux [F] 56 H6
Cuisery [F] 56 G6
Cujmir [RO] 146 E1
Çukurhisar [TR] 150 H5
Çukurköi [TR] 150 B2
Çukurköy [TR] 152 G5
Çukurören [TR] 152 G2
Culan [F] 56 B5
Culdaff [IRL] 2 F1
Culemborg [NL] 16 E5
Cúllar [E] 102 G3
Cullen [GB] 6 F5
Cullera [E] 98 F5
Cullompton [GB] 12 E4
Culoz [F] 68 H3
Cuma [I] 120 D3
Cumbernauld [GB] 8 D3
Cumbres de S. Bartolomé [E] 94 F4
Cumbres Mayores [E] 94 F4
Čumić [SCG] 146 B2
Cumnock [GB] 8 D4
Cunault [F] 54 E2
Cúneo [I] 108 F3
Čunski [HR] 112 E3
Cuntis [E] 78 B3
Cuorgnè [I] 70 D5
Cupar [GB] 8 F2
Cupello [I] 116 E5
Cupra Marittima [I] 116 D2
Cupramontana [I] 116 B1
Ćuprija [SCG] 146 C2
Cura, Santuari de- [E] 104 E5
Curel [F] 108 C3
Curia [P] 80 B6
Ćurlovac [HR] 74 G5
Curon Venosta / Graun im Vinschgau [I] 72 B2
Curraghmore [IRL] 4 E5
Curtatone [I] 110 E1
Curtea De Argeş [RO] 204 D5
Curtici [RO] 76 G4
Curtis [E] 78 D2
Čurug [SCG] 142 G1
Cusset [F] 68 D1
Custonaci [I] 126 B2
Cutigliano [I] 110 E4
Cutro [I] 124 F5
Cutting [F] 44 F5
Çüvenli [TR] 150 C2
Cuveşdia [RO] 76 H5
Cuvilly [F] 28 E6
Cuxhaven [D] 18 D3
Cuzzola [I] 118 E3
Cvikov [CZ] 48 G2
Cwmbran [GB] 12 F2
Cybinka [PL] 34 G3
Cycöw [PL] 38 F5
Cytonium [TR] 152 C2
Czajków [PL] 36 E5
Czaplinek [PL] 22 A5
Czarna Białostocka [PL] 24 F5
Czarna Dąbrówka [PL] 22 C2
Czarna Górna [PL] 52 F5
Czarna Woda [PL] 22 D4
Czarne [PL] 22 B4
Czarnków [PL] 36 C1
Czarnożyły [PL] 36 F6
Czarny Dunajec [PL] 50 H5
Czastry [PL] 36 E6
Czchów [PL] 52 B4
Czechowice-Dziedzice [PL] 50 G4
Czeladź [PL] 50 G3
Czemierniki [PL] 38 E4
Czempiń [PL] 36 C3
Czeremcha [PL] 38 F2
Czerniejewo [PL] 36 D2
Czernikowo [PL] 36 F1
Czersk [PL] 22 D4
Czersk [PL] 38 C3
Czerwieńsk [PL] 34 H4
Częstochowa [PL] 50 G1
Człopa [PL] 20 H6
Człuchów [PL] 22 C4
Czorsztyn [PL] 52 B5
Czudec [PL] 52 D4
Czyżew-Osada [PL] 38 D1

D

Daaden [D] 32 C6
Dabarska Spilja [BIH] 142 B3
Dabas [H] 76 C2
Dabern [D] 34 E4
Dąbie [PL] 20 F5
Dąbie [PL] 36 F3
Dabilja [MK] 128 G2
Dąbki [PL] 22 A2
Dąbki [PL] 36 C5
Dabo [F] 44 G5
Dabo, Roch. de- [F] 44 G5
Dăbovo [BG] 148 C4
Dąbrowa [PL] 36 E1
Dąbrowa [PL] 36 F4
Dąbrowa [PL] 38 E2
Dąbrowa [PL] 50 E2
Dąbrowa Białostocka [PL] 24 F4
Dąbrowa Górnicza [PL] 50 G3
Dąbrowa Tarnowska [PL] 52 C3
Dąbrówca Warszawska [PL] 38 C5
Dabrówka [PL] 52 E2
Dąbrówka Kościelna [PL] 24 E6
Dąbrówka Leśna [PL] 36 C2
Dąbrówka Wielkopolska [PL] 36 A3
Dąbrówno [PL] 22 G5
Dăbuleni [RO] 146 G2
Dachau [D] 60 E4
Dachnów [PL] 52 F3
Dachsteinhöhlen [A] 62 A6
Dačice [CZ] 62 D2
Dädesjö [S] 162 E4
Dåfnes [GR] 132 F6
Dáfni [GR] 130 D5
Dáfni [GR] 130 F6
Dafní [GR] 134 C6
Dáfni [GR] 136 D2
Dafnónas [GR] 130 E2
Dafnotí [GR] 132 D2
Dağakça [TR] 150 F5
Dagali [N] 170 F4
Dağardı [TR] 152 F1
Dagda [LV] 198 G6
Dagebüll [D] 156 B5
Dağkızılca [TR] 152 D4
Dahlen [D] 34 D5
Dahlenburg [D] 18 G5
Dahme [D] 18 H2
Dahme [D] 34 E4
Dahmen [D] 20 C4
Dahn [D] 44 H4
Dähre [D] 32 H1
Daia [RO] 148 C1
Daikanvik [S] 190 F4
Daimiel [E] 96 F4
Daimoniá [GR] 136 F5
Daingean [IRL] 2 E6
Đakovica / Gjakove [SCG] 146 B6
Đakovo [HR] 142 D1
Daksti [LV] 198 E4
Dal [N] 170 F6
Dal [N] 172 C5
Dala [S] 166 F6
Dala-Floda [S] 172 G4
Dala-Husby [S] 174 D5
Dala-Järna [S] 172 G4
Dalama [TR] 152 E5
Dalaman [TR] 154 E2
Dalarö [S] 168 E3
Dalbeattie [GB] 8 D5
Dalberg [D] 44 H2
Dalby [DK] 156 G3
Dalby [S] 158 C3
Dalbyn [S] 172 H3
Dale [GB] 12 D1
Dale [N] 164 E3
Dale [N] 170 B1
Dale [N] 170 B3
Dale [N] 180 C4
Dalen [N] 164 E2
Dalen [N] 180 F3
Daleszyce [PL] 52 C1
Dalfors [S] 172 H2
Dalhem [S] 162 F1
Dalhem [S] 168 G4
Dalholen [N] 180 H5
Dalías [E] 102 F5
Daliowa [PL] 52 D5
Dalj [HR] 142 E1
Dalkeith [GB] 8 E3
Dalkey [IRL] 2 F6
Dalmose [DK] 156 F3
Daløy [N] 170 A2
Dalry [GB] 8 C3
Dalsbruk / Taalintehdas [FIN] 176 E6
Dalselv [N] 190 E2
Dalseter [N] 170 G1
Dalseter [N] 180 H4
Dalsjöfors [S] 162 B2
Dalskog [S] 166 D4
Dals Långed [S] 166 D4
Dals Rostock [S] 166 D4
Daluis, Gorges de- [F] 108 E3
Dalum [S] 162 C1
Dalvík [IS] 192 C2
Daly [CY] 154 G5
Dalyan [TR] 130 H6
Dalyan [TR] 154 E2
Damási [GR] 132 F1
Damaskiniá [GR] 128 E5
Damasławek [PL] 36 D1
Damba [N] 180 B5
Dambaslar [TR] 150 C3
Dambeck [D] 20 C5
Dammartin-en-Goële [F] 42 G3
Damme [D] 32 D1
Dammen [N] 164 G2
Dammendorf [D] 34 G3
Damno [PL] 22 C2
Damp 2000 [D] 18 F1
Damparis [F] 56 H4
Dampierre [F] 42 E4
Dampierre [F] 58 A5
Dampierre-sur-Boutonne [F] 54 D5
Dampierre-sur-Salon [F] 58 A4
Damville [F] 26 H5
Damvillers [F] 44 D3
D. Andrijevci [HR] 142 D2
Dăneasa [RO] 148 A1
Daneţi [RO] 146 G2
Dångebo [S] 162 E5
Dangé-St-Romain [F] 54 F3
Danilov [RUS] 202 F1
Danilovgrad [SCG] 144 E4
Danişment [TR] 150 D5
Daniszyn [PL] 36 D5
Danków [PL] 34 H1
Dannäs [S] 162 C4
Dannemarie [F] 58 D4
Dannenberg [D] 18 H5
Dannenwalde [D] 20 D6
Dannike [S] 162 B2
Dánszentmiklós [H] 76 D2
Daon [F] 40 H5
Daoulas [F] 40 B2
Darabani [RO] 204 D3
Darány [H] 74 H5
Darbėnai [LT] 200 D4
Darbu [N] 164 G1
Darda [HR] 76 C6
Dardesheim [D] 32 H3
Dardhë [AL] 128 D5
Darfo [I] 72 B5
Dargilan, Grotte de- [F] 106 E2
Dargun [D] 20 C3
Darıca [TR] 150 D5
Darıca [TR] 150 F3
Darıçayırı [TR] 150 H2
Dariveren [TR] 152 G6
Därligen [CH] 70 E1
Darlington [GB] 10 F2
Darłówko [PL] 22 A2
Darłowo [PL] 22 A2
Darmstadt [D] 46 C3
Darney [F] 58 B2
Darnius [E] 92 G2
Daroca [E] 90 D5
Darque [P] 78 A6
Darro [E] 102 E3
Dartford [GB] 14 E4
Dartmouth [GB] 12 E5
Dartsel [S] 190 H3
Daruvar [HR] 74 G6
Darvas [H] 76 G2
Darwen [GB] 10 E3
Dasburg [D] 44 F1
Dašice [CZ] 50 B4
Dasing [D] 60 D3
Daskalovo [BG] 146 F5
Dasochóri [GR] 130 E3
Dassel [D] 32 F4
Dassow [D] 18 H3
Dasswang [D] 46 H6
Daszyna [PL] 36 G3
Datça [TR] 154 C2
Datteln [D] 30 H2
Daugai [LT] 24 G2
Daugård [DK] 156 C2
Daugavpils [LV] 200 H3
Dauguli [LV] 198 E4
Daun [D] 30 G6
Dautphetal [D] 32 D6
Daventry [GB] 14 D2
Daviá [GR] 136 D2
Davik [N] 180 B5
Daviot [GB] 6 D5
Davle [CZ] 48 F4
Dávleia [GR] 132 H5
Davlós (Kaplıca) [CY] 154 G4
Davos [CH] 72 A2
Davutlar [TR] 152 D5
Dawlish [GB] 12 E5
Dax [F] 66 B6
Dazkırı [TR] 152 H4
Ddrinci [BG] 148 F2
Deal [GB] 14 G5
Deão [P] 78 A6
Deauville [F] 26 G3
Debar [MK] 128 C2
Debeburnu [TR] 152 D2
Debelets [BG] 148 C3
Dębe Wielkie [PL] 38 C3
Dębica [PL] 52 D3
Dębina [PL] 50 E3
Deblin [PL] 38 D5
Debnevo [BG] 148 B4
Dębnica Kaszubska [PL] 22 B2
Dębno [PL] 34 G1
Dębno [PL] 52 B4
Debno [PL] 52 B5
Debovo [BG] 148 B2
Debowo [PL] 24 E4
Debrc [SCG] 142 F3
Debrecen [H] 64 G6
Debrznica [PL] 34 H3
Debrzno [PL] 22 C5
Debür [BG] 148 C6
Dęby [PL] 24 C5
Dečani [SCG] 146 B5
Decazeville [F] 68 A5
Dechtice [SK] 62 H3
Decimomannu [I] 118 C7
Děčín [CZ] 48 F2
Decines [F] 68 G3
Decize [F] 56 D4
De Cocksdorp [NL] 16 D2
Dedaj [AL] 144 E4
Dedebağı [TR] 152 G6
Dedemsvaart [NL] 16 G4
Dédestapolcsány [H] 64 E4
Dedinci [BG] 148 D3
Dedovichi [RUS] 202 B2
Defile de L'Ecluse [F] 70 A2
Dég [H] 76 B3
Degaña [E] 78 F4
Degeberga [S] 158 D2
Degerby [FIN] 168 G1
Degerby [FIN] 176 G5
Degerfors [S] 166 G3
Degerhamn [S] 162 G6
Degerndorf [D] 60 F5
Degernes [N] 166 C3
Degersjö [S] 190 G6
Deggendorf [D] 60 G2
Değirmenalanı [TR] 152 F6
Değirmendere [TR] 150 G3
Değirmendere [TR] 152 C5
Değirmisaz [TR] 152 F1
Dego [N] 194 D1
De Haan [B] 28 F1
Dehesa de Campoamor [E] 104 D3
Deià / Deyá [E] 104 E4
Deidesheim [D] 46 B5
Deifontes [E] 102 E3
Deining [D] 46 H6
Deinze [B] 28 G2
Deizisau [D] 58 H1
Dej [RO] 204 C4
Deje [S] 166 F2
Dekéleia [CY] 154 G5
De Koog [NL] 16 D2
De Kooy [NL] 16 D2
Dekov [BG] 148 B2
Delary [S] 162 C5
Delbrück [D] 32 D3
Delčevo [MK] 128 G1
Delden [NL] 16 G5
Delebäck [S] 166 F4
Deleitosa [E] 96 C1
Đelekovec [HR] 74 G4
Delémont [CH] 58 D5
Delfoí [GR] 132 G5
Delfoí [GR] 132 G5
Delft [NL] 16 C5
Delfzijl [NL] 16 H2
Délia [I] 126 E4
Delianuova [I] 124 C7
Deliatyn [UA] 204 C3
Deliblato [SCG] 142 H2
Deliler [TR] 152 E3
Delitzsch [D] 34 C5
Delle [F] 58 D4
Delme [F] 44 F5
Delmenhorst [D] 18 D5
Delnice [HR] 112 F1
Delouze-Rosières [F] 44 D5
Delsbo [S] 184 D6
Delvin [IRL] 2 E5
Delvina [AL] 132 B1
Delvináki [GR] 132 C1
Demandice [SK] 64 C4
Demänová [SK] 64 D2
Demänovská Jaskyňa Slobody [SK] 64 D2
Demidov [RUS] 202 C4
Demigny [F] 56 G5
Demirci [TR] 150 F5
Demirci [TR] 152 E2
Demirhanlı [TR] 150 B2
Demir Kapija [MK] 128 G2
Demirköy [TR] 150 C1
Demirköy [TR] 150 G5
Demirören [TR] 152 G3
Demirtaş [TR] 150 F4
Demjansk [RUS] 202 C2
Demmin [D] 20 C3
Demoiselles, Grotte des- [F] 106 E3
Demre [TR] 154 H3
Denain [F] 28 G4
Denbigh [GB] 10 C4
Den Burg [NL] 16 D2
Dendermonde [B] 28 H2
Denekamp [NL] 16 G4
Đeneral Janković [SCG] 146 C6
Den Haag [NL] 16 C5
Den Helder [NL] 16 D2
Dénia [E] 104 F1
Denizgören [TR] 150 B5
Denizkent [TR] 150 C5
Denizler [TR] 152 G4
Denizli [TR] 152 G5
Denkendorf [D] 60 E2
Denkingen [D] 58 H3
Den Oever [NL] 16 E2
Denzlingen [D] 58 E3
De Panne [B] 28 F1
Derbent [TR] 152 E4
Derby [GB] 10 E5
Derebağ [TR] 152 E6
Derecske [H] 76 G1
Dereham [GB] 14 G2
Dereköy [TR] 150 C1
Dereköy [TR] 152 E4
Dereköy [TR] 152 F2
Dereköy [TR] 152 G6
Dereköy [TR] 152 H5
Dereli [TR] 150 E6
Deringaj [HR] 112 H4
Dermantsi [BG] 148 A3
Dermbach [D] 46 F1
Dermulo [I] 72 C4
Derneburg [D] 32 G3
Derreada [P] 94 B3
Deruta [I] 116 A2
Derval [F] 40 F5
Dervéni [GR] 132 G6
Derventa [BIH] 142 D2
Dervishka mogila [BG] 150 A1
Descartes [F] 54 F3
Desenzano del Garda [I] 72 B6
Deset [N] 172 C2
Desfína [GR] 132 G5
Desimirovac [SCG] 146 C2
Desio [I] 70 G4
Deskáti [GR] 132 F1
Deskle [SLO] 72 H5
Desmond's Castle [IRL] 4 D3
Desná [CZ] 48 H2
Dešov [CZ] 62 E2
Despeñapperos [E] 96 F6
Despotovac [SCG] 146 C2
Despotovo [SCG] 142 F1
Dessau [D] 34 C4
Destriana [E] 78 G6
Désulo [I] 118 D5
Desvres [F] 28 D2
Deszk [H] 76 E4
Deta [RO] 204 B5
Detk [H] 64 E5
Detkovo [RUS] 198 G2
Detmold [D] 32 E3
Dettelbach [D] 46 F4
Dettifoss [IS] 192 C2
Detva [SK] 64 D3
Deurne [NL] 30 F2
Deutschkreutz [A] 62 F6
Deutschlandsberg [A] 74 D3
Deutsch-Wagram [A] 62 F4
Deva [E] 82 H4
Deva [RO] 204 C5
Dévaványa [H] 76 F2
Devčići [HR] 112 F3
Devecikonağı [TR] 150 E5
Devecser [H] 74 H2
Devene [BG] 146 G3
Deventer [NL] 16 F5
Deveselu [RO] 148 A1
Devetaki [BG] 148 B3
Devin [BG] 130 D1
Devizes [GB] 12 G3
Devnya [BG] 148 F3
Dewsbury [GB] 10 F4
Deyá / Deià [E] 104 E4
Deza [E] 90 C4
Dezzo [I] 72 B4
Dhërmi [AL] 128 B6
Diafáni [GR] 140 H2
Diagučiai [LT] 200 G4
Diakoftó [GR] 132 G6
Dialampí [GR] 130 F3
Diamante [I] 124 C3
Dianalund [DK] 156 F3
Diano Marina [I] 108 G4
Diarvialiai [LT] 200 F4
Diásello [GR] 132 F1
Diatlovo [BY] 202 A6
Diavatá [GR] 128 H4
Dicomano [I] 110 F5
Didcot [GB] 14 D3
Didesti [RO] 148 B1
Dídyma [GR] 136 F2
Didymóteicho [GR] 130 H1
Die [F] 68 G6
Dieburg [D] 46 C3
Diego Alvaro [E] 88 D4
Diekirch [L] 44 F2
Diemelstadt [D] 32 E4
Dienne [F] 68 B4
Dienten [A] 72 G1
Diepholz [D] 32 D1
Dieppe [F] 28 C4
Dierdorf [D] 46 B1
Dieren [NL] 16 F5
Dierzki [PL] 22 H4
Diesdorf [D] 32 H1
Diessen [D] 60 D5
Diest [B] 30 D4
Dietenheim [D] 60 B4
Dietfurt [D] 46 H6
Dietikon [CH] 58 F5
Dietmannsdorf [A] 74 D3
Dietmannsried [D] 60 C5
Dieue-sur-Meuse [F] 44 D4
Dieulefit [F] 68 F6
Dieulouard [F] 44 E5
Dieuze [F] 44 F5
Dieveniškės [LT] 200 G6
Diever [NL] 16 G3
Diez [D] 46 B2
Differdange [L] 44 E3
Digerberget [S] 182 G4
Digermulen [N] 192 D4
Digernes [N] 180 D3
Dignac [F] 66 E2
Dignano [I] 72 G4
Digne-les-Bains [F] 108 D3
Digny [F] 26 H6
Digoin [F] 56 E5
Dijon [F] 56 G4
Dikaia [GR] 150 A2
Dikanäs [S] 190 F4
Dikance [SCG] 128 C1
Dikili [TR] 152 C3
Dikli [LV] 198 E4
Diksmuide [B] 28 F2
Diktaío Ántro [GR] 140 F5
Diktýnaion [GR] 140 B4
Dilesi [GR] 134 C5
Dillenberg [D] 32 D6
Dillingen [D] 44 F3
Dillingen [D] 60 C3
Dilos [GR] 138 E2
Dilwyn [GB] 12 G1
Dímaina [GR] 136 F2
Dimaro [I] 72 C4
Dímitra [GR] 132 G1
Dimitrovgrad [BG] 148 C6
Dimitrovgrad [SCG] 146 E4
Dimmelsvik [N] 170 B5
Dimovo [BG] 146 E2
Dinami [I] 124 D6
Dinan [F] 26 C5
Dinant [B] 30 D6
Dinar [TR] 152 H4
Dinard [F] 26 C4
Dingelstädt [D] 32 G5
Dingle [S] 166 C5
Dingle / An Daingean [IRL] 4 A3
Dingli [M] 126 C6
Dingolfing [D] 60 F3
Dingwall [GB] 6 D4
Dinkelsbühl [D] 46 F6
Dinklage [D] 18 C6
Dinozé [F] 58 C2
Dinslaken [D] 30 G2
Dio [S] 162 D5
Dion [GR] 128 G6
Diosgyőr [H] 64 F4
Dipkarpaz (Rizokárpasox) [CY] 154 H4
Dipótamos [GR] 130 D2
Dippoldiswalde [D] 48 E1
Dirgenler [TR] 154 H3
Disenå [N] 172 C5
Disentis / Mustér [CH] 70 G1
Disneyland [F] 42 G3
Dispilí [GR] 128 E5
Diss [GB] 14 G2
Distomo [GR] 132 H5
Dístrato [GR] 128 D6
Ditzingen [D] 58 G1
Diva Slatina [BG] 146 F3
Divci [SCG] 146 A1
Divčibare [SCG] 146 A2
Dívčí Hrady [CZ] 62 F2

E

Fasterholt [DK] 156 C1
Fastov [UA] 202 D7
Fatezh [RUS] 202 F5
Fátima [E] 100 H4
Fátima [P] 86 C3
Fatjas [S] 190 H1
Fättjaur [S] 190 E3
Faucille, Col de la- [F] 70 B1
Faucogney-et-la-Mer [F] 58 C3
Faulensee [CH] 70 E1
Faulquemont [F] 44 F4
Fausa [N] 180 D4
Fauske [N] 192 D6
Fauville [F] 26 H2
Fåvang [N] 170 H1
Favara [E] 98 E5
Favara [I] 126 D4
Faverges [F] 70 B3
Faverney [F] 58 B3
Favignana [I] 126 A2
Favone [F] 114 B5
Favorite [D] 46 B6
Favrholt [DK] 160 C6
Fawley [GB] 12 H5
Fayence [F] 108 D4
Fayet [F] 106 D3
Fayl-Billot [F] 58 A3
Fayón [E] 90 G5
Fay-sur-Lignon [F] 68 E5
Feakle [IRL] 2 C6
Fécamp [F] 26 G2
Feda [N] 164 C5
Fedje [N] 170 A2
Feengrotten [D] 46 H2
Fefor [N] 170 G1
Fegen [S] 162 B4
Feggeklit [DK] 160 C4
Fegyvernek [H] 76 F1
Fehrbellin [D] 34 D1
Fehring [A] 74 E2
Feigumfoss [N] 170 E1
Feios [N] 170 D2
Feiring [N] 172 C4
Feistritz [A] 74 E2
Feitos [P] 78 A6
Feketić [SCG] 76 D6
Felanitx [E] 104 F5
Felben [A] 72 F1
Felber-tauern Tunnel [A] 72 F2
Feld [A] 72 H3
Feldafing [D] 60 D5
Feldbach [A] 74 E2
Feldballe [DK] 160 E6
Feldberg [D] 20 D5
Feldberg [D] 58 F3
Feldkirch [A] 58 H5
Feldkirchen [A] 74 B3
Feldkirchen [D] 60 E5
Feldsted [DK] 156 C4
Felechosa [E] 82 B3
Feletto [I] 70 D5
Felgueiras [P] 80 C3
Felgyö [H] 76 E3
Félix [E] 104 B4
Felixstowe [GB] 14 G3
Felizzano [I] 70 E6
Fellbach [D] 58 H1
Fellern [A] 72 F1
Felletin [F] 68 B1
Fellingsbro [S] 168 A3
Felnac [RO] 76 G4
Felonica [I] 110 F2
Felsengarten [D] 46 G3
Felsoleperd [H] 76 B4
Felsonyárád [H] 64 F4
Felsoszentiván [H] 76 C4
Felsotárkány [H] 64 E5
Felsozsolca [H] 64 F4
Feltre [I] 72 E5
Femsjö [S] 162 B4
Femundsenden [N] 182 D6
Fenagh [IRL] 2 E4
Fenais da Ajuda [P] 100 E3
Fene [E] 78 D2
Fenékpuszta [H] 74 G3
Fener [I] 72 E5
Fenestrelle [I] 70 C5
Fénétrange [F] 44 G5
Feneu [F] 40 H6
Fénis [I] 70 D4
Fenit [IRL] 4 B3
Fenstad [N] 172 C5
Fer a Cheval, Cirque du- [F] 58 A5
Feragen [N] 182 D4
Féraklos [GR] 154 D4
Ferbane [IRL] 2 D5
Ferdinandshof [D] 20 E4
Fére [GR] 132 H2
Fère, Château de- [F] 44 A3
Fère-Champenoise [F] 44 B4
Fère-en-Tardenois [F] 44 A3
Ferentino [I] 116 B6
Ferento [I] 114 H3
Féres [GR] 130 H3
Ferez [E] 104 B1
Feria [E] 94 G3
Feričanci [HR] 142 D1
Ferizli [TR] 150 H2
Ferla [I] 126 G5
Ferlach [A] 74 B3
Ferleiten [A] 72 G1
Fermignano [I] 110 H6
Fermo [I] 116 C2
Fermoselle [E] 80 G5
Fermoy [IRL] 4 D4
Fernancaballero [E] 96 E4
Fernán Núñez [E] 102 C2
Ferns [IRL] 4 F4
Fernstein [A] 60 C6
Ferovac [HR] 142 C1
Ferrandina [I] 122 D4
Ferrara [I] 110 G2
Ferreira [E] 78 E2
Ferreira do Alentejo [P] 94 D3
Ferreira do Zêzere [P] 86 D3
Ferreries [E] 104 G4
Ferreruela de Huerva [E] 90 D5
Ferrette [F] 58 D4
Ferriere [I] 110 C3
Ferrières [F] 42 G6
Ferrières-sur-Sichon [F] 68 D2
Ferring [DK] 160 B5
Ferrol [E] 78 D1
Fertöd [H] 62 G6
Fertorákos [H] 62 F6
Fertoszentmiklós [H] 62 G6
Festenburg [A] 74 E1
Festøy [N] 180 D4
Festung Königstein [D] 48 F1
Festvåg [N] 192 D5
Fethard [IRL] 4 E4
Fethard [IRL] 4 F5
Fethiye [TR] 154 F2
Fetsund [N] 166 C1
Feu, Roche du- [F] 40 B3
Feucht [D] 46 G5
Feuchtwangen [D] 46 F6
Feurs [F] 68 E2
Fevåg [N] 190 B6
Fevik [N] 164 E5
Fiamignano [I] 116 B4
Fiastra, Abbadia di- [I] 116 C2
Fibiş [RO] 76 G5
Fíchti [GR] 136 E2
Ficulle [I] 114 H3
Fidenza [I] 110 D2
Fidje [N] 164 E4
Fieberbrunn [A] 60 F6
Fier [AL] 128 A4
Fier, Gorges du- [F] 70 A3
Fiera di Primiero [I] 72 E4
Fiesch [CH] 70 E2
Fieschi, Basilica dei- [I] 110 B3
Fiésole [I] 110 F5
Fiesso Umbertiano [I] 110 G2
Figaléia [GR] 136 D3
Figari [F] 114 B6
Figeac [F] 66 H5
Figeholm [S] 162 G3
Figgjo [N] 164 B3
Figline Valdarno [I] 110 F6
Figueira da Foz [P] 80 A6
Figueira de Castelo Rodrigo [P] 80 E6
Figueiró dos Vinhos [P] 86 D3
Figueres / Figueras [E] 92 G2
Fiholm [S] 168 C3
Fiksdal [N] 180 D3
Filadélfi [GR] 130 B4
Filadélfia [I] 124 D6
Fil'akovo [SK] 64 D4
Filatova Gora [RUS] 198 G3
Filevo [BG] 148 C6
Filey [GB] 10 G3
Filia [GR] 134 G2
Filiaşi [RO] 204 C6
Filiátes [GR] 132 C2
Filiatrá [GR] 136 C3
Filipovci [BG] 146 E4
Filipów [PL] 24 D3
Filippiáda [GR] 132 D3
Filippoi [GR] 130 D3
Filipstad [S] 166 F2
Filisur [CH] 70 H2
Filitosa [F] 114 A5
Fillan [N] 190 A6
Fillefjell Pass [N] 170 E2
Fillýra [GR] 130 G2
Filótas [GR] 128 F4
Filóti [GR] 138 F3
Filottrano [I] 116 C1
Filskov [DK] 156 B2
Filyriá [GR] 128 G4
Filzmoos [A] 72 H1
Finale Emília [I] 110 F2
Finale Lígure [I] 108 H3
Fiñana [E] 102 F4
Finby / Särkisalo [FIN] 176 E5
Finderup [DK] 156 B1
Finestrat [E] 104 E2
Fingerbora [S] 166 H2
Finike [TR] 154 H3
Finiq [AL] 132 B1
Finisterre / Fisterra [E] 78 A2
Finja [S] 158 C1
Finnäs [S] 190 H4
Finnbo [S] 174 C4
Finnea [IRL] 2 E5
Finneby [S] 182 H5
Finneid [N] 192 D6
Finneidfjord [N] 190 D2
Finnentrop [D] 32 C5
Finnerödja [S] 166 G4
Finnhöle [S] 174 E5
Finnøy [N] 192 D5
Finnsäter [S] 190 D6
Finnsnes [N] 192 F3
Finnstad [N] 182 C5
Finntorp [S] 166 D3
Finnvelta [N] 172 D5
Finow [D] 34 E1
Finsand [N] 170 H4
Finsjö [S] 162 G4
Finspång [S] 168 A5
Finsta [S] 168 E2
Finsterwalde [D] 34 E5
Finström [FIN] 176 A5
Fionnay [CH] 70 D3
Fionnphort [GB] 8 B1
Fiorenzuola d'Arda [I] 110 C2
Fira / Thíra [GR] 138 F5
Firbis Castle [IRL] 2 C3
Firenze [I] 110 F5
Firenzuola [I] 110 F4
Firkeel [IRL] 4 A5
Firlej [PL] 38 E4
Firminy [F] 68 E3
Fiscal [E] 84 E5
Fischamend [A] 62 F5
Fischbach [D] 44 H4
Fischbach [D] 44 H2
Fischbeck [D] 32 F3
Fischbeck [D] 34 C2
Fischen [D] 60 B6
Fischerbócsa [H] 76 D3
Fishguard [GB] 4 H6
Fisíni [GR] 130 F6
Fiska [N] 180 C4
Fiskárdo [GR] 132 C5
Fiskebäckskil [S] 166 C6
Fiskebøl [N] 192 D4
Fiskevollen [N] 182 C5
Fiskö [FIN] 176 C4
Fismes [F] 44 A3
Fisterra / Finisterre [E] 78 A2
Fistıklı [TR] 150 E4
Fitero [E] 84 A6
Fitjar [N] 170 A5
Fiuggi [I] 116 B6
Fiumefreddo Bruzio [I] 124 D4
Fiumefreddo di Sicilia [I] 124 B8
Fiumicino [I] 114 H6
Fivemiletown [NIR] 2 F3
Fivizzano [I] 110 D4
Fjæra [N] 170 C5
Fjærland [N] 170 D1
Fjäl [S] 182 H2
Fjälkinge [S] 158 D2
Fjällåsen [S] 192 G5
Fjällbacka [S] 166 C5
Fjällgården [S] 182 G4
Fjällnäs [S] 182 D4
Fjaltring [DK] 160 B5
Fjand Gårde [DK] 160 B5
Fjäras [S] 160 H3
Fjärdhundra [S] 168 C2
Fjell [N] 170 A4
Fjellbu [N] 192 F4
Fjellerup [DK] 160 E5
Fjellheim [N] 170 F3
Fjellsrud [N] 166 C1
Fjelstrup [DK] 156 C3
Fjenneslev [DK] 156 F3
Fjerritslev [DK] 160 D3
Fjon [N] 170 B2
Fjone [N] 164 E3
Fjordgård [N] 192 F2
Fjugesta [S] 166 G3
Flå [N] 170 G4
Fladdabister [GB] 6 G4
Fladungen [D] 46 F2
Flaine [F] 70 C3
Flaka [FIN] 168 G1
Flakaberg [S] 194 A8
Flakaträsk [S] 190 F3
Flakk [N] 182 B1
Flakkstadvågen [N] 192 E3
Flåm [N] 170 D3
Flampouráři [GR] 132 D1
Flaran [F] 66 E6
Flärke [S] 184 G1
Flatabø [N] 170 C4
Flateby [N] 166 C1
Flateland [N] 164 E4
Flåten [N] 192 G1
Flåtestøa [N] 172 C2
Flatmark [N] 180 F4
Flatøydegard [N] 170 G3
Flatråker [N] 170 B5
Flätsbo [S] 174 C3
Flätt [N] 190 C4
Flattnitz [A] 74 B2
Flauenskjold [DK] 160 E3
Flaugeac [F] 66 E4
Flavigny-sur-Moselle [F] 44 E5
Fléchin [F] 28 E3
Flecken-berg [D] 32 D5
Fleckenstein, Château de- [F] 44 H4
Fleetwood [GB] 10 D3
Flehingen [D] 46 C6
Flekke [N] 170 B1
Flekkefjord [N] 164 C5
Flemma [N] 180 F2
Flen [S] 168 C4
Flensburg [D] 156 C5
Flerahopp [S] 162 F5
Flers [F] 26 E4
Flesberg [N] 164 G1
Flesnes [N] 192 E3
Fleurance [F] 84 G2
Fleuré [F] 54 F4
Fleurier [CH] 58 C6
Fleurus [B] 30 C5
Fleury [F] 28 C6
Flims [CH] 70 G1
Flims Waldhaus [CH] 70 G1
Flins [F] 42 F3
Flirsch [A] 72 B1
Flisa [N] 172 D4
Flisbrua [N] 172 D4
Flisby [S] 162 E2
Fliseryd [S] 162 G4
Flix [E] 90 H5
Flize [F] 44 C2
Floby [S] 162 C1
Floda [S] 160 H2
Floda [S] 172 H5
Floda [S] 190 H5
Flögåsen [S] 172 F2
Flogned [S] 166 D1
Flogny-la-Chapelle [F] 56 F1
Flöha [D] 48 D1
Flon [S] 182 E4
Flor [S] 182 H5
Florac [F] 68 D6
Florange [F] 44 E3
Florennes [B] 30 C5
Florenville [B] 44 D2
Floreşti [MD] 204 E3
Florídia [I] 126 G5
Flórina [GR] 128 E4
Flornes [N] 182 C1
Florø [N] 180 B5
Florstadt [D] 46 D2
Florvåg [N] 170 A3
Flostrand [N] 190 D2
Flötningen [S] 182 D6
Fluberg [N] 170 H3
Flüelen [CH] 58 F6
Fluglafjørdur [FR] 160 B1
Flühli [CH] 58 E6
Flumeri [I] 120 F2
Flumet [F] 70 B3
Fluminimaggiore [I] 118 B6
Flums [CH] 58 H6
Fluren [S] 174 D1
Flykälen [S] 190 E6
Flymen [S] 162 F6
Flyn [S] 184 D1
Flystveit [N] 164 D4
Flytåsen [S] 174 C2
Fnideq [MAR] 100 G6
Foça [TR] 152 B4
Foča-Srbinje [BIH] 144 D2
Fockbek [D] 18 F2
Focşani [RO] 204 E4
Fódele [GR] 140 E4
Foeni [RO] 76 F6
Fogdö [S] 168 C3
Fóggia [I] 120 G1
Föglö [FIN] 168 H1
Fohnsdorf [A] 74 C2
Foiano di Chiana [I] 114 G1
Foinikoúntas [GR] 136 D4
Foix [F] 84 H5
Fojnica [BIH] 142 C4
Fojnica [BIH] 144 D2
Fokstugu [N] 180 G5
Földeák [H] 76 F4
Foldereid [N] 190 C4
Földes [H] 76 G1
Foldingbro [DK] 156 B3
Folégandros [GR] 138 E4
Folelli [F] 114 C3
Folgaria [I] 72 C5
Folgarida [I] 72 C4
Folgoso [E] 78 E4
Foliá [GR] 130 D4
Foligno [I] 116 A2
Folkärna [S] 174 D5
Folkestad [N] 180 C4
Folkestone [GB] 14 F5
Folladal [N] 190 C5
Follafoss [N] 190 C5
Folldal [N] 180 H5
Follina [I] 72 E5
Föllinge [S] 190 E6
Follónica [I] 114 E2
Folmava [CZ] 48 D5
Fölsbyn [S] 166 D2
Folwarki [PL] 36 G6
Folyás [H] 64 G5
Fondamente [F] 106 D3
Fondi [I] 120 C1
Fondo [I] 72 C3
Fönebo [S] 184 E6
Fonfría [E] 80 G4
Fonfría [E] 90 D5
Fonni [I] 118 D5
Fonseca, Castillo de- [E] 88 E3
Fontainebleau [F] 42 G5
Fontaine-de-Vaucluse [F] 106 H3
Fontaine-Française [F] 56 H3
Fontaine Guérard, Abbaye de- [F] 28 C6
Fontaine Henry, Château de- [F] 26 F3
Fontaine-le-Dun [F] 26 H2
Fontaine-sur-Coole [F] 44 B4
Fontanellato [I] 110 D2
Fontanelle [I] 72 F5
Fontanosas [E] 96 D4
Fonte Avellana, Monastero di- [I] 116 B1
Fontecha [E] 82 G5
Fonte Colombo, Convento di- [I] 116 B4
Fontedias [E] 78 C3
Fontenay, Abbaye de- [F] 56 F2
Fontenay-le-Comte [F] 54 C4
Fontenay-Trésigny [F] 42 G4
Fontevraud-l'Abbaye [F] 54 E2
Fontfroide, Abbaye de- [F] 106 C5
Fontgombault [F] 54 G4
Fontinha [P] 86 C2
Fontioso [E] 88 G1
Fontiveros [E] 88 D3
Font-Romeu [F] 92 E1
Fontstown [IRL] 4 F3
Fontvieille [F] 106 G4
Fonyód [H] 74 H3
Fonzaso [I] 72 E5
Fóppolo [I] 70 H3
Föra [S] 162 G4
Forbach [D] 58 F1
Forbach [F] 44 G4
Forbes, Castle- [IRL] 2 D4
Forcall [E] 98 F1
Forcalquier [F] 108 C3
Forcarei [E] 78 C4
Forchheim [D] 46 G4
Forchtenstein [A] 62 F6
Ford [GB] 8 C2
Førde [N] 164 B1
Førde [N] 180 C6
Fordingbridge [GB] 12 G4
Fordongianus [I] 118 C5
Forenza [I] 120 H3
Forfar [GB] 8 F2
Forges-les-Eaux [F] 28 C5
Forino [I] 120 E3
Forio [I] 120 D3
Førland [N] 164 C5
Forlì [I] 110 G4
Forlì del Sánnio [I] 116 D6
Forlimpopoli [I] 110 G4
Formazza [I] 70 F2
Formby [GB] 10 D3
Formerie [F] 28 D5
Formia [I] 120 C2
Formigine [I] 110 E3
Formiguères [F] 92 E1
Formofoss [N] 190 C5
Fornaci di Barga [I] 110 D4
Fornalutx [E] 104 E4
Fornelli [I] 118 B2
Fornells [E] 104 H4
Forni Avoltri [I] 72 F3
Forni di Sopra [I] 72 F4
Forni di Sotto [I] 72 F4
Forno Alpi Graie [I] 70 C5
Forno di Zoldo [I] 72 E4
Fornos de Algodres [P] 80 D6
Fornovo di Taro [I] 110 D3
Foros Do Arrão [P] 86 D5
Forøy [N] 190 D1
Forráskút [H] 76 E4
Forres [GB] 6 E5
Fors [S] 166 D6
Fors [S] 174 D5
Fors [S] 184 G1
Forsbacka [S] 174 E4
Forsby / Koskenkylä [FIN] 178 B4
Forserum [S] 162 D2
Forset [N] 170 H2
Forshaga [S] 166 F2
Forsheda [S] 162 C4
Forshem [S] 166 E5
Forslöv [S] 162 B6
Forsmark [S] 174 F5
Forsmo [S] 184 E2
Forsnacken [S] 190 F3
Forsnäs [S] 190 G3
Forsnäs [S] 190 G2
Forsnes [N] 180 F1
Forsøl [N] 194 B2
Forssa [FIN] 176 F3
Forst [D] 34 G4
Forsvik [S] 166 G5
Fort Augustus [GB] 6 D5
Forte dei Marmi [I] 110 D5
Forte di Bibbiona [I] 114 E1
Forth [D] 46 G5
Fort-Mahon-Plage [F] 28 D3
Fortrose [GB] 6 E4
Fortun [N] 170 E1
Fortuna [E] 104 C2
Fortuneswell [GB] 12 F5
Fort William [GB] 6 C6
Forvik [N] 190 D3
Fos [F] 84 F5
Fösked [S] 166 F2
Foskros [S] 182 E5
Føskvallen [S] 182 E6
Fosnavåg [N] 180 C4
Fosnes [N] 190 C4
Fossano [I] 108 G2
Fossanova, Abbazia di- [I] 120 C1
Fossbakken [N] 192 F3
Fossby [N] 166 C3
Fossen [N] 180 D6
Fosser [N] 166 C1
Fosses [B] 30 C5
Fossland [N] 190 C5
Fossombrone [I] 112 B6
Fos-sur-Mer [F] 106 G5
Foteiná [GR] 128 G5
Foucarmont [F] 28 C4
Fouesnant [F] 40 B3
Fougères [F] 26 D5
Fougerolles [F] 58 C3
Foulain [F] 56 H2
Foulum [DK] 160 D5
Fouras [F] 54 C5
Fourcès [F] 66 D6
Fourfourás [GR] 140 D5
Foúrka [GR] 128 D6
Fourmies [F] 28 G5
Fourná [GR] 132 F3
Fourneaux [F] 54 H6
Fournels [F] 68 C5
Fournés [GR] 140 C4
Foúrnoi [GR] 138 H1
Fourquet [F] 66 F6
Fours [F] 56 E4
Foústani [GR] 128 G3
Fowey [GB] 12 C5
Foxford [IRL] 2 C3
Foynes [IRL] 4 C3
Foz [E] 78 E2
Foz do Arelho [P] 86 B3
Foz Giraldo [P] 86 E3
Frabosa Soprana [I] 108 G3
Fraga [E] 90 G5
Fragkísta [GR] 132 E4
Fragkokástello [GR] 140 C5
Fraize [F] 58 D2
Framley [DK] 156 D1
Framlingham [GB] 14 G3
Frammersbach [D] 46 D3
Frammestad [S] 166 D6
Framnäs [S] 190 H1
Frampol [PL] 52 F2
Framzelle [F] 14 G6
Francardo [F] 114 B3
Francavilla al Mare [I] 116 D4
Francavilla di Sicilia [I] 124 A8
Francavilla Fontana [I] 122 F4
Francelos [P] 80 B4
Francofonte [I] 126 G4
Frändefors [S] 166 D5
Franeker [NL] 16 F2
Frangy [F] 70 A2
Frankenberg [D] 32 E5
Frankenburg [A] 60 H4
Frankenmarkt [A] 60 H5
Frankenthal [D] 46 B4
Frankfurt (Oder) [D] 34 G3
Frankfurt am Main [D] 46 C3
Frankrike [S] 190 D6
Fränsta [S] 184 D4
Františkovy Lázně [CZ] 48 C3
Franzburg [D] 20 C3
Frasassi, Grotte di- [I] 116 B1
Frascati [I] 116 A6
Frasdorf [D] 60 F5
Fraserburgh [GB] 6 G5
Frashër [AL] 128 C5
Frasno, Puerto de- [E] 90 D4
Frassino [I] 108 F2
Frassinoro [I] 110 E4
Frasso [I] 120 E2
Fratel [P] 86 E4
Fratte Polesine [I] 110 G2
Frauenau [D] 60 H2
Frauenberg [D] 46 D1
Frauenburg [A] 74 B2
Frauenfeld [CH] 58 G4
Frauenkirch [CH] 72 A2
Frauenstein [A] 62 B5
Frauenstein [D] 48 E1
Frauschereck [A] 60 H4
Frayssinet [F] 66 G4
Frechen [D] 30 G4
Frechilla [E] 82 C6
Freckenhorst [D] 32 C3
Fredensborg [DK] 156 G2
Fredericia [DK] 156 C2
Frederiks [DK] 160 C5
Frederiksberg [DK] 156 F3
Frederikshavn [DK] 160 E3
Frederikssund [DK] 156 G2
Frederiksværk [DK] 156 G2
Frednowy [PL] 22 F4
Fredrika [S] 190 G5
Fredriksberg [S] 172 G5
Fredrikshamn / Hamina [FIN] 178 D3
Fredrikstad [N] 166 B3
Fredriksten [N] 166 C3
Fregenal de la Sierra [E] 94 G3
Fregene [I] 114 H5
Freiberg [D] 48 E1
Freiburg [D] 18 E3
Freiburg im Breisgau [D] 58 E3
Freiensteinau [D] 46 D2
Freihung [D] 48 B5
Freilassing [D] 60 G5
Freising [D] 60 E3
Freistadt [A] 62 C3
Freital [D] 48 E1
Freixedas [P] 80 E6
Freixianda [P] 86 D3
Freixo de Espada à Cinta [P] 80 F5
Frejev [DK] 160 D4
Frejlev [DK] 20 B1
Fréjus [F] 108 D5
Fréjus, Tunnel de- [EUR] 70 B5
Frenchpark [IRL] 2 D4
Frenštát pod Radhoštěm [CZ] 50 E5
Freren [D] 32 C1
Freshford [IRL] 4 E4
Fresnay-sur-Sarthe [F] 26 F6
Fresnes [F] 28 F4
Fresnes [F] 58 B3
Fresnes-en-Woëvre [F] 44 E4
Fresno Alhándiga [E] 88 C4
Fresno de la Ribera [E] 88 D1
Fresvik [N] 170 D2
Fréteval [F] 42 D6
Fretigney-et-Velloreille [F] 58 B4
Fretzdorf [D] 20 C6
Freudenberg [D] 32 C6
Freudenberg [D] 46 D4
Freudenstadt [D] 58 F2
Freundsberg [A] 72 E1
Frévent [F] 28 E3
Frey [N] 180 F2
Freyburg [D] 34 B5
Freyenstein [D] 20 B5
Freyming Merlebach [F] 44 F4
Freystadt [D] 46 G6
Freyung [D] 60 H2
Frías [E] 82 F5
Fribourg [CH] 58 D6
Frick [CH] 58 E4
Fridafors [S] 162 D6
Fridingen [D] 58 G3
Friedberg [A] 74 E1
Friedberg [D] 46 C2
Friedberg [D] 60 D3
Friedburg [A] 60 H5
Friedeburg [D] 18 C4
Friedersdorf [D] 34 F3
Friedewald [D] 32 F6
Friedland [D] 20 D4
Friedland [D] 32 F5
Friedland [D] 34 F3
Friedrichroda [D] 46 F1
Friedrichshafen [D] 58 H4
Friedrichskoog [D] 18 E3
Friedrichsort [D] 18 G2
Friedrichstadt [D] 18 E2
Friedrichswalde [D] 20 D6
Friedstein [A] 62 B6
Friesach [A] 74 B2
Friesack [D] 34 D1
Friesoythe [D] 18 C5
Frifelt [DK] 156 B3
Friggesund [S] 184 D6
Frihetsli [N] 192 G3
Frillesås [S] 160 H3
Frinkenberg [A] 72 E1
Frinnaryd [S] 162 E1
Friol [E] 78 D3
Fristad [S] 162 B2
Fritsla [S] 162 B2
Fritzlar [D] 32 E5
Fröderyd [S] 162 E3
Frödinge [S] 162 F2
Frohburg [D] 34 C6
Frohnleiten [A] 74 D1
Froissy [F] 28 D5
Fröjel [S] 168 F5
Frombork [PL] 22 F2
Frome [GB] 12 G4
Fromental [F] 26 F5
Frómista [E] 82 D5
Fromy [F] 44 D2
Fronsac [F] 84 F4
Fronteira [P] 86 E5
Frontenhausen [D] 60 F3
Frontera [E] 100 A5
Frontignan [F] 106 E4
Fronton [F] 84 H2
Fröseke [S] 162 F4
Frosinone [I] 116 C6
Fröskog [S] 166 D4
Frösö [S] 182 G2
Frosolone [I] 120 E1
Frosta [N] 190 B6
Frostavallen [S] 158 C2
Frösthult [S] 168 C2
Frøstrup [DK] 160 C3
Frösunda [S] 168 E2
Frøvik [S] 166 H2
Fruges [F] 28 E3
Frutigen [CH] 70 D1
Fry [GR] 140 G3
Frýdek-Místek [CZ] 50 F5
Frýdlant [CZ] 48 G1
Frýdlant nad Ostravicí [CZ] 50 F5
Frýdštejn [CZ] 48 H2
Frygnowo [PL] 22 G5
Frymburk [CZ] 62 B3
Fryšták [CZ] 50 D6
Frysztak [PL] 52 D4
Ftéri [GR] 132 F6
Fubine [I] 70 E6
Fucécchio [I] 110 E5
Fuencalderas [E] 84 C5
Fuencaliente [E] 96 D5
Fuencaliente de la Palma [E] 100 A4
Fuencaliente de Lucio [E] 82 E4
Fuencarral [E] 88 F5
Fuendejalón [E] 90 D3
Fuendetodos [E] 90 E4
Fuengirola [E] 102 B5
Fuenlabrada [E] 88 F6
Fuenlabrada de los Montes [E] 96 C3
Fuenmayor [E] 82 G6
Fuensalida [E] 96 E1
Fuensanta [E] 104 C3
Fuente Álamo [E] 98 C6
Fuente Álamo de Murcia [E] 104 C4
Fuentecén [E] 88 G2
Fuente Dé [E] 82 D3
Fuente de Cantos [E] 94 G3
Fuente del Arco [E] 94 H4
Fuente del Maestre [E] 94 G3
Fuente del Obispo [E] 102 E2
Fuente de Santa Cruz [E] 88 E3
Fuente el Fresno [E] 96 F3
Fuente el Sauz [E] 88 G5
Fuente el Sol [E] 88 D3
Fuenteguinaldo [E] 86 H2
Fuentelapeña [E] 88 D2
Fuentelcésped [E] 88 G2
Fuentelespino de Haro [E] 96 H3
Fuentelespino de Moya [E] 98 D3
Fuentemilanos [E] 88 F4
Fuente Obejuna [E] 96 B5
Fuente Palmera [E] 102 B1
Fuentepinilla [E] 90 B3
Fuenterrabía / Hondarribia [E] 84 B2
Fuentes [E] 98 C2
Fuentesaúco [E] 80 H6
Fuentes de Andalucía [E] 102 A2
Fuentes de Ayódar [E] 98 F3
Fuentes de Ebro [E] 90 E4
Fuentes de Jiloca [E] 90 D4
Fuentes de León [E] 94 G4
Fuentes de Nava [E] 82 C6
Fuentes de Oñoro [E] 86 H2
Fuentes de Ropel [E] 82 A5
Fuentidueña de Tajo [E] 96 H1
Fuerte del Rey [E] 102 E2
Fügen [A] 72 E1
Fuglebjerg [DK] 156 F3
Fuglem [N] 182 C2
Fuhrberg [D] 32 G1
Fulda [D] 46 E2
Fulgem [N] 182 C2
Fulnek [CZ] 50 E5
Fülöpszállás [H] 76 C3
Fulpmes [A] 72 D1
Fulunäs [S] 172 E2
Fumay [F] 30 C6
Fumel [F] 66 F5
Funäsdalen [S] 182 E4
Funchal [P] 100 A3
Fundão [P] 86 F2
Fundres / Pfundres [I] 72 E2
Furadouro [P] 80 B4
Furculeşti [RO] 148 B2
Fure [N] 170 B1
Furnes (Veurne) [B] 28 F1
Fürnitz [A] 72 H3
Furset [N] 180 E2
Fürstenau [D] 32 C1
Fürstenberg [D] 20 D5
Fürstenfeld [A] 74 E2
Fürstenfeldbruck [D] 60 D4
Fürstenwalde [D] 34 F2
Fürstenwerder [D] 20 D5
Fürstenzell [D] 60 H3
Furta [H] 76 G2
Furtan [S] 166 E2
Fürth [D] 46 G5
Furth im Wald [D] 48 D6
Furtwangen [D] 58 F3
Furuby [S] 162 E4
Furudal [S] 172 H2
Furuflaten [N] 192 G2
Furusjö [S] 162 D1
Furusund [S] 168 F2
Furutangvik [N] 190 D4

Goričan [HR] 74 F4
Goricë [AL] 128 D4
Gorinchem [NL] 16 D5
Gorino Veneto [I] 110 H3
Goritsy [RUS] 202 E2
Göritz [D] 20 E5
Gorízia [I] 72 H5
Gørlev [DK] 156 F3
Gorlice [PL] 52 C5
Görlitz [D] 34 G6
Gormanston Castle [IRL] 2 F5
Gormund [CH] 58 F5
Gorna Beshovica [BG] 146 G3
Gorna Cerovene [BG] 146 F3
Gorna Kremena [BG] 146 G3
Gorna Mitropoliya [BG] 148 A3
Gorna Oryakhovitsa [BG] 148 C3
Gorna Studena [BG] 148 C3
Gorni Tsibur [BG] 146 F2
Gornja Grabovica [BIH] 144 C2
Gornjak, Manastir- [SCG] 146 C1
Gornja Klina [SCG] 146 B5
Gornja Ploča [HR] 112 G4
Gornja Radgona [SLO] 74 E3
Gornja Sabanta [SCG] 146 C2
Gornja Toponica [SCG] 146 D3
Gornja Tuzla [BIH] 142 E3
Gornji Lapac [HR] 112 H4
Gornji Milanovac [SCG] 146 B2
Gornji Podgradci [BIH] 142 B2
Gornji Ravno [BIH] 144 B1
Górno [PL] 52 C1
Gorno Alexandrovo [BG] 148 E4
Gorno Novo Selo [BG] 148 C5
Gorno Yabălkovo [BG] 148 E5
Gorobinci [MK] 128 F1
Gorodets [RUS] 198 H2
Gorodno [RUS] 198 H3
Górowo Iławeckie [PL] 22 G2
Gorreana [P] 100 E3
Gorredijk [NL] 16 F2
Gorron [F] 26 E5
Gørslev [DK] 156 G3
Gort [IRL] 2 C5
Górtys [GR] 136 D2
Górtys [GR] 140 E5
Görükle [TR] 150 E4
Gorv [N] 180 B5
Görvik [S] 184 C1
Gorzanów [PL] 50 C3
Görzke [D] 34 C3
Gorzkowice [PL] 36 G6
Gorzków-Osada [PL] 38 F6
Górzna [PL] 22 B5
Górzno [PL] 22 F6
Górzno [PL] 36 E4
Gorzów Śląski [PL] 50 F1
Gorzów Wielkopolski [PL] 34 H2
Górzyca [PL] 34 G2
Gorzyce [PL] 52 D2
Gorzyń [PL] 36 B2
Goržžam [N] 194 D3
Gosaldo [I] 72 E4
Gosau [A] 60 H6
Göschenen [CH] 70 F1
Gościno [PL] 20 G3
Gosdorf [A] 74 E3
Goslar [D] 32 G3
Goślice [PL] 36 H2
Gospari [LV] 198 F6
Gospić [HR] 112 G4
Gosport [GB] 12 H5
Gossau [CH] 58 H5
Gosselies [B] 30 C5
Gossensass / Colle Isarco [I] 72 D2
Gössl [A] 62 B6
Gössweinstein [D] 46 G4
Gosticy [RUS] 198 G1
Gostilicy [RUS] 178 G5
Gostivar [MK] 128 D1
Gostkow [PL] 36 F4
Göstling [A] 62 C5
Gostomia [PL] 22 A6
Gostycyn [PL] 22 C5
Gostyń [PL] 36 C4
Gostynin [PL] 36 G2
Goszcz [PL] 36 D5
Goszczanowo [PL] 36 A2
Göteborg [S] 160 G2
Götene [S] 166 E5
Gotha [D] 32 H6
Gothem [S] 168 G4
Götlunda [S] 168 A3
Gotse Delchev [BG] 130 C1
Gottböle [FIN] 186 A4
Gottby [FIN] 176 A5
Gotthard Tunnel [CH] 70 F2
Göttingen [D] 32 F4
Gottne [S] 184 G1
Gottolengo [I] 110 D1
Gottröra [S] 168 E2
Göttweig [A] 62 D4
Götzis [A] 58 H5
Gouarec [F] 26 A5
Gouda [NL] 16 D5
Goules, Col des- [F] 68 C2
Gouménissa [GR] 128 G3
Goumois [CH] 58 C5
Gourdon [F] 66 G4
Gourin [F] 40 C3
Gournay-en-Bray [F] 28 C5
Goúrnes [GR] 140 E4
Gourniá [GR] 140 G5
Gourville [F] 54 D6
Gout-Rossignol [F] 66 E2
Gouveia [P] 80 D6
Goúves [GR] 140 F4
Gouvets [F] 26 E4
Gouviá [GR] 132 B2
Gouzon [F] 56 B6
Govedartsi [BG] 146 G6
Govedjari [HR] 144 B3
Gøvstdal [N] 170 F5
Goworowo [PL] 24 C6
Gowran [IRL] 4 F4
Göynükbelen [TR] 150 F5
Gózd [PL] 52 B1
Gozdnica [PL] 34 H5
Gözler [TR] 152 G4
Graal-Müritz [D] 20 B2
Grab [BIH] 144 D4
Grab [PL] 36 D4
Grabaţ [RO] 76 F5
Graberje [HR] 142 A1
Gråbo [S] 160 H2
Gråborg [S] 162 G5
Grabow [D] 20 A5
Grabów [PL] 36 F3
Grabowiec [PL] 52 G1
Grabówka [PL] 24 F5
Grabownica Starzeńska [PL] 52 E4
Grabów n Prosną [PL] 36 E5
Grabowskie [PL] 24 D5
Gračac [HR] 112 H4
Gračanica [BIH] 142 D3
Gračanica [SCG] 146 C5
Graçay [F] 54 H3
Grächen [CH] 70 E2
Gračišće [HR] 112 D2
Gračišče [SLO] 72 H6
Gradac [BIH] 144 C3
Gradac [HR] 144 B3
Gradac [SCG] 144 E4
Gradac [SCG] 144 E2
Gradac, Manastir- [SCG] 146 B3
Gradačac [BIH] 142 D2
Graddis [N] 190 F1
Gräddö [S] 168 F2
Gradec [BG] 146 E2
Gradefes [E] 82 C4
Graderas, Cueva de las- [E] 90 E6
Gradešnika [MK] 128 F3
Gradets [BG] 148 D4
Gradignan [F] 66 C3
Gradina [HR] 112 F3
Gradina [SCG] 146 E4
Gradisca d'Isonzo [I] 72 H5
Gradishte [BG] 148 B3
Gradište [HR] 142 E2
Gradište [SCG] 146 E3
Grado [E] 78 G3
Grado [I] 72 G6
Gradsko [MK] 128 F2
Græsted [DK] 156 G1
Grafenau [D] 60 H2
Gräfenberg [D] 46 G4
Grafenegg [A] 62 E4
Gräfenhainichen [D] 34 C4
Grafenwöhr [D] 48 B4
Grafing [D] 60 E4
Grafrath [D] 60 D4
Gräfsnäs [S] 160 H1
Graglia, Santuário di- [I] 70 E4
Gragnano [I] 120 E3
Grahovo [SCG] 144 D4
Graiguenamanagh [IRL] 4 F4
Grainetière, Abbaye de la- [F] 54 C3
Graja, Cueva de la- [E] 102 E2
Grajewo [PL] 24 D4
Gralhos [P] 80 D3
Gralla [A] 74 D3
Grallagh [IRL] 2 D4
Gram [DK] 156 B3
Gramada [BG] 146 E2
Gramat [F] 66 G4
Gramatikovo [BG] 148 F5
Grametten [A] 62 D2
Gramkow [D] 20 A3
Grammatikó [GR] 132 G3
Gramméni Oxyá [GR] 132 F4
Gramméno [GR] 132 C2
Grammichele [I] 126 F4
Gram Slot [DK] 156 B3
Gramzda [LV] 198 B6
Gramzow [D] 20 E5
Gran [N] 172 B4
Granada [E] 102 E4
Granadilla de Abona [E] 100 B5
Granard [IRL] 2 E4
Granarolo dell'Emilia [I] 110 F3
Granåsen [S] 190 F5
Granátula de Calatrava [E] 96 F4
Granberget [S] 190 F5
Granboda [FIN] 176 B6
Grancey-le-Château [F] 56 G3
Grandas de Salime [E] 78 F3
Grandcamp-Maisy [F] 26 E2
Grand-Champ [F] 26 A6
Grand Chartreuse, Couvent de la- [F] 68 H4
Grande-Fougeray [F] 40 F5
Grandjouan [F] 40 F5
Grândola [P] 94 C2
Grandpré [F] 44 C3
Grandrieu [F] 68 D5
Grand Roc [F] 66 F3
Grand-Rozoy [F] 42 H3
Grandson [CH] 58 C6
Grand-St-Bernard, Col du- [EUR] 70 C3
Grandvilliers [F] 28 D5
Grañén [E] 90 F3
Grangärde [S] 172 H5
Grange [IRL] 2 D3
Grange-Bleneau, Château de la- [F] 42 G4
Grange-le-Bocage [F] 42 H5
Grängesberg [S] 172 H6
Granges-sur-Vologne [F] 58 D2
Grängsjö [S] 184 E5
Granhult [S] 192 H6
Graninge [S] 184 E2
Granitola Torretta [I] 126 B3
Granitz, Jagdschloss- [D] 20 E2
Granja [P] 80 B4
Granja [P] 94 E3
Granja de Moreruela [E] 80 H4
Granja de Torrehermosa [E] 96 B5
Grankulla / Kauniainen [FIN] 176 H5
Grankullavik [S] 162 H3
Granlunda [S] 168 C1
Gränna [S] 162 D1
Grannäs [S] 190 F3
Granne [PL] 38 E2
Grannes [N] 190 E3
Gränningen [S] 184 C2
Granollers [E] 92 E4
Granön [S] 190 H5
Granowo [PL] 36 C3
Gransee [D] 20 D6
Gränsgård [S] 190 G3
Gransherad [N] 164 F1
Gransjö [S] 196 A2
Gränsjön [S] 166 D2
Gran Tarajal [E] 100 E6
Grantham [GB] 10 F6
Grantown-on-Spey [GB] 6 E5
Granträsk [S] 190 G5
Granvik [S] 166 G5
Granvika [N] 182 C5
Granville [F] 26 D4
Granvin [N] 170 C3
Granvollen [N] 172 B4
Grao / el Grau [E] 98 F6
Grasbakken [N] 194 E2
Gräsberg [S] 172 H5
Gräsmark [S] 166 E1
Gräsmyr [S] 190 H6
Gräso [S] 174 F5
Grassano [I] 122 C4
Grassau [D] 60 F5
Grasse [F] 108 E4
Grässjön [S] 184 C3
Grästen [DK] 156 C4
Grästorp [S] 166 D6
Gratangen [N] 192 F4
Gråtanliden [S] 190 F4
Gratkorn [A] 74 D2
Gråträsk [S] 190 H3
Graulhet [F] 106 B3
Graus [E] 90 H3
Grava [S] 166 E2
Grávalos [E] 84 A5
Gravberget [N] 172 D3
Gravdal [N] 164 B4
Gravdal [N] 192 C4
Grave [NL] 16 E6
Gravedona [I] 70 G3
Gravelines [F] 14 H6
Gravellona Toce [I] 70 F3
Gravens [DK] 156 C2
Gravesend [GB] 14 F4
Gravhaug [N] 180 C5
Graviá [GR] 132 G4
Gravina in Púglia [I] 122 D3
Gravitsa [GR] 132 E3
Gravmark [S] 196 A5
Gravoúna [GR] 130 E3
Gray [F] 58 A4
Graz [A] 74 D2
Grazalema [E] 100 H4
Gražiškiai [LT] 24 E2
Grazzanise [I] 120 D2
Grazzano Visconti [I] 110 C2
Grčak [SCG] 146 C3
Grdelica [SCG] 146 D4
Greaca [RO] 148 D1
Greaker [N] 164 H2
Great Dunmow [GB] 14 F3
Great Malvern [GB] 12 G2
Great Torrington [GB] 12 D3
Great Yarmouth [GB] 14 H2
Grebbestad [S] 166 B4
Grebenhain [D] 46 D2
Grebenstein [D] 32 F5
Grębkowo [PL] 38 D3
Grębocin [PL] 22 E6
Greding [D] 46 G6
Greencastle [NIR] 2 F5
Greenock [GB] 8 D3
Greetsiel [D] 16 H1
Gregolímano [GR] 132 H4
Greifenburg [A] 72 G3
Greiffenberg [D] 20 E6
Greifswald [D] 20 D3
Greillenstein [A] 62 D3
Grein [A] 62 C4
Greiz [D] 48 C2
Grenaa [DK] 160 F5
Grenade [F] 66 C6
Grenade [F] 84 H2
Grenchen [CH] 58 D5
Grenctale [LV] 198 E6
Grenoble [F] 68 H4
Grense-Jakobselv [N] 194 F3
Grenzland-Turm [CZ] 48 C4
Gréolières [F] 108 E4
Gréoux-les-Bains [F] 108 C4
Gressoney-la-Trinité [I] 70 E3
Gressoney-St-Jean [I] 70 E4
Gresten [A] 62 D5
Gretna Green [GB] 8 E5
Greussen [D] 32 H5
Greux [F] 44 D6
Grevbäck [S] 166 G6
Greve in Chianti [I] 110 F6
Greven [D] 32 C2
Grevená [GR] 128 E6
Grevenbroich [D] 30 G4
Grevenbrück [D] 32 C5
Grevenmacher [L] 44 F2
Grevesmühlen [D] 18 H3
Greve Strand [DK] 156 G3
Greyabbey [NIR] 2 H4
Greystones [IRL] 4 G3
Grez-en-Bouère [F] 40 H5
Grezzana [I] 72 C6
Grianan of Aileach [IRL] 2 F2
Gries-am-Brenner [A] 72 D2
Griesbach [D] 60 H3
Gries in Sellrain [A] 72 D1
Grieskirchen [A] 62 A4
Griffen [A] 74 C3
Grignan [F] 106 H2
Grignols [F] 66 D5
Grillby [S] 168 C2
Grimaldi [I] 124 D5
Grimaud [F] 108 D5
Grimdalen [N] 164 E2
Grimma [D] 34 D6
Grimmen [D] 20 D3
Grimo [N] 170 C4
Grimsås [S] 162 C3
Grimsbu [N] 180 H5
Grimsby [GB] 10 G4
Grimsdalshytta [N] 180 H5
Grimslöv [S] 162 D5
Grímsstaðir [IS] 192 C2
Grimstad [N] 164 E5
Grindaheim [N] 170 F2
Grindavík [IS] 192 A3
Grindelwald [CH] 70 E1
Grindjorda [N] 192 E4
Grindsted [DK] 156 B2
Grinkiškis [LT] 200 F4
Griñón [E] 88 F6
Grinzane Cavour [I] 108 G2
Gripenberg [S] 162 E1
Gripenberg [S] 162 E1
Grisignano di Zocco [I] 72 D6
Grisolles [F] 84 H2
Grisslehamn [S] 174 G6
Grivitsa [BG] 148 B3
Grizáno [GR] 132 F2
Grižkabūdis [LT] 200 E5
Grøa [N] 180 G3
Gröbers [D] 34 C5
Grobina [LV] 198 B6
Gröbming [A] 74 B1
Grocka [SCG] 142 H3
Gródek [PL] 24 F5
Gródek [PL] 38 G1
Gródek nad Dunajcem [PL] 52 C4
Gröditz [D] 34 E5
Gródki [PL] 52 F1
Grodków [PL] 50 D2
Grodno [PL] 50 B2
Grodzeń [PL] 36 G1
Grodziec [PL] 36 A6
Grodziec [PL] 50 F4
Grodzisk Mazowiecki [PL] 38 B3
Grodzisk Wielkopolski [PL] 36 B3
Groenlo [NL] 16 G5
Groix [F] 40 C4
Grojdibodu [RO] 148 A2
Grójec [PL] 36 D3
Grójec [PL] 38 B4
Grömitz [D] 18 H3
Gromnik [PL] 52 C4
Gromo [I] 72 A4
Gromovo [RUS] 178 G2
Gromovo [RUS] 200 D5
Grøna [N] 180 F5
Gronau [D] 16 G5
Gronau [D] 32 F3
Grönbo [S] 196 A4
Grønbua [N] 180 F6
Grøndal [N] 180 B5
Grong [N] 190 C5
Grönhögen [S] 158 G1
Grønhøj [DK] 160 C5
Gröningen [D] 34 A3
Groningen [NL] 16 G2
Grønlja [N] 190 B6
Grønnes [N] 180 E3
Grönskåra [S] 162 F4
Grönsö [S] 168 C2
Gropen [S] 166 G3
Grósio [I] 72 B4
Grossarl [A] 72 G1
Grossbeeren [D] 34 E2
Grossbreitenbach [D] 46 G2
Grossburgwedel [D] 32 G2
Grossenbrode [D] 18 H2
Grossenhain [D] 34 E5
Grossenkneten [D] 18 C5
Grossenzersdorf [A] 62 F4
Grosseto [I] 114 F3
Gross-Gerau [D] 46 C3
Gross-Gerungs [A] 62 C3
Grossharras [A] 62 F3
Grosshöchstetten [CH] 58 E6
Gross Mohrdorf [D] 20 C2
Gross Oesingen [D] 32 H1
Gross-Pertenschlag [A] 62 C4
Gross-Pertholz [A] 62 C3
Grosspetersdorf [A] 74 F2
Grossraming [A] 62 C5
Gross Räschen [D] 34 F5
Gross Schönebeck [D] 34 E1
Gross-Siegharts [A] 62 D3
Gross-Umstadt [D] 46 D3
Grostenquin [F] 44 F4
Grosuplje [SLO] 74 C5
Grøtavær [N] 192 E3
Grötholen [S] 182 E6
Grotli [N] 180 E5
Grottaglie [I] 122 F4
Grottaminarda [I] 120 F2
Grottammare [I] 116 D2
Grotteria [I] 124 D7
Grouw [NL] 16 F2
Grövelsjön [S] 182 D5
Grovfjord [N] 192 E4
Grovo [N] 164 F3
Grozd'ovo [BG] 148 F3
Grožnjan [HR] 112 D1
Grua [N] 172 B5
Grubben [N] 190 E3
Gruda [HR] 144 D4
Grude [BIH] 144 B2
Grude [S] 162 B1
Grudusk [PL] 22 H6
Grudziądz [PL] 22 E5
Gruemirë [AL] 144 E5
Gruia [RO] 146 E1
Gruibingen [D] 60 B3
Gruissan [F] 106 D5
Grumentum [I] 120 H5
Grums [S] 166 E3
Grünau [A] 62 B5
Grünberg [D] 46 D1
Grünburg [A] 62 B5
Grundfors [S] 190 E4
Grundfors [S] 190 G4
Grundforsen [S] 172 E2
Grundlsee [A] 62 A6
Grundsel [S] 190 H3
Grundsjö [S] 190 F5
Grundsjö [S] 190 F4
Grundsjön [S] 184 C5
Grundsund [S] 166 C6
Grundsunda [S] 184 H2
Grundtjärn [S] 184 E1
Grünenplan [D] 32 F3
Grungedal [N] 164 E1
Grünheide [D] 34 F2
Grünstadt [D] 46 B4
Grunwald [PL] 22 G5
Grupčin [MK] 128 D1
Grüsch [CH] 58 H6
Gruškovje [SLO] 74 E4
Gruta de Sant Josep [E] 98 F4
Gruvberget [S] 174 D3
Gruyères [CH] 70 C1
Gruža [SCG] 146 B2
Gruzdžiai [LT] 200 E3
Grybów [PL] 52 C5
Grycksbo [S] 172 H4
Gryfice [PL] 20 G4
Gryfino [PL] 20 F5
Gryfów Śląski [PL] 48 H1
Grykë [AL] 128 A4
Gryllefjord [N] 192 E2
Grymyr [N] 170 H5
Gryneion [TR] 152 C3
Gryt [S] 168 C4
Gryt [S] 168 C6
Gryta [N] 190 A6
Grytgöl [S] 166 H4
Grythyttan [S] 166 G2
Grytsjö [S] 190 E4
Grytstorp [S] 166 H5
Gryzy [PL] 24 D3
Grzmiąca [PL] 22 A4
Grzybno [PL] 22 F5
Gschnitz [A] 72 D2
Gschwend [D] 46 E6
Gstaad [CH] 70 D2
Gstadt [D] 60 F5
Gsteig [CH] 70 D2
Guadahortuna [E] 102 E3
Guadajoz [E] 94 H6
Guadalajara [E] 88 G5
Guadalcanal [E] 94 H4
Guadalcázar [E] 102 B1
Guadalerzas [E] 96 F3
Guadalest [E] 104 E2
Guadalmez [E] 96 C4
Guadalmina [E] 102 A5
Guadalupe [E] 96 C2
Guadalupe, Monasterio de- [E] 96 C2
Guadalupe, Santuario de- [E] 102 F1
Guadamur [E] 96 E2
Guadarrama [E] 88 F5
Guadix [E] 102 F4
Guagno [F] 114 B4
Gualdo Tadino [I] 116 B2
Guarcino [I] 116 C6
Guarda [CH] 72 B2
Guarda [P] 86 G2
Guardamar del Segura [E] 104 D3
Guardavalle [I] 124 D6
Guardiagrele [I] 116 D5
Guardialfiera [I] 116 E6
Guardia Lombardi [I] 120 F3
Guardia Piemontese [I] 124 C4
Guardia Sanframondi [I] 120 E2
Guardias Viejas [E] 102 F5
Guardo [E] 82 C4
Guareña [E] 94 H2
Guarromán [E] 96 E6
Guasila [I] 118 C6
Guastalla [I] 110 E2
Gubanitsy [RUS] 178 G6
Gubbhögen [S] 190 E5
Gúbbio [I] 116 A1
Gubbmyran [S] 172 E2
Gubbträsk [S] 190 G4
Guben [D] 34 G4
Guberevac [SCG] 146 B2
Gubin [PL] 34 G4
Guča [SCG] 146 B2
Gücenoluk [TR] 152 H1
Gudavac [BIH] 142 A2
Guddal [N] 170 B1
Guderup [DK] 156 C4
Gudhjem [DK] 158 E4
Gudow [D] 18 G4
Gudvangen [N] 170 D2
Guebwiller [F] 58 D3
Güéjar Sierra [E] 102 E4
Guémené-Penfao [F] 40 F5
Guémené-sur-Scorff [F] 40 D3
Guenange [F] 44 F3
Guer [F] 26 B6
Guérande [F] 40 D6
Guéret [F] 54 H6
Guérigny [F] 56 D4
Guethary [F] 84 C2
Gueugnon [F] 56 E5
Güglingen [D] 46 C6
Guglionesi [I] 116 F5
Gugny [PL] 24 E5
Guía de Isora [E] 100 B5
Guichen [F] 26 C6
Guidonia [I] 116 A5
Guíglia [I] 110 E3
Guignes [F] 42 G4
Guijuelo [E] 88 C4
Guillaumes [F] 108 E3
Guillena [E] 94 G5
Guillestre [F] 108 E2
Guilvinec [F] 40 B3
Güímar [E] 100 C5
Guimarães [P] 80 C3
Guimiliau [F] 40 C2
Guincho [P] 86 A5
Guînes [F] 14 G6
Guingamp [F] 26 A4
Guipry [F] 40 F4
Guísamo [E] 78 D2
Guisborough [GB] 10 G2
Guise [F] 28 G5
Guissény [F] 40 B1
Guissona [E] 92 C3
Guitiriz [E] 78 D2
Guîtres [F] 66 D3
Gujan-Mestras [F] 66 B3
Gükçeyazı [TR] 152 D1
Gulbene [LV] 198 F4
Guldborg [DK] 156 F5
Gülec [TR] 150 C5
Gulgofjorden [N] 194 D1
Gulla [N] 180 G2
Gullabo [S] 162 F6
Gullaskruv [S] 162 F4
Gullbrå [N] 170 C2
Gulleråsen [S] 172 H3
Gullfoss [IS] 192 B3
Gullhaug [N] 164 H2
Gullringen [S] 162 F2
Gullsby [S] 172 E6
Gullspång [S] 166 F4
Gullstein [N] 180 F1
Güllü [TR] 152 F4
Güllüce [TR] 150 E5
Güllük [TR] 154 C1
Gülpınar [TR] 134 G1
Gulsele [S] 190 F6
Gulsrud [N] 170 H5
Gulsvik [N] 170 G4
Gülübintsi [BG] 148 D5
Gülübovo [BG] 148 D5
Gulyantsi [BG] 148 B2
Gumboda [S] 196 A5
Gumhöjden [S] 166 F1
Gumiel de Hizán [E] 88 G2
Gumlösa [S] 158 D1
Gummersbach [D] 32 C5
Gumpoldskirchen [A] 62 F5
Gumtow [D] 20 B6
Gümüldür [TR] 152 C5
Gümüşpınar [TR] 150 D2
Gümüşsu [TR] 152 H4
Gümüşyeni [TR] 150 G5
Gümzovo [BG] 146 E2
Gundelfingen [D] 60 C3
Gundelsheim [D] 46 D5
Güneşli [TR] 152 E2
Güney [TR] 152 F4
Güney [TR] 152 G5
Güngör (Koutsovéntis) [CY] 154 G5
Güngörmez [TR] 152 D1
Gunja [HR] 142 E2
Günlüce [TR] 152 F1
Gunnarn [S] 190 G4
Gunnarp [S] 162 B4
Gunnarsbyn [S] 196 B2
Gunnarskog [S] 166 D1
Gunnarskulla [FIN] 176 G5
Gunnarvattnet [S] 190 E5
Gunnebo [S] 162 G2
Gunnilbo [S] 168 B2
Gunten [CH] 70 E1
Güntersberge [D] 32 H4
Guntersblum [D] 46 C4
Guntersdorf [A] 62 E3
Guntertshausen [A] 60 G4
Guntín [E] 78 D3
Günzburg [D] 60 C3
Gunzenhausen [D] 46 F6
Güre [TR] 152 F3
Güre [TR] 152 H3
Güreci [TR] 150 B5
Gurgazu [F] 114 B6
Gurk [A] 74 B2
Gurkovo [BG] 148 C4
Gurlevo [RUS] 178 F6
Gürpinar [TR] 150 E3
Gurrea de Gállego [E] 90 F3
Gürsu [TR] 150 F4
Gurtnellen [CH] 70 F1
Gusev [RUS] 24 D1
Gusinje [SCG] 146 A5
Gusmar [AL] 128 B6
Gúspini [I] 118 C6
Gusselby [S] 166 H2
Güssing [A] 74 F2
Gusswerk [A] 62 D6
Gustavberg [S] 190 H4
Gustavfors [S] 172 F5
Gustavs / Kustavi [FIN] 176 C4
Gustavsberg [S] 168 E3
Gustavsfors [S] 166 D3
Güstrow [D] 20 B4
Gusum [S] 168 B6
Gusvattnet [S] 190 E5
Guta [BY] 202 D6
Gutcher [GB] 6 H3
Gutenstein [A] 62 E5
Gütersloh [D] 32 D3
Gutštejn [CZ] 48 D4
Guttannen [CH] 70 F1
Gützkow [D] 20 D3
Güvercinlik [TR] 154 C1
Güzelbahçe [TR] 152 C4
Güzelpinar [TR] 152 G4
Güzelyalı (Vavylás) [CY] 154 F5
Güzelyurt (Mórfou) [CY] 154 F5
Guzet-Neige [F] 84 H5
Gvardeiskoye [RUS] 22 H2
Gvardeysk [RUS] 24 B1
Gvarv [N] 164 F2
Gvozd [HR] 112 H1
Gvozd [SCG] 144 E3
Gwatt [CH] 70 D1
Gwda Wielka [PL] 22 B4
Gy [F] 58 B4
Gya [N] 164 B4
Gyermely [H] 64 B6
Gyl [N] 180 F2
Gylien [S] 194 B8
Gylling [DK] 156 D2
Gýmeš [SK] 64 B4
Gymnó [GR] 134 C5
Gyomaendrod [H] 76 F2
Gyömro [H] 76 D1
Gyöngyös [H] 64 E5
Gyöngyöspata [H] 64 D5
Gyönk [H] 76 B3
Gyor [H] 62 H6
Gysinge [S] 174 E5
Gýtheio [GR] 136 E4
Gyttorp [S] 166 G2
Gyueshevo [BG] 146 E6
Gyula [H] 76 G3
Gzy [PL] 38 B1

H

Häädemeeste [EST] 198 D3
Haag [A] 62 C4
Haag [D] 60 F4
Haag am Hausruck [A] 62 A4
Haaksbergen [NL] 16 G5
Haapajärvi [FIN] 196 D6
Haapajoki [FIN] 196 C4
Haapa-Kimola [FIN] 178 B3
Haapakylä [FIN] 186 G3
Haapala [FIN] 196 D3
Haapamäki [FIN] 186 E4
Haapamäki [FIN] 188 D3
Haapamäki [FIN] 188 D1
Haapamäki [FIN] 196 E6
Haapasalmi [FIN] 188 F4
Haapavesi [FIN] 196 D5
Haapsalu [EST] 198 D2
Haar [D] 60 E4
Haarajoki [FIN] 176 H4
Haarala [FIN] 186 G2
Haaraoja [FIN] 196 D4
Haarby [DK] 156 D3
Haaren [D] 32 E4
Haarlem [NL] 16 D4
Haavisto [FIN] 186 F5
Habartice [CZ] 48 G1
Habay [B] 44 E2
Hablingbo [S] 168 F5
Habo [S] 162 D2
Håbol [S] 166 D4
Habry [CZ] 48 H4
Håby [S] 166 C5
Häby [S] 166 C5
Hachdorf [D] 58 G2
Hachenburg [D] 46 B1
Hachmühlen [D] 32 F2
Hackås [S] 182 G3
Häckeberga [S] 158 C3
Hacketstown [IRL] 4 F4
Hacksjö [S] 190 G5
Håcksvik [S] 162 B3
Hadamar [D] 46 B2
Hädanberg [S] 184 F1
Haddington [GB] 8 F3
Haderslev [DK] 156 C3
Haderup [DK] 160 C5
Hadiach [UA] 202 F7
Hadım [TR] 152 G4
Hadleigh [GB] 14 G3
Hadmersleben [D] 34 B3
Hadsten [DK] 160 D6
Hadsund [DK] 160 E4
Hadzhidimovo [BG] 130 C2
Hadžići [BIH] 144 C1
Hægeland [N] 164 D5
Hærland [N] 166 C2
Hafsmo [N] 180 G1
Haftorsbygget [S] 172 F1
Haga [N] 172 C5
Hagafoss [N] 170 F3
Hagby [S] 162 F5
Hagby [S] 168 D2
Hagebro [DK] 160 C5
Hagen [D] 18 D4
Hagen [D] 32 C4
Hagenow [D] 18 H5
Hageri [EST] 198 D2
Hagetmau [F] 84 E2
Hagfors [S] 172 F6
Häggås [S] 190 F5
Häggemåla [S] 162 G4
Häggenås [S] 182 H1
Häggsåsen [S] 182 G2
Häggsjöbränna [S] 182 E1
Häggsjömon [S] 190 G5
Häggsjövik [S] 190 E6
Haglebu [N] 170 G4
Hagondange [F] 44 E4
Hagudi [EST] 198 E2
Haguenau [F] 44 H5
Håhellarhytta [N] 164 D3
Hahn [D] 18 C4
Hahnbach [D] 46 H5
Hahót [H] 74 G3
Haid [A] 62 B4
Haiger [D] 32 D6
Haigerloch [D] 58 G2
Häijää [FIN] 176 E1
Hailsham [GB] 14 E6
Hailuoto / Karlö [FIN] 196 D4
Haina [D] 32 E6
Hainburg [A] 62 G4
Hainfeld [A] 62 E5
Hainichen [D] 48 D1

Kimito / Kemiö [FIN] 176 E5
Kimméria [GR] 130 E2
Kímolos [GR] 138 D4
Kimonkylä [FIN] 178 B3
Kimovaara [RUS] 196 H5
Kimry [RUS] 202 E2
Kincardine [GB] 8 E3
Kindberg [A] 62 D6
Kindelbrück [D] 32 H5
Kinding [D] 46 G6
Kindsjön [S] 172 E4
Kinéta [GR] 134 B6
Kingisepp [RUS] 198 G1
Kingsbridge [GB] 12 D5
Kingscourt [IRL] 2 F5
King's Lynn [GB] 14 F1
Kingston upon Hull [GB] 6 F5
Kington [GB] 12 F1
Kınık [TR] 150 F5
Kınık [TR] 152 C2
Kınık [TR] 154 F3
Kınık [TR] 154 G1
Kınıkyeri [TR] 152 G6
Kinlochbervie [GB] 6 D2
Kinlochewe [GB] 6 C4
Kinlochleven [GB] 6 C6
Kinlough [IRL] 2 D3
Kinna [S] 162 B3
Kinnadoohy [IRL] 2 B4
Kinnarp [S] 162 C1
Kinnbäck [S] 196 B4
Kinnegad [IRL] 2 E5
Kinni [FIN] 178 C1
Kinnitty [IRL] 2 D6
Kinnula [FIN] 186 F1
Kinnuranlahti [FIN] 188 C1
Kinross [GB] 8 E2
Kinsale [IRL] 4 C5
Kinsarvik [N] 170 C4
Kintai [LT] 200 D4
Kintaus [FIN] 186 F4
Kinvarra [IRL] 2 C5
Kióni [GR] 132 D5
Kiónia [GR] 138 E2
Kipen' [RUS] 178 G5
Kipi [EST] 198 C3
Kipilahti [FIN] 178 B4
Kipina [FIN] 196 E3
Kipoureío [GR] 132 E1
Kirakkaköngäs [FIN] 194 D4
Kiralan [TR] 152 G4
Királyegyháza [H] 76 A5
Kıranköy [TR] 152 F3
Kirawsk [BY] 202 C5
Kiraz [TR] 152 E4
Kirazlı [TR] 150 B5
Kirbla [EST] 198 D2
Kircasalih [TR] 150 B2
Kirchbach [A] 72 G3
Kirchbach [A] 74 E2
Kirchberg [A] 60 F6
Kirchberg [D] 44 H2
Kirchberg [D] 46 E5
Kirchberg an der Pielach [A] 62 D5
Kirchdorf [D] 32 E1
Kirchdorf an der Krems [A] 62 B5
Kirchenlamitz [D] 48 B3
Kirchen-tellinsfurt [D] 58 H2
Kirchenthumbach [D] 46 H4
Kirchhain [D] 32 E6
Kirchheim [D] 32 F6
Kirchheimbolanden [D] 46 B4
Kirchheim unter Teck [D] 58 H1
Kirchlauter [D] 46 F3
Kirchlinteln [D] 18 E6
Kirchschlag [A] 62 F6
Kirchundem [D] 32 C5
Kirchzell [D] 46 D4
Kircubbin [NIR] 2 H4
Kireç [TR] 152 E1
Kiriküla [EST] 198 D1
Kırıklar [TR] 152 C1
Kiriou, Roche de- [F] 40 D2
Kiriši [RUS] 202 C1
Kirjaluokta [S] 192 F5
Kırkağaç [TR] 152 D2
Kirkby Lonsdale [GB] 10 E2
Kirkcaldy [GB] 8 E3
Kirkcudbright [GB] 8 D5
Kirkeby [N] 182 D1
Kirkehamn [N] 164 B5
Kirke Hvalsø [DK] 156 F3
Kirkenær [N] 172 D4
Kirkenes [N] 194 E3
Kirkholt [DK] 160 E3
Kírki [GR] 130 G3
Kirkjubæjarklaustur [IS] 192 B3
Kirkjubøur [FR] 160 B2
Kirkkolati [RUS] 188 H4
Kirkkonummi / Kyrkslätt [FIN] 176 G5
Kırklareli [TR] 150 B1
Kirkonkylä [FIN] 176 E4
Kırkpınar [TR] 152 H6
Kirkvollen [N] 182 D2
Kirkwall [GB] 6 G2
Kirn [D] 44 H2
Kirov [RUS] 202 E4
Kirovohrad [UA] 202 E8
Kirovsk [RUS] 202 B1
Kirovskoye [RUS] 178 G3
Kirriemuir [GB] 8 F2
Kirtorf [D] 46 D1
Kiruna [S] 192 G5
Kisa [S] 162 F1
Kisbér [H] 64 A6
Kisdobsza [H] 74 H5
Kiseljak [BIH] 144 C1
Kishartyán [H] 64 D5
Kisielice [PL] 22 F4
Kisielnica [PL] 24 D5
Kisko [FIN] 176 F5
Kisköre [H] 64 F6
Kiskőrös [H] 76 D3
Kiskundorozsma [H] 76 E4
Kiskunfélegyháza [H] 76 E3
Kiskunhalas [H] 76 D4
Kiskunlacháza [H] 76 C2
Kiskunmajsa [H] 76 D4
Kişla [TR] 152 F3
Kisláng [H] 76 B2
Kisslegg [D] 60 B5
Kisszállás [H] 76 D4
Kist [D] 46 E4
Kistanje [HR] 112 H5
Kistelek [H] 76 E4
Kisterenye [H] 64 D5
Kisújszállás [H] 76 F1
Kisvárda [H] 64 H4
Kiszkowo [PL] 36 D2
Kiszombor [H] 76 F4
Kitajaur [S] 190 H2
Kitee [FIN] 188 G4
Kiten [BG] 148 F5
Kition [CY] 154 G5
Kitkiöjärvi [S] 194 B6
Kitkiöjoki [S] 194 B6
Kítros [GR] 128 G5
Kitsi [FIN] 196 H6
Kittelfjäll [S] 190 E4
Kittendorf [D] 20 C4
Kittilä [FIN] 194 C6
Kittsee [A] 62 G5
Kitula [FIN] 176 F4
Kitula [FIN] 186 G5
Kitzbühel [A] 60 F6
Kitzingen [D] 46 F4
Kitzloch-Klamm [A] 72 G1
Kiukainen [FIN] 176 D2
Kiurujärvi [FIN] 194 E6
Kiuruvesi [FIN] 196 E6
Kiutaköngäs [FIN] 194 F8
Kivadár [H] 74 H5
Kivéri [GR] 136 E2
Kivesjärvi [FIN] 196 E4
Kiviapaja [FIN] 188 E5
Kivijärvi [FIN] 186 F2
Kivik [S] 158 D3
Kivikangas [FIN] 186 E1
Kivilahti [FIN] 188 G1
Kivilompolo [FIN] 194 B5
Kivilompolo [FIN] 194 C8
Kivioja [FIN] 194 C8
Kiviõli [EST] 198 F1
Kivisalmi [FIN] 186 H3
Kivisuo [FIN] 186 G5
Kivivaara [FIN] 196 G5
Kivi-Vigala [EST] 198 D2
Kivotós [GR] 128 E6
Kıyıkışlacık [TR] 154 C1
Kıyıköy [TR] 150 D1
Kızılca [TR] 152 G6
Kızılcabölük [TR] 152 F5
Kızılcasöğüt [TR] 152 G3
Kızılinler [TR] 150 H5
Kızılkoltuk [TR] 152 F2
Kızılören [TR] 152 H3
Kızılyaka [TR] 154 D1
Kjeeringvika [N] 192 E4
Kjelda [N] 190 C4
Kjeldebotn [N] 192 E4
Kjelfossen [N] 170 D2
Kjellerup [DK] 160 D6
Kjellmyra [N] 172 D4
Kjernmoen [N] 172 D3
Kjerringvoll [N] 182 C3
Kjerret [N] 166 D1
Kjerringvåg [N] 190 A6
Kjerringvik [N] 190 C6
Kjøllefjord [N] 194 D1
Kjølsdal [N] 180 C5
Kjøpsvik [N] 192 E4
Kjøra [N] 180 H1
Kjulo / Köyliö [FIN] 176 D2
Klacka-Lerberg [S] 166 G2
Kläckeberga [S] 162 G5
Kladanj [BIH] 142 E4
Kladnica [SCG] 146 A3
Kladnice [HR] 142 A5
Kladno [CZ] 48 F3
Kladruby [CZ] 48 D4
Klæbu [N] 182 B1
Klagenfurt [A] 74 B3
Klaipėda [LT] 200 D4
Klakegg [N] 180 D6
Klaksvík [FR] 160 B1
Klamila [FIN] 178 D3
Klana [HR] 112 E1
Klanac [HR] 112 G3
Klanxbüll [D] 156 B4
Kläpen [N] 192 E3
Kläppen [S] 190 G3
Kläppsjö [S] 190 F6
Klarabro [S] 172 E4
Klärke [S] 184 E3
Klarup [DK] 160 E4
Klašnice [BIH] 142 C2
Klässbol [S] 166 E2
Klášterec nad Ohří [CZ] 48 D3
Klášter Teplá [CZ] 48 D4
Kláštor pod Znievom [SK] 64 C2
Klatovy [CZ] 48 D5
Klaukkala [FIN] 176 G4
Klaus an der Pyhrnbahn [A] 62 B5
Klausdorf [D] 20 D2
Klausdorf [D] 34 E3
Klausen / Chiusa [I] 72 D3
Klazienaveen [NL] 16 H3
Klazomenai [TR] 152 C4
Kłębowiec [PL] 22 A5
Kłecko [PL] 36 D2
Kleczew [PL] 36 E3
Klein Glödnitz [A] 74 B3
Kleinhau [D] 30 F5
Kleinhaugsdorf [A] 62 E3
Kleinzell [A] 62 E5
Kleisoúra [GR] 132 D3
Kleive [N] 180 E3
Kleivegrend [N] 164 E2
Kleivstua [N] 170 H5
Klejniki [PL] 24 F6
Klemensker [DK] 158 E4
Klempenow [D] 20 D4
Klenčí pod Čerchovem [CZ] 48 D5
Klenike [SCG] 146 D5
Klenjë [AL] 128 C2
Klenovica [HR] 112 F2
Kleppe [N] 164 A3
Kleppestø [N] 170 A3
Klerken [B] 28 F2
Kleśno [PL] 36 A1
Kleszczele [PL] 38 F2
Kletnya [RUS] 202 E5
Klevar [N] 164 F2
Kleve [D] 16 F6
Klevshult [S] 162 D3
Klezeno [RUS] 198 G4
Kliczków [PL] 34 H5
Klietz [D] 34 C1
Klimátia [GR] 132 C2
Kliment [BG] 148 E2
Klimontów [PL] 52 B3
Klimontów [PL] 52 D2
Klimovo [RUS] 178 F3
Klimpfjäll [S] 190 E4
Klin [RUS] 202 E2
Klina [SCG] 146 B5
Klinča Sela [HR] 74 E6
Klingenbach [A] 62 F6
Klingenmunster [D] 46 B5
Klingenthal [D] 48 C3
Klink [D] 20 C5
Klintehamn [S] 168 F5
Klintfors [S] 196 A4
Klintholm [DK] 156 G4
Klintsy [RUS] 202 D5
Kliplev [DK] 156 C4
Klippan [S] 158 C1
Klippen [S] 190 E3
Klippen [S] 190 G5
Klippinge [DK] 156 G3
Klírou [CY] 154 G5
Klis [HR] 144 A2
Klisino [PL] 50 E3
Klisura [BG] 148 A4
Klisura [SCG] 146 E5
Klisura Sutjeske [BIH] 144 D2
Klitmøller [DK] 160 C3
Klixbüll [D] 156 B4
Kljajićevo [SCG] 76 D6
Ključ [BIH] 142 B3
Klobouky u Brna [CZ] 62 G2
Kłobuck [PL] 50 F1
Klobuczyn [PL] 36 B5
Klobuk [BIH] 144 B2
Klockestrand [S] 184 F3
Kłoczew [PL] 38 D4
Kłodawa [PL] 34 H1
Kłodawa [PL] 36 F3
Kłodzko [PL] 50 C3
Kløfta [N] 172 B5
Klokkarvik [N] 170 A4
Klokkervik [N] 194 C2
Klokočevac [SCG] 146 D1
Klokočevci [HR] 76 B6
Klokotnica [BIH] 142 D3
Kloogaranna [EST] 198 D1
Klos [AL] 128 B1
Klos [AL] 128 B2
Kloštar Ivanić [HR] 74 F6
Kloštar Podravski [HR] 74 G5
Kloster [S] 174 D5
Kloster Arnstein [D] 46 B2
Kloster Chorin [D] 34 F1
Klosterkirche in Altenmarkt [D] 60 G3
Klösterle [A] 72 B1
Klosterneuburg [A] 62 F4
Klosterruiner [N] 180 B4
Klosters [CH] 72 A2
Kloster Schäftlarn [D] 60 E5
Kloster Zella [D] 32 G5
Kloster Zinna [D] 34 D3
Kloten [S] 166 H1
Klötze [D] 34 A1
Klöverträsk [S] 196 B3
Kløvimoen [N] 190 D3
Klövsjö [S] 182 G4
Kl. Plasten [D] 20 C4
Kluczbork [PL] 50 E1
Klucze [PL] 50 G3
Kluczewsko [PL] 50 H1
Kluis [D] 20 D2
Kluki [PL] 22 C1
Kluki [PL] 36 G5
Klukowa Huta [PL] 22 D3
Klupe [BIH] 142 C3
Klusy [PL] 24 D4
Klutsjön [S] 182 E5
Klütz [D] 18 H3
Klyastsitsy [BY] 198 H6
Knaben [N] 164 C4
Knäm [S] 166 B4
Knapphus [N] 164 B1
Knappogue Castle [IRL] 2 C6
Knäred [S] 162 B5
Knaresborough [GB] 10 F3
Knarvik [N] 170 B3
Knåsjö [S] 190 G6
Knätten [S] 182 G5
Knebel [DK] 160 E6
Knetzgau [D] 46 F3
Kneža [SLO] 72 H4
Kneževi Vinogradi [HR] 76 C6
Kneževo [HR] 76 B5
Knezha [BG] 146 G3
Knić [SCG] 146 B2
Knídi [GR] 128 F6
Knidos [TR] 154 B3
Kniebis [D] 58 F2
Knighton [GB] 10 C6
Knights Town [IRL] 4 A4
Knin [HR] 142 A4
Knislinge [S] 158 D1
Knittelfeld [A] 74 C2
Knivsta [S] 168 D2
Knjaževac [SCG] 146 E3
Knock [IRL] 2 C4
Knockcroghery [IRL] 2 D5
Knocknalina [IRL] 2 C2
Knocktopher [IRL] 4 E4
Knokke-Heist [B] 28 G1
Knosós [GR] 140 E4
Knottingley [GB] 10 F4
Knudshoved [DK] 156 E3
Knurów [PL] 50 F3
Knurowiec [PL] 38 C1
Knutby [S] 168 E1
Knutsford [GB] 10 D4
Knyazevo [RUS] 198 H5
Knyazhevo [BG] 148 E5
Knyazhicy [RUS] 198 G3
Knyszyn [PL] 24 E5
Kobarid [SLO] 72 H4
Kobbelveid [N] 192 E5
Kobeliaky [UA] 202 F7
København [DK] 156 H2
Koberg [S] 166 D6
Kobeřice [CZ] 50 E4
Kobiele Wlk. [PL] 36 H6
Kobilyane [BG] 130 F1
Kobišnica [SCG] 146 E1
Koblenz [D] 30 H6
Kobola [FIN] 194 F7
Kobryn [BY] 38 G2
Kobułty [PL] 24 B4
Kobylany [PL] 38 F3
Kobylin [PL] 36 D4
Kobyłka [PL] 38 C2
Kobyl'nik [BY] 200 H5
Kocaali [TR] 150 H2
Kocabaş [TR] 152 G5
Kocaçeşme [TR] 150 B4
Kocaeli (İzmit) [TR] 150 G3
Kocakaymaz [TR] 150 G2
Kočani [MK] 128 G1
Kocapınar [TR] 150 D5
Koçarlı [TR] 152 D5
Kocbeře [CZ] 50 A2
Koceljevo [SCG] 146 A1
Kočerin [BIH] 144 B2
Kočevje [SLO] 74 C6
Kochel [D] 60 D5
Kocherinovo [BG] 146 F6
Kocherov [UA] 202 D7
Kochmar [BG] 148 F2
Kock [PL] 38 E4
Kocs [H] 64 B6
Kocsér [H] 76 E2
Kocsiújfalu [H] 64 F6
Kocsola [H] 76 B4
Koczała [PL] 22 B4
Kodal [N] 164 H3
Kodeń [PL] 38 F3
Kodersdorf [D] 34 G6
Kodesjärvi [FIN] 186 B5
Kodrąb [PL] 36 H6
Koetschette [L] 44 E2
Kofçaz [TR] 150 B1
Köflach [A] 74 D2
Kögbo [S] 174 E4
Køge [DK] 156 G3
Kogila [MK] 128 E3
Kogula [EST] 198 C3
Kohfidisch [A] 74 F2
Kohila [EST] 198 D2
Kohtla-Järve [EST] 198 F1
Koigi [EST] 198 E2
Koijärvi [FIN] 176 F3
Koikkala [FIN] 188 D5
Koiliáda [GR] 136 F3
Koilovtsi [BG] 148 B3
Kõima [EST] 198 D2
Köinge [S] 162 B4
Koirakoski [FIN] 196 F6
Koisjärvi [FIN] 176 G4
Koíta [GR] 136 E5
Koivu [FIN] 194 C8
Koivulahti / Kvevlax [FIN] 186 B2
Koivumäki [FIN] 188 E3
Kojetín [CZ] 50 D6
Kojola [FIN] 196 D6
Kökar [FIN] 168 H1
Kokava nad Rimavicou [SK] 64 D3
Kokemäki / Kumo [FIN] 176 D2
Kokin Brod [SCG] 146 A3
Kokkála [GR] 136 E5
Kokkário [GR] 152 C5
Kokkila [FIN] 176 E5
Kókkina (Erenköy) [CY] 154 F5
Kókkino Neró [GR] 132 H1
Kokkola / Karleby [FIN] 196 C6
Kokkolahti [FIN] 188 F4
Koklë [AL] 128 C4
Koklioí [GR] 132 C1
Koknese [LV] 198 E5
Kokonvaara [FIN] 188 E2
Kokorevo [RUS] 198 H3
Kokořín [CZ] 48 G3
Koksijde-Bad [B] 28 F1
Köla [S] 166 D1
Kołacz [PL] 20 H4
Kołacze [PL] 38 F5
Koláka [GR] 134 A5
Koláre [SK] 64 C5
Kolari [FIN] 194 B7
Kolari [SCG] 142 H3
Kolárovo [SK] 64 A5
Kolasen [S] 190 D6
Kolašin [SCG] 144 E3
Kolbäck [S] 168 B2
Kołbacz [PL] 20 F5
Kołbaskowo [PL] 20 F5
Kolbermoor [D] 60 F5
Kołbiel [PL] 38 C3
Kolbotn [N] 166 B1
Kolbudy Górne [PL] 22 D3
Kolbuszowa [PL] 52 D3
Kolby [DK] 156 E2
Kolby Kås [DK] 156 E2
Kołczewo [PL] 20 F3
Kołczygłowy [PL] 22 C3
Koldby [DK] 160 B4
Kolding [DK] 156 C3
Koleczkowo [PL] 22 D2
Koler [S] 196 A3
Kölesd [H] 76 B4
Kolešino [MK] 128 H2
Kolga-Jaani [EST] 198 E2
Kolho [FIN] 186 E5
Koli [FIN] 188 F1
Kolín [CZ] 48 H4
Kolin [PL] 20 G5
Kolind [DK] 160 E6
Kolindrós [GR] 128 G5
Kolinec [CZ] 48 E6
Kölingared [S] 162 C1
Kõljala [EST] 198 C3
Kolka [LV] 198 C4
Kolkonpää [FIN] 188 E5
Kolkontaipale [FIN] 188 D4
Kolky [UA] 202 B7
Kölleda [D] 34 A5
Kollerud [S] 172 E5
Kollínes [GR] 136 E3
Kollund [DK] 156 C4
Kolmården [S] 168 B5
Kolm-Saigurn [A] 72 G2
Köln [D] 30 G4
Kolnica [PL] 50 D2
Kolno [PL] 24 C5
Kolo [BIH] 144 B1
Koło [PL] 36 F3
Kołobrzeg [PL] 20 G3
Kolokolovo [RUS] 198 G2
Kolomyia [UA] 204 C3
Kolonia Korytnica [PL] 38 D4
Kolonjë [AL] 128 B4
Kolonowskie [PL] 50 F2
Kolophon [TR] 152 C5
Kolossai [TR] 152 G5
Kolossi [CY] 154 F6
Koloveč [CZ] 48 D5
Kolpino [RUS] 202 B1
Kolsätter [S] 182 G5
Kölsillre [S] 182 H4
Kolsjön [S] 184 D5
Kolsva [S] 168 B2
Kolta [SK] 64 B5
Kolu [FIN] 186 E3
Kolunič [BIH] 142 A3
Koluszki [PL] 36 H4
Kolut [SCG] 76 C5
Kolvasozero [RUS] 196 G5
Kolvereid [N] 190 C4
Kolymvári [GR] 140 B4
Komádi [H] 76 G2
Komagvær [N] 194 F2
Koman [AL] 128 B1
Komańcza [PL] 52 E5
Kómara [GR] 130 H1
Komarevo [BG] 148 A2
Komárno [SK] 64 B5
Komarno [UA] 52 G4
Komárom [H] 64 A6
Komar Prolaz [BIH] 142 C4
Koma Tou Yialou (Kumyalı) [CY] 154 G4
Komenda [SLO] 74 C4
Kómi [GR] 134 G5
Kómi [GR] 138 E1
Komi Kebir (Büyükkonuk) [CY] 154 G4
Komin [HR] 74 F5
Kómito [GR] 134 D6
Komiža [HR] 116 H2
Komjáti [H] 64 F3
Komló [H] 64 E6
Komló [H] 76 B4
Komméno [GR] 132 D3
Kommerniemi [FIN] 188 E5
Kommunary [RUS] 178 G2
Komnes [N] 164 G2
Komniná [GR] 128 F5
Komniná [GR] 130 E2
Komninádes [GR] 128 D5
Komorane [SCG] 146 C5
Komorzno [PL] 36 E6
Komossa [FIN] 186 C2
Komotiní [GR] 130 F2
Kömpöc [H] 76 E4
Kompolje [HR] 112 G3
Kompóti [GR] 132 D3
Komsomol'skoye [RUS] 178 F2
Komula [FIN] 196 F5
Komunari [BG] 148 F3
Kömürköy [TR] 150 C2
Konak [SCG] 142 H1
Konakpınar [TR] 152 D1
Konarevo [SCG] 146 B3
Konarzyny [PL] 22 C4
Končanica [HR] 74 G6
Konče [MK] 128 G2
Konchansko-Suvorovskoye [RUS] 202 D1
Kondolovo [BG] 148 F5
Kondorfa [H] 74 F2
Kondoros [H] 76 F3
Kondrić [HR] 142 D1
Koněpruské Jeskyně [CZ] 48 F4
Køng [DK] 156 F4
Konga [S] 162 E6
Köngäs [FIN] 194 C6
Köngäs [FIN] 194 D6
Kongasmäki [FIN] 196 E4
Kongensgruve [N] 164 G1
Kongensvollen [N] 190 A6
Kongerslev [DK] 160 E4
Kong Humbles Grav [DK] 156 E5
Konginkangas [FIN] 186 G3
Kongsberg [N] 164 G1
Kongsvea [N] 192 D4
Kongsfjord [N] 194 E1
Kongshavn [N] 164 F5
Kongsmoen [N] 190 D4
Kongsnes [N] 170 C2
Kongsvinger [N] 172 D5
Konice [CZ] 50 C5
Koniecpol [PL] 50 H2
Konieczna [PL] 52 D5
König-Otto-Höhle [D] 46 H5
Königsbrück [D] 34 F6
Königsbrunn [D] 60 D4
Königsee [D] 46 G2
Königsfeld [D] 58 F3
Königshofen [D] 46 E4
Königslutter [D] 32 H2
Königssee [D] 60 G6
Königsstuhl [D] 20 D2
Königstein [D] 46 C2
Königstein [D] 48 F1
Königswartha [D] 34 F5
Königswiesen [A] 62 C4
Königswinter [D] 30 H5
Königs-Wusterhausen [D] 34 E3
Konin [PL] 36 E3
Koniščina [HR] 74 E5
Koniskós [GR] 132 F1
Konispol [AL] 132 B2
Kónitsa [GR] 128 D6
Köniz [CH] 58 D6
Konjic [BIH] 144 C1
Konjsko [BIH] 144 D4
Könnern [D] 34 B4
Konnerud [N] 164 H1
Konnevesi [FIN] 186 G3
Könni [FIN] 186 C3
Könnu [EST] 198 E1
Konopiště [CZ] 48 G4
Konotop [PL] 20 H5
Konotop [PL] 36 B4
Końskie [PL] 38 A6
Konsko [MK] 128 G3
Konsmo [N] 164 D5
Konstancin-Jeziorna [PL] 38 B3
Konstantynów [PL] 38 E3
Konstantynów Łodzki [PL] 36 G4
Konstanz [D] 58 G4
Kontiainen [FIN] 186 D2
Kontiás [GR] 130 F6
Kontinjoki [FIN] 196 F5
Kontiolahti [FIN] 188 F2
Kontiomäki [FIN] 196 F4
Kontiovaara [FIN] 188 G1
Kontkala [FIN] 188 F2
Kontokáli [GR] 132 B2
Kontopoúli [GR] 130 F6
Konttajärvi [FIN] 194 C7
Konush [BG] 148 C6
Konyavo [BG] 146 F5
Konyshevka [RUS] 202 F6
Konz [D] 44 F2
Koonga [EST] 198 D2
Kööritilä [FIN] 186 B6
Koosa [EST] 198 F2
Koparnes [N] 180 C4
Kópasker [IS] 192 C2
Köpenick [D] 34 E2
Koper [SLO] 72 H6
Köpernitz [D] 20 C6
Kopervik [N] 164 A2
Kópháza [H] 62 F6
Kopidlno [CZ] 48 H3
Köping [S] 168 B2
Köpingsvik [S] 162 G4
Kopisto [FIN] 196 C5
Koplik [AL] 144 E5
Köpmanholmen [S] 184 G2
Köpmannebro [S] 166 D4
Koporin, Manastir- [SCG] 146 C1
Kopor'ye [RUS] 178 F5
Koppang [N] 172 C1
Koppangen [N] 192 G2
Kopparberg [S] 166 H1
Kopperå [N] 182 D1
Kopperby [D] 18 F1
Koppom [S] 166 D2
Koprivets [BG] 148 C3
Koprivlen [BG] 130 C2
Koprivnica [HR] 74 G5
Koprivnica [SCG] 146 E2
Koprivshtitsa [BG] 148 A5
Köprübaşi [TR] 152 E3
Köprübaşı [TR] 152 F5
Köprühisar [TR] 150 G4
Köprüören [TR] 152 G1
Koprzywnica [PL] 52 D2
Kopsa [FIN] 196 D4
Kõpu [EST] 198 E3
Korbach [D] 32 E5
Korbevac [SCG] 146 D5
Korbielów [PL] 50 G5
Korbu [MD] 204 E2
Korçë [AL] 128 D5
Korčula [HR] 144 B3
Korczew [PL] 38 E2
Korczyców [PL] 34 G3
Korczyna [PL] 52 D4
Korenica [HR] 112 H3
Korenita [SCG] 142 F3
Korentovaara [FIN] 188 H1
Korespohja [FIN] 186 G5
Korfantów [PL] 50 D2
Körfez [TR] 150 G3
Kórfos [GR] 136 F2
Korgen [N] 190 D2
Korgene [LV] 198 D4
Koria [FIN] 178 C3
Korinós [GR] 128 G5
Korinth [DK] 156 D4
Kórinthos [GR] 136 F1
Kórinthos, Arhéa- [GR] 136 F1
Korisós [GR] 128 E5
Korissía [GR] 138 C2
Korita [BIH] 144 D3
Korita [HR] 144 C4
Koritata [BG] 130 E2
Koriten [BG] 148 F1
Koríthi [GR] 136 A1
Korkea [FIN] 196 G5
Korkeakangas [FIN] 188 G4
Korlátka [SK] 62 H3
Körmend [H] 74 F2
Kormu [FIN] 176 G3
Korne [PL] 22 C3
Korneuburg [A] 62 F4
Kornevo [RUS] 22 G2
Kórnik [PL] 36 C3
Kornsjø [N] 166 C4
Kornwestheim [D] 58 H1
Kornye [H] 64 B6
Koromačno [HR] 112 E2
Koróni [GR] 136 D4
Kóronos [GR] 138 F3
Koronoúda [GR] 128 H3
Koronowo [PL] 22 D5
Korop [UA] 202 E6
Koropí [GR] 136 H1
Körösladány [H] 76 G2
Köröstarcsa [H] 76 G2
Korosten' [UA] 202 C7
Korostyshiv [UA] 202 D7
Korpavár [H] 74 G4
Korpi [FIN] 196 C6
Korpijärvi [FIN] 188 C6
Korpikå [S] 196 B2
Korpilahti [FIN] 186 G5
Korpilombolo [S] 194 B7
Korpo / Korppoo [FIN] 176 C5
Korpoström [FIN] 176 C5
Korppinen [FIN] 186 G1
Korppoo / Korpo [FIN] 176 C5
Korrigans [F] 40 D6
Korrö [S] 162 E5
Korsåsen [S] 172 H2
Korsberga [S] 162 E3
Korsberga [S] 166 F6
Korsen [N] 190 C5
Korsholm [S] 158 C2
Korsholm / Mustasaari [FIN] 186 B2
Korskrogen [S] 184 C6
Korsmo [N] 172 C5
Korsnäs [FIN] 186 A3
Korsø [DK] 160 C3
Korsør [DK] 156 E3
Korsun'-Shevchenkivs'kyi [UA] 202 E8
Korsveien [N] 182 B2
Korsvoll [N] 180 F1
Korsze [PL] 24 B3
Körteke [TR] 152 F6
Korten [BG] 148 D4
Kortenberg [B] 30 C4
Kortesjärvi [FIN] 186 C1
Kortevaara [FIN] 196 G5
Kórthi [GR] 138 D1
Kortrijk (Courtrai) [B] 28 G2
Korucu [TR] 152 C2
Koruköy [TR] 150 C1
Korup [DK] 156 D3
Koruše [HR] 142 A5
Korva [S] 194 B8
Korvala [FIN] 194 D7
Korvaluoma [FIN] 186 C5
Korvenkylä [FIN] 196 D5
Korvensuu [FIN] 176 D4
Koryčany [CZ] 62 G2
Korycin [PL] 24 E4
Korydallós [GR] 132 E1
Koryfási [GR] 136 C4
Korytnica-Kúpele [SK] 64 C2
Korytno [RUS] 198 G2
Korzeniste [PL] 24 D5
Korzunovo [RUS] 194 F3
Korzybie [PL] 22 B2
Korzyst-Kowice [PL] 34 H4
Kos [GR] 154 B2
Kosanica [SCG] 144 E2
Košarovce [SK] 52 D6
Kościan [PL] 36 C3
Kościelec [PL] 36 F3
Kościerzyna [PL] 22 D3
Kose [EST] 198 E1
Kösedere [TR] 134 G1
Kosel [MK] 128 D3
Koserow [D] 20 E3
Košetice [CZ] 48 G5
Košice [SK] 64 G3
Kosik [RUS] 202 E5
Kosjerić [SCG] 146 A2
Kösk [TR] 152 E5
Koška [HR] 142 D1
Koskeby [FIN] 186 B2
Koskela [FIN] 186 D2
Koskenkorva [FIN] 186 C3
Koskenkylä [FIN] 188 C2
Koskenkylä / Forsby [FIN] 178 B4
Koskenniska [FIN] 194 C4
Koskenpää [FIN] 186 F5
Koski [FIN] 176 E4
Koski [FIN] 176 F2
Koski [FIN] 196 E6
Koskimäki [FIN] 186 B3
Kóskina [GR] 134 D5
Koskolovo [RUS] 178 F6
Koškovce [SK] 52 E6
Koskue [FIN] 186 C4
Koskullskulle [S] 192 G6
Kosmás [GR] 136 E3
Kósmio [GR] 130 F2
Kosmo [N] 192 D6
Kosmonosy [CZ] 48 G3
Kosola [FIN] 186 C2
Kosovo Polje [SCG] 146 C5
Kosovska Mitrovica [SCG] 146 C4
Kosów Lacki [PL] 38 D2
Kössen [A] 60 F5
Kost [CZ] 48 H2
Kósta [GR] 136 F3
Kosta [S] 162 E5
Kostanjevac [HR] 74 D6

Kosta Perchevo [BG] 146 E2
Kostelec [CZ] 48 H6
Kostelec nad Černými [CZ] 48 G4
Kostelec nad Labem [CZ] 48 G3
Kostelec nad Orlicí [CZ] 50 B3
Kostelec na Hané [CZ] 50 C5
Kostenets [BG] 146 G5
Kostinbrod [BG] 146 F4
Kostomłoty [PL] 36 C6
Kostomuksha [RUS] 196 G4
Kostopil' [UA] 202 B7
Kóstos [GR] 138 E3
Kostów [PL] 36 E6
Kostrzyn [PL] 34 G2
Kostrzyn [PL] 36 D2
Kosturino [MK] 128 G2
Košumberk [CZ] 50 B4
Košutovo [SCG] 146 B4
Koszalin [PL] 20 H3
Koszęcin [PL] 50 F2
Koszeg [H] 74 F1
Kosztowo [PL] 22 C6
Koszuty [PL] 36 D3
Koszyce [PL] 52 B3
Kótaj [H] 64 H4
Kotala [FIN] 186 E4
Kótas [GR] 128 E4
Kotë [AL] 128 B5
Kotel [BG] 148 D4
Kotelec [H] 76 E1
Köthen [D] 34 C4
Kotila [FIN] 196 F4
Kotka [FIN] 178 C4
Kotlarnia [PL] 50 F3
Kotlin [PL] 36 D4
Kotly [RUS] 178 F6
Kotor [SCG] 144 D4
Kotorsko [BIH] 142 D2
Kotor Varoš [BIH] 142 C3
Kotovs'k [UA] 204 E3
Kotowice [PL] 50 G2
Kótronas [GR] 136 E5
Kötschach-Mauthen [A] 72 G3
Kotten [NL] 16 G6
Köttkulla [S] 162 C2
Kotvala [FIN] 186 F1
Kötzting [D] 48 D6
Koufália [GR] 128 G4
Koufós [GR] 130 C6
Kouhi [FIN] 186 H5
Koúklia [CY] 154 F6
Koukounariés [GR] 134 B3
Koúmanis [GR] 136 C2
Koúndouros [GR] 138 C2
Koúrenta [GR] 132 C2
Kourion [CY] 154 F6
Kournás [GR] 140 C5
Kouroúta [GR] 136 B2
Koutsó [GR] 130 E3
Koutsóchero [GR] 132 G2
Koutsourás [GR] 140 G5
Koutsovéntis (Güngör) [CY] 154 G5
Kouvola [FIN] 178 C3
Kovachevica [BG] 130 C1
Kovachevtsi [BG] 146 F5
Kovachica [BG] 146 F2
Kovačica [SCG] 142 G2
Kovarskas [LT] 200 G4
Kovel' [UA] 202 A7
Kovero [FIN] 188 G2
Kovin [SCG] 142 H2
Kovland [S] 184 E4
Kövra [S] 182 G3
Kowal [PL] 36 G2
Kowale Oleckie [PL] 24 D3
Kowalewo Pomorskie [PL] 22 E6
Kowary [PL] 50 A2
Köyceğiz [TR] 154 E1
Köyhänperä [FIN] 196 D6
Köyliö / Kjulo [FIN] 176 D2
Köysivaara [FIN] 194 D5
Koyunhis [TR] 150 F4
Koyunköy [TR] 150 G4
Kozağaci [TR] 154 G1
Kozak [TR] 152 C2
Kozan [TR] 150 G4
Kozáni [GR] 128 F5
Kozarac [BIH] 142 B2
Kozarac [HR] 76 B6
Kozar Belene [BG] 148 B3
Kozel [CZ] 48 E5
Kozel'sk [RUS] 202 F4
Koziatyn [UA] 202 C8
Kozica [HR] 144 B2
Koziebrody [PL] 36 H1
Koziegłowy [PL] 50 G2
Kozienice [PL] 38 C4
Kozí Hrádek [CZ] 48 G5
Kozina [SLO] 74 A6
Kozine [LV] 198 G4
Kozjak [MK] 128 D3
Kozlar [TR] 152 G6
Kozloduí [BG] 146 G2
Kozlov Bereg [RUS] 198 G2
Kozłowo [PL] 22 G5
Kozluk [BIH] 142 E3
Kozly [RUS] 198 G4
Koźmin [PL] 36 D4
Kozojedy [CZ] 48 E4
Kozolupy [CZ] 48 D4
Kozpınar [TR] 150 G5
Kożuchów [PL] 36 A4
Kozy [PL] 50 G4
Kozyürük [TR] 150 B3
Kräkkiö [FIN] 176 F2
Krabbesholm [DK] 160 C5
Krabi [EST] 198 F4
Kräckelbäcken [S] 172 G2
Kraddsele [S] 190 F3
Kraftverk Härspränget [S] 190 H1
Krąg [PL] 22 B3
Kragelund [DK] 160 E3
Kragenæs [DK] 156 F4
Kragerø [N] 164 F4
Kragujevac [SCG] 146 C2
Krahës [AL] 128 B5
Krajenka [PL] 22 B5
Krajišnik [SCG] 142 H1
Krajn [AL] 128 B1
Krajna [SLO] 74 E3
Krajná Pol'ana [SK] 52 D5
Krajnik Gorny [PL] 20 E6
Krakača [BIH] 112 H2
Kråkan [S] 184 H1
Kråkeland [N] 164 C4
Krakės [LT] 200 F4
Krakhella [N] 170 B1
Kräklingbo [S] 168 G5
Kråklivollen [N] 182 C2
Kråkmo [N] 192 E5
Krakol'ye [RUS] 178 E6
Krakovec [UA] 202 A8
Krakovets' [UA] 52 F3
Kraków [PL] 50 H4
Krakow am See [D] 20 B4
Kråksmåla [S] 162 F4
Krakvik [S] 192 G5
Králíky [CZ] 50 C4
Kraljeva Sutjesca [BIH] 142 D4
Kraljevica [HR] 112 E2
Kraljevo [SCG] 146 B3
Kral'ovany [SK] 50 G6
Král'ov Brod [SK] 64 A5
Královec [CZ] 50 B2
Kralovice [CZ] 48 E4
Král'Ovský Chlmec [SK] 64 H3
Kralupy nad Vltavou [CZ] 48 F3
Kramfors [S] 184 F3
Kramolin [BG] 148 B3
Krampenes [N] 194 E2
Kråmvik [N] 164 E1
Kramvik [N] 194 F2
Kraneá [GR] 132 E2
Kranenburg [D] 16 F6
Kranevo [BG] 148 G2
Krångede [S] 184 D2
Kraní [MK] 128 D4
Kraniá [GR] 132 E1
Kraniá Elassónas [GR] 132 F1
Kranichfeld [D] 46 G1
Kranídi [GR] 136 F3
Kranj [SLO] 74 B4
Kranjska Gora [SLO] 72 H3
Krapina [HR] 74 E5
Krapinske Toplice [HR] 74 E5
Krapkowice [PL] 50 E2
Krapperup [S] 156 G1
Krasen [BG] 148 F1
Krasiczyn [PL] 52 F4
Krasikovshchina [RUS] 198 G3
Krāslava [LV] 198 G6
Kraslice [CZ] 48 C3
Krásna Hôrka [SK] 64 F3
Krásná Lípa [CZ] 48 G1
Krasnaya Hora [RUS] 202 D5
Krasne Folwarczne [PL] 24 E5
Krašniczyn [PL] 38 F6
Kraśnik [PL] 52 E1
Krasnogorodskoye [RUS] 198 G5
Krasnogorsk [RUS] 202 F3
Krasnohryvka [UA] 202 D8
Krásno nad Kysucou [SK] 50 F5
Krasnoperekops'k [UA] 204 H3
Krasnopol [PL] 24 E3
Krasnopol'e [BY] 202 D5
Krasnopol'e [UA] 202 F6
Krasnosielc [PL] 24 B6
Krasnovo [BG] 148 A5
Krasnoye [RUS] 198 H5
Krasnoye [RUS] 200 D5
Krasnoye Selo [RUS] 178 H5
Krasnoznamensk [RUS] 200 E5
Krasnye Prudy [RUS] 198 G4
Krasnyje Gory [RUS] 198 H1
Krasnystaw [PL] 38 F6
Krasnyy Bor [RUS] 24 B1
Krasnyy Kholm [RUS] 202 E1
Krasocin [PL] 52 A1
Krašov [CZ] 48 E4
Krastë [AL] 128 C2
Krasznokvajda [H] 64 F3
Krátigos [GR] 134 H2
Kratovo [MK] 146 E6
Kratovska Stena [SCG] 146 A2
Krauchenwies [D] 58 H3
Kraushöhle [A] 62 C6
Krautheim [D] 46 E5
Kravaře [CZ] 48 F2
Kravaře [CZ] 50 E4
Kravarsko [HR] 74 E6
Kravik [N] 170 F5
Kravnsø [DK] 156 A2
Kraymorie [BG] 148 F4
Kražiai [LT] 200 E4
Kreba-Neudorf [D] 34 G5
Krefeld [D] 30 G3
Kregme [DK] 156 G2
Krekila [FIN] 196 C6
Kremastí [GR] 136 F4
Kremastí [GR] 154 D3
Kremenchuk [UA] 202 F8
Kremenets' [UA] 202 B8
Kremmen [D] 34 D1
Kremna [SCG] 144 E1
Kremnica [SK] 64 C3
Krems [A] 62 E4
Kremsmünster [A] 62 B5
Křemže [CZ] 62 B2
Krenkerup [DK] 20 B1
Křenov [CZ] 50 C5
Krępa [PL] 36 F4
Krepcha [BG] 148 D2
Krepoljin [SCG] 146 D1
Kresna [BG] 130 B1
Kréstena [GR] 136 C2
Krestsy [RUS] 202 C2
Kretinga [LT] 200 D4
Kreuth [D] 60 E5
Kreuzenstein [A] 62 F4
Kreuzlingen [CH] 58 G4
Kreuztal [D] 32 C6
Kreva [BY] 200 H6
Kriakėnava [LT] 200 F4
Krichim [BG] 148 B6
Kričov [BY] 202 D5
Kriebstein [D] 34 D6
Krieglach [A] 62 D6
Kriezá [GR] 134 C5
Kríkello [GR] 132 F4
Krimml [A] 72 E1
Krimmler Wasserfälle [A] 72 E1
Křinec [CZ] 48 H3
Kringla [N] 170 B2
Krinídes [GR] 130 D3
Kristall-Höhle [D] 46 C2
Kristalopig [GR] 128 E5
Kristberg [S] 166 H5
Kristdala [S] 162 G3
Kristianopel [S] 158 G1
Kristiansand [N] 164 D5
Kristianstad [S] 158 D2
Kristiansund [N] 180 F2
Kristiinankaupunki / Kristinestad [FIN] 186 A5
Kristineberg [S] 172 E1
Kristineberg [S] 190 G4
Kristinefors [S] 172 E5
Kristinehamn [S] 166 F3
Kristinehov [S] 158 D2
Kristinestad / Kristiinankaupunki [FIN] 186 A5
Kristoffervalen [N] 192 G1
Kristóni [GR] 128 H3
Kristvallabrunn [S] 162 F5
Kritinía [GR] 154 C4
Kritsá [GR] 140 F5
Kriva Feja [SCG] 146 E5
Kriváň [SK] 64 D3
Kriva Palanka [MK] 146 E6
Kriva reka [BG] 148 E2
Krivelj [SCG] 146 D1
Krivi Dol [MK] 128 F1
Krivodol [BG] 146 F3
Krivogaštani [MK] 128 E3
Křivoklát [CZ] 48 E4
Krivolak [MK] 128 F2
Kriz [HR] 74 F6
Křižanov [CZ] 50 B6
Križevci [HR] 74 F5
Krk [HR] 112 E2
Krka [SLO] 74 C5
Krklja [MK] 146 E6
Krnjak [HR] 112 G1
Krnjeuša [BIH] 142 A3
Krnov [CZ] 50 D4
Krobia [PL] 36 C4
Kroczyce [PL] 50 G2
Krøderen [N] 170 G5
Krogsbølle [DK] 156 D2
Krokan [N] 170 E6
Krokebol [N] 166 C1
Krokeés [GR] 136 E4
Krokek [S] 168 B5
Kroken [N] 190 E3
Kroknes [N] 194 F2
Krokom [S] 182 G2
Krokowa [PL] 22 D1
Kroksjö [S] 190 G5
Kroksjö [S] 196 A5
Krokstad [S] 166 C5
Krokstadelva [N] 164 G1
Krokstadøra [N] 180 H1
Krokstrand [N] 190 E2
Kroksund [N] 166 C2
Kroktorp [S] 172 G5
Krokvåg [S] 184 D2
Krolevets' [UA] 202 E6
Królewiec [PL] 38 A6
Królowy Most [PL] 24 F5
Kroměříž [CZ] 50 D6
Kromerowo [PL] 22 H4
Krompachy [SK] 64 F2
Kromy [RUS] 202 F5
Kronach [D] 46 H3
Kronegg [A] 62 C4
Kronoby / Kruunupyy [FIN] 196 C6
Kronshtadt [RUS] 178 G4
Kropa [SLO] 74 B4
Kröpelin [D] 20 B3
Kropp [D] 18 F2
Kroppenstedt [D] 34 B3
Kropstädt [D] 34 D3
Krościenko [PL] 52 F5
Krościenko nad Dunajcem [PL] 52 B5
Krosna [LT] 24 F2
Krośniewice [PL] 36 G3
Krosno [PL] 22 F3
Krosno [PL] 52 D4
Krosno Odrzańskie [PL] 34 H3
Krossbu [N] 180 E6
Krossen [N] 164 D6
Krostiz [D] 34 C5
Krote [LV] 198 B6
Krotoszyn [PL] 36 D4
Krouna [CZ] 50 B4
Kršete [HR] 112 D1
Krško [SLO] 74 D5
Krstac [SCG] 144 D3
Krstac [SCG] 144 E5
Kručov [SK] 52 D6
Kruglovo [RUS] 22 G1
Kruiningen [NL] 28 H1
Kruisland [NL] 16 C6
Krujë [AL] 128 B2
Kruk [N] 170 G2
Krukowo [PL] 24 B5
Krumbach [A] 62 E6
Krumbach [D] 60 C4
Krumë [AL] 146 B6
Krummendorf [D] 20 B3
Krumovgrad [BG] 130 F1
Krumpendorf [A] 74 B3
Krün [D] 60 D6
Krupá [CZ] 48 E3
Krupac [BIH] 144 C2
Krupac [BIH] 144 D1
Krupaja [SCG] 146 C1
Krupa na Vrbasu [BIH] 142 B3
Krupanj [SCG] 142 F3
Krupe [PL] 38 F6
Krupina [SK] 64 C4
Krupište [MK] 128 F1
Krupnik [BG] 128 H1
Krupp [RUS] 198 G3
Kruså [DK] 156 C4
Krušedol, Manastir- [SCG] 142 F2
Kruševac [SCG] 146 C3
Kruševo [MK] 128 E2
Krusha [BG] 146 E4
Krushari [BG] 148 F1
Krushevets [BG] 148 F5
Krushovene [BG] 148 A2
Krushovica [BG] 146 G2
Kruszwica [PL] 36 E2
Kruszyna [PL] 50 G1
Krutcy [RUS] 198 H4
Krute [SCG] 128 A1
Krutneset [N] 190 E3
Kruunupyy / Kronoby [FIN] 196 C6
Kruusila [FIN] 176 F4
Krya [TR] 154 E2
Kryakusa [RUS] 198 G3
Krýa Vrýsi [GR] 128 G4
Kryekuq [AL] 128 A4
Krylbo [S] 174 D6
Kryle [DK] 160 B6
Krylovo [RUS] 24 C2
Krymne [UA] 38 H4
Krynica [PL] 52 C5
Krynica Morska [PL] 22 F2
Krynki [PL] 24 F5
Kryopigí [GR] 130 C6
Kryspinów [PL] 50 H4
Kryve Ozero [UA] 204 F2
Kryvyi Rih [UA] 204 G2
Krzęcin [PL] 20 G6
Krzczów [PL] 36 F6
Krzelów [PL] 36 C5
Krzepice [PL] 50 F1
Krzeszów [PL] 50 B2
Krzeszów [PL] 52 E2
Krzeszowice [PL] 50 H3
Krzeszyce [PL] 34 G2
Krzyewo [PL] 24 B6
Krzynowłoga Mała [PL] 22 H6
Krzywiń [PL] 36 C4
Krzyż Wlkp. [PL] 36 B1
Ksar-Es-Seghir [MAR] 100 G6
Książ [PL] 50 B1
Książ Wielki [PL] 52 A2
Ktísmata [GR] 132 C1
Kubbe [S] 184 F1
Küblis [CH] 70 H1
Kubrat [BG] 148 D2
Kuç [AL] 128 B6
Kučevo [SCG] 146 D1
Kuchl [A] 60 G6
Kućište [SCG] 146 A5
Kucovë [AL] 128 B4
Küçükbahçe [TR] 134 H4
Küçükçekmece [TR] 150 E3
Küçükkuyu [TR] 134 H1
Kuddby [S] 168 B5
Kudever' [RUS] 198 H5
Kudirkos Naumiestis [LT] 24 E1
Kudowa-Zdrój [PL] 50 B3
Kufstein [A] 60 F6
Kuggeboda [S] 158 F1
Kuggerud [N] 172 C5
Kuha [FIN] 196 E2
Kuhanen [FIN] 188 D2
Kühlungsborn [D] 20 B3
Kuhmalahti [FIN] 176 G1
Kuhmo [FIN] 196 G5
Kuhmoinen [FIN] 176 H1
Kühsen [D] 18 G4
Kuhstedt [D] 18 E4
Kühtai [A] 72 C1
Kuimetsa [EST] 198 E2
Kuivajärvi [FIN] 196 G4
Kuivaniemi [FIN] 196 D3
Kuivanto [FIN] 178 B3
Kuivasjärvi [FIN] 186 C5
Kuivasmäki [FIN] 186 F4
Kuivastu [EST] 198 D3
Kukës [AL] 128 C1
Kukina [PL] 20 H3
Kukko [FIN] 186 E3
Kukko [FIN] 186 E3
Kukkola [FIN] 176 G2
Kukkulankoski [FIN] 196 C2
Kuklin [PL] 22 H5
Kuks [CZ] 50 B3
Kukujevci [SCG] 142 F2
Kükür [TR] 154 F4
Kukurečani [MK] 128 E3
Kula [BG] 146 E2
Kula [SCG] 76 D6
Kulalar [TR] 152 E2
Kula Novinska [HR] 144 C3
Kulaši [BIH] 142 C3
Kulata [BG] 130 B2
Kuldīga [LV] 198 C5
Ku'Le [RUS] 198 G3
Kuleli [TR] 150 B2
Kulennoinen [FIN] 188 F5
Kulen Vakuf [BIH] 112 H4
Kulhuse [DK] 156 G2
Kuliai [LT] 200 D4
Kullaa [FIN] 176 D1
Kulla Gunnarstorp [S] 156 H1
Kullo / Kulloo [FIN] 178 A4
Kulloo / Kullo [FIN] 178 A4
Küllstedt [D] 32 G5
Kulmbach [D] 46 H3
Kuloharju [FIN] 196 E2
Kultaranta [FIN] 176 D4
Kulvemäki [FIN] 196 F5
Kulykiv [UA] 52 H3
Kumafşarı [TR] 152 G6
Kumafşarı [TR] 152 G6
Kumane [SCG] 76 E6
Kumanica [SCG] 146 B3
Kumanovo [MK] 146 D6
Kumarlar [TR] 150 B5
Kumbağ [TR] 150 C3
Kümbet [TR] 150 H5
Kumburk [CZ] 48 H2
Kumburun [TR] 130 H6
Kumkale [TR] 130 H5
Kumköy [TR] 150 E2
Kumla [S] 166 H3
Kumlinge [FIN] 176 B5
Kummayuopio [S] 192 G3
Kummeren [N] 192 D6
Kumo / Kokemäki [FIN] 176 D2
Kumola [RUS] 188 G6
Kumpuvaara [FIN] 196 E2
Kumreut [D] 60 H3
Kumrovec [HR] 74 E5
Kumuu [FIN] 196 G4
Kumyalı (Koma Tou Yialou) [CY] 154 G4
Kunadacs [H] 76 D2
Kunágota [H] 76 G4
Kuncsorba [H] 76 F2
Kunda [EST] 198 F1
Kunes [N] 194 C2
Kunfehértó [H] 76 D4
Kungälv [S] 160 G1
Kungsängen [S] 168 D2
Kungsäter [S] 160 H3
Kungsbacka [S] 160 H3
Kungsberg [S] 174 D4
Kungsfors [S] 174 D4
Kungshället [S] 168 C3
Kungshamn [S] 166 B5
Kungsör [S] 168 B3
Kunhegyes [H] 76 F1
Kunín [CZ] 50 E5
Kunmadaras [H] 76 F1
Kunovice [CZ] 62 H2
Kunów [PL] 52 C1
Kunowo [PL] 36 C4
Kunpeszér [H] 76 C2
Kunrau [D] 34 A2
Kunštát [CZ] 50 C5
Kunszentmárton [H] 76 E3
Kunszentmiklós [H] 76 C2
Kunžak [CZ] 48 H6
Künzelsau [D] 46 E5
Kuohatti [FIN] 196 G5
Kuohenmaa [FIN] 176 F2
Kuoksu [S] 192 H5
Kuolayarvi [RUS] 194 F7
Kuolio [FIN] 196 F2
Kuona [FIN] 196 D6
Kuopio [FIN] 188 D2
Kuora [FIN] 188 G1
Kuortane [FIN] 186 D3
Kuosku [FIN] 194 E6
Kup [H] 74 H2
Kup [PL] 50 E2
Kupferberg [D] 46 H3
Kupferzell [D] 46 E5
Kupirovo [HR] 112 H4
Kupiškis [LT] 200 G4
Kupjak [HR] 112 F1
Kupkovo [RUS] 198 G2
Kupli [LV] 198 D5
Küplü [TR] 130 H2
Küplü [TR] 150 G4
Kuprava [LV] 198 G4
Kupres [BIH] 142 C4
Kurbinovo [MK] 128 D4
Kurbnesh [AL] 128 B1
Kurchatov [RUS] 202 F6
Kurd [H] 76 B4
Kŭrdzhali [BG] 130 F1
Kurejoki [FIN] 186 D2
Kuremäe [EST] 198 F1
Kuressaare [EST] 198 C3
Kurevere [EST] 198 C3
Kurgolovo [RUS] 178 E5
Kurianka [PL] 24 F4
Kurikka [FIN] 186 C4
Kurilo [BG] 146 F4
Kuřim [CZ] 50 B6
Kurjala [FIN] 188 D3
Kurkiyeki [RUS] 188 G6
Kurkkio [FIN] 194 C6
Kurkkio [S] 192 H5
Kŭrnare [BG] 148 B4
Kürnüç [TR] 150 H4
Kurobaşı [TR] 134 G1
Kurola [FIN] 188 D4
Kurolanahti [FIN] 188 C2
Kurów [PL] 38 D5
Kurowice [PL] 36 H4
Kurozwęki [PL] 52 C2
Kurravaara [S] 192 G5
Kuršėnai [LT] 200 E4
Kursīši [LV] 198 C6
Kursu [FIN] 194 E7
Kuršumlija [SCG] 146 C4
Kuršumlijska Banja [SCG] 146 C4
Kurşunlu [TR] 150 D4
Kurşunlu [TR] 150 F4
Kurtakko [FIN] 194 C6
Kurtbey [TR] 150 B3
Kurtköy [TR] 150 G3
Kurtköyü [TR] 150 H2
Kurtti [FIN] 196 F3
Kuru [FIN] 176 F1
Kuru [FIN] 186 D6
Kurvinen [FIN] 196 F2
Kurzeszyn [PL] 38 A4
Kurzętnik [PL] 22 F5
Kuşadası [TR] 152 D5
Kuşçayır [TR] 150 B6
Kusel [D] 44 H3
Kushalino [RUS] 202 E2
Kushevanda [RUS] 196 G2
Kuside [SCG] 144 D3
Kusmark [S] 196 A4
Küssnacht [CH] 58 F6
Kustavi / Gustavs [FIN] 176 C4
Kuşu [TR] 152 F2
Kut [HR] 142 A1
Kuta [SCG] 144 E3
Kütahya [TR] 152 G1
Kutemajärvi [FIN] 186 H5
Kutina [HR] 142 B1
Kutjevo [HR] 142 D1
Kutná Hora [CZ] 48 H4
Kutno [PL] 36 G3
Kuttanen [FIN] 194 B5
Kuttura [FIN] 194 D5
Kuuksenvaara [FIN] 188 H2
Kuurtola [FIN] 196 F3
Kuusaa [FIN] 186 G4
Kuusaa [FIN] 196 D5
Kuusajoki [FIN] 194 C6
Kuusalu [EST] 198 E1
Kuusamo [FIN] 194 F8
Kuusankoski [FIN] 178 C3
Kuusiniemi [RUS] 196 H3
Kuusjärvi [FIN] 188 E2
Kuusjoki [FIN] 176 F4
Kuuttila [FIN] 186 B2
Kuvaskangas [FIN] 186 B6
Kuvshinovo [RUS] 202 D2
Kuyubaşi [TR] 150 G4
Kuyucak [TR] 150 H5
Kuyucak [TR] 152 E5
Kuzemki [RUS] 202 E4
Kuzma [SLO] 74 E3
Kuzmin [SCG] 142 F2
Kuźmina [PL] 52 E5
Kuznechnoye [RUS] 178 G1
Kuznetsovo [RUS] 198 H1
Kuznetsovs'k [UA] 202 B7
Kuźnia Raciborska [PL] 50 E3
Kuźnica [PL] 24 F4
Kuzovo [RUS] 198 H3
Kuzuluk [TR] 150 H3
Kvænangsbotn [N] 192 H2
Kværndrup [DK] 156 D4
Kvål [N] 182 B2
Kvalsund [N] 194 B2
Kvalsvik [N] 180 C3
Kvalvåg [N] 170 A5
Kvalvåg [N] 180 F2
Kvam [N] 180 H6
Kvam [N] 190 C5
Kvammen [N] 180 G2
Kvamsøy Gml. Kirke [N] 170 C2
Kvanndal [N] 170 C4
Kvanne [N] 180 F2
Kvantenburg [S] 166 D5
Kvarnåsen [S] 190 H4
Kvarnberg [S] 172 G2
Kvarsebo [S] 168 C5
Kvarstadseter [N] 172 B2
Kvås [N] 164 C5
Kvasilov [UA] 202 B7
Kveaunet [N] 190 D5
Kvėdarna [LT] 200 D4
Kveejdet [N] 190 D5
Kveina [N] 190 C4
Kvelde [N] 164 G3
Kvelia [N] 190 D5
Kvenvær [N] 190 A6
Kvernessetra [N] 172 C1
Kvetkai [LT] 198 E6
Kvevlax / Koivulahti [FIN] 186 B2
Kvicksund [S] 168 B2
Kvikkjokk [S] 190 G1
Kvikne [N] 182 B4
Kvilda [CZ] 48 E6
Kvilldal [N] 164 C1
Kville [S] 166 C5
Kvillsfors [S] 162 F3
Kvinesdal [N] 164 C5
Kvinlog [N] 164 C4
Kvisler [N] 172 D4
Kvissleby [S] 184 E5
Kvistgård [DK] 156 G2
Kvisvik [N] 180 F2
Kviteseid [N] 164 E2
Kvitnes [N] 180 F2
Kvitten [N] 182 D4
Kwiatkowice [PL] 36 G4
Kwidzyn [PL] 22 E4
Kwilcz [PL] 36 B2
Kybartai [LT] 24 E1
Kyburg [CH] 58 G5
Kycklingvattnet [S] 190 E5
Kyffhäuser -Denkmal [D] 34 A5
Kyiv [UA] 202 D7
Kyjov [CZ] 62 G2
Kyläinpää [FIN] 186 B3
Kylänlahti [FIN] 196 G6
Kylemore Abbey [IRL] 2 B4
Kyle of Lochalsh [GB] 6 C5
Kyliia [UA] 204 F4
Kyllaj [S] 168 G4
Kylland [N] 164 D4
Kyllburg [D] 44 F1
Kyllíni [GR] 136 B1
Kylmäkoski [FIN] 176 F2
Kylmälä [FIN] 196 E4
Kylmämäki [FIN] 186 H4
Kymbo [S] 162 C1
Kyme [TR] 152 C3
Kými [GR] 134 C4
Kýmina [GR] 128 H4
Kymönkoski [FIN] 186 G2
Kynšperk Nad Ohří [CZ] 48 C3
Kypäräjärvi [FIN] 188 E3
Kypäravaara [FIN] 196 F4
Kyparissía [GR] 136 C3
Kyriáki [GR] 132 H5
Kyritz [D] 20 B6
Kyrkhult [S] 162 D6
Kyrkjebygdi [N] 164 E3
Kyrksæterøra [N] 180 G1
Kyrkslätt / Kirkkonummi [FIN] 176 G5
Kyrkstad [S] 196 B5
Kyrksten [S] 166 G2
Kyrö [FIN] 176 E4
Kyrönlahti [FIN] 186 D6
Kyröskoski [FIN] 176 E1
Kyrping [N] 170 B6
Kyšice [CZ] 48 F3
Kysucké Nové Mesto [SK] 50 F6
Kytäjä [FIN] 176 G4
Kýthira [GR] 136 F6
Kýthnos [GR] 138 C2
Kytömäki [FIN] 196 F4
Kyustendil [BG] 146 E6
Kyyjärvi [FIN] 186 E2
Kyynämöinen [FIN] 186 F4
Kyzikos [TR] 150 D4
Kyznecovo [RUS] 202 B1

L

Laa an der Thaya [A] 62 F3
Laage Weitendorf [D] 20 B3
Laája [FIN] 196 F4
Laajoki [FIN] 176 D3
Laakajärvi [FIN] 196 F5
Laakirchen [A] 62 A5
La Alameda [E] 96 E5
La Alamedilla [E] 88 E4
La Alberca [E] 88 B4
La Alberca de Záncara [E] 98 A3
La Albuera [E] 94 G2
La Algaba [E] 94 G6
La Almarcha [E] 98 B3
La Almolda [E] 90 F4
La Almudena [E] 104 B2
La Almunia de Doña Godina [E] 90 D4
Laamala [FIN] 188 E6
Laanila [FIN] 194 D5
La Antilla [E] 94 E6
Laarbruch [D] 30 F2
Laas [A] 72 G3
Laasala [FIN] 186 E3
La Azohía [E] 104 C4
Labacolla [E] 78 C3
Labajos [E] 88 E4
la Balme [F] 68 G5
La Baña [E] 78 F6
La Bañeza [E] 78 G6
La Barca de la Florida [E] 100 G4
La Barrela [E] 78 D4
La Bassée [F] 28 F3
la Bastide [F] 108 D4
Labastide-d'Armagnac [F] 66 D6
La Bastide de-Sérou [F] 84 H5
Labastide-Murat [F] 66 G4
La Bastide-Puylaurent [F] 68 D6
Labastide-Rouairoux [F] 106 C4
La Bastie d'Urfé [F] 68 E2
La Bâtiaz [CH] 70 C2
La Bâtie-Neuve [F] 108 D2
La Baule [F] 40 E6
La Bazoche-Gouet [F] 42 D5
Łabędzie [PL] 20 H4
la Bégude-de-Mazenc [F] 68 F6
La Belle Etoile [F] 44 A5
Labenne [F] 66 A6
La Bérarde [F] 70 A5
L'Aber-Wrac'h [F] 40 B1
La Bien Aparecida [E] 82 F3
Labin [HR] 112 E2
Labinot Fushë [AL] 128 C3
La Bisbal de Falset [E] 90 H5
Łabiszyn [PL] 36 E1
Labjana [SCG] 146 C5
Lábod [H] 74 H4
Laboe [D] 18 G2
Laborel [F] 108 C2
Labouheyre [F] 66 B5
La Bourboule [F] 68 C2
La Bóveda de Toro [E] 88 D2
Labrags [LV] 198 B5
Labraunda [TR] 152 E6
Labrède [F] 66 C3
La Bresse [F] 58 D3
La Brillanne [F] 108 C3
Labrit [F] 66 C5
Łabunie [PL] 52 G1
Läby [S] 174 F6
Laç [AL] 128 B2
La Cabrera [E] 88 G4
La Caillere-St-Hilaire [F] 54 C3
La Calahorra [E] 102 F4
La Calera [E] 100 B5
La Caleta [E] 100 E5
La Caleta [I] 118 E3
Lacalm [F] 68 C5
La Calzada de Calatrava [E] 96 E5
La Calzada de Oropesa [E] 88 C6
La Campana [E] 102 A2
La Campana [E] 104 B4
La Cañada de Cañepla [E] 102 H3
Lacanau [F] 66 C2
Lacanau-Océan [F] 66 B2
La Canonica [F] 114 C3
La Canonja [E] 92 C5
La Canourgue [F] 68 C6
La Capelle [F] 28 G5
Lacapelle-Marival [F] 66 H4
La Capte [F] 108 C6
Laćarak [SCG] 142 F2
La Caridad [E] 78 F2
La Carlota [E] 102 B2
La Carolina [E] 96 E6
La Cartuja [E] 100 F3
Lacaune [F] 106 C3
La Cavalerie [F] 106 D3
Lacave [F] 66 G4
Lacco Ameno [I] 120 D3
Lacedonia [I] 120 G2
La Celle-Dunoise [F] 54 H5

Lac - Laz
271

Lăceni [RO] 148 B1
La Cerca [E] 82 F4
Láces [I] 72 C3
La Chaise-Dieu [F] 68 D3
La Chambre [F] 70 B4
Lachamp [F] 68 C5
Lachanás [GR] 130 B3
Lachaniá [GR] 154 D4
La Chapelle [F] 68 F1
La Chapelle-d'Angillon [F] 56 C3
la Chapelle-en-Valgaudemar [F] 70 A6
La Chapelle-en-Vercors [F] 68 G5
La Chapelle-Glain [F] 40 G5
la-Chapelle-Laurent [F] 68 C4
La Charité-sur-Loire [F] 56 D3
La Chartre-sur-le-Loir [F] 42 C6
La Châtaigneraie [F] 54 D3
La Châtre [F] 54 H5
La Chaux-de-Fonds [CH] 58 C5
Lachendorf [D] 32 G1
La-Chevignerie [F] 40 E6
la Chèze [F] 26 B5
Lachowo [PL] 24 D4
La Ciotat [F] 108 B5
La Ciudad Encantada [E] 98 C2
Łąck [PL] 36 G2
Läckeby [S] 162 G5
Läckö [S] 166 E5
La Clayette [F] 56 F6
la Clisse [F] 54 C6
La Clusaz [F] 70 B3
La Cluse [F] 68 H2
La Cluse-et-Mijoux [F] 58 B6
La Codosera [E] 86 F5
La Colle Noire [F] 108 E5
Lacona [I] 114 D3
La Concepción [E] 102 C4
Láconi [I] 118 D5
La Coquille [F] 66 G2
La Coronada [E] 96 B3
La Corrèze [F] 66 H3
La Coruña / A Coruña [E] 78 C2
La Côte-St-André [F] 68 G4
Lacourt [F] 84 G5
La Courtine [F] 68 B2
la Couvertoirade [F] 106 E3
Lacq [F] 84 D3
La Croisière [F] 54 G5
La Croix Ferrée [F] 66 H1
La Croixille [F] 26 D6
La Croix-Valmer [F] 108 D6
La Cueva Santa [E] 98 E3
La Cumbre [E] 96 B1
La Cure [F] 70 B1
Lad [H] 74 H5
Ląd [PL] 36 E3
Ladapeyre [F] 54 H5
Ladbergen [D] 32 C2
Ladby [DK] 156 E3
Ladek-Zdroj [PL] 50 C3
Ládi [GR] 130 H1
Ladíspoli [I] 114 H5
Ladoeiro [P] 86 F3
Ladon [F] 42 F6
Ladoye, Cirque de- [F] 58 A6
Ladushkin [RUS] 22 G2
Ladyzhyn [UA] 204 E2
La Encinilla y El Rubio [E] 100 G3
Lærdalsøyri [N] 170 E2
Laerma [GR] 154 D4
La Espina [E] 78 G3
La Estrella [E] 96 D1
La Felipa [E] 98 C5
La Fère [F] 28 F6
la Ferrière [F] 42 C6
la Ferrière [F] 70 A4
La Ferrière-en-Parthenay [F] 54 E3
Laferté [F] 58 B3
La Ferté-Bernard [F] 42 C5
La Ferté-Gaucher [F] 42 H4
la-Ferté-Loupière [F] 56 E1
La Ferté-Macé [F] 26 F5
La Ferté-Milon [F] 42 H3
La Ferté-sous-Jouarre [F] 42 H3
La Ferté-St-Aubin [F] 56 B1
La Ferté-Vidame [F] 26 H5
La-Feuille [F] 28 C5
Laffrey [F] 68 H5
Láfka [GR] 136 E1
La Flèche [F] 42 B6
La Florida [E] 78 G3
La Flotte [F] 54 B4
La Font de la Figuera [E] 98 D6
la Foresta, Convento- [I] 116 B4
Laforsen [S] 182 H6
Lafortunada [E] 84 E5
Lafrançaise [F] 66 F6
La Fregeneda [E] 80 E5
La Fresneda [E] 90 F6
La Frua [I] 70 F2
La Fuente de San Esteban [E] 80 F6
Lăga [BG] 148 A4
La Gacilly [F] 40 E5
Lagan [S] 162 C4
Laganás [GR] 136 B2
Lagarde [F] 44 F5
La Garde-Freinet [F] 108 D5
La Garriga [E] 92 E4
La Garrovilla [E] 94 G1
Lage [D] 32 E3
Łagiewniki [PL] 50 C2
Laginá [GR] 130 B4
La Gineta [E] 98 B5
L'Agiot Élancourt [F] 42 F3
Lagkáda [GR] 134 G4
Lagkáda [GR] 136 E4
Lagkadás [GR] 130 B4
Lagkádia [GR] 136 D2
Lagkadíkia [GR] 130 B4
Lagnieu [F] 68 G2
Lagnö [S] 168 C6
Lagny [F] 42 G3
Lagoa [P] 94 B5
Lagodaž [BG] 146 F6
Lagonegro [I] 120 G5
Lagonísi [GR] 136 H1
Lágos [GR] 130 F3
Lagos [P] 94 B5
Lagosanto [I] 110 H3
Łagów [PL] 34 H3
Łagów [PL] 52 C1
La Granada de Rio Tinto [E] 94 F4
la Granadella [E] 90 H5
La Grand-Combe [F] 106 F2
La Grande-Motte [F] 106 F4
La Granja [E] 88 F4
La Granjuela [E] 96 B5
Lagrasse [F] 106 C5
La Grave [F] 70 B5
Lägsta [S] 190 G6
La Guardia / A Guarda [E] 78 A5
La Guardia / A Guarda [E] 96 G2
Laguardia / Biasteri [E] 82 G6
La Guardia de Jaén [E] 102 E2
Laguarres [E] 90 H3
Laguarta [E] 84 E5
Laguépie [F] 66 H6
La Guerche-de-Bretagne [F] 40 G4
La Guerche-sur-l'Aubois [F] 56 D4
Laguiole [F] 68 B5
Laguna de Duero [E] 88 E2
Laguna del Marquesado [E] 98 C2
Laguna de Negrillos [E] 82 B5
Laguna Negra [E] 90 B2
Lagunas De Villafáfila [E] 82 A6
Lagýna [GR] 128 H4
La Haba [E] 96 B3
Lahane [F] 66 B5
la Haye [F] 28 C5
La Haye-du-Puits [F] 26 D2
Lahdenperä [FIN] 186 F2
La Hermida [E] 82 D3
Laheycourt [F] 44 C4
Lahinch [IRL] 2 B5
Lahnajärvi [S] 194 B7
Lahnasjärvi [FIN] 196 F5
Lahnberg [A] 72 F2
Lahnstein [D] 30 H6
Laholm [S] 162 B5
Laholuoma [FIN] 186 C5
La Horra [E] 88 G2
Lahoysk [BY] 202 B5
La Hoz de la Vieja [E] 90 E6
Lahr [D] 58 E2
Lähteenkylä [FIN] 176 D2
Lahti / Lahtis [FIN] 178 B2
Lahtis / Lahti [FIN] 178 B2
La Hutte [F] 26 F6
Laibgaliai [LT] 200 G3
Laichingen [D] 60 B3
Laifour, Roches de- [F] 44 C1
L'Aigle [F] 26 G5
La Iglesuela del Cid [E] 98 F2
Laignes [F] 56 F2
Laiguéglia [I] 108 G4
L'Aiguillon [F] 54 B4
Laihela / Laihia [FIN] 186 B3
Laihia / Laihela [FIN] 186 B3
Laikko [FIN] 188 F6
Laïliás [GR] 130 C2
Laimbach [A] 62 D4
Laimoluokta [S] 192 G4
Lainate [I] 70 G4
Lainbach [A] 62 C6
Lainijaur [S] 190 G4
Lainio [S] 192 H5
Lairg [GB] 6 E3
Laisbäck [S] 190 F4
La Isla [E] 82 C2
Laissac [F] 68 B6
Laïsta [GR] 132 D1
Laisvall [S] 190 F2
Laitikkala [FIN] 176 G2
Laitila [FIN] 176 D3
Laitineva [FIN] 196 D4
Laize-la-Ville [F] 26 F4
la-Jaille-Yvon [F] 40 H5
La Jana [E] 98 G2
Lajares [E] 100 E6
La Javie [F] 108 D3
Lajes [P] 100 D3
Lajes das Flores [P] 100 B4
Lajes do Pico [P] 100 C3
Lajkovac [SCG] 146 A1
la Jonquera [E] 92 G2
Lajoskomárom [H] 76 B3
Lajosmizse [H] 76 D2
Lak [H] 64 F4
Lakaluoma [FIN] 186 D3
Lakaniemi [FIN] 186 D2
Łaka Prudnicka [PL] 50 D3
Lakatnik [BG] 146 F4
Lakaträsk [S] 194 A8
Lakavica [MK] 128 G2
Lakfors [N] 190 D3
Lakhdenpokh'ya [RUS] 188 G6
Laki [MK] 128 G1
Lakitelek [H] 76 E3
Lákka [GR] 132 B3
Lakkí [GR] 154 A2
Lákkoi [GR] 140 C4
Lákkoma [GR] 130 G4
Lakkópetra [GR] 132 E6
Lakolk [DK] 156 A3
Laksåvik [N] 190 A6
Lakselv [N] 194 C3
Laktaši [BIH] 142 C2
La Lantejuela [E] 102 B2
Lalapaşa [TR] 150 B1
Lálas [GR] 136 C2
l'Albagés [E] 90 H5
L'Albi [E] 92 B4
l'Alcora / Alcora [E] 98 F3
L'Alcúdia [E] 98 E5
L'Alcúdia (Ilice) [E] 104 D2
L'Alcúdia de Crespins [E] 98 E6
L'Aldea [E] 92 B5
l'Alguenya [E] 104 D2
La Lima [I] 110 E4
Lalín [E] 78 C4
Lalinde [F] 66 F4
La Línea de la Concepción [E] 100 H5
Lalm [N] 180 G6
La Loupe [F] 26 H6
Lalouvesc [F] 68 F4
La Louvière [B] 28 H4
L'Alpe-d'Huez [F] 70 A5
Lalueza [E] 90 F3
La Luisiana [E] 102 B2
Lam [D] 48 D6
La Machine [F] 56 D4
La Maddalena [I] 118 E2
Lama dei Peligni [I] 116 D5
La Magdalena [E] 78 G5
La Malène [F] 68 C6
Lamalou-les-Bains [F] 106 D4
Lamarche [F] 58 B2
Lamargelle [F] 56 G3
La Marina [E] 104 D3
Lamarosa [P] 86 C5
Lamarque [F] 66 C2
Lamas do Vouga [P] 80 B5
Lamastre [F] 68 F5
La Mata [E] 104 D3
La Matanza [E] 82 B5
La Maucarrière [F] 54 E3
Lambach [A] 62 B4
Lamballe [F] 26 B4
Lambesc [F] 106 H4
Lamborn [S] 174 C3
Lambrecht [D] 46 B5
Lamego [P] 80 D4
la-Melleraye-de-Bretagne [F] 40 F5
L'Ametlla de Mar [E] 92 B5
Lamezia Terme [I] 124 D5
Lamía [GR] 132 G4
Lammhult [S] 162 D4
Lammi [FIN] 176 H2
Lammi [FIN] 186 D1
Lamminaho [FIN] 196 D6
Lamminkylä [FIN] 188 G3
Lamminkylä [FIN] 196 F2
Lamminkyulya [RUS] 188 F6
Lamminmaa [FIN] 186 C4
La Molina [E] 92 E2
La Mongie [F] 84 F4
La Mota [E] 102 D3
La Mothe-Achard [F] 54 B3
La-Mothe-St-Héray [F] 54 D4
Lamotte-Beuvron [F] 56 B2
La Motte-Chalancon [F] 108 B2
la Motte-du-Caire [F] 108 C2
Lamouroux, Grottes de- [F] 66 G3
Lampaanjärvi [FIN] 186 H1
Lampaul [F] 40 A1
Lampaul-Plouarzel [F] 40 A1
Lampedusa [I] 126 A6
Lámpeia [GR] 136 C1
Lampeland [N] 164 G1
Lamperila [FIN] 188 C2
Lampeter [GB] 10 B6
Lampinsaari [FIN] 196 D5
L'Ampolla [E] 92 B5
Lamppi [FIN] 176 C1
Lamprechtshausen [A] 60 G5
Lamprechtsofenloch [A] 60 G6
Lämsänkylä [FIN] 196 F2
Lamsfeld [D] 34 F4
Lamstedt [D] 18 E4
La Mudarra [E] 88 E1
La Muela [E] 90 E4
La Mure [F] 68 H5
Lamure-sur-Azergues [F] 68 F2
La Murta [E] 98 E6
Lana [I] 72 C3
Lanaja [E] 90 F4
La Napoule-Plage [F] 108 E5
Lanark [GB] 8 D4
La Nava [E] 94 F4
La Nava de Ricomalillo [E] 96 D1
La Nava de Santiago [E] 86 G6
Lancaster [GB] 10 D2
Lanciano [I] 116 E5
Łańcut [PL] 52 E3
Landau [D] 46 B5
Landau [D] 60 G3
Landeck [A] 72 C1
Landedo [P] 80 F3
Landendorf [A] 62 F3
Landepéreuse [F] 26 G4
Landerneau [F] 40 B2
Landersfjorden [N] 194 D2
Landeryd [S] 162 B4
Landesbergen [D] 32 E1
Landete [E] 98 D3
Landévennec [F] 40 B2
Landivisiau [F] 40 C2
Landivy [F] 26 D5
Landkirchen [D] 18 H2
Landön [S] 182 G1
Landquart [CH] 58 H6
Landrecies [F] 28 G4
Landsberg [D] 34 C5
Landsberg [D] 60 D4
Landsbro [S] 162 E3
Landshut [D] 60 F3
Landshut, Ruine- [D] 44 G2
Landskrona [S] 156 H2
Landštejn [CZ] 62 D2
Landstuhl [D] 44 H3
Landudec [F] 40 B3
Landvetter [S] 160 H2
Lane [N] 170 C1
Lanersbach [A] 72 E1
Lanesborough [IRL] 2 D5
La Neuve-Lyre [F] 26 H5
La Neuveville [CH] 58 D5
Langa [DK] 160 D5
Långå [S] 182 F4
Langa de Duero [E] 88 H2
Långåminne [FIN] 186 B3
Langangen [N] 164 G3
Langballig [D] 156 C5
Långban [S] 166 G1
Långbo [S] 174 D2
Langdal [N] 180 E4
Langeac [F] 68 D4
Langeais [F] 54 F2
Langehauk [N] 170 F3
Langeid [N] 164 D3
Länge Jan [S] 158 G1
Längelmäki [FIN] 186 F6
Langelsheim [D] 32 G3
Långemåla [S] 162 G4
Langen [A] 72 B1
Langen [D] 18 D4
Langen [D] 46 C3
Langenargen [D] 58 H4
Långenäs [FIN] 166 E1
Langenau [D] 60 B3
Langenburg [D] 46 E5
Langenes [N] 192 D3
Längenfeld [A] 72 C2
Langenfeld [D] 30 G4
Langenhahn [D] 46 B1
Langenhorn [D] 156 B5
Langenisarhofen [D] 60 G3
Langenlois [A] 62 E4
Langennaundorf [D] 34 E5
Langenselbold [D] 46 D3
Langenthal [CH] 58 E5
Langenwang [A] 62 E6
Langenzenn [D] 46 F5
Langeoog [D] 18 B3
Langeskov [DK] 156 E3
Langesø [DK] 156 D3
Langesund [N] 164 G3
Langevåg [N] 164 A1
Langevåg [N] 180 C3
Langewiese [D] 32 D5
Langfjord [N] 192 H1
Langfjordnes [N] 194 D1
Långflon [S] 172 E3
Langhirano [I] 110 D3
Langholm [GB] 8 E5
Långlöt [S] 162 G5
Långnäs [FIN] 176 B5
Langnau im Emmental [CH] 58 E6
Langø [DK] 156 E5
Langogne [F] 68 D5
Langoiran [F] 66 D3
Langon [F] 66 D4
Langquaid [D] 60 F2
Langreo [E] 78 H4
Langres [F] 56 H2
Långron [S] 184 H1
Långsel [S] 194 A8
Långsele [S] 184 E2
Långsele [S] 190 F5
Långserud [S] 166 D3
Långshyttan [S] 174 D5
Långsjöby [S] 190 F4
Langstrand [N] 194 B2
Långträsk [S] 190 H4
Långträsk [S] 196 A3
Languidou, Chapelle de- [F] 40 B3
Langula [D] 32 G5
Långvattnet [S] 190 H4
Langviken [S] 196 A4
Långviksmon [S] 184 G1
Långvind [S] 174 E2
Langwarden [D] 18 D4
Langwedel [D] 18 E6
Langweid [D] 60 D3
Langwies [CH] 70 H1
Lanhelas [P] 78 A5
Lanjarón [E] 102 E5
Lankas [LV] 198 B5
Lankila [FIN] 178 D3
Länkipohja [FIN] 186 F6
Lankojärvi [FIN] 194 C7
Lankosi [FIN] 186 B6
Lanleff, Temple de- [F] 26 A3
Lanmeur [F] 40 C1
Lanna [S] 162 C3
Länna [S] 168 C3
Lannabruk [S] 166 G3
Lannavaara [S] 192 H4
Lannemezan [F] 84 F4
Lannevesi [FIN] 186 F3
Lannilis [F] 40 B1
Lannion [F] 40 D1
Lanobre [F] 68 B3
La Noguera [E] 98 D1
Lanouaille [F] 66 G2
Lansån [S] 194 B8
Lansikylä [FIN] 186 D3
Länsi-Vuokka [FIN] 196 F6
Lansjärv [S] 194 A8
Lanškroun [CZ] 50 C4
Lanslebourg-Mont-Cenis [F] 70 C5
Lanšperk [CZ] 50 B4
Lantosque [F] 108 F4
Lanusei [I] 118 E5
Lanvollon [F] 26 A4
Lánycsók [H] 76 B5
Lanzá [E] 78 C2
Lanzendorf [A] 62 F5
Lanžhot [CZ] 62 G3
Lanzo d'Intelvi [I] 70 G3
Lanzo Torinese [I] 70 D5
Lao [EST] 198 D3
Laodikeia [TR] 152 G5
La Oliva [E] 84 B5
La Oliva [E] 100 E6
Laon [F] 28 G6
La Orotava [E] 100 B5
La Paca [E] 104 B3
La Pacaudière [F] 68 E1
Lapalisse [F] 56 D6
La Pallice [F] 54 B4
La Palma [E] 104 C4
La Palma del Condado [E] 94 F6
Lapalme [F] 106 D5
La Palud-sur-Verdon [F] 108 D4
la Panouse [F] 68 D5
Łapanów [PL] 52 B4
Lápas [GR] 132 E6
La Pelechaneta / Pelejaneta [E] 98 F3
La Peraleja [E] 98 B1
la Péruse [F] 54 E6
La Petite-Pierre [F] 44 G5
Lapeyrade [F] 66 D5
Lapinjärvi / Lappträsk [FIN] 178 B3
Lapinlahti [FIN] 188 C1
Lapinsaari [FIN] 186 C3
Lapistó [H] 76 E3
Lápithos (Lâpta) [CY] 154 F5
La Plagne [F] 70 B4
La Plaza / Teverga [E] 78 G4
Laplume [F] 66 E5
la Pobla de Lillet [E] 92 E2
La Pobla de Massaluca [E] 90 G6
la Pobla de Segur [E] 92 C1
la Pobla de Vallbona [E] 98 E4
La Poblallarga [E] 98 E5
la Pobla Tornesa [E] 98 G3
La Pola de Gordón [E] 78 H5
La Portera [E] 98 D4
Lapoutroie [F] 58 D2
Lapovo [SCG] 146 C2
Lappach / Lappago [I] 72 E2
Lappago / Lappach [I] 72 E2
Lappajärvi [FIN] 186 D2
Lappäjärvi [FIN] 194 B5
Läppe [S] 168 B3
Lappeenranta / Villmanstrand [FIN] 178 E2
Lappfjärd / Lapväärtti [FIN] 186 B5
Lappfors [FIN] 186 C1
Lappi [FIN] 176 D3
Lappo [FIN] 176 C5
Lappo / Lapua [FIN] 186 C2
Lappohja / Lappvik [FIN] 176 F6
Lappträsk [S] 196 C2
Lappträsk / Lapinjärvi [FIN] 178 B3
Lappvattnet [S] 196 A5
Lappvik / Lappohja [FIN] 176 F6
La Primaude [F] 68 B6
Lapseki [TR] 150 B5
Lâpta (Lápithos) [CY] 154 F5
Laptevo [RUS] 198 H5
Lapua / Lappo [FIN] 186 C2
La Puebla de Almoradiel [E] 96 G3
La Puebla de Cazalla [E] 102 A3
La Puebla de Híjar [E] 90 F5
La Puebla de los Infantes [E] 96 B6
La Puebla del Río [E] 94 G6
La Puebla de Montalbán [E] 96 E1
La Puebla de Valdavia [E] 82 D4
La Puebla de Valverde [E] 98 E2
La Pueblanueva [E] 96 D1
La Puerta del Segura [E] 102 G1
La Punt [CH] 72 A3
Lapväärtti / Lappfjärd [FIN] 186 B5
Łapy [PL] 24 E6
Laqueuille [F] 68 C2
L'Aquila [I] 116 C4
La Rábita [E] 102 E5
Laracha [E] 78 C2
Laragh [IRL] 4 G3
Laragne-Montéglin [F] 108 C2
La Rambla [E] 102 C2
l'Arbre [F] 54 E6
L'Arbresle [F] 68 F2
Lärbro [S] 168 G4
Larceveau-Arros-Cibits [F] 84 C3
Larche [F] 66 G3
Larche [F] 108 E2
Lårdal [N] 164 E2
Lardaro [I] 72 C4
Larderello [I] 114 F1
Lardero [E] 82 G6
Lárdos [GR] 154 D4
Lardosa [P] 86 F3
Laredo [E] 82 F3
La Réole [F] 66 D4
La Restinga [E] 100 A5
Largentière [F] 68 E6
L'Argentière-la-Bessée [F] 70 B6
Largs [GB] 8 C3
La Rhune [E] 84 B2
Lariano [I] 116 B6
La Rinconada [E] 94 G6
Larino [I] 116 F6
Larionovo [RUS] 178 G2
Lárisa [GR] 132 G2
Larissa [TR] 152 C3
Larkollen [N] 166 B3
L'Armelliere [F] 106 G4
Larmor [F] 40 C4
Lárnaka [CY] 154 G5
Larne [NIR] 2 G3
La Robla [E] 78 H5
La Roca de la Sierra [E] 86 G6
la Roca del Vallès [E] 92 E4
la Roche [CH] 70 D1
La Roche-Bernard [F] 40 E5
La Roche-Chalais [F] 66 E2
la Roche-de-Rame [F] 70 B6
La Roche-en-Ardenne [B] 30 E6
La Rochefoucauld [F] 54 E6
La Rochelle [F] 54 C4
La Roche-Posay [F] 54 F3
La Roche-sur-Foron [F] 70 B2
La Roche-sur-Yon [F] 54 B3
La Rochette [F] 70 A4
Larochette [L] 44 F2
La Roda [E] 98 B4
La Roda de Andalucía [E] 102 B3
Laroquebrou [F] 68 A4
La Roquebrussanne [F] 108 C5
Laroque-des-Arcs [F] 66 G5
Laroque-d'Olmes [F] 106 A5
La Roque-Gageac [F] 66 G4
La Rouche-Courbon [F] 54 C5
Larraga [E] 84 B4
Larrau [F] 84 D3
Larret [F] 58 A3
Larroque [F] 106 B2
Larsmo / Luoto [FIN] 196 C6
Larsnes [N] 180 C4
l'Artigue [F] 84 H5
La Rubia [E] 90 B2
Laruns [F] 84 D4
Larvik [N] 164 G3
Lárymna [GR] 134 B5
La Salceda [E] 88 F4
la Salles-les Alpes [F] 70 B6
La Salvetat [F] 66 H6
La Salvetat-sur-Agout [F] 106 C3
Läsänkoski [FIN] 188 C5
Las Anorias [E] 98 C6
Lasarte-Oria [E] 84 B2
La Sauceda [E] 100 G4
Las Bárdenas Reales [E] 84 B6
Las Batuecas [E] 88 B4
Låsby [DK] 160 D6
Las Cabezas de San Juan [E] 100 G3
Las Caldas de Besaya [E] 82 E3
Lascaux, Grotte de- [F] 66 G3
la Selve [F] 106 C2
la Sénia [E] 92 A6
Lasenice [CZ] 62 C2
La Señuela [E] 100 G2
La Serna del Monte [E] 88 G4
la Seu d'Urgell [E] 92 D1
La Seyne [F] 108 C6
Las Fuentes [E] 98 C5
Las Huelgas [E] 82 E6
Łasin [PL] 22 E5
Łask [PL] 36 G5
Łaskarzew [PL] 38 C4
Łasko [PL] 20 H6
Laško [SLO] 74 D5
Laskowa [PL] 52 B4
Laskowice [PL] 22 D5
Laskowice [PL] 50 D3
Laslovo [HR] 142 E1
Las Marías [E] 102 F5
Las Médulas [E] 78 E5
Las Mesas [E] 96 H3
Las Navas de la Concepción [E] 96 B6
Las Navas del Marqués [E] 88 E5
Las Negras [E] 102 H5
La Solana [E] 96 G4
La Souterraine [F] 54 G5
Lasovo [SCG] 146 D2
Las Palas [E] 104 C4
Las Palmas de Gran Canaria [E] 100 C6
Las Pedroñeras [E] 96 H3
La Spézia [I] 110 C4
Las Rozas [E] 88 F5
Lassan [D] 20 E3
Lassay [F] 26 E5
Lassemoen [N] 190 D4
Lassigny [F] 28 E6
Las Torcas [E] 98 C2
Las Torres de Cotillas [E] 104 C3
Lastovo [HR] 144 A3
Lastra a Signa [I] 110 E5
Lastres [E] 82 C2
Lästringe [S] 168 D4
Lastrup [D] 18 C6
Lastuk [FIN] 188 D1
Lastulahti [FIN] 188 D1
Lastva [BIH] 144 D4
La Suze-sur-Sarthe [F] 42 B5
Lašva [BIH] 142 D4
Las Veguillas [E] 88 C3
Las Ventas con Peña Aguilera [E] 96 E2
Las Ventas de S. Julián [E] 88 C6
Łaszczów [PL] 52 G2
Laszki [PL] 52 F3
la Tannière [F] 26 D5
Lätefossen [N] 170 C5
Laterza [I] 122 D4
Lathen [D] 16 H3
La Thuile [I] 70 C4
Latiano [I] 122 F4
Latikberg [S] 190 F5
Latina [I] 120 B1
Latinac [SCG] 146 D3
Latisana [I] 72 G5
Lató [GR] 140 F5
Latorpsbruk [S] 166 H3
La Torre [E] 98 D4
la Torre Baixa [E] 98 D2
La Torresaviñán [E] 90 A5
La Tour-du-Pin [F] 68 G3
La Tranche-sur-Mer [F] 54 B4
La Trimouille [F] 54 G4
La Trinité [F] 40 D5
La Trinité-Porhoët [F] 26 B5
Latronico [I] 120 H5
Latronquière [F] 66 H4
Latte, Fort la- [F] 26 B4
Latteluokta [S] 192 G4
Lattuna [FIN] 194 E6
La Turbie [F] 108 F4
Latva [FIN] 196 D5
Latvalampi [FIN] 188 E3
Latvaset [FIN] 196 D6
Laubrières [F] 40 G5
Laucha [D] 34 B5
Lauchdorf [D] 60 C4
Lauchhammer [D] 34 E5
Laudal [N] 164 D5
Lauder [GB] 8 F4
Laudio / Llodio [E] 82 G6
Laudona [LV] 198 F5
Lauenau [D] 32 F2
Lauenbrück [D] 18 F5
Lauenburg [D] 18 G5
Lauenstein [D] 48 E2
Lauf [D] 46 G5
Laufen [CH] 58 D4
Laufen [D] 60 G5
Laufenburg [CH] 58 F4
Laufenburg (Baden) [D] 58 F4
Lauffen [D] 46 D6
Laugratte [F] 66 E4
Lauingen [D] 60 C3
Laujar de Andarax [E] 102 F5
Laukaa [FIN] 186 G4
Laukeland [N] 170 B1
Laukka [FIN] 196 D4
Laukkala [FIN] 186 G1
Lauksundskaret [N] 192 G1
Laukuluspa [S] 192 G5
Laukuva [LT] 200 E4
Laukvik [N] 192 F2
Laukvik [N] 194 B3
Laukvika [N] 192 D5
Launceston [GB] 12 D4
La Unión [E] 104 C4
Laupen [CH] 58 D6
Laupheim [D] 60 B4
Lauragh [IRL] 4 B5
Laureana di Borrello [I] 124 D6
Laurencetown [IRL] 2 D5
Laurenzana [I] 120 H4
Lauria [I] 120 H5
Laurière [F] 54 G6
Laurino [I] 120 G4
Lausanne [CH] 70 C1
Laussig [D] 34 D5
Lautaporras [FIN] 176 F3
Lautemburg [D] 30 F4
Lauter [S] 168 H3
Lauterbach [D] 46 E1
Lauterbourg [F] 46 B6
Lauterbrunnen [CH] 70 E1
Lautere [LV] 198 F5
Lauterecken [D] 44 H3
Lauterhofen [D] 46 H5
Lautrec [F] 106 B3
Lauvåsen [N] 182 B2
Lauvsjølia [N] 190 D5
Lauvsnes [N] 190 C5
Lauvstad [N] 180 C4
Lauvuskylä [FIN] 196 G5
Lauvvik [N] 164 B3
Lauwersoog [NL] 16 G1
Lauzerte [F] 66 F5
Lauzun [F] 66 E4
Lavagna [I] 110 B3
Laval [F] 26 E6
la Vall d'Uixó [E] 98 F4
Lavamünd [A] 74 C3
Lavangnes [N] 192 E3
Lávara [GR] 130 H2
Lavardac [F] 66 E5
Lavardin [F] 42 C6
Lavarone [I] 72 D5
Lavaur [F] 106 B3
La Vecilla [E] 82 B3
Lavelanet [F] 106 A5
Lavello [I] 120 H3
Lavelsloh [D] 32 E2
La Venta [E] 102 F4
La Verna [I] 110 G6
la Veurdre [F] 56 D4
Lavia [FIN] 176 E1
Laviano [I] 120 G3
Lavik [N] 170 B2
la Vila Joiosa / Villajoyosa [E] 104 E2
la Villa / Stern [I] 72 E3
Lavinio-Lido di Enea [I] 120 A1
La Virgen del Camino [E] 78 H5
Lavis [I] 72 C4
Lavit [F] 66 F6
Lavong [N] 190 D2
Lavos [P] 86 C2
La Voulte-sur-Rhône [F] 68 F5
Lavoûte-Chilhac [F] 68 D4
Lavoûte-Polignac, Château de- [F] 68 D4
Lavoûte-sur-Loire [F] 68 D4
Lavoye [F] 44 D4
Lavre [P] 86 C6
Lávrio [GR] 136 H1
Lavry [RUS] 198 G4
Lavsjö [S] 190 F5
La Wantzenau [F] 44 H6
Laxå [S] 166 G4
Laxe [E] 78 B2
Laxne [S] 168 C3
Laxsjö [S] 190 E6
Laxsjön [S] 184 E3
Laxtjärn [S] 172 G5
Laxviken [S] 190 E6
La Yedra [E] 102 F2
La Yesa [E] 98 E3
Läyliäinen [FIN] 176 G4
La Yunta [E] 90 C5
Laza [E] 78 D6
Lazarevac [SCG] 146 B1
Lazarevo [SCG] 142 G1
Lazdijai [LT] 24 F2
Laži [LV] 198 C4
Lazise [I] 72 C6
Łaziska Górne [PL] 50 F3
Lazisko [SK] 64 D2
Lazkao [E] 84 A3
Lázně Bělohrad [CZ] 48 H3
Lázně Kynžvart [CZ] 48 C4
La Zubia [E] 102 E4
Łazy [PL] 22 A2

Molkom [S] 166 F2
Mollafeneri [TR] 150 F3
Mollas [AL] 128 D5
Möllbrücke [A] 72 G2
Mölle [S] 160 H6
Molledo [E] 82 E3
Möllenbeck [D] 20 D5
Mollerussa [E] 92 C3
Mollet del Vallès [E] 92 E4
Molliens [F] 28 D4
Mollina [E] 102 C3
Mölln [D] 18 G4
Mollösund [S] 160 G1
Mölltorp [S] 166 G5
Mölnbo [S] 168 D4
Mölndal [S] 160 G2
Mölnlycke [S] 160 H2
Mołodycz [PL] 52 F3
Mólos [GR] 132 G4
Moloskovitsy [RUS] 178 F6
Moloy [F] 56 G3
Molpe / Moikipää [FIN] 186 A3
Molsheim [F] 44 G6
Molveno [I] 72 C4
Molvotitsy [RUS] 202 C2
Mombaroccio [I] 112 B5
Mombeltrán [E] 88 D5
Mombuey [E] 80 G3
Momchilgrad [BG] 130 F1
Momin Prohod [BG] 146 G5
Mommark [DK] 156 D4
Momo [I] 70 F4
Momrak [N] 164 E3
Monachil [E] 102 E4
Monaco [MC] 108 F4
Monaghan [IRL] 2 F4
Monäs [FIN] 186 B1
Monasterace Marina [I] 124 E6
Monasterboice [IRL] 2 F5
Monasterevin [IRL] 2 E6
Monasterio De Caaveiro [E] 78 D2
Monasterio de Leyre [E] 84 C4
Monasterio del Palancar [E] 86 H4
Monasterio De Moreruela [E] 80 H4
Monasterio De Ribas Do Miño [E] 78 D4
Monasterio De San Clodio [E] 78 C4
Monasterio De San Leonardo [E] 88 C3
Monasterio De Santo Estevo [E] 78 D5
Monasterio De S.Ginés De La Jara [E] 104 C4
Monastir [I] 118 C6
Monastiráki [GR] 130 G3
Monastiráki [GR] 132 D4
Monbiel [CH] 72 A2
Moncalieri [I] 70 D6
Moncalvo [I] 70 E6
Monção [P] 78 B5
Moncarapacho [P] 94 C5
Moncayo [E] 90 C3
Mönchdorf [A] 62 C4
Mönchengladbach [D] 30 G3
Mönchhof [A] 62 G5
Mónchio d. Cortio [I] 110 D3
Monchique [P] 94 B4
Monclova [E] 102 B2
Moncófa [E] 98 F4
Moncontour [F] 26 B5
Moncoutant [F] 54 D3
Mondariz [E] 78 B5
Mondariz–Balneario [E] 78 B5
Mondaye, Abbaye de– [F] 26 E3
Mondéjar [E] 88 G6
Mondello [I] 126 C1
Mondelos [SCG] 142 F2
Mondim de Basto [P] 80 D4
Mondolfo [I] 112 C6
Mondoñedo [E] 78 E2
Mondorf–les–Bains [L] 44 F3
Mondoubleau [F] 42 C5
Mondovì [I] 108 G3
Mondragone [I] 120 D2
Mondsee [A] 60 H5
Monéglia [I] 110 C4
Monegrillo [E] 90 F4
Monemvasía [GR] 136 F5
Monesi [I] 108 F3
Monesterio [E] 94 G4
Monestier–de–Clermont [F] 68 G5
Monestir De Benifassá [E] 98 G2
Monêtier–Allemont [F] 108 C2
Moneygall [IRL] 2 D6
Moneymore [NIR] 2 F3
Monfalcone [I] 72 H5
Monfarracinos [E] 80 H5
Monfero [E] 78 D2
Monflanquin [F] 66 F5
Monforte [P] 86 E5
Monforte da Beira [P] 86 F4
Monforte de Lemos [E] 78 D4
Mongstad [N] 170 A2
Monguelfo / Welsberg [I] 72 E3
Monheim [D] 30 G4
Monheim [D] 60 D2
Moní [CY] 154 G6
Moni Ap. Andreas [CY] 154 H4
Mönichkirchen [A] 62 E6
Moní Elónis [GR] 136 F3
Moni Panagias Eleousas [CY] 154 H4
Möniste [EST] 198 F4
Monistrol–d'Allier [F] 68 D4
Monistrol de Montserrat [E] 92 D4
Monistrol–sur–Loire [F] 68 E4
Monivea [IRL] 2 C5
Mońki [PL] 24 E5
Monmouth [GB] 12 G2
Monnai [F] 26 G4
Mönni [FIN] 188 F2
Monnickendam [NL] 16 D4
Monninkylä [FIN] 178 A4
Monodéndri [GR] 132 C1
Monódryo [GR] 134 C4
Monólithos [GR] 154 C4
Monopoli [I] 122 E3
Monor [H] 76 D1
Monóvar / Monòver [E] 104 D2
Monòver / Monóvar [E] 104 D2
Monpazier [F] 66 F4
Monplaisir [F] 42 C5
Monreal [E] 96 G2
Monreal / Elo [E] 84 B4
Monreal del Campo [E] 90 D6
Monreale [I] 126 C2
Monroy [E] 86 H5
Monroyo [E] 98 G1
Monrupino [I] 72 H6
Mons (Bergen) [B] 28 G4
Monsanto [P] 86 G3
Monsaraz [P] 94 E2
Monschau [D] 30 F5
Monségur [F] 66 D4
Monsélice [I] 110 G1
Mons En Baroeul [F] 28 F3
Monsheim [D] 46 B4
Mønsted [DK] 160 C5
Mönsterås [S] 162 G4
Monsummano Terme [I] 110 E5
Montabaur [D] 46 B2
Montagnac [F] 106 E4
Montagnana [I] 110 F1
Montaigu [F] 54 C2
Montaigu–de–Quercy [F] 66 F5
Montaigut [F] 56 C6
Montaione [I] 110 E6
Montalbán [E] 90 E6
Montalbán [E] 96 E2
Montalbano Elicona [I] 124 A7
Montalbano Jonico [I] 122 D5
Montalbo [E] 98 A2
Montalcino [I] 114 G2
Montaldo di Cosola [I] 110 B2
Montalegre [P] 78 C6
Montalieu [F] 68 G3
Montalivet–les–Bains [F] 66 C1
Montallegro [I] 126 C4
Montalto delle Marche [I] 116 C2
Montalto di Castro [I] 114 G4
Montalto Ligure [I] 108 G4
Montalto Uffugo [I] 124 D4
Montalvão [P] 86 E4
Montalvo [P] 94 C1
Montamarta [E] 80 H4
Montana [BG] 146 F3
Montana [CH] 70 D2
Montañana [E] 90 E4
Montánchez [E] 86 H6
Montanejos [E] 98 E3
Montaren [F] 106 G3
Montargil [P] 86 D5
Montargis [F] 42 F6
Montargull / Artesa de Segre [E] 92 C2
Montastruc la–Conseillère [F] 106 A3
Montauban [F] 26 C5
Montauban [F] 66 F6
Montbard [F] 56 F2
Montbazens [F] 66 H5
Montbazon [F] 54 F2
Montbéliard [F] 58 C4
Montbenoît [F] 58 C5
Montblanc [E] 92 C4
Mont–Blanc, Tunnel du– [EUR] 70 C3
Montbonnot [F] 68 H4
Montbrison [F] 68 E3
Montbron [F] 66 F1
Montbrun–les–Bains [F] 108 B3
Montceau–les–Mines [F] 56 F5
Montchanin [F] 56 F5
Montcornet [F] 28 G6
Montcuq [F] 66 F5
Mont–de–Marsan [F] 66 C6
Montdidier [F] 28 E5
Mont–Dol [F] 26 C4
Montealegre [E] 82 C6
Montealegre del Castillo [E] 98 C6
Monte Arabí, Cueva de– [E] 98 C6
Montebelluna [I] 72 E5
Montebourg [F] 26 D2
Montebruno [I] 110 B3
Monte–Carlo [MC] 108 F4
Montecassino, Abbazia di– [I] 120 D1
Montecatini–Terme [I] 110 E5
Montécchio [I] 112 B5
Montecchio Emilia [I] 110 D3
Montécchio Maggiore [I] 72 D6
Montech [F] 66 F6
Montechiaro, Castello di– [I] 126 D4
Montecorice [I] 120 F5
Montecorvino Rovella [I] 120 F4
Monte da Pedra [P] 86 E4
Monte Do Trigo [P] 94 E2
Montefalco [I] 116 A2
Montefalcone nel Sannio [I] 116 E6
Montefiascone [I] 114 H3
Montefiorentino, Convento di– [I] 110 H6
Montefiorino [I] 110 E4
Monteforte Irpino [I] 120 E3
Montefrío [E] 102 D3
Montegabbione [I] 114 H2
Montegiordano Marina [I] 122 D5
Montegiorgio [I] 116 C2
Monte Gordo [P] 94 D5
Montegrotto Terme [I] 110 G1
Montehermoso [E] 86 H3
Monteil [F] 68 F5
Monte Isola [I] 72 A5
Montejícar [E] 102 E3
Montelaver [P] 86 B5
Montel–de–Gelat [F] 68 C1
Montélimar [F] 68 F6
Montella [I] 120 F3
Montellano [E] 100 H3
Montemaggiore Belsito [I] 126 D2
Monte Maria, Abbazia di– / Marienberg, Kloster– [I] 72 B2
Montemiccioli, Torre di– [I] 114 F1
Montemolín [E] 94 G4
Montemor–o–Novo [P] 86 C6
Montemor–o–Velho [P] 86 D2
Montemurlo [I] 110 E5
Montendre [F] 66 D2
Montenegro de Cameros [E] 90 B2
Montenero di Bisáccia [I] 116 E5
Monte Oliveto Maggiore, Abbazia di– [I] 114 G2
Montepulciano [I] 114 G2
Monterde [E] 90 C5
Montereale [I] 116 B4
Montereale Valcellina [I] 72 F4
Montereau [F] 56 C1
Montereau–Faut–Yonne [F] 42 G5
Monte Redondo [P] 86 C2
Monterenzio [I] 110 F4
Monteriggioni [I] 114 F1
Monteroda [D] 32 G5
Monteroni d'Arbia [I] 114 G1
Monteroni di Lecce [I] 122 G5
Monterosso al Mare [I] 110 C4
Monterosso Almo [I] 126 F5
Monterosso Grana [I] 108 F2
Monterotondo [I] 116 A5
Monterotondo Marittimo [I] 114 E1
Monterroso [E] 78 D4
Monterrubio de la Serena [E] 96 B4
Monte San Biagio [I] 120 C1
Montesano sulla Marcellana [I] 120 G5
Monte San Savino [I] 114 G1
Monte Sant' Angelo [I] 116 H6
Monte Santiago [E] 82 G4
Montesarchio [I] 120 E2
Montescaglioso [I] 122 D4
Montesclaros [E] 88 D6
Monte Senario, Convento– [I] 110 F5
Montesilvano Marina [I] 116 D4
Montesinos, Cueva de– [E] 96 G5
Montesquieu–Volvestre [F] 84 H4
Montesquiou [F] 84 F3
Montevarchi [I] 110 F6
Monteverde [I] 120 G3
Monte Vergine, Santuario di– [I] 120 E3
Montevil [P] 94 C1
Montfaucon–en–Velay [F] 68 E4
Montferrat [F] 108 D4
Montfort [F] 26 C6
Montfort–en–Chalosse [F] 66 B6
Montfort l'Amaury [F] 42 E3
Mont Gargan [F] 66 H2
Montgat [E] 92 E4
Montgenèvre [F] 70 B6
Montgenèvre, Col de– [EUR] 70 B6
Montgeoffroy, Château de– [F] 40 H6
Montgiscard [F] 106 A3
Montguyon [F] 66 D2
Monthermé [F] 44 C1
Monthey [CH] 70 C2
Monthois [F] 44 C3
Monthureux–sur–Saône [F] 58 B2
Monti [I] 118 D3
Monticelli Terme [I] 110 D3
Montichiari [I] 72 B6
Monticiano [I] 114 F2
Montiel [E] 96 G5
Montier–en–Der [F] 44 C5
Montignac [F] 66 G3
Montigny–le–Roi [F] 58 A2
Montigny–sur–Aube [F] 56 G2
Montijo [P] 86 B5
Montilla [E] 102 C2
Monti–Sion, Santuari de– [E] 104 E5
Montivilliers [F] 26 G3
Montizón [E] 96 G6
Montlieu–la–Garde [F] 66 D2
Mont–Louis [F] 92 E1
Montluçon [F] 56 C5
Montluel [F] 68 G2
Montmajour, Abbaye de– [F] 106 G4
Montmarault [F] 56 C6
Montmédy [F] 44 D3
Montmélian [F] 70 A4
Montmeyan [F] 108 C4
Montmirail [F] 42 C5
Montmirail [F] 42 H4
Montmirey [F] 56 H4
Montmoreau–St–Cybard [F] 66 E2
Montmorillon [F] 54 F4
Montmort [F] 44 A4
Montoire–sur–le–Loir [F] 42 C6
Montoito [P] 94 E2
Montorio [E] 82 E5
Montorio al Vomano [I] 116 C3
Montoro [E] 102 D1
Montoy–Flanville [F] 44 F4
Montpellier [F] 106 E4
Montpellier–le–Vieux [F] 106 E2
Montpezat–de–Quercy [F] 66 G6
Montpon–Ménestérol [F] 66 E3
Montpont–en–Bresse [F] 56 G6
Montréal [F] 56 F3
Montréal [F] 66 D6
Montréal [F] 106 B4
Montredon–Labessonnie [F] 106 C3
Montréjeau [F] 84 F4
Montrésor [F] 54 G3
Montresta [I] 118 B4
Montret [F] 56 G5
Montreuil [F] 28 D3
Montreuil–aux–Lions [F] 42 H3
Montreuil–Bellay [F] 54 E2
Montreux [CH] 70 C1
Montrevault [F] 54 C1
Montrevel–en–Bresse [F] 68 G1
Montrichard [F] 54 G2
Montrøen [N] 182 C4
Montroi / Montroy [E] 98 E5
Mont–roig del Camp [E] 90 H6
Montrond–les–Bains [F] 68 E3
Montrose [GB] 8 F2
Montroy / Montroi [E] 98 E5
Montsalvy [F] 68 B5
Montsauche–les–Settons [F] 56 F3
Montségur [F] 106 A5
Montseny [E] 92 E3
Montserrat [E] 92 D4
Montsoreau [F] 54 E2
Mont–sous–Vaudrey [F] 56 H5
Monts–s–Guesnes [F] 54 E3
Mont–Ste–Odile [F] 44 G6
Montsûrs [F] 26 E6
Montuenga [E] 88 E3
Monturque [E] 102 C2
Monza [I] 70 G4
Monze [F] 106 C5
Monzón [E] 90 G3
Monzón de Campos [E] 82 D6
Monzuno [I] 110 F4
Moon–sur–Elle [F] 26 E3
Moordorf [D] 18 B4
Moosburg [D] 60 F3
Moosham [A] 72 H2
Moosinning [D] 60 E4
Moos in Passeier / Moso in Passiria [I] 72 D2
Mór [H] 76 B1
Mora [E] 96 F2
Mora [E] 96 F2
Mora [P] 86 D5
Mora [S] 172 G3
Mora [S] 174 C5
Mora, Puerto de la– [E] 102 E4
Morača, Manastir– [SCG] 144 E3
Móra d'Ebre [E] 90 H6
Mora de Rubielos [E] 98 E2
Moradillo de Roa [E] 88 G2
Morąg [PL] 22 G3
Mórahalom [H] 76 E4
Moraïtika [GR] 132 B2
Morakovo [SCG] 144 E3
Morakowo [PL] 36 D1
Móra la Nova [E] 90 H6
Moral de Calatrava [E] 96 F5
Moraleda de Zafayona [E] 102 D4
Moraleja [E] 86 G3
Morales del Vino [E] 80 H5
Morano Cálabro [I] 120 H6
Mora Stenar [S] 168 D2
Morasverdes [E] 88 B3
Moratalla [E] 104 B2
Moravče pri Gabrovki [SLO] 74 C5
Moravice [HR] 112 F1
Morávka [CZ] 50 F5
Moravská Třebová [CZ] 50 C4
Moravské Budějovice [CZ] 62 E2
Moravské Lieskové [SK] 62 H3
Moravský Beroun [CZ] 50 D4
Moravský Krumlov [CZ] 62 F2
Morawica [PL] 52 B2
Morbach [D] 44 G2
Mörbacka [S] 172 E4
Morbegno [I] 70 H3
Mörbisch [A] 62 F6
Mörbylånga [S] 162 G5
Morcenx [F] 66 B5
Morciano di Romagna [I] 112 B5
Morcone [I] 120 E2
Morcote [CH] 70 G3
Mordelles [F] 26 C6
Mordoğan [TR] 152 B4
Mordy [PL] 38 E3
Morecambe [GB] 10 D2
Moreda [E] 102 E3
Morella [E] 98 G1
Morella la Vella [E] 98 G1
Moreno, Col de la– [F] 68 C2
Móres [I] 118 C3
Morestel [F] 68 G3
Moret–sur–Loing [F] 42 G5
Moretta [I] 108 F1
Moreuil [F] 28 E5
Morez [F] 70 B1
Mörfelden [D] 46 C3
Mórfi [GR] 132 C3
Mórfou (Güzelyurt) [CY] 154 F5
Morgantina [I] 126 F4
Morgat [F] 40 B2
Morgedal [N] 164 E2
Morges [CH] 70 B1
Morgex [I] 70 C3
Morgins [CH] 70 C2
Morgongåva [S] 168 C1
Morhange [F] 44 F5
Mori [I] 72 C5
Moriani–Plage [F] 114 C3
Mórichida [H] 62 H6
Morigny Champigny [F] 42 F4
Morimondo, Abbazia di– [I] 70 F5
Moritzburg [D] 34 C6
Moritzburg [D] 34 E6
Moritzburg, Schloss– [D] 34 E6
Moriville [F] 44 F6
Morjärv [S] 196 B2
Mørk [N] 166 B2
Morkarla [S] 174 F6
Mørke [DK] 160 E6
Mørkøv [DK] 156 F2
Morkovice Slížany [CZ] 50 D6
Mörkret [S] 172 E1
Mørkveden [N] 192 C5
Morla [E] 78 F6
Morlaàs [F] 84 E3
Morlaix [F] 40 C2
Mörlunda [S] 162 F3
Mormanno [I] 120 H6
Mormant [F] 42 G4
Mornay–Berry [F] 56 D4
Mornese [I] 110 A2
Morón de Almazán [E] 90 B4
Morón de la Frontera [E] 100 H3
Morosaglia [F] 114 B3
Morovič [SCG] 142 E2
Morøya [N] 192 D5
Morozzo [I] 108 G2
Morpeth [GB] 8 G5
Morra [I] 114 H1
Morral de Cabrafeixet [E] 92 B5
Mørriaunet [N] 190 B5
Morro del Jable [E] 100 D6
Mörrum [S] 158 E1
Mörsburg [CH] 58 G4
Mörsil [S] 182 F2
Morskoga krog [S] 166 H2
Mörskom / Myrskylä [FIN] 178 B3
Morskoye [RUS] 200 D5
Morsum [D] 156 A4
Mørsvikbotn [N] 192 E5
Mortagne–au–Perche [F] 26 G5
Mortagne–sur–Sèvre [F] 54 C2
Mortágua [P] 80 B6
Mortain [F] 26 E5
Mortara [I] 70 F5
Mörtberg [S] 194 A8
Morteau [F] 58 C5
Mortegliano [I] 72 G5
Mörtfors [S] 162 G3
Mortier–Crolle, Château de– [F] 40 G5
Mortrée [F] 26 F5
Mörtschach [A] 72 G2
Morud [DK] 156 D3
Morup [S] 160 H4
Moryń [PL] 34 G1
Morzine [F] 70 C2
Morzycyn [PL] 20 F5
Mosal'sk [RUS] 202 E4
Mosås [S] 166 H3
Mosätt [S] 182 G5
Mosbach [D] 46 D5
Mosbekk [N] 166 D1
Mosby [N] 164 D5
Moscavide [P] 86 B5
Moščenica [HR] 142 A1
Moščenice [HR] 112 E2
Moščenička Draga [HR] 112 E2
Moschendorf [A] 74 F2
Moschopótamos [GR] 128 G5
Moscufo [I] 116 D4
Mosėdis [LT] 200 D3
Moshult [S] 162 B4
Mosina [PL] 36 C3
Mosjö [S] 184 F2
Mosjøen [N] 190 D3
Moškanjci [SLO] 74 E4
Moskaret [N] 182 B5
Mosko [BIH] 144 D3
Moskog [N] 180 C6
Moskosel [S] 190 H3
Moskva [RUS] 202 F3
Moslavina [HR] 76 A6
Moso in Passiria / Moos in Passeier [I] 72 D2
Mosonmagyaróvár [H] 62 G5
Mosqueruela [E] 98 F2
Moss [N] 166 B2
Mossiberg [S] 172 F1
Mössingen [D] 58 G2
Most [CZ] 48 E2
Mosta [M] 126 C6
Mostar [BIH] 144 C2
Mosteiros [P] 100 E2
Mosterhamn [N] 170 A6
Mostesquiu [E] 92 E2
Mostki [PL] 52 C2
Most na Soči [SLO] 72 H4
Móstoles [E] 88 F6
Mostowo [PL] 22 A3
Mosty [PL] 38 F4
Mostys'ka [UA] 52 F4
Mosune [HR] 112 F2
Moszczanka [PL] 38 D4
Mota, Cast. de la– [E] 88 E2
Mota del Cuervo [E] 96 H3
Mota del Marqués [E] 88 D1
Motala [S] 166 G5
Motherwell [GB] 8 D3
Motilla del Palancar [E] 98 B3
Motjärnshyttan [S] 166 F1
Motko [RUS] 196 H6
Motovun [HR] 112 D1
Motricoux [F] 66 G6
Motril [E] 102 E5
Motta di Livenza [I] 72 F5
Motta Visconti [I] 70 F5
Motte–Glain, Château de la– [F] 40 G5
Móttola [I] 122 E4
Möttönen [FIN] 186 E2
Mou [DK] 160 E4
Mouchard [F] 58 A5
Moudon [CH] 70 C1
Moúdros [GR] 130 F6
Mougins [F] 108 E5
Mouhijärvi [FIN] 176 E1
Moulherne [F] 54 E1
Moulins [F] 56 D5
Moulins–Engilbert [F] 56 E4
Moulins–la–Marche [F] 26 G5
Moulismes [F] 54 F5
Moult [F] 26 F4
Mountallen [IRL] 2 D4
Mount Bellew [IRL] 2 D5
Mount Charles [IRL] 2 E2
Mountmellick [IRL] 2 E6
Mountrath [IRL] 2 D6
Mountshannon [IRL] 2 C6
Moura [P] 94 E3
Mourão [P] 94 E2
Mouriés [GR] 128 H3
Mouros, Castelo dos– [P] 86 A5
Mourujärvi [FIN] 194 E8
Moustiers–Ste–Marie [F] 108 D4
Mouthe [F] 58 B6
Mouthier [F] 58 B5
Mouthoumet [F] 106 C5
Moutier [CH] 58 D5
Moutier–d'Ahun [F] 54 H6
Moutiers [F] 54 B3
Moûtiers [F] 70 B4
Mouton–Rothschild [F] 66 C2
Moutoullás [CY] 154 F5
Moutsoúna [GR] 138 F3
Mouy [F] 28 D6
Mouzakaíoi [GR] 132 D2
Mouzáki [GR] 132 E2
Mouzáki [GR] 136 C2
Mouzon [F] 44 D2
Moville [IRL] 2 F2
Moy [NIR] 2 F3
Moyenvic [F] 44 F5
Moynalty [IRL] 2 F5
Moyne Abbey [IRL] 2 C3
Moyuela [E] 90 E5
Moyvore [IRL] 2 E5
Mozhaysk [RUS] 202 E3
Mozia [I] 126 B2
Mozirje [SLO] 74 C4
Mozyr' [RUS] 24 C2
Mpalí [GR] 140 D4
Mpampalió [GR] 132 E4
Mpampíni [GR] 132 D5
Mpatsí [GR] 134 E6
Mpenítses [GR] 132 B2
Mpórsio [GR] 136 C1
Mpoúkka [GR] 132 D4
Mprálos [GR] 132 G4
Mrągowo [PL] 24 B4
Mrakovica [BIH] 142 B2
Mrazovac [BIH] 112 H2
Mrčajevci [SCG] 146 B2
Mrežičko [MK] 128 F3
Mrkonjić–Grad [BIH] 142 B3
Mrkopalj [HR] 112 F1
Mrocza [PL] 22 C5
Mroczeń [PL] 36 E6
Mrzeżyno [PL] 20 G3
Mrzygłód [PL] 52 E4
Mšeno [CZ] 48 G3
Mshinskaya [RUS] 198 H1
Mstislavl' [BY] 202 D5
Mstów [PL] 50 G1
Mszana Dolna [PL] 52 A5
Mszczonów [PL] 38 B4
Mt–Dauphin [F] 108 E1
Mt. Melleray Monastery [IRL] 4 D4
Mtsensk [RUS] 202 F4
Mt. St. Joseph Abbey [IRL] 2 D6
Muć [HR] 144 A1
Muccia [I] 116 B2
Much [D] 30 H4
Mücheln [D] 34 B5
Muchówka [PL] 52 B4
Muckross [IRL] 4 B4
Muckross House [IRL] 4 B4
Mudanya [TR] 150 E4
Mudau [D] 46 D4
Mudela, Castillo de– [E] 96 F5
Müden [D] 18 F6
Mudiske [EST] 198 E2
Müdrets [BG] 148 D5
Muel [E] 90 E4
Muela de Cortes [E] 98 D5
Muelas del Pan [E] 80 H4
Muezerskiy [RUS] 196 H5
Muff [IRL] 2 F2
Muge [P] 86 C4
Mügeln [D] 34 D6
Muggendorf [D] 46 G4
Múggia [I] 72 H6
Mugiro [E] 84 B3
Muğla [TR] 154 D1
Müglizh [BG] 148 C4
Mugnano [I] 114 H2
Mugron [F] 66 C6
Mühlacker [D] 46 C6
Mühlbach [A] 72 G1
Mühlberg [D] 34 E5
Mühldorf [D] 60 F4
Mühlhausen [D] 32 G5
Mühlhausen [D] 60 B3
Muhola [FIN] 186 F1
Muhos [FIN] 196 D4
Muhovo [BG] 148 A5
Muine Bheag / Bagenalstown [IRL] 4 F4
Muiños [E] 78 C6
Muir of Ord [GB] 6 D5
Mujejärvi [FIN] 196 G5
Mukacheve [UA] 204 B3
Mula [E] 104 B3
Mulazzo [I] 110 C4
Mulba [E] 94 H5
Mulegns [CH] 70 H2
Mülheim [D] 30 G3
Mülheim [D] 44 G2
Mulhouse [F] 58 D3
Muljula [FIN] 188 G4
Müllheim [D] 58 E3
Mullinavat [IRL] 4 E4
Mullingar [IRL] 2 E5
Müllrose [D] 34 G3
Mullsjö [S] 162 C2
Mullyttan [S] 166 G3
Mulseryd [S] 162 C2
Multia [FIN] 186 F4
Multrå [S] 184 E2
Mumor [H] 74 F3
Muñana [E] 88 D4
Münchberg [D] 48 B3
Müncheberg [D] 34 F2
München [D] 60 E4
Münchhausen [D] 34 E4
Mundaka [E] 82 H3
Munderkingen [D] 60 B4
Mundheim [N] 170 B4
Munera [E] 96 H5
Mungia [E] 82 G3
Muniaczkowice [PL] 52 B3
Muñico [E] 88 D4
Muniesa [E] 90 E5
Munka–Ljungby [S] 156 H1
Munkebo [DK] 156 E3
Munkedal [S] 166 C5
Munkelven [N] 194 E3
Munkflohögen [S] 182 H1
Munkfors [S] 166 F1
Münnerstadt [D] 46 F3
Munsala [FIN] 186 C1
Münsingen [CH] 58 D6
Münsingen [D] 58 H2
Munsö [S] 168 D3
Münster [CH] 70 E2
Munster [D] 18 F6
Münster [D] 32 C3
Munster [F] 58 D3
Münstertal [D] 58 E3
Münzenberg [D] 46 C2
Münzkirchen [A] 62 A3
Muodoslompolo [S] 194 B6
Muonio [FIN] 194 B6
Muotkalahti [RUS] 194 F6
Muotkavaara [FIN] 194 C6
Muradiye [TR] 152 C3
Murakeresztúr [H] 74 G4
Muráň [SK] 64 E3
Murano [I] 72 E6
Muras [E] 78 E2
Murat [F] 68 C4
Muratdere [TR] 150 G5
Murati [EST] 198 F4
Muratlar [TR] 150 B6
Muratlar [TR] 152 F6
Muratlı [TR] 150 C3
Murato [F] 114 C3
Murat–sur–Vèbre [F] 106 D3
Murau [A] 74 B2
Muravera [I] 118 E6
Murazzano [I] 108 G2
Murça [P] 80 E4
Mürchevo [BG] 146 F3
Murchin [D] 20 E3
Murcia [E] 104 C3
Murciélagos, Cueva de los– [E] 102 C2
Murcielagos, Cueva de los– [E] 102 E5
Murczyn [PL] 36 E1
Mur–de–Barrez [F] 68 B4
Mur–de–Bretagne [F] 26 A5
Mureck [A] 74 E3
Mürefte [TR] 150 C4
Muret [F] 84 H3
Murga [H] 76 B4
Murgados [E] 78 D1
Murgaševo [MK] 128 E3
Murgia / Murguía [E] 82 G5
Murg–Kraftwerk [D] 58 F1
Murguía / Murgia [E] 82 G5
Muri [CH] 58 F5
Murias de Paredes [E] 78 G4
Murieta [E] 82 H6
Murighiol [RO] 204 F5
Murino [SCG] 146 A5
Muriquan [AL] 128 A1
Murjek [S] 196 A2
Murlo [I] 114 F2
Murnau [D] 60 D5
Muro [E] 104 E4
Muro [F] 114 B3
Muro de Alcoy / Muro del Comtat [E] 104 E1
Muro del Comtat / Muro de Alcoy [E] 104 E1
Murole [FIN] 186 E6
Muro Lucano [I] 120 G3
Murony [H] 76 G3
Muros [E] 78 B3
Murowana Goślina [PL] 36 C2
Mürren [CH] 70 E2
Murrhardt [D] 46 D6
Murrisk Abbey [IRL] 2 B4
Murru [EST] 198 D3
Murska Sobota [SLO] 74 E3
Mursko Središće [HR] 74 F4
Murta [RO] 146 G2
Murtas [E] 102 E5
Murten [CH] 58 D6
Murter [HR] 112 G6
Murtinheira [P] 80 A6
Murtosa [P] 80 B5
Murtovaara [FIN] 196 F2
Murtovaara [FIN] 196 F2
Murvica [HR] 112 G5
Mürzsteg [A] 62 D6
Mürzzuschlag [A] 62 E6
Musamaa [FIN] 186 C2
Musetrene [N] 180 G6
Mussalo [FIN] 178 C4
Musselkanaal [NL] 16 H3
Mussidan [F] 66 E3
Mussomeli [I] 126 D3
Mussy [F] 56 G2
Mustafa Kemal Paşa [TR] 150 E5
Müstair [CH] 72 B3
Mustajärvi [FIN] 186 E5
Mustajõe [EST] 198 G1
Mustalahti [FIN] 186 F5
Mustasaari / Korsholm [FIN] 186 B2
Mustér / Disentis [CH] 70 G1
Mustikkaperä [FIN] 186 F2
Mustinmäki [FIN] 188 D3
Mustinsalo [FIN] 188 D3
Mustjala [EST] 198 C3
Mustla [EST] 198 E3
Mustola [FIN] 194 E4

Paldiski [EST] 198 D1
Pale [BIH] 144 D1
Pāle [LV] 198 E4
Palena [I] 116 D5
Palencia [E] 82 C6
Palermo [AL] 128 B6
Palermo [I] 126 C2
Palestrina [I] 116 B5
Pálháza [H] 64 G3
Páli [H] 74 G1
Palić [SCG] 76 D5
Palikkala [FIN] 176 F3
Palín [SK] 64 H3
Palinuro [I] 120 G5
Paliouriá [GR] 132 E1
Palioúrion [GR] 130 C6
Paliseul [B] 44 D1
Paljakka [FIN] 178 C2
Paljakka [FIN] 196 F4
Paljakka [FIN] 196 F1
Pälkäne [FIN] 176 G2
Palkino [RUS] 198 G4
Palkisoja [FIN] 194 D5
Pallanza [I] 70 F3
Pallarés [E] 94 G4
Pallaruelo de Monegros [E] 90 F4
Pallas Grean [IRL] 4 D3
Pallestrina [I] 110 H1
Pallíni [GR] 134 C6
Pallosenvaara [FIN] 196 H6
Palluau [F] 54 B2
Palma del Río [E] 102 B1
Palma de Mallorca [E] 104 E5
Palma di Montechiaro [I] 126 D4
Palmadula [I] 118 B3
Palma Nova [E] 104 D5
Palmanova [I] 72 G5
Pálmas Arboreá [I] 118 C5
Palmela [P] 86 B6
Palmi [I] 124 C7
Palo del Colle [I] 122 D2
Palohuornas [S] 192 H6
Páloi [GR] 154 B3
Palojärvi [FIN] 194 B5
Palojoensuu [FIN] 194 B5
Palokastër [AL] 128 C6
Palokka [FIN] 186 G4
Palokki [FIN] 188 E3
Palomäki [FIN] 196 F6
Palomares [E] 104 A5
Palomares del Campo [E] 98 A2
Palomas [E] 94 H2
Palombara Sabina [I] 116 B5
Palonurmi [FIN] 188 D1
Palos de la Frontera [E] 94 E6
Palota [SK] 52 E6
Pålsboda [S] 166 H4
Pålsträsk [S] 196 A3
Paltamo [FIN] 196 F4
Paltanen [FIN] 186 H4
Paltaniemi [FIN] 196 E5
Pal'tsevo [RUS] 178 F3
Palus [FIN] 176 D1
Paluzza [I] 72 G3
Palvainen [FIN] 188 D4
Pāmark / Pomarkku [FIN] 176 D1
Pamhagen [A] 62 G6
Pamiątkowo [PL] 36 C2
Pamiers [F] 106 A4
Pamiętowo [PL] 22 C5
Pamma [EST] 198 C3
Pampaneira [E] 102 E5
Pamparato [I] 108 G3
Pampilhosa da Serra [P] 86 E2
Pamplona / Iruña [E] 84 B4
Pamporovo [BG] 130 E1
Pamucak [TR] 152 D5
Pamukça [TR] 152 D1
Pamukçu [TR] 152 D1
Pamukkale [TR] 152 G5
Pamukova [TR] 150 G3
Pamukyazı [TR] 152 D5
Panagía [GR] 128 F6
Panagía [GR] 130 E4
Panagía [GR] 134 C5
Panagiá [GR] 140 F5
Panagia Aphendrika [CY] 154 H4
Panagia Chrysorrogiatissa [CY] 154 F6
Panagia Tou Kykkou [CY] 154 F5
Panagyurishte [BG] 148 A5
Panaitólio [GR] 132 E5
Panajë [AL] 128 A5
Panasówka [PL] 52 F2
Panassac [F] 84 G3
Panayır [TR] 152 E2
Pancar [TR] 152 C4
Pančevo [SCG] 142 H2
Pancharevo [BG] 146 F5
Pancorbo, Garganta de- [E] 82 F5
Pancorvo [E] 82 F5
Pandėlys [LT] 198 E6
Pandino [I] 70 G5
Pandrup [DK] 160 D3
Panenský Týnec [CZ] 48 F3
Panes [E] 82 D3
Panevėžys [LT] 200 F4
Panicale [I] 114 H2
Paničkovo [BG] 148 C6
Paniza [E] 90 D4
Paniza, Puerto de- [E] 90 D5
Panjavaara [FIN] 196 F6
Pankajärvi [FIN] 196 G6
Pankakoski [FIN] 196 G6
Pankala [FIN] 196 C5
Panki [PL] 50 F1
Pannohalma [H] 62 H6
Pannonhalma [H] 62 H6
Panoias [P] 80 D4
Páno Léfkara [CY] 154 G5
Páno Panagiá [CY] 154 F6
Páno Plátres [CY] 154 F6
Panormítis [GR] 154 C3
Pánormos [GR] 138 E1
Pánormos [GR] 140 D4
Pantalica, Necropoli di- [I] 126 G4
Pantánassa [GR] 136 F5
Päntäne [FIN] 186 B4
Pantelej [MK] 128 G1
Pantelej, Manastir- [MK] 128 G1
Pantelleria [I] 126 A4
Pantón [E] 78 D4
Pantów [PL] 52 C1
Panxón [E] 78 B5
Páola [I] 124 D4
Pápa [H] 74 H1
Papadiánika [GR] 136 F5
Paparzyn [PL] 22 E5
Papasidero [I] 120 H6
Pape [LV] 200 D3
Papenburg [D] 18 B5
Papile [LT] 198 C6
Papilys [LT] 198 E6
Paplin [PL] 38 D2
Papowo Biskupie [PL] 22 E5
Papozze [I] 110 G2
Pappenheim [D] 60 D2
Paprotnia [PL] 38 E2
Parábita [I] 122 G5
Paraćin [SCG] 146 C2
Parád [H] 64 E5
Parada del Sil [E] 78 D5
Paradas [E] 100 H2
Paradeísi [GR] 154 D3
Paradeísia [GR] 136 D3
Parádeisos [GR] 130 E3
Paradela [P] 78 C6
Paradies [D] 60 B6
Paradisgård [S] 166 F2
Paradyż [PL] 38 A5
Parainen / Pargas [FIN] 176 D5
Parakka [S] 192 H5
Parákoila [GR] 134 G2
Paralía [GR] 128 G5
Paralía [GR] 132 F6
Paralía [GR] 132 H6
Paralía [GR] 136 F4
Paralía Akrátas [GR] 132 G6
Paralía Iríon [GR] 136 F2
Paralía Kýmis [GR] 134 C4
Paralía Platánou [GR] 132 G6
Paralía Skotínas [GR] 128 H6
Paralímni [CY] 154 G5
Paralío Ástros [GR] 136 E3
Páramo del Sil [E] 78 F4
Paramythiá [GR] 132 C2
Paranésti [GR] 130 D2
Parantala [FIN] 186 F3
Parapótamos [GR] 132 C2
Parassapuszta [H] 64 C5
Parata, Tour de la- [F] 114 A5
Paravóla [GR] 132 E5
Paray-le-Monial [F] 56 E6
Parcent [E] 104 F1
Parcé Sur Sarthe [F] 42 A5
Parchim [D] 20 B5
Parczew [PL] 38 E4
Pardubice [CZ] 50 A4
Paredes [E] 78 D5
Paredes [P] 80 C4
Paredes de Coura [P] 78 B5
Paredes de Nava [E] 82 C6
Paredes de Sigüenza [E] 90 A4
Parentis-en-Born [F] 66 B4
Paretón [E] 104 B4
Parey [D] 34 C2
Párga [GR] 132 C3
Pargas / Parainen [FIN] 176 D5
Pargny-sur-Saulx [F] 44 C4
Pargolovo [RUS] 178 H4
Parikkala [FIN] 188 F5
Paris [F] 42 F3
Parisot [F] 66 G6
Parkajoki [S] 194 B6
Parkalompolo [S] 194 B6
Parkano [FIN] 186 D5
Parkkila [FIN] 196 D5
Parkkima [FIN] 196 D6
Parknasilla [IRL] 4 B4
Parkumäki [FIN] 188 E5
Parla [E] 88 F6
Parłówko [PL] 20 F4
Parma [I] 110 D2
Parndorf [A] 62 G5
Pärnu [EST] 198 D3
Pärnu-Jaagupi [EST] 198 D2
Parola [FIN] 178 C2
Páros [GR] 138 E3
Paroveia [LT] 198 E6
Parpan [CH] 70 H1
Parsberg [D] 46 H6
Partakko [FIN] 194 D4
Partakoski [FIN] 178 D1
Partanna [I] 126 B3
Partenen [A] 72 B2
Parthenay [F] 54 D3
Parthéni [GR] 136 E2
Parthéni [GR] 154 A1
Partille [S] 160 H2
Partinello [F] 114 A3
Partinico [I] 126 C2
Partizani [SCG] 146 B1
Partizánske [SK] 64 B3
Partizanske Vode [SCG] 146 A3
Partry [IRL] 2 C4
Pårup [DK] 160 C6
Parychy [BY] 202 C6
Påryd [S] 162 F5
Pasaia [E] 84 B2
Pasaköy (Asha) [CY] 154 G5
Pasá Limáni [GR] 134 G5
Paşayiğit [TR] 150 B3
Paşcani [RO] 204 D3
Pas de la Casa [AND] 84 H6
Pasęk [PL] 22 F3
Pas-en-Artois [F] 28 E4
Pasewalk [D] 20 E5
Pasi [FIN] 178 C2
Pasiecznik [PL] 50 A1
Pasiene [LV] 198 G5
Pasjak [HR] 112 E1
Pasjane [SCG] 146 D5
Påskallavik [S] 162 G4
Pasmajärvi [FIN] 194 C7
Pašman [HR] 112 G5
Paspolo [TR] 150 C1
Passage East [IRL] 4 E5
Passage West [IRL] 4 D5
Passandra [TR] 152 B2
Passau [D] 60 H3
Passignano sul Trasimeno [I] 114 H2
Pastavy [BY] 200 H4
Pastena, Grotte di- [I] 120 C1
Pastor [E] 78 C3
Pastoriza [E] 78 E2
Pastra [BG] 146 F6
Pastrana [E] 88 H6
Păstrovo [BG] 148 C5
Pasvalys [LT] 198 E6
Pasym [PL] 22 H4
Pásztó [H] 64 D5
Pasztowa Wola [PL] 38 C6
Patana [FIN] 186 D1
Patara [TR] 154 F3
Patavesi [FIN] 186 F6
Patay [F] 42 E5
Paterek [PL] 22 C6
Patergassen [A] 74 A3
Paterna [E] 98 E4
Paterna del Madera [E] 96 H6
Paterna de Rivera [E] 100 G4
Paternion [A] 72 H3
Paternò [I] 126 G3
Paternopoli [I] 120 F3
Patersdorf [D] 60 G2
Patio [RUS] 178 D3
Patiópoulo [GR] 132 E3
Patitíri [GR] 134 C3
Patlangıç [TR] 154 G1
Pátmos [GR] 138 H2
Pątnów [PL] 36 F6
Pato [FIN] 176 D3
Patos [AL] 128 B4
Pátra [GR] 132 F6
Patreksfjörður [IS] 192 A1
Patrickswell [IRL] 4 D3
Patrikka [FIN] 188 H2
Patsch [A] 72 D1
Pattada [I] 118 D3
Pattensen [D] 32 F2
Patterdale [GB] 10 D1
Patti [I] 124 A7
Pattijoki [FIN] 196 D4
Pătulele [RO] 146 E1
Páty [H] 64 C6
Pau [F] 84 E3
Pauillac [F] 66 C2
Paukarlahti [FIN] 188 D3
Paularo [I] 72 G3
Paulhaguet [F] 68 D4
Paulilatino [I] 118 C5
Paulinzella [D] 46 G1
Păuliş [RO] 76 H4
Paulistrōm [S] 162 F3
Pauls-Kirche [D] 44 G2
Paulstown [IRL] 4 F4
Paupys [LT] 200 E5
Pauträsk [S] 190 G4
Pävalsby [FIN] 176 E5
Pavel [BG] 148 C3
Pavel Banya [BG] 148 C5
Pavia [I] 70 G6
Pavia [P] 86 D5
Pavia, Certosa di- [I] 70 G5
Pavilly [F] 28 B5
Pāvilosta [LV] 198 B5
Pávliani [GR] 132 G4
Pavlice [CZ] 62 E2
Pavlikeni [BG] 148 C3
Pávlos [GR] 134 A5
Pavlovsk [RUS] 178 H5
Pavullo nel Frignano [I] 110 E4
Pavy [RUS] 198 H3
Pawłowo Żonskie [PL] 36 D1
Pawłowiczki [PL] 50 E3
Pawłowo [PL] 22 G5
Pawonków [PL] 50 F2
Paxoí [GR] 132 C3
Payerne [CH] 58 C6
Paymogo [E] 94 E4
Payrac [F] 66 G4
Pazardzhik [BG] 148 A6
Pazarköy [TR] 150 C6
Pazarköy [TR] 152 B1
Pazaryeri [TR] 150 G5
Pazin [HR] 112 D2
Pazo de Oca [E] 78 C3
P. Cachorro [P] 100 C3
Pchelino [RUS] 178 F3
Pchelnik [BG] 148 F3
Pčinja [MK] 128 E1
Peal de Becerro [E] 102 F2
Péaule [F] 40 E5
Péc / Peje [SCG] 146 B5
Pećane [HR] 112 H3
Peccioli [I] 110 E6
Pechenga [RUS] 194 F3
Pechina [E] 102 G5
Pech-Merle, Grotte du- [F] 66 G5
Pecica [RO] 76 G4
Pecineaga [RO] 148 G1
Pecka [SCG] 142 F4
Peckelsheim [D] 32 E4
Pecorini a Mare [I] 124 A5
Pečory [RUS] 198 G3
Pec pod Sněžkou [CZ] 50 A2
Pécs [H] 76 B5
Pécsvárad [H] 76 B5
Pedaso [I] 116 D2
Pederobba [I] 72 E5
Pedersker [DK] 158 E4
Pedersöre [FIN] 196 C6
Pedési [GR] 154 C3
Pedoulás [CY] 154 F5
Pedrafita do Cebreiro, Puerto- [E] 78 E4
Pedralba [E] 98 E4
Pedraza [E] 88 G3
Pedreguer [E] 104 F1
Pedreira [E] 78 D2
Pedrera [E] 96 F3
Pedrizas, Puerto de las- [E] 102 C4
Pedro Abad [E] 102 D1
Pedro Andrés [E] 102 H2
Pedro Bernardo [E] 88 D5
Pedrógão [P] 86 C2
Pedrógão [P] 94 E3
Pedro Martínez [E] 102 F3
Pedro Muñoz [E] 96 G3
Pedrosillo el Ralo [E] 80 H6
Peebles [GB] 8 E4
Peel [GBM] 10 B1
Peenemünde [D] 20 E3
Peera [FIN] 192 G3
Péfkos [GR] 128 D5
Péfkos [GR] 140 F5
Pega [P] 86 G2
Pegau [D] 34 C6
Pégeia [CY] 154 F6
Peggau [A] 74 D2
Pegli [I] 110 A3
Pegnitz [D] 46 H4
Pego [E] 104 F1
Pegões [P] 86 C6
Peguera [E] 104 D5
Pehčevo [MK] 128 H1
Pehlivanköy [TR] 150 B2
Peine [D] 32 G2
Peïra-Cava [F] 108 F4
Peiraías [GR] 134 C6
Peiss [D] 60 E5
Peissenberg [D] 60 D5
Peiting [D] 60 D5
Peitz [D] 34 F4
Peje / Péc [SCG] 146 B5
Pejo [I] 72 C3
Pekkala [FIN] 194 D8
Pelasgía [GR] 132 H4
Pelatikovo [BG] 146 F6
Pełczyce [PL] 20 G6
Pełczyn [PL] 36 C5
Pelejaneta / La Pelechaneta [E] 98 F3
Pélekas [GR] 132 B2
Peleshi [RUS] 198 G2
Peletá [GR] 136 F4
Pelhřimov [CZ] 48 H5
Peliciego, Cueva de- [E] 104 C1
Pelince [MK] 146 D6
Pelitözu [TR] 150 G4
Pelkosenniemi [FIN] 194 E7
Pélla [GR] 128 G4
Péllaro [I] 124 C7
Pellegrino Parmense [I] 110 C2
Pellegrue [F] 66 E4
Pellesmäki [FIN] 188 C2
Pellinge / Pellinki [FIN] 178 B5
Pellinki / Pellinge [FIN] 178 B5
Pello [FIN] 194 C7
Pello [S] 194 C7
Pellosniemi [FIN] 178 C1
Pelovo [BG] 148 A3
Pelplin [PL] 22 E4
Peltosalmi [FIN] 196 E6
Pélussin [F] 68 F3
Pély [H] 64 E6
Pemaninos [TR] 150 D5
Pemar / Paimio [FIN] 176 E4
Pembroke [GB] 12 D2
Pembroke Dock [GB] 12 D2
Peñacerrada [E] 82 G5
Penacova [P] 86 E2
Peña Escrita, Cuevas de- [E] 96 D5
Peñafiel [E] 88 F2
Peñaflor [E] 102 B1
Penaguiao [P] 80 D4
Peñalén [E] 90 B6
Peñalsordo [E] 96 C4
Penalva do Castelo [P] 80 D6
Penamacor [P] 86 G3
Peñaranda de Bracamonte [E] 88 D3
Peñaranda de Duero [E] 88 H2
Peñarroya, Castillo de- [E] 96 G4
Peñarroya-Pueblonuevo [E] 96 B5
Penarth [GB] 12 F3
Peñascosa [E] 96 H6
Peñas de San Pedro [E] 98 B6
Peñausende [E] 80 H5
Penc [H] 64 C5
Pendik [TR] 150 F3
Pendine [GB] 12 D2
Pendus, Rocher des- [F] 68 B4
Penedono [P] 80 D5
Penela [P] 86 D2
Penestin [F] 40 E5
Peniche [P] 86 B3
Penicuik [GB] 8 E3
Penig [D] 48 D1
Peníscola / Peñíscola [E] 98 G2
Peñíscola / Peníscola [E] 98 G2
Penkum [D] 20 E5
Penmarch, Pointe de- [F] 40 B3
Pennabilli [I] 110 H5
Pennala [FIN] 178 B3
Penne [I] 116 D4
Penne [N] 164 B5
Penningby [S] 168 E2
Peno [RUS] 202 D3
Penrith [GB] 8 E6
Penryn [GB] 12 C5
Pensala [FIN] 186 C1
Pentagioí [GR] 132 F5
Pentálofo [GR] 128 E6
Pentálofo [GR] 132 E5
Pénte Vrýses [GR] 130 B4
Pentrez-Plage [F] 40 B2
Penzance [GB] 12 B5
Penzberg [D] 60 D5
Penzlin [D] 20 D5
Pępowo [PL] 36 C4
Peqin [AL] 128 B3
Pér [H] 62 H6
Perachóra [GR] 132 H6
Péra Chorion [CY] 154 G5
Perafita [P] 80 B3
Peraía [GR] 128 H5
Perälä [FIN] 186 B4
Peraleda del Zaucejo [E] 96 B4
Peralejos de las Truchas [E] 90 C6
Perales del Alfambra [E] 98 E1
Peralta [E] 84 B5
Pérama [GR] 132 D2
Pérama [GR] 140 D4
Peranka [FIN] 196 F3
Peränkylä [FIN] 176 C2
Peränne [FIN] 186 E4
Perä-Posio [FIN] 194 E8
Peräseinäjoki [FIN] 186 C4
Peräseinäjoki [FIN] 186 D4
Perast [SCG] 144 D4
Perchauer Sattel [A] 74 B2
Perchtoldsdorf [A] 62 F5
Percy [F] 26 D4
Perdasdefogu [I] 118 D6
Perdifumo [I] 120 F5
Perdigão [P] 86 E4
Pérdika [GR] 132 C3
Pérdika [GR] 132 D2
Pereda de Ancares [E] 78 F4
Père de Montfort, Grotte du- [F] 54 C3
Peredo [P] 80 F4
Pereiaslav-Khmel'nyts'kyi [UA] 202 E7
Pereiro [P] 94 D5
Peremozhne [UA] 52 H5
Peremyshl' [RUS] 202 F4
Pereruela [E] 80 H5
Pereshchepyne [UA] 204 H1
Pereslavl'-Zalesskiy [RUS] 202 F2
Pereta [I] 114 F3
Peretu [RO] 148 B1
Perevolok [RUS] 198 G1
Perfugas [I] 118 C3
Perg [A] 62 C4
Pergamos (Beyarmudu) [CY] 154 G5
Pérgine Valsugana [I] 72 D4
Pergola [I] 112 B6
Perho [FIN] 186 E2
Periam [RO] 76 F5
Périers [F] 26 D3
Pérignác [F] 54 C6
Périgueux [F] 66 F3
Perii Broşteni [RO] 148 B1
Periš [SCG] 146 E3
Perişoru [RO] 146 F1
Perissa [GR] 138 F5
Peristerá [GR] 130 B4
Peristeróna [CY] 154 F5
Perivóli [GR] 132 D1
Perjasica [HR] 112 G1
Perjen Tunnel [A] 72 C1
Perkáta [H] 76 C2
Perkpolder [NL] 28 H1
Perle [LV] 198 F5
Perleberg [D] 20 B6
Perlez [SCG] 142 G1
Perly [PL] 24 C2
Përmet [AL] 128 C6
Pernaa [FIN] 186 C2
Pernacha de Cima [P] 86 D5
Pernaja / Pernå [FIN] 178 B4
Pernaja-Pernå [FIN] 178 B4
Pernat [HR] 112 E2
Pernek [SK] 62 G4
Pernes [P] 86 C4
Pernes-les-Fontaines [F] 106 H3
Pernik [BG] 146 F5
Perniö / Bjärnå [FIN] 176 F5
Pernitz [A] 62 E5
Pernštejn [CZ] 50 B5
Pernu [FIN] 194 E8
Pérolles, Pont de- [CH] 58 D6
Peron [F] 70 A2
Péronne [F] 28 F5
Perosa Argentina [I] 70 C6
Pérouges [F] 68 G2
Perpignan [F] 92 G1
Perrero [I] 70 C6
Perros-Guirec [F] 40 D1
Persberg [S] 166 G2
Persenbeug [A] 62 D4
Pershagen [S] 168 D3
Perskogen [N] 192 G3
Persön [S] 196 B3
Perstorp [S] 158 C1
Perth [GB] 8 E2
Pertisau [A] 60 E6
Pertoča [SLO] 74 E3
Pertosa, Grotta di- [I] 120 G4
Pertoúli [GR] 132 E2
Perttaus [FIN] 194 C7
Pertteli [FIN] 176 F4
Pertuis [F] 108 B4
Pertunmaa [FIN] 178 B1
Pertusa [E] 90 G3
Peruc [CZ] 48 F3
Perúgia [I] 116 A2
Perunika [BG] 130 G1
Perushtica [BG] 148 B6
Perušić [HR] 112 G3
Péruwelz [B] 28 G3
Pervomais'k [UA] 204 F2
Pervomais'ke [UA] 204 H3
Pervomajskoye [RUS] 178 G3
Perwez [B] 30 D4
Pesadas de Burgos [E] 82 F5
Pesados [TR] 154 C1
Pésaro [I] 112 B5
Pescaglia [I] 110 D5
Pescara [I] 116 D4
Pescasseroli [I] 116 C6
Peschici [I] 116 H5
Peschiera del Garda [I] 72 B6
Pescia [I] 110 E5
Pescina [I] 116 C5
Pescocostanzo [I] 116 D5
Pescolanciano [I] 116 D6
Pescopagano [I] 120 G3
Peshkëpija [AL] 128 B5
Peshkopi [AL] 128 C2
Peshtera [BG] 148 A6
Pesio, Certosa di- [I] 108 F3
Pesmes [F] 56 H4
Pesnica pri Mariboru [SLO] 74 E3
Pesočani [MK] 128 D3
Pesochnyy [RUS] 178 H4
Peso da Régua [P] 80 D4
Pesoz [E] 78 F3
Pesquera del Duero [E] 88 F2
Pesqueza [E] 86 G4
Pessáni [GR] 130 G2
Pessin [D] 34 D2
Peštani [MK] 128 D4
Pestovo [RUS] 202 D1
Pešurići [BIH] 144 E1
Petäiskylä [FIN] 196 G5
Petäjäkylä [FIN] 186 G1
Petäjämäki [FIN] 188 C3
Petäjävesi [FIN] 186 F4
Petalídi [GR] 136 D4
Petaloúdes [GR] 154 D3
Pétange [L] 44 E3
Petehi [HR] 112 D2
Peteranec [HR] 74 G4
Peterborough [GB] 14 E2
Peterhead [GB] 6 G5
Peterlee [GB] 10 F1
Petersburg [A] 72 C1
Petersdorf [D] 18 H2
Petersdorf [D] 20 B3
Petersfield [GB] 14 D5
Petershagen [D] 32 E2
Petershagen [D] 34 F2
Petershausen [D] 60 E3
Pétervására [H] 64 E5
Pétifürdo [H] 76 B2
Petikträsk [S] 190 H4
Petilia Policastro [I] 124 E5
Petino [RUS] 24 B1
Petko Karavelov [BG] 148 C3
Petko Slaveykov [BG] 148 B4
Petkula [FIN] 194 D6
Petkus [D] 34 E3
Petlovac [HR] 76 B6
Petlovača [SCG] 142 F3
Petoháza [H] 62 G6
Petoúsi [GR] 132 C2
Petra [E] 104 E5
Pétra [GR] 128 G6
Pétra [GR] 134 G2
Petralia Soprana [I] 126 E3
Petrálona [GR] 130 B5
Petraná [GR] 128 F5
Petra Tou Romiou [CY] 154 F6
Petrelë [AL] 128 B3
Petrella Tifernina [I] 116 E6
Petrelle [I] 114 H1
Petrer [E] 104 D2
Petreto-Bicchisano [F] 114 B5
Petrich [BG] 130 B2
Petrikov [BY] 202 C6
Petrila [RO] 204 C5
Petrina [SLO] 112 F1
Petrinja [HR] 142 A1
Petrodvorets [RUS] 178 G5
Petrohan [BG] 146 F4
Petróla [E] 98 C6
Petromäki [FIN] 188 D3
Petronell-Carnuntum [A] 62 G5
Petroşani [RO] 204 C5
Petrosino [I] 126 B3
Petrotá [GR] 150 A2
Petroússa [GR] 130 C2
Petrovac [SCG] 144 E5
Petrovac [SCG] 146 C1
Petrovaradin [SCG] 142 F1
Petrove [UA] 202 F8
Petrovice [CZ] 48 E6
Petrovice [CZ] 48 F5
Petrovići [BIH] 144 B2
Petřvald [CZ] 50 E5
Petsákoi [GR] 132 F6
Petsikko [FIN] 194 D3
Pettenbach [A] 62 B5
Pettigo [NIR] 2 E3
Peuerbach [A] 62 A4
Peura [FIN] 194 C8
Peurajärvi [FIN] 196 G5
Peurasuvanto [FIN] 194 D6
Pevensey [GB] 14 E6
Peypin [F] 108 B5
Peyrat-le-Chateaux [F] 66 H1
Peyrehorade [F] 84 D2
Peyrolles [F] 108 B4
Peyruis [F] 108 C3
Peyrusse-le-Roc [F] 66 H5
Pézenas [F] 106 E4
Pezinok [SK] 62 G4
Pezoúla [GR] 130 E3
Pezovo [MK] 146 D6
Pezuela de las Torres [E] 88 G6
Pfaffendorf [D] 46 G3
Pfaffenhausen [D] 60 C4
Pfaffenhofen [D] 60 E3
Pfaffen-Hoffen [F] 44 H5
Pfäffikon [CH] 58 G5
Pfäffikon [CH] 58 G5
Pfafflar [A] 72 C1
Pfalzfeld [D] 44 H1
Pfalzgrafen Weller [D] 58 G2
Pfänder Tunnel [A] 60 B6
Pfarrkirchen [D] 60 G3
Pfatter [D] 60 F2
Pfeffenhausen [D] 60 F3
Pforzheim [D] 46 C6
Pfreimd [D] 48 C5
Pfronten [D] 60 C6
Pfullendorf [D] 58 H3
Pfullingen [D] 58 H2
Pfundres / Fundres [I] 72 E2
Pfunds [A] 72 C2
Pfungstadt [D] 46 C4
P.gynaikókastro [GR] 128 H3
Phalsbourg [F] 44 G5
Phellos [TR] 154 G3
Philippeville [B] 30 C6
Philippsreut [D] 62 A2
Philippsthal [D] 32 F6
Phokaia [TR] 152 B3
Phönike [AL] 132 B1
Piacenza [I] 70 H6
Piádena [I] 110 D1
Piaggine [I] 120 G4
Piana [F] 114 A4
Piana Crixia [I] 108 H2
Piana degli Albanesi [I] 126 C2
Pian Castagna [I] 108 H2
Pian d'Alma [I] 114 E2
Piàn di Scò [I] 110 F6
Pianella [I] 114 G1
Pianello Val Tidone [I] 70 G6
Piani Resinelli [I] 70 G4
Pianoro [I] 110 F4
Pianotolli-Caldarello [F] 114 B6
Pias [P] 94 E2
Pias [P] 94 E3
Piasecznik [PL] 20 G5
Piaseczno [PL] 20 F6
Piaseczno [PL] 38 B3
Piaski [PL] 36 C4
Piaski [PL] 38 E6
Piastów [PL] 38 B3
Piaszczyna [PL] 22 C3
Piątek [PL] 36 G3
Piatra [RO] 148 B2
Piatra Neamţ [RO] 204 D4
Piazza al Serchio [I] 110 D4
Piazza Armerina [I] 126 E4
Piazza Brembana [I] 70 H4
Piazzatorre [I] 70 H3
Piazzola sul Brenta [I] 72 D6
Pićan [HR] 112 E2
Picassent [E] 98 E5
Picerno [I] 120 G4
Pichoux, Gorges de- [CH] 58 D5
Pickering [GB] 10 G3
Pico [I] 120 C1
Picquigny [F] 28 D4
Pidna [GR] 128 G5
Piechowice [PL] 48 H1
Piecki [PL] 24 C4
Piedade, Ponta da- [P] 94 B5
Piedicavallo [I] 70 E4
Piedicroce [F] 114 C3
Piediluco [I] 116 B4
Piedimonte Etneo [I] 124 A8
Piedimonte Matese [I] 120 E2
Piedimulera [I] 70 E3
Piedra, Monasterio de- [E] 90 C4
Piedrabuena [E] 86 F5
Piedrabuena [E] 96 E4
Piedrafita de Babia [E] 78 G4
Piedrahita [E] 88 C4
Piedralaves [E] 88 D5
Piedras Albas [E] 86 G4
Piekary Śląskie [PL] 50 F3
Pieksämäki [FIN] 188 C4
Pielavesi [FIN] 186 H1
Pieniężno [PL] 22 G3
Piennes [F] 44 E3
Pieńsk [PL] 34 G6
Pienza [I] 114 G2
Pierre-Buffière [F] 66 G2
Pierre-de-Bresse [F] 56 H5
Pierrefitte-Nestalas [F] 84 E4
Pierrefitte-sur-Aire [F] 44 D4
Pierrefonds [F] 42 G2
Pierrefort [F] 68 B4
Pierrefort, Château de- [F] 44 E5
Pierrelatte [F] 106 G2
Pierroton [F] 66 C3
Piertinjaure [S] 190 H1
Piesalankylä [FIN] 186 F4
Pieski [PL] 34 H2
Pieskowa Skała [PL] 50 H3
Piessling Urspr. [A] 62 B6
Piešťany [SK] 62 H3
Pieszyce [PL] 50 C2
Pietarsaari / Jakobstad [FIN] 196 B6
Pietra Bismantova [I] 110 D3
Pietragalla [I] 120 H3
Pietralba [F] 114 B3
Pietra Ligure [I] 108 G3
Pietralunga [I] 116 A1
Pietramelara [I] 120 D2
Pietraperzia [I] 126 E4
Pietrasanta [I] 110 D5
Pietravairano [I] 120 D2
Pietrowice [PL] 50 D3
Pietrzwałd [PL] 22 G4
Pieve di Bono [I] 72 B5
Pieve di Cadore [I] 72 F3
Pieve di Teco [I] 108 G4
Pievepelago [I] 110 E4
Pieve Santo Stefano [I] 110 G6
Pieve S. Giacomo [I] 110 D1
Pigádi [GR] 132 H3
Pigés [GR] 132 E3
Pigí [GR] 132 F5
Pigna [I] 108 F4
Pignola [I] 120 H4
Pihkainmäki [FIN] 188 C2
Pihkala [FIN] 196 D5
Pihlajalahti [FIN] 186 E5
Pihlajalahti [FIN] 188 E5
Pihlajavaara [FIN] 188 H1

Raslavice [SK] 52 D6
Řásná [CZ] 48 H6
Rasony [BY] 198 H6
Rasovo [BG] 146 F2
Raspay [E] 104 C2
Rasquera [E] 90 H6
Rast [RO] 146 F2
Rastatt [D] 46 B6
Råsted [DK] 160 D5
Rastede [D] 18 C5
Rastenfeld [A] 62 D3
Rasteš [MK] 128 D1
Rasti [FIN] 188 F4
Rastošnica [BIH] 142 E3
Rasueros [E] 88 D3
Raszków [PL] 36 D4
Rätan [S] 182 G4
Ratan [S] 196 A5
Rateče [SLO] 72 H3
Ratekau [D] 18 G3
Rathangen [IRL] 2 E6
Rathcoole [IRL] 2 F6
Rathcormack [IRL] 4 D5
Rathcroghan [IRL] 2 D4
Rathdrum [IRL] 4 G4
Rathenow [D] 34 C2
Rathfran Abbey [IRL] 2 C3
Rathfriland [NIR] 2 G4
Rathkeale [IRL] 4 C3
Rath Luirc / Charleville [IRL] 4 C4
Rathmelton [IRL] 2 F2
Rathmolyon [IRL] 2 F5
Rathmullan / Rathmullen [IRL] 2 F2
Rathmullen / Rathmullan [IRL] 2 F2
Rathnew [IRL] 4 G4
Rath of Mullamast [IRL] 4 F3
Rathvilty [IRL] 4 F4
Ratiboř [CZ] 50 E6
Ratingen [D] 30 G3
Ratipera [FIN] 186 E2
Ratkovo [SCG] 142 F1
Ratne [UA] 38 H4
Ratsichy [BY] 24 F4
Rattenberg [A] 60 E6
Ratten-Unterdorf [A] 74 E1
Rattersdorf [A] 74 F1
Rattosjärvi [FIN] 194 C7
Rättvik [S] 172 H3
Ratzeburg [D] 18 G4
Raubling [D] 60 F5
Raudaskylä [FIN] 196 D5
Raudeberg [N] 180 B4
Raudlia [N] 190 E2
Raufaröfn [IS] 192 C2
Raufoss [N] 172 B3
Rauha [FIN] 178 E1
Rauhala [FIN] 194 C6
Rauhala [FIN] 196 G6
Rauhaniemi [FIN] 188 E5
Raulach [F] 68 B4
Rauland Høyfjellshotell [N] 164 E1
Rauma / Raumo [FIN] 176 C2
Raumala [FIN] 176 E5
Raumo / Rauma [FIN] 176 C2
Raumünzach [D] 58 F1
Rauna [LV] 198 E4
Rauris [A] 72 G1
Rautajärvi [FIN] 176 G1
Rautalampi [FIN] 186 H3
Rautaniemi [FIN] 176 E2
Rautas [S] 192 G5
Rautavaara [FIN] 196 F6
Rautila [FIN] 176 D4
Rautio [FIN] 196 C5
Rautjärvi [FIN] 178 F1
Rauvatn [N] 190 E2
Ravanica, Manastir- [SCG] 146 C2
Ravanička Pećina [SCG] 146 D2
Ravanusa [I] 126 E4
Rava-Rus'ka [UA] 52 G3
Ravatn [N] 190 D3
Ravattila [FIN] 178 E2
Ravča [HR] 144 B2
Ravda [BG] 148 F4
Ravel [F] 68 D2
Ravello [I] 120 E4
Rävemåla [S] 162 E5
Ravenglass [GB] 10 D2
Ravenna [I] 110 H4
Ravensbrück [D] 20 D5
Ravensburg [D] 46 C6
Ravensburg [D] 58 H4
Ravioskorpi [FIN] 178 B1
Rävmarken [S] 166 C4
Ravna Dubrava [SCG] 146 E4
Ravna Reka [SCG] 146 D2
Ravne [SLO] 74 C3
Ravnholt [DK] 156 E3
Ravno [BIH] 144 C3
Ravno Selo [SCG] 142 F1
Rawa Mazowiecka [PL] 38 A4
Rawicz [PL] 36 C5
Rayleigh [GB] 14 F4
Rayol [F] 108 D6
Räyrinki [FIN] 186 D1
Räyskälä [FIN] 176 G3
Rayvio [RUS] 188 G5
Razboj [BIH] 142 C2
Razbojna [SCG] 146 C3
Razbojna Dupka [MK] 128 E2
Razdol'e [UA] 204 H3
Razdol'ye [RUS] 178 G3
Razdrto [SLO] 74 B6
Razgrad [BG] 148 D2
Razhanka [BY] 24 H4
Razkrižje [SLO] 74 F4
Razlovci [MK] 128 G1
Reading [GB] 14 D4
Réalmont [F] 106 B3
Realp [CH] 70 F1
Reanaclogheen [IRL] 4 D5
Réau, Ancient Abbaye de la- [F] 54 F5
Réaup-Lisse [F] 66 D6
Reay [GB] 6 E2
Rebais [F] 42 H4
Rebolledo de la Torre [E] 82 D4
Reboly [RUS] 196 G5
Rebordelo [P] 80 E3
Rebrovo [BG] 146 F4
Rebürkovo [BG] 146 G4
Reç [AL] 128 C1
Recanati [I] 116 C1
Rečane [SCG] 146 C6
Recas [E] 96 F1
Recaş [RO] 76 H5
Recea [RO] 146 E1
Recey-sur-Ource [F] 56 G2
Rechnitz [A] 74 F1
Rechytsa [BY] 202 D6
Recke [D] 32 C2
Recklinghausen [D] 30 H2
Recoaro Terme [I] 72 C5
Recologne [F] 58 B4
Recsk [H] 64 E5
Recz [PL] 20 G5
Ręczno [PL] 36 H6
Reda [PL] 22 D2
Redalen [N] 172 B3
Redcar [GB] 10 G2
Redditch [GB] 12 H1
Redea [RO] 148 A1
Redefin [D] 18 H5
Rédics [H] 74 F3
Redipuglia [I] 72 H5
Redon [F] 40 E5
Redondela [E] 78 B4
Redondo [P] 94 E1
Redruth [GB] 12 C5
Rędzikovo [PL] 22 B2
Rees [D] 16 F6
Reetz [D] 20 B5
Refnes [N] 192 E3
Reftele [S] 162 C4
Regalbuto [I] 126 F3
Regéc [H] 64 G4
Regen [D] 60 H2
Regensburg [D] 48 B6
Regenstauf [D] 48 B6
Reggello [I] 110 F6
Réggio di Calábria [I] 124 C7
Reggiolo [I] 110 E2
Réggio nell'Emilia [I] 110 E3
Reghin [RO] 204 C4
Regis-Breitingen [D] 34 C6
Regkínio [GR] 132 H4
Regna [S] 168 A4
Regonkylä [FIN] 186 C3
Regozero [RUS] 196 G2
Reguengos de Monsaraz [P] 94 E2
Rehau [D] 48 B3
Rehborn [D] 44 H3
Rehden [D] 32 E1
Rehna [D] 18 H4
Reichéa [GR] 136 F4
Reichenau [D] 58 G4
Reichenau an der Rax [A] 62 E6
Reichenbach [D] 32 F5
Reichenbach [D] 34 G6
Reichenbach [D] 48 C2
Reichenberg [D] 34 F2
Reichertshausen [D] 60 E3
Reichertshofen [D] 60 E3
Reichstett [F] 44 H6
Reigate [GB] 14 E5
Reigersburg [A] 62 E2
Reignier [F] 70 B2
Reijola [FIN] 188 F3
Reila [FIN] 176 C3
Reillanne [F] 108 C3
Reims [F] 44 B3
Rein [A] 74 D2
Reinach [CH] 58 E4
Reinach [CH] 58 F5
Reinberg [D] 20 D3
Reine [N] 192 C5
Reinfeld [D] 18 G3
Reinhardshagen [D] 32 F4
Reinheim [D] 46 C3
Reinosa [E] 82 E4
Reinsfeld [D] 44 G2
Reinsvik [N] 180 F2
Reinsvoll [N] 172 B4
Reirat [N] 190 D4
Reisach [A] 72 G3
Reisbach [D] 60 G3
Reischach [D] 60 G4
Reischenhart [D] 60 F5
Reisjärvi [FIN] 196 D6
Reitan [N] 182 C3
Reit im Winkl [D] 60 F5
Reittiö [FIN] 188 D1
Reitzehain [D] 48 D2
Rejmyre [S] 168 B4
Rejowiec [PL] 38 F6
Rejowiec Fabryczny [PL] 38 F6
Rejštejn [CZ] 48 E6
Reka [HR] 74 F5
Reka [SLO] 74 A5
Rekeland [N] 164 B5
Reken [D] 16 G6
Rekijoki [FIN] 176 F4
Rekovac [SCG] 146 C2
Rekvik [N] 192 F2
Rel' [RUS] 198 G1
Rely [F] 28 E3
Remagen [D] 30 H5
Rémalard [F] 26 G6
Remels [D] 18 C4
Remeskylä [FIN] 196 E5
Remetea Mare [RO] 76 G5
Remich [L] 44 F3
Remígia, Cova- [E] 98 G2
Remiremont [F] 58 C3
Remmarn [S] 190 G6
Remmet [S] 182 G5
Remnes [N] 190 D2
Remolinos [E] 90 E3
Remouchamps [B] 30 E5
Remoulins [F] 106 G3
Remscheid [D] 30 H4
Remte [LV] 198 C5
Rémuzat [F] 108 B2
Rena [N] 172 C2
Renaison [F] 68 E2
Renaix (Ronse) [B] 28 G3
Renälandet [S] 190 E6
Renbygda [N] 182 C3
Rencēni [LV] 198 E4
Renchen [D] 58 F1
Renda [LV] 198 C5
Rendal [N] 180 G2
Rende [I] 124 D4
Rendsburg [D] 18 F2
Renfors [S] 190 H4
Rengsjö [S] 174 D2
Reni [UA] 204 E4
Renko [FIN] 176 G3
Renkum [NL] 16 E5
Rennebu [N] 180 H3
Rennerod [D] 46 B1
Rennes [F] 26 C6
Rennweg [A] 72 H2
Renon / Ritten [I] 72 D3
Rens [DK] 156 B4
Renså [N] 192 E4
Rentería / Errenteria [E] 84 B2
Rentína [GR] 130 C4
Rentína [GR] 132 F3
Rentjärn [S] 190 G4
Renträsk [S] 190 H3
Répáshuta [H] 64 F5
Répcelak [H] 74 G1
Repino [RUS] 178 G4
Replot / Raippaluoto [FIN] 186 A2
Repo-Aslak [FIN] 194 D4
Repojoki [FIN] 194 C5
Reposaari [FIN] 176 C1
Reppen [N] 190 D1
République, Col de la- [F] 68 F4
Repvåg [N] 194 C2
Requena [E] 98 D4
Réquista [F] 106 C2
Rerik [D] 20 A3
Reşadiye [TR] 154 C2
Resana [I] 72 E6
Resavska Pećina [SCG] 146 D2
Resele [S] 184 E2
Resen [MK] 128 D3
Reshetylivka [UA] 202 F7
Reşiţa [RO] 204 B5
Resko [PL] 20 G4
Resmo [S] 162 G5
Resna [SCG] 144 D4
Reso / Raisio [FIN] 176 D4
Ressons [F] 28 E6
Reszel [PL] 24 B3
Retama [E] 96 D3
Retama, Garganta de- [E] 96 D3
Retamal de Llerena [E] 96 A4
Retamar [E] 102 G5
Retamosa [E] 96 C1
Retford [GB] 10 F5
Rethel [F] 44 C2
Rethem [D] 18 E6
Réthymno [GR] 140 D4
Retie [B] 30 D3
Retiers [F] 40 G4
Retortillo de Soria [E] 90 A3
Retournac [F] 68 E4
Rétság [H] 64 C5
Retuerta [E] 88 H1
Retuerta del Bullaque [E] 96 E2
Retuneri [FIN] 188 E2
Retz [A] 62 E3
Reuilly [F] 56 B3
Reus [E] 92 C5
Reusel [NL] 30 E3
Reuterstadt Stavenhagen [D] 20 C4
Reutlingen [D] 58 H2
Reutte [A] 60 C6
Revel [F] 106 B4
Révigny-sur-Ornain [F] 44 C4
Revin [F] 44 C1
Revište [SK] 64 B3
Řevničov [CZ] 48 E3
Revò [I] 72 C3
Revonkylä [FIN] 188 G2
Revonlahti [FIN] 196 D4
Revsnes [N] 170 D2
Revsnes [N] 190 B5
Revsund [S] 182 H3
Revúca [SK] 64 E3
Rewal [PL] 20 F3
Rexbo [S] 172 H4
Reykjalið [IS] 192 C2
Reykjavík [IS] 192 A3
Rey Moro, Cueva del- [E] 98 D6
Rēzekne [LV] 198 G5
Rezovo [BG] 148 G5
Rgotina [SCG] 146 E2
Rhade [D] 18 E5
Rhayader [GB] 10 C6
Rheda [D] 32 D3
Rhede [D] 16 G6
Rheinau [D] 44 H6
Rheinbach [D] 30 G5
Rheinberg [D] 30 G2
Rheinböllen [D] 44 H2
Rheindahlen [D] 30 F3
Rheine [D] 16 H5
Rheinfall [D] 58 F4
Rheinfelden [CH] 58 E4
Rheinfelden (Baden) [D] 58 E4
Rheinsberg [D] 20 C6
Rhein-Weser-Turm [D] 32 D5
Rheinzabern [D] 46 B5
Rhêmes N.D. [I] 70 C4
Rhenen [NL] 16 E5
Rhens [D] 30 H6
Rheydt [D] 30 G3
Rhinau [F] 58 E2
Rhinow [D] 34 C1
Rho [I] 70 G5
Rhoon [NL] 16 C5
Rhosneigr [GB] 10 B4
Rhyl [GB] 10 C4
Rhynern [D] 32 C4
Ría Formosa [P] 94 C6
Riaillé [F] 40 G6
Riaño [E] 82 C3
Rians [F] 108 C4
Rianxo [E] 78 B3
Riaza [E] 88 G3
Ribabellosa [E] 82 G5
Ribadavia [E] 78 C5
Ribadelago [E] 78 E6
Ribadeo [E] 78 F2
Ribadesella [E] 82 C2
Ribaflecha [E] 90 C1
Ribaforada [E] 84 B6
Ribarci [SCG] 146 E5
Ribariće [SCG] 146 B4
Ribaritsa [BG] 148 A4
Riba-roja de Túria [E] 98 E4
Ribarska Banja [SCG] 146 D3
Ribas de Sil [E] 78 E5
Ribe [DK] 156 B3
Ribeauville [F] 58 D2
Ribécourt [F] 28 E6
Ribeira Brava [P] 100 A3
Ribeira de Pena [P] 80 D3
Ribeira Grande [P] 100 E3
Ribeiras [P] 100 C3
Ribeirinha [P] 100 C3
Ribemont [F] 28 F5
Ribera [I] 126 C3
Ribérac [F] 66 E2
Ribera de Cardós [E] 84 G6
Ribera del Fresno [E] 94 H3
Ribes de Freser [E] 92 E2
Ribnica [BIH] 142 D3
Ribnica [SLO] 74 B6
Ribnica [SLO] 74 C6
Rîbniţa [MD] 204 E3
Ribnitz-Damgarten [D] 20 C2
Ribolla [I] 114 F2
Ricadi [I] 124 C6
Říčany [CZ] 48 G4
Riccia [I] 120 F1
Riccione [I] 112 B5
Richelieu [F] 54 F3
Richmond [GB] 10 F2
Richtenberg [D] 20 C3
Rickarum [S] 158 D2
Rickling [D] 18 G3
Ricla [E] 90 D4
Ricse [H] 64 H4
Riddarhyttan [S] 166 H2
Ridderkerk [NL] 16 D5
Ridjica [SCG] 76 C5
Riebini [LV] 198 F6
Ried [A] 72 C2
Riedenburg [D] 60 E2
Rieder [D] 60 C5
Riedern [D] 58 F4
Ried im Innkreis [A] 60 H4
Riedlingen [D] 58 H3
Riegel [D] 34 F5
Riegel [D] 58 E2
Riegersburg [A] 74 E2
Riekki [FIN] 196 F2
Riello [E] 78 G5
Rieneck [D] 46 E3
Riesa [D] 34 E5
Riesi [I] 126 E4
Riestedt [D] 34 B5
Rietavas [LT] 200 D4
Rietberg [D] 32 D3
Rieti [I] 116 B4
Rietschen [D] 34 G5
Rieumes [F] 84 H3
Rieupeyroux [F] 66 H6
Rieussec [F] 106 C4
Rieux [F] 84 H4
Riez [F] 108 C4
Riezlern [A] 60 B6
Rīga [LV] 198 D5
Rígaio [GR] 132 G2
Rigáni [GR] 132 F5
Rignac [F] 68 A5
Rignano Flaminio [I] 116 A4
Riihimäki [FIN] 176 G3
Riihivaara [FIN] 196 G5
Riihivalkama [FIN] 176 F3
Riiho [FIN] 186 E4
Riipi [FIN] 194 D6
Riispyy [FIN] 186 B5
Riistavesi [FIN] 188 D2
Rijeka [BIH] 142 D4
Rijeka [HR] 112 E1
Rijeka Crnojevića [SCG] 144 E4
Rijssen [NL] 16 G5
Říkonín [CZ] 50 B6
Riksgränsen [S] 192 F4
Rila [BG] 146 F6
Rillé [F] 54 F1
Rillo [E] 90 D6
Rilski Man. [BG] 146 F6
Rima [I] 70 E3
Rimaucourt [F] 44 D6
Rimavská Sobota [SK] 64 E4
Rimbach [D] 60 G3
Rimbo [S] 168 E2
Rimella [I] 70 E3
Rimforsa [S] 162 F1
Rímini [I] 110 H5
Rimito / Rymättylä [FIN] 176 D5
Rimske Toplice [SLO] 74 D5
Rincón de la Victoria [E] 102 C5
Rincón de Soto [E] 84 A5
Rindal [N] 180 G2
Rindown Castle [IRL] 2 D5
Ring / An Rinn [IRL] 4 E5
Ringamala [S] 162 E6
Ringarum [S] 168 B6
Ringaskiddy [IRL] 4 D5
Ringe [DK] 156 D3
Ringebu [N] 170 H1
Ringkøbing [DK] 160 B6
Ringnäs [S] 172 F2
Ringnes [N] 170 G5
Ringøy [N] 170 D4
Ringstad [S] 168 B5
Ringsted [DK] 156 F3
Ringwood [GB] 12 G5
Rinkilä [FIN] 188 E5
Rinna [S] 166 G6
Rinøya [N] 192 E4
Rinteln [D] 32 E2
Río [GR] 132 F5
Riobianco / Weissenbach [I] 72 D2
Río de Losa [E] 82 F4
Ríofrío [E] 78 G5
Riola Sardo [I] 118 B5
Riolobos [E] 86 H4
Riolo Terme [I] 110 G4
Riom [F] 68 C2
Riomaggiore [I] 110 C4
Rio Maior [P] 86 C4
Riomar [E] 92 B6
Rio Marina [I] 114 E2
Rio Mau [P] 80 B3
Riom-ès-Montagnes [F] 68 B3
Rion-des-Landes [F] 66 B5
Rionegro del Puente [E] 80 G3
Rionero in Vúlture [I] 120 G3
Riópar [E] 96 H6
Riós [E] 78 D6
Riosa [E] 78 H4
Rio Saliceto [I] 110 E2
Rioseco de Tapia [E] 78 G5
Rio Torto [P] 80 D6
Rioz [F] 58 B4
Ripač [BIH] 112 H3
Ripacandida [I] 120 G3
Ripanj [SCG] 142 G3
Riparbella [I] 114 E1
Ripatransone [I] 116 C2
Ripats [S] 192 G6
Ripky [UA] 202 D6
Ripley [GB] 10 E5
Ripoll [E] 92 E2
Ripon [GB] 10 F3
Riposto [I] 124 B8
Ripsa [S] 168 C4
Riquewihr [F] 58 D2
Risan [SCG] 144 D4
Risasvallen [S] 182 E4
Risbäck [S] 190 E4
Risberg [S] 172 F3
Riscle [F] 84 E2
Riseberga [S] 158 C1
Riseberga Kloster [S] 166 G3
Risede [S] 190 E5
Rish [BG] 148 E3
Risinge [S] 168 B5
Risliden [S] 190 H4
Risnes [N] 164 C4
Risnes [N] 170 B2
Rišňovce [SK] 64 A4
Risør [N] 164 F4
Risøyhamn [N] 192 E3
Rissa [N] 190 B6
Rissna [S] 182 H2
Risti [EST] 198 D2
Ristiina [FIN] 188 C6
Ristijärvi [FIN] 196 F4
Ristilä [FIN] 186 H4
Ristinge [DK] 156 E5
Ristinkylä [FIN] 188 E3
Ristna [EST] 198 C2
Ristovac [SCG] 146 D5
Risträsk [S] 190 G4
Risulahti [FIN] 188 D6
Risum-Lindholm [D] 156 B5
Risuperä [FIN] 186 E2
Ritíni [GR] 128 G5
Ritola [FIN] 186 D3
Ritsem [S] 192 F5
Rittmanshausen [D] 32 G6
Riuttala [FIN] 176 D1
Riva-Bella [F] 26 F3
Riva dei Tarquini [I] 114 G4
Riva del Garda [I] 72 C5
Riva di Solto [I] 72 A5
Rivarolo Canavese [I] 70 D5
Rivarolo Mantovano [I] 110 E2
Riva Valdobbia [I] 70 E3
Rive-de-Gier [F] 68 F3
Rivergaro [I] 110 C2
Rivesaltes [F] 92 G1
Rivinperä [FIN] 196 E5
Rivne [UA] 202 B7
Rivoli [I] 70 D5
Rizári [GR] 128 F4
Rízia [GR] 150 A2
Rizokárpaso (Dipkarpaz) [CY] 154 H4
Rízoma [GR] 132 E2
Rizómata [GR] 128 G5
Rizómylos [GR] 132 H2
Rizómylos [GR] 136 D4
Rjånes [N] 180 C4
Rjukan [N] 170 F6
Ro [I] 110 G2
Roa [E] 88 G2
Roa [N] 172 B5
Roald [N] 180 C3
Røan [N] 180 G2
Roana [I] 72 D5
Roanne [F] 68 E2
Roasjö [S] 162 B2
Roavvegieddi [N] 194 D3
Robăneştii de Jos [RO] 146 G1
Robbio [I] 70 F5
Röbel [D] 20 C5
Robella [I] 70 E5
Røberg [N] 182 B1
Robertingue [F] 14 G6
Robertsfors [S] 196 A5
Robleda [E] 86 H2
Robledillo de Gata [E] 86 H3
Robledo [E] 96 H5
Robledo de Chavela [E] 88 E5
Robledo del Buey [E] 96 D2
Robles de la Valcueva [E] 78 H5
Robliza de Cojos [E] 88 B3
Robres [E] 90 F3
Robres del Castillo [E] 90 C1
Robru [N] 170 F3
Rocamadour [F] 66 G4
Roccabianca [I] 110 D2
Roccadáspide [I] 120 F4
Rocca di Cambio [I] 116 C4
Rocca di Mezzo [I] 116 C4
Rocca di Neto [I] 124 F5
Rocca Imperiale [I] 122 D5
Roccalbegna [I] 114 G3
Roccalumera [I] 124 B8
Rocca Malatina, Sassi di- [I] 110 E4
Roccamonfina [I] 120 D2
Roccanova [I] 122 C5
Roccapalumba [I] 126 D2
Rocca Pia [I] 116 D5
Roccaraso [I] 116 D6
Rocca San Casciano [I] 110 G5
Rocca Sinibalda [I] 116 B4
Roccastrada [I] 114 F2
Rocca Vecchia [I] 122 H5
Roccaverano [I] 108 H2
Roccella Iónica [I] 124 D7
Roccelletta del Vescovo di Squillace [I] 124 E5
Rocche di Cusa [I] 126 B3
Rocchetta Belbo [I] 108 G2
Rocella Valdemonte [I] 124 A8
Rochdale [GB] 10 E4
Roche [E] 100 F4
Rochebloine, Château de- [F] 68 E5
Rochechouart [F] 54 F6
Rochecourbière, Grotte de- [F] 106 H2
Rochefort [B] 30 D6
Rochefort [F] 54 C5
Rochefort, Grotte de- [F] 40 H5
Rochefort-en-Terre [F] 40 E5
Rochefort-s-Nenon [F] 56 H4
Rochehaut [B] 44 D2
Rochemaure [F] 68 F6
Rocher, Château du- [F] 26 E6
Rocherolle, Château de la- [F] 54 G4
Rochers, Château des- [F] 26 D6
Rocheservière [F] 54 B2
Rochester [GB] 14 F4
Rochlitz [D] 34 D6
Rochsburg [D] 48 D1
Rociana del Condado [E] 94 F6
Rockcorry [IRL] 2 F4
Rockenhausen [D] 46 B4
Rockhammar [S] 166 H2
Rockneby [S] 162 G5
Rocroi [F] 28 H5
Róda [GR] 132 B1
Rodach [D] 46 G2
Roda de Isábena [E] 84 F6
Rodaljice [HR] 112 H5
Rodange [L] 44 E3
Ródão, Portas de- [P] 86 E4
Rødberg [N] 170 F5
Rødby [DK] 20 A1
Rødbyhavn [DK] 20 A1
Rødding [DK] 156 B3
Rødding [DK] 160 C5
Rödeby [S] 158 F1
Rodeiro [E] 78 C4
Rødekro [DK] 156 C4
Roden [NL] 16 G2
Rodenkirchen [D] 18 D4
Rodewald [D] 32 F1
Rodewisch [D] 48 C2
Rodez [F] 68 B6
Rodgau [D] 46 C3
Rødhus Klit [DK] 160 D3
Rodiá [GR] 132 G1
Rodi Gargánico [I] 116 G5
Roding [D] 48 C6
Rødkærsbro [DK] 160 D5
Rodolívos [GR] 130 C3
Rodópoli [GR] 128 H2
Ródos [GR] 154 D3
Rodovoye [RUS] 198 G4
Rodrigatos de la Obispalía [E] 78 G5
Rodrigo, Castelo- [P] 80 E6
Rødsjøen [N] 190 B6
Rødven [N] 180 E3
Rødvig [DK] 156 G4
Roela [EST] 198 F1
Roermond [NL] 30 F3
Roeselare (Roulers) [B] 28 F2
Roeulx [B] 28 H3
Roflaschlucht [CH] 70 G2
Röfors [S] 166 G4
Rofrano [I] 120 G5
Rogač [HR] 142 A6
Rogačica [SCG] 142 F4
Rogalice [PL] 50 D1
Rogalin [PL] 36 C3
Rogaška Slatina [SLO] 74 D4
Rogatec [SLO] 74 E4
Rogatica [BIH] 144 E1
Rogätz [D] 34 B2
Rogil [P] 94 B4
Røgind [DK] 156 A1
Rögla [S] 158 C3
Rogliano [F] 114 C2
Rogliano [I] 124 D5
Rognac [F] 106 H5
Rognan [N] 192 D6
Rogne [N] 170 G2
Rognes [N] 182 B2
Rogovka [LV] 198 G5
Rogovo [RUS] 198 G4
Rogowo [PL] 36 D2
Rogozhinë [AL] 128 B3
Rogoznica [HR] 116 H1
Rogoźno [PL] 36 C2
Rogozno [PL] 36 F5
Roguszyn [PL] 38 D2
Rohan [F] 26 A5
Rohatec [CZ] 62 G2
Rohatyn [UA] 204 C2
Rohr [A] 72 E1
Rohrbach [A] 62 B3
Rohrbach-lès-Bitche [F] 44 G4
Rohrberg [D] 34 A1
Rohr i. Niederb. [D] 60 F2
Rohuküla [EST] 198 D2
Rohuneeme [EST] 198 D1
Roisel [F] 28 F5
Roja [LV] 198 C4
Rojales [E] 104 D3
Röjan [S] 182 G4
Rojão Grande [P] 80 C6
Röjdåfors [S] 172 E5
Rojiştea [RO] 146 G1
Rök [S] 166 G6
Röka [S] 190 G4
Röke [S] 158 C1
Rokiciny [PL] 36 H4
Rokietnica [PL] 52 F4
Rokiškis [LT] 200 G3
Rokity [PL] 22 C2
Rökkum [N] 180 F2
Røkland [N] 190 E1
Roknäs [S] 196 A3
Rokua [FIN] 196 E4
Rokycany [CZ] 48 E4
Rolandstorp [S] 190 E4
Rold [DK] 160 D4
Røldal [N] 170 C5
Rolle [CH] 70 B1
Roltstorp [S] 160 H4
Rølvåg [N] 190 D3
Rolvsøy [N] 166 B3
Roma [I] 116 A5
Romagnano Sésia [I] 70 E4
Romakkajärvi [FIN] 194 C7
Romakloster [S] 168 G4
Roman [BG] 146 G3
Roman [RO] 204 D3
Romangordo [E] 88 B6
Romanija [BIH] 144 D1
Romanshorn [CH] 58 H4
Romans-sur-Isère [F] 68 F5
Romashki [RUS] 178 G2
Rombas [F] 44 E4
Rom By [DK] 160 B5
Romena, Castello di- [I] 110 G5
Romena, Pieve di- [I] 110 G5
Romeral [E] 96 G2
Romfartuna [S] 168 B2
Romilly-sur-Seine [F] 44 A5
Romny [UA] 202 E7
Romont [CH] 70 C1
Romorantin-Lanthenay [F] 54 H2
Romppala [FIN] 188 F1
Romsey [GB] 12 H4
Romtemplom [H] 64 C6
Røn [N] 170 G2
Roncade [I] 72 E6
Roncadelle [I] 72 A6
Roncal / Erronkari [E] 84 C4
Roncegno [I] 72 D4
Roncesvalles [E] 84 C3
Ronchamp [F] 58 C3
Ronchi dei Legionari [I] 72 H5
Ronciglione [I] 114 H4
Ronco Canavese [I] 70 D4
Roncofreddo [I] 110 H5
Ronco Scrivia [I] 110 B3
Ronda [E] 102 A4
Rønde [DK] 160 E6
Ronehamn [S] 168 G5
Rong [N] 170 A3
Rõngu [EST] 198 F3
Ronkeli [FIN] 196 G5
Rönnäng [S] 160 G1
Rønne [DK] 158 E4
Ronneburg [D] 48 C1
Ronneby [S] 158 F1
Rønnede [DK] 156 G4
Rönnigsåsen [S] 182 F4
Rönnliden [S] 190 H3
Rönnöfors [S] 190 D6
Rönnskär [S] 196 A4
Rönnynkylä [FIN] 186 F1
Rönö [S] 168 C5
Ronse (Renaix) [B] 28 G3
Roodeschool [NL] 16 G1
Roonah Quay [IRL] 2 B3
Roosendaal [NL] 16 C6
Roosky [IRL] 2 D4
Ropa [PL] 52 C5
Ropaži [LV] 198 E5
Ropczyce [PL] 52 D3
Ropeid [N] 164 B1
Ropinsalmi [FIN] 192 H3
Ropotovo [MK] 128 E2
Ropsha [RUS] 178 E6
Roque, Pointe de la- [F] 26 G3
Roquebillière [F] 108 F4
Roquebrune-Cap-Martin [F] 108 F4
Roquefort [F] 66 C5
Roquefort-sur-Soulzon [F] 106 D3
Roquemaure [F] 106 G3
Roquesteron [F] 108 E4
Roquetaillade, Château de- [F] 66 D4
Roquetas de Mar [E] 102 F5
Roquetes [E] 92 A5
Røra [N] 190 C6
Rörbäcksnäs [S] 172 E3
Rore [BIH] 142 B4
Roron [S] 182 G3

284 Ror - San

Røros [N] 182 C4
Rorschach [CH] 58 H5
Rörum [S] 158 D3
Rørvig [DK] 156 F2
Rørvik [N] 164 C5
Rørvik [N] 182 B1
Rørvik [N] 190 C4
Ros' [BY] 24 G5
Rosais [P] 100 C3
Rosala [FIN] 176 E6
Rosal de la Frontera [E] 94 E3
Rosa Marina [I] 122 F3
Rosans [F] 108 B2
Rosapenna [IRL] 2 E1
Rosarno [I] 124 C6
Rosbach [D] 46 C2
Rosche [D] 18 G6
Rościszewo [PL] 36 H1
Roscoff [F] 40 C1
Roscommon [IRL] 2 D5
Roscrea [IRL] 2 D6
Rosdorf [D] 32 F4
Rosegg [A] 74 B3
Roselle [I] 114 F2
Roselle Módica [I] 126 G6
Rosen [BG] 148 F4
Rosenberg [D] 46 E6
Rosenburg [A] 62 E3
Rosendal [N] 170 B5
Rosendal [S] 156 H1
Rosenheim [D] 60 F5
Rosenhof [A] 62 C3
Rosenholm [DK] 160 E6
Rosentorp [S] 172 H2
Rosersberg [S] 168 D2
Roses / Rosas [E] 92 G2
Roseto degli Abruzzi [I] 116 D3
Roseto Valfortore [I] 120 F2
Roshchino [RUS] 178 G4
Rosica [BG] 148 F1
Rosice [CZ] 50 B6
Rosignano-Marittimo [I] 110 D6
Rosignano Solvay [I] 114 E1
Rosino [BG] 148 B4
Roşiori [RO] 76 H1
Roşiori de Vede [RO] 148 B1
Roşiori De Vede [RO] 204 D6
Roskilde [DK] 156 G2
Rosko [PL] 36 B1
Roslags-Bro [S] 168 E1
Roslags kulla [S] 168 E2
Roslavl' [RUS] 202 D5
Roslev [DK] 160 C4
Rosli [N] 180 G5
Rosmaninhal [P] 86 F4
Rosnowo [PL] 22 A3
Rosny Sur Seine [F] 42 E3
Rosolina Mare [I] 110 H2
Rosolini [I] 126 G5
Rosoman [MK] 128 F2
Rosporden [F] 40 C3
Ross Abbey [IRL] 2 C4
Rossano [I] 124 E4
Rossas [P] 80 C5
Ross Carbery [IRL] 4 C5
Rosscor [NIR] 2 E3
Rosserk Abbey [IRL] 2 C3
Rosses Point [IRL] 2 D3
Rossfjord [N] 192 F2
Rosshaupten [D] 60 C5
Rossiglione [I] 108 H2
Rossio [P] 86 D4
Rossla [D] 34 A5
Rossland [N] 170 A3
Rosslare Harbour [IRL] 4 F5
Rosslau [D] 34 C4
Rosslea [NIR] 2 F4
Rossnes [N] 170 A3
Rossön [S] 190 F6
Ross-on-Wye [GB] 12 G2
Rossosz [PL] 38 F4
Rossoszyca [PL] 36 F4
Røssvassbukt [N] 190 E3
Röstånga [S] 158 C2
Rostassac [F] 66 F5
Roštejn [CZ] 48 H6
Roštejn [CZ] 50 A6
Röster [S] 168 B6
Rostock [D] 20 B3
Rostov [RUS] 202 F2
Rostrenen [F] 40 D3
Rostrevor [NIR] 2 G4
Röström [S] 190 F5
Røstvollen [N] 182 D5
Rosvik [N] 192 D5
Rosvik [S] 196 B3
Rosyth [GB] 8 E3
Röszke [H] 76 E4
Roszki-Wodźki [PL] 24 E6
Rot [S] 172 F2
Rota [E] 100 F3
Rotberget [N] 172 D4
Roteberg [S] 168 C1
Rotemo [N] 164 D2
Rotenburg [D] 18 E5
Rotenburg [D] 32 F6
Rotenfels [D] 46 B3
Rotgülden [A] 72 H2
Roth [D] 46 G5
Rötha [D] 34 C6
Rothemühl [D] 20 E4
Rothenburg [D] 34 G5
Rothenburg, Ruine- [D] 46 G5
Rothenburg ob der Tauber [D] 46 E5
Rothéneuf [F] 26 C4
Rothenstein [D] 60 D2
Rotherham [GB] 10 F4
Rothes [GB] 6 E5
Rothesay [GB] 8 C3
Rotondella [I] 122 D5
Rótova [E] 98 E6
Rotsjö [S] 184 D3
Rott [D] 60 D5
Rott [D] 60 F5
Rottach [D] 60 E5
Rötteln [D] 58 E4
Rottenbach [D] 46 G2
Rottenbuch [D] 60 D5
Rottenburg [D] 58 G2
Rottenburg [D] 60 F3
Rottenmann [A] 62 B6
Rotterdam [NL] 16 C5
Rotthalmünster [D] 60 H4
Röttingen [D] 46 E5
Rottne [S] 162 E4
Rottneros [S] 166 E1
Rottweil [D] 58 G3
Rotvoll [N] 182 D2
Rötz [D] 48 C5
Roubaix [F] 28 F3
Rouchovany [CZ] 62 E2
Roudnice nad Labem [CZ] 48 F3
Rouen [F] 28 B5
Rouffach [F] 58 D3
Rouffignac, Grotte de- [F] 66 F3
Rougé [F] 40 F5
Rougemont [F] 58 C4
Rougemont [F] 58 D3
Rouillac [F] 54 D6
Roujan [F] 106 D4
Roukavichy [BY] 202 D5
Roulers (Roeselare) [B] 28 F2
Roundstone [IRL] 2 B4
Roundwood [IRL] 4 G3
Roússa [GR] 130 G2
Roussillon [F] 106 H4
Rouvres-en-Xaintois [F] 44 E6
Rovakka [S] 194 B7
Rovaniemi [FIN] 194 D8
Rovanjska [HR] 112 G4
Rovastinaho [FIN] 196 D2
Rovato [I] 72 A6
Roverbella [I] 110 E1
Rovereto [I] 72 C5
Röverhagen [D] 20 B3
Roverud [N] 172 D5
Roviés [GR] 134 B4
Rovigo [I] 110 G2
Rovinj [HR] 112 D2
Rovišće [HR] 74 F5
Rovjok [N] 192 G3
Rovte [SLO] 74 B5
Rów [PL] 20 F6
Rowy [PL] 22 B1
Royan [F] 54 B6
Royat [F] 68 C2
Royaumont, Abbaye de- [F] 42 F3
Roybon [F] 68 G4
Roye [F] 28 E5
Royère-de-Vassivière [F] 68 A1
Royken [N] 164 H1
Røyrvik [N] 190 D4
Røyse [N] 170 H5
Røysheim [N] 180 F6
Royston [GB] 14 E3
Roza [BG] 148 D5
Rožaj [SCG] 146 B5
Rózan [PL] 24 C6
Rożanki [PL] 34 H1
Rožanstvo [SCG] 146 A3
Rozay-en-Brie [F] 42 G4
Rozdil [UA] 52 H5
Roženski Manastir [BG] 130 B2
Rožmberk nad Vltavou [CZ] 62 B3
Rožmitál pod Třemšínem [CZ] 48 E5
Rožňava [SK] 64 E3
Rožnov pod Radhoštěm [CZ] 50 E5
Rożnów [PL] 52 B4
Rozogi [PL] 24 C5
Rozoy [F] 28 G6
Rozprza [PL] 36 H5
Roztoky [CZ] 48 F3
Rožupe [LV] 198 F6
Rozvadov [CZ] 48 C4
Rozzano [I] 70 G5
Rrëshen [AL] 128 B1
Rtanj [SCG] 146 D2
Ru [E] 78 D3
Rubbestadneset [N] 170 A5
Rubena [E] 82 E6
Rubielos de Mora [E] 98 E2
Rubiera [I] 110 E3
Rucava [LV] 200 D3
Ruciane-Nida [PL] 24 C4
Rud [N] 164 H1
Rud [N] 170 H5
Rud [S] 166 F3
Ruda [S] 162 F4
Ruda Maleniecka [PL] 38 A6
Rudare [SCG] 146 C4
Rudawica [PL] 34 H5
Ruda Wolińska [PL] 38 D3
Rudelsburg [D] 34 B6
Rudenica [SCG] 146 C3
Rüdersdorf [D] 34 F2
Rüdesheim [D] 46 B3
Rūdiškės [LT] 24 H1
Rudka [PL] 38 E1
Rudka [PL] 38 G5
Rudkøbing [DK] 156 E4
Rudna [PL] 22 C5
Rudna [PL] 36 B5
Rudna Glava [SCG] 146 D1
Rudnica [SCG] 144 E2
Rudnica [SCG] 146 B4
Rudnik [BG] 148 F3
Rudnik [PL] 50 E3
Rudnik [SCG] 146 B5
Rudnik [SCG] 146 B2
Rudniki [PL] 50 F1
Rudnik nad Sanem [PL] 52 E2
Rudnik Szlachecki-Kol. [PL] 38 D6
Rudno [PL] 22 E4
Rudno [SLO] 74 B4
Rudnya [RUS] 202 C4
Rudolphstein [D] 46 H2
Rudolstadt [D] 46 H1
Rudozem [BG] 130 E1
Rudsgrendi [N] 164 F1
Rudsjön [S] 190 F6
Rudskoga [S] 166 G4
Ruds-Vedby [DK] 156 F3
Rudy [PL] 50 F3
Rudzāti [LV] 198 F5
Rue [F] 28 D3
Rueda [E] 88 E2
Rueda, Monasterio de- [E] 90 F5
Rueda de Jalón [E] 90 D3
Ruelle-sur-Touvre [F] 66 E1
Ruen [BG] 148 F4
Ruffano [I] 122 G6
Ruffec [F] 54 E5
Ruffieux [F] 68 H3
Rugāji [LV] 198 G5
Rugby [GB] 14 D2
Rugeley [GB] 10 E6
Rugldalen [N] 182 C3
Rugles [F] 26 H5
Ruha [FIN] 186 C3
Ruhällen [S] 168 C1
Rühen [D] 32 H2
Ruhland [D] 34 F5
Ruhmannsfelden [D] 60 G2
Ruhpolding [D] 60 G5
Ruidera [E] 96 G4
Ruinas Romanas [E] 96 D1
Ruínas Romanas [P] 94 D2
Rūjiena [LV] 198 E3
Ruju, Nuraghe- [I] 118 D3
Ruka [FIN] 194 F8
Rullbo [S] 182 H6
Rülzheim [D] 46 B5
Rum [H] 74 G2
Ruma [SCG] 142 F2
Rumboci [BIH] 144 B1
Rumburk [CZ] 48 G1
Rumelifeneri [TR] 150 E2
Rumia [PL] 22 D2
Rumigny [F] 28 H5
Rumilly [F] 70 A3
Rummen [B] 30 D4
Rummukkala [FIN] 188 E3
Rumo [FIN] 196 F5
Rumont [F] 44 D4
Rumpani [LV] 198 F4
Runcorn [GB] 10 D4
Rundfloen [N] 172 E3
Rundvik [S] 184 H1
Runni [FIN] 196 E6
Runović [HR] 144 B2
Ruokojärvi [FIN] 194 C7
Ruokojärvi [S] 194 B8
Ruokolahti [FIN] 178 E1
Ruokto [S] 192 F6
Ruona [FIN] 186 D3
Ruopsa [FIN] 194 E7
Ruorasmäki [FIN] 186 H6
Ruotaanmäki [FIN] 196 E6
Ruoti [I] 120 G3
Ruotsinpyhtää Strömfors [FIN] 178 C4
Ruovesi [FIN] 186 E5
Rupa [HR] 112 E1
Rupea [RO] 204 D4
Rupt [F] 58 C3
Rus [E] 102 F1
Rus2 [BY] 202 B7
Rus2 [BY] 202 B7
Rusalka [BG] 148 G2
Rusanivka [UA] 202 F7
Rùscio [I] 116 B3
Rusdal [N] 164 B4
Ruse [BG] 148 C2
Ruše [SLO] 74 D4
Rusele [S] 190 G4
Ruševo [HR] 142 D1
Rusfors [S] 190 G4
Rush [IRL] 2 F6
Rushden [GB] 14 E2
Rusiec [PL] 36 F5
Rusinovo [PL] 20 G4
Rusinowo [PL] 22 A6
Rusjasi [MK] 128 D2
Ruskeala [RUS] 188 G4
Ruski Krstur [SCG] 76 D6
Ruskila [FIN] 188 D2
Rusksand [S] 190 F6
Rusksele [S] 190 G4
Ruskträsk [S] 190 G4
Rusnė [LT] 200 D5
Rusokastro [BG] 148 F4
Rüsselsheim [D] 46 C3
Russi [I] 110 G4
Russliseter [N] 180 G6
Rust [A] 62 F5
Rust [D] 58 E2
Rustad [N] 172 B5
Rustefjelbma [N] 194 D2
Rusvekk [N] 172 D4
Ruswil [CH] 58 E6
Ruszów [PL] 34 H5
Rutalahti [FIN] 186 G5
Rute [E] 102 C3
Rutenbrock [D] 16 H3
Rüthen [D] 32 D4
Ruthin [GB] 10 C4
Rüti [CH] 58 G6
Rüti [CH] 58 G5
Rutigliano [I] 122 E3
Rutka-Tartak [PL] 24 E2
Rutki [PL] 24 D6
Rutledal [N] 170 B2
Rutvik [S] 196 B3
Ruukki [FIN] 196 D4
Ruunaa [FIN] 196 G6
Ruurlo [NL] 16 F5
Ruutana [FIN] 176 F1
Ruutana [FIN] 196 E6
Ruuvaoja [FIN] 194 E6
Ruvanaho [FIN] 194 F7
Ruvasiahtio [FIN] 188 F2
Ruvo di Púglia [I] 122 D2
Ruwer [D] 44 G2
Ruza [RUS] 202 E3
Ruzhany [BY] 24 H6
Ruzhintsi [BG] 146 E3
Ruzhyn [UA] 202 D8
Růžkovy Lhotice [CZ] 48 G5
Ružomberok [SK] 64 C2
Rvíziana [GR] 132 D3
Ry [DK] 156 D1
Ryå [DK] 160 D3
Ryakhovo [BG] 148 D1
Ryákia [GR] 128 G5
Rybachiy [RUS] 200 C5
Rybarzowice [PL] 50 G5
Rybinsk [RUS] 202 F1
Rybnik [PL] 50 F4
Rybník [SK] 64 E3
Rybno [PL] 22 G5
Ryboły [PL] 24 F6
Rychliki [PL] 22 F3
Rychmburk [CZ] 50 B4
Rychnov nad Kněžnou [CZ] 50 B3
Rychnowo [PL] 22 G4
Rychtal [PL] 36 E6
Rychwał [PL] 36 E3
Ryczywół [PL] 38 C4
Ryd [S] 162 D6
Rydaholm [S] 162 D4
Ryde [GB] 12 H5
Rydet [S] 160 G3
Rydland [N] 182 B6
Rydsnäs [S] 162 E2
Rydułtowy [PL] 50 F4
Rydzyna [PL] 36 C4
Rye [GB] 14 F5
Ryen [N] 164 E5
Ryfoss [N] 170 F2
Rygge [N] 166 B2
Rygozy [RUS] 198 H5
Ryhälä [FIN] 188 E5
Ryhäntä [FIN] 196 F4
Rykene [N] 164 E5
Ryki [PL] 38 D4
Ryl'sk [RUS] 202 F6
Rymań [PL] 20 G3
Rymanów [PL] 52 D5
Rýmařov [CZ] 50 D4
Rymättylä / Rimito [FIN] 176 D5
Rýmnio [GR] 128 F6
Ryn [PL] 24 C3
Rynarzewo [PL] 22 D6
Ryomgård [DK] 160 E5
Rypefjord [N] 194 B2
Rypin [PL] 22 F6
Ryslinge [DK] 156 D3
Ryssby [S] 162 D4
Rysum [D] 16 H2
Rytel [PL] 22 C4
Rytinki [FIN] 196 E2
Rytkynkylä [FIN] 196 D5
Rytro [PL] 52 B5
Ryuttyu [RUS] 188 H4
Rýzmberk [CZ] 48 D5
Rząśnik [PL] 38 C1
Rzeczenica [PL] 22 B4
Rzeczyca [PL] 38 A5
Rzęgnowo [PL] 22 H6
Rzemień [PL] 52 D3
Rzepin [PL] 34 G3
Rzesznikowo [PL] 20 G4
Rzeszów [PL] 52 E3
Rzewnowo [PL] 20 F3
Rzgów [PL] 36 G4
Rzhev [RUS] 202 D3
Rzhishchiv [UA] 202 E7

S

Sääksjärvi [FIN] 186 D2
Sääksmäki [FIN] 176 F2
Saal [D] 60 F2
Saalbach [A] 72 F1
Saalburg [D] 46 C2
Saales [F] 44 G6
Saalfeld [D] 46 H2
Saalfelden [A] 60 G6
Saamatti [FIN] 176 F5
Saananmaja [FIN] 192 G3
Saanen [CH] 70 D1
Saarbrücken [D] 44 G4
Saarburg [D] 44 F3
Sääre [EST] 198 C4
Saare [EST] 198 F2
Saarela [FIN] 186 G1
Saarela [FIN] 196 G5
Saarenkylä [FIN] 194 D8
Saarenmaa [FIN] 176 D2
Saaresmäki [FIN] 196 E5
Saari [FIN] 188 F5
Saarijärvi [FIN] 186 F3
Saarikko [FIN] 176 F3
Saarikoski [FIN] 192 H3
Saarinen [FIN] 196 F4
Saario [FIN] 188 G3
Saarivaara [FIN] 188 G3
Saariväara [FIN] 196 G4
Saarlouis [D] 44 F3
Saas Almagell [CH] 70 E3
Saas-Fee [CH] 70 E3
Saas Grund [CH] 70 E3
Sääskijärvi [FIN] 196 E2
Sääskjärvi [FIN] 178 B3
Sababurg [D] 32 F4
Šabac [SCG] 142 F2
Sabadell [E] 92 E4
Sabaro [E] 82 C4
Sabáudia [I] 120 B2
Sabbioneta [I] 110 E2
Sabbucina [I] 126 E3
Sabile [LV] 198 C5
Sabiñánigo [E] 84 D5
Sabinosa [E] 100 A5
Sabinov [SK] 52 C6
Sabiote [E] 102 F2
Sables-d'Or-les-Pins [F] 26 B4
Sablé-sur-Sarthe [F] 42 A5
Såbole [S] 182 F1
Saborsko [HR] 112 G2
Sabres [F] 66 C5
Sabrosa [P] 80 D4
Sabugal [P] 86 G2
Sabuncu [TR] 150 H6
Saby [S] 162 E1
Šaca [SK] 64 G3
Săcălaz [RO] 76 G5
Sacavém [P] 86 B5
Sacecorbo [E] 90 B5
Sacedón [E] 88 H6
Saceruela [E] 96 D4
Sacile [I] 72 F5
Sacra di San Michele [I] 70 C5
Sádaba [E] 84 B5
Sadala [EST] 198 F2
Sadikov Bunar [SCG] 146 E4
Sadina [BG] 148 D2
Sadki [PL] 22 C6
Sadova [RO] 146 G2
Sadovets [BG] 148 A3
Sadovo [BG] 148 B6
Sądów [PL] 34 G3
Sadowne [PL] 38 C2
Sadrazamköy (Livera) [CY] 154 F5
S. Adriano [I] 110 G4
Sadská [CZ] 48 G3
Sädvaluspen [S] 190 F2
Sæbø [N] 170 D4
Sæbø [N] 180 D4
Sæbøvik [N] 170 B5
Sæby [DK] 160 E3
Sæd [DK] 156 B4
SÄedinenie [BG] 148 B5
SÄedinenie [BG] 148 C5
Saelices [E] 96 H2
Sælvig [DK] 156 E2
Saepinum [I] 120 E1
Saerbeck [D] 32 C2
Sætra [N] 192 E2
Sætre [N] 164 H2
Sætre [N] 172 C2
Sætteråsen [N] 190 B6
Saeul [L] 44 E2
Sævareid [N] 170 B4
Sævråsvåg [N] 170 B3
Safa [TR] 150 G5
Safara [P] 94 E3
Säffle [S] 166 E3
Saffron Walden [GB] 14 F3
Safonovo [RUS] 202 D4
Sagard [D] 20 D2
S'Agaró [E] 92 G4
S. Agata di Esaro [I] 124 C3
Saggrenda [N] 164 G2
Sagiáda [GR] 132 B2
Sågmyra [S] 172 H4
Sagone [F] 114 A4
Sagres [P] 94 A5
Şagu [RO] 76 G5
Sagu / Sauvo [FIN] 176 E5
Sagunt / Sagunto [E] 98 F4
Sagunto / Sagunt [E] 98 F4
Sagvåg [N] 170 A5
Ságvár [H] 76 A3
Sahagún [E] 82 C5
Sahalahti [FIN] 176 G1
Sahankylä [FIN] 186 C4
Sahavaara [S] 194 B7
Sahilköy [TR] 150 F2
Şahin [TR] 150 B3
Sahrajärvi [FIN] 186 F4
Šahy [SK] 64 C5
Saignelégier [CH] 58 D5
Saija [FIN] 194 E7
Saikari [FIN] 186 H3
Saillagouse [F] 92 E1
Sailly Flibeaucourt [F] 28 D4
Säimen [FIN] 188 F4
Sains [F] 28 G5
Saint Albain [F] 56 G6
Sainte-Lucie-de-Tallano [F] 114 B5
Sainte-Marie-Siché [F] 114 B5
Saintes [F] 54 C6
Saintfield [NIR] 2 G4
Saint-Ghislain [B] 28 G3
Saint Hilaire de la Côte [F] 68 G4
Saint-Jacques [I] 70 D3
Sairinen [FIN] 176 D4
Saissac [F] 106 B4
Saittarova [S] 192 H6
Saivomuotka [S] 194 B5
Sajaniemi [FIN] 176 G3
Sajenek [PL] 24 E3
Šajkaš [SCG] 142 G1
Sajószentpéter [H] 64 F4
Sakar [TR] 150 H4
Sakaravaara [FIN] 196 F4
Sakarya (Adapazari) [TR] 150 H3
Šakiai [LT] 200 E5
Säkinmäki [FIN] 186 H3
Sakıremer [TR] 152 D6
Sakızlık [TR] 150 G5
Sakowczyk [PL] 52 E5
Sakskøbing [DK] 20 B1
Saky [UA] 204 H4
Säkylä [FIN] 176 D3
Sala [S] 168 C1
Šal'a [SK] 64 A4
Salaberg [A] 62 C5
Salacgrīva [LV] 198 D4
Sala Consilina [I] 120 G4
Saladamm [S] 168 C1
Salahmi [FIN] 196 E5
Salamajärvi [FIN] 186 E1
Salamanca [E] 80 H6
Salamína [GR] 134 B6
Salamis [CY] 154 G5
Salantai [LT] 200 D4
Salaóra [GR] 132 D4
Salar [E] 102 D4
Sălard [RO] 76 H1
Salardú [E] 84 G5
Salas [E] 78 G3
Salaš [SCG] 146 E2
Salas de los Infantes [E] 88 H1
Salaspils [LV] 198 E5
Salau [F] 84 G5
Salbohed [S] 168 B1
Salbris [F] 56 B2
Salcia [RO] 146 E1
Šalčininkai [LT] 200 G6
Salcombe [GB] 12 D5
Sălcuța [RO] 146 F1
Saldaña [E] 82 C5
Salduba [E] 90 E3
Saldus [LV] 198 C5
Sale [I] 70 F6
Saleby [S] 166 E5
Salem [D] 58 H4
Salema [P] 94 A5
Salemi [I] 126 B2
Sälen [S] 172 E2
Salernes [F] 108 D4
Salerno [I] 120 F4
Salers [F] 68 B4
S. Alessio Siculo [I] 124 B8
Saletta [I] 70 C5
Salgótarján [H] 64 D4
Šalgovík [SK] 64 G2
Salhus [N] 170 B3
Sali [HR] 112 F5
Salice [F] 114 B4
Salice Terme [I] 70 F6
Salies-de-Béarn [F] 84 D2
Salies-du-Salat [F] 84 G4
Salignac-Eyvigues [F] 66 G4
Salihli [TR] 152 E4
Salihorsk [BY] 202 B6
Salinas [E] 78 H3
Salinas [E] 104 D2
Salinas de Pinilla [E] 96 H5
Salinas de Pisuerga [E] 82 D4
Saline di Volterra [I] 114 F1
Sälinkää [FIN] 176 H3
Salins-les-Bains [F] 58 A5
Salir [P] 94 C5
Salisbury [GB] 12 G4
Salka [SK] 64 C5
Salkoluokta [S] 192 F6
Salla [FIN] 194 E7
Sallanches [F] 70 B3
Sallent de Gállego [E] 84 D4
Sälleryd [S] 158 G1
Salles [F] 66 C4
Salles-Curan [F] 68 B6
Salles-s.-l'Hers [F] 106 A4
Sällinge [S] 166 H2
Sallmunds [S] 168 G6
Salme [EST] 198 C3
Salmenkylä [FIN] 186 E4
Salmenniemi [FIN] 186 F2
Salmerón [E] 90 A6
Salmi [FIN] 186 D3
Salmi [S] 194 B7
Salmivaara [FIN] 194 E7
Sal'miyarvi [RUS] 194 F3
Salmoral [E] 88 D4
Salo [FIN] 176 E4
Salò [I] 72 B6
Salobreña [E] 102 D5
Saločiai [LT] 198 E6
Saloinen [FIN] 196 C4
Salon [F] 44 B5
Salona [HR] 144 A2
Salon-de-Provence [F] 106 H4
Salonta [RO] 76 H3
Salorino [E] 86 F5
Salou [E] 92 C5
Salovci [SLO] 74 F3
Salsåker [S] 184 F3
Salsbruket [N] 190 C4
Salse di Nirano [I] 110 E3
Salses-le-Château [F] 106 C6
Salsnes [N] 190 C4
Salsomaggiore Terme [I] 110 D2
Salsta [S] 168 D1
Salt [E] 92 F3
Saltash [GB] 12 D5
Saltbæk [DK] 156 E2
Saltrød [N] 164 F5
Saltsjöbaden [S] 168 E3
Saltum [DK] 160 D3
Saltvik [FIN] 176 B5
Saltvik [S] 162 G3
Saluböle [S] 184 H1
Saluzzo [I] 108 F2
Salvacañete [E] 98 D2
Salvada [P] 94 D3
Salvagnac [F] 106 B2
Salvarola, Terme di- [I] 110 E3
Salvaterra de Magos [P] 86 C5
Salvaterra de Miño [E] 78 B5
Salvatierra [E] 96 E5
Salvatierra / Agurain [E] 82 H5
Salvatierra de los Barros [E] 94 G2
Salviac [F] 66 G4
Salzburg [A] 60 G5
Salzburg [D] 46 F2
Salzgitter-Bad [D] 32 G3
Salzgitter-Lebenstedt [D] 32 G3
Salzhausen [D] 18 F5
Salzkotten [D] 32 D4
Salzwedel [D] 18 H6
Salzweg [D] 60 H3
Sama de Langreo [E] 78 H4
Samadet [F] 66 C6
Samadet [F] 84 E2
Samailli [TR] 152 E5
Samandıra [TR] 150 F3
Samarína [GR] 128 D6
Samassi [I] 118 C6
Samatan [F] 84 G3
Sambiase [I] 124 D5
Sambir [UA] 52 G5
Sambuca di Sicília [I] 126 C3
Sambucheto [I] 116 B3
Sambuci [I] 116 B5
Sambucina, Abbazia della- [I] 124 D4
Samedan [CH] 72 A3
Samer [F] 28 D2
Sámi [GR] 132 C6
Samitier [E] 84 E6
Şamlı [TR] 150 D6
Sammakkola [FIN] 196 F6
Sammakkovaara [FIN] 188 E2
Sammatti [FIN] 186 D4
Sammi [FIN] 186 B6
Samnaun [CH] 72 B2
Samo [I] 124 C7
Samobor [HR] 74 E6
Samoëns [F] 70 C3
Samokłęski [PL] 38 E5
Samokov [BG] 146 G5
Samokov [MK] 128 D2
Samolva [RUS] 198 G3
Samoranovo [BG] 146 F6
Šamorín [SK] 62 G5
Samos [E] 78 E4
Sámos [GR] 152 C5
Samoš [SCG] 142 H1
Samos, Monasterio de- [E] 78 E4
Samostan Pleterje [SLO] 74 D6
Samothráki [GR] 130 F4
Samovodene [BG] 148 C3
Sampatikí [GR] 136 F3
Samper [E] 84 E6
Samper de Calanda [E] 90 F5
Sampéyre [I] 108 F2
Samtens [D] 20 D2
Samugheo [I] 118 C5
Saná [GR] 130 B5
San Adrián [E] 84 A5
San Agustín [E] 98 C3
San Agustín [E] 100 C6
San Andrés [E] 78 D1
San Anton Leitza [E] 84 B3
Sanary-sur-Mer [F] 108 C6
San Asensio [E] 82 G6
Sanat Eufemia [E] 82 D4
San Bartolomé [E] 100 E6
San Bartolomé de las Abiertas [E] 96 D1
San Bartolomé de la Torre [E] 94 E5
San Bartolomeo in Galdo [I] 120 F1
San Benedetto dei Marsi [I] 116 C5
San Benedetto del Tronto [I] 116 D2
San Benedetto in Alpe [I] 110 G5
San Benedetto Po [I] 110 E2
San Bernardino [CH] 70 G2
San Bernardino, Tunnel del- [EUR] 70 G2
San Biagio di Callalta [I] 72 F6
San Biágio Plátani [I] 126 D3
San Bonifácio [I] 72 C6
San Bruzio [I] 114 F3
San Calogero [I] 126 C3
San Cándido / Innichen [I] 72 E3
San Carlos del Valle [E] 96 G5
San Casciano dei Bagni [I] 114 G2
San Casciano in Val di Pesa [I] 110 F6
San Cataldo [I] 122 G4
San Cataldo [I] 126 E3
Sancergues [F] 56 D3
Sancerre [F] 56 D3
Sancey-le-Grand [F] 58 C5
Sanchidrián [E] 88 E4
San Cipirello [I] 126 C2
San Claudio al Chienti [I] 116 C1
San Clemente [E] 98 A4
San Clemente a Casuria [I] 116 D4
San Clemente al Vomano [I] 116 D3
Sancoins [F] 56 D4
San Cosme / Barreiros [E] 78 E2
San Cristóbal de la Laguna [E] 100 C5
San Cristóbal de la Vega [E] 88 E3
Sancti Petri [E] 100 F4
Sancti-Spíritus [E] 88 A3
Sancti Spiritus, Convent del- [E] 98 F4
Sand [N] 164 B1
Sand [N] 172 C4
Sånda [N] 164 E4
Sanda [N] 164 F4
Sanda [S] 174 G6
San Damiano d'Asti [I] 70 E6
Sandane [N] 180 C5
San Daniele del Friuli [I] 72 G4
San Daniele Po [I] 110 D2
Sandanski [BG] 130 B2
Sandared [S] 162 B2
Sandarne [S] 174 E2
Sandau [D] 34 C1
Sandaucourt [F] 44 E6
Sandbach [GB] 10 D5
Sande [D] 18 C4
Sande [N] 164 H2
Sande [N] 170 C1
Sandefjord [N] 164 H3
Sandeid [N] 164 B1
Sandem [N] 166 C2
San Demetrio Corone [I] 124 D4
Sanden [N] 164 F2
Sander [N] 172 C5
Sandhem [S] 162 C1
Sandias [E] 78 C5
Sandıklı [TR] 152 H3

San - Sav 285

Sand in Taufers / Campo Túres [I] 72 E2
Sandizell [D] 60 D3
Sandl [A] 62 C3
Sandla [EST] 198 C3
Sandnäset [S] 184 D4
Sandnes [N] 164 B3
Sandnes [N] 164 F3
Sandnes [N] 194 D2
Sandness [GB] 6 G3
Sandnessjøen [N] 190 D2
Sando [E] 80 G6
Sandö Bro [S] 184 F3
Sandomierz [PL] 52 D2
San Dónaci [I] 122 G4
San Donà di Piave [I] 72 F6
San Donato Milanese [I] 70 G5
Sandøreng [N] 190 E3
Sándorfalva [H] 76 E4
Sandown [GB] 12 H5
S. Andrea [I] 120 D2
S. Andrea Apostolo dello Iónio [I] 124 E6
S. Andrés del Rabanedo [E] 78 H5
Sandrigo [I] 72 D6
Šandrovac [HR] 74 G5
Sandsbraten [N] 170 G5
Sandsjö [S] 172 G1
Sandsjö [S] 190 G5
Sandsjön [S] 166 F1
Sandsjönas [S] 190 G4
Sandslån [S] 184 F3
Sandsletta [N] 192 D4
Sandsøy [N] 192 E3
Sandstad [N] 172 D4
Sandstad [N] 190 A6
Sandstedt [D] 18 D4
Sandur [FR] 160 A2
Sandvatn [N] 164 C4
Sandve [N] 164 A2
Sandvig [DK] 158 E4
Sandvik [S] 162 G4
Sandvika [N] 164 H1
Sandvika [N] 190 C6
Sandvika [N] 190 D2
Sandvikal [N] 164 C5
Sandviken [S] 174 E4
Sandviken [S] 190 D6
Sandvikvåg [N] 170 A5
Sandwich [GB] 14 G5
San Emiliano [E] 78 G4
San Esteban [E] 84 B3
San Esteban de Gormaz [E] 88 H3
San Fele [I] 120 G3
San Felice Circeo [I] 120 B2
San Felice in Balsignano [I] 122 D2
San Felice sul Panaro [I] 110 F2
San Ferdinando di Púglia [I] 120 H2
San Fernando [E] 100 F4
San Francisco [E] 82 B6
San Fratello [I] 126 F2
San Fruttuoso [I] 110 B3
Sånga [S] 184 F2
San Galgano, Abbazia di- [I] 114 F2
Sangarcía [E] 88 E4
San Gavino Monreale [I] 118 C6
Sangazi [TR] 150 F3
San Gemini [I] 116 A3
San Gemini Fonte [I] 116 A3
Sangerhausen [D] 34 B5
San Germano [I] 70 E5
San Gimignano [I] 110 E6
San Ginesio [I] 116 C2
Sanginkylä [FIN] 196 E4
San Giorgio di Livenza [I] 72 F6
San Giórgio di Nogaro [I] 72 G5
San Giorgio Iónico [I] 122 F4
San Giovanni, Grotta- [I] 122 F4
San Giovanni, Grotta di- [I] 118 B6
San Giovanni al Mavone [I] 116 C4
San Giovanni A Piro [I] 120 G5
San Giovanni di Sinis [I] 118 B5
San Giovanni in Croce [I] 110 D2
San Giovanni in Fiore [I] 124 E4
San Giovanni in Persiceto [I] 110 F3
San Giovanni in Venere [I] 116 E4
San Giovanni Lupatoto [I] 72 C6
San Giovanni Rotondo [I] 116 G6
San Giovanni Suergiu [I] 118 B7
San Giovanni Valdarno [I] 110 F6
San Giovenale [I] 114 H4
Sangis [S] 196 C2
Sangis [S] 196 C2
San Giuliano Terme [I] 110 D5
San Giuseppe Jato [I] 126 C2
San Giustino [I] 110 G6
San Giusto [I] 116 B2
Sangla [EST] 198 F3
Sangonera la Verde [E] 104 C3
Sangüesa / Zangoza [E] 84 C5
Sanguinet [F] 66 B4
Sáni [GR] 130 B6
San Ignacio de Loiola [E] 82 H4
Sanitz [D] 20 C3
San Javier [E] 104 D4
San José [E] 102 G6
San José / Sant Josep [E] 104 C5
San José del Valle [E] 100 G4
San Juan de Alicante / Sant Joan d'Alacant [E] 104 E2
San Juan del Olmo [E] 88 D4
San Juan de los Terreros [E] 104 B4
San Juan del Puerto [E] 94 E6
San Juan de Muskiz [E] 82 G3
San Juan De Ortega [E] 82 F6
Sankovo [RUS] 202 E1
Sankt Magdalena / Santa Maddalena Vallalta [I] 72 E2
Sankt-Michaelisdonn [D] 18 E3
Sankt-Peterbürg [RUS] 178 H4
Sankt-Peterburg [RUS] 202 B1
Sankt Valentin auf der Haide / San Valentino alla Muta [I] 72 B2
San Lazzaro di Savena [I] 110 F3
San Leo [I] 110 H5
San Leonardo [I] 120 H1
San Leonardo de Yagüe [E] 90 A2
San Leonardo in Passiria / Sankt Leonhard in P. [I] 72 D2
San Lorenzo [I] 124 C8
San Lorenzo de Calatrava [E] 96 E5
San Lorenzo de El Escorial [E] 88 F5
San Lorenzo de la Parrilla [E] 98 B2
San Lorenzo in Campo [I] 112 B6
San Lorenzo Nuovo [I] 114 G3
San Luca [I] 124 C7
Sanlúcar de Barrameda [E] 100 F3
Sanlúcar la Mayor [E] 94 G6
San Lúcido [I] 124 D4
Sanluri [I] 118 C6
San Marcello Pistoiese [I] 110 E4
San Marco Argentano [I] 124 D4
San Marco dei Cavoti [I] 120 F2
San Marco in Lamis [I] 116 G6
San Marino [RSM] 110 H5
Sânmartin [RO] 76 H2
San Martín de la Vega [E] 88 F6
San Martín del Pedroso [E] 80 G4
San Martín de Pusa [E] 96 E1
San Martín de Unx [E] 84 B5
San Martín de Valdeiglesias [E] 88 E5
San Martino Buon Albergo [I] 72 C6
San Martino della Battaglia [I] 72 C6
San Martino delle Scale [I] 126 C2
San Martino di Castrozza [I] 72 E4
San Martino di Lupari [I] 72 E6
San Mateo de Gállego [E] 98 G2
San Matteo de Gállego [E] 90 E3
San Mauro Castelverde [I] 126 E2
San Michele all'Ádige [I] 72 C4
San Michele di Plaianu [I] 118 C3
San Michele Salentino [I] 122 F4
San Miguel de Bernúy [E] 88 G3
San Miguel de las Dueñas [E] 78 F5
San Miguel de Salinas [E] 104 D3
San Millan [E] 82 F5
San Millán de la Cogolla [E] 82 G6
San Miniato [I] 110 E6
Sänna [EST] 198 F3
Sänna [S] 166 G4
S. Anna [S] 168 C6
Sånna [S] 174 E1
S.Anna di Alfaedo [I] 72 C5
Sannazzaro de' Burgondi [I] 70 F6
Sannenmöser [CH] 70 D1
Sannicandro di Bari [I] 122 D3
Sannicandro Gargánico [I] 116 G6
San Nicolás de Tolentino [E] 100 C6
Sânnicolau Mare [RO] 76 F5
San Nicolò [I] 110 G3
San Nicolò di Trullas [I] 118 C4
San Nicolò Gerrei [I] 118 D6
Sannidal [N] 164 F3
Sanniki [PL] 36 H3
Sanok [PL] 52 E5
San Pancrazio Salentino [I] 122 F4
San Paolo di Civitate [I] 116 F6
San Paolo di Peltuino [I] 116 C4
San Pedro [E] 82 C2
San Pedro [E] 98 A5
San Pedro de Alcántara [E] 102 A5
San Pedro De Arlanza [E] 88 H1
San Pedro De La Nave [E] 80 H4
San Pedro del Arroyo [E] 88 D4
San Pedro del Pinatar [E] 104 D4
San Pelayo [E] 88 G1
San Pellegrino in Alpe [I] 110 D4
San Pellegrino Terme [I] 70 H4
San Piero a Sieve [I] 110 F5
San Pietro, Badia di- [I] 112 D6
San Pietro di Simbranos [I] 118 C3
San Pietro di Sorres [I] 118 C3
San Pietro in Casale [I] 110 F3
San Pietro in Valle [I] 116 B3
San Pietro Vernotico [I] 122 G4
San Polo d'Enza [I] 110 D3
San Priamo [I] 118 D7
San Prospero [I] 110 F2
Sanquhar [GB] 8 D4
San Quírico d'Orcia [I] 114 G2
San Rafael [E] 88 F4
San Rafael del Río [E] 92 A6
San Remo [I] 108 F4
San Roman de Cameros [E] 90 B1
San Roque [E] 78 C2
San Roque [E] 100 G5
San Roque de Riomera [E] 82 F3
San Rufo [I] 120 G4
San Sadurniño [E] 78 D1
San Salvo [I] 116 E5
San Sebastián de la Gomera [E] 100 B5
San Sebastiano Curone [I] 110 B2
Sansepolcro [I] 110 G6
San Servando, Castillo de- [E] 96 F2
San Severino Marche [I] 116 B2
San Severo [I] 116 F6
Sanski Most [BIH] 142 B3
San Sosti [I] 124 D3
Santa, Cova- [E] 104 C5
Santa Amalia [E] 96 A2
Santa Ana de Cambas [P] 94 D4
Santa Bárbara [E] 94 E4
Santa Bárbara [P] 100 D3
Santacara [E] 84 B5
Santa Caterina di Pittinuri [I] 118 B4
Santa Caterina Valfurva [I] 72 B3
Santa Caterina Villarmosa [I] 126 E3
Santa Cesarea Terme [I] 122 H5
Santa Clara-a-Velha [P] 94 B4
Santa Coloma [AND] 84 H6
Santa Coloma de Farners [E] 92 F3
Santa Coloma de Queralt [E] 92 C4
Santa Colomba de Somoza [E] 78 F5
Santa Comba [E] 78 B2
Santa Comba Dão [P] 80 C6
Santa Comba de Rossas [P] 80 F4
Santa Cristina / St Christina [I] 72 D3
Santa Cristina d'Aro [E] 92 G3
Santa Croce Camerina [I] 126 F5
Santa Croce di Magliano [I] 116 F6
Santa Croce d. Sannio [I] 120 E1
Santa Croce sull'Arno [I] 110 E5
Santa Cruz [P] 100 A3
Santa Cruz da Graciosa [P] 100 D2
Santa Cruz das Flores [P] 100 C4
Santa Cruz de Campezo / Santi Kurutze Kanpezu [E] 82 H6
Santa Cruz de la Palma [E] 100 B4
Santa Cruz de la Serós [E] 84 D5
Santa Cruz de la Sierra [E] 96 B2
Santa Cruz de la Zarza [E] 96 G2
Santa Cruz del Retamar [E] 88 E6
Santa Cruz de Moya [E] 98 D3
Santa Cruz de Mudela [E] 96 F5
Santa Cruz de Tenerife [E] 100 C5
Santadi [I] 118 C7
Santa Elena [E] 96 F6
Santaella [E] 102 B2
Santa Eufemia [E] 96 C4
Santa Eulalia [E] 78 H3
Santa Eulalia [E] 98 D1
Santa Eulália [P] 86 F6
Santa Eulalia del Río / Santa Eulària des Riu [E] 104 C5
Santa Eulalia de Oscos [E] 78 F3
Santa Eulària des Riu / Santa Eulalia del Río [E] 104 C5
Santa Fé [E] 102 E4
Sant'Àgata de' Goti [I] 120 E2
Sant'Ágata di Militello [I] 126 F2
Sant'Agata di Púglia [I] 120 G2
Santa Gertrude / Sankt Gertraud [I] 72 C3
Sant'Agostino [I] 110 F3
Sant Agusti de Lluçanes [E] 92 E2
Santa Iria [P] 94 E3
Santa Justa [P] 86 D6
Sant'Alberto di Butrio [I] 110 B2
Santa Luce [I] 110 D6
Santa Lucía [E] 100 C6
Santa Lucia del Mela [I] 124 B7
Santa Luzia [P] 78 A6
Santa Luzia [P] 94 C3
Santa Maddalena Vallalta / Sankt Magdalena [I] 72 E2
Santa Magdalena de Polpis [E] 98 G2
Santa Margalida [E] 104 E5
Santa Margarida de Montbui [E] 92 D4
Santa Margarida do Sado [P] 94 C2
Santa Margherita [I] 118 C7
Santa Margherita di Bélice [I] 126 C3
Santa Margherita Lígure [I] 110 B3
Santa María [E] 104 E5
Santa Maria a Pié di Chienti [I] 116 C1
Santa Maria Arabona [I] 116 D4
Santa Maria Cápua Vetere [I] 120 E2
Santa Maria da Feira [P] 80 B4
Santa Maria d'Anglona [I] 122 D5
Santa María de Cayón [E] 82 F3
Santa María de Huerta [E] 90 B4
Santa Maria dei Lattani [I] 120 D2
Santa María de las Hoyas [E] 90 A2
Santa María del Campo [E] 82 E6
Santa María del Páramo [E] 78 G6
Santa María de Nieva [E] 102 H4
Santa Maria di Bressanoro [I] 70 H5
Santa Maria di Corte, Abbazia di- [I] 118 C4
Santa Maria di Portonovo [I] 112 D6
Santa Maria di Propezzano [I] 116 D3
Santa Maria di Rambona [I] 116 C2
Santa Maria di Ronzano [I] 116 C4
Santa Maria di Siponto [I] 120 H1
Santa Maria in Valle Porclaneta [I] 116 C5
Santa María la Real de Nieva [E] 88 E3
Santa Maria Maggiore [I] 70 F3
Santa María Mayor [P] 80 C4
Santa Maria Navarrese [I] 118 E5
Santa Maria Nuova [I] 116 C1
Santa Marinella [I] 114 G5
Santa Marta [E] 94 G2
Santa Marta [E] 98 B4
Santa Marta de Tormes [E] 88 C3
Santana [P] 100 A3
Santana da Serra [P] 94 C4
Santana do Mato [P] 86 C5
Santander [E] 82 F3
Sant'Andrea [I] 122 H5
Sant'Andrea Bagni [I] 110 D2
Sant' Andrea di Conza [I] 120 G3
Sant' Andrea Frius [I] 118 D6
Sant' Ángelo in Vado [I] 110 H6
Sant'Angelo Lodigiano [I] 70 G5
Santa Ninfa [I] 126 B2
Sant'Anna, Santuario di- [I] 108 E3
Sant'Anna Arresi [I] 118 B7
Sant'Antimo, Abbazia di- [I] 114 G2
Sant' Antine, Nuraghe- [I] 118 C4
Sant' Antíoco [I] 118 B7
Sant Antoni de Portmany [E] 104 C5
Sant'António di Gallura [I] 118 D2
Santanyí [E] 104 E6
Santa Olalla [E] 88 E6
Santa Olalla del Cala [E] 94 G4
Santa Pola [E] 104 D3
Sant'Apollinare in Classe [I] 110 H4
Santa Ponça [E] 104 D5
Sant'Arcangelo [I] 122 C5
Santarcángelo di Romagna [I] 110 H5
Santarém [P] 86 C4
Santa Sabina, Nuraghe- [I] 118 C4
Santa Severa [F] 114 C2
Santa Severa [I] 114 G5
Santas Martas [E] 78 H6
Santa Sofia [I] 110 G5
Santa Susanna [E] 92 F4
Santa Teresa di Riva [I] 124 B8
Santa Teresa Gallura [I] 118 D2
Santa Uxía de Ribeira [E] 78 B3
Santa Vitória [P] 94 D3
Sant Boi de Llobregat [E] 92 D4
Sant Carles de la Ràpita [E] 92 A6
Sant Celoni [E] 92 F4
Sant Cugat Sesgarrigues [E] 92 D4
Sant. de la Encarnación [E] 98 B6
Sant. de Ródanas [E] 90 D4
Santed [E] 90 D5
Sant'Elia a Pianisti [I] 120 F1
Sant'Elia Fiumerapido [I] 120 D1
San Telmo [E] 94 F4
Santena [I] 70 D6
San Teodoro [I] 118 E3
Santéramo in Colle [I] 122 D3
Santes Creus [E] 92 C4
Sant' Eufémia Lamézia [I] 124 D5
Sant'Eutizio, Abbazia di- [I] 116 B3
Sant Feliu de Codines [E] 92 E4
Sant Feliu de Guíxols [E] 92 G4
Sant Feliu de Llobregat [E] 92 E4
Sant Ferran de Ses Roquetes [E] 104 C6
Sant Francesc de Formentera [E] 104 C6
Sant Grau [E] 92 F4
Santhià [I] 70 E5
Sant Hilari Sacalm [E] 92 F3
Sant Hipòlit de Voltregà [E] 92 E3
Santiago [P] 80 F5
Santiago, Cuevas de- [E] 94 H4
Santiago de Alcántara [E] 86 F4
Santiago de Calatrava [E] 102 D2
Santiago de Compostela [E] 78 C3
Santiago de la Espada [E] 102 G2
Santiago de la Ribera [E] 104 D4
Santiago del Campo [E] 86 H5
Santiago do Cacém [P] 94 B2
Santiago do Escoural [P] 94 D1
Santibáñez [E] 82 D4
Santibáñez de la Sierra [E] 88 B4
Santibáñez de Vidriales [E] 80 H3
Santibáñez Zarzaguda [E] 82 E5
Santi Kurutze Kanpezu / Santa Cruz de Campezo [E] 82 H6
Santillana del Mar [E] 82 E3
Santimamiñe [E] 82 H4
Santiponce [E] 94 G6
Santissima Trinitá di Saccargia [I] 118 C3
Santisteban del Puerto [E] 102 F1
Sant Joan d'Alacant / San Juan de Alicante [E] 104 E2
Sant Joan de les Abadesses [E] 92 E2
Sant Joan de Llabritja [E] 104 C5
Sant Joan de Vilatorrada [E] 92 D3
Sant Josep / San José [E] 104 C5
Sant Julià de Lória [AND] 84 H6
Sant Llorenç de Morunys [E] 92 D2
Sant Lluís [E] 104 H5
Sant Martí Sarroca [E] 92 D4
Sant Mateu [E] 98 G2
Sant Miquel de Balansat [E] 104 C5
Santo Aleixo [P] 86 E6
Santo André [P] 94 B2
Santo Domingo [E] 96 C6
Santo Domingo de la Calzada [E] 82 G6
Santo Domingo de Silos [E] 88 H1
Santo Estevão [P] 86 G2
Santo Estevo [E] 78 D5
Santok [PL] 34 H2
S. Antolín [E] 82 D2
Santomera [E] 104 C3
Santoméri [GR] 136 C1
Santoña [E] 82 F3
S. Antonio di Santadi [I] 118 B5
Santo Stefano Belbo [I] 108 H2
Santo Stéfano di Cadore [I] 72 F3
Santo Stefano di Camastra [I] 126 F2
Santo Stéfano Quisquina [I] 126 D3
Santo Stino di Livenza [I] 72 F5
Santo Tirso [P] 80 C3
Santo Tomé [E] 102 F2
Santo Tomé del Puerto [E] 88 G3
Santovenia [E] 82 A6
Santovenia de Pisuerga [E] 88 E1
Sant Pau de Seguries [E] 92 F2
Sant Pere de Rodes [E] 92 G2
Sant Pere Pescador [E] 92 G3
Sant Pol de Mar [E] 92 F4
Sant Quirze de Besora [E] 92 E2
Sant Quirze De Colera [E] 92 G2
Sant Rafel [E] 104 C5
Sant Sadurní d'Anoia [E] 92 D4
Sant Salvador [E] 104 F5
Sant Tomàs [E] 104 G4
Santuari de Núria [E] 92 E2
Santuario De Estíbaliz [E] 82 H5
Santuario De Torreciudad [E] 90 H3
Santu Lussúrgiu [I] 118 C4
Santurce / Santurtzi [E] 82 G3
Santurtzi / Santurce [E] 82 G3
Sant Vicenç de Castellet [E] 92 D3
Sant Vicent del Raspeig / San Vicente del Raspeig [E] 104 E2
Sant Vicent de sa Cala [E] 104 C5
San Urbez, Santuario de- [E] 84 D6
San Valentino alla Muta / Sankt Valentin auf der Haide [I] 72 B2
San Venanzo [I] 114 H3
San Vicente de Alcántara [E] 86 F5
San Vicente de la Barquera [E] 82 E3
San Vicente del Raspeig / Sant Vicent del Raspeig [E] 104 E2
San Vincenzo [I] 114 E2
San Vincenzo, Abbazia di- [I] 116 D6
San Vito [I] 118 D6
San Vito al Tagliamento [I] 72 F5
San Vito Chietino [I] 116 E4
San Vito dei Normanni [I] 122 F4
San Vito di Cadore [I] 72 E3
San Vito lo Capo [I] 126 B1
San Vito Romano [I] 116 B5
San Vittore delle Chiuse [I] 116 B1
Sanxay [F] 54 E4
Sanxenxo [E] 78 B4
Sanza [I] 120 G5
Sanzay [F] 54 D2
São Barnabé [P] 94 C4
São Bartolomeu de Messines [P] 94 C5
São Brás de Alportel [P] 94 C5
São Cristóvão [P] 94 D1
São Domingos [P] 94 C3
São Francisco da Serra [P] 94 C2
São Gregório [P] 78 C5
São Jacinto [P] 80 B5
São João [P] 100 C3
São João da Madeira [P] 80 B4
São João da Pesqueira [P] 80 E5
São João da Serra [P] 80 C5
São João dos Caldeireiros [P] 94 D4
São Luis [P] 94 B3
São Manços [P] 94 E2
São Marcos [P] 80 B6
São Marcos da Ataboeira [P] 94 D4
São Marcos da Serra [P] 94 C4
São Martinho [P] 86 E2
São Martinho das Amoreiras [P] 94 C4
São Martinho do Porto [P] 86 B3
São Mateus [P] 100 C3
São Mateus da Calheta [P] 100 D3
São Matias [P] 94 D3
São Miguel de Acha [P] 86 F3
São Miguel de Machede [P] 94 E1
São Miguel do Pinheiro [P] 94 D4
São Pedro [P] 86 E2
São Pedro da Cadeira [P] 86 B4
São Pedro de Balsemão [P] 80 D4
São Pedro de Muel [P] 86 C2
São Pedro de Solis [P] 94 D4
São Pedro do Sul [P] 80 C5
Saorge [F] 108 F4
São Romão [P] 86 C6
São Romão [P] 94 C2
São Sebastião [P] 100 D3
São Teotónio [P] 94 B4
Saou [F] 68 F6
São Vicente [P] 100 A3
São Vicente da Beira [P] 86 F3
Sapakpınar [TR] 150 G3
Sapanca [TR] 150 G3
Sapareva Banya [BG] 146 F5
Sapernoye [RUS] 178 G2
Sápes [GR] 130 G3
Şaphane [TR] 152 F2
Säpilä [FIN] 176 D2
Šapjane [HR] 112 E1
sa Pobla [E] 104 E4
Sappada [I] 72 F3
Sappee [FIN] 176 G2
Sappee [FIN] 176 H1
Sappemeer [NL] 16 G2
Sappen [N] 192 G2
Sappisaasi [S] 192 H5
Sappu [FIN] 188 E3
Sapri [I] 120 G5
Saqués [E] 84 D5
Saraby [N] 194 B2
Sarafovo [BG] 148 F4
Säräisniemi [FIN] 196 E4
Sarajevo [BIH] 144 D1
Sarakíniko [GR] 134 B4
Sarakinoí [GR] 128 F4
Saramon [F] 84 G3
Sáránd [H] 76 H1
Saranda [AL] 132 B1
Saransko [BG] 148 E5
Sarantsi [BG] 146 G4
Sarata [UA] 204 F4
Saray [TR] 150 D2
Saraycık [TR] 152 E3
Sarayköy [TR] 152 F5
Šarbanovac [SCG] 146 D2
Sarbia [PL] 36 C1
Sarbinowo [PL] 20 H3
Sarbinowo [PL] 34 G2
Sárbogárd [H] 76 B3
Sarby Doine [PL] 50 D2
Sarceda [E] 82 E3
Sárdara [I] 118 C6
Sardara, Terme di- [I] 118 C6
Sardes [TR] 152 E4
Sardínia [GR] 132 E4
S'Arenal [E] 104 E5
S'Arenal d'en Castell [E] 104 H4
Šarengrad [HR] 142 E1
Sarentino / Sarnthein [I] 72 D3
Sărenz [BG] 148 F1
Sarga, Cova de la- [E] 104 E1
Sargans [CH] 58 H6
Sári [H] 76 C2
Sarıbeyler [TR] 152 D2
Sarıcakaya [TR] 150 H4
Sari d'Orcino [F] 114 A4
Sarıgöl [TR] 152 F4
Sarıkaya [TR] 152 E4
Sarıköy [TR] 150 C5
Sarılar [TR] 150 C3
Sariñena [E] 90 G4
Šarišský Hrad [SK] 64 F2
Sarısu [TR] 150 G3
Sariyer [TR] 150 E2
Sarkad [H] 76 G3
Sarkadkeresztúr [H] 76 G3
Sárkeresztúr [H] 76 B2
Särkijärvi [FIN] 196 E4
Särkilahti [FIN] 186 G6
Särkilahti [FIN] 188 F6
Särkisalmi [FIN] 188 F5
Särkisalo [FIN] 186 G3
Särkisalo / Finby [FIN] 176 E5
Särkkä [FIN] 196 F6
Šarkovo [BG] 150 B1
Şarköy [TR] 150 C4
Sarlat-la-Canéda [F] 66 G4
Sarmizegetuza [RO] 204 C5
Särna [S] 172 E1
Sarnaki [PL] 38 E2
Sarnano [I] 116 C2
Sarnate [LV] 198 B5
Sarnen [CH] 58 F6
Sarnes [E] 82 C2
Sárnico [I] 72 A5
Sărnino [BG] 148 G1
Sarno [I] 120 E3
Sarnowa [PL] 36 C5
Sarnówek [PL] 38 C6
Sarny [UA] 202 B7
Särö [S] 160 G3
Saronída [GR] 136 H1
Saronno [I] 70 G4
Sárospatak [H] 64 G4
Šarovce [SK] 64 B5
Sarpsborg [N] 166 B3
Sarracín [E] 82 E6
Sarral [E] 92 C4
Sarralbe [F] 44 G4
Sarrebourg [F] 44 G5
Sarreguemines [F] 44 G4
Sárrétudvari [H] 76 G1
Sarre-Union [F] 44 G5
Sarria [E] 78 E4
Sarrión [E] 98 E2
Sarroch [I] 118 C7
Sarron [F] 84 E2
Sarsıla İskele [TR] 154 E2
Sársina [I] 110 G5
Sarstedt [D] 32 G2
Sarteano [I] 114 G2
Sartène [F] 114 B5
Sárti [GR] 130 D6
Sartilly [F] 26 D4
Sartmustafa [TR] 152 E4
Saruhanli [TR] 152 D3
Sárvár [H] 74 G2
Sarvela [FIN] 186 C5
Sarvijoki [FIN] 186 B3
Sarvikumpu [FIN] 188 E3
Sarvinki [FIN] 188 G2
Sarvisvaara [S] 194 A8
Särvsjön [S] 182 F4
Sarzana [I] 110 C4
Sarzeau [F] 40 D5
Sarzedas [P] 86 E3
Sasa [MK] 146 E6
Sa Savina [E] 104 C6
Sásd [H] 76 A4
Šášov [SK] 64 C3
Sassari [I] 118 C3
Sassello [I] 108 H3
Sassenage [F] 68 H4
Sassenberg [D] 32 D3
Sassenheim [NL] 16 D4
Sassnitz [D] 20 D2
Sassocorvaro [I] 110 H5
Sassoferrato [I] 116 B1
Sassofortino [I] 114 F2
Sasso Marconi [I] 110 F4
Sassonero [I] 110 F4
Sassuolo [I] 110 E3
Šaštin- Stráže [SK] 62 G3
Sastmola / Merikarvia [FIN] 186 B6
Såtåhaugvoll [N] 182 C3
Sataniv [UA] 202 B8
Sátão [P] 80 D5
Sätenäs [S] 166 D5
Säter [S] 166 F5
Säter [S] 174 C5
Sätila [S] 160 H2
Satırlar [TR] 152 D3
Sätofta [S] 158 C2
Sátoraljaújhely [H] 64 G3
Satovcha [BG] 130 C1
Satow [D] 20 B3
Satra brunn [S] 168 B1
Sátres [GR] 130 E2
Satrup [D] 18 F1
Sattajärvi [S] 194 B7
Sattanen [FIN] 194 D6
Satter [S] 192 H6
Satu Mare [RO] 204 C3
Saturn [RO] 148 G1
Saturnia [I] 114 G3
Saturnia, Terme di- [I] 114 G3
Saucats [F] 66 C4
Sauda [N] 164 C1
Saudasjøen [N] 164 C1
Saudron [F] 44 D5
Saue [EST] 198 D1
Sauerbrunn [A] 74 C2
Sauerlach [D] 60 E5
Saugos [LT] 200 D4
Saugues [F] 68 D4
Saujon [F] 54 C6
Saukkola [FIN] 176 G4
Saukonkylä [FIN] 186 D2
Sauðárkrókur [IS] 192 B2
Sauland [N] 164 F1
Saulgau [D] 58 H3
Saulieu [F] 56 F3
Saulkrasti [LV] 198 D4
Sault [F] 108 B3
Saulx [F] 58 B3
Saulxures [F] 58 C3
Saumur [F] 54 E2
Saunajärvi [FIN] 196 G5
Saunakylä [FIN] 186 C5
Saunalahti [FIN] 188 C3
Saunavaara [FIN] 194 E7
Saus [N] 190 D3
Sausheim [F] 58 D3
Sauvagnat [F] 68 B2
Sauve [F] 106 F3
Sauveterre-de-Béarn [F] 84 D2
Sauveterre-de-Guyenne [F] 66 D4
Sauviant-sur-Vige [F] 54 G6
Sauvo / Sagu [FIN] 176 E5
Sauxillanges [F] 68 D3
Sauze d'Oulx [I] 70 C5
Sauzet [F] 66 F5
Sauzé-Vaussais [F] 54 E5
Sauzon [F] 40 C5
Sava [BG] 148 F3
Sava [I] 122 F4
Sävar [S] 196 A6
Sävast [S] 196 B3
Savaştepe [TR] 152 D2
Savci [SLO] 74 E4
Save [S] 160 G2
Savelletri [I] 122 F3
Savelli [I] 124 E4
Savenaho [FIN] 186 G5
Savenay [F] 40 G6
Saverdun [F] 84 H4
Saverne [F] 44 G5
Savero [FIN] 178 C3
Savi [FIN] 176 E1
Säviä [FIN] 186 H1
Savigliano [I] 108 F2
Savignac-les-Eglises [F] 66 F3
Savignano Irpino [I] 120 F2
Savignano sul Rubicone [I] 110 H5
Savigny-sur-Braye [F] 42 C5
Savijärvi [FIN] 196 G5
Savikoski [FIN] 176 F2
Savikylä [FIN] 196 F6
Savines-le-Lac [F] 108 D2
Savine Vode [SCG] 146 B5
Saviniemi [FIN] 176 F3
Savino Selo [SCG] 142 F1
Saviore dell'Adamello [I] 72 B4
Savitaipale [FIN] 178 D2

St-Leger [F] 56 F4
St.-Léon, Chapelle- [F] 44 G5
St-Léonard-de-Noblat [F] 66 H1
St Leonhard [A] 62 D4
St-Leu-d'Esserent [F] 42 F2
St-Lizier [F] 84 G4
St-Lô [F] 26 E3
St Lorenzen [A] 72 F3
St-Louis [F] 58 E4
St-Loup-sur-Semouse [F] 58 C3
St-Luc [CH] 70 D2
St-Lunaire [F] 26 C4
St-Lys [F] 84 H3
St-Macaire [F] 66 D4
St-Maclou [F] 26 G3
St-Maixent-l'Ecole [F] 54 D4
St.Malm [S] 168 B4
St-Malo [F] 26 C4
St-Mamest [F] 66 F3
St. Marcel [F] 70 B4
St-Marcellin [F] 68 G4
St. Marcellin-en-Forez [F] 68 E3
St. Marein [A] 74 E2
St Margaret's Hope [GB] 6 G2
St Märgen [D] 58 F3
St. Maria [D] 46 E6
St. Maria zu den Engeln [CH] 58 G5
St-Mars-la-Jaille [F] 40 G6
St. Martin [F] 40 E5
St-Martin-d'Auxigny [F] 56 C3
St-Martin-de-Londres [F] 106 E3
St. Martin-d'Entraunes [F] 108 E3
St-Martin-de-Ré [F] 54 B4
St.-Martin-du-Canigou [F] 92 F1
St-Martin-Vésubie [F] 108 F3
St-Martory [F] 84 G4
St-Mathieu [F] 66 F1
St.-Mathieu, Pointe de- [F] 40 A2
St-Mathieu-de-Tréviers [F] 106 E3
St-Maurice [CH] 70 C2
St.Maurice la Sotterraine [F] 54 G5
St-Maurice-Navacelles [F] 106 E3
St Maurice-sur-Moselle [F] 58 C3
St Mawes [GB] 12 C5
St-Maximin-la-Ste-Baume [F] 108 C5
St-Méen [F] 26 B5
St. Meinrad [CH] 58 G5
St. Mellösa [S] 166 H3
St Michael [A] 74 C1
St Michael [A] 74 F2
St Michael i. Lungau [A] 72 H2
St Michel / Mikkeli [FIN] 188 C6
St.-Michel-de Cuxa [F] 92 F1
St-Michel-de-Maurienne [F] 70 B5
St.Michel de Rieufret [F] 66 C4
St-Michel-en-Grève [F] 40 D1
St-Michel-en-l'Herm [F] 54 C4
St-Michel-Mont-Mercure [F] 54 C3
St-Mihiel [F] 44 D4
St. Miquel del Fai [E] 92 E3
St-Morand [F] 58 D4
St Moritz [CH] 70 H2
St-Nazaire [F] 40 E6
St.nazaire Les Eymes [F] 68 H4
St-Nectaire [F] 68 C2
St Neots [GB] 14 E2
St.-Nicodème [F] 26 A5
St-Nicolas [F] 40 E5
St Nicolas-de-Port [F] 44 E5
St-Nicolas-du-Pélem [F] 26 A4
St-Niklaas [B] 28 H2
St Niklaus [CH] 70 E2
St Nikolai [A] 74 B1
Støa [N] 172 E2
Stobeč [HR] 144 A2
Stobi [MK] 128 F2
Stoby [S] 158 D1
Stocka [S] 184 E6
Stockach [D] 58 G4
Stockaryd [S] 162 D3
Stockbridge [GB] 12 H4
Stöcke [S] 196 A6
Stockelsdorf [D] 18 G3
Stockerau [A] 62 F4
Stockheim [D] 46 G3
Stockholm [S] 168 D3
Stockport [GB] 10 E4
Stocksbo [S] 174 C1
Stockton on Tees [GB] 10 F2
Stoczek Klasztorny [PL] 22 H3
Stoczek Łukowski [PL] 38 D3
Stod [CZ] 48 D5
Stod [N] 190 C5
Stöde [S] 184 D4
Stødi [N] 190 E1
St Oedenrode [NL] 30 E2
Stojan Mikhaylovski [BG] 148 E2
Stojmirovo [MK] 128 H1
Stoke-on-Trent [GB] 10 E5
Stokke [N] 164 H3
Stokkemarke [DK] 156 F5
Stokkland [N] 164 F2
Stokkvågen [N] 190 D2
Stokmarknes [N] 192 D4
Štoky [CZ] 48 H5
Stola [S] 166 E5
Stolac [BIH] 144 C3
Stolberg [D] 30 F4
Stolbovo [RUS] 198 G5
Stolbzy [BY] 202 B5
Stolin [BY] 202 B7
Stollberg [D] 48 C2
Stollberg [D] 48 D2
Stöllet [S] 172 E5
Stolno [PL] 22 E5
St Olof [S] 158 D3
Stolpe [D] 20 E6
Stolpe [D] 34 E2
Stolpen [D] 34 F6
Stołpie [PL] 38 F5
Stolzenau [D] 32 E1
St-Omer [F] 28 E2
Stómio [GR] 132 G1
Stömne [S] 166 E2
Ston [HR] 144 C3
Stonařov [CZ] 48 H6
Stone [GB] 10 E5
Stonehaven [GB] 8 G1
Stongfjorden [N] 180 B6
Stonglandseidet [N] 192 E3
Stønjumfoss [N] 170 E2
Stopanja [SCG] 146 C3
Stopnica [PL] 52 C2
Stora [PL] 36 H6
Storå [S] 166 H2
Storå / Isojoki [FIN] 186 B5
Stora Bläsjön [S] 190 E4
Storås [N] 180 H2
Stora Sjöfallet [S] 192 F5
Storbäck [S] 190 F4
Storborgaren [S] 190 G6
Storby [FIN] 174 H5
Stord [N] 170 B5
Stordal [N] 180 D4
Stordalen [S] 192 F4
Storebro [S] 162 F2
Storebru [N] 180 B6
Store Darum [DK] 156 B3
Storehaug [N] 170 C1
Store Heddinge [DK] 156 G3
Storekorsnes [N] 194 B2
Storelv [N] 194 A2
Storelvavoll [N] 182 D3
Store Merløse [DK] 156 F3
Store Molvik [N] 194 D1
Store Molvik [N] 194 E1
Støren [N] 182 B2
Storestandal [N] 180 D4
Storestølen [N] 170 E3
Stor-Evdal [N] 172 C1
Storfall [S] 190 H6
Storfjellseter [N] 182 B6
Storfjord [N] 192 G3
Storfors [S] 166 G2
Storforshei [N] 190 E2
Storfossen [N] 192 F4
Storfossen [N] 194 C4
Storhallaren [N] 190 A6
Storhögen [S] 182 H2
Storholmsjö [S] 190 E6
Storjola [S] 190 E4
Storjord [N] 190 E1
Storjord [N] 190 E1
Storjorda [N] 190 E1
Storkow [D] 34 F3
Storkyro / Isokyrö [FIN] 186 B2
Storlägda [N] 182 C5
Storli [N] 180 G3
Storlien [S] 182 D2
Stormi [FIN] 176 E2
Störnaset [S] 190 F5
Stornes [N] 192 G2
Stornorrfors [S] 190 H6
Stornoway / Steornabhagh [GB] 6 C2
Storo [I] 72 B5
Storoddan [N] 180 G1
Storsätern [S] 182 D5
Storsävarträsko [S] 190 H5
Storseterfossen [N] 180 E4
Storsjö [S] 182 E3
Storslett [N] 192 G2
Storstein [N] 192 G1
Storsteinnes [N] 192 F3
Storsund [S] 196 A3
Stortinden [N] 194 B2
Storuman [S] 190 F4
Storvallen [S] 182 D2
Storvik [S] 174 D4
Storvika [N] 190 B5
Storvollen [N] 180 H4
Storvorde [DK] 160 E4
Storvreta [S] 168 D1
Stössen [D] 34 B6
St Oswald [A] 62 C3
St. Oswald [A] 74 D3
St.-Oswald [F] 44 F3
Stotel [D] 18 D4
Sto. Toribio de Liébana [E] 82 D3
Stotternheim [D] 32 H6
St. Ottilien [D] 60 D4
Stouby [DK] 156 C2
St-Ouen [F] 28 D4
Stourbridge [GB] 10 D6
Stournaraíika [GR] 132 E2
Støvring [DK] 160 D4
Støvringgård [DK] 160 E5
Stowbtsy [BY] 202 B5
Stowmarket [GB] 14 G3
Stow-on-the-Wold [GB] 12 H2
Stozher [BG] 148 F2
St-Palais [F] 84 D3
St-Palais-sur-Mer [F] 54 B6
St. Pankraz [A] 62 B5
St-Pardoux-la-Rivière [F] 66 F2
St Paul [A] 74 C3
St-Paul [F] 108 E2
St-Paul [F] 108 E4
St-Paul-Cap-de-Joux [F] 106 B3
St-Paul-de-Fenouillet [F] 106 C6
St-Pauliene [F] 68 D4
St-Paul-lès-Dax [F] 66 B6
St-Pé [F] 84 E4
St-Péray [F] 68 F5
St-Père [F] 56 E3
St-Père-en-Retz [F] 40 E6
St. Peter [A] 74 B3
St Peter-Ording [D] 18 D2
St-Peter Port [GBG] 26 C2
St-Philbert [F] 54 B2
St-Pierre-d'Albigny [F] 70 A4
St-Pierre-de-Chartreuse [F] 68 H4
St-Pierre-de-Chignac [F] 66 F3
St.Pierre d'Extravache [F] 70 C5
St-Pierre-d'Oléron [F] 54 B5
St-Pierre-Église [F] 26 E2
St-Pierre-le-Moûtier [F] 56 D4
St-Pierre-Quiberon [F] 40 C5
St-Pierre-sur-Dives [F] 26 F4
St-Pois [F] 26 E4
St-Pol-de-Léon [F] 40 C1
St-Pol-sur-Ternoise [F] 28 E3
St Pölten [A] 62 E4
St-Pons-de-Thomieres [F] 106 C4
St-Porchaire [F] 54 C5
St-Pourçain sur-Sioule [F] 56 D6
St.Priest [F] 68 G3
St-Privat [F] 68 A3
St-Quay-Portrieux [F] 26 B4
St.-Quen-en-Belin [F] 42 B5
St-Quentin [F] 28 F5
St. Quirin [D] 48 C4
Strå [I] 110 G1
Straach [D] 34 D3
Strabane [NIR] 2 F2
Strachówka [PL] 38 C2
Stracia [I] 124 C8
Stracin [MK] 146 D6
Stradalen [S] 182 E5
Stradalovo [BG] 146 F6
Stradbally [IRL] 4 B3
Stradbally [IRL] 4 F3
Stradella [I] 70 G6
Stradone [IRL] 2 E4
Strádov [CZ] 50 A4
Straduny [PL] 24 D3
Straelen [D] 30 F3
Strakonice [CZ] 48 E6
Straldzha [BG] 148 E4
Stralki [BY] 198 G6
Strålsnäs [S] 166 H6
Stralsund [D] 20 D2
St-Rambert [F] 68 E3
St-Rambert-d'Albon [F] 68 F4
St-Rambert-en-Bugey [F] 68 G2
Stramnes [N] 170 B3
Strand [N] 172 C2
Strand [N] 192 D3
Strand [S] 190 E6
Stranda [N] 180 D4
Stranda [N] 194 C2
Strandby [DK] 160 C4
Strandby [DK] 160 E2
Strandcally Castle [IRL] 4 D5
Strande [D] 18 G2
Strandebarm [N] 170 B4
Strandhill [IRL] 2 D3
Strandlykkja [N] 172 C4
Strangford [NIR] 2 G4
Strängnäs [S] 168 C3
Strängsered [S] 162 C2
Strångsjö [S] 168 B4
Strání [CZ] 62 H2
Stranice [SLO] 74 D4
Stranorlar [IRL] 2 E2
Stránov [CZ] 48 G3
Stranraer [GB] 8 C5
St-Raphaël [F] 108 D5
Strasbourg [F] 44 H6
Strasburg [D] 20 E5
Stråsjö [S] 174 D1
Strassburg [A] 74 B2
Strassengel [A] 74 D2
Strassfurt [D] 34 B4
Strasswalchen [A] 60 H5
Stratford-upon-Avon [GB] 12 H2
Strathaven [GB] 8 D3
Stratinska [BIH] 142 B2
Stratóni [GR] 130 C4
Stratoníki [GR] 130 C4
Strátos [GR] 132 E5
Straubing [D] 60 G2
Straum [N] 190 D2
Straume [N] 164 E1
Straume [N] 164 F3
Straume [N] 170 A4
Straumen [N] 180 F1
Straumen [N] 190 C4
Straumen [N] 190 D2
Straumen [N] 192 D6
Straumfjorden [N] 192 D5
Straumsjøen [N] 192 D3
Straumsnes [N] 192 D4
Straumsnes [N] 192 E2
Straupitz [D] 34 F4
Strausberg [D] 34 F2
Straussfurt [D] 32 H5
Stravaj [AL] 128 C4
Straža [SCG] 146 D2
Strazh [RUS] 202 D5
Stražica [BG] 148 D3
Strážky [SK] 52 B6
Strážnice [CZ] 62 G2
Strážný [CZ] 62 A2
Strážske [SK] 64 H2
Štrba [SK] 64 E2
Štrbské Pleso [SK] 52 A6
Street [GB] 12 F4
Strehaia [RO] 204 C6
Strehla [D] 34 E5
Streitberg [D] 46 G4
Strękowa Góra [PL] 24 E5
Strelcha [BG] 148 A5
Strelci [BG] 148 B5
Střeliště [CZ] 50 A6
Strel'na [RUS] 178 H5
Strem [A] 74 F2
St-Rémy-de-Provence [F] 106 G4
St-Renan [F] 40 B2
Strenči [LV] 198 E4
Strendene [N] 190 D3
Strengberg [A] 62 C4
Stresa [I] 70 F3
S. Tresund [S] 190 F4
St.-Révérien [F] 56 E3
Strezimirovci [SCG] 146 E4
Strezovce [SCG] 146 D6
Strib [DK] 156 C2
Stříbro [CZ] 48 D4
Strilky [UA] 52 F5
Strimasund [S] 190 E2
St-Riquier [F] 28 D4
Strittjomvare [S] 190 G3
Strittmat [D] 58 E4
Striževac [SCG] 146 E4
Strmica [HR] 142 A4
Strmilov [CZ] 48 H6
Strobl [A] 60 H5
Strøby Egede [DK] 156 G3
Stroevo [BG] 148 B5
Strofyliá [GR] 134 B4
Ströhem [D] 32 E1
Strokestown [IRL] 2 D4
Strøm [N] 190 A6
Ström [S] 166 D2
Strömåker [S] 190 F5
St.-Roman, Abbaye de- [F] 106 G3
Strömbacka [S] 184 E6
Stromberg [D] 46 B3
Strómboli [I] 124 C5
St-Rome-de-Tarn [F] 106 D2
Strömfors [S] 196 A4
Strömholm [S] 190 G3
Strømmen [N] 166 B1
Strømmen [N] 190 C6
Strömmen [S] 182 E5
Strömnäs [S] 190 F4
Strompdalen [N] 190 D4
Strömsbruk [S] 184 E6
Stromsfors [S] 168 B5
Strömsholm [S] 168 B2
Strömsillret [S] 172 E1
Strömsnäs [S] 184 D2
Strömsnäsbruk [S] 162 C5
Strömsrum [S] 162 G4
Strömstad [S] 166 B4
Strömsund [S] 190 E6
Strömsund [S] 190 F3
Strond [N] 164 E3
Strongoli [I] 124 F4
Stronie Śląskie [PL] 50 C3
Stroove [IRL] 2 F2
Stropkov [SK] 52 D6
Stroppo [I] 108 E2
Stroud [GB] 12 G3
Strövles [GR] 140 B5
Stróża [PL] 50 H4
Str. Pole [PL] 22 F3
Strub Pass [A] 60 G6
Strücklingen [D] 18 C5
Struer [DK] 160 B5
Struga [MK] 128 D3
Strugi-Krasnyye [RUS] 198 H2
Struhařov [CZ] 48 G4
Struino [BG] 148 E2
Strumica [MK] 128 G2
Strumień [PL] 50 F4
Strupina [PL] 36 C5
Stružec [HR] 142 B1
Stryama [BG] 148 B5
Strycksele [S] 190 H5
Stryj [UA] 52 H5
Stryjów [PL] 52 F1
Stryków [PL] 36 G4
Stryn [N] 180 D5
Strzałkowo [PL] 36 E3
Strzegocin [PL] 38 B2
Strzegom [PL] 50 B1
Strzelce [PL] 34 H1
Strzelce [PL] 36 G3
Strzelce Krajeńskie [PL] 36 A1
Strzelce Małe [PL] 36 H6
Strzelce Opolskie [PL] 50 E2
Strzelin [PL] 50 C2
Strzelno [PL] 36 E2
Strzyżów [PL] 38 G6
Strzyżów [PL] 52 D4
St.-Sabin, Chapelle- [F] 66 D5
St-Saëns [F] 28 C5
St. Salvator [A] 74 B2
St.-Samson-la-Poterie [F] 28 D5
St-Satur [F] 56 D3
St-Saturnin-lès-Apt [F] 108 B3
St-Saulge [F] 56 E4
St-Sauvant [F] 54 E4
St-Sauveur-en-Puisaye [F] 56 D2
St-Sauveur-le-Vicomte [F] 26 D2
St-Sauveur-sur-Tinée [F] 108 E3
St-Savin [F] 66 D2
St-Savin-sur-Gartempe [F] 54 F4
St-Seine-l'Abbaye [F] 56 G3
St-Sernin-sur-Rance [F] 106 C3
St-Sever [F] 26 E4
St-Sever [F] 66 C6
St-Sulpice [F] 106 B3
St. Sulpice-Les-Feuilles [F] 54 G5
St. Sundby [S] 168 B3
St-Symphorien [F] 66 C4
St-Symphorien-de-Lay [F] 68 E2
St-Symphorien-d'Ozon [F] 68 F3
St-Symphorien-sur-Coise [F] 68 F3
St-Thégonnec [F] 40 C2
St-Thiébault [F] 58 A2
St-Trivier-de-Courtes [F] 56 G6
St-Tropez [F] 108 D5
St.-Truiden (St.-Trond) [B] 30 D4
Stubbekøbing [DK] 156 G5
Stubbergård [DK] 160 C5
Stuben [A] 72 B1
Štubik [SCG] 146 E1
Stubline [SCG] 142 G3
Studánky [CZ] 62 B3
Studena [BG] 146 F5
Studená [CZ] 48 H6
Studenec [CZ] 48 H2
Studenica [SCG] 146 B3
Studénka [CZ] 50 E5
Studenzen [A] 74 E2
Studsviken [S] 190 G6
Studzienice [PL] 22 C3
Stugudal [N] 182 D3
Stugufläten [N] 180 F4
Stugun [S] 184 C2
Stuguvollmoen [N] 182 D3
Stühlingen [D] 58 F4
Stukenbrock [D] 32 E3
Stülpe [D] 34 E3
St.-Ulrich, Château- [F] 58 D2
St Ulrich / Ortisei [I] 72 D3
Stupava [SK] 62 G4
Stupinigi [I] 70 D6
Stupnik [HR] 74 E6
Stuposiany [PL] 52 F6
Sturehov [S] 168 D3
Štúrovo [SK] 64 B5
St-Ursanne [CH] 58 D4
Stuttgart [D] 58 H1
St-Vaast-la-Hougue [F] 26 E2
St Valentin [A] 62 C4
St-Valery-en-Caux [F] 26 H2
St-Valery-sur-Somme [F] 28 D4
St-Vallier-de-Thiey [F] 108 E4
St-Vallier-sur-Rhône [F] 68 F4
St-Vaury [F] 54 H5
St Veit [A] 74 B3
St-Véran [F] 108 E1
St Vigil / Marebbe [I] 72 E3
St-Vincent [I] 70 D4
St-Vincent, Grotte de- [F] 108 D3
St-Vincent-de-Tyrosse [F] 66 A6
St. Vincent-du-Lorouër [F] 42 C6
St-Vincent-les-Forts [F] 108 D2
St Vith [B] 30 F6
St-Vivien-de-Médoc [F] 66 C1
St-Wandrille [F] 26 H3
St Wendel [D] 44 G3
St Wolfgang [A] 60 H5
St-Yan [F] 56 E6
Stykkishólmur [IS] 192 A2
Stylída [GR] 132 G4
Stymfalía [GR] 136 E1
St-Yorre [F] 68 D1
Stýpsi [GR] 134 G2
Stýra [GR] 134 D5
Styri [N] 172 C5
St-Yrieix-la-Perche [F] 66 G2
Styrnäs [S] 184 F2
Styrsö [S] 160 G2
Suadiye [TR] 150 G3
Suances [E] 82 E3
Suaredda [I] 118 E3
Subačius [LT] 200 F4
Subaşi [TR] 150 D2
Subaşı [TR] 152 D5
Subate [LV] 198 F6
Subbiano [I] 110 G6
Suben [A] 60 H4
Subiaco [I] 116 B5
Subkowy [PL] 22 E3
Subotica [SCG] 76 D5
Subotište [SCG] 142 G2
Sučany [SK] 64 C2
Suceava [RO] 204 D3
Sucha Beskidzka [PL] 50 H4
Suchań [PL] 20 G5
Suchdol nad Lužnicí [CZ] 62 C2
Suchedniów [PL] 38 B6
Suchorze [PL] 22 B3
Suchowola [PL] 24 E4
Suchożebry [PL] 38 D3
Süchteln [D] 30 G3
Sucina [E] 104 C3
Sućuraj [HR] 144 B3
Sudbø [N] 164 E1
Sudbury [GB] 14 F3
Suddesjaur [S] 190 H2
Süden [D] 18 E1
Süderbrarup [D] 18 F1
Süderende [D] 156 A4
Süderlügum [D] 156 B4
Sudok [S] 196 A2
Sudova Vyshnia [UA] 52 G4
Sudzha [UA] 202 F6
Sueca [E] 98 E5
Suelli [I] 118 D6
Suenskby [FIN] 176 F5
Sugères [F] 68 D3
Süğütlü [TR] 150 H2
Suhinichi [RUS] 202 E4
Suhl [D] 46 G2
Suho Polje [BIH] 142 E3
Suhopolje [HR] 74 H6
Šuica [BIH] 144 B1
Suijavaara [S] 194 B5
Suikka [FIN] 178 E1
Suinula [FIN] 176 F1
Suinula [FIN] 186 F5
Suio, Terme di- [I] 120 D2
Suippes [F] 44 C3
Sukeva [FIN] 196 E5
Sukoły [PL] 24 E6
Sukopokh'ya [RUS] 188 G5
Sukošan [HR] 112 G5
Sükösd [H] 76 C4
Sukovo [SCG] 146 E4
Sul [N] 190 C6
Šula [SCG] 144 E2
Sulåmo [N] 182 D1
Suldal [N] 164 C1
Suldalseid [N] 164 C1
Suldalsosen [N] 164 C1
Sulden / Solda [I] 72 C3
Suldrup [DK] 160 D4
Sulechów [PL] 36 A3
Sulęcin [PL] 34 H2
Sulęczyno [PL] 22 C3
Sulejów [PL] 36 H5
Sulejówek [PL] 38 C3
Sulesund [N] 180 C3
Süleymanlı [TR] 152 D3
Sulina [RO] 204 F4
Sulingen [D] 32 E1
Suliszewo [PL] 20 G6
Sulitjelma [N] 192 E6
Sulkava [FIN] 188 F5
Sulkava [FIN] 196 E6
Sulkavanjärvi [FIN] 186 G1
Sulkavankylä [FIN] 186 D4
Sulkavanpera [FIN] 196 D6
Sułkowice [PL] 50 H4
Süller [TR] 152 G4
Sully [F] 56 F4
Sully-sur-Loire [F] 56 C1
Sulmierzyce [PL] 36 D5
Sulmierzyce [PL] 36 G6
Sulmona [I] 116 D5
Süloğlu [TR] 150 B1
Sul'Ovské Skaly [SK] 50 F6
Sulów [PL] 36 D5
Sultançayırı [TR] 150 D5
Sultanhisar [TR] 152 E5
Sultanköy [TR] 130 H2
Sultanköy [TR] 150 D3
Sülümenli [TR] 152 G4
Sulva / Solf [FIN] 186 B2
Sulviken [S] 190 D6
Sülysáp [H] 76 D1
Sulz [D] 58 G2
Sulzbach [A] 74 E3
Sulzbach [D] 46 D6
Sulzbach-Rosenberg [D] 46 H5
Sumacarcer [E] 98 E5
Sumartin [HR] 144 A2
Sumba [FR] 160 A3
Sümeg [H] 74 G2
Sumer [BG] 146 F3
Sumiainem [FIN] 186 G3
Sumiswald [CH] 58 E6
Summa [FIN] 178 D3
Šumperk [CZ] 50 C4
Sumsa [FIN] 196 G4
Šumvald [CZ] 50 D4
Sumy [UA] 202 F6
Sund [FIN] 176 B5
Sund [N] 192 D3
Sund [S] 166 C3
Sund [S] 184 C5
Sundborn [S] 174 C4
Sundby [FIN] 196 B6
Sundbyberg [S] 168 D3
Sundbyholm [S] 168 C3
Sunde [N] 170 B5
Sunde [N] 180 C6
Sunde [N] 190 A6
Sunde bru [N] 164 F4
Sunder [S] 190 D6
Sunderland [GB] 8 G6
Sundern [D] 32 C5
Sundhultsbrunn [S] 162 E1
Sundklakk [N] 192 D4
Sundnäs [S] 190 G2
Sundö [S] 190 H5
Sundre [S] 168 F6
Sunds [DK] 160 C6
Sundsbø [N] 180 D3
Sundsli [N] 164 E3
Sundsøre [DK] 160 C4
Sundsvall [S] 184 E4
Sundsvoll [N] 190 C3
Sundvollen [N] 170 H5
Sungurlare [BG] 148 E4
Suni [I] 118 C4
Sunja [HR] 142 B1
Sunnanå [S] 182 G6
Sunnansjö [S] 172 G5
Sunnaryd [S] 162 C4
Sunndal [N] 170 C5
Sunndalsøra [N] 180 F3
Sunne [S] 166 E1
Sunnemo [S] 166 F1
Sunnersta [S] 168 D2
Suntaži [LV] 198 E5
Suodenniemi [FIN] 176 E1
Suojoki [FIN] 186 B5
Suokonmäki [FIN] 186 D3
Suolahti [FIN] 186 G3
Suolovuobme [N] 194 B3
Suomenlinna / Sveaborg [FIN] 176 H5
Suomenniemi [FIN] 178 D1
Suomijärvi [FIN] 186 C5
Suomusjärvi [FIN] 176 F4
Suomussalmi [FIN] 196 F3
Suonenjoki [FIN] 188 C3
Suontaka [FIN] 176 D3
Suopelto [FIN] 176 H1
Suoperya [RUS] 196 G2
Suorva [S] 192 F5
Šuoššjávri [N] 194 B4
Suotuperä [FIN] 196 D5
Suovanlahti [FIN] 186 G2
Superga [I] 70 D5
Supetar [HR] 144 A2
Supino [I] 116 B6
Suprašl [PL] 24 F5
Supru [FIN] 194 E3
Surahammar [S] 168 B2
Šurany [SK] 64 B5
Suraż [PL] 24 E6
Surazh [BY] 202 C4
Surčin [SCG] 142 G2
Surduk [SCG] 142 G2
Surdulica [SCG] 146 E5
Surgères [F] 54 C5
Súria [E] 92 D3
Šurice [SK] 64 E4
Surju [EST] 198 E3
Šurlane [SCG] 146 D6
Surnadalsöra [N] 180 G2
Sūrnitsa [BG] 130 C1
Sursee [CH] 58 E5
Surtainville [F] 26 D2
Surte [S] 160 H2
Survilliers [F] 42 G3
Susa [I] 70 C5
Šušara [SCG] 142 H2
Susch [CH] 72 B2
Suscinio, Château de- [F] 40 D5
Susek [SCG] 142 F1
Suševo [MK] 128 G2
Sushitsa [BG] 148 C3
Sušice [CZ] 48 E6
Suso y Yuso, Monasterios de- [E] 82 G6
Süssen [D] 60 B2
Susurluk [TR] 150 D5
Susz [PL] 22 F4
Sutivan [HR] 144 A2
Sutjeska [SCG] 142 H1
Sütlaç [TR] 152 H4
Sutomore [SCG] 144 E5
Sutri [I] 114 H4
Sutrieu [F] 68 H2
Sutton Coldfield [GB] 10 E6
Süttorf [D] 18 G6
Suure-Jaani [EST] 198 E2
Suurejõe [EST] 198 E2
Suuremõisa [EST] 198 C2
Suurlahti [FIN] 178 D1
Suurmäki [FIN] 188 E3
Suva Reka [SCG] 146 C6
Suvekas [LT] 200 G3
Suvereto [I] 114 E2
Suvorovo [BG] 148 F2
Suvorovo [RUS] 202 E3
Suwałki [PL] 24 E3
Suystamo [RUS] 188 H4
Suzzara [I] 110 E2
Svabensverk [S] 174 C3
Svalöv [S] 158 C2
Svalyava [UA] 204 C3
Svanabyn [S] 190 F5
Svaneholm [S] 158 C3
Svanehölm [S] 166 H6
Svaneke [DK] 158 E4
Svanesund [S] 166 C6
Svängsta [S] 158 E1
Svaningen [S] 190 E5
Sv. Anna [CZ] 50 A5
Svannäs [S] 190 G2
Svanskog [S] 166 D3
Svanstein [S] 194 B8
Svanvik [N] 194 F3
Svappavaara [S] 192 G5
Svarar [FIN] 186 B3
Svärdsjo [S] 174 D4
Svarstad [N] 164 G2
Svartå [S] 166 G3
Svärta [S] 168 C4
Svartå Mustio [FIN] 176 F5
Svartberget [S] 194 B8
Svartbyn [S] 194 B8
Svarte [S] 158 C3
Svärtinge [S] 168 B5
Svartisdalen [N] 190 E2
Svartlå [S] 196 A2
Svartnäs [S] 174 D3
Svartnäs [S] 190 H4
Svartnes [N] 192 D6
Svartnes [N] 194 F2
Svarttjärn [S] 190 F3
Svartvik [S] 184 E5
Svatá Hora [CZ] 48 F5
Svatá Kateřina [CZ] 48 C4
Svategjel [N] 170 E2
Svätý Anton [SK] 64 C4
Svätý Jur [SK] 62 G4
Svatý Mikuláš [CZ] 50 B4
Sv. Barbora [CZ] 48 G6
Svedala [S] 158 C3
Svedasai [LT] 200 G4
Svedje [S] 184 E5
Svedje [S] 184 G1
Svedje [S] 190 E5
Sveg [S] 182 G5
Sveindal [N] 164 D4
Sveio [N] 164 A1
Švėkšna [LT] 200 D4
Svelgen [N] 180 B5
Svellingen [N] 190 A6
Svelvik [N] 164 H2
Svenarum [S] 162 D3
Švenčionėliai [LT] 200 H4
Švenčionys [LT] 200 H5
Svendborg [DK] 156 E4
Svenes [N] 164 E4
Svenkerud [N] 170 G3
Svenljunga [S] 162 B3
Svennevad [S] 166 H4
Svensby [N] 192 G2
Svenstavik [S] 182 G3
Svenstorp [S] 158 C2
Svenstrup [DK] 160 D4
Sveom [N] 180 G5
Švermov [CZ] 48 F3
S. Vero Milis [I] 118 C5
Sveta Petka [SCG] 146 D2
Sveti Andrejaš [MK] 128 E1
Sveti Ivan Žabno [HR] 74 F5
Sveti Jovan Bigorski [MK] 128 C2
Sveti Naum [AL] 128 D4
Sveti Nikita [MK] 146 C6
Sveti Nikole [MK] 128 F1
Sveti Pantelejmon [MK] 128 E1
Sveti Rok [HR] 112 G4
Sveti Stefan [SCG] 144 E5
Světlá nad Sázavou [CZ] 48 H5
Svetlen [BG] 148 D3

Svetlice [SK] 52 E6
Svetlina [BG] 148 D5
Svetlina [BG] 148 E5
Svetlogorsk [RUS] 200 C5
Svetlyy [RUS] 22 G1
Svetlyy [RUS] 194 E4
Svetogorsk [RUS] 178 F2
Svetozar Miletic [SCG] 76 C5
Svetvinčenat [HR] 112 D2
Svežen [BG] 148 B5
Svib [HR] 144 B2
S.Vicente de la Cabeza [E] 80 G4
Svidník [SK] 52 D5
Švihov [CZ] 48 D5
Svilajnac [SCG] 146 C1
Svilengrad [BG] 150 A2
Svilojevo [SCG] 76 C6
Svinesund [S] 166 C3
Svingstad [N] 170 H3
Svingvoll [N] 170 H2
Svinhult [S] 162 E2
Svinná [SK] 64 B3
Svinndal [N] 166 B2
Svinninge [DK] 156 F2
Svir [BY] 200 H5
Svishtov [BG] 148 C2
Svislach [BY] 24 G5
Svitavy [CZ] 50 B4
Svitlovods'k [UA] 202 F8
Sv. Juraj [HR] 112 F2
Sv. Jurij [SLO] 74 E3
Sv. Nikola [SCG] 128 A1
Svoboda [RUS] 24 C2
Svobodnoye [RUS] 178 F2
Svode [BG] 146 G4
Svodje [SCG] 146 E4
Svoge [BG] 146 F4
Svolvær [N] 192 D4
Svorkmo [N] 180 H2
Svormuseet [N] 180 D5
Svratka [CZ] 50 B5
Svrčinovec [SK] 50 F5
Svrljig [SCG] 146 D3
Svullrya [N] 172 D5
Svyetlahorsk [BY] 202 C6
Swaffham [GB] 14 G2
Swalmen [NL] 30 F3
Swanage [GB] 12 G5
Swanlinbar [IRL] 2 E4
Swansea [GB] 12 E2
Swarożyn [PL] 22 E3
Swarzędz [PL] 36 C2
Swarzewo [PL] 22 D1
Świdnica [PL] 34 H4
Świdnica [PL] 50 B1
Swidnik [PL] 38 E5
Świdwin [PL] 20 H4
Świeba [PL] 20 F4
Świebodzice [PL] 50 B1
Świebodzin [PL] 36 A3
Świecie [PL] 22 D5
Świecko [PL] 34 G3
Świeradów-Zdrój [PL] 48 H1
Świerczów [PL] 50 E1
Świerki [PL] 50 B2
Świerzawa [PL] 50 B1
Świerzno [PL] 20 F3
Święta Anna [PL] 50 G1
Święta Lipka [PL] 24 B3
Święte [PL] 36 E3
Świętno [PL] 36 B4
Swindon [GB] 12 H3
Swinford [IRL] 2 C4
Świnoujście [PL] 20 E3
Swords [IRL] 2 F6
Swory [PL] 38 E3
Syalyets [BY] 38 G2
Sybaris-Copia [I] 124 D3
Sychevka [RUS] 202 E3
Sycow [PL] 36 D6
Sydanmää [FIN] 176 D2
Sykaminéa [GR] 134 G2
Sykäräinen [FIN] 196 D6
Syke [D] 18 D6
Sykéa [GR] 136 F4
Sykéa [GR] 140 G5
Sykiá [GR] 130 D6
Sykiá [GR] 132 F1
Sykióna [GR] 136 E1
Sykkylven [N] 180 D4
Sykoúri [GR] 132 G1
Sylling [N] 164 H1
Sylte [N] 180 E2
Symbister [GB] 6 H4
Sými [GR] 154 C3
Synsiö [FIN] 186 H5
Syötekylä [FIN] 196 E2
Sypniewo [PL] 22 C5
Sypniewo [PL] 24 C6
Syrau [D] 48 C2
Syrävaara [FIN] 196 G5
Sysmä [FIN] 178 A1
Sysslebäck [S] 172 E4
Syston [GB] 10 F6
Syväjärvi [FIN] 194 D7
Syvänniemi [FIN] 188 C2
Syvärinpää [FIN] 196 F6
Syvde [N] 180 C4
Sývota [GR] 132 C2
Syvsten [DK] 160 E3
Syyspohja [FIN] 178 E1
Szabadegyháza [H] 76 B2
Szabadszállás [H] 76 C3
Szabolcsbáka [H] 64 H4
Szada [H] 64 D6
Szadek [PL] 36 F4
Szakály [H] 76 B4
Szakcs [H] 76 B3
Szakmár [H] 76 C4
Szalánta [H] 76 B5
Szalkszentmárton [H] 76 C2
Szalonna [H] 64 F3
Szamocin [PL] 22 B6
Szamotuły [PL] 36 C2
Szandaszőlős [H] 76 E2
Szany [H] 74 G1
Szápár [H] 76 A1
Szarvas [H] 76 F2
Szarvasi Arboretum [H] 76 F2
Szarvasko [H] 64 E5
Szászvár [H] 76 B4
Százhalombatta [H] 76 C1
Szczaniec [PL] 36 A3
Szczawnica [PL] 52 B5
Szczebrzeszyn [PL] 52 F1
Szczecin [PL] 20 F5
Szczecinek [PL] 22 B4
Szczekociny [PL] 50 H2
Szczerców [PL] 36 G5
Szczucin [PL] 52 C3
Szczuczyn [PL] 24 D4
Szczurowa [PL] 52 B3
Szczyrk [PL] 50 G5
Szczytna [PL] 50 B3
Szczytno [PL] 24 B4
Szécsény [H] 64 D5
Szederkény [H] 76 B5
Szedres [H] 76 B4
Szeged [H] 76 E4
Szeghalom [H] 76 G2
Szegvár [H] 76 E3
Székely [H] 64 H4
Székesfehérvár [H] 76 B2
Székkutas [H] 76 F3
Szekszárd [H] 76 C4
Szendro [H] 64 F4
Szentendre [H] 64 C6
Szentes [H] 76 E3
Szentlászló [H] 74 G3
Szentlászló [H] 76 A5
Szentlőrinc [H] 76 A5
Szerencs [H] 64 G4
Szestno [PL] 24 B3
Sztetlew [PL] 36 E3
Szigetszentmiklós [H] 76 C1
Szigetvár [H] 76 A5
Szigliget [H] 74 H3
Szikszó [H] 64 F4
Szil [H] 62 G6
Szilvágy [H] 74 F3
Szilvásvárad [H] 64 E4
Szklarska Poreba [PL] 48 H1
Szklary [PL] 52 E4
Szklary Górne [PL] 36 B5
Szlichtyngowa [PL] 36 B4
Szłum [PL] 22 E4
Szob [H] 64 C5
Szolnok [H] 76 E2
Szombathely [H] 74 F2
Szonowice [PL] 50 E3
Szony [H] 64 B6
Szpetal Górny [PL] 36 G2
Szprotawa [PL] 34 H5
Szreńsk [PL] 22 G6
Sztabin [PL] 24 E4
Sztutowo [PL] 22 F2
Szubin [PL] 22 C6
Szulmierz [PL] 22 H6
Szumirad [PL] 50 E1
Szumowo [PL] 24 D6
Szurdokpüspöki [H] 64 D5
Szwecja [PL] 22 B5
Szydłów [PL] 36 G5
Szydłowiec [PL] 38 B6
Szydłowo [PL] 22 B6
Szymbark [PL] 22 F4
Szypliszki [PL] 24 E2

T

Taalintehdas / Dalsbruk [FIN] 176 E6
Taastrup [DK] 156 G2
Taavetti [FIN] 178 D2
Tab [H] 76 A3
Tabaja [BIH] 144 C3
Tábara [E] 80 H4
Taberg [S] 162 D2
Tabernas [E] 102 G5
Tabiano Bagni [I] 110 D2
Taboada [E] 78 D4
Tábor [CZ] 48 G5
Tábua [P] 86 E2
Tabuaço [P] 80 D5
Tabuenca [E] 90 D3
Täby [S] 168 D2
Tachov [CZ] 48 C4
Tackåsen [S] 172 H2
Tadcaster [GB] 10 F3
Tafalla [E] 84 B4
Tafira [E] 100 C6
Tafjord [N] 180 E4
Täfteå [S] 184 G2
Täfteå [S] 196 A6
Tagaranna [EST] 198 C3
Tagenac [F] 68 C4
Taggia [I] 108 G4
Taghmon [IRL] 4 F5
Tagliacozzo [I] 116 B5
Táglio di Po [I] 110 H2
Tahal [E] 102 G4
Tahiche [E] 100 E6
Tahitótfalu [H] 64 C6
Tahivilla [E] 100 G5
Tahtacı [TR] 152 C2
Tahtaköprü [TR] 150 G5
Tai di Cadore [I] 72 F4
Tailfingen [D] 58 G2
Taillebois [F] 26 F4
Taimoniemi [FIN] 186 G2
Tain [GB] 6 E4
Taininiemi [FIN] 196 D2
Tain-l'Hermitage [F] 68 F4
Taipadas [P] 86 C5
Taipale [FIN] 176 E1
Taipale [FIN] 186 F3
Taipale [FIN] 186 H2
Taipale [FIN] 196 E6
Taipaleenharju [FIN] 196 E3
Taipaleenkyla [FIN] 186 D4
Taipalsaari [FIN] 178 D2
Tairbeart / Tarbert [GB] 6 B3
Taivalkoski [FIN] 196 F3
Taivalmaa [FIN] 186 C4
Taivassalo / Tövsala [FIN] 176 C4
Taizé [F] 56 F6
Tajada, Cuevas de la- [E] 98 D2
Tajcy [RUS] 178 H5
Tajo de las Figuras, Cueva del- [E] 100 G5
Takácsi [H] 74 H1
Takamaa [FIN] 176 F1
Takene [S] 166 F3
Takmak [TR] 152 F3
Taksony [H] 74 G4
Taksony [H] 76 C1
Talachyn [BY] 202 C5
Talalaïvka [UA] 202 F6
Talamone [I] 114 F3
Talarrubias [E] 96 C3
Talaván [E] 86 H4
Talavera de la Reina [E] 88 D6
Talavera la Real [E] 94 G1
Talaveruela [E] 88 C5
Talayuela [E] 88 B6
Talayuelas [E] 98 D3
Talcy [F] 42 D6
Tali [EST] 198 E3
Táliga [E] 94 F2
Talinen [S] 194 B7
Talla [I] 110 G6
Tallaght [IRL] 2 F6
Tallaki [RUS] 24 B1
Tallard [F] 108 D2
Tällas [S] 190 G3
Tallåsen [S] 172 D3
Tallåsen [S] 184 D6
Tällberg [S] 172 H3
Tallberg [S] 190 H6
Tallhed [S] 172 G2
Tallinn [EST] 198 D1
Talloires [F] 70 B3
Tallow [IRL] 4 D5
Tallsjö [S] 190 G5
Tallträsk [S] 190 G5
Talluskylä [FIN] 186 H2
Tallvik [S] 194 B8
Tállya [H] 64 G4
Talmont [F] 54 C6
Talmont-St-Hilaire [F] 54 B3
Talsi [LV] 198 C5
Talvik [N] 192 H1
Tamajón [E] 88 H4
Tamames [E] 88 B3
Tamanes [N] 194 D2
Tamarë [AL] 144 F4
Tamarino [BG] 148 E5
Tamarite de Litera [E] 90 H4
Tamási [H] 76 B3
Tambohuse [DK] 160 C4
Taminaschlucht [CH] 58 H6
Tammela [FIN] 176 F3
Tammensiel [D] 18 E1
Tammerfors / Tampere [FIN] 176 F1
Tammijärvi [FIN] 186 G5
Tammisaari / Ekenäs [FIN] 176 F6
Tamnič [SCG] 146 E2
Tampere / Tammerfors [FIN] 176 F1
Tamsalu [EST] 198 E1
Tamsweg [A] 72 H2
Tämta [S] 162 B1
Tamworth [GB] 10 E6
Tanabru [N] 194 D2
Tanágra [GR] 134 B5
Tananger [N] 164 A3
Tancarville [F] 26 G3
Tanda [SCG] 146 D1
Tandö [S] 172 F3
Tandragee [NIR] 2 G4
Tandsbyn [S] 182 G3
Tandsjöborg [S] 172 G1
Tänga [S] 156 H1
Tängaberg [S] 160 H3
Tangen [N] 166 B3
Tangen [N] 166 C1
Tangen [N] 172 C4
Tanger [AFR] 100 F6
Tangerhütte [D] 34 B2
Tangermünde [D] 34 C2
Tanhua [FIN] 194 E6
Taninges [F] 70 B2
Tankolampi [FIN] 186 G3
Tanlay [F] 56 F2
Tann [D] 46 F1
Tannåker [S] 162 C4
Tännäs [S] 182 E4
Tänndalen [S] 182 D4
Tanne [D] 32 H4
Tannenhof [D] 20 C5
Tännforsen [S] 182 E1
Tannheim [A] 60 C6
Tannila [FIN] 196 D3
Tänno [S] 162 D4
Tanowo [PL] 20 F5
Tanttila [FIN] 176 H2
Tanum [N] 164 G3
Tanum [S] 166 C4
Tanumshede [S] 166 C4
Tanvald [CZ] 48 H2
Taormina [I] 124 B8
Tapa [EST] 198 E1
Tapanivaara [FIN] 196 F4
Tapfheim [D] 60 C2
Tapia de Casariego [E] 78 F2
Tapionkylä [FIN] 194 C7
Tápiószecso [H] 76 D1
Tápiószele [H] 76 D1
Tápiószentmárton [H] 76 D1
Tápiószőlős [H] 76 D1
Tapojärvi [FIN] 194 B6
Tapolca [H] 74 H3
Tapolcafo [H] 74 H1
Taponas [F] 68 F2
Tapperøje [DK] 156 G4
Taps [DK] 156 C3
Tara [IRL] 2 F5
Taraguilla [E] 100 G5
Tarajalejo [E] 100 D6
Tara Kanjon [SCG] 144 E2
Tara Kanjon [SCG] 144 E3
Taraklı [TR] 150 H4
Taramundi [E] 78 F2
Tarancón [E] 96 H2
Táranto [I] 122 E4
Tarare [F] 68 F2
Tarascon [F] 106 G4
Tarascon-sur-Ariège [F] 84 H5
Tarasp [CH] 72 B2
Tarazona [E] 84 A6
Tarazona de la Mancha [E] 98 B4
Tårbæk [DK] 156 H2
Tarbert [IRL] 2 B6
Tarbert / Tairbeart [GB] 6 B3
Tarbes [F] 84 F3
Tarbet [GB] 8 D2
Tarcento [I] 72 G4
Tarčin [BIH] 144 C1
Tarczyn [PL] 38 B4
Tardets-Sorholus [F] 84 D3
Tardienta [E] 90 F3
Tärendö [S] 194 B7
Târgovişte [RO] 204 D5
Târgu Frumos [RO] 204 D3
Târgu Jiu [RO] 204 C5
Târgu Lăpuş [RO] 204 C3
Târgu Mureş [RO] 204 C4
Târgu Neamţ [RO] 204 D3
Târgu Secuiesc [RO] 204 D4
Tarhos [H] 76 G3
Tarhos [H] 76 G3
Tarifa [E] 100 G6
Tarján [H] 64 B6
Tarlo [PL] 38 E5
Tarm [DK] 156 B1
Tarmstedt [D] 18 E5
Tärna [S] 168 C1
Tärnaby [S] 190 E3
Tarnala [FIN] 188 G5
Tarnalelesz [H] 64 E5
Tarnaméra [H] 64 E6
Tärnamo [S] 190 E3
Tarnaszentmiklós [H] 64 E6
Târnăveni [RO] 204 C4
Tarnawa Duża [PL] 52 F1
Tarnawatka [PL] 52 G2
Tarnawka [PL] 52 E1
Tärnet [N] 194 F3
Tarnobrzeg [PL] 52 D2
Tarnogród [PL] 52 F2
Tárnok [H] 76 C1
Tarnos [F] 66 A6
Târnova [RO] 76 H4
Tărnovci [BG] 148 D1
Tarnów [PL] 34 G1
Tarnów [PL] 38 C4
Tarnów [PL] 52 C4
Tarnowo Podgórne [PL] 36 C2
Tarnowskie Góry [PL] 50 F3
Tärnsjö [S] 174 E5
Tărnvik [N] 192 D5
Tarouca [P] 80 D5
Tarp [D] 18 F1
Tarquínia [I] 114 G4
Tarquinia [I] 114 G4
Tarquinia Lido [I] 114 G4
Tarragona [E] 92 C5
Tärrajur [S] 190 H2
Tàrrega [E] 92 C3
Tårs [DK] 156 E4
Tårs [DK] 160 E3
Tarsia [I] 124 D3
Tartas [F] 66 B6
Tartu [EST] 198 F3
Tårup [DK] 156 E3
Tarutino [UA] 204 F4
Tarvainen [FIN] 176 D4
Tarvasjoki [FIN] 176 E4
Tarvisio [I] 72 H3
Tarvola [FIN] 186 D2
Tasapää [FIN] 188 G4
Taşbükü [TR] 154 D2
Täsch [CH] 70 E3
Täsjö [S] 190 F5
Taşköy [TR] 152 F3
Taşkule [TR] 152 C3
Taşlıca [TR] 154 D3
Tassjö [S] 162 B6
Tata [H] 64 B6
Tatabánya [H] 64 B6
Tataháza [H] 76 D4
Tatarbunary [UA] 204 F4
Tatárszentgyörgy [H] 76 D2
Tatlısu (Akanthoú) [CY] 154 G5
Tatranská Kotlina [SK] 52 B6
Tatranská Lomnica [SK] 52 B6
Tau [N] 164 B3
Taubenlochschlucht [CH] 58 D5
Tauberbischofsheim [D] 46 E4
Taucha [D] 34 C5
Tauerntunnel [A] 72 G2
Tauern Tunnel [A] 72 H1
Taufers / Tubre [I] 72 B3
Taufkirchen [A] 60 H4
Taufkirchen [D] 60 F4
Taujėnai [LT] 200 G4
Taüll [E] 84 G6
Taunton [GB] 12 F4
Taunusstein [D] 46 B3
Tauplitz [A] 62 B6
Taurage [LT] 200 E5
Taurasi [I] 120 F3
Taurianova [I] 124 C7
Taurine, Terme- [I] 114 G5
Taurisano [I] 122 G6
Taurkains [LV] 198 E5
Tauste [E] 90 E3
Tauves [F] 68 B2
Tavaklı [TR] 134 G1
Tavannes [CH] 58 D5
Tavarnelle Val di Pesa [I] 110 F6
Tavas [TR] 152 G5
Tavascan [E] 84 G6
Tavastehus / Hämeenlinna [FIN] 176 G3
Tavastila [FIN] 178 C3
Tavastkenka [FIN] 196 E5
Tavastkyro / Hämeenkyro [FIN] 176 E1
Tavaux [F] 56 H4
Tavelsjö [S] 190 H5
Taverna [I] 124 E5
Tavernelle [I] 114 H2
Tavernes [F] 108 C4
Tavernes de la Valldigna [E] 98 E6
Taviano [I] 122 G6
Tavira [P] 94 D5
Tavistock [GB] 12 D4
Tavole Palatine [I] 122 D4
Tavşancil [TR] 150 F3
Tavşanlı [TR] 152 G1
Täxan [S] 190 F6
Taxenbach [A] 72 G1
Taxiarchón, Moní- [GR] 138 D3
Tayfur [TR] 150 B5
Taytan [TR] 152 E3
Tăzha [BG] 148 B4
Tázlár [H] 76 D3
Tazones [E] 82 C1
Tczew [PL] 22 E3
Tczów [PL] 38 C5
Teano [I] 120 D2
Tearce [MK] 146 C6
Teascu [RO] 146 G1
Techendorf [A] 72 G3
Teck [D] 58 H2
Tecklenburg [D] 32 C2
Tecuci [RO] 204 E4
Teerijärvi / Terjärv [FIN] 196 C6
Teféli [GR] 140 E5
Tefenni [TR] 152 H6
Tegéa [GR] 136 E3
Tegelen [NL] 30 F3
Tegelträsk [S] 190 G6
Tegernsee [D] 60 E5
Teggiano [I] 120 G4
Téglás [H] 64 H5
Teglaszin [H] 74 F2
Teglio [I] 72 A4
Tegra, Monte de Santa [E] 78 A5
Teguise [E] 100 E6
Tehi [FIN] 176 H1
Teichel [D] 46 H1
Teichiussa [TR] 152 D6
Teignmouth [GB] 12 E5
Teillay [F] 40 F5
Teillet [F] 106 C3
Teisendorf [D] 60 G5
Teisko [FIN] 186 E6
Teixeiro [E] 78 D2
Tejeda [E] 100 C6
Tejn [DK] 158 E4
Teke [TR] 150 F2
Tekeriš [SCG] 142 F3
Tekin [TR] 152 H4
Tekirdağ [TR] 150 C3
Tekmen [TR] 154 F4
Tekovské Lužany [SK] 64 B5
Telana [I] 118 E5
Telavåg [N] 170 A4
Telč [CZ] 48 H6
Teldau [D] 18 G5
Telde [E] 100 C6
Teleborg [S] 162 E5
Telekháza [H] 64 F6
Telese Terme [I] 120 E2
Telford [GB] 10 D6
Telgte [D] 32 C3
Telheiro [P] 94 B3
Telish [BG] 148 A3
Teljo [FIN] 196 G5
Tellingstedt [D] 18 E2
Tellskap [CH] 58 F6
Telmessos [TR] 154 F2
Telšiai [LT] 200 E4
Telti [I] 118 D3
Tembleque [E] 96 G2
Temelín [CZ] 48 F6
Temerin [SCG] 142 F1
Temmes [FIN] 196 D4
Temnata Dupka [BG] 146 F4
Témpi [GR] 132 G1
Témpio Pausánia [I] 118 D3
Templemore [IRL] 4 E3
Templetouhy [IRL] 4 E3
Templin [D] 20 D6
Templom [H] 64 C5
Temse [B] 28 H2
Temska [SCG] 146 E3
Tenala / Tenhola [FIN] 176 F5
Tenby [GB] 12 D2
Tence [F] 68 E4
Tenda, Colle di - / Tende, Col de- [EUR] 108 F3
Tende [F] 108 F3
Tendilla [E] 88 H6
Tenebrón [E] 88 A3
Tenevo [BG] 148 E5
Tenhola / Tenala [FIN] 176 F5
Tenhult [S] 162 D2
Tenja [HR] 142 E1
Tenk [H] 64 E6
Tennänget [S] 172 F3
Tennevol [N] 192 F3
Tenterden [GB] 14 F5
Tentudia, Mon. de- [E] 94 G4
Teo / Ramallosa [E] 78 C3
Teofipol' [UA] 202 B8
Teolo [I] 110 G1
Teos [TR] 152 C5
Tepasto [FIN] 194 C6
Tepecik [TR] 150 E5
Tepecik [TR] 150 F3
Tepecik [TR] 150 F5
Tepecik [TR] 152 G1
Tepeköy [TR] 152 E4
Tepelenë [AL] 128 B6
Tepeören [TR] 150 F3
Teplá [CZ] 48 D4
Teplice [CZ] 48 E2
Teplice nad Metují [CZ] 50 B2
Tepsa [FIN] 194 C6
Téramo [I] 116 C3
Ter Apel [NL] 16 H3
Teratyn [PL] 38 G6
Terchová [SK] 50 G6
Terebiń [PL] 52 G1
Terebišče [RUS] 198 G3
Terebovlia [UA] 202 B8
Teremia Mare [RO] 76 F5
Terena [P] 94 E2
Teresin [PL] 38 A3
Terespol [PL] 38 F3
Terezín [CZ] 48 F2
Terezino Polje [HR] 74 H5
Tergnier [F] 28 F6
Terjärv / Teerijärvi [FIN] 196 C6
Terkoz [TR] 150 E2
Terland [N] 164 B4
Terlizzi [I] 122 D2
Termal [TR] 150 F3
Termas de Monfortinho [P] 86 G3
Terme di Lurisia [I] 108 F3
Terme di Valdieri [I] 108 F3
Terme Luigiane [I] 124 C4
Termes-d'Armagnac [F] 84 F2
Terme S. Lucia [I] 116 C2
Terme Vigliatore [I] 124 A7
Términi Imerese [I] 126 D2
Terminillo [I] 116 B4
Terminón [E] 82 E5
Térmoli [I] 116 F5
Termolovo [RUS] 178 G3
Termonfeckin [IRL] 2 F5
Terndrup [DK] 160 E4
Terneuzen [NL] 28 H1
Terni [I] 116 A3
Ternitz [A] 62 E6
Ternopil' [UA] 202 B8
Térovo [GR] 132 D2
Terpan [AL] 128 B5
Terpezita [RO] 146 F1
Terpilitsy [RUS] 178 G6
Terpní [GR] 130 B3
Terracina [I] 120 C2
Terradillos de los Templarios [E] 82 C5
Terråk [N] 190 D4
Terralba [I] 118 C5
Terra Mala [I] 118 D7
Terra Mitica [E] 104 E2
Terranova di Pollino [I] 122 C6
Terrassa / Tarrasa [E] 92 E4
Terrasson-la-Villedieu [F] 66 G3
Terrateig [E] 98 E6
Terrazos [E] 82 F5
Terriente [E] 98 D2
Terskanperä [FIN] 196 D5
Tersløse [DK] 156 F3
Tertenía [I] 118 E6
Teruel [E] 98 E2
Tervahauta [FIN] 176 E1
Tervakoski [FIN] 176 G3
Tervel [BG] 148 F1
Tervo [FIN] 186 H2
Tervola [FIN] 196 C2
Tervuren [B] 30 C4
Terz [A] 62 D5
Terzaga [E] 90 C6
Tesejerague [E] 100 D6
Těškovice [CZ] 50 E4
Teslić [BIH] 142 C3
Teslui [RO] 146 G1
Tessenberg [A] 72 F3
Tesseosen [N] 180 G6
Tessin [D] 20 C3
Tessy sur-Vire [F] 26 E4
Tét [H] 62 H6
Tetbury [GB] 12 G3
Teterow [D] 20 C4
Teteven [BG] 148 A4
Tetovo [BG] 148 D2
Tetovo [MK] 128 D1
Tetrálofo [GR] 128 F5
Tettnang [D] 58 H4
Teuchrania [TR] 152 C3
Teufelshöhle [D] 46 H4
Teufen [CH] 58 H5
Teulada [E] 104 F2
Teulada [I] 118 C7
Teupitz [D] 34 E3
Teurnia [A] 72 H3
Teuro [FIN] 176 F3
Teuva / Östermark [FIN] 186 B4
Tevaniemi [FIN] 186 D6
Tevel [H] 76 B4
Tevfikiye [TR] 130 H5
Tewkesbury [GB] 12 G2
Tewli [BY] 38 G2
Texeiro [E] 78 E3
Teysset [F] 66 E5
Thal [A] 72 F3
Thale [D] 34 A4
Thalfang [D] 44 G2
Thalheim [D] 48 D2
Thalmässing [D] 46 G6
Thalwil [CH] 58 F5
Thame [GB] 14 D3
Thann [F] 58 D3
Thannhausen [D] 60 C3
Tharandt [D] 48 E1
Tharigné-sur-Dué [F] 42 C5
Thárros [I] 118 B5
Tharsis [E] 94 E5
Thásos [GR] 130 E4
Thatcham [GB] 12 H4
Thaumiers [F] 56 C4
Theessen [D] 34 C3
Them [DK] 156 C1
Themar [D] 46 F2
Thénezay [F] 54 E3
Thenon [F] 66 F3
Theológos [GR] 130 E4
Theológos [GR] 134 A4
Théoule [F] 108 E5
Thera [TR] 154 E2
Thermá [GR] 130 G4
Thérma [GR] 138 G1
Thérmi [GR] 130 B4
Thermí [GR] 134 H2
Thermisía [GR] 136 G2
Thérmo [GR] 132 F5
Thermopýles [GR] 132 G4
Thermopýles [GR] 132 G4
Thernberg [A] 62 E6
Thérouanne [F] 28 E2
Thespiés [GR] 134 A5
Thesprotía [GR] 132 C2
Thessaloníki [GR] 128 H4
Thetford [GB] 14 G2
The Turoe Stone [IRL] 2 C5
Theuley [F] 58 B3
Theux [B] 30 E5
Thevet-St-Julien [F] 56 B4
Theze [F] 84 E3
Thiaucourt-Regniéville [F] 44 E4
Thiberville [F] 26 G4
Thiélbemont-Farémont [F] 44 C5
Thiendorf [D] 34 E5
Thiene [I] 72 D5
Thiers [F] 68 D2
Thiersee [A] 60 F6
Thiersheim [D] 48 C3
Thiesi [I] 118 C3
Thiessow [D] 20 E2
Thingvellir [IS] 192 A3
Thionville [F] 44 E3
Thíra [GR] 138 F5
Thíra / Firá [GR] 138 F5
Thirette [F] 68 H1
Thirsk [GB] 10 F3
Thisted [DK] 160 C4
Thísvi [GR] 132 H5
Thíva [GR] 134 B5
Thivars [F] 42 D4
Thiviers [F] 66 F2
Thizy [F] 68 F2
Tho, Pieve del- [I] 110 G4
Thoissey [F] 68 G1
Tholey [D] 44 G3
Tholó [GR] 136 C3
Thomasberg [A] 62 E6
Thomas Street [IRL] 2 D5
Thomastown [IRL] 4 E4
Thônes [F] 70 B3
Thonon-les-Bains [F] 70 B2
Thorens-Glières, Château de- [F] 70 B3
Thorigné-en-Charnie [F] 42 A5
Thorikó [GR] 136 H1
Thörl [A] 62 D6
Thornbury [GB] 12 G3
Thorney [GB] 14 F2
Thornhill [GB] 8 D4
Thoronet, Abbaye du- [F] 108 D5
Thors [F] 44 C6
Thórshöfn [IS] 192 C2
Thouarcé [F] 54 D2
Thouars [F] 54 E2
Thouría [GR] 136 D4
Thoúrio [GR] 130 H1
Thueyts [F] 68 E5
Thuin [B] 28 H4
Thuir [F] 92 G1
Thum [D] 48 D2
Thun [CH] 70 D1
Thuret [F] 68 D2
Thürkow [D] 20 C4
Thurles / Durlas [IRL] 4 E3
Thurnau [D] 46 H3
Thurn Pass [A] 72 F1
Thurso [GB] 6 F2
Thury-Harcourt [F] 26 F4
Thusis [CH] 70 H1
Thyborøn [DK] 160 B4
Thymariá [GR] 130 H3
Thymianá [GR] 134 G5
Thyregod [DK] 156 C1
Tiana [I] 118 D5
Tibaes [P] 80 C3
Tibarrié [F] 106 C3
Tibava [SK] 64 H2
Tiberio, Grotta di- [I] 120 E2
Tibro [S] 166 F5
Ticha [BG] 148 D3
Tidaholm [S] 166 F6
Tidan [S] 166 F5
Tidersrum [S] 162 F1
Tidö [S] 168 B2
Tiefenbronn [D] 58 G1
Tiefencastel [CH] 70 H2
Tiefensee [D] 34 F2
Tiel [NL] 16 E5
Tielt [B] 28 G2
Tiemassaari [FIN] 188 D4
Tienen (Tirlemont) [B] 30 D4
Tiengen [D] 58 F4
Tiercé [F] 40 H6
Tierga [E] 90 D3
Tiermas [E] 88 H3
Tierp [S] 174 F5
Tieva [FIN] 194 C6
Tighina [MD] 204 F3
Tigkáki [GR] 154 B2
Tignes [F] 70 C4
Tihany [H] 76 A2
Tihilä [FIN] 196 E5
Tihusniemi [FIN] 188 D4
Tiironkyla [FIN] 186 F2
Tiistenjoki [FIN] 186 D3
Tijarafe [E] 100 A4

Tulcea [RO] 204 F5
Tul'chyn [UA] 204 E2
Tuliszków [PL] 36 E3
Tulla [IRL] 2 C6
Tullamore [IRL] 2 E6
Tulle [F] 66 H3
Tullebølle [DK] 156 E4
Tulleråsen [S] 182 G1
Tullgarn [S] 168 D4
Tullinge [S] 168 D3
Tullins [F] 68 G4
Tulln [A] 62 E4
Tullow [IRL] 4 F4
Tułowice [PL] 50 D2
Tulppio [FIN] 194 F6
Tulsk [IRL] 2 D4
Tum [PL] 36 G3
Tumba [S] 168 D3
Tumulus de Gavrinis [F] 40 D5
Tun [S] 166 D5
Tuna [S] 162 F3
Tunaberg [S] 168 C5
Tuna Hästberg [S] 172 H5
Tunbridge Wells [GB] 14 E5
Tunby [S] 184 E5
Tunçbilek [TR] 150 G6
Tune [DK] 156 G3
Túnel del Cadí [E] 92 E2
Túnel de Viella [E] 84 F5
Tunge [S] 160 H1
Tungelsta [S] 168 E4
Tungozero [RUS] 196 G2
Tunhovd [N] 170 F4
Tunnerstad [S] 162 D1
Tunnsjørørvika [N] 190 D4
Tunø By [DK] 156 D1
Tuntsa [FIN] 194 F6
Tunvågen [S] 182 G3
Tuohikotti [FIN] 178 C2
Tuohittu [FIN] 176 F5
Tuomioja [FIN] 196 D4
Tuonj [HR] 112 G2
Tuorila [FIN] 186 B6
Tuornoel, Château de- [F] 68 C2
Tupadły [PL] 36 E2
Tupitsyno [RUS] 198 G2
Tuplice [PL] 34 G4
Tuppurinmäki [FIN] 188 D3
Tura [H] 64 D6
Turan [TR] 150 F4
Turanlı [TR] 152 C2
Turany [SK] 50 G6
Türas [TR] 150 G2
Turbe [BIH] 142 C4
Turčianske Teplice [SK] 64 C2
Turckheim [F] 58 D3
Turda [RO] 204 C4
Turégano [E] 88 F3
Turek [PL] 36 F4
Turenki [FIN] 176 G3
Turenne [F] 66 G3
Turgeliai [LT] 200 G6
Tŭrgovishte [BG] 148 D3
Turgut [TR] 152 E6
Turgutbey [TR] 150 C2
Turgutlu [TR] 152 D4
Turgutreis [TR] 154 B2
Turhala [FIN] 196 E6
Türi [EST] 198 E2
Turi [I] 122 E3
Turiis'k [UA] 38 H5
Turís / Torís [E] 98 E5
Turjaci [HR] 144 A1
Turjak [SLO] 74 C5
Turka [PL] 38 G5
Turka [UA] 52 F6
Türkeli [TR] 150 C4
Túrkeve [H] 76 F2
Türkheim [D] 60 C4
Türkmen [TR] 152 C3
Turku / Åbo [FIN] 176 D4
Turleque [E] 96 F2
Turlough [IRL] 2 C4
Turňa nad Bodvou [SK] 64 F3
Turnberry [GB] 8 C4
Turnhout [B] 30 D3
Türnitz [A] 62 D5
Turnov [CZ] 48 H2
Turnu Măgurele [RO] 148 B2
Turo [FIN] 194 D4
Turobin [PL] 52 F1
Túrony [H] 76 B5
Turośl [PL] 24 C5
Turów [PL] 38 E4
Turrach [A] 74 A2
Turre [E] 102 H5
Turriff [GB] 6 F5
Turtagrø [N] 170 E1
Turtel [MK] 128 G1
Turtola [FIN] 194 C8
Turunç [TR] 154 D2
Turunçova [TR] 154 H3
Turzovka [SK] 50 F5
Tusa [I] 126 E2
Tusby / Tuusula [FIN] 176 H4
Tuscánia [I] 114 G4
Tušilovic [HR] 112 G1
Tustervatnet [N] 190 D3
Tuszów Narodowy [PL] 52 D2
Tuszyn [PL] 36 G5
Tutajev [RUS] 202 F1
Tutin [SCG] 146 B4
Tutjunniemi [FIN] 188 F3
Tutrakan [BG] 148 D1
Tutting [D] 60 H4
Tuttlingen [D] 58 G3
Tütugi [E] 102 G3
Tutzing [D] 60 D5
Tützpatz [D] 20 D4
Tuukkala [FIN] 186 H6
Tuukkala [FIN] 188 C6
Tuulos [FIN] 176 G2
Tuupovaara [FIN] 188 G3
Tuuruniemi [FIN] 194 D4
Tuusjärvi [FIN] 188 D2
Tuuski [FIN] 178 C4
Tuusniemi [FIN] 188 E2
Tuusula / Tusby [FIN] 176 H4
Tuv [N] 170 F3
Tuvaltnet [S] 190 E6
Tuvas [FIN] 186 B4
Tuvnes [N] 190 A6
Tuzi [SCG] 144 E4
Tuzla [BIH] 142 E3
Tuzla [TR] 134 G1
Tuzla [TR] 150 F3
Tuzlata [BG] 148 G2
Tuzsér [H] 64 H4
Tvååker [S] 160 H4
Tväråbäck [S] 190 H5
Tvärålund [S] 190 H5
Tväråträsk [S] 190 G4
Tvärskog [S] 162 F5
Tvarud [S] 166 D1
Tvede [DK] 160 E5
Tvedestrand [N] 164 F4
Tveita [N] 170 B4
Tveitsund [N] 164 E3
Tver' [RUS] 202 E2
Tverai [LT] 200 D4
Tverrå [N] 190 E2
Tverrelvmo [N] 192 G3
Tversted [DK] 160 E2
Tvinde [N] 170 C3
Tvindehaugen [N] 170 F1
Tving [S] 158 F1
Tvis [DK] 160 C5
Tvøroyri [FR] 160 A3
Tvrdošovce [SK] 64 A5
Tv-Torony [H] 74 G3
Tvŭrditsa [BG] 148 D4
Twann-Schlucht [CH] 58 D5
Twardogóra [PL] 36 D5
Tweng [A] 72 H1
Twimberg [A] 74 C2
Twist [D] 16 H4
Twistringen [D] 18 D6
Tworków [PL] 50 E4
Tworóg [PL] 50 F2
Tyamsha [RUS] 198 G3
Tychowo [PL] 22 A4
Tychy [PL] 50 G3
Tyczyn [PL] 52 E4
Tyfjord [N] 194 D1
Tyfors [S] 172 G5
Tyholland [NIR] 2 F4
Tyin [N] 170 F2
Tyinosen [N] 170 E2
Tykocin [PL] 24 E5
Tylawa [PL] 52 D5
Tylisos [GR] 140 E4
Tylldal [N] 182 B5
Tylösand [S] 162 B5
Tylstrup [DK] 160 E3
Tymfristós [GR] 132 F4
Tympáki [GR] 140 D5
Tyndaris [I] 124 A7
Tynderö [S] 184 F4
Tyndrum [GB] 8 D2
Týnec Nad Labem [CZ] 48 H4
Tynemouth [GB] 8 G6
Tyngsjö [S] 172 F5
Tyniec [PL] 50 H4
Týniště nad Orlicí [CZ] 50 B3
Tynkä [FIN] 196 C5
Týn nad Vltavou [CZ] 48 F6
Tynnelsö [S] 168 C3
Tynset [N] 182 B4
Typpö [FIN] 196 C5
Tyresö [S] 168 E3
Tyringe [S] 158 C1
Tyrislöt [S] 168 C6
Tyristrand [N] 170 H5
Tyrjänsaari [FIN] 188 G1
Tyrnävä [FIN] 196 D4
Týrnavos [GR] 132 G1
Tyrós [GR] 136 F3
Týřov [CZ] 48 E4
Tyrrellspass [IRL] 2 E5
Tyry [FIN] 186 F6
Tysken [N] 172 D4
Tysse [N] 170 B4
Tyssebotn [N] 170 B3
Tyssedal [N] 170 C5
Tystberga [S] 168 C4
Tyszki-Nadbory [PL] 24 D6
Tytuvėnai [LT] 200 E4
Tyulenovo [BG] 148 G2
Tyvsen [DK] 156 B4
Tywyn [GB] 10 B5
Tzermiádo [GR] 140 F5
Tzummarum [NL] 16 F2

U

Ub [SCG] 146 A1
Úbeda [E] 102 F2
Ubergsmoen [N] 164 F4
Überlingen [D] 58 G4
Ubli [HR] 144 A3
Ubrique [E] 100 H4
Uçarı [TR] 154 F4
Uccellina, Torre dell-' [I] 114 F3
Uchanie [PL] 38 G6
Uchorowo [PL] 36 C2
Uchte [D] 32 E1
Uckange [F] 44 E3
Uckfield [GB] 14 E5
Uclés [E] 96 H2
Üçpınar [TR] 152 D3
Ucria [I] 124 A7
Udbina [HR] 112 H4
Udbyhøj [DK] 160 E5
Udbyhøj Vasehuse [DK] 160 E5
Uddeholm [S] 166 F1
Uddel [NL] 16 F4
Uddel [NL] 16 F4
Udden [S] 166 D5
Uddevalla [S] 166 C5
Uddheden [S] 166 E1
Uden [NL] 16 E6
Udine [I] 72 G5
Údlice [CZ] 48 E2
Udorpie [PL] 22 C3
Udovo [MK] 128 G2
Ūdrupij [LV] 198 F4
Udvar [H] 76 B5
Ueckermünde [D] 20 E4
Ueffeln [D] 32 C1
Uelsen [D] 16 G4
Uelzen [D] 18 G6
Uetersen [D] 18 F4
Uetze [D] 32 G2
Uffenheim [D] 46 F5
Uga [E] 100 E6
Ugāle [LV] 198 C5
Ugao [SCG] 146 A4
Ugao-Miraballes [E] 82 G4
Ugento [I] 122 G6
Ugerløse [DK] 156 F3
Uggdal [N] 170 B5
Uggerby [DK] 160 E2
Uggersjev [DK] 156 D3
Ugglarpshavsbad [S] 160 H4
Ugijar [E] 102 F5
Ugine [F] 70 B3
Uglich [RUS] 202 F1
Ugljan [HR] 112 F5
Ugljane [HR] 144 A2
Ugrinovci [SCG] 146 B2
Ugŭrchin [BG] 148 A4
Uğurluca [TR] 152 G2
Uğurlutepe [TR] 130 G5
Uherčice [CZ] 62 E2
Uherse Mineralne [PL] 52 E5
Uherské Hradiště [CZ] 62 H2
Uherský Brod [CZ] 62 H2
Uherský Ostroh [CZ] 62 H2
Uhlířské Janovice [CZ] 48 G4
Uhniv [UA] 52 G2
Uhříněves [CZ] 48 G4
Uhrovec [SK] 64 B3
Uhrovský Hrad [SK] 64 B3
Uhyst [D] 34 G5
Uig [GB] 6 B4
Újhartyán [H] 76 D2
Uimaharju [FIN] 188 G1
Uimila [FIN] 178 B2
Uithoorn [NL] 16 D4
Uithuizen [NL] 16 G1
Ujazd [PL] 36 H5
Ujazd [PL] 50 E3
Ujazd [PL] 52 C2
Újfehértó [H] 64 H5
Újiráz [H] 76 G2
Újkígyós [H] 76 G3
Újléta [H] 64 H6
Ujma [PL] 36 F2
Ujście [PL] 22 B6
Újszász [H] 76 E1
Ujué [E] 84 B5
Ukk [H] 74 G2
Ukkola [FIN] 188 F1
Ukmergė [LT] 200 G5
Ukonvaara [FIN] 188 E1
Ukri [LV] 198 D6
Ukta [PL] 24 C4
Ula [BY] 202 C4
Ula [TR] 154 D1
Ul'anka [SK] 64 C3
Ulan Majorat [PL] 38 E4
Ulanów [PL] 52 E2
Ulaş [TR] 150 G2
Ulbjerg [DK] 160 D5
Ulcinj [SCG] 144 E5
Uldum [DK] 156 C2
Ulefoss [N] 164 F2
Uleila del Campo [E] 102 H4
Ulëzë [AL] 128 B2
Ulhówek [PL] 52 G2
Úlibice [CZ] 48 H3
Ulinia [PL] 22 C1
Uljanik [HR] 142 B1
Uljma [SCG] 142 H2
Ullånger [S] 184 F3
Ullapool [GB] 6 D3
Ullared [S] 162 B4
Ullatti [S] 192 H6
Ullava [FIN] 196 C6
Ulldecona [E] 92 A6
Ulldemolins [E] 90 H5
Ullene [S] 166 E6
Ullerslev [DK] 156 E3
Üllés [H] 76 E4
Ullisjaur [S] 190 F4
Üllő [H] 76 D1
Ulm [D] 60 B3
Ulme [P] 86 D4
Ulmen [D] 44 G1
Ulmeni [RO] 148 D1
Ulnes [N] 170 G2
Ulog [BIH] 144 D2
Ulpiana [SCG] 146 C5
Ulpia Traiana [RO] 204 C5
Ulricehamn [S] 162 C2
Ulrika [S] 162 E1
Ulriksfors [S] 190 E6
Ulsberg [N] 180 H3
Ulsrud [N] 166 C1
Ulsted [DK] 160 E4
Ulsteinvik [N] 180 C4
Ulstrup [DK] 156 E2
Ulstrup [DK] 160 D5
Uluabat [TR] 150 E5
Ulubey [TR] 152 G3
Ulüçayır [TR] 150 H5
Uludağ [TR] 150 F5
Ulukışla (Marathóvounos) [CY] 154 G5
Ulukÿy [TR] 150 H6
Ulvåila [N] 172 D3
Ulvåsa [S] 166 H5
Ulverston [GB] 10 D2
Ülvesbüll [D] 18 E1
Ulvestad [N] 170 D1
Ulvik [N] 170 D3
Ulvika [N] 192 E4
Ulvila / Ulvsby [FIN] 176 D2
Ulvsby / Ulvila [FIN] 176 D2
Ulvsjön [S] 172 G1
Ulvsvåg [N] 192 E4
Umag [HR] 112 D1
Uman' [UA] 202 D8
Umasjö [S] 190 E2
Umbertide [I] 116 A1
Umbukta [N] 190 E2
Umčari [SCG] 142 H3
Umeå [S] 196 A6
Umfors [S] 190 E2
Umgransele [S] 190 G4
Umka [SCG] 142 G3
Umurbey [TR] 150 B5
Umurbey [TR] 150 F4
Umurlu [TR] 152 E5
Uña [E] 98 C2
Unaja [FIN] 176 C3
Unari [FIN] 194 D7
Unbyn [S] 196 B3
Uncastillo [E] 84 C5
Undenäs [S] 166 G5
Undersåker [S] 182 F2
Undva [EST] 198 C3
Úněšov [CZ] 48 D4
Ungheni [MD] 204 E3
Unhošť [CZ] 48 F3
Unichowo [PL] 22 C3
Uničov [CZ] 50 C4
Uniejów [PL] 36 F4
Unirea [RO] 146 F1
Unisław [PL] 22 D6
Unna [D] 32 C4
Unnaryd [S] 162 C4
Unserfrau / Madonna di Senales [I] 72 C2
Unset [N] 182 C5
Unsholtet [N] 182 C3
Untamala [FIN] 186 C2
Unterach [A] 60 H5
Unterbergen [A] 74 E1
Unterlüss [D] 18 G6
Unter Pfaffenhofen [D] 60 D4
Unterradlberg [A] 62 E4
Unterschächen [CH] 70 G1
Unter-Schleissheim [D] 60 E4
Unteruhldingen [D] 58 H4
Unterwasser [CH] 58 H5
Unterweissenbach [A] 62 C4
Unterwössen [D] 60 F5
Untorp [S] 172 G2
Uors [CH] 70 G1
Úpice [CZ] 50 B2
Upiłka [PL] 22 C4
Upper Largo [GB] 8 F3
Upphärad [S] 166 D6
Upplands Väsby [S] 168 D2
Uppsala [S] 168 D1
Uppsete [N] 170 D3
Upyna [LT] 200 E4
Urachi, Nuraghe s'- [I] 118 C5
Úras [I] 118 C6
Ura Vajgurore [AL] 128 B4
Urbánia [I] 110 H6
Urbino [I] 112 B6
Urbise [F] 56 E6
Urçay [F] 56 C5
Urda [E] 96 F3
Urdaibai [E] 82 H3
Urdos [F] 84 D4
Uriage-les-Bains [F] 68 H5
Uriz / Arze-Arce [E] 84 C4
Urjala [FIN] 176 F2
Urk [NL] 16 E3
Urla [TR] 152 C4
Urlingford [IRL] 4 E3
Urnäsch [CH] 58 H5
Urnes [N] 170 D1
Uroševac [SCG] 146 C6
Urpila [FIN] 186 F1
Urroz [E] 84 B4
Urshult [S] 162 E5
Ursus [PL] 38 B3
Urtimjaur [S] 196 A1
Ürünlü [TR] 150 B2
Ururi [I] 116 F6
Ury [F] 42 F5
Urzędów [PL] 38 D6
Urzelina [P] 100 C3
Urziceni [RO] 204 E5
Urzicuța [RO] 146 F2
Urzulei [I] 118 E5
Usagre [E] 94 H3
Uşak [TR] 152 G3
Ušće [SCG] 146 B3
Uście Gorlickie [PL] 52 C5
Usedom [D] 20 E4
Ushakovo [RUS] 22 G2
Uši [MK] 128 F2
Usingen [D] 46 C2
Uskali [FIN] 188 G3
Uskedal [N] 170 B5
Uskopolje [BIH] 144 B1
Üsküdar [TR] 150 E3
Usküp [TR] 150 C1
Usküpdere [TR] 150 C1
Uslar [D] 32 F4
Usma [LV] 198 C5
Usmate Velate [I] 70 G4
Úsov [CZ] 50 C4
Uspen'ye [RUS] 202 B3
Ussé [F] 54 F2
Usseglio [I] 70 C5
Ussel [F] 68 B2
Ussel [I] 70 D4
Usseln [D] 32 D5
Usson-du-Poitou [F] 54 F5
Usson-en-Forez [F] 68 E3
Usson-les-Bains [F] 106 B6
Ustaoset [N] 170 E4
Ustaritz [F] 84 C2
Úštěk [CZ] 48 F2
Uster [CH] 58 G5
Ústí [CZ] 50 E6
Ustibar [BIH] 144 E2
Ústí nad Labem [CZ] 48 F2
Ústí nad Orlicí [CZ] 50 B4
Ustiprača [BIH] 144 E1
Ustjuzha [RUS] 202 E1
Ustka [PL] 22 B2
Ust'-Luga [RUS] 178 E6
Ustrem [BG] 150 A1
Ustroń [PL] 50 F5
Ustronie Morskie [PL] 20 H3
Ustrzyki Dolne [PL] 52 F5
Ustrzyki Górne [PL] 52 F6
Ustyluh [UA] 38 G6
Ususău [RO] 76 H5
Usvaty [RUS] 202 C4
Utajärvi [FIN] 196 E4
Utåker [N] 170 B5
Utansjö [S] 184 F3
Utbjoa [N] 164 B1
Utebo [E] 90 E3
Utena [LT] 200 G4
Uthlede [D] 18 D4
Utiel [E] 98 D4
Utne [N] 170 C4
Utrecht [NL] 16 D5
Utrera [E] 100 G2
Utrillas [E] 90 E6
Utrine [SCG] 76 E5
Utsjö [S] 172 F4
Utsjoki [FIN] 194 D3
Utstein [N] 164 A2
Uttendorf [A] 60 G4
Uttendorf [A] 72 F1
Uttermossa [FIN] 186 B5
Uttersberg [S] 168 A2
Utti [FIN] 178 C3
Utting [D] 60 D4
Uttoxeter [GB] 10 E5
Utula [FIN] 178 E1
Utvalnäs [S] 174 E4
Utvängstorp [S] 162 C1
Utvik [N] 180 D5
Utvorda [N] 190 C4
Uukuniemen Kk. [FIN] 188 G5
Uurainen [FIN] 186 F4
Uuro [FIN] 186 B5
Uuro [FIN] 196 G6
Uusijoki [FIN] 194 E5
Uusikaarlepyy / Nykarleby [FIN] 186 C1
Uusikaupunki [FIN] 176 C3
Uusikaupunki / Nystad [FIN] 176 C3
Uusikylä [FIN] 178 B3
Uusi-Värtsilä [FIN] 188 G3
Uutela [FIN] 194 D6
Uva [FIN] 196 F4
Uvac [BIH] 144 E1
Úvaly [CZ] 48 G4
Uvanå [S] 172 F5
Uvarovka [RUS] 202 E3
Uvdal [N] 170 F4
Uyeasound [GB] 6 H3
Uzdowo [PL] 22 G5
Uzel [F] 26 A5
Uzerche [F] 66 G2
Uzès [F] 106 G3
Uzeste [F] 66 D4
Uzhorod [UA] 204 B3
Užice [SCG] 146 A2
Uzlovoye [RUS] 200 E5
Užokski, pereval- [UA] 52 F6
Užpaliai [LT] 200 G4
Üzümlü [TR] 154 F2
Uzunköprü [TR] 150 B3
Uzunkuyu [TR] 152 B4
Uzunpinar [TR] 152 G4
Uzuntarla [TR] 150 G3
Užventis [LT] 200 E4

V

Vå [N] 164 E1
Vä [S] 158 D2
Vaajakoski [FIN] 186 G4
Vaajasalmi [FIN] 186 H3
Vääkiö [FIN] 196 F3
Vääksy [FIN] 178 A2
Vaala [FIN] 196 E4
Vaalajärvi [FIN] 194 D6
Vaalimaa [FIN] 178 D3
Vaarakylä [FIN] 196 F5
Vaaraniva [FIN] 196 F3
Väärinmaja [FIN] 186 E5
Vaas [F] 42 B6
Vaasa / Vasa [FIN] 186 B2
Vaassen [NL] 16 F4
Väätäiskylä [FIN] 186 E3
Vabalninkas [LT] 200 F3
Vác [H] 64 C5
Vacha [D] 46 F1
Váchartyán [H] 64 C6
Väckelsång [S] 162 E5
Vad [S] 168 A1
Vădastra [RO] 148 A2
Vadé-Puszta [H] 76 A3
Väderstad [S] 166 G6
Vadheim [N] 170 C1
Vadili (Vatili) [CY] 154 G5
Vadna [H] 64 F4
Vado Ligure [I] 108 H3
Vadsø [N] 194 E2
Vadstena [S] 166 G5
Vaduz [FL] 58 H6
Væggerløse [DK] 20 B1
Vafaíika [GR] 130 E3
Vafiochóri [GR] 128 G3
Vág [H] 74 G1
Vågåmo [N] 180 G5
Vagan [BIH] 142 B4
Våge [N] 164 A1
Våge [N] 164 C6
Våge [N] 170 B5
Vage [N] 180 E3
Vågen [N] 190 A6
Vägeva [EST] 198 E2
Vaggeryd [S] 162 D3
Vaggsvik [N] 192 F3
Vágia [GR] 134 B5
Vagiónia [GR] 140 E5
Vaglio Basilicata [I] 120 H4
Vagnhärad [S] 168 D4
Vagos [P] 80 B5
Vågsbygd [N] 164 D6
Vägsele [S] 190 G5
Vägsjöfors [S] 172 E5
Vågslid [N] 164 D1
Vágur [FR] 160 A3
Vähäkyro / Lillkyro [FIN] 186 B2
Vahanka [FIN] 186 E3
Vahastu [EST] 198 E2
Vaheri [FIN] 186 G5
Vái [GR] 140 H4
Vaiano [I] 110 F5
Vaiges [F] 40 H5
Vaiguva [LT] 200 E4
Vaihingen [D] 46 C6
Väike-Maarja [EST] 198 F1
Väike Rakke [EST] 198 F3
Vaikko [FIN] 196 F6
Vailly [F] 56 C2
Vainikkala [FIN] 178 E2
Vainupea [EST] 198 E1
Vainutas [LT] 200 D5
Vaison-la-Romaine [F] 106 H3
Vaite [F] 58 A3
Vajmat [S] 190 H2
Vajnede [LV] 198 C6
Vajont [I] 72 F4
Vajszló [H] 76 A5
Vajza [AL] 128 B5
Vakarel [BG] 146 G5
Vakern [S] 172 F5
Vakiflar [TR] 150 C2
Vaksdal [N] 170 B3
Vaksevo [BG] 146 F6
Vålådalen [S] 182 E2
Valajanaapa [FIN] 196 D2
Valajaskoski [FIN] 194 D8
Valandovo [MK] 128 G2
Valanhamn [N] 192 G1
Valareña [E] 84 B6
Valaská Belá [SK] 64 B2
Valašská Polanka [CZ] 50 E6
Valašské Klobouky [CZ] 50 E6
Valašské Meziříčí [CZ] 50 E5
Valbella [CH] 70 H1
Valberg [F] 108 E3
Vålberg [S] 166 E3
Valbiska [HR] 112 E2
Valbo [S] 174 E4
Valbondione [I] 72 A4
Valbonë [AL] 146 A5
Valbonnais [F] 68 H5
Vâlcani [RO] 76 F5
Valcarlos / Luzaide [E] 84 C3
Val-Claret [F] 70 C4
Valcum [H] 74 G3
Valdagno [I] 72 D6
Valdahon [F] 58 B5
Valdaj [RUS] 202 D2
Valdalen [N] 182 D5
Valdeazores [E] 96 D2
Valdecaballeros [E] 96 C2
Valdecabras [E] 98 C2
Valdecarros [E] 88 C3
Valdedios [E] 82 C2
Valdeganga [E] 98 C5
Valdelacas de Tajo [E] 96 C1
Val del Charco del Agua Amarga, Cueva de la- [E] 90 F6
Valdeltormo [E] 90 G6
Valdemārpils [LV] 198 C4
Valdemarsvik [S] 168 C6
Valdemorillo [E] 88 F5
Valdemoro [E] 88 F6
Valdemoro Sierra [E] 98 C2
Valdenoceda [E] 82 F4
Valdepeñas [E] 96 F5
Valdepeñas de Jaén [E] 102 E3
Valdepolo [E] 82 C4
Valderas [E] 82 B5
Valderice [I] 126 B2
Valderöy [N] 180 C3
Valderrobres [E] 98 G1
Valdesalor [E] 86 H5
Val d'Esquières [F] 108 D5
Valdeverdeja [E] 96 C1
Valdieri [I] 108 F3
Val d'Isère [F] 70 C4
Val-d'Izé [F] 26 D6
Valdobbiádene [I] 72 E5
Valdoviño [E] 78 D1
Valdštejn [CZ] 48 H2
Valdunquillo [E] 82 B6
Valea lui Mihai [RO] 204 B3
Valea Rea [RO] 148 F1
Valebø [N] 164 F2
Valečov [CZ] 48 G2
Vale Da Rosa [P] 94 C5
Vale de Açor [P] 94 D3
Vale de Cambra [P] 80 C5
Vale de Lobos [P] 94 C5
Vale do Arco [P] 86 D4
Vale do Côa, Parque Arqueológico do- [P] 80 E5
Vale do Poço [P] 94 D4
Valega [P] 80 B5
Valéggio sul Míncio [I] 110 E1
Valen [N] 170 B5
Valença do Minho [P] 78 B5
Valençay [F] 54 H3
Valence [F] 66 E6
Valence [F] 66 F6
Valence [F] 68 F5
Valence d'Albigeois [F] 106 C2
Valencia [E] 98 E4
Valencia de Alcántara [E] 86 F5
Valencia de Don Juan [E] 82 B5
Valencia de las Torres [E] 94 H3
Valencia del Ventoso [E] 94 G3
Valencia de Mombuey [E] 94 F3
Valenciennes [F] 28 G4
Văleni [RO] 148 B1
Vălenii De Munte [RO] 204 D5
Valensole [F] 108 C4
Valentano [I] 114 G3
Valentigney [F] 58 C4
Valenza [I] 70 F6
Våler [N] 166 B2
Våler [N] 172 D4
Valeria [E] 98 B3
Valevåg [N] 170 B6
Valfàbbrica [I] 116 A2
Valga [EST] 198 F4
Valgeristi [EST] 198 D2
Valgrisenche [I] 70 C4
Valguarnera Caropepe [I] 126 F3
Välijoki [FIN] 178 D2
Välijoki [FIN] 194 D8
Välikylä [FIN] 196 C6
Valimítika [GR] 132 G6
Välivaara [FIN] 196 G6
Valjevo [SCG] 146 A1
Valjimena [E] 88 C4
Valjok [N] 194 C3
Valka [LV] 198 F4
Valkeakoski [FIN] 176 F2
Valkeala [FIN] 178 C2
Valkeavaara [FIN] 188 G4
Valkenburg [NL] 30 F4
Valkenswaard [NL] 30 E3
Valkiamäki [FIN] 188 E6
Valkininkai [LT] 24 H2
Valko / Valkom [FIN] 178 B4
Valkom / Valko [FIN] 178 B4
Valla [S] 182 F1
Valla [S] 184 D3
Vallada [E] 78 F4
Valladolid [E] 88 E2
Vallåkra [S] 156 H2
Vallargärdet [S] 166 F2
Vallata [I] 120 F3
Vallbona de les Monges [E] 92 C4
Valldal [N] 180 E4
Valldemossa [E] 104 E4
Valle [LV] 198 E6
Valle [N] 164 D2
Valle de Abdalajís [E] 102 B4
Valle de Cabuérniga [E] 82 E3
Valle dei Templi [I] 126 D4
Valle de la Serena [E] 96 A3
Valle de los Caidos [E] 88 F5
Valle de Matamoros [E] 94 F3
Valledoria [I] 118 C2
Vallehermoso [E] 100 B5
Vallelunga Pratameno [I] 126 D3
Vallen [S] 184 D1
Vallentuna [S] 168 E2
Valleraugue [F] 106 E2
Valles de Ortega [E] 100 E6
Vallet [F] 54 C2
Valletta [M] 126 C6
Vallfogona de Ripollès [E] 92 E2
Vallheim [N] 190 D4
Vallivana [E] 98 G2
Vallo di Lucania [I] 120 F5
Valloire [F] 70 B5
Valloires, Abbaye de- [F] 28 D3
Vallombrosa [I] 110 F5
Vallon-en-Sully [F] 56 C5
Vallon-Pont-d'Arc [F] 68 E6
Vallorbe [CH] 58 B6
Vallorcine [F] 70 C3
Vallø Slot [DK] 156 G3
Vallouise [F] 70 B6
Vallrun [S] 190 E6
Valls [E] 92 C4
Vallsbo [S] 174 D3
Vallset [N] 172 C4
Vallsta [S] 174 D1
Vallter 2000 [E] 92 E2
Vallvig [S] 174 E2
Valmadrid [E] 90 E4
Valmiera [LV] 198 E4
Valmigère [F] 106 C5
Valmojado [E] 88 E6
Valmontone [I] 116 B6
Valmorel [F] 70 B4
Val Moutier [CH] 58 D5
Valö [S] 174 F5
Valognes [F] 26 D2
Valongo [P] 80 C4
Valoria la Buena [E] 88 F1
Valøy [N] 190 C4
Valøya [N] 190 C5
Valozhyn [BY] 200 H6
Valpaços [P] 80 E3
Valpelline [I] 70 D3
Valporquero de Torío [E] 78 H5
Valpovo [HR] 76 B6
Valras-Plage [F] 106 D5
Valréas [F] 106 H2
Vals [CH] 70 G2
Valsamónero [GR] 140 E5
Valsebo [S] 166 C3
Valset [N] 190 B6
Valsjöbyn [S] 190 E5
Valsjön [S] 184 D5
Valskog [S] 168 B3
Vals-les-Bains [F] 68 E6
Valsøybotn [N] 180 G2
Välsta [S] 184 E6
Val-Suzon [F] 56 G3
Valtesíniko [GR] 136 D2
Val Thorens [F] 70 B5
Valtiendas [E] 88 G3
Valtierra [E] 84 B5
Valtimo [FIN] 196 F5
Valtjom [S] 184 E4
Valtola [FIN] 178 C2
Váltos [GR] 130 H1
Valtournenche [I] 70 D3

Vila Velha de Ródão [P] 86 E4
Vila Verde [P] 78 B6
Vila Verde [P] 80 F3
Vila Verde da Raia [P] 80 E3
Vila Verde de Ficalho [P] 94 E3
Vila Viçosa [P] 86 E6
Vilches [E] 102 F1
Vildbjerg [DK] 160 C6
Vilémov [CZ] 48 H4
Vilhelmina [S] 190 F5
Vília [GR] 134 B6
Vilinska Jama [HR] 74 D6
Viljakkala [FIN] 186 D6
Viljandi [EST] 198 E3
Viljolahti [FIN] 188 E4
Vilkaviškis [LT] 24 E1
Vilkija [LT] 200 F5
Villa Adriana [I] 116 B5
Villa Bartolomea [I] 110 F2
Villablanca [E] 94 D5
Villablino [E] 78 G4
Villabona [E] 84 B2
Villacañas [E] 96 G2
Villacarrillo [E] 102 F1
Villa Castelli [I] 122 F4
Villacastín [E] 88 E4
Villach [A] 72 H3
Villacidro [I] 118 C6
Villada [E] 82 C5
Villadangos del Páramo [E] 78 G6
Villa del Prado [E] 88 E6
Villa del Río [E] 102 D1
Villa de Ves [E] 98 D5
Villadiego [E] 82 E5
Villadoro [I] 126 E3
Villadossola [I] 70 E3
Villa Estense [I] 110 G2
Villafranca del Bierzo [E] 78 F5
Villafranca del Cid / Vilafranca del Maestrat [E] 98 F2
Villafranca de los Barros [E] 94 G3
Villafranca de los Caballeros [E] 96 G3
Villafranca di Verona [I] 110 E1
Villafranca Montes de Oca [E] 82 F6
Villafranca Piemonte [I] 70 D6
Villafranca Tirrena [I] 124 B7
Villafrati [I] 126 D2
Villafrechós [E] 82 B6
Villafruela [E] 88 G1
Villafuerte [E] 88 F2
Village, Roche aux- [F] 44 C1
Villaggio Aplui [I] 122 E3
Villaggio Mancuso [I] 124 E5
Villagonzalo Pedernales [E] 82 E6
Villagordo [E] 102 E2
Villagrains [F] 66 C4
Villagrande Strisaili [I] 118 E5
Villaharta [E] 96 C6
Villahermosa [E] 96 G5
Villahoz [E] 88 G1
Villaines la Gonais [F] 42 C5
Villaines-la-Juhel [F] 26 F6
Villajos, Ermita de- [E] 96 G3
Villajoyosa / la Vila Joiosa [E] 104 E2
Villala [FIN] 188 F4
Villalba Alta [E] 78 E2
Villalba de Guardo [E] 82 C4
Villalba de la Sierra [E] 98 C2
Villalba de los Barros [E] 94 G2
Villalcázar de Sirga [E] 82 D5
Villalgordo del Marquesado [E] 98 A3
Villa Literno [I] 120 D3
Villalón de Campos [E] 82 C6
Villalpando [E] 82 B6
Villalpardo [E] 98 C4
Villaluenga [E] 96 F1
Villamalea [E] 98 C4
Villamañán [E] 78 H6
Villamanín de la Tercia [E] 78 H5
Villamanrique [E] 96 G6
Villamanrique de la Condesa [E] 94 F6
Villamar [I] 118 C6
Villamartín [E] 100 G3
Villamartín de Campos [E] 82 C6
Villamassargia [I] 118 B7
Villamayor [E] 80 H6
Villamayor de Santiago [E] 96 H2
Villamediana de Iregua [E] 82 H6
Villamesías [E] 96 B2
Villa Minozzo [I] 110 D3
Villandraut [F] 66 D4
Villandry [F] 54 F2
Villanova [I] 122 F3
Villanova d'Asti [I] 70 D6
Villanova Monteleone [I] 118 B3
Villanova Tulo [I] 118 D5
Villanúa [E] 84 D5
Villanubla [E] 88 E1
Villanueva de Alcardete [E] 96 H3
Villanueva de Argaño [E] 82 E5
Villanueva de Cañedo [E] 80 H6
Villanueva de Córdoba [E] 96 C5
Villanueva de Gállego [E] 90 E3
Villanueva de Huerva [E] 90 E4
Villanueva del Aceral [E] 88 E3
Villanueva de la Fuente [E] 96 H5
Villanueva de la Jara [E] 98 B4
Villanueva de la Reina [E] 102 E1
Villanueva del Arzobispo [E] 102 G1
Villanueva de las Cruces [E] 94 E5
Villanueva de la Serena [E] 96 B3
Villanueva de la Sierra [E] 86 H3
Villanueva de Las Torres [E] 102 F3
Villanueva de las Torres [E] 102 F3
Villanueva de la Vera [E] 88 C5
Villanueva del Campo [E] 82 B6
Villanueva del Duque [E] 96 C5
Villanueva del Fresno [E] 94 F2
Villanueva de los Castillejos [E] 94 E5
Villanueva de los Infantes [E] 96 G5
Villanueva del Rey [E] 96 B5
Villanueva del Río Segura [E] 104 C2
Villanueva del Río y Minas [E] 94 H5
Villanueva del Trabuco [E] 102 C4
Villanueva de San Carlos [E] 104 H5
Villanueva de Sigena [E] 90 G4
Villány [H] 76 B5
Villa Opicina [I] 72 H6
Villapalacios [E] 96 H6
Villapiana Scalo [I] 122 D6
Villaplana [I] 122 D6
Villa Potenza [I] 116 C1
Villaputzu [I] 118 E6
Villaquejida [E] 82 B5
Villaquilambre [E] 78 H5
Villarcayo [E] 82 F4
Villard-de-Lans [F] 68 G5
Villardebelle [F] 106 B5
Villar de Cantos [E] 98 B3
Villar de Ciervo [E] 80 E6
Villardeciervos [E] 80 G3
Villar de Domingo García [E] 98 B1
Villardefrades [E] 88 D1
Villar del Arzobispo [E] 98 E3
Villar del Pedroso [E] 96 C1
Villar del Pozo [E] 98 B5
Villar del Rey [E] 86 F6
Villar de Olalla [E] 98 B2
Villar de Rena [E] 96 B3
Villar de Río [E] 90 C2
Villarejo de Fuentes [E] 96 H2
Villarejo de Salvanés [E] 96 G1
Villares de la Reina [E] 80 H6
Villares del Saz [E] 98 B2
Villargordo del Cabriel [E] 98 C4
Villaricos [E] 104 A5
Villariño de Conso [E] 78 D6
Villarluengo [E] 98 F1
Villarmayor [E] 80 G6
Villa Romana del Casale [I] 126 E4
Villarosa [I] 126 E3
Villarquemado [E] 98 D1
Villarramiel [E] 82 C6
Villarreal de San Carlos [E] 88 A6
Villarreal - la Vila Reial [E] 98 F3
Villarrobledo [E] 96 H4
Villarroga de los Pinares [E] 98 F1
Villarroja [E] 84 A5
Villarroya de la Sierra [E] 90 C4
Villarrubia de los Ojos [E] 96 F3
Villars [CH] 70 C2
Villars-les-Dombes [F] 68 G2
Villars-sur-Var [F] 108 E4
Villarta [E] 98 C4
Villarta de los Montes [E] 96 D3
Villarta de San Juan [E] 96 F3
Villarubia de Santiago [E] 96 G1
Villasalto [I] 118 D6
Villasana de Mena [E] 82 F4
Villa San Giovanni [I] 124 C7
Villa Santa Maria [I] 116 D5
Villasante [E] 82 F4
Villa Santina [I] 72 G4
Villaseco de los Gamitos [E] 80 G6
Villaseco de los Reyes [E] 80 G5
Villasequilla [E] 96 F2
Villasimius [I] 118 D7
Villa S.Lucia degli Abruzzi [I] 116 D4
Villasor [I] 118 C6
Villasrubias [E] 86 H3
Villastar [E] 98 D2
Villatobas [E] 96 G2
Villatoro [E] 82 E6
Villatoya [E] 98 C4
Villava [E] 84 B4
Villavelayo [E] 90 A1
Villaverde del Río [E] 94 H5
Villaverde de Trucios [E] 82 G3
Villaviciosa [E] 82 C2
Villaviciosa [E] 96 C6
Villavieja [E] 80 F6
Villa Vomano [I] 116 C3
Villé [F] 58 D2
Villebois-Lavalette [F] 66 E2
Ville-Devant-Chaumont [F] 44 D3
Villedieu-les-Poêles [F] 26 D4
Ville-en-Tardenois [F] 44 B3
Villefagnan [F] 54 E5
Villefontaine [F] 68 G3
Villefort [F] 68 D6
Villefranche [F] 108 F4
Villefranche-d'Albigeois [F] 106 C2
Villefranche-de-Conflent [F] 92 F1
Villefranche-de-Lauragais [F] 106 A4
Villefranche-de-Lonchat [F] 66 E3
Villefranche-de-Panat [F] 106 D2
Villefranche-de-Rouergue [F] 66 H5
Villefranche-du-Périgord [F] 66 F4
Villefranche-sur-Cher [F] 54 H2
Villefranche-sur-Saône [F] 68 F2
Villegats [F] 54 E5
Villel [E] 98 D2
Villemur [F] 106 A2
Villena [E] 104 D1
Villenauxe-la-Grande [F] 42 H5
Villeneuve [F] 66 H5
Villeneuve [F] 106 G3
Villeneuve d'Ascq [F] 28 F3
Villeneuve-de-Berg [F] 68 E6
Villeneuve-de-Marsan [F] 66 C6
Villeneuve-l'Archevêque [F] 42 H6
Villeneuve-Loubet [F] 108 E4
Villeneuve-sur-Allier [F] 56 D5
Villeneuve-sur-Lot [F] 66 E5
Villeneuve-sur-Yonne [F] 42 G6
Villerbon [F] 42 D6
Villeréal [F] 66 F4
Villers [B] 30 C5
Villers [F] 26 G3
Villers-Bocage [F] 26 E3
Villers-Bretonneux [F] 28 E5
Villers-Cotterêts [F] 42 H3
Villersexel [F] 58 C4
Villers-le-Lac [F] 58 C5
Villerville [F] 26 G3
Villeseque [F] 66 G5
Ville-sur-Illon [F] 58 C2
Villetta Barrea [I] 116 D6
Villiers-St-Georges [F] 42 H4
Villingen [D] 58 F3
Villingsberg [S] 166 G3
Villmanstrand / Lappeenranta [FIN] 178 E2
Villnäs / Askainen [FIN] 176 D4
Villoldo [E] 82 C5
Villon [F] 56 F2
Villorba [I] 72 E5
Villoria [E] 88 D3
Villoslada de Cameros [E] 90 B1
Villstad [S] 162 C3
Villvattnet [S] 190 H5
Vilmajor [H] 76 F3
Vilnius [LT] 200 G5
Vilobacka [FIN] 186 C1
Vilovo [SCG] 142 G1
Vilppula [FIN] 186 E5
Vils [DK] 160 C4
Vilsbiburg [D] 60 F3
Vilseck [D] 46 H5
Vilshofen [D] 60 H3
Vilshult [S] 162 D6
Vilsund [DK] 160 C4
Vilunai [LT] 24 G1
Vilusi [SCG] 144 D3
Viluste [EST] 198 F3
Vilyeyka [BY] 202 B5
Vimianzo [E] 78 B2
Vimieiro [P] 86 D6
Vimioso [P] 80 G4
Vimmerby [S] 162 F2
Vimoutiers [F] 26 G4
Vimpeli [FIN] 186 D2
Vimperk [CZ] 62 A2
Vina [SCG] 146 D4
Vinac [BIH] 142 C4
Vinádio [I] 108 E3
Vinaixa [E] 92 C4
Vinaròs [E] 92 A6
Vinay [F] 68 G4
Vinça [F] 92 F1
Vinchiaturo [I] 120 E1
Vinci [I] 110 E5
Vindbyholt [DK] 156 G4
Vindelgransele [S] 190 G4
Vindeln [S] 190 H5
Vinderslev [DK] 160 D6
Vinderup [DK] 160 C5
Vindsvik [N] 164 C2
Vinebre [E] 90 H6
Vinga [RO] 76 G5
Vingåker [S] 168 B4
Vingelen [N] 182 C4
Vingnes [N] 172 B2
Vingrau [F] 106 C6
Vingrom [N] 170 H2
Vinhais [P] 80 F3
Vinica [BG] 148 E3
Vinica [MK] 128 G1
Vinica [SLO] 112 G1
Viničani [MK] 128 F2
Viniegra de Abajo [E] 90 B1
Vinishte [BG] 146 F3
Vinjani [HR] 144 B2
Vinje [N] 164 E1
Vinje [N] 170 C3
Vinjeøra [N] 180 G2
Vinkovci [HR] 142 E1
Vinliden [S] 190 G5
Vinnytsia [UA] 202 C8
Vinon-sur-Verdon [F] 108 C4
Vinslöv [S] 158 D1
Vinsnes [N] 164 E3
Vinsternes [N] 180 F1
Vinstra [N] 170 H1
Vintgar [SLO] 74 B4
Vintjärn [S] 174 D3
Vintrosa [S] 166 G3
Viñuelas [E] 88 G5
Vinuesa [E] 90 B2
Vinzelberg [D] 34 B2
Violès [F] 106 H3
Vipava [SLO] 74 A5
Vipiteno / Sterzing [I] 72 D2
Vira [HR] 144 A2
Virányos [H] 64 G4
Virdois / Virrat [FIN] 186 D4
Vire [F] 26 E4
Viré [F] 56 G6
Vire Court [F] 40 B3
Vireda [S] 162 D1
Vireši [LV] 198 F4
Virestad [S] 162 D5
Virgen [A] 72 F2
Virgen de Criptana [E] 96 G3
Virgen de la Cabeza [E] 96 E6
Virgen De La Cabeza [E] 98 B4
Virgen de la Cabeza [E] 102 G2
Virgen de la Montaña [E] 86 H5
Virgen de la Muela [E] 96 G2
Virgen de la Peña [E] 90 H3
Virgen De La Peña [E] 94 E4
Virgen del Castillo [E] 88 F3
Virginia [IRL] 2 E5
Virieu [F] 68 G4
Virieu-le-Grand [F] 68 H3
Virje [HR] 74 G5
Virkby / Virkkala [FIN] 176 G5
Virkkala / Virkby [FIN] 176 G5
Virklund [DK] 156 C1
Virmaanpää [FIN] 186 H3
Virmaila [FIN] 176 H1
Virmutjoki [FIN] 178 E1
Virojoki [FIN] 178 D3
Virolahti [FIN] 178 D3
Vironvay [F] 28 C6
Virovitica [HR] 74 H5
Virpazar [SCG] 144 E5
Virrat / Virdois [FIN] 186 D4
Virsbo [S] 168 B1
Virsbo bruk [S] 168 B1
Virserum [S] 162 F3
Virtaniemi [FIN] 194 E4
Virtasalmi [FIN] 188 D4
Virton [B] 44 E2
Virtsu [EST] 198 D3
Virttaa [FIN] 176 E3
Viru-Jaagupi [EST] 198 F1
Virvoru [RO] 146 F1
Vis [HR] 116 H2
Visaginas [LT] 200 H4
Visbek [D] 18 C6
Visby [DK] 156 B4
Visby [S] 168 G4
Visé [B] 30 E4
Višegrad [BIH] 144 E1
Visegrád [H] 64 C5
Viseu [P] 80 C6
Vishnyeva [BY] 200 H6
Vishovgrad [BG] 148 C3
Vishtytis [LT] 24 D2
Visiedo [E] 90 D6
Vişina Veche [RO] 148 A2
Visingsborg [S] 162 D1
Viskafors [S] 162 B2
Viskinge [DK] 156 F2
Viškovci [HR] 142 D1
Viškovo [HR] 112 E1
Visland [N] 164 C4
Vislanda [S] 162 D5
Višnja Gora [SLO] 74 C5
Visočka Ržana [SCG] 146 E4
Viso del Marqués [E] 96 F5
Visoka [SCG] 146 A3
Visoki Dečani, Manastir- [SCG] 146 B5
Visoko [BIH] 142 D4
Visoko [SLO] 74 B4
Visp [CH] 70 E2
Vissefjärda [S] 162 F5
Visselhövede [D] 18 E6
Visseltofta [S] 162 C6
Vissenbjerg [DK] 156 D3
Visso [I] 116 B2
Vistdal [N] 180 F3
Vistheden [S] 196 A3
Vistino [RUS] 178 F5
Visuvesi [FIN] 186 E5
Visz [H] 76 A3
Vitalahti [FIN] 186 G5
Vitănești [RO] 148 C1
Vitanovac [SCG] 146 B3
Vitberget [S] 190 H2
Vitemölla [S] 158 D2
Viterbo [I] 114 H4
Viterbo, Bagni di- [I] 114 H4
Vithkuq [AL] 128 C5
Vitigudino [E] 80 F6
Vitina [BIH] 144 B2
Vitina [SCG] 146 C6
Vitis [A] 62 D3
Vitkov [CZ] 50 E4
Vitkovo [SCG] 146 C3
Vitolište [MK] 128 F3
Vitomirica [SCG] 146 B5
Vitoria-Gasteiz [E] 82 G5
Vitré [F] 26 D6
Vitry-le-François [F] 44 C5
Vitsand [S] 172 E5
Vitskøl Kloster [DK] 160 D4
Vitsyebsk [BY] 202 C4
Vittangi [S] 192 H5
Vittarp [DK] 156 A2
Vittaryd [S] 162 C4
Vitteaux [F] 56 G3
Vittel [F] 58 B2
Vittinge [S] 168 C1
Vittjärn [S] 172 D5
Vittjärv [S] 196 B3
Vittória [I] 126 F5
Vittoriosa [M] 126 C6
Vittório Véneto [I] 72 E5
Vitträsk [S] 194 A8
Vittsjö [S] 162 C6
Vittskövle [S] 158 D2
Vitvattnet [S] 190 H6
Vitvattnet [S] 196 C2
Vitznau [CH] 58 F6
Viù [I] 70 D5
Vivario [F] 114 B4
Viveiro [E] 78 E1
Vivel del Río Martín [E] 90 E6
Viver [E] 98 E3
Viverone [I] 70 E5
Viveros [E] 96 H5
Vivier, Château du- [F] 42 G4
Viviers [F] 68 F6
Vivonne [F] 54 E4
Vivungi [S] 192 H5
Vixia Herbeira [E] 78 D1
Vize [TR] 150 C2
Vizille [F] 68 H5
Vižinada [HR] 112 D1
Vizovice [CZ] 50 E6
Vizsoly [H] 64 G4
Vizzavona [F] 114 B4
Vizzini [I] 126 F4
Vjazy [RUS] 178 E3
Vjetrenica [BIH] 144 C3
Vlaardingen [NL] 16 C5
Vlacháva [GR] 132 E1
Vlacherná [GR] 132 D3
Vlachiótis [GR] 136 E4
Vlachokerasiá [GR] 136 E3
Vlachovo Březí [CZ] 48 E6
Vladičin Han [SCG] 146 D5
Vlădila [RO] 148 A1
Vladimir [SCG] 128 A1
Vladimirescu [RO] 76 G4
Vladimirovac [SCG] 142 H2
Vladimirovka [RUS] 178 H2
Vladimirovo [BG] 146 F3
Vladimirovo [BG] 148 F2
Vladimirskiy [RUS] 198 H3
Vlagtweed [NL] 16 H3
Vlahovo [BG] 130 E1
Vlas [BG] 148 F4
Vlasenica [BIH] 142 E4
Vlašim [CZ] 48 G5
Vlasin [RO] 148 C1
Vlasina Okruglica [SCG] 146 E5
Vlasotince [SCG] 146 D4
Vlieland [NL] 16 E1
Vlissingen [NL] 16 B6
Vlkava [CZ] 48 G3
Vlkolinec [SK] 64 C2
Vlochós [GR] 132 F2
Vlorë [AL] 128 A5
Vlotho [D] 32 E2
Vlychó [GR] 132 D5
Voćin [HR] 74 H6
Vöcklabruck [A] 62 A5
Vodice [HR] 112 H6
Vodice [SLO] 74 B4
Vodinci [HR] 142 E1
Voditsa [BG] 148 D3
Vodňany [CZ] 48 F6
Vodnjan [HR] 112 D2
Vodskov [DK] 160 E3
Voergård [DK] 160 E3
Voerså [DK] 160 E3
Vogatsikó [GR] 128 E5
Vogelsdorf [D] 34 F2
Voghera [I] 70 F6
Vognillan [N] 180 H3
Vogogna [I] 70 E3
Vogorno [CH] 70 F3
Vogorno [CH] 70 G2
Vogošća [BIH] 144 D1
Vohburg [D] 60 E2
Vohenstrauss [D] 48 C5
Võhma [EST] 198 C3
Võhma [EST] 198 E2
Vöhringen [D] 60 B4
Void [F] 44 D5
Voikoski [FIN] 178 C2
Voïnka [UA] 204 H3
Voiron [F] 68 H4
Voise [F] 42 E4
Võiske [EST] 198 D3
Voitsberg [A] 74 D2
Voix [F] 108 C3
Vojakkala [FIN] 176 G3
Vojany [SK] 64 H3
Vojčice [SK] 64 G3
Vojens [DK] 156 C3
Vojlovica [SCG] 142 H2
Vojmån [S] 190 F4
Vojnić [HR] 112 H1
Vojnik [SLO] 74 D4
Vojtanov [CZ] 48 C3
Vojtjajaure [S] 190 E3
Voknavolok [RUS] 196 G3
Voláda [GR] 140 H2
Vólakas [GR] 130 C2
Volary [CZ] 62 B2
Volda [N] 180 C4
Voldby [DK] 160 F5
Volders [A] 72 D1
Volendam [NL] 16 E4
Volfštejn [CZ] 48 D4
Volgosovo [RUS] 198 G2
Volimes [GR] 136 A2
Volissós [GR] 134 G4
Volkach [D] 46 F4
Völkermarkt [A] 74 C3
Volkhov [RUS] 202 C1
Völklingen [D] 44 G4
Volkmarsen [D] 32 E5
Volkovija [MK] 128 D2
Vollenhove [NL] 16 F3
Volmsjö [S] 190 G5
Volochys'k [UA] 202 B8
Volodarka [UA] 202 D8
Volodymyr-Volyns'kyi [UA] 38 H6
Volokolamsk [RUS] 202 E3
Voloma [RUS] 196 H5
Vólos [GR] 132 H2
Voloshovo [RUS] 198 H2
Volosovo [RUS] 178 G6
Volovo [BG] 148 C2
Volpiano [I] 70 D5
Volterra [I] 114 F1
Volterraio [I] 114 E2
Voltri [I] 110 A3
Voltti [FIN] 186 C2
Volturara Appula [I] 120 F1
Volvic [F] 68 C2
Volyně [CZ] 48 E6
Vonesha voda [BG] 148 C4
Võnitsa [GR] 132 D4
Võnnu [EST] 198 F3
Vönöck [H] 74 G1
Voorschoten [NL] 16 C4
Voorst [NL] 16 F5
Vopnafjörður [IS] 192 C2
Vörå / Vöyri [FIN] 186 B2
Vorau [A] 74 E1
Vorbasse [DK] 156 B2
Vorbourg [CH] 58 D4
Vorchdorf [A] 62 B5
Vörden [D] 32 D1
Vordernberg [A] 62 C6
Vorderriss [D] 60 D6
Vordingborg [DK] 156 F4
Vorë [AL] 128 B3
Voreinó [GR] 128 F3
Voreppe [F] 68 H4
Vorey [F] 68 E4
Vøringsfossen [N] 170 D4
Vormsele [S] 190 G4
Vormstad [N] 180 H2
Vormsund [N] 172 C5
Voronkova Niva [RUS] 198 H4
Vorontsovo [RUS] 198 H4
Vorsfelde [D] 32 H2
Võru [EST] 198 F3
Voskopojë [AL] 128 C5
Voss [N] 170 C3
Vossijatskoje [UA] 204 G2
Votice [CZ] 48 G5
Votonósi [GR] 132 D1
Vouillé [F] 54 E4
Voukoliés [GR] 140 B4
Voúla [GR] 136 G1
Vouliagméni [GR] 136 G1
Voúlpi [GR] 132 E3
Vourkári [GR] 138 C2
Vourvouroú [GR] 130 C5
Voutás [GR] 134 A4
Vouvant [F] 54 C3
Vouvray [F] 54 G2
Vouzela [P] 80 C5
Vouziers [F] 44 C3
Voves [F] 42 E5
Vovoúsa [GR] 132 D1
Vowpa [BY] 24 G5
Voxna [S] 174 C2
Voxtorp [S] 162 D4
Vöylä [FIN] 194 D4
Voynica [BG] 146 E2
Voynitsa [RUS] 196 G3
Voynovo [BG] 148 F1
Vöyri / Vörå [FIN] 186 B2
Vozarci [MK] 128 F2
Voznesens'k [UA] 204 F2
Vozrozhdenie [RUS] 178 F2
Vrå [DK] 160 E3
Vrå [S] 162 C5
Vrabinec [CZ] 48 F2
Vráble [SK] 64 B4
Vrachnaíika [GR] 132 F6
Vrådal [N] 164 E2
Vråliosen [N] 164 E2
Vrams Gunnarstorp [S] 156 H1
Vrana [HR] 112 E3
Vrana [HR] 112 G5
Vranduk [BIH] 142 D4
Vranino [BG] 148 G2
Vranja [HR] 112 E1
Vranjak [HR] 112 F3
Vranje [SCG] 146 D5
Vranjska Banja [SCG] 146 D5
Vranov nad Dyjí [CZ] 62 E2
Vranov Nad Topl'Ou [SK] 64 G2
Vransko [SLO] 74 C4
Vrapčići [BIH] 144 C2
Vrapčište [MK] 128 D1
Vrástama [GR] 130 C5
Vratarnica [SCG] 146 E2
Vrátna [SK] 50 G6
Vratna, Manastir- [SCG] 146 E1
Vratnica [MK] 146 C6
Vratno [HR] 74 E4
Vratsa [BG] 146 G3
Vravróna [GR] 134 C6
Vražogrnac [SCG] 146 E2
Vrba [SLO] 74 B4
Vrbanja [HR] 142 E2
Vrbanje [SCG] 144 D4
Vrbas [SCG] 76 D6
Vrbaška [BIH] 142 C2
Vrbnica [SCG] 146 B6
Vrbnik [HR] 112 F2
Vrbno pod Pradědem [CZ] 50 D3
Vrboska [HR] 144 A2
Vrbové [SK] 62 H3
Vrbovec [HR] 74 F5
Vrbovsko [HR] 112 F1
Vrchlabí [CZ] 50 A2
Vrčice [SLO] 74 D6
Vrčin [SCG] 142 G3
Vrdnik [SCG] 142 F2
Vreden [D] 16 G5
Vrees [D] 18 C5
Vrelo [HR] 112 G3
Vrelo Bune [BIH] 144 C2
Vrena [S] 168 C4
Vreoci [SCG] 146 B1
Vresovo [BG] 148 E4
Vresse [B] 44 D1
Vreta Kloster [S] 166 H5
Vretstorp [S] 166 G4
Vrgorac [HR] 144 B2
Vrhnika [SLO] 74 B5
Vrhpolje [BIH] 142 B3
Vriezenveen [NL] 16 G4
Vrigny [F] 44 B3
Vrigstad [S] 162 D3
Vrilisia [GR] 134 C6
Vrilissia [GR] 132 G3
Vrin [CH] 70 G1
Vříšek [CZ] 48 G2
Vrlika [HR] 142 A4
Vrnjačka Banja [SCG] 146 C3
Vron [F] 28 D3
Vrontádos [GR] 134 G4
Vrontoú [GR] 128 G6
Vroomshoop [NL] 16 G4
Vrosína [GR] 132 C2
Vrouchás [GR] 140 F4
Vroutek [CZ] 48 E3
Vroville [F] 44 E6
Vrpolje [HR] 112 H6
Vršani [BIH] 142 E2
Vrsar [HR] 112 D2
Vrtoče [BIH] 142 A3
Vrtojba [SLO] 72 H5
Vrútky [SK] 50 F6
Vrŭv [BG] 146 E1
Vrýses [GR] 140 C4
Vrysoúla [GR] 132 C3
Vrýtaina [GR] 132 H3
Vsetín [CZ] 50 E6
V. Sjulsmark [S] 196 A5
V. Torsas [S] 162 D5
V. Trgovišce [HR] 74 E5
Vučitrn [SCG] 146 C5
Vučjavas [SLO] 74 E3
Vučkovci [BIH] 142 D2
Vuckovica [SCG] 146 B2
Vue [F] 54 B1
Vufflens, Château de- [CH] 70 B1
Vught [NL] 16 E6
Vŭglevtsi [BG] 148 C4
Vujanovo [SCG] 146 D4
Vuka [HR] 142 D1
Vukovar [HR] 142 E1
Vukovec [HR] 74 F5
Vuku [N] 190 C6
Vulcăneşti [MD] 204 E4
Vŭlchedrŭm [BG] 146 F2
Vŭlchidol [BG] 148 F2
Vulci [I] 114 G4
Vuobmaved [FIN] 194 C4
Vuohtomäki [FIN] 196 E6
Vuojalahti [FIN] 186 H5
Vuojärvi [FIN] 194 D7
Vuokatti [FIN] 196 F5
Vuolenkoski [FIN] 178 B2
Vuolijoki [FIN] 196 E5
Vuolle [FIN] 196 C5
Vuollerim [S] 196 A2
Vuonislahti [FIN] 188 F1
Vuorenkylä [FIN] 186 G6
Vuorenmaa [FIN] 176 E3
Vuorenmaa [FIN] 188 D5
Vuorijärvi [FIN] 186 C5
Vuorilahti [FIN] 186 F2
Vuoriniemi [FIN] 188 F5
Vuostimojärvi [FIN] 194 E7
Vuotner [S] 190 H3
Vuotsino [FIN] 194 E7
Vuotso [FIN] 194 D5
Vuottas [S] 194 A8
Vuottolahti [FIN] 196 E5
Vŭrbitsa [BG] 148 E3
Vŭrshets [BG] 146 F3
Vyanta [LT] 198 C6
Vyartsilya [RUS] 188 G3
Vyaz'ma [RUS] 202 E3
Vybor [RUS] 198 H4
Vyborg [RUS] 178 F3
Vyerkhnyadzvinsk [BY] 202 B4
Vyhonochy [RUS] 202 E5
Vynohradiv [UA] 204 C3
Vyra [RUS] 178 H6
Vyritsa [RUS] 178 H6
Vyróneia [GR] 130 B2
Vyshgorodok [RUS] 198 G4
Vyshhorod [UA] 202 D7
Vyshniy Volochek [RUS] 202 D2
Vyskatka [RUS] 198 G1
Vyškov [CZ] 50 C6
Vyšná Revúca [SK] 64 C2
Vysock [RUS] 178 E3
Vysoká [CZ] 48 H4
Vysoká u Příbr. [CZ] 48 E5
Vysokaye [BY] 38 F2
Vysoké Mýto [CZ] 50 B4
Vysokoe [RUS] 24 C1
Vysokoye [RUS] 198 G2
Vysoký Chlumec [CZ] 48 F5
Vysoký Hrádek [CZ] 62 C2
Vyšší Brod [CZ] 62 B3
Vyssineá [GR] 128 E5
Vytína [GR] 136 D2

W

Waabs [D] 18 F1
Waalwijk [NL] 16 D6
Wabern [D] 32 E5
Wąbrzeźno [PL] 22 E5
Wachenroth [D] 46 F4
Wąchock [PL] 38 B6
Wachow [D] 34 D2
Wächtersbach [D] 46 D2
Wachtum [D] 18 C6
Wackersdorf [D] 48 C5
Wadebridge [GB] 12 C4
Wädenswil [CH] 58 F5
Wadlew [PL] 36 G5
Wadowice [PL] 50 G4
Wagenfeld [D] 32 E1
Wageningen [NL] 16 E5
Waging [D] 60 G5
Wagrain [A] 72 G1
Wągrowiec [PL] 36 D1
Wahlwies [D] 58 G4
Wahrenholz [D] 32 H1
Waiblingen [D] 58 H1
Waidhaus [D] 48 C5
Waidhofen an der Thaya [A] 62 D3
Waidhofen an der Ybbs [A] 62 C5
Waidring [A] 60 F6
Waischenfeld [D] 46 G4
Wakefield [GB] 10 F4
Walbeck [D] 34 A2
Wałbrzych [PL] 50 B2
Walchensee [D] 60 D6
Walchsee [A] 60 F5

Walcourt [B] 28 H4
Wałcz [PL] 22 A5
Wald [A] 72 E1
Wald [CH] 58 G5
Wald-angelloch [D] 46 C5
Waldbröl [D] 32 C6
Waldburg [D] 60 B5
Waldeck [D] 32 E5
Waldenbuch [D] 58 H1
Waldenburg [D] 46 D5
Waldenburg [D] 48 C1
Waldfischbach [D] 44 H4
Waldheim [D] 34 D6
Waldkirch [D] 58 E3
Waldkirchen [D] 62 A3
Waldkraiburg [D] 60 F4
Waldmünchen [D] 48 C5
Waldowice [PL] 34 H2
Waldsassen [D] 48 C4
Waldshut [D] 58 F4
Walenstadt [CH] 58 H6
Walhalla [D] 48 C6
Wallasey [GB] 10 D4
Walldorf [D] 46 C5
Walldürn [D] 46 D4
Wallenfels [D] 46 H3
Wallersdorf [D] 60 G3
Wallerstein [D] 60 C2
Wallfahrtskirche [D] 60 C2
Wallingford [GB] 14 D3
Wallsbüll [D] 156 B4
Wals [A] 60 G5
Walsall [GB] 10 E6
Walsrode [D] 18 E6
Waltrop [D] 30 H2
Waltsberg [A] 74 E3
Wambach [D] 32 E6
Wambierzyce [PL] 50 B2
Wanderup [D] 18 E1
Wandlitz [D] 34 E1
Wanfried [D] 32 G5
Wangen [D] 60 B5
Wangenbourg [F] 44 G6
Wangerooge [D] 18 C3
Wangersen [D] 18 E4
Wängi [CH] 58 G5
Wankendorf [D] 18 G2
Wantage [GB] 12 H3
Wanzleben [D] 34 B3
Warburg [D] 32 E4
Wardenburg [D] 18 C5
Ware [GB] 14 E3
Waregem [B] 28 G2
Wareham [GB] 12 G5
Waremme [B] 30 E4
Waren [D] 20 C4
Warendorf [D] 32 D3
Warin [D] 20 A4
Warka [PL] 38 C4
Warlubie [PL] 22 E4
Warmbad Villach [A] 72 H3
Warmensteinach [D] 46 H4
Warminster [GB] 12 G4
Warnemünde [D] 20 B3
Warner Bros Park [E] 88 F6
Warnice [PL] 20 F5
Warnice [PL] 34 G1
Warnsveld [NL] 16 F5
Warrenpoint [NIR] 2 G4
Warrington [GB] 10 D4
Warstein [D] 32 D4
Warszawa [PL] 38 B3
Warszkowo [PL] 22 B2
Warta [PL] 36 F4
Warta Bolesławiecka [PL] 36 A6
Wartburg [D] 32 G6
Wartensee [CH] 58 F5
Wartenstein [A] 62 E6
Warth [A] 72 B1
Wartha [D] 32 G6
Warwick [GB] 12 H2
Washington [GB] 8 G6
Wasigenstein, Château de- [F] 44 H4
Wasilków [PL] 24 E5
Wąsosz [PL] 24 D4
Wąsosz [PL] 36 C5
Wasselonne [F] 44 G6
Wassen [CH] 70 F1
Wassenaar [NL] 16 C4
Wassenberg [D] 30 F4
Wasseralfingen [D] 60 C2
Wasserbillig [L] 44 F2
Wasserburg [D] 60 F4
Wasserfall Groppenstn. [A] 72 G2
Wasserkuppe [D] 46 E2
Wasserleonberg [A] 72 H3
Wasserschloss [D] 32 C3
Wasserschloss [D] 34 D4
Wassertrüdingen [D] 46 F6
Wassy [F] 44 C5
Wasungen [D] 46 F1
Waterford / Portlairge [IRL] 4 E5
Watergrasshill [IRL] 4 D5
Waterloo [B] 30 C4
Waterlooville [GB] 12 H5
Waterville [IRL] 4 A4
Watford [GB] 14 E4
Watten [F] 14 H6
Wattens [A] 72 D1
Watton [GB] 14 G2
Wattwil [CH] 58 G5
Watzelsdorf [A] 62 E3
Waulsort [B] 30 D6
Wavre (Waver) [B] 30 D4
Waxenberg [A] 62 B3
Waxweiler [D] 44 F1
Ważne Młyny [PL] 36 G6
Wda [PL] 22 D4
Wdzydze Kiszewskie [PL] 22 D3
Węchadłów [PL] 52 B2
Wechselburg [D] 34 D6
Weddelsborg [DK] 156 C3
Wedel [D] 18 F4
Wedemark [D] 32 F1
Weener [D] 18 B5
Weert [NL] 30 E3
Weesen [CH] 58 G6
Weeze [D] 30 F2
Wegberg [D] 30 F3
Wegeleben [D] 34 A4
Wegenstedt [D] 34 B2
Weggis [CH] 58 F6
Węgliniec [PL] 34 H6
Węgorzewo [PL] 24 C2
Węgorzyno [PL] 20 G5
Węgrów [PL] 38 D2
Węgrzynice [PL] 34 H3
Wegscheid [D] 62 A3
Wehr [D] 30 H4
Wehr [D] 58 E4
Weichselboden [A] 62 D6
Weichshofen [D] 60 F3
Weida [D] 48 C1
Weiden [D] 48 C4
Weidenberg [D] 46 H4
Weidenstetten [D] 60 B3
Weigetschlag [A] 62 B3
Weikersheim [D] 46 E5
Weil [D] 58 G1
Weilar [D] 46 F1
Weilburg [D] 46 C2
Weilheim [D] 60 D5
Weilmünster [D] 46 C2
Weimar [D] 32 D6
Weimar [D] 34 A6
Weinfelden [CH] 58 G4
Weingarten [D] 60 B5
Weinheim [D] 46 C4
Weinsberg [D] 46 D5
Weintor [D] 46 B5
Weirenstein [A] 72 F2
Weismain [D] 46 G3
Weissbriach [A] 72 G3
Weissenbach [A] 60 C6
Weissenbach / Riobianco [I] 72 D2
Weissenburg [D] 46 G6
Weissenegg [A] 74 D2
Weissenfels [D] 34 C6
Weissenhorn [D] 60 B3
Weissenkirchen [A] 62 D4
Weissensee [D] 32 H5
Weissenstadt [D] 48 B3
Weissenstein [D] 46 G4
Weisskirchen [A] 74 C2
Weisstannen [CH] 58 H6
Weisswasser [D] 34 G5
Weitersfelden [A] 62 C3
Weitra [A] 62 C3
Weiz [A] 74 D2
Wejherowo [PL] 22 D2
Welden [D] 60 C3
Wełdkowo [PL] 22 A3
Well [NL] 30 F2
Wellaune [D] 34 D5
Welle [D] 18 F5
Wellin [B] 30 D6
Wellingborough [GB] 14 E2
Wellington [GB] 12 F4
Wells [GB] 12 F4
Wells-next-the-Sea [GB] 10 H6
Wels [A] 62 B4
Welsberg / Monguelfo [I] 72 E3
Welschofen / Nova Levante [I] 72 D3
Welshpool [GB] 10 C5
Weltenburg [D] 60 E2
Welwyn Garden City [GB] 14 E3
Welzheim [D] 60 B2
Wemding [D] 60 D2
Wemperhaardt [L] 30 F6
Wenddorf [D] 34 B2
Wendlingen [D] 58 H1
Wenecja [PL] 36 D1
Wengen [CH] 70 E1
Wenns [A] 72 C1
Wépion [B] 30 D5
Weppersdorf [A] 62 F6
Werben [D] 34 C1
Werbomont [B] 30 E5
Werdau [D] 48 C2
Werder [D] 34 D2
Werdohl [D] 32 C5
Werfen [A] 60 G6
Werl [D] 32 C4
Werlte [D] 18 B6
Wermelskirchen [D] 30 H4
Wernberg [D] 48 C5
Werne [D] 32 C4
Werneck [D] 46 E3
Werneuchen [D] 34 F2
Wernigerode [D] 32 H4
Wertach [D] 60 C5
Wertheim [D] 46 D4
Werther [D] 32 D3
Wertingen [D] 60 C3
Wesel [D] 30 G2
Wesenberg [D] 20 C5
Wesendorf [D] 32 H1
Wesoła [PL] 52 C3
Wesselburen [D] 18 E2
Wessobrunn [D] 60 D5
West Bridgford [GB] 10 F5
West Bromwich [GB] 10 E6
Westbury [GB] 12 G4
Westende-Bad [B] 28 F1
Westendorf [A] 60 F6
Westenholz [D] 18 F6
Westensee [D] 18 F2
Westerhever [D] 18 D2
Westerholt [D] 18 B3
Westerland [D] 156 A4
Westerlo [B] 30 D3
Westerstede [D] 18 C4
Westkapelle [NL] 16 B6
Weston-super-Mare [GB] 12 F3
Westport [IRL] 2 C4
West Sandwick [GB] 6 H3
West-Terschelling [NL] 16 E1
Wetherby [GB] 10 F3
Wetlina [PL] 52 E6
Wetter [D] 30 H3
Wetter [D] 32 D6
Wetteren [B] 28 H2
Wettringen [D] 16 H5
Wetzikon [CH] 58 G5
Wetzlar [D] 46 C1
Wexford / Loch Garman [IRL] 4 F5
Weyer [A] 74 D1
Weyerburg [A] 72 F1
Weyer-Markt [A] 62 C5
Weyhausen [D] 32 G1
Weymouth [GB] 12 F5
Weyregg [A] 60 H5
Whitby [GB] 10 G2
Whitchurch [GB] 10 D5
Whitegate [IRL] 4 D5
Whitehead [NIR] 2 H3
Whithorn [GB] 8 C5
Whiting Bay [GB] 8 C3
Whitley Bay [GB] 8 G6
Whitstable [GB] 14 F5
Wiartel [PL] 24 C4
Wiązownica [PL] 52 F3
Wiblingen [D] 60 B3
Wicimice [PL] 20 G4
Wick [GB] 6 F3
Wickham Market [GB] 14 G3
Wicklow [IRL] 4 G4
Wicko [PL] 22 C1
Widawa [PL] 36 C6
Widawa [PL] 36 F5
Widdern [D] 46 D5
Widnes [GB] 10 D4
Widoma [PL] 52 A3
Widuchowa [PL] 20 E6
Więcbork [PL] 22 C5
Wiechowice [PL] 50 E4
Wiedenbrück [D] 32 D3
Wiefelstede [D] 18 C5
Wiehe [D] 34 B5
Wiehler Tropfsteinhöle [D] 30 H4
Wiek [D] 20 D1
Większyce [PL] 50 E3
Wielbark [PL] 22 H5
Wiele [PL] 22 D4
Wieleń [PL] 36 B1
Wielgie [PL] 36 F5
Wielgie [PL] 38 C6
Wielichowo [PL] 36 B3
Wieliczka [PL] 52 A4
Wieliczki [PL] 24 D3
Wielka Piaśnica [PL] 22 D1
Wielogłowy [PL] 52 B5
Wielogóra [PL] 38 C5
Wielowieś [PL] 50 F2
Wieluń [PL] 36 F6
Wien [A] 62 F4
Wiener Neustadt [A] 62 F5
Wienhausen [D] 32 G1
Wieniawa [PL] 38 B5
Wiepke [D] 34 B2
Wierden [NL] 16 G4
Wieruszów [PL] 36 E6
Wierzbica [PL] 38 B5
Wierzbice [PL] 50 C1
Wierzbowo [PL] 22 G5
Wierzchowo [PL] 22 B4
Wierzchucin Krolewski [PL] 22 C5
Wierzchucino [PL] 22 D1
Wies [D] 60 D5
Wiesau [D] 48 C4
Wiesbaden [D] 46 B3
Wiesberg [A] 72 B1
Wieselburg [A] 62 D4
Wiesen [CH] 70 H1
Wiesenburg [D] 34 C3
Wiesentheid [D] 46 F4
Wieskirche [D] 60 D5
Wiesloch [D] 46 C5
Wiesmath [A] 62 F6
Wiesmoor [D] 18 C4
Wietze [D] 32 G1
Wietzendorf [D] 18 F6
Wigan [GB] 10 D4
Wigston [GB] 10 F6
Wigton [GB] 8 E6
Wigtown [GB] 8 C5
Wijhe [NL] 16 F4
Wikingerburg [D] 44 F2
Wil [CH] 58 G5
Wilanów [PL] 38 B3
Wilczków [PL] 36 C6
Wilczkowo [PL] 22 G3
Wilczyska [PL] 52 C5
Wildalpen [A] 62 C6
Wildbad [D] 58 G1
Wildberg [D] 58 G1
Wildeck [D] 46 D6
Wildenburg [D] 44 G2
Wildenburg [D] 46 D4
Wildenrath [D] 30 F4
Wildenstein [CH] 58 E4
Wildenstein [D] 58 G3
Wildenstein Wasserfall [A] 74 C3
Wildeshausen [D] 18 D6
Wildhaus [CH] 58 H5
Wildkirchli [CH] 58 H5
Wildon [A] 74 D3
Wilfersdorf [A] 62 F3
Wilga [PL] 38 C4
Wilhelmsburg [A] 62 D5
Wilhelmsh [D] 32 F5
Wilhelmshaven [D] 18 C4
Wilhelmsthal [D] 32 F5
Wilhering [A] 62 B4
Wilków [PL] 38 B4
Willebroek [B] 30 C3
Willemstad [NL] 16 C6
Willingen [D] 32 D5
Willisau [CH] 58 E5
Wilnsdorf [D] 32 C6
Wilsin [NL] 16 D4
Wilster [D] 18 E3
Wilton [GB] 12 G4
Wiltz [L] 44 E2
Wimborne Minster [GB] 12 G5
Wimereux [F] 14 G6
Wincanton [GB] 12 G4
Winchester [GB] 12 H4
Windeck [D] 32 C6
Windermere [GB] 10 D2
Windisch [D] 48 C4
Windischgarsten [A] 62 B6
Windsbach [D] 46 G5
Winklern [A] 72 G2
Winnenden [D] 58 H1
Winnica [PL] 38 B2
Winnigstedt [D] 32 H3
Winnweiler [D] 46 B4
Winschoten [NL] 16 H2
Winsen [D] 18 G5
Winsen [D] 32 G1
Wińsko [PL] 36 C5
Winsum [NL] 16 G2
Winterberg [D] 32 D5
Winterfeld [D] 34 B1
Wintermoor [D] 18 F5
Winterstein [D] 32 G6
Winterswijk [NL] 16 G5
Winterthur [CH] 58 G4
Wipperfürth [D] 30 H4
Wippra [D] 34 A4
Wiry [PL] 50 C1
Wisbech [GB] 14 F2
Wischhafen [D] 18 E3
Wisełka [PL] 20 F3
Wiskitki [PL] 38 A3
Wisła [PL] 50 F5
Wiślica [PL] 52 B3
Wismar [D] 20 A3
Wiśniewo Ełckie [PL] 24 D4
Wiśniowa [PL] 52 A4
Wiśniowa [PL] 52 D4
Wissant [F] 14 G6
Wissembourg [F] 46 B6
Wissen [D] 32 C6
Wisznice [PL] 38 F4
Witham [GB] 14 F4
Withernsea [GB] 10 H4
Witków [PL] 52 H2
Witkowice [PL] 50 G1
Witkowo [PL] 36 E2
Witney [GB] 12 H3
Witnica [PL] 34 G2
Witnica [PL] 34 G1
Witostowice [PL] 50 C2
Witowo [PL] 36 F2
Wittdün [D] 18 D1
Witten [D] 30 H3
Wittenberge [D] 20 A6
Wittenburg [D] 18 H4
Wittgenstein [D] 46 B4
Wittichenau [D] 34 F5
Wittingen [D] 32 H1
Wittlich [D] 44 G2
Wittmund [D] 18 C4
Wittstock [D] 20 C5
Witzenhausen [D] 32 F5
Wiżajny [PL] 24 E2
Wizna [PL] 24 D5
Władysławowo [PL] 22 D1
Wleń [PL] 50 A1
Włocławek [PL] 36 G2
Włodawa [PL] 38 F4
Włoszczowa [PL] 50 H1
Wodzisław [PL] 52 B2
Wodzisław Śląski [PL] 50 F4
Woerden [NL] 16 D5
Woerth [F] 44 H5
Woesten [B] 28 F2
Wohlen [CH] 58 F5
Woijtowice [PL] 50 D2
Wojcieszków [PL] 38 D4
Wojcieszów [PL] 50 B1
Wojnicz [PL] 52 C4
Wojsławice [PL] 38 F6
Wojtakiemie [PL] 24 E2
Woking [GB] 14 D4
Wola Idzikowska [PL] 38 F6
Wola Klasztorna [PL] 38 D5
Wola Obszańska [PL] 52 F2
Wola Rakowa [PL] 36 G4
Wola Uhruska [PL] 38 G5
Wola Wierzbowska [PL] 22 H6
Wolbórz [PL] 36 H5
Wolbrom [PL] 50 H3
Wołczyn [PL] 50 E1
Woldegk [D] 20 D5
Wolfach [D] 58 F2
Wolfegg [D] 60 B5
Wolfen [D] 34 C4
Wolfenbüttel [D] 32 H3
Wolfhagen [D] 32 E5
Wolframs-Eschenbach [D] 46 F6
Wolfratshausen [D] 60 E5
Wolfsberg [A] 74 C3
Wolfsburg [D] 32 H2
Wolfstein [D] 44 H3
Wolgast [D] 20 E3
Wolhusen [CH] 58 E6
Wolibórz [PL] 50 C2
Wolica [PL] 52 B2
Wolin [PL] 20 F4
Wólka [PL] 52 A1
Wólka Dobryńska [PL] 38 F3
Wólka Łabuńska [PL] 52 G2
Wolkenstein [D] 48 D2
Wolkenstein in Gröden / Selva di Val Gardena [I] 72 E3
Wolkersdorf [A] 62 F4
Wollenberg [D] 34 F1
Wöllersdorf [A] 62 E5
Wollin [D] 34 C3
Wolmirstedt [D] 34 B3
Wolnzach [D] 60 E3
Wołomin [PL] 38 C2
Wołow [PL] 36 C5
Wolsingham [GB] 8 F6
Wolsztyn [PL] 36 B3
Wolvega [NL] 16 F3
Wolverhampton [GB] 10 D6
Woodbridge [GB] 14 G3
Woodford [IRL] 2 C6
Wooler [GB] 8 F4
Wooton Bassett [GB] 12 G3
Worb [CH] 58 D6
Worbis [D] 32 G5
Worcester [GB] 12 G2
Wörgl [A] 60 F6
Workington [GB] 8 D6
Worksop [GB] 10 F5
Workum [NL] 16 E2
Wörlitz [D] 34 C4
Wormerveer [NL] 16 D4
Wormhout [F] 14 H6
Worms [D] 46 C4
Wörnitz [D] 46 F5
Worpswede [D] 18 E5
Wörrstadt [D] 46 B3
Wörth [A] 72 G1
Wörth [D] 46 B6
Wörth [D] 46 D4
Wörth [D] 60 F2
Worthing [GB] 14 D5
Wozławki [PL] 22 H3
Woźniki [PL] 50 G2
Wożuczyn [PL] 52 G2
Wragby [GB] 10 G5
Wręczyca Wielka [PL] 50 F1
Wredenhagen [D] 20 C5
Wrexham [GB] 10 D5
Wriezen [D] 34 F2
Wróblew [PL] 36 F5
Wroblewo [PL] 36 B2
Wrocki [PL] 22 F5
Wrocław [PL] 36 C6
Wroniniec [PL] 36 B4
Wronki [PL] 24 D3
Wronki [PL] 36 B2
Wrząca Wielka [PL] 36 F3
Września [PL] 36 D3
Wschowa [PL] 36 B4
Wulfen [D] 30 H2
Wulkau [D] 34 C1
Wullowitz [A] 62 C3
Wünnenberg [D] 32 D4
Wunsiedel [D] 48 B3
Wunstorf [D] 32 F2
Wuppertal [D] 30 H3
Würgau [D] 46 G4
Wurmlinger Kapelle [D] 58 G2
Wurzbach [D] 46 H2
Würzbrunnen [CH] 58 E6
Würzburg [D] 46 E4
Wurzen [D] 34 D5
Wust [D] 34 C2
Wusterhausen [D] 34 D1
Wüstermarke [D] 34 E4
Wustrow [D] 20 C2
Wuustwezel [B] 30 D2
Wybcz [PL] 22 D6
Wydminy [PL] 24 D3
Wygoda [PL] 52 D4
Wyk [D] 156 A5
Wymondham [GB] 14 G2
Wyrzysk [PL] 22 C6
Wyśmierzyce [PL] 38 B4
Wysoka [PL] 22 B6
Wysokie [PL] 52 F1
Wysokie Mazowieckie [PL] 24 D6
Wysowa [PL] 52 C5
Wyszanów [PL] 36 E5
Wyszki [PL] 24 E6
Wyszków [PL] 38 C2
Wyszogród [PL] 38 A2
Wyszyna [PL] 36 F3

X

Xàbia / Jávea [E] 104 F1
Xabier / Javier [E] 84 C4
Xanten [D] 30 G2
Xánthi [GR] 130 E2
Xanthos [TR] 154 F3
Xàtiva [E] 98 E6
Xeraco [E] 98 F6
Xeresa [E] 98 E6
Xert [E] 98 G2
Xerta [E] 92 A5
Xertigny [F] 58 C2
Xesta, Puerto de la- [E] 78 E2
Xhoffraix [B] 30 F5
Xilopároiko [GR] 132 E2
Xinzo de Limia / Ginzo de Limia [E] 78 C6
Xirokámpi [GR] 136 E4
Xirókampos [GR] 154 A2
Xixona / Jijona [E] 104 E2
Xove [E] 78 E1
Xubia [E] 78 D1
Xunqueira de Ambia [E] 78 D5
Xunqueira de Espadanedo [E] 78 D5
Xylaganí [GR] 130 F3
Xylofagou [CY] 154 G5
Xylókastro [GR] 132 H6
Xylópoli [GR] 130 B3
Xyniás [GR] 132 G3
Xynó Neró [GR] 128 F4

Y

Yablanitsa [BG] 148 A4
Yablanovo [BG] 148 D3
Yablonovka [RUS] 178 H2
Yacimiento De Botorrita [E] 90 E4
Yacimientos De Icnitas [E] 90 C2
Yağcılar [TR] 152 E1
Yağcılı [TR] 152 D2
Yağlılar [TR] 152 C1
Yagoda [BG] 148 C5
Yahotyn [UA] 202 E7
Yaiza [E] 100 E6
Yakimovo [BG] 146 F2
Yakkima [RUS] 188 G4
Yakoruda [BG] 146 G6
Yalakdere [TR] 150 F3
Yalıkavak [TR] 154 B1
Yalıköy [TR] 150 D2
Yalova [TR] 150 F3
Yalta [UA] 204 H4
Yaman [TR] 152 G4
Yambol [BG] 148 E5
Yamm [RUS] 198 G2
Yampil' [UA] 202 B8
Yampil' [UA] 202 E6
Yampil' [UA] 204 E2
Yancıklar [TR] 150 C2
Yanguas [E] 90 C2
Yanjukalns [LV] 198 F5
Yannikyanniyemi [RUS] 188 G5
Yantarnyy [RUS] 22 G1
Yaraş [TR] 154 D1
Yarbasan [TR] 152 F2
Yarema [BG] 146 F5
Yarımca [TR] 150 G3
Yariş [TR] 152 G1
Yarm [GB] 10 F2
Yarmolyntsi [UA] 204 D2
Yarmouth [GB] 12 H5
Yasen [BG] 148 A3
Yasna Polyana [BG] 148 F5
Yassiören [TR] 150 E2
Yassiören [TR] 152 F1
Yatağan [TR] 152 E6
Yavorets [BG] 148 B4
Yavoriv [UA] 52 G3
Yaylabayır [TR] 152 E2
Yaylaköy [TR] 152 H6
Yazhelbitsy [RUS] 202 C2
Yazıkent [TR] 152 E5
Yazıköv [TR] 154 B3
Yazıköy [TR] 152 H5
Yazır [TR] 152 G6
Yazır [TR] 154 H2
Yazırköy [TR] 152 F5
Ybbs an der Donau [A] 62 D4
Ybbsitz [A] 62 C5
Ychoux [F] 66 B4
Yderby [DK] 156 F1
Ýdra [GR] 136 G3
Ydrefors [S] 162 F2
Yecla [E] 104 D1
Yecla de Yeltes [E] 80 F6
Yeleğen [TR] 152 F4
Yelizavetino [RUS] 178 G6
Yel'na [RUS] 202 D4
Yelverton [GB] 12 D5
Yemel'yanovka [RUS] 196 H5
Yemikaraağac [TR] 150 E4
Yemişendere [TR] 152 F6
Yemişli [TR] 152 F2
Yenibogaziçi (Ay. Seryios) [CY] 154 G5
Yenice [TR] 150 C5
Yenice [TR] 150 C1
Yenice [TR] 150 D4
Yenice [TR] 152 F5
Yenice [TR] 152 H2
Yenicekent [TR] 152 F4
Yeniçiftlik [TR] 150 D3
Yenicöy [TR] 152 D3
Yenierenköy (Aigialoúsa) [CY] 154 G4
Yenifoça [TR] 152 C3
Yeni Karpuzlu [TR] 130 H3
Yeniköy [TR] 130 H6
Yeniköy [TR] 150 C3
Yeniköy [TR] 150 D6
Yeniköy [TR] 150 E2
Yeniköy [TR] 150 F6
Yeniköy [TR] 150 F4
Yeniköy [TR] 150 G3
Yeniköy [TR] 152 E3
Yeniköy [TR] 152 F2
Yeniköy [TR] 154 G3
Yenipazar [TR] 150 H4
Yenipazar [TR] 152 E5
Yenişakran [TR] 152 C3
Yenisarıbey [TR] 150 D5
Yenişehir [TR] 150 G4
Yenişehir [TR] 152 F3
Yenişehir [TR] 152 F3
Yenne [F] 68 H3
Yeovil [GB] 12 F4
Yerkesik [TR] 154 D1
Yershi [RUS] 202 E4
Yerville [F] 26 H3
Yesa / Esa [E] 84 C4
Yeşilçay / Ağva [TR] 150 G2
Yeşilköy [TR] 150 E3
Yesilköy [TR] 152 F2
Yesilköy [TR] 154 G3
Yeşiller [TR] 150 F5
Yeşilova [TR] 150 D5
Yeşilova [TR] 152 H5
Yeşilvadi [TR] 150 F2
Yeşilyurt [TR] 152 F4
Yeşilyurt [TR] 154 D1
Yeşilyuva [TR] 152 G5
Yeste [E] 102 H1
Yevpatoria [UA] 204 H4
Yezyaryshcha [BY] 202 C4
Yiğitler [TR] 152 B1
Yılmazköy (Skylloura) [CY] 154 F5
Yılmazlı [TR] 154 G1
Yitteräng [S] 190 D6
Ylakiai [LT] 198 C6
Ylä-Kuona [FIN] 188 F4
Ylä-Luosta [FIN] 196 F6
Ylämaa [FIN] 178 E3
Ylämylly [FIN] 188 F2
Yläne [FIN] 176 D3
Ylihärmä [FIN] 186 C2
Yli-Ii [FIN] 196 D3
Yli-Kärppä [FIN] 196 D2
Ylikiiminki [FIN] 196 D4
Ylikylä [FIN] 186 B4
Ylikylä [FIN] 186 C2
Ylikylä [FIN] 186 E1
Yli-Lesti [FIN] 186 E1
Yli-Ii [FIN] 196 D3
Ylimarkku / Övermark [FIN] 186 B4
Yli-Nampa [FIN] 194 D7
Yli-Olhava [FIN] 196 D3
Ylistaro [FIN] 186 C3
Ylitornio / Övertorneå [FIN] 194 B8
Ylivieska [FIN] 196 D5
Ylläsjärvi [FIN] 194 C6
Ylöjärvi [FIN] 176 F1
Ylönkylä [FIN] 176 E5
Yngsjö [S] 158 D2
Yoğuntaş [TR] 150 B1
Yolüstü [TR] 152 F5
Yordankino [BG] 146 G4
York [GB] 10 F3
Youghal [IRL] 4 D5
Ypéria [GR] 132 G2
Yport [F] 26 G2
Yppäri [FIN] 196 C5
Ypres (Ieper) [B] 28 F2
Ýpso [GR] 132 B2
Ypsoús [GR] 136 D2
Yquem, Château- [F] 66 D4
Yrittäperä [FIN] 196 E3
Yrkje [N] 164 B2
Yrouerre [F] 56 F2
Yset [N] 182 B4
Ysjö [S] 190 F6
Yssandon, Puy d'- [F] 66 G3
Yssingeaux [F] 68 E4
Ystad [S] 158 D3
Ystebrød [N] 164 B4
Yterturingen [S] 182 H4
Ytre Arna [N] 170 B3
Ytre Enebakk [N] 166 B1
Ytre Kjæs [N] 194 C2
Ytre Snillfjord [N] 180 G1
Ytterån [S] 182 G2
Ytterås [N] 182 C1
Ytteråträsk [S] 196 A5
Ytterberg [S] 182 G5
Ytterboda [S] 172 H4
Ytterby [S] 160 G1
Ytterhogdal [S] 182 H5
Ytterjeppo [FIN] 186 C1
Yttermalung [S] 172 F4
Ytterselö [S] 168 C3
Yttervik [S] 190 E3
Yukarıkızılca [TR] 152 D4
Yukhavichy [BY] 198 H6
Yukhnov [RUS] 202 E4
Yuncos [E] 96 F1
Yundola [BG] 146 G6
Yunquera [E] 102 B4
Yunquera de Henares [E] 88 H5
Yuntdağ [TR] 152 C3
Yunuseli [TR] 150 F4
Yuratsishki [BY] 200 H6
Yüreğil [TR] 152 E2
Yürücekler [TR] 150 F5
Yuste, Monasterio de- [E] 88 B5
Yusufça [TR] 152 G6
Yuvacık [TR] 154 D2
Yverdon-les-Bains [CH] 58 C6
Yvetot [F] 26 H3
Yvoir [B] 30 D5
Yvoire [F] 70 B2
Yxnerum [S] 168 B6

Z

Zaandam [NL] 16 D4
Zabalats' [BY] 24 H3
Žabalj [SCG] 142 G1
Zăbalt [RO] 76 H5
Zabar [H] 64 E4
Žabari [SCG] 146 C1
Żabice [PL] 36 B5
Zabierzów [PL] 50 H3
Zabki [PL] 38 B3
Ząbkowice Śląskie [PL] 50 C2
Zablaće [HR] 112 H6
Žabljak [SCG] 144 E2
Zabłudów [PL] 24 F6
Żabno [PL] 52 C3
Zabok [HR] 74 E6
Zabolottia [UA] 38 G4
Zabór [PL] 36 A4
Zăbrani [RO] 76 H5
Zábřeh [CZ] 50 C4
Zabrodzie [PL] 38 C2
Zabrze [PL] 50 F3
Zabrzeż [PL] 52 B5
Zacháro [GR] 136 C3
Zachloroú [GR] 132 G6
Zadar [HR] 112 G5
Zadvarje [HR] 144 A2
Zadzyezhzha [BY] 198 H6
Zafferana Etnea [I] 126 G3
Zafirovo [BG] 148 E1
Zafra [E] 94 G3
Žaga [SLO] 72 H4
Żagań [PL] 34 H5
Zagare [LT] 198 D6
Zagkliveri [GR] 130 B4
Zaglav [HR] 112 F5
Zaglavak [SCG] 146 A2
Zagorá [GR] 132 H2
Zagorje [HR] 112 G1
Zagorje [SLO] 74 C5
Zagórów [PL] 36 E3
Zagórz [PL] 52 E5
Zagoska [RUS] 198 H3
Zagreb [HR] 74 E6
Žagubica [SCG] 146 D1
Zagvozd [HR] 144 B2
Zagwiździe [PL] 50 E1
Zagyva Palfalva [H] 64 D5
Zahara [E] 100 H3

Zahara de los Atunes [E] 100 G5
Zahinos [E] 94 F3
Zahna [D] 34 D4
Zahody [RUS] 198 G3
Záhoří [CZ] 48 F6
Záhorská Ves [SK] 62 G4
Zaiceva [LV] 198 G4
Zajas [MK] 128 D2
Zaječar [SCG] 146 E2
Zákas [SCG] 128 E6
Zakliczyn [PL] 52 C4
Zaklików [PL] 52 E1
Zakopane [PL] 50 H6
Zakroczym [PL] 38 B2
Zakrós [GR] 140 H5
Zakrós [GR] 140 H5
Zakrzewo [PL] 36 F1
Zakrzówek [PL] 38 C5
Zákupy [CZ] 48 G2
Zákynthos [GR] 136 B2
Zalaapáti [H] 74 G3
Zalabaksa [H] 74 G3
Zalabér [H] 74 G2
Zalaegerszeg [H] 74 G3
Zalakaros [H] 74 G3
Zalakomár [H] 74 G4
Zalalövo [H] 74 F3
Zalamea de la Serena [E] 96 B4
Zalamea la Real [E] 94 F5
Zalaszabar [H] 74 G3
Zalaszántó [H] 74 G3
Zalaszentbalázs [H] 74 G3
Zalaszentgrót [H] 74 G2
Zălau [RO] 204 C4
Žalec [SLO] 74 D4
Zalewo [PL] 22 F4
Zalęże [PL] 22 H5
Zalishchyky [UA] 204 D2
Zalla [E] 82 G4
Zaltbommel [NL] 16 E6
Załuski [PL] 38 A2
Załuż [PL] 52 E5
Zalużnica [HR] 112 G3
Zamárdi [H] 76 A3
Zamarte [PL] 22 C4
Žamberk [CZ] 50 B4
Zambrana [E] 82 G5
Zambrów [PL] 24 D6
Zambujal [P] 86 B6
Zambujeira do Mar [P] 94 B4
Zamora [E] 80 H5
Zamość [PL] 24 C6
Zamość [PL] 24 C6
Zamość [PL] 52 F1
Zamostne [PL] 22 D2
Zandhoven [B] 30 D3
Zandvoort [NL] 16 D4
Zaniemyśl [PL] 36 D3
Zánka [H] 74 H3

Zante [LV] 198 C5
Zaorejas [E] 90 B5
Zaostrog [HR] 144 B3
Zaostrov'ye [RUS] 178 H2
Zaozernoye [RUS] 24 C2
Zapadnaja Dvina [RUS] 202 D3
Zapałów [PL] 52 F3
Zapfendorf [D] 46 G3
Zaplusy'ye [RUS] 198 H2
Zapole [PL] 36 F5
Zapol'E [RUS] 198 H2
Zapolyarnyy [RUS] 194 F3
Zapol'ye [RUS] 202 B2
Zaporizhzhia [UA] 204 H2
Zaporozhskoye [RUS] 178 H3
Záppeio [GR] 132 G2
Zapponeta [I] 120 H1
Zaprešić [HR] 74 E5
Zaprudy [BY] 38 H2
Zapyškis [LT] 200 F5
Zaragoza [E] 90 E4
Zárakes [GR] 134 D5
Zarańsko [PL] 20 H5
Zarasai [LT] 200 H4
Zarautz [E] 84 A2
Zarcilla de los Ramons [E] 104 B3
Zaręby–Warchoły [PL] 38 D1
Zarech'E [RUS] 198 H4
Zarenthien [D] 18 H6
Żarki [PL] 50 G2
Zárkos [GR] 132 F2
Zärneşti [RO] 204 D5
Žarnovica [SK] 64 B3
Żarnów [PL] 38 A6
Żarnowiec [PL] 50 H2
Zarós [GR] 140 E5
Żarów [PL] 50 B1
Zarrentin [D] 18 H4
Żarska Wies [PL] 34 H6
Zarszyn [PL] 52 E5
Zaruch'e [RUS] 198 G1
Żary [PL] 34 H5
Zarza-Capilla [E] 96 C4
Zarza de Alange [E] 94 H2
Zarzadilla de Totana [E] 104 B3
Zarza la Mayor [E] 86 G4
Zarzecze [PL] 52 E2
Zás [E] 78 B2
Zasa [LV] 198 F6
Zasieki [PL] 34 G4
Žatec [CZ] 48 E3
Zatom [PL] 20 H6
Zator [PL] 50 G4
Zaube [LV] 198 E5
Zauchwitz [D] 34 D3
Zavala [BIH] 144 C3

Zavet [BG] 148 D2
Zavidovići [BIH] 142 D3
Zavlaka [SCG] 142 F3
Zavoya [BG] 130 F2
Zavrc [SLO] 74 E4
Zawada [PL] 36 A4
Zawada [PL] 50 E2
Zawady [PL] 50 F1
Zawadzkie [PL] 50 F2
Zawichost [PL] 52 D1
Zawidów [PL] 48 G1
Zawiercie [PL] 50 G2
Zawoja [PL] 50 H5
Zawonia [PL] 36 D5
Zawroty [PL] 22 G4
Zayan'e [SCG] 64 B5
Zayan'ye [RUS] 198 G2
Zaytsevo [RUS] 178 F2
Žažina [HR] 142 A1
Zázriva [SK] 50 G6
Zbąszyń [PL] 36 B3
Zbąszynek [PL] 36 A3
Zblewo [PL] 22 D4
Zbojno [PL] 22 F6
Zborov [SK] 52 D5
Zborowice [PL] 52 C4
Zbrachlin [PL] 22 D5
Zbraslav [CZ] 48 F4
Zbraslavice [CZ] 48 H4
Zbrašovske Aragonitové Jeskyně [CZ] 50 D5
Zbucz [PL] 38 F1
Zbuczyn Poduchowny [PL] 38 D3
Zdala [HR] 74 G5
Zdánice [CZ] 48 E3
Ždár [CZ] 48 E3
Žďár nad Sázavou [CZ] 50 B5
Zdenci [HR] 76 A6
Zdiby [CZ] 48 F3
Zdice [CZ] 48 F4
Ždírec nad Doubrava [CZ] 50 A5
Zdounky [CZ] 50 D6
Zdunje [MK] 128 D1
Zduńska Wola [PL] 36 F5
Zduny [PL] 36 D5
Zduny [PL] 36 H3
Zdziechowice [PL] 52 E1
Zdzieszowice [PL] 50 E3
Żebrák [CZ] 48 E4
Zebreira [P] 86 G4
Zebrzydowa [PL] 34 H6
Zeddiani [I] 118 C5
Žednik [SCG] 76 D5
Zeebrugge [B] 28 G1
Zefyría [GR] 138 D4
Żegiestów [PL] 52 C5
Zegorje [RUS] 198 G1
Zehdenick [D] 20 D6
Zeil [D] 60 B5
Zeist [NL] 16 E5

Zeitz [D] 34 C6
Żelazna [PL] 22 D1
Żelazna Góra [PL] 22 G2
Żelechów [PL] 38 D4
Zelená Hora [CZ] 48 E5
Zelena morava [BG] 148 D3
Zelenika [SCG] 144 D4
Zelenogorsk [RUS] 178 G4
Zelenogradsk [RUS] 200 C5
Żeletava [CZ] 50 A6
Železná Ruda [CZ] 48 D6
Železnik [SCG] 142 G3
Železniki [SLO] 74 B4
Železný Brod [CZ] 48 H2
Zelhem [NL] 16 F5
Żeliezovce [SK] 64 B5
Želin [SLO] 74 A5
Zelina [HR] 74 F5
Zélio [GR] 132 H4
Želiv [CZ] 48 H5
Želizna [PL] 38 E4
Želkowo [PL] 22 C2
Zell [A] 62 A4
Zell [D] 44 G2
Zell [D] 58 E4
Zella [D] 32 G5
Zella–Mehlis [D] 46 G2
Zell am See [A] 72 F1
Zell am Ziller [A] 72 E1
Želnava [CZ] 62 B2
Zelów [PL] 36 G5
Zeltini [LV] 198 F4
Zeltweg [A] 74 C2
Želva [LT] 200 G5
Zelwa [PL] 24 F3
Zelzate [B] 28 H1
Žemaičiu Naumiestis [LT] 200 D5
Žemberovce [SK] 64 C4
Zemblak [AL] 128 D4
Zeme [I] 70 F5
Zemen [BG] 146 F5
Zemite [LV] 198 C5
Zemplíriská Teplica [SK] 64 G3
Zemun [SCG] 142 G2
Zenica [BIH] 142 D4
Žepa [BIH] 142 E4
Zepče [BIH] 142 D3
Zerbst [D] 34 C3
Zerczyce [PL] 38 E2
Zerevna [BG] 148 D4
Zerf [D] 44 F3
Zeri [I] 110 C3
Zerind [RO] 76 G3
Zermatt [CH] 70 D3
Zernez [CH] 72 B2
Zernien [D] 18 H6
Zerniki [PL] 36 C6
Zerqan [AL] 128 C2

Zestoa / Cestona [E] 84 A2
Zetel [D] 18 C4
Zeulenroda [D] 48 B2
Zeven [D] 18 E5
Zevenaar [NL] 16 F5
Zevenergen [NL] 16 C6
Zevgaráki [GR] 132 E5
Zeybekçayırı [TR] 150 C6
Zeytinbaği [TR] 150 E4
Zeytindağ [TR] 152 C3
Zeytinli [TR] 152 C1
Zgierz [PL] 36 G4
Zgníłocha [PL] 22 H4
Zgórsko [PL] 52 C3
Zgorzelec [PL] 34 G5
Zg. Polskava [SLO] 74 D4
Zhabinka [BY] 38 G2
Zhaludok [BY] 24 H4
Zhashkiv [UA] 202 D8
Zhedricy [RUS] 198 H4
Zhelezna [BG] 146 F5
Zheleznitsa [BG] 146 F5
Zheleznodorozhnyj [RUS] 24 B2
Zheleznogorsk [RUS] 202 F5
Zheleznya [RUS] 202 F4
Zhilentsi [BG] 146 E6
Zhilino [RUS] 200 D5
Zhitosvyat [BG] 148 E4
Zhlobin [BY] 202 C6
Zhmerynka [UA] 202 C8
Zhodzina [BY] 202 C5
Zhovkva [UA] 52 H3
Zhovten' [UA] 204 F3
Zhuprany [BY] 200 H6
Zhvtkavichy [BY] 202 C6
Zhydachiv [UA] 52 H5
Zhytomyr [UA] 202 C7
Žiar nad Hronom [SK] 64 C3
Zicavo [F] 114 B5
Zickhusen [D] 20 A4
Zidani Most [SLO] 74 D5
Židlochovice [CZ] 62 F2
Ziębice [PL] 50 C2
Ziegenrück [D] 46 H2
Zieleniek [PL] 24 B5
Zielona Chocina [PL] 22 C4
Zielona Góra [PL] 34 H4
Zielonka [PL] 38 B3
Zieluń–Osada [PL] 22 G6
Ziemupe [LV] 198 B5
Zierenberg [D] 32 E5
Zierikzee [NL] 16 B6
Ziersdorf [A] 62 E3
Zierzow [D] 20 A5
Ziesar [D] 34 C3
Ziethen [D] 20 D4
Žiežmariai [LT] 200 F5
Žiguri [LV] 198 G4

Zijpe [NL] 16 C6
Žilina [SK] 50 F6
Zilupe [LV] 198 G5
Zimandu Nou [RO] 76 G4
Zimma Woda [PL] 22 H5
Zimnicea [RO] 148 C2
Zimnitsa [BG] 148 E4
Zinal [CH] 70 D3
Zingst [D] 20 C2
Zinnowitz [D] 20 E3
Zinnwald–Georgenfeld [D] 48 E2
Zinzulusa, Grotta– [I] 122 H5
Zipári [GR] 154 B2
Zirc [H] 76 A2
Zirchow [D] 20 E4
Žiri [SLO] 74 B5
Zirl [A] 72 D1
Žíros [GR] 140 G5
Žirovnice [CZ] 48 G6
Zistersdorf [A] 62 F3
Žitište [SCG] 142 G1
Žitkovac [SCG] 146 D3
Žitomislići [BIH] 144 C2
Žitoradja [SCG] 146 D4
Žitsa [GR] 132 C2
Zittau [D] 48 G1
Živaja [HR] 142 B1
Živinice [BIH] 142 E3
Živogošće [HR] 144 B2
Ziyamet (Leonarisso) [CY] 154 G4
Zizers [CH] 70 H1
Zlata [SCG] 146 D4
Zlatá Baňa [SK] 64 G2
Zlatá Koruna [CZ] 62 B2
Zlatar [BG] 148 E3
Zlatar Bistrica [HR] 74 E5
Zlatarevo [BG] 128 H2
Zlatari [SCG] 146 C3
Zlaté Hory [CZ] 50 D3
Zlaté Klasy [SK] 62 H4
Zlaté Moravce [SK] 64 B4
Zlatitsa [BG] 148 A4
Zlati voyvoda [BG] 148 D4
Zlatna Panega [BG] 148 A4
Zlatni Pyasŭtsi [BG] 148 G2
Zlatograd [BG] 130 E2
Žleby [CZ] 48 H4
Zliechov [SK] 64 B2
Zlín [CZ] 50 D6
Złocieniec [PL] 20 H5
Złoczew [PL] 36 F5
Zlonice [CZ] 48 F3
Zlot [SCG] 146 D2
Złotniki Kujawskie [PL] 36 E1
Złotoryja [PL] 36 B6
Złotów [PL] 22 B5
Zlotska Pećina [SCG] 146 D2

Złoty Stok [PL] 50 C3
Žlutice [CZ] 48 D3
Zlynka [RUS] 202 D6
Zmajevac [HR] 76 C5
Zmievka [RUS] 202 F5
Żmigród [PL] 36 C5
Żminj [HR] 112 D2
Zmysłowo [PL] 36 C4
Znamenka [RUS] 198 G3
Znamensk [RUS] 24 B1
Znamianka [UA] 202 F8
Zniev [SK] 64 B2
Żnin [PL] 36 D1
Znojmo [CZ] 62 E3
Zoetermeer [NL] 16 C5
Zoeterwoude [NL] 16 C5
Zofingen [CH] 58 E5
Zolder [B] 30 E4
Żółki [PL] 24 E5
Żółkiewka–Osada [PL] 38 E6
Żółkow [D] 20 B4
Zollchow [D] 20 E5
Zolotonosha [UA] 202 E7
Zomba [H] 76 B4
Zona Volcànica de la Garrotxa [E] 92 F2
Zonza [F] 114 B5
Zoo Svatý Kopeček [CZ] 50 D5
Zörbig [D] 34 C4
Zorge [D] 32 H4
Zorita [E] 96 B2
Zorneding [D] 60 E4
Zornitsa [BG] 148 E5
Żory [PL] 50 F4
Zossen [D] 34 E3
Zoutkamp [NL] 16 G2
Zoutleeuw [B] 30 D4
Zoúzouli [GR] 128 D6
Zovka [RUS] 198 G2
Zreče [SLO] 74 D4
Zrenjanin [SCG] 142 G1
Zrinski Topolovac [HR] 74 F5
Zrmanja [HR] 112 H5
Zrnovci [MK] 128 G1
Zruč nad Sázavou [CZ] 48 G4
Zrze [SCG] 146 B6
Zsadány [H] 76 G2
Zsámbék [H] 64 C6
Zsana [H] 76 D4
Zschopau [D] 48 D2
Zuani [F] 114 C4
Zuberec [SK] 50 H6
Zubin Potok [SCG] 146 B4
Zubiri [E] 84 B3
Zubné [SK] 52 E6
Zubřič [CZ] 50 E5
Zubrzyca Górna [PL] 50 H5
Zubtsov [RUS] 202 E3

Zudar [D] 20 D2
Zuera [E] 90 E3
Zug [CH] 58 F5
Zuidhorn [NL] 16 G2
Zuidlaren [NL] 16 G2
Zújar [E] 102 F3
Żukowo [PL] 22 D2
Žulová [CZ] 50 C3
Zülpich [D] 30 G5
Zumaia / Zumaya [E] 84 A2
Zumarraga [E] 82 H4
Zundert [NL] 30 D2
Zuoz [CH] 72 A3
Žur [SCG] 146 B6
Zurawica [PL] 52 F4
Zürich [CH] 58 F5
Żuromin [PL] 22 G6
Żurrieq [M] 126 C6
Zürs [A] 72 B1
Zurzach [CH] 58 F4
Zusmarshausen [D] 60 C3
Züssow [D] 20 A3
Züssow [D] 20 D3
Žuta Lokva [HR] 112 F2
Zutphen [NL] 16 F5
Zuyevo [RUS] 202 C1
Žužemberk [SLO] 74 C5
Zvečka [SCG] 142 G3
Zvenyhorodka [UA] 202 E8
Zverevo [RUS] 178 F3
Zvěřínek [CZ] 48 F5
Zvezdel [BG] 130 F1
Zvezdets [BG] 148 F5
Zvíkov [CZ] 48 F5
Zvolen [SK] 64 C3
Zvonce [SCG] 146 E4
Zvornik [BIH] 142 E3
Zweibrücken [D] 44 G4
Zweisimmen [CH] 70 D1
Zwettl [A] 62 D3
Zwettl an der Rodl [A] 62 B3
Zwickau [D] 48 C2
Zwiefalten [D] 58 H3
Zwierzno [PL] 22 F3
Zwierzyniec [PL] 52 F2
Zwiesel [D] 60 H2
Zwijndrecht [NL] 16 D5
Zwingenberg [D] 46 D5
Zwoleń [PL] 38 C5
Zwolle [NL] 16 F4
Zychlin [PL] 36 G3
Zyciny [PL] 52 C2
Żydowo [PL] 36 D2
Zyel'va [BY] 24 H5
Żygi [CY] 154 G6
Zyrardów [PL] 38 A3
Żywiec [PL] 50 G5
Żywocice [PL] 50 E3

7th edition October 2005

© ISTITUTO GEOGRAFICO DE AGOSTINI, Novara and
© Automobile Association Developments Limited, Basingstoke.

Original edition printed 1996

Ordnance Survey® This product includes mapping data licensed from Ordnance Survey® with the permission of the Controller of Her Majesty's Stationery Office. © Crown copyright 2005. All rights reserved. Licence number 399221

This product includes mapping based upon data licensed from Ordnance Survey of Northern Ireland ® reproduced by permission of the Chief Executive, acting on behalf of the Controller of Her Majesty's Stationery Office. © Crown copyright 2005. Permit No. 40454.

Republic of Ireland mapping based on Ordnance Survey Ireland. Permit No. MP000105 © Ordnance Survey Ireland and Government of Ireland

Published by ISTITUTO GEOGRAFICO DE AGOSTINI, Novara and Automobile Association Developments Limited whose registered office is Fanum House, Basing View, Basingstoke, Hampshire, RG21 4EA, UK. Registered number 1878835

ISBN-10: 0 7495 4710 3 (flexibound)
ISBN-13: 978 0 7495 4710 3
ISBN-10: 0 7495 4709 X (spiral bound)
ISBN-13: 978 0 7495 4709 7

A CIP catalogue record for this book is available from The British Library.

Printed in Italy by Canale & C. S.p.A., Torino

ROAD DISTANCES
DISTANZE STRADALI
DISTANCIAS KILOMÉTRICAS
DISTANCES ROUTIÈRES
STRASSENENTFERNUNGEN

Frankfurt am Main-Ljubljana = 804 km

	Amsterdam	Athína	Barcelona	Belfast	Beograd	Berlin	Bern	Birmingham	Bordeaux	Bratislava	Brussel/Bruxelles	Bucureşti	Budapest	Dublin	Edinburgh	Frankfurt am Main	Genève	Göteborg	Hamburg	Helsinki/Helsingfors	İstanbul	København	Köln	Kyïv	Lisboa	Ljubljana	London	Luxembourg
Athína	2760																											
Barcelona	1557	2520																										
Belfast	1312	3520	2265																									
Beograd	1718	1044	1981	2816																								
Berlin	655	2288	1863	1868	1247																							
Bern	838	1971	944	1725	1363	922																						
Birmingham	738	3285	1691	582	2244	1295	1152																					
Bordeaux	1091	3049	552	1815	2007	1634	852	1241																				
Bratislava	1225	1618	1866	2324	577	671	938	1750	1879																			
Brussel/Bruxelles	206	2568	1355	1148	1673	763	637	574	883	1181																		
Bucureşti	2181	1106	2597	3279	619	1646	1893	2706	2613	977	2136																	
Budapest	1398	1429	1897	2497	388	864	1111	1923	2053	194	1353	788																
Dublin	1088	3455	2041	164	2594	1644	1502	358	1585	2101	925	3057	2274															
Edinburgh	1190	3557	2143	305	2695	1746	1603	460	1686	2203	1026	3159	2376	468														
Frankfurt am Main	445	2323	1323	1545	1281	565	423	971	1150	788	400	1744	961	1321	1422													
Genève	908	2372	778	1683	1331	1072	165	1109	687	1088	706	1946	1261	1457	1561	573												
Göteborg	1178	3131	2479	2412	2090	823	1637	1839	2185	1514	1307	2490	1708	2187	2290	1214	1787											
Hamburg	463	2602	1763	1696	1561	294	910	1123	1470	985	591	1961	1178	1471	1574	487	1059	728										
Helsinki/Helsingfors	2580	3590	3788	3792	2641	1959	2847	3220	3551	2208	2687	2483	2252	3567	3670	2489	2996	982	2192									
İstanbul	2649	1092	2913	3748	935	2179	2294	3175	2929	1509	2605	681	1320	3522	3626	2213	2261	3022	2493	3164								
København	920	2873	2220	2153	1832	564	1378	1580	1927	1255	1048	2231	1449	1928	2031	955	1528	269	469	1123	2764							
Köln	265	2506	1342	1352	1464	575	585	778	1062	972	208	1928	1145	1126	1230	192	735	1141	425	2500	2396	882						
Kyïv	2016	1994	3093	3228	1322	1398	2190	2655	2988	1251	2123	888	1123	3003	3106	1884	2340	2211	1681	1595	1569	1952	1935					
Lisboa	2296	3787	1237	3019	3188	2838	2150	2446	1202	3090	2095	3804	3103	2793	2897	2355	1989	3397	2681	4764	4119	3138	2273	4199				
Ljubljana	1241	1572	1455	2294	530	999	836	1721	1471	435	1153	1146	443	2069	2173	804	803	1916	1203	2623	1462	1656	987	1565	2661			
London	533	2910	1486	766	2039	1090	947	193	1030	1546	370	2502	1719	541	645	766	905	1634	918	3015	2970	1375	574	2450	2243	1537		
Luxembourg	386	2355	1149	1355	1469	762	431	782	946	1010	213	1965	1183	1129	1233	240	500	1326	610	2687	2401	1066	188	2081	2159	956	582	
	1800	3145	614	2523	2573	2343	1535	1950	706	2458	1599	3189	2489	2298	2402	1859	1374	2901	2185	4268	3505	2642	1778	3684	619	2046	1750	1662
	868	3415	1821	461	2374	1425	1282	138	1365	1881	705	2837	2054	310	339	1101	1240	1969	1253	3350	3305	1710	909	2785	2578	1872	323	911
	1236	2567	505	2003	1526	1541	623	1429	654	1419	1034	2141	1441	1778	1881	1003	422	2158	1442	3467	2457	1899	1025	2564	1711	999	1230	832
	1077	1218	977	1963	1026	1033	350	1390	985	919	876	1642	942	1737	1841	662	317	1833	1120	2959	1958	1574	823	2064	2182	499	1190	669
	1742	2448	2878	2955	1513	1124	1938	2381	2714	1178	1850	1341	1125	2729	2833	1620	2088	1938	1408	1183	2023	1678	1662	557	3927	1593	2181	1817
	2449	2864	3584	3661	2084	1830	2644	3088	3420	1885	2556	1758	1831	3435	3539	2326	2794	2643	2114	1116	2440	2385	2368	871	4364	2300	2888	2523
	827	1990	1370	1880	949	585	442	1297	1278	466	739	1421	639	1655	1759	390	591	1502	789	2511	1880	1242	573	1718	2576	435	1107	521
	1859	597	1555	2746	1483	1693	1132	2173	1704	1376	1658	2099	1399	2521	2624	1444	1085	2586	1874	3563	2415	2327	1606	2521	2761	956	1973	1476
	1490	3443	2790	2723	2402	1134	1949	2150	2497	1826	1618	2801	2019	2498	2601	1525	2098	315	1039	1030	3333	580	1446	2522	3710	2248	1950	1636
	525	2465	1039	1248	1800	1068	592	659	583	1340	324	2295	1513	1023	1126	604	529	1626	910	2993	2732	1367	502	2428	1796	1287	475	407
	2094	4028	1076	2818	2986	2637	1948	2244	1000	2889	1893	3602	2902	2592	2696	2153	1788	3196	2480	4563	3918	2936	2072	3997	300	2459	2044	1956
	891	1946	1709	2045	904	341	769	1471	1601	328	902	1304	522	1820	1923	510	919	1186	657	2178	1836	927	693	1389	2814	664	1272	731
	1618	2807	2825	2830	1766	996	1885	2257	2590	1333	1725	1676	1378	2604	2708	1527	2035	1760	1230	962	2357	1501	1537	1029	3803	1748	2057	1724
	1658	1190	1354	2545	1282	1493	932	1972	1503	1175	1457	1898	1198	2320	2423	1243	884	2386	1673	3363	2214	2126	1405	2321	2560	755	1772	1275
	2180	3190	3388	3393	2241	1558	2447	2819	3152	1809	2288	2084	1853	3167	3271	2089	2597	2284	1793	387	2765	2063	2099	1196	4365	2223	2619	2286
	1727	1121	1990	2826	303	1389	1372	2252	2007	707	1682	824	539	2600	2704	1290	1339	2402	1644	2791	1113	2143	1474	1601	3196	539	2052	1478
	2277	3998	998	3000	2957	2838	1919	2427	1183	2842	2076	3573	2873	2775	2878	2299	1759	3378	2662	4763	3889	3119	2255	4068	403	2430	2227	2128
	2139	654	2402	3237	424	1668	1783	2664	2418	998	2094	598	809	3012	3115	1702	1750	2512	1982	3061	781	2253	1885	1485	3608	951	2464	1890
	2095	735	2358	3193	380	1624	1739	2620	2375	954	2050	372	765	2968	3071	1658	1707	2468	1938	2854	555	2209	1841	1259	3564	907	2420	1846
	1534	3488	2835	2768	2446	1175	1993	2195	2541	1870	1663	2846	2064	2543	2646	1570	2143	481	1084	505	3378	624	1497	2566	3755	2293	1995	1681
	1920	3105	3127	3132	2063	1298	2187	2559	2892	1631	2027	1973	1675	2907	3011	1829	2337	2062	1533	90	2654	1803	1839	1326	4105	2046	2359	2026
	2333	454	2597	3432	619	1862	1978	2858	2613	1193	2288	656	1004	3207	3310	1896	1945	2707	2177	3139	642	2447	2080	1543	3802	1145	2658	2085
	2103	735	2366	3201	606	1765	1748	2628	2383	1083	2058	886	915	2976	3163	1666	1715	2778	2020	3167	1069	2518	1849	1773	3572	915	2428	1854
	3071	4692	4371	4304	3743	2715	3529	3731	4078	3311	3199	3586	3355	4114	4182	3106	3679	1949	2620	1360	4267	2160	3033	2698	5291	3829	3531	3217
	1897	3363	363	2603	2322	2202	1283	2030	803	2206	1695	2937	2237	2378	2482	1663	1123	2819	2103	4128	3253	2560	1686	3433	894	1795	1830	1492
	1636	2550	2776	2849	1509	1018	1836	2275	2608	1077	1744	1384	1121	2623	2727	1518	1986	1733	1203	1142	2066	1474	1555	738	3821	1492	2075	1715
	1202	2097	2342	2414	1056	584	1402	1841	2174	643	1309	1240	668	2189	2293	1084	1552	1397	868	1566	1922	1138	1121	815	3387	1057	1641	1281
	1148	1664	1789	2246	622	629	861	1673	1802	66	1103	1022	240	2021	2125	711	1010	1473	943	2246	1554	1214	895	1319	3016	378	1473	933
	1326	1435	1586	2424	394	988	968	1852	1603	417	1281	1009	347	2199	2302	889	936	2001	1243	2604	1325	1741	1073	1470	2793	135	1647	1074